THE MASTER
OF THE
UNICORN

THE MASTER
OF THE
UNICORN

THE LIFE AND WORK
OF JEAN DUVET

Colin Eisler

ABARIS BOOKS • NEW YORK

This publication was supported by le Centre National de la Recherche Scientifique, Paris.

ISBN 0-913870-46-3
Library of Congress Card Number 77-086223

First published 1977 by Abaris Books, Inc.
24 West 40th Street, New York, N.Y. 10018
Printed in the United States of America
A Joel Walker Production

This book is for Benita

CONTENTS

PREFACE

Jean Duvet's oeuvre is eminently compatible with today's taste. Yet,
we are led to wonder how were these strange works received by his contemporaries? It is not easy to know. At first glance, these wild compositions,
reminiscent of Dürer and Marcantonio, also recalling Gothic architecture,
overshadowed by the beginning of the Reformation, must have shocked the
viewers of the day. Often they are worlds apart from the purity of the work
of his contemporary Etienne Delaune, although both printmakers were active
as goldsmiths. Duvet was highly esteemed in Burgundy as in Switzerland,
for he embodied a romantic current. His allegories, which we are hard put
to understand today, were readily comprehensible to people of the sixteenth
century. The unicorn, symbol of Henri II and Diane de Poitiers, was no more
extraordinary than the elephant with *fleur de lys* or Vercingetorix with a
pomegranate, symbolizing François I, in the gallery named after him in the
Château de Fontainebleau.

We are amazed that Duvet was not rediscovered by the Symbolists in
the nineteenth century. Probably, this is due to the extreme scarcity of his
works. A Huysmans or a Robert de Montesquiou would have pronounced
him *"l'inextricable graveur"* as they have characterized Rodolphe Bresdin for
a similar amalgam of malaise and enchantment.

Duvet's works are imbued with the turbulent poetry, mystery, and faith
of his times, as Colin Eisler so eloquently demonstrates in these revealing
pages.

Jean Adhémar

Curator Emeritus of Prints
Bibilothèque Nationale, Paris

ACKNOWLEDGMENTS

The distinguished art historian Louis Réau, though aware of Duvet's special fire, criticized the engraver for his failure to master "l'art des sacrifices." This study, initiated as a Harvard dissertation for Jakob Rosenberg, and inspired by all the relentless aspirations to omniscience of that academic exercise, has since changed somewhat from both sacrificial pruning and new findings of links between France and Geneva; possible ties between Duvet and the alchemical dimension; and his role as architect. I have been fortunate enough to receive funds from Harvard University to conduct this investigation, from the Ford Foundation to present its findings in Paris, from New York University and the Centre National de la Recherche Scientifique for its revision and preparation for publication.

The author is indebted to the late Charles Seymour Jr. for his spirited sustenance at Yale, where the unforgettable Elizabeth Gee's universal rapport with prints was delightfully instructive. Egbert Haverkamp Begemann proved a hospitable counselor. I am grateful to Natalie Zemon Davis for her special knowledge of book production in the Renaissance. Jean Adhémar has generously provided advice and the Preface. Pierre Quarré and his wife were of constant help and encouragement in Dijon's museum and its library. Bengt Dahlbeck and Per Bjurström generously allowed the reproduction of the fête designs which they discovered and ascribed to Duvet. The staffs of the great European print rooms were always unfailingly kind. I hope none of these many helpers ever thought I took their hard and patient labors for granted.

Anne Hoy's mastery of Neo-Platonic theory was of great value. Rosemarie Garipoli's scrupulous editorial assistance, with the aid of Barbara Giella, Ann Plogsterth, Joy Kestenbaum and Eric Zafran, helped prepare the manuscript for publication. My thanks to Walter L. Strauss and Carol Sobelsohn for their good offices at Abaris Books. Pierre Berès kindly applied to the Centre National on my behalf; Mmes. Sylvia Winter and Myra Orth proved instrumental in making the manuscript available for publication.

Melancholia, so closely linked with creativity and imagination and the black art of printmaking has taken a tragic toll of Duvet's earlier scholars. I hope this work may prove partially worthy of their labors, and those of E. Jullien de la Boullaye, whose archival research and first study are fundamental to our knowledge of the artist.

Colin Eisler
Robert Lehman Professor
New York University
Institute of Fine Arts

THE MASTER
OF THE
UNICORN

ABBREVIATIONS

A   Albertina, Vienna
AIC   Art Institute, Chicago
B   Bartsch, Adam van. *Le peintre-graveur.* Vienna, 1803-1828.
BM   British Museum, London
BN   Bibliothèque Nationale, Paris
IFF   Inventaire du Fonds Français, Paris
NG   National Gallery, Washington
LC   Library of Congress, Washington
RD   Robert-Dumesnil, A.P.F. *Le peintre-graveur français,* V. Paris, 1841

I.

LIFE AND TIMES OF JEAN DUVET

By the end of the fifteenth century, Dijon had long occupied a unique place in European art. The art of the Burgundian capital was distinguished by a precise opulence, and an intricate fusion of Northern and Southern talents drawn there by the prodigious wealth of its ducal court. Abounding in craftsmen ready to produce the most richly devised works to suit a royal fancy, Dijon dwindled into a depressed economy after the killing of Charles the Bold, defeated at the battle of Nancy in 1477. Gunsmiths rather than goldsmiths were the order of the day. Surrounded by monuments of past glories — the sculpture of Sluter, the vast number of abbeys, chapels, and churches — Dijon was characterized both by nostalgia for past splendor and anxiety for the uncertain future as the fifteenth century drew to a close. Into this shrinking Burgundian world, Jean Duvet was born in 1485, the same year as Luther, whose faith he was to follow, and two years after Raphael, whose works he was to copy.

The earliest known French engraver, Jean Duvet created an intensely personal yet strongly derivative oeuvre that developed over six decades, providing an uniquely comprehensive artistic odyssey through the worlds of late Gothic, Renaissance and Mannerist styles. He was first active in Dijon and in Langres, the nearby episcopal seat and bastion. Curiously, Langres has documents of the first French woodcutter, who cut the coat of arms or emblem of Tours in 1365. Burgundy has continued to be notable for its early concern with this reproductive art. In 1393, the Comptes des Ducs de Bourgogne cited a Jehan Baudet, *charpentier*, who followed designs by Jean Beaumetz, the Netherlandish painter active at the Chartreuse de Champmol, near Dijon.[1]

Jean's father, Drouot Duvet, a prominent goldsmith and resident of the parish of St.-Médard, apprenticed him to the celebrated if declining school of the Burgundian *orfèvrerie*. In addition to their skills as jewelers and sculptors of precious metals, goldsmiths were often familiar with other techniques such as gilding, engraving, enameling, damascening. Some of these versatile craftsmen were also employed as coin and medal-makers, their repertoire occasionally encompassing those of the graphic artist and designer of armor. As we shall see, these various skills allowed Duvet the freedom to move in whatever circle he chose.

The dissolution of the ducal court, coupled with the Wars of Succession, created further economic crises in Burgundy. By the end of the century, many local craftsmen petitioned Dijon for tax reductions, stressing their financial straits. Among these appeals was one from Drouot Duvet (App. E, Doc. 2) who, despite having received a major commission from the abbey of St.-Etienne in 1495 (App. E, Doc. 1). characterized himself as a poor man, unable to make a living.

Splendor of contemporary triumphal entries and other official pageantry seems to have been in inverse ratio to the economic depression then prevalent in Burgundy. The government policy preferred staging circuses to distributing bread.[2] One such entry was planned six years after Drouot Duvet made his plea for tax reduction. The Officials of Dijon commissioned him to make two silver-gilt sweetmeat dishes which were to be presented to Louis XII and Anne de Bretagne (App. E, Doc. 5). This event was described by an anonymous chronicler as an unusually magnificent enterprise, since it celebrated the first local appearance of the new monarch.[3] Five special open air stages or *échafauds*, located at strategic points along the processional route were built for the occasion. *Tableaux-vivants*, complete with mechanically operated mythological beasts, and elaborately costumed groups symbolizing classical, Biblical, and historical heroes, virtues, and victories were assembled on these stages to reflect and enhance the celebrated arrival of the new king and queen. These allegorical representations, known as *mystères*, employed many participants who were often seen against a painted or tapestried backdrop. While the triumphal entry officially culminated in a great service at the cathedral, the popular high-point of the ceremony occurred when the king came to a stage from which the actress personifying Dijon stepped down to present the monarch with the rich silver gift wrought by Drouot Duvet. This demonstrated the fealty and regard in which Louis XII was held.

Jean's father, who may have been one of the most esteemed craftsmen of Dijon, also had a hand in planning the five *tableaux-vivants* that showed Louis XII uniting in his exalted person the classical virtues of antiquity with those of Christianity. The five major phases of world history were presented in dramatic form. Each was described by an identifying inscription—the *escriteau* below. In later years, Jean Duvet also became an accomplished producer of the intricate, elaborate scenery for the program of the triumphal entry and its *mystères*. Most probably, he received his first lessons in scenic design from his father.

One goldsmith and assayer to the Mint, Philibert Duvet, is also listed in 1506 as living in Drouot Duvet's parish. (App. E, Doc. 6), near the abbey of St.-Etienne which belonged to the diocese of Langres and employed both the Drouot, first father, then son. Jean, who is known to have worked in the Mint in Geneva, also executed coinage for Gruyère toward the middle of the century. This is discussed again in Chapter III. Jean may well have been trained in these skills by his neighboring relative Philibert, at whose address he appears to have resided in 1520 (App. E, Doc. 13).

In 1509, Jean, together with his older brother Loys Duvet, received his *lettres de maîtrise* as a master craftsman of Dijon. It was on this occasion, when at the age of twenty-four, Jean Duvet is recorded as the son of "Drouot DuVay" (App. E, Doc. 7) and as receiving free admission to the guild where his older brother was already a member. By this time, if not earlier, he may have been active as a print-maker, although no surviving works are dated before 1520. On stylistic grounds, several smaller engravings seem to stem from the first decades of the century (Cats. 1-10). These prints, which are signed with the artist's initials, in Gothic letters, show him to have been in close contact with contemporary Netherlandish and German graphic arts. They represent the first engravings securely identified as the work of a French artist, and were probably prepared when Duvet was in his mid-twenties.

In 1513, Drouot Duvet was again in financial difficulty and appealed to the town council for aid, claiming that he had neither "ceuses, ni rentes dont il puisse nourrir lui, sa femme, et son mesnaige, sinon de son' mestier au jour de la journée" (App. E, Doc. 9). In that year the Battle of Dijon brought many Northern troops to Burgundy, including the great Swiss graphic artist Urs Graf. Remunerative commissions were hard to come by; once obtained, they were subject to royal review and approval. Combined with the economic depression, this probably accounts for the goldsmiths turning toward related crafts and techniques involving less costly media. In 1506, Louis XII required that every important goldsmith's project be submitted for royal approval. Strong protests, especially from provincial goldsmiths who were the hardest hit by this edict, forced its repeal in 1510.

Pages of learned Burgundian journals have been filled with lengthy disputes as to whether Jean Duvet should be regarded as a native son of Langres or Dijon. The fact that he described himself in 1555 as "Aurifaber Lingon" (goldsmith of Langres) on the frontispiece of the *Apocalypse* Series (Cat. 65) encourages local historians of this small citadel to claim him as their own. However, the word "Lingon" in no way implies birth within the episcopal seat.[4] Jean Duvet's early training took place in Dijon in the diocese of Langres. Dijon was his probable birthplace and that of his ancestors. At that time, Langres was very large and included Burgundy, the Comté and most of the Champagne. The archival entries for the engraver's residence in Geneva refer to him as a Dijon citizen (App. E, Doc. 40), and indicate that that city was his birthplace.

Bishop Boudet of Langres, who ruled from 1512 to 1529 purchased a *hôtel* in Dijon which he bequeathed to his domain. Both he and his successor Claude de Longvy, the future Cardinal de Givry, were abbots of St.-Bénigne and St.-Etienne in Dijon, providing further links between Dijon and Langres. Since the engraver's father was employed by the two abbeys (App. E, Doc. 2, 11), he may have first brought Jean Duvet in touch with Langres. Boudet, an important figure at the court of Louis XII was in contact with advanced currents of humanistic thought. Appointed bishop of Langres in 1512, Boudet was praised two years later in Budé's *De asse et partibus* and appears to have been a patron of Oronce Finé, who dedicated a mathematical study to him. Both Nicolas Bourbon and Etienne Templier inscribed poems to Boudet, who was also an associate of Cardinal Aleandro, an important propagator of humanistic studies in France.[5] From about 1513-19 Duvet adapted Italian works of the late fifteenth century such as plaquettes by Moderno (Text fig. 1).

Boudet's episcopal court was one of the many French provincial centers of religion distinguished for its sympathy for the new learning in the early decades of the sixteenth century, recalling the milieu of the Franciscan abbey of Fontenay-le-Comte and the Benedictine cloister of Maizellais where a similar but more cautious concern with Renaissance thought contributed to the formation of François Rabelais. Duvet's first signed and dated work, the brilliant *Annunciation of 1520* (Cat. 12), is without French parallel for its accomplished, audacious use of Italian High Renaissance form. It may have been partially inspired by the cosmopolitan character of Boudet's episcopal court and by a possible Italian journey.

The major relic of Langres' cathedral of St.-Mammès, the head of its titular saint, is recorded as having been placed in a new setting of precious metal by Jean Duvet (App. E, Doc. 17). Unfortunately, it no longer exists. According to a copy of the original document pertaining to the costly project, many donations were needed for it to be commenced in 1500. This date would preclude the engraver's taking a leading role in the work, since at the time he was only fifteen. However, as his father is known to have received important commissions from the two Dijon abbeys under the direction of Langres, it was probably Drouot Duvet who began the lengthy task of devising an appropriately splendid setting for this relic, and Jean who completed it in 1524. Furthermore, although the year 1500 is often discounted due to the seemingly inordinate length of time needed for the reliquary's manufacture, it may be correct as these lavishly planned projects were much delayed because further donations were needed. These schemes often necessitated time-consuming changes in design. The only surviving work to resemble the description of the St.-Mammès head is a reliquary bust of Saint Lambert at Liège, which was begun under the Chancellor of Burgundy in 1469.[6] Over thirty-six years elapsed before the project really got under way, and even with the collaboration of several craftsmen, seven additional years of labor were needed for its completion.

When François Ier made his first major formal entry at Langres in 1519 to survey the fortifications initiated by his father-in-law Louis XII, Duvet's name was not mentioned in any of the reports connected with this important event.[7] As these entries usually necessitated the participation of all skilled craftsmen in the vicinity, especially in a town the size of Langres, the omission of his name from the accounts suggests that Duvet was not in Burgundy at the time. If the artist made an Italian journey, the year 1519, when he had every reason to be employed at Langres, provides the most logical date for this trip, coming as it does just one year before the unprecedented Italianate *Annunciation of 1520* (Cat. 12). He may also have gone with French troops to Italy at an earlier date, to acquire or develop important skills in military engineering.

Duvet's interest in armor and fortifications emerges from his engravings and

1. *Moderno*, Saint Sebastian, *London, Victoria and Albert Museum.*

2. *Raphael*, Two Sibyls, *1516, Rome, Sta. Maria della Pace.*

suggests that he accompanied the French armies to Italy at some point between 1500-25. Support for this assumption lies in the Lombard aesthetic orientation of several of his prints. The "Milanese" style accounts for the fact that four engravings which originate in that region have long been regarded as Duvet's own (App. I, 1-4). Duvet's expertise in damascening—an usual craft for France but current in Northern Italy—coupled with his donation of various weapons probably wrought for a Langres war chest in 1524 (App. E, Doc. 18), also indicate familiarity with military life. The drastic stylistic change from early, *Kleinmeister*-like engravings such as the *Entry of Christ into Jerusalem* and *Expulsion of the Moneychangers* (Cats. 1-2) to a full-blown High Renaissance form may also point to an Italian journey. Several of his rarest early Renaissance engravings are in Pavia and Florence, and may even have been executed in their environs.

The brilliant *Annunciation of 1520* (Cat. 12) has all the qualities of heroic classical pageantry one would expect from a designer of *entrées solennelles*. It confers on the thirty-five year old Duvet the unofficial title of the most proficient and inventive master of Italian High Renaissance art in France. Further support of Duvet's precocity is found in his reproduction of Raphael's *Cumaean Sibyl* (Text fig. 2) which has an illegible date scratched on it reading 1517 or 1519 (Cat. 8).[8] Very possibly Duvet was in Italy in that year, working directly after Raphael's Roman fresco of 1516 in the Chigi Chapel, of Santa Maria della Pace.

It is only after Drouot Duvet began his work for St.-Bénigne in 1520 (App. E, Doc. 11) that there is documentation of Duvet's own activity in Langres. He is recorded as assistant to Nicolas Ladmiral, the *facteur* or pageant-master for the second triumphal entry of François Ier, in April 1521.[9] The artists met to decide on what gifts they would prepare for the royal presentation, and also to plan a series of allegorical *tableaux-vivants*. The town of Langres held a dinner for all those who had been consulted in the production of the "mistères qui se feraient à l'entrée du roy nostre seigneur" (App. E, Doc. 14). Langres—best known as a center for cutlery—lacked a distinguished goldsmith of its own, although "Perrenot l'argentier et Guyot fils de celui-ci, orfevres" were included among those who conferred with Duvet about the gift presentation. Previously entrusted with the completion of the town's most important goldsmith's commission, the reliquary head of St. Mammès, Jean Duvet was regarded as the most qualified to make the royal presentation gift. In 1521, Duvet was still listed as maintaining a residence in the parish of St.-Médard in Dijon. (App. E. Doc. 13). He was probably called to Langres for the entry preparations.

Upon the occasion of this 1521 entry, François Ier may well have appointed the thirty-six year old artist *orfèvre du roi*.[10] It is likely he knew of Duvet's exceptional skill as a goldsmith. On the other hand, the engraver could have received this honor during either of the royal visits of 1529 or 1534, where there is evidence of his having assumed a still more important role.[11] For the 1521 entry Duvet worked together with Etienne Thomas, an otherwise unknown painter, and two goldsmiths, under the direction of Nicolas Ladmiral, who wrote and produced the program. Deliberation over the most suitable gift for presentation ceased when a silver heart set within a lily was chosen to symbolize how Langres, a "royal" diocese, put all her heart into protecting the *fleur-de-lys*.

Two great columns were erected at the city gates, probably emblematic of the Pillars of Hercules and royal power. Langres was the foremost fortress of France's eastern border. The wooden columns were nineteen feet tall, crowned by richly ornamented bronzed capitals three feet high. This theme of strength was also represented to the right of the gate by a personification of *Force aliée à Prudence*—a maiden clad *à l'antique*, one foot resting on a gilt wooden lion (Force), the other upon a serpent (Prudence). She signified the supremacy of Langres: excellent fortifications, martial spirit, prudence and good government. *Ferme Foi*, at the left column, held a sword in her right hand and a *fleur-de-lys* in the other, indicating Langres' loyalty to the king and her maintenance of the Royal Standard. An allegory of this type anticipates Duvet's own later engravings, such as *Henri II as the Victorious Saint Michael* (Cat. 62).

Above the portal were two pillars forming a tabernacle sheltering a triumphal throne in a bower, where a little girl, symbolizing Diligence, held a silver bowl filled with violets, rosemary, mint, laurel, and orange leaves. These she scattered over the royal cortège as they entered the citadel.[12]

A gorgeously costumed maiden, representing Langres, was seated upon a throne brilliant in its decoration. Her two attendants were clad in silver-gilt armor, bearing silver batons. These metal trappings, like the bowl held by Diligence, may have been fashioned by Jean Duvet. As the king passed the stage upon which Langres was seated, she rose to recite a *rondeau* and to present him with the silver gift. François Ier had previously received identical *objets* from Dijon and Mâcon, but managed a grateful smile nonetheless, according to a contemporary account.[13]

The final stage for the entry of 1521 bore a hundred-twenty little boys who held miniature wooden halberds. When the king and his court were received by Bishop Boudet at the portal of the cathedral, they cried "Vive le Roy." The bells rang out, accompanied by cannon fire, the sounding of trumpets and the roar of drums, all of which contributed to the gladsome noise. That evening the king climbed the foundations of the future ramp tower known as the Tour d'Orval and examined the fortifica-

5

tions of Langres whose construction may have been designed by Duvet (See App. G), as his engravings show great concern with armor and military architecture.

Three years after the entry of 1521, the great reliquary head of St.-Mammès, quite literally Duvet's *chef-d'oeuvre*, was finished (App. E, Docs. 3, 17). Working within an essentially late medieval program, the goldsmith followed a model opposed by recent taste, reflecting an enforced continuity with the past.

Duvet demonstrated his knowledge of dye-making and metal-casting by designing and presumably executing a commemorative medal of Pope Adrian VI in 1524. What appears to be a preparatory print shows the pope's portrait bust (after Marcantonio) on one side and an allegory of the Triumph of Divinity on the other. (Cats. 13, 14). Only the unique impressions of the engravings for this medal are preserved. These prints, together with the coins Duvet minted during his Genevan period (App. E, Doc. 57) and a seal and *jeton* (Text fig. 3) for Cardinal de Givry (App. D, 1-2), are the sole surviving visual evidence of his documented activity as *médailleur* and *tailleur de la monnaie*.

3. *Jean Duvet,* Silver Medal, *for Chambre de Comptes of Langres, Paris, Bibliothèque Nationale, Cabinet des Médailles.*

By 1524, Duvet's residence in Langres is assured by the inclusion of his name on a list of *bourgeois* contributors of military equipment to a war chest (App. E, Doc. 18). It may seem unlikely for a goldsmith to have made military equipment, shovels, and hatchets, but it was well within his ability to do so and in keeping with Duvet's concern for fortifications. As a goldsmith, he was familar with certain aspects of the armorer's craft, such as gilding, casting, and engraving.

Between 1522 and 1525 Duvet received payment for a silver casket bearing the arms of Langres to contain the town council's seals (App. E, Doc. 19), which were probably designed and executed by the artist as well. The exact location of Duvet's residence in 1527 is given on an assessment list made for the payment of François Ier's Spanish ransom. (App. E, Doc. 2). Negotiations for the king's release were conducted by Amiral Chabot, governor of Burgundy and a probable patron of the artist.

Duvet's most important local source for Renaissance thought may well have been Federico Fregoso, who was appointed abbot of the ancient Benedictine abbey of St.-Bénigne at Dijon by François Ier for ten years beginning circa 1527.[14] A native of Genoa, where his brother was first elected Doge in 1513 and then appointed governor by the king of France, Fregoso was a friend of Bembo and Sadoleto and included in Castiglione's *Cortegiano* (Book I, 5) as one of the intellectual ornaments of the court of Urbino. He is known to have commissioned magnificent choir stalls "tout à l'antique" for his abbey in 1527.[15] Fregoso may have shown Duvet Italian engravings or other models in order to give the goldsmith an idea of how he wished his donations to look.

Duvet probably continued his father's association with the Treasury of St.-Bénigne (App. E, Doc. 11) after the latter's death in 1530.

In 1528 Duvet executed four dated engravings: *Saint John the Baptist and Saint John the Evangelist* (Cat. 24), *Allegory of the Power of Love* (Cat. 26), *The Entombment* (Cat. 25), and *Rest on the Flight into Egypt* (Cat. 23). His mature style was fully realized by the age of forty-two, when, judging from the style and technique of these engravings alone, he must have been equally conversant with the graphic arts of both Italy and the Lowlands. The subject matter of the *Allegory of the Power of Love* (Cat. 26), indicates a knowledge of contemporary translations of classical texts. It also suggests employment of the new humanistic studies developed by the erudite canons at Bishop Boudet's court of Langres, as well as Fregoso's abbey in Dijon.

During the late 1520's and throughout the succeeding decade, one of the first major Renaissance buildings in Burgundy was under construction—the château of Pagny, situated twenty-three miles south of Dijon. Pagny was built for the Longvy family, two of whose members, Claude and Françoise, uncle and niece were to be of great importance for the development of Langres.[16] By her marriage to Philippe Chabot in 1527, Françoise united her already influential family to one of the most powerful men in France. Outstanding as soldier, statesman, governor, and ambassador, Chabot was for many years almost as important a figure as the Connétable de France, Anne de Montmorency.[17] Claude was to become Cardinal de Givry.

The far-flung, eventful careers of both Chabot and his uncle by marriage, Cardinal de Givry (who was in Langres by 1530), brought the episcopal seat of Langres and Dijon close to the center of French authority in the third and fourth decades of the sixteenth century. While Chabot's patronage of art was not comparable to that of Montmorency, the major surviving indication of his taste, the magnificant screen of 1538 from his chapel at Pagny (Philadelphia Museum of Art) is certainly one of the most important early monuments of the French Renaissance (Text figs. 4, 5).[18] Equally indicative of

4. Choir Screen, *1530-40, from Château de Pagny, Philadelphia Museum of Art.*

5. Detail of Choir Screen: Tempietto on Canopy of the Virgin, *from Chapel at Château de Pagny, Philadelphia Museum of Art.*

the sophistication of Chabot's patronage was the park surrounding his château, which included a grotto of 1529 whose walls were painted with scenes from Ovid's *Metamorphoses* and depictions of the Four Seasons, a marble Bacchus within. Like the splendid grotto still surviving at Bastie d'Urfé, the garden architecture of Pagny suggests that its rustic style may have been in advance of French royal taste.[19] As Givry contributed heavily to the embellishment of Pagny, the château and its chapel must also indicate the Cardinal's *avant-garde* inclinations.

Thus, for artists and craftsmen active in the patronage circles of Chabot and Givry in the 1530s and 1540s, the environs of Dijon may have offered a cosmopolitan milieu, comparable in scope if not in quality to the ducal commissions at the beginning of the preceding century and a worthy successor to the breadth of scholarly and cultural concern evinced by Langres' Bishop Boudet and Abbot Fregoso in the previous decades of the sixteenth century.

In 1529, the name of the forty-four year old engraver appears on the *Compte deuxième* of Claude Haligre, "trésorier des menuz plaisers et affaires de la chambre du Roy nostre signeur" (App E. Doc. 23), for a bowl commissioned by the king, decorated with gold and silver inlay "à la moresque." François Ier purchased the damascened bowl on the occasion of his second visit to Dijon. Its technique was introduced to the French court by Milanese armorers of the early sixteenth century and was still regarded as a foreign craft in 1529.[20] The phrase "démourant à Dijon" on the receipt of payment for the damascened bowl suggests that the engraver may have lived with his parents there, while maintaining a separate residence in Langres where a major change in patronage had taken place, due to the death of Bishop Michel Boudet.

In the year 1530, Drouot Duvet's widow petitioned to reduce her tax payments by half, the remainder payable by her son, now residing in Langres (App. E, Docs. 24, 25). His father's death and the appointment of Claude de Longvy (previously bishop of Mâcon) at Langres may explain Duvet's decision to again center his activities in the little episcopal town, which under Longvy's leadership was rapidly developing a reputation for discriminating patronage of the arts and letters.

François Ier made another triumphal entry to Langres in 1533, accompanied by Eléonore d'Autriche and his three sons from his previous marriage: the Dauphin François, duc de Bretagne; Charles, duc d'Angoulême; and Henri, duc d'Orléans, who was to be Duvet's future patron. On this occasion, "Jehan Duvet di Drouot" is again recorded as having made gifts for presentation to the queen and the three dukes, functioning once more as the expert organizer of pageants. While the archives fail to contain any description of the gifts, Duvet's first biographer, the archivist Boullaye discovered five receipts signed by the engraver for funds and materials given him by the town council early in January 1533 for the preparation of of the gifts (App. E, Docs. 26-30), made with the assistance of a goldsmith from Chaumont.

Boullaye's research reveals Duvet to have been very much in command of the entry preparations. The Langres carpenters, who were to construct the three temporary outdoor stages, recalled that the decisions as to where and how these platforms were to be erected were "déliberée en la Chambre de ladite ville, en presence de Jehan Drouot qui guidoit et conduisoit ledit affaire" (App. E, Doc. 32). Costumes, sets, even special mechanical effect and purchases of materials were under Duvet's supervision.

Working together with a poet, sculptor, painter, embroiderer, and several other artists, Duvet brought to life the emblematic imagery of poet and playwright. Renaissance courtly imagery may have been popularized in Burgundy by Fregoso, who was described by Castiglione as excelling in the "emblem game" when at the court of Urbino.[21] Goldsmith's work, like so many other art forms of the sixteenth century, was often a fusion of these "devyses," an assemblage of appropriate symbols. The very specific reference to "Drouhot l'argentier" as having originated "le devys" of a little boy clad in black silk as the personification of Peace, characterizing the mourning for those lost in the recent war, indicated that Duvet assisted the anonymous poet who is known to have participated in the planning of the *mystère*. The *Allegory of the Power of Love* (Cat. 26), engraved by Duvet three years earlier, probably illustrated a classical text. Either he himself was familiar with such literature or else worked in close association with a learned member of the episcopal court at Langres. Jean Lefèvre, Cardinal de Givry's secretary, may have prepared some of the "devyses." Translator of the first French edition of Alciati's *Emblèmes*, published three years after the entry of 1533, the ingenious Lefèvre is known to have been interested in painting and clockmaking and was a likely source of literary inspiration.[22]

Another possible source for Duvet's dramatic subjects may have been Canon Guillaume Flameng. Born in Flanders in the mid- fifteenth century, Flameng was attached to Langres prior to Bishop Boudet, whose triumphal entry he directed in 1512, composing and staging a special *bérgèrie allégorique* for the occasion.[23] Contributor to most of the dramatic productions at Langres, Flameng wrote *La Vie et Passion de Saint Didier* in 1482, the most elaborate mystery play to that date.[24] Employing almost as many mechanical staging devices as it did actors, the drama exhausted the facilities of even the Parisian theaters.[25] Flameng, with his Netherlandish background, must have been of interest to Duvet, whose earliest engravings follow those of the North. Much of the artist's engraved oeuvre drew upon such literary sources as Flameng. Canon Flameng, provided the program for Cardinal Givry's great *jubé* in the cathedral of St. Mammès, suggesting that it be made "en arch triomphal à trois arcades," the victorious motif which arch triomphal à trois arcades," the victorious motif which characterizes the bulk of

Givry, as bishop of Mâcon, had sponsored works on Ovid and studies of local Roman antiquities,[27] and thus may well have been interested in the abundant Roman ruins in his new diocese (Text fig. 6). Indicative of the relatively tolerant atmosphere at the episcopal court of Langres was Claude de Longvy's patronage of the Latin poet Nicholas Bourbon, whose clearly Protestant sympathies are discernible in the *Nugae Poeticae* of 1533, two of which are dedicated to Givry. The poet may well have been an associate of Duvet's since both were linked to Langres and Lyons, mutually concerned with the Reformation and the graphic arts.[28]

6. Roman Triumphal Arch, *formerly visible at Langres.*

Langres' most splendid *entrée solennelle*, which began on January 12, 1533, lasted fifteen days and was preceded by almost as many months of preparation.[29] Not only was this the royal entry of François Ier, but it also heralded the first appearance of Claude de Longvy as Cardinal de Givry since receiving the hat of Sant 'Agnese in Agone from Clement VII at Marseilles. The event was far more explicitly a Roman triumph than its predecessors, even though they had stressed the martial aspects of the episcopal bastion. The first visual tribute of Langres to François Ier in 1533 was a temporary tower designed and erected by Duvet at the base of the recently rebuilt Porte des Moulins, the reconstruction of which, like most contemporary military architecture of Langres, may have been in the artist's charge (See App. G). The gold-lettered plaque at the base of the festival tower was inscribed TURRIS FORTITUDINIS A FACIE INIMICI. The first of three stages, forty feet in length and hung with tapestries, appeared nearby, decorated with painted festoons and gold-lettered inscriptions. Enthroned upon the stages were three ladies of Langres, representing Juno, Pallas, and the citadel, each holding an identifying shield and clad in an antique style. Their splendid mantles of gold cloth lined with white damask were lent by three of the local churches. The character of the French provincial Renaissance is captured by this classical trinity whose costumes came from church vestments. The coexistence of antique and Christian motifs of triumph extended to include Judith bearing the head of Holofernes and brandishing a scimitar.

The second and most important stage was placed at Champeaux; eighty feet in length, it supported a "montagne," created by a great "lys artificiel" twenty feet in height, with the arms of the king, queen and three princes, surrounded by their orders and topped by a tiara. Trees bearing forty *écussons blassonnés des princes chrétiens* were placed at each side of the giant lily for support, Ceres, sheaves of golden wheat in her hair, held a silver-gilt cornucopia, de Givry's emblem; both may have been made by Duvet. She was seated on a golden throne set in a tabernacle hung with cloth of gold taken from the "chappe et habite diaconnau de Saint Martin," "depecé" for the royal visit, a drastic reversal of the miracle of the Gallican saint. The goddess was shown with Bacchus, both symbolized the rich harvest of Burgundy and were surrounded by a circle of Langres' infants dressed or undressed as vine-wreathed putti rattling their *thyrsoi*. The wealth of classical allusions in this infant bacchanal again suggests the participation of Jean Lefèvre in the planning of the entry. His translation of the first French edition of Alciati's celebrated emblem book contains a little woodcut that is very close to the description of this scene, with staging reminiscent of the *tableau-vivant* enacted two years before its publication.[30]

The traditional *Vergier de Paix* was shown occupied by a windmill "à roue ailée en mouvement, dont la monture était représentée par du bresy et la farine par des feuilles d'or et d'argent." These leaves of gold and silver, in the precious garden "toute verdoyante," also appear to have been made by Duvet's workshop.[31] The windmill was not only decorative but also probably drove a pump for the elaborate water circulation machinery, the "ceuilx de beuf," designed by Duvet for Mars' galleon nearby. Duvet's talents as an engineer must have proved useful for the construction of these aquatic special effects.

Mars, clad in golden armor, stood at the helm of the galleon, a variation of the popular Ship of Fortune motif. The wooden galleon in full sail came to a tragic end, engulfed by a fiery abyss. Thereupon *Discorde* appeared, carrying a golden apple and a severed head which she threw into the abyss after the sinking ship. Seven *écriteaux* were ranged above the eight-foot-long stage, with the names *Amour, Paix, Concorde, Bacchus, Ceres, Mars, Discorde*.

The third platform presented the seven cardinal and theological virtues, placed before the church of the local martyr Saint Didier.

Duvet also designed and executed three decorative crowns for the king, queen and dauphin. François Ier's included the Order of St. Michael, and his queen's the royal crest. A recently discovered Duvet engraving after Agostino Veneziano *St. Michael Victorious* (Cat. 9 and Text fig. 7) may reflect the imagery of this triumphal entry in which the Order of Saint Michael, also carved on the walls of the Tour St.-Jean (Text fig. 8) was prominent. The relief may well have been conceived by Duvet, who appears to have played a decisive role in designing the fortifications of Langres and Geneva (see Appendix G).

The triumphal entry of 1533 staged for François Ier by Jean Duvet at Langres was the last documented activity of the engraver in France until 1544. Thus, at the age of forty-eight, the artist either left Burgundy or maintained a very low profile for over a decade. Officially recognized as pageant master and *orfèvre du roi,* entrusted with the most important local commissions, and probably closely involved with Burgundian fortifications, the biography of the pioneer engraver of the French Renaissance is hardly one to suggest a prolonged period of retirement at the height of his powers.

Upon François Ier's return to Paris after his triumphal visit to Langres, he began a drastic revision of governmental policies toward the suppression of Protestantism in France.[32] Earlier that year he had conferred with Clement VII at Marseilles, concerning the restriction of local opposition to the Catholic Church and indirectly to his own power. A special committee was set up in Paris to investigate and prosecute all forms of heresy in 1534, when Duvet seems to have left Langres. The artist may have been encouraged to do so by Calvinist missionaries who came to Langres from Meaux at just about this time, their leader leaving France in 1535.[33] With the ambivalence and calculations that characterized many of François Ier's political activities, he persecuted local Protestants, while claiming to offer them amnesty with the Treaty of Coucy (1536-38), in a diplomatic gesture toward a hoped-for German alliance. When the plans for the latter collapsed, so did the amnesty, if not sooner. Duvet's disappearance from the Langres archives in 1534 coincides with the *Affaire des Placards,* the sudden, fiercely repressive measures taken against Protestantism following the ill-timed and inflammatory *Articles véritables sur les horribles grands et importables abuz de la Messe Papale* posted all over Paris, Orléans, Tours, Rouen, Blois, and the gate of François Ier's château at Amboise during the night of Saturday-Sunday, October 18.[34] The papal legate in the city, the humanist and friend of Bishop Boudet of Langres, Gerolamo Aleandro, noted "There are thirty thousand Lutherans in Paris."[35]

Considering the turbulence of the times, the emergence of Jean Duvet's name in

7. *Agostino Veneziano,* St. Michael Victorious, *engraving after Raphael.*

8. Order of Saint Michael, *relief on Langres fortifications. Tour Saint-Jean (de Navarre)*

the archives of the four-year-old Republic of Geneva in 1540 (App. E, Doc. 34) is not as wildly implausible as it might appear. Geneva had a long history of Burgundian association in that it was allied to the duchy as early as 1475. Late nineteenth and early twentieth century scholars refused to admit that the Jean Duvets in Geneva and Langres were identical, dismissing the correspondence of name and craft as a coincidence. It was not until Henri Naef's work emerged that the Genevan and Burgundian information and activity began to be integrated.[36] The engraver's name is to be found in the records of Geneva and Langres over the next twenty-three years, entrusted with major commissions in the militant centers of Catholicism and Calvinism; and valued as a member of both communities in which he occupied important roles in civic and religious organizations. The Counter-Reformation within France was erratic and inconsistent. Total disagreement prevailed within the royal family itself. Protestant sympathizers were plagued by continual "cat and mouse" changes in policy, whose chief function seems to have been the insurance of a permanent state of anxiety and insecurity conducive to the most fervent display of orthodoxy and persecution.

In the late fifteenth and early sixteenth centuries there was considerable French resentment toward Rome; artists and writers, printers and producers were all relatively free to caricature and satirize, to publish and to perform works rife with anticlericalism. This liberal climate was marked by a major French commitment to the new humanism—the foundation of innovative academies designed to further studies of classical and Biblical languages and literature. Many members of the aristocracy and upper bourgeoisie became sympathetic to new theological and other scholarly currents, which were even more enthusiastically supported by the printers and other skilled craftsmen and artists. Those concerned with words and images and their communication seem to have been especially committed to the new thought of Calvin and Luther, although this may be simply due to the fact that their expression of faith was often recorded while that of the less professionally expressive groups was lost in anonymity and persecution. In the early 1530s, when an increasingly rigid opposition to Reformation became French policy, thousands were placed in the tragic situation of having to choose a life without their new faith or its exercise in exile.

Despite the hazards of joining the new faith, a reliable estimate shows that toward the middle of the sixteenth century two-thirds of the people of Burgundy were Protestant; this includes almost all the artists and craftsmen.[37] Nearby Lyon, the capital of French printing and an international mercantile center, was among the earliest and certainly the most outspoken centers of Protestant thought. In 1524, François Ier had already written the Pope of the menace posed by the new religious thought to both their reigns, singling out Lyons where "a vast number of people have been seduced and misled from the true and sound doctrine.[38] In that year the Dominican Aimé Meigret, member of the prominent Lyonnais family, was arrested by order of Claude de Lonvy, then bishop of Mâcon. The circumstances of the preacher's arrest illustrate the complexity of contemporary French attitudes toward the Reformation, since on the one hand Meigret received the support and protection of François Ier's sister Marguerite d' Angoulême, while on the other, this was crushed by the opposition of the conservative Queen Mother Louise de Savoie, with the bishop's counsel.[39] Additional members of Meigret's family joined the Reformation, as did several of the leading mercantile figures of Lyons who established themselves or their relatives in Geneva in the later 1520s and 1530s.

A major attempt to consolidate the Counter-Reformation forces was undertaken by the Council of Lyon convened by Pope Clement VII and including both Bishops Boudet and Longvy. The latter set up a new series of sixteen *décrets de foi* specifically designed to oppose Luther's theology. They included *De venerations sacrarum imaginum*,[40] but it was precisely among the image-makers and craftsmen that Calvinism had the greatest appeal.[41] Almost without exception, the distinguished French artists of the first half of the sixteenth century were, in varying degrees, sympathetic to the Reformation. Pierre Bontemps,[42] Jean Goujon,[43] Bernard Palissy,[44] Ligier Richier,[45]

Jean Cousin, were all associated with Protestantism. The outstanding mid-century print-makers were also linked to the Calvinist cause. In his craft of enameling, Limousin seems to have prepared a pantheon of portraits of Protestant theologians.[46] A Master of the Mint and goldsmith as well as a brilliant engraver, Etienne Delaune fled Paris in 1557, spending the following years in Strasbourg and Augsburg before returning to France and royal favor.[47] Son of a prosperous goldsmith and a member of the Lorraine aristocracy, Pierre Woeriot was the engraver of many portraits of Protestant writers and illustrated their works.[48]

Another aspect of the French artists' participation in the Reformation can be seen in the career of the sculptor Ligier Richier,[49] who worked in Lorraine, which was open to German influence. Especially famous for highly realistic, life-size, sculptural recreations of the Lamentation and the Entombment, his dramatic art appealed to many religious communities throughout Northeastern France. During this period when he carved these Catholic devotional images, Richier was a Calvinist. In 1543 he was elected mayor of St.-Mihiel. Richier designed triumphal entries; he prepared one for Charles IX in 1539. The following year he declared himself a Calvinist and for the next two years, actively campaigned for freedom of worship in Lorraine. By 1564 Richier was established in Geneva. His son, like Duvet's and Estienne's, remained in France working as a sculptor in his father's stead. Unable to practice his trade in Calvin's community, Richier used his substantial savings to establish himself as a money-lender. Thanks to his drastic change of profession, Richier was one of the very few French artists who managed to remain economically solvent while so near the fountainhead of their new faith.

The Edict of Fountainbleau, a severely restrictive decree of 1540, established a spy system throughout the country designed to root out all traces of Protestant thought and practice. Orders were given for the clergy to be closely watched, since they were suspected of laxity in the prosecution of Protestantism. The humanistically-inclined episcopal court at Langres may have been under suspicion, as it was situated on the "underground railway" escape route to Geneva. Even Cardinal de Givry's Vicar General of Burgundy was arrested for preaching heretical doctrine, and Antoine Franchot, who occupied the still more important post of Regent of the College of Dijon, fled to the Republic of Geneva in 1541.[50]

Duvet probably came to Geneva slightly more than two years before the major wave of immigration began in 1542. Geneva was only eighty miles away from Dijon, and once there Duvet took up residence near Calvin's home.[51] In addition to the imperatives of faith, the goldsmith could have left France to avoid the new restrictions imposed upon craftsmen in 1540 by François Ier, who repeated his earlier gesture in an attempt to control their output.[52] Immigration of artisans from Langres was not a rarity; between 1549 and 1560, at least fourteen Calvinists from the small episcopal seat took refuge in Geneva.[53] However, while her persecution of Protestants was approaching its peak, France was careful to maintain diplomatic relations with Geneva because the Republic functioned as an important international military clearing house. France and Geneva signed a treaty of perpetual peace in 1515. The Genevan printing industry, source of the Republic's only significant export, was careful to respect the French royal *privilèges* (copyrights).[54] These two areas were attracted by their mutual opposition to Charles V. Development of the Republic's fortifications was viewed with disinterest, if not benevolence, by France. The more impregnable Geneva became, the better it might function as a protection to French territory. Geneva's position as a buffer between the other Swiss and the French was accentuated by its republican status, evolved during the 1520s and achieved in 1536. Duvet is documented as being as closely concerned with the design of Geneva's fortifications as he appears to have been with those of Langres, and may have been engaged to work on the protection of Calvin's city with the tacit approval of François Ier and Givry. Committed to zealous opposition to the Reformation at home, king and cardinal might have closed their eyes to Duvet's strategic activities abroad. The engraver could scarcely have hoped to keep his appointment to the Conseil des Deux-Cents in 1546 (App. E, Doc. 51) a secret from France, nor could his and his wife's admission to the archconservative

Confrérie du Saint-Sacrement in Langres about four years later remain (App. E, Doc. 56) hidden from his Republican colleagues.

Duvet was closely associated with the most influential and aristocratic of Calvin's French adherents in Geneva, known as "les hommes Nouveaux." They were the reformer's militant avant-garde, who had advocated Calvin's spiritual leadership since the mid-1530s.[55] Outstanding among these were Laurent Meigret, known as *Le Magnifique*, and Claude Perrin. Shortly after Duvet's arrival in Geneva, Perrin was delegated by the Conseil des Deux-Cents to persuade Calvin, who was expelled from the city with Farel in 1538, to return permanently. Perrin succeeded in 1540,[56] when he was also Duvet's guarantor in October for partial payment given to the artist for his earliest known Geneva commission, minting coins. (App. E, Doc. 35). During the preceding month or earlier, Duvet had already been appointed *tailleur de la monnaie* from 1539, according to Henri Naef, who points out that Duvet's arrival must have been forwarded by "une reputation flatteuse" to merit such an important appointment from the Petit Conseil before even having received the rights of citizenship.[57]

It is typical of the innumerable paradoxes of the Reformation that Perrin, probably most responsible for bringing Duvet to Geneva, should have been that city's first and foremost iconoclast, whose destruction of devotional art in 1535 was instrumental in establishing the Reformation there.[58] Few artists drawn to Geneva could have hoped to exercise their skills in making religious images, since on Sunday, 21 May 1536, the Conseil General voted to adhere to Protestantism. All members did "promis et juré à Dieu par l'éslevation des mains en l'air que tous, unanimement, avec l'aide de Dieu, ainsi au'elle nous est annoncée, veuillans declaisser toutes messes et autres ceremonies et abusions papales, imaiges at idoles, vivre en union et obeissance de justice.[59]

Calvin's humanistic education included juridical studies under Alciati, the chief propagator of emblems, at Bourges in 1529.[60] These educational experiences coupled with his great mastery of literary style, are among the factors which may have kept him from sharing Zwingli's view that "We should be taught only by the Word of God; but the indolent priests, who should have been teaching us without respite, have painted doctrines on the walls, and we, poor simple ones, have been robbed of teaching thereby, and have fallen back upon images and have worshipped them.[61] Being Zwingli's junior by a generation, Calvin was far less willing to jettison the arts. It was under Calvin's direction that stained glass windows were ordered for the cathedral of St. Peter, which may have been designed by Duvet. The latter is also known to have prepared designs for the Church of the Magdalen and tapestries for the Maison de la Ville (App. E, Doc. 48).

In 1541, Duvet was paid "pource qu'il est homme expers az diviser des forteresses et dejaz as servye appres" (App. E, Doc. 36). He was also instructed to participate in the manufacture of a new series of *écus d'or,* an issue which has not yet come to light. Duvet's work pleased the Conseil, which voted him further payment and admission as bourgeois "gratis," characterizing him as an "home d'esperit" (App. E, Doc.39).

Jehan Droz, orpheuvre, Lequelt az vacqué az plesieurs journees az comprendre les forteresses de laz ville et en peintures en laz moyson de laz ville sans estre satisfayct . . . ;
Et pource qu'il est home d'esperit et sert vien en laz ville, resoluz qu'il soyt admys az borgeoys et juré de Geneva, gratis. Et az promys et juré.

Henri Naef pointed out that "comprendres les forteresses de la ville" meant architectural draftsmanship, a skill that was at a premium in Geneva and one for which the Conseil was always willing to grant rights of a bourgeois "gratis"; the Swiss scholar believed that the few surviving remnants of decorative wall painting at the Maison de la Ville were executed by Duvet.[62] The artist was probably also designer of the ramp associated with the same building (see App. G). In view of his extensive activities as pageant master and set-decorator at Langres, Duvet must have been well-qualified for the Maison's paintings. The style of these remaining fragments is a weak reflection of contemporary French work from this period, close to the ruined decorations of the château of Ancy-le-Franc, in the diocese of Langres.[63] Construction of the château commenced in 1555, at just about the time Duvet is known to have left Geneva permanently.[64] When the artist may have resumed his French residence, the château would have been ready for interior decoration. Therefore, he could have been associated with both buildings.

Duvet's occupation as *tailleur de la monnaie* and fortifications designer did not prevent him from also working as a goldsmith. On 13 August 1541, he received funds from the *trésorier d'état* to make a ring for Pierre Cullier of Basel, as a token of appreciation for his services as arbiter between Geneva and Berne. (App. E, Doc. 38). Three years later, Duvet was given a commission by the *Scindicques et Conseyl de Geneva* for two enamels (App. E, Doc. 43). The receipt of payment for these is especially important as it bears a signature in Duvet's own hand which is close to the monogram engraved on the double tablets in his prints (App. E, Doc. 44).[65]

Several months later another commission was contracted in which Duvet was referred to as *Jo. Dro, Dorier*, for three armorial enamels to be worn by the heralds of the *Seigneurie* (App. E, Doc. 45). Duvet depended on payment of thirty *écus* for his labor, but the Conseil was only willing to pay twenty-five (App. E, Doc. 46). Although a compromise was finally reached, considerable conflict must have existed when native Genevan thrift, coupled with Calvinist austerity, encountered lavish Burgundian craftsmanship accustomed to relatively unrestricted expenditure.

The year following Duvet's association with Perrin, the artist found himself working with Laurent Meigret, another outstanding French resident of Geneva, where he was an early champion of Calvin's cause.[66] Meigret was one of four extraordinarily dynamic and gifted sons of a Lyonnais notary. The others included Lambert, who was *trésorier et controleur général des guerres* by 1522. Jean, *avocat* at the Parlement de Paris, and Aimé, a brilliant Dominican preacher, were well-known for their Protestant sympathies. Following his older half-brother Lambert, Laurent became a favorite at the court of François Ier, where he soon became very rich as a money lender, probably using funds advanced by his father. Meigret's soaring wealth and popularity aroused the jealousy of the Connétable Anne de Montmorency who accused him of eating meat during Lent and on other prohibited days, a common charge at the time. As Meigret's half-brother Aimé was already identified with the Protestant cause, he was found guilty and imprisoned in 1532, the same year as was the poet, Clément Marot. After two years in jail Meigret was released; however, his property was confiscated, and he was banished for five years.

Meigret remained in contact with the French court when he took refuge in Geneva. He arrived there in 1536, when it was besieged by Charles III, Duke of Savoy, under whose dominion it had long existed. Meigret enlisted the military support of Bern which counterbalanced French power and led to the establishment of the Republic. In addition to his familiarity with fortifications, Meigret was concerned with alchemy and was listed as metal-worker in the Geneva archives in order to conform with the city's requirement that all immigrants be versed in a specific craft. Metalwork was no doubt a euphemism for Meigret's real interest, alchemy, which was not a highly regarded endeavor in Geneva, as it was associated there with the black arts and counterfeiting.[67]

Long concerned with the defense of Geneva, Meigret was entrusted with the inspection, maintenance, and improvement of fortifications in 1535, when construction workers were in short supply and military engineers even scarcer. Appointed to the Conseil des Deux-Cents in 1541, Meigret, together with another member of the mercantile aristocracy from Lyon, named Baudichon de Maisonneuve, was assigned to work together with Jean Duvet, "Jo droz expers en tel cas" (App. E, Doc. 37), on the building of a great earth work or *belluars* toward Pallex. Duvet may well have known both Meigret and Baudichon de Maisonneuve in France. Prior acquaintance with the latter is especially likely as he was closely connected with the printing industry and the dissemination of Protestant publications. The Republic maintained a diplomatic representative in Lyon. Both Geneva and the French city, connected by the Rhône were centers for book production where workers in this field went back and forth with relative impunity. Characterized as an "homme entreprenant, luthérien de la première heure et politician assez maladroit," Baudichon, an outstanding merchant in Geneva, had been arrested in 1534 at the Lyon trade fair when he was found to have several Protestant publications in his possession.[68]

On 8 June 1543, Duvet joined a "commission d'étude," which included Perrin, Claude Pertemps and Pernet DesFosses, appointed by the Conseil in order to study the fortification at Dôle, preparatory to designing additional ramparts for Geneva (App. E, Doc. 42). Pertemps and Pernet DesFosses were also among the Calvinist avant garde of Geneva. Appointed Treasurer in 1534, Pertemps became a part of the Petit Conseil two years later. Described in Bonivard's *Chronique* as "Homme d'ung grand esprit commun, sans soy estre adonné à l'estude des lettres, mais principalment en art de bastiment ou d'architecture,"[69] he sounds much like Duvet in character.

Among Naef's many discoveries in the Geneva archives was the record of a discussion in 1542 revealing the intensity of Duvet's participation in the beliefs of the Reformation, showing him to be the "home d'esprit" he had been characterized as in the preceding year (App. E, Doc. 39). On a summer evening in August, the artist was in a tavern together with his predecessor at the Mint, discussing the Gospel with a monk named Frère Noël from Cluse. Duvet must have convinced the latter of the Calvinist cause as he requested further instruction; this fact was reported to the Conseil. It was resolved that "monsieur Calvin et altres predicans doyae converser aveque luy et l'instruyre à vraye verité, affin de la povoyer retyre à Dieu et à sa parolle" (App. E, Doc. 41).

Two years later, Duvet returned to the heart of conservative Catholicism, taking part in a Langres cortège celebrating the Treaty of Crespy which was to end the conflicts between Charles V and François Ier freeing them both to fight the Turks (App. E, Doc. 47). The Treaty, which was bitterly opposed by the Dauphin, was of great importance to Burgundy since Charles V renounced the Burgundian claim in exchange for French withdrawal of all Italian territorial claims. Bringing about the conclusive union of Burgundy and France, the Treaty must have been an occasion for great panoply. It demanded Duvet's experience as a pageant master.[70] The Hapsburg accord initiated a new wave of Protestant persecution, since François Ier no longer concerned himself with propitiating Lutheran allies. He destroyed two Protestant centers: the towns of Calrières and Merindol in 1544.[71]

France and Geneva were deeply involved in fence-mending at just this time. The Republic sent agents from all levels, from ambassadorial to espionage to facilitate trade and provide strategic military information. These new negotiations and investigations involved Duvet's associates: Perrin, Meigret, and others, and very possibly included the artist himself. On 26 March 1544, Ami Perrin, together with J.A. Curtet was appointed to represent Geneva in a conference at Chambèry, Perrin reluctantly undertook this diplomatic commission.[72]

The Republicans were received with extreme cordiality at Chambèry and assured that "le roi aimoit fort une ville de Genève pour le plaisirs qu'en icelle on a fait à ses gens." By the phrase "his people," the king presumably meant the Swiss mercenaries which Geneva was willing to lodge en route to French service. Such hospitality was extended at considerable risk; the Republic and the Swiss cantons were often bitterly opposed.[73] It was suggested to Perrin that he seize Geneva with the aid of François Ier's troops in the name of France. Could Duvet's surprising appearance at Langres in 1544 have been merely coincidental when there was a resolution in Geneva that the Conseil send spies to Burgundy in the very same year, in order to obtain data concerning François' military plans in that region?[74]

Another reason Duvet may have returned was to see his eldest son Mammès, who was a French goldsmith (App. E, Doc. 73). Another son, Jean, was born in Geneva at an unknown date.[75] Moreover, the artist's considerable talents as pageant master could not have had much exposure in Geneva. Paradoxically, some of the creative pursuits forbidden in France as pro-Reformation were the same as those even more drastically curtailed in Geneva since they were opposed to Calvinist doctrine. Just as the great dramatic productions at the Hôtel de Bourgogne in Paris were discouraged, so were they in Geneva. Only one such drama, inspired by the Acts of the Apostles, was permitted public performance in 1546, no doubt because the playwright, the pastor Abel Pupin, was highly esteemed by Calvin.[76] Despite Calvin's authorization, the drama was attacked by the local clergy who came before the Conseil on July 12. They requested that the funds originally relegated to the production go to the poor instead.[77] The Conseil agreed to suspend any further performances of such plays, which might have provided Duvet with employment, until "le temps le plus propre," but this never came.[78]

Along with Duvet, several other outstanding printer-scholars, artists, and craftsmen of the mid-sixteenth century were forced to move back and forth between Geneva and France to earn a living, combining Catholic employment in a state repressing their new faith with residence in Geneva, which in turn, censored or condemned their native forms of expression and livelihood. Robert Estienne's career typifies their complex lives.[79] Son of the first French classical printer, Estienne was born in Paris in 1503. After apprenticeship he established his own highly successful press. Estienne went to Geneva just after publishing the New Testament in Greek in 1546. His son remained in Paris to carry on the business. In similar fashion, Duvet left his son Mammès in Langres when he went to Geneva. Throughout Estienne's self-imposed exile, the printer made many journeys to France, and as has been trenchantly observed, his "voyages frequents de Genève à Paris et de Paris à Genève, selon qu'il avait plus a craindre de l'intolerance des protestants ou de celle des catholiques."[80] The necessarily two-faced role of the contemporary artist and craftsman is most amusingly indicated by Plantin's publication of the annual Index which regularly included his own underground publications among the books prohibited. More than sixty French printers and book sellers came to Geneva between 1550 and 1557.[81]

After Duvet's participation in the Langrois cortège celebrating the Treaty of Crespy in 1544, his name next appears in Geneva on a contract of 1545 through which he accepted an orphan for four years' apprenticeship (App. E, Doc. 49). Further proof of Duvet's manifold activities in the Republic is found in a contract dated October 1, 1545 (App. E, Doc. 48) for designs of painted glass windows for the church of the Magdelen and tapestries for the Maison de la Ville. His style in such decorative media may be inferred from his mature engravings where the influence of the *peintre-verrier* is prominent. Unfortunately, the windows of the church were all destroyed and the tapestries of the Maison de la Ville have also vanished. Just as the very form and style of the *Apocalypse* Series (Cat. 36-65) anticipate evidence of window designs, so do the form and style of his Unicorn Series (Cat. 32-34, 66-68) imply a parallel participation in tapestry design. The latter may have been initiated under the prospective patronage of Henri II as a secular celebration of the king's love for Diane de Poiters and the chase, to be completed many years later as a mystical allegory.

The very considerable patronage Duvet received in Geneva should not be regarded as typical of the treatment accorded emigré artists. In the city's account of 1544, the smallest sum is that of thirty and a half florins, spent for painters, glassmakers, locksmiths, and saddlers.[82]

Compared to her sister Reformation center, Zurich, Geneva seemed hospitable to the arts, although Calvin agreed with Zwingli that there should be no images of God or any other representations of religious subject matter that could possibly be conducive to idolatry, devoting the eleventh and twelfth chapters of the first part of his Institutions to the subject. By 1523, Zwingli had articulated his total opposition to any form of art associated with worship; not until the mid-1530s could the new religious leaders of Geneva restrict the making or veneration of religious imagery.[83]

Both reformers agreed upon the legitimacy of history painting—what Zwingli referred to as "geschichteswyss"—as long as it was kept outside the places of worship and could not give rise to veneration.[54] Although Calvin was drawn to handsome civic architecture and had no basic objection to painting and sculpture, he had little use for the visionary and imaginative, stating "one should neither paint nor carve what could not be seen—that the gift of art was one for the transcription of the created."[55]

In 1545 Duvet applied for a more responsible appointment at the Mint or perhaps one concerned with fortifications, a confidential position that was usually reserved for citizens of Geneva. The records show him to have been somewhat grudgingly accepted on a temporary basis (App. E, Doc. 50). The following year he was elected to the important Conseil des Deux-Cents, to which he belonged intermittently until 1556 (App. E, Doc. 51) when he was seventy-one years of age.

Despite his activities in Langres, Duvet retained the confidence of the Geneva Conseil. This was evident from the artist's continued employment for fortification projects in 1546 (App. E, Doc. 52). Unable to hold the post of *essayeur de la monnaie*, Duvet maintained the office of *tailleur de la monnaie* until 1556. In this capacity he requested the Conseil to authorize the purchase of equipment formerly owned by the duke of Savoy (App. E, Doc. 54). In May 1549 and April 1550 he made requests for the "retaillon" scraps of gold and silver, the mint "sweep" (App. E, Doc. 54).

Since the *Privilège* (App. E. Doc. 68 and Text fig. 9), for Jean Duvet's engraved *Apocalypse*, dated 1556, stated that the artist began the Series ten years earlier at the request of François Ier, it would seem that the artist must have made another French journey around 1546. The *Apocalypse* was published in 1561 (Text fig. 10). At about

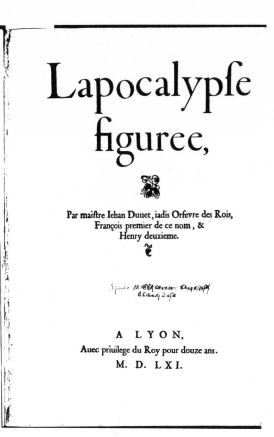

9. *Jean Duvet,* Privilège du Roi *from* L'Apocalypse figurée, *1561 edition, The Cleveland Museum of Art, Gift of Hanna Fund.*

10. *Jean Duvet,* Title Page *from* L'Apocalypse figurée, *1561 edition, The Cleveland Museum of Art, Gift of Hanna Fund.*

this time, if not earlier, he began his most ambitious secular project– the tapestry-like Unicorn Series. Apparently initiated in the late 1540s to suit the taste of Henri II and Diane de Poitiers, the chivalric cycle recalls the romantic revival of such texts as Amadis de Gaule, two editions of which were dedicated to the king's sophisticated mistress. It follows the style set by the print center at Fontainebleau in circa 1542 and found in the tapestries designed for the cathedral of Langres by Jean Cousin in the following year. (Text figs. 11, 12, 13)[86] but was probably started after 1547, when Luca Penni's biblical subjects were reproduced in print form.

11. *Jean Cousin*, Saint Mammès Preaching the Gospel to the Wild Beasts, *1543, tapestry, Langres, Cathedral St.-Mammès.*

12. *Jean Cousin*, Saint Mammès before the Tribunal of Cappadocia, *1543, tapestry, Langres, Cathedral of St.-Mammès.*

13. *Jean Cousin*, The Martyrdom of Saint Mammès, *1543, tapestry, Langres, Cathedral St.-Mammès.*

The engraver may have been in Langres in 1547 when, in the year of his death, the king conducted a last tour of inspection of the fortifications for which he had for so long shown so much concern. The monarch rode to the very top of the ramp of the Tour de Navarre, which was probably designed by Duvet. The construction of this edifice had been Francois Ier's special interest over the preceding decades.[87] At just this time, the diplomatic negotiations between France and Geneva were at their height, and Duvet's sponsor Perrin went on a mission in June 1547 concerning French taxation of textile vendors from Geneva. He brought letters to Cardinal de Givry's associates, Cardinal du Bellay, Marguerite de Navarre, the duc de Guise, Montmorency and Olivier. Perrin's mission proved successful; he was given royal patents forbidding Burgundy and the Dauphine from taxing the Republican merchants. Moreover, Perrin was invited to attend the coronation of Henri II at Reims, where Duvet's Langres sponsor, Cardinal de Givry, together with the Bishop of Beauvais and that of Reims, were the king's major attendants.[88] Upon Perrin's return to Geneva with a pension (his due from the deceased François Ier), his enemies had him jailed, claiming the fund to be a compromising gift from Henri II. Due to Meigret's intervention the venerable origin of the pension was established and Perrin was freed.[89]

According to other accounts, Meigret and Perrin were in conflict. Meigret may have operated as a double agent for Calvin and François Ier. An intimate friend of the first and former courtier, Meigret's informed liasions could have been to the mutual interest of all. His multitudinous business activities, whose precise nature has defied scholarly solution, might have operated as a cover for the transfer of funds or information. Enjoying access to French diplomatic pouches en route to their Swiss embassy, Meigret's many transactions gave rise to concern among his Republican colleagues and to wrath in Bern. Both he and Perrin were imprisoned for treason in the fall and winter of 1547 and were tried separately. Possession of an alchemical furnace was among the charges held against Meigret. Both men evinced interest in the same cause—stronger links with France. As each viewed himself as the exclusive agent for this mission, they frustrated one another. Meigret, more suave and intelligent than Perrin, probably exploited his knowledge of Perrin's somewhat muddled activities, informing upon them to the Petit Conseil to prove his own redoubtable citizenship. Three jurists were called from the other cantons for consultation. They freed Perrin but deprived him of all offices and banished him for two years and found Meigret to have been the French spy. Calvin, at great personal risk, came to the latter's defense before the Conseil des Deux-Cents which was largely opposed to Meigret. Three days later both Perrin and Meigret were reinstated. Conflict between the two flared up again in the next decade when it was Perrin who accused Meigret of French subversion.

Although Duvet's name does not appear among the artists participating in the entry of Henri II to Dijon on 1 July 1548, the engraver certainly had his king in mind, engraving the several prints relating to François's death (Cat. 63) and his son's coronation (Cat. 62) and role as saviour of the church (Cat. 64). Duvet's prints which are almost Counter-Reformation in iconography, because they include such archaic nationalistic references as the miracle of the dove at Clovis' coronation (Cat. 64), certainly parallel his new royal patron's mood; they were engraved afterwards with the *Apocalypse* Series begun under François Ier. The young king spoke at Saint-Bénigne—the church whose portal inspired Duvet's *Moses Surrounded by the Patriarchs* (Cat. 36)—making the highly conservative address expected by the Burgundians.

Almost four years after receiving the *Privilège* and completing the prints honoring Henri II, Jean Duvet is again documented in Langres, where he and his wife Jeanne were listed circa 1550 as members of the most conservative and elite Confrérie du Saint-Sacrement. This group was established about two years earlier (App. E, Doc. 56).[90] A distinguished historian, Canon Marcel, admitted that Jean Duvet of Geneva and Jean Duvet of Langres might well be one and the same. But, he insisted, if such were the case, Duvet's joining of the confraternity must have been an act of conclusive reconversion. Subsequent archival discoveries by Naef demonstrated that Duvet's Calvinist career was far from over.[91]

The artist may have been drawn to the confraternity by one of its functions, preserving holy images from destruction, including his masterpiece, the reliquary head of St. Mammès.[92] The confraternity met in a chapel built upon the site of the house used for secret Protestant services. The owner was condemned to death at the stake in Paris in 1548; his effigy was burnt at Langres. His followers who were for the most part artisans, met an equally ghastly fate, death by strangulation near the house where they had met.[93] Their bodies and condemned books were burnt, and their property, which reverted to the crown, was partially used for the chapel's construction. The confraternity was established by a doctor in 1548, shortly after Paul II had given major support to the chief chapter at the Dominican church of Sta. Maria sopra Minerva in Rome. He commissioned the major local monument of the High Renaissance, a splendid wooden Man of Sorrows attributed to François Gentil. The confraternity's "headquarters" in Rome housed Michelangelo's statue of the same subject.[94] The society's dedication to the veneration of the Eucharist, encouraged them to devote all funds to ostensories—elaborate reliquaries in which the Host was carried for Corpus Christi processions and other events. Duvet was probably included in the confraternity so that his talents as a goldsmith and pageant master might be exploited on its behalf.[95] The name appearing after those of the engraver and his wife Jeanne is that of "Jean Senault, peintre" (also possibly in the confraternity's employ), followed by that of Jean d'Amoncourt, the nobleman who was godfather to Jean Duvet's grandson.[96]

Shortly after his admission to the orthodox, Catholic lay society in Langres, Duvet's name reappears in Geneva, where he is again brought into a circle of aristocratic patronage. It was at this point that the Comte de Gruyère petitioned the Conseil des Deux Cents to allow Duvet to mint coinage for his principality in 1551 (App. E, Doc. 57).[97] This work may have come to Duvet through his association with Meigret who had successfully negotiated the establishment of good relations between Geneva and Gruyère. The count, upon discovering that his own minter, an alchemist called Battonat, was also a counterfeiter, turned to the Republic in 1552 for assistance in the production of his coinage. Duvet's work is of slight stylistic significance, conventional in design and crude in execution. It was withdrawn from circulation almost immediately upon issue in 1552, hence the coins are extremely rare (App. D.4).

A rather pretentious and unstable person, the Comte de Gruyère arranged secret meetings in 1547 with Henri II, Diane de Poitiers, and the Connétable de Montmorency to witness the wonders of his Alchemist.[98] Meigret, who was also interested in alchemy and in France at this time, might have known Battonat as well. As Master of the Mint in Geneva, Duvet was summoned to Battonat's trial as an expert witness (App. E, Doc. 61); his own alchemical concerns will be discussed in the next chapter.

"Jehan Drouhot, orphebvre" appears on a Langres tax record of 1552 and points to his return to the town in that year (App. E, Doc. 60). Artists and craftsmen such as Robert and Henri II Estienne and Ligier Richier also traveled between Geneva and their former French work-centers without injury. But such journeys involved great risk, judging by the case of an eyeglass-maker who, returning to France from Geneva, was arrested in Dijon in 1553, and executed.[99] The playwright Jean Michel met the same fate.[100] Duvet's special protection extended by both his French and Swiss patrons was probably due to his invaluable ability as designer of fortifications, and may have been implied in the text of his *Privilège* for the *Apocalypse figurée* (App. E, Doc. 68).

The careers of two mid-sixteenth century print-makers, Pierre Eskrich and Mathias Gerung, provide several parallels to Duvet's. Painter, print-maker, typographer and designer of embroidery, Eskrich was active in Lyon. He was employed by Guillaume Rouille, one of the few printers known for his staunch Catholicism.[101] Eskrich left for Geneva in 1552. He could not support his large family, and because of his battle with the governors of the poor fund when they refused him aid, he was jailed for his bellicosity. Pierre returned to Lyons alone in 1564 and worked as a pageant master on the triumphal entry of Charles IX[102] Eskrich had been employed in Geneva to illustrate Simon du Rosier's anti-Catholic polemic, and was engaged without hesitation by Rouillé in

Lyon to design several Books of Hours.[103] Despite his extended residence in Lyon, Eskrich was listed on Geneva records as a *bourgeois* and seems to have had no difficulties going back and forth between the two cities.

Gerung combined Catholic and Lutheran patronage with extraordinary facility, first working on a series of biblical illuminations at Nördlingen for the conservative Catholic Pfalzgraf Otto Heinrich. Gerung was also a tapestry designer like Duvet, and prepared cartoons for the Nördlingen Rathaus in 1551. His major work, a series of twenty-six Apocalypse woodcuts, was commissioned by Otto Heinrich in the very year that Duvet began his engravings on the same subject.[104] While engaged on the *Apocalypse*, Gerung was also working on a series of the most scurriously anti-papal caricatures of the time, the *Spottbilder* of 1548.[105]

Duvet's seeming theological schizophrenia or opportunist duplicity, when seen in the light of his contemporaries' similar lives, loses much of its improbability. By the middle of the sixteenth century, French Catholics depended upon a generation of artists for the creation and reproduction of images essential for its preservation and prestige, many of whom were secret Calvinists or his sympathizers. It is not to be wondered at that they could not make a break with their native faith and patronage. Such an act would often have involved acute financial deprivation by the sacrifice of their accustomed livelihood, as well as physical uprooting to Geneva whose intolerance was almost as extreme as that of France. Caught between the opposing tyrannies of Catholicism and Calvinism, Duvet struck his own bargain with both in his search for patronage and peace of mind. His complex career is paralleled by that of his twentieth century American confrères, the pageant masters and "moniteurs de mystères" of the cinema, many of whom, like the "Hollywood Ten," were persecuted and exiled for left-wing sympathies. This extraordinary climate of complicity and fear, limited in the Cold War years to "communications" industries, must in sixteenth century France have existed for the greater part of the artisan class, without whose works the "show" of the Renaissance culture could not have gone on.

Further evidence of the engraver's continued activity at the Genevan Mint is seen in an archival entry ordering that "honneste Jean Dro monstré la portray de aulcunes pieces" which were supposed to be struck in 1554 (App. E, Doc. 62).

14. Jean Duvet, Baton de Justice, *1555, Geneva, Maison de Ville.*

The final commission known to have been given to Duvet by the Conseil took place on 31 October 1553, when "syre Jehan de Vett die Dro" received seven florins for having prepared the baton of Geneva (App. E, Doc. 65). Naef has succeeded in locating what may well be this very baton (App. D.1 and Text fig. 14), the sole surviving example of Duvet's *oeuvre* as goldsmith.

That same year, the aged Duvet portrayed himself as a man of seventy on the Frontispiece to his *Apocalypse figurée* (Cat. 65). He was haunted by images of impending death yet sustained by the knowledge of victory over mortality in the completion of his greatest graphic work. In the guise of Saint John the Evangelist, Duvet is seated on an island before a heavily fortified city, which may represent the artist's self-imposed exile and lakeside residence "en la Revière dessous" (App. E, Doc. 51), where he lived from 1546 to 1553. In the next year, he and his wife moved "sus la pont du Rosne" (App. E, Doc. 67), conveniently located just to the left of the Mint. Inscribed "IOH. DVVT AURIFABER LINGON. ANOR. 70" who "HAS. HIST. PER FECIT. 1555," the print is Duvet's most important biographical document. The same year also witnessed the commencement of what may prove to have been his major architectural undertaking, the great ramp tower by the Maison de la Ville in Geneva, whose design was derived from that of the Tour de Navarre at Langres (see App. G)

Duvet's petition for the use of two rooms at the mint as a residence was entered on October 11 and granted on October 15, 1556 (App. E, Doc. 64). Last recorded as *tailleur de cuings des monnoyes* in September 1556, symptons of Duvet's enroaching weakness first noted in the *Apocalypse* Frontispiece of the preceding year, led the Conseil to give the ailing artist funds (App. E, Doc. 70). Later in the month, his wife also fell ill and both received alms (App. E, Doc. 71).

Duvet's declining health during his last years in Geneva may have been aggravated by the quarrels between his earliest French associates there. Perrin, mentioned before as a man of zealously independent spirit, came to find the reformer's autocratic manner as well as the prying spirit of the Republic hard to bear. By the mid-1530s the anti-Calvinist faction was known locally as that of the "perrenites" and by their enemies as the *libertins* or *libertins spirituels*, indentifying Perrin's relative liberalism with that of a mystical pantheistic sect. To further complicate matters, the Perrin circle did not, as might have been expected, welcome any relaxation of tension between France and Geneva. Despite Perrin's own relatively successful diplomatic negotiations at the court of Henri II for the Republic, he was fiercely opposed to Meigret, the Genevan officer most concerned with establishing *rapprochment* with France, accusing him of a French sell-out. Duvet left Geneva in 1556, a year after the collapse of Perrin's disastrous uprising against Meigret's pro-French faction. The rebel leader and his family escaped; those who could not were executed.[106]

The very last record of Duvet's life in Geneva is the response to the indigent engraver's request for further alms from the Conseil, received on November 5, 1556 (App. E, Doc. 72). To what extent Duvet realized the wishes for a good recovery given by the Conseil is unknown.

Characterized as a man of spirit by his contemporaries in Geneva, as he grew older, Duvet may have found the repressive climate of that city hard to bear, despite, or perhaps because of the charity that had been extended toward the ailing artist and his wife. With Perrin, Meigret and Baudichon de Maisonneuve, Duvet belonged to an older generation than Calvin's. Though reared in a conservative Catholic culture, they were accustomed to a certain aristocratic *laissez faire* approach alien to the resolutely middle-class theocracy of Geneva. Duvet was there before Calvin's reestablishment in 1541. By 1558, none of the magistrates of the Petit Conseil active in that body since 1536 remained; a third of their children lived in exile. Beginning in 1549, Geneva was suddenly swamped with refugees. Of the 2,247 newcomers, 1,536 were craftsmen, among them 67 goldsmiths and 113 printers and booksellers. In addition to his old age and ill health, his new competitors may well have discouraged the old Duvet and contributed to his desire to return to France.[107] He must have returned to France in 1556, as he was granted the *Privilège* for his *Apocalypse* publication on June 3 of that year at Fontaine-bleau. Duvet was described as living at Langres, and as the current goldsmith of Henri II and that of his father François Ier, who had ordered the publication of the engraved work ten years before.

The generous, unusually comprehensive *Privilège* refers to the unspecified "outre considerations à ce que nous mouuans" which may well include consideration for the artist's poverty, poor health and advancing blindness, alluded to in the inscribed Frontispiece of 1555, engraved a year before the *Privilège* was granted. The other considerations could perhaps be royal cognizance of services rendered in the course of Duvet's double duty between France and Geneva. According to Marcel, 1556 must have been the year in which Henri II appointed the seventy-one year old engraver his *orfèvre du Roi.*[108] Perhaps this purely honorific designation entitled Duvet to special funds.

The church register of St.-Pierre in Langres lists in 1557 the baptism of a "Jehan fils de honorable homme Mammès Duvet orfebvre" (App. E, Doc. 73). He was probably the engraver's grandson and namesake, whose father's given name was that of Langres' patron saint, Mammès' profession as a goldsmith also suggests he was the engraver's son. This is further confirmed by the fact that the infant's godfather was Jean d'Amoncourt, archdeacon of Langres, who was very well acquainted with Duvet both as an outstanding local art patron and as a fellow member of the Confrèrie du Saint Sacrement.[109]

In 1561 the *Apocalypse* plates were issued in Lyon with a poorly printed accompanying text, described on the title page as "Lapocalypse figuree par Jehan Duuet, iadis Orfevre des Rois, Francois premier de ce nom & Henri deuxieme. A Lyon. Avec privilege du Roy pour douze ans. MDLXI "(Text fig. 10). As Duvet's name is the only one to appear in the *Apocalypse figurée*, he must have undertaken its preparation, since royal decree made the absence of identification of a printer or publisher a criminal offense. What is also clear from the text of the *Privilège*, which records that the artist himself had prepared "caractaires pour Imprimer," is that the aged engraver was himself responsible for the typography as well as the engravings. The text pages of the *Apocalypse figurée* look too amateurish to have emerged from Lyon, the center of French printing. They are poorly aligned and inferior in quality, but can be explained by Duvet's typographical inexperience and poor eyesight in his seventy-sixth year. The artist was involved in another, abortive publication, that of his Unicorn Series with text, known from a unique impression of the *Capture of the Unicorn* (Cat. 33), with a typeset caption below, probably set by the old engraver himself. The hitherto unobserved number "61" scratched into the most mystical, concluding plate of the Unicorn Series (Cat. 67), also establishes that Duvet was creating important works in the year that the *Apocalypse* was printed. His name is listed at a Langres town meeting in 1562 (App. E, Doc. 76);[110] when he was seventy-seven.

The artist may have spent his final years in Lyon, a center of French Protestantism and the graphic arts, noted for its erudition and liberal thought.[111] Not only could Lyon have offered the engraver a relatively safe haven, but its location also would have made it easier for Duvet's sons in Langres and Geneva to have contributed to his financial support. Writers have referred to the possibility of the artist's activity in Paris in the 1540s and 1550s.[112] If the engraver had spent the end of his life in that city, he would in all likelihood have been employed in the extensive coinage campaign initiated by Henri II in 1559. But this is unrecorded.[113] He may have returned to France permanently only after Henri's II death in July of that year, prompted by the conciliatory moves made toward Protestants during the beginning of Charles IX's reign, when the Prince de Condé was converted to Calvinism in 1561.[114]

New pleas for tolerance and understanding were placed in vain before Henri II, that devoté of the Chambre Ardente. Among the most beautiful is one found in S. Châteillon's preface to his French bible translation, printed in Basel in 1555 and dedicated to the king:[115]

Quand in bataille la nuit survient, on cesse de combattre jusqu'au jour, de peur qu'en frappant à l'aventure on ne tue ses amis au lieu des ennemis. . . . Le Monde est aujourd'hui dans de grands troubles et brouilles, principalement touchant la Religion; et il n'y eut jamais tant de maux et de méchancetés. ... Par conséquent, ce seroit le meilleur, tandis que les choses sont tant douteuses, ou tant brouillées d'attendre de décrocher, jusqu'à ce que le jour lève, de peur que parmi ces ténèbres on ne fasse quelque chose de laquelle il faille dire après: "Je ne pensai pas le faire."

On November 23, 1570, a request for tax emption was made in Geneva by "Jehanne, relaissé de Jehan Droz" (App. E, Doc. 78). It not only furnishes a rough date for Duvet's death, but it also provides his wife's first name, offering another link proving his identity as a resident of Burgundy and Geneva, since his wife's name is given as Jeanne in the register of the Confrérie du Saint-Sacrement of Langres (App. E, Doc. 56). It is clear that the artist did not die in the Republic by the absence of his name from the city's death records.[116]

Such late engravings as the *Despair and Suicide of Judas* (Cat. 72) and *Moses and St. Peter* (Cat. 73) proclaim Duvet's passionately individual approach to faith and conscience, and speak of his lonely pilgrimage without definitive orthodox guidance from Rome or Geneva. Much of his *oeuvre* suggests that the engraver's character may have resembled that of his Lyonnais contemporary and fellow pageant master Maurice Scève, who was described as "compliqué, savant, singulier, obscur, avec une sorte d'ardeur intime qui soulève parfois le lourd apareil des allusions érudites et de la forme laborieuse."[117] Like those of Michelangelo, Duvet's final images are illuminated by a desperate sense of the isolation of man before God. Perhaps the engraver's end resembled that of his follower Hugues Sambin who, long a Calvinist, died a Catholic.[118] Religious ambiguity and ultimate repudiation are found among kings as well as craftsmen—Maximilian II, though officially Catholic, was a Lutheran sympathizer and refused Catholic last rites in 1576. A man of many skills and interests, embracing metal work, pageantry, theology, numismatics, typography, military engineering, and probably alchemical knowledge, the engraver established his own way of faith. As suggested by Didier, Duvet may have been more a humanist in search of liberty than a "reform convaincu."[119] With Marot, who planned to return to France from his Italian refuge, Duvet might also have found France to be the only place where he could be himself despite the terrors of religious persecution. This poet's declaration of faith, written in 1526 from his Parisian prison shortly before exile, anticipates by three decades Duvet's feelings upon his final return to France:

> . . . Point ne suis Lutheriste
> Ne Zwinglien, & moins Anabatiste:
> Je suis de Dieu par son filz Jesu christ.
> Je suis celluy qui ay faict maint escript,
> Dont ung seul vers on n'en scauroit extraire
> Qui a Loy divine soit contraire.
> Je suis celluy qui prends plaisir & peine
> A louer Christ & sa Mere tant pleine
> De grace infuse; & pour bien l'esprouver
> On le pourra par mes escriptz trouver.[120]

NOTES

1. Pierre Louis Duchartre and René Saulnier, *L'Imagerie Populaire, Les Images de toutes les provinces françaises du XV siècle au Second Empire,* Paris, 1925, p. 21.

2. For a discussion of local poverty, financial depression and restrictions, see L. E. Marcel, *Le Cardinal de Givry, évêque de Langres,* Paris, 1926, II, pp. 340-341, "le pauperisme," followed, significantly enough, by "Le décor brillant," pp. 342-44. This work will be referred to hereafter as Marcel.

3. For the description of this entry, see Cyprien Monget, *La Chartreuse de Dijon,* Montreuil-sur-Mer, 1898-1905, II, pp. 202-203.

4. A probable colleague of Duvet's, the Latin poet Nicholas Bourbon characterized himself as "Poeta Lingonensis," since he was born in the diocese of Langres, as was Duvet himself in all likelihood. See V. L. Saulnier, "Recherches sur Nicolas Bourbon," *Bibliothèque d'humanisme et renaissance,* XVI, 1954, p. 184.

5. See J. Paquier, *Gérôme Aleandro,* Paris, 1914, p. 91; also Marcel, II, p. 187.

6. The Saint Lambert head was made by the father of a distinguished Flemish print-maker, Lambert Suavius, its face "peint en carnation" (polychromy in flesh tones) follows the prevalent Burgundian fashion. For a detailed description and illustration of this reliquary, see Jules Helbig, *La sculpture en les arts plastiques au pays de Liège,* Bruges, 1890, Pl. XXI, pp. 149-151. For the St.-Mammès reliquary head, see App. E., Docs. 3, 17.

7. See E. Jullien de la Boullaye, "Entrées et séjours de François Ier à Langres," *Bulletin de la Société historique et archéologique de Langres,* I, 1880, pp. 68-100 (hereafter referred to as Boullaye, 1880), esp. p. 95. See also Léonce de Piépape, *Histoire militaire du pays de Langres,* Langres, 1884, *passim.*

8. Boullaye, *Etude sur la vie et sur l'oeuvre de Jean Duvet dit le maître à la licorne,* Paris 1876, p. 6, has read the curiously blurred numerals scratched on the base plate mark of the proof impressions of the *Marriage of Adam and Eve* (Cat. 35) and *Moses Surrounded by the Patriarchs* (Cat. 36) as 1517, but this reading is not possible. The publication will be referred to as Boullaye.

9. Boullaye, 1880, pp. 74 ff.; Marcel, II, p. 284.

10. Marcel II, p. 428. Boullaye (p. 7) believed that François Ier would have seen and been duly impressed by the splendor of the unfinished reliquary head of Saint Mammès when he made his tour of inspection and devotion to examine the Tresor of the Cathedral.

11. Even though Duvet may have occupied a subsidiary role in the preparation of the 1521 triumphal entry, a comparison between a similar position—that of Hugues Sambin as "lambroisseur" in the ceremonies for the Dijon entry in 1550 of the Duc d'Aumale, governor of Burgundy—shows that such secondary appointments may nonetheless have determined the style of the festivity. The contract for a sculptor participating in the same entry stated that the statues were to be executed "selon l'art et les pourtraicts et ordonnances que luy a seront pour ce bailles par pre Hugues Sambin," suggesting that the latter's function was far more significant than was his official designation; this was no doubt true for Duvet as well. See David DuBon, "Hugues Sambin as Architect and Designer of Woodwork," M. A. thesis, New York University, Institute of Fine Arts, 1959, pp. 4-5; Noel Garnier, "Contribution à l'histoire de Hugues Sambin," *Mémoires de la Société bourguignonne de geographie et d'histoire,* 1891, p. 33. The sculptor's contract was published by Henri David, *De Sluter à Sambin,* Paris, 1933, II, p. 221.

12. Boullaye, 1880, p. 95.

13. *Ibid.*

14. Marcel, II, pp. 82-85, 294; *Enciclopedia italiana,* Milan, XVI, 1932, p. 55.

15. Marcel, II, p. 84. For Fregoso see also David, *De Sluter à Sambin, op. cit.,* II, pp. 353-359, "La renaissance". His uncle was the Duke of Urbino. In 1522 the Spanish capture of Genoa (governed by his brother Ottaviano, an appointee of François Ier) forced Federico into exile He was given the Dijon abbacy by the king.

16. Marcel, II, pp. 1-143. Their contribution has been exhaustively studied in L. E. Marcel's monograph on Claude, the future Cardinal de Givry.

17. Marcel, I, pp. 85 ff. Imprisoned in Madrid with François Ier after the French defeat at Pavia, Chabot was released first, and with Montmorency arranged for the king's ransom. His successful negotiations gained Chabot the title *Amiral de France* in 1526. He married Françoise de Longvy the following year. Her uncle Claude de Longvy, after several years as bishop of Mâcon, was chosen, probably through Cabot's influence at court, to succeed Boudet as bishop of Langres in 1529. The diocese was considerably enlarged for the new bishop, to include Pothières, part of Yonne, the Aube, Mussy, Luzy, and Gurgy. Chabot spent years in completing the plans for the return of François Ier's sons from Charles V's imprisonment in Spain and also went to Italy to ratify the Treaty of Cambrai. In 1532 Chabot and Claude de Longvy went to England to cement the alliance of François Ier and Henry VIII against Charles V; it was upon this occasion that the *Amiral* received the Order of the Garter. With the failure of his invasion of Piedmont, Chabot's career declined while Montmorency's prospered. Opposed by Montmorency and Diane de Poitiers, Chabot's property, offices, and titles were removed in 1541. Reinstated the following year, he died in 1543 at the age of fifty-one.

18. For an excellent study of this screen and its setting, see David DuBon, *The Chapel of the Château of Pagny,* Philadelphia Museum of Art, n.d. For further bibliography, see DuBon, p. 35, n. 2. See also Marcel, II, pp. 88-143.

19. See Louis Hautecoeur, *Histoire de l'architecture en France,* Paris, 1943, I, p. 142; see also Olga Raggio, "Vignole, Fra Damiano et Gerolamo Siciolante à la chapelle de la Bastie d'Urfé," *Revue de l'Art,* No. 15, 1972, pp. 29-52.

20. See Léon de Laborde, *Notice des émaux, bijoux et objets divers exposés dans les galeries du Musée du Louvre,* Paris, 1853, p. 93; Spire Blondel, "La damasquinerie," *Gazette des beaux-arts industriels au moyen âge et à l'époque de la renaissance,* Paris, 1864-66, IV, p. 38. H. Chabeuf, "Jehan Duvet, était il dijonnais ou langrois?" *Mémoires de l'académie des sciences, arts, et belles-lettres de Dijon,* 5ème Sér., II, pp. 7-12.

21. Baldassare Castiglione, *Libro del Cortegiano,* I, 5.

22. See Marcel, II, pp. 213-228, for Lefèvre's biography. For Alciati in France, see *Storia di Milano, VII: Tra Francia e Spagna 1500-1535,* Milan, 1957, pp. 444-447. For the publication history of Alciati's *Emblemata,* see Mario Praz, *Studies in Seventeenth-Century Imagery,* Rome, 1964, pp. 248-252.

23. Marcel, II, p. 33, quoting Artur Daguin, *Les évêques de Langres,* Nogent, 1880-83, pp. 42-45.

24. Play edited by J. Carnadet, Paris, 1855. See also Donald Clive Stuart, *Stage Decoration in France in the Middle Ages,* New York, 1910, pp. 180, 182.

25. Carnadet, *op. cit.,* p. viii.

26. Marcel, II, p. 381.

27. Pierre de la Vigne, a Dominican from Langres, dedicated his moralized Ovid to Givry in 1510 when he was bishop of Mâcon. Jean Fustaillier followed suit with his *Antiquités de Mâcon* in 1520. (Marcel, I, p. 19). For the classical antiquities of Langres, see Earle Wilbur Dow, "The Roman City of Langres in the Early Middle Ages," *Annual Report of the American Historical Association,* I, 1899, pp. 485-511.

28. Marcel, II, pp. 199-205; V. L. Saulnier, "Recherches sur Nicolas Bourbon," *Bibliothèque d'humanisme et renaissance,* XVI, 1954, pp. 172-191; Natalie Zemon Davis, "Holbein's Pictures of Death at Lyons," *Studies in the Renaissance,* I, 1954, pp. 97-130, esp. pp. 112-114. The *Nugae* of 1538 praise the engraver Woeriot along with Holbein. Bourbon was a friend of Holbein, whose portrait of the poet is now at Windsor. They worked in collaboration on the verses and woodcuts for a Dance of Death which was also to have references favorable to Protestantism.

29. All the information pertaining to this entry is taken from Boullaye, 1880, pp. 68-100.

30. *Livret des Emblèmes de Maistre André Alciat,* printed by Chrestien Wechel, Paris,

1536. Bacchus and Ceres symbolize the rich agriculture of Burgundy: its
bounteous grape and wheat harvests; for François Ier's entry at Angers in 1518,
Bacchus praised the grapes of Anjou. See Louis Petit de Julleville, *Les mystères*,
Paris, 1880, II, p. 158.

31. Boullaye, 1880, p. 93.

32. Marcel, I, pp. 330-430, "Les débuts du Protestantisme dans l'ancien diocèse de
Langres: I - Partie bourguignonne. II - Partie comtoise. Rôle du Cardinal de Givry."

33. E. Henry, *La Réforme et la ligue en Champagne et à Reims*, Saint-Nicolas, 1869,
Chapter I, quoted in Marcel, I, p. 412, n. 4.

34. Important new evidence and a reproduction of the rediscovered original placard,
the only one known to survive is given by Gabrielle Berthoud, "Les placards de
1534," in G. Berthoud et al., *Aspects de la propagande religieuse (Travaux
d'humanisme et renaissance, 28)*, Geneva, 1957, pp. 78-154, reproduction on p. 78.

35. Quoted, *ibid.*, p. 92, n. 1., from a letter in the Bibliotheca Vaticana, urb. 1035 -
28.2.1534.

36. Henri Naef, "La vie et les travaux de Jean Duvet le Maître à la Licorne," *Bulletin
de la Société de l'histoire de l'art françois*, 1934, p. 120. Naef discovered the
Duvet references contained within the Geneva archives. Marcel, II, p. 430, rejecting the possibility of identity, wrote, "Ce pourrait être un de ses parents, du
même nom, ou un simple homonyme de Dijon. On a vu qu'en 1509 Jean Duvet
avait été reçu maître avec son frère Louis. Le Jean Duvet en question pourrait
être fils de ce dernier. D'après le *Dict. des artistes suisses* du Dr. Ch. Brun, Vol.
I, 1902, p. 406, il vivait encore en 1575." The latter date may be an error of
Brun's and probably refers to the death date of Duvet's son. Edmond Belle, in
his article "La Réforme à Dijon," *Revue bourguignonne de l'Université de Dijon*,
XXI, No. 1, 1911, p. 17, quoted Duvet's entry in the Livre des Bourgeois but
did not associate him with the engraver active at Langres. Naef also wrote "Un
artiste français du XVIe siècle, bourgeois de Genève: Jehan Duvet, le Maître à
la licorne," *Bulletin de la Société d'histoire et d'archéologie de Genève*, V, 1925,
pp. 30 ff. Naef's research into the possible identification between the Jean Duvet
of Geneva and the Jean Duvet of Langres was probably stimulated by A. Covelle's
publication *Livre des bourgeois de l'ancienne republique de Genève*, Geneva, 1897,
p. 122, where, quoting from the Register of Foreigners for November 15, 1541,
Covelle lists a "Jehan Duvet, filz de feuz Louys Duvet, alias Drouot, de Dijon."
Naef observed that Duvet's rapid rise in Geneva suggested that the engraver "était
précédé d'une reputation flatteuse, car le Petit Conseil l'occupa tout de suite dans
l'un des postes les plus importants de la Seigneurie. Drouhot fut nommé graveur,
ou, comme on disait, tailleur de la monnaie." Writing in 1917, Louis Marcel observed the following concerning the probability of identity of the Jean Duvets of
Langres and Geneva, "Disons-le très franchement: a priori, la chose ne parait pas
absolument invraisemblable. Beaucoup des artistes et des ouvriers d'art du XVIe
siècle, contrairement à leur intérêt materiel qui était de rester fidèles à l'Église qui
utilisait ou qui, du moins, était susceptible d'utiliser à l'avenir leur talent et leur
savoir-faire, embarasserent avec passion les idées nouvelles, et il n'y avait pas lieu de
s'étonner, extraordinairement, si le père de la gravure au burin avait imité leur
example." (Canon Louis Marcel, "Pierre Guyot de Giey, sa vie, sa maison, ses
collections," *Bulletin de la Société historique et archéologique de Langres*, VII,
1917, pp. 302 ff). However, Marcel believed that if Jean Duvet had gone to
Geneva, when he returned to Langres to join the Confraternity of the Holy Sacrament, this must have been a definitive and permanent reconversion. In order to
solve this knotty problem, the Burgundian scholar also wondered whether there
may not have been two Jean Duvets in Dijon, one Catholic, the other Protestant.

37. Belle, *op. cit.*, p. 17.

38. Marcel, I, p. 317.

39. H. Hours, "Procés d'hérésie contre Aimé Meigret, Lyon, Grenoble, 1524," *Bibliothèque d'humanisme et renaissance*, XIX, 1957, pp. 14-43.

40. Marcel, I, pp. 477-479.

41. E. Müntz, "Le protestantisme et l'art," *Revue des revues*, March 1, 1900, pp. 488 ff.

42. See Maurice Roy, *Artistes et monuments de la renaissance en France*, Paris, 1934,
I, pp. 199, 399. Bontemps left Paris after the completion of his work for the

entry of Charles IX into Paris in 1561. See also Roy, "Le sculpteur Pierre Bontemps (1505-1568)," *Mémoires de la Société des antiquaires de France,* LXX, 1911, pp. pp. 265-371.

43. See Tommaso Sandoninni and Anatole de Montaiglon, "Jean Goujon, la verité sur sa religion et sur sa morte," *Bulletin de la Société de l'histoire du protestantisme français,* XXXV, 1886, pp. 376-386.

44. For an important Protestant text printed by Palissy, see "Bernard Palissy consideré comme evangeliste ou predicateur de la Reforme et comme écrivain: son récit de la fondation de l'église réforme de Saintes, d'après l'édition originale et avec les notes manuscrites de l'exemplaire de la B.N. (z 2, 122, E)," *Bulletin de la Société de l'histoire du protestantisme français,* I, 1853, pp. 88-91. For biography of Palissy by E. W. Braun, see Thieme-Becker, *Künstler-Lexikon,* XXVI, pp. 160-162.

45. Müntz, *op. cit.,* p. 488.

46. See E. Doumergue, *Iconographie calvinienne,* Lausanne, 1909, p. 13, and Cat. 484. Limoisin seems to have done a series of portraits of Protestant leaders in enamel including Calvin, Luther, Bèze, and Melanchthon. The authenticity of the portrait of Calvin, signed L.L. and dated 1535, the year of the publication of his *Institutes* has been questioned.

47. See the biography by Stöcklein in Thieme-Becker, *Künstlerlexikon,* IX, pp. 2-3.

48. He was once regarded as a possible pupil of Duvet. E. Doumergue, *op. cit.,* Chap. IV, "Les Woeriot," quoted J. Renouvier, who described Woeriot as "le graveur le plus intime de la forte race des calvinistes français." His portrait of Calvin was the frontispiece for Theodore de Bèze's *Receuil des opuscules,* printed in Geneva by Baptiste Pinereul in 1566. N. Rondot (*Les graveurs sur bois à Lyon au XVIe siècle,* Paris, 1897, p. 40) stated that Woeriot's engravings of Barthélèmy Aneau and Georgette de Montenay also indicate his sympathy for the Reformation.

49. See Müntz, *op. cit.,* p. 488.

50. See Belle, *op. cit.,* pp. XLI, 11.

51. Amédée Roget, *Histoire du peuple de Genève,* Geneva, II, 1870, p. 52; Naef, 1946, p. 16, n. 2.

52. See Paul Mantz, "L'orfèvrèrie française," *Gazette des Beaux-Arts,* IX, 1861, pp. 15, 141.

53. See Paul F. Geisendorf, *Le livre des habitants de Genève* (I, 1540-1560), Geneva, 1957, pp. 5, 11, 26, 36, 105, 106, 160, 170, 177, 186, 218, 219. For a fine introduction to the subject, see E. William Monter, *Calvin's Geneva,* New York, 1967. See also Antony Babel, *Histoire économique de Genève des origines au début du XVIe siècle,* Geneva, 1963, I, pp. 514-521. Of the one hundred seventy-four French who migrated to Geneva between 1501 and 1536, one hundred twenty-four came from Burgundy.

54. See Elizabeth Armstrong, *Robert Estienne, Royal Printer,* Cambridge, 1954, pp. 237-238. For diplomatic ties between France and Switzerland, see the exhibition catalogue *Les grandes heures de l'amitié franco suisse,* Paris, Hôtel de Rohan, 1967. It is worth remembering that Geneva itself was not in accord with the other cantons characterized with disdain as "les allemands."

55. Roget, *op. cit.,* I, p. 27.

56. *Ibid.,* p. 291.

57. See note 36.

58. For an account of the raid and its consequences, see the publication issued by the Comité G. Farel, *Guillaume Farel 1489-1565,* Neufchâtel-Paris, 1930, p. 326.

59. Roget, *op. cit.,* I, p. 2.

60. Paul Emile Viard, *André Alciat 1492-1550,* Paris, 1926, p. 76. However, Calvin opposed Alciati's views and provided a preface to Nicholas Duchemin's *Antapologia,* Paris, 1529.

61. *A Brief Christian Introduction,* 656, 15-19; cf. 708, 18-22. "By Sunday, July 3, 1524, scarcely a statue, a painting, a crucifix, a votive lamp, a reliquary, a shrine, or image or decoration of any sort was to be seen anywhere in in the Zurich churches." (Quoted by Charles Garside, *Zwingli, and the Arts,* New Haven, 1966, p. 160).

62. Naef, p. 122.

63. *Ibid.*, pp. 122-123, described the decorations framing the walled-in door formerly leading to the room of the Conseil d'Etat as consisting of "fronton, bordure lineaire, s'entremêlant a des rinceaux, pilastres le long desquels pendent en cordon des fruits stylisés, tout rappelle l'ornementation française de la première moitié du XVIe siècle, celle d'Ancy-le-Franc, par example." The wall-paintings are illustrated by Camille Martin in his thorough study "La maison de ville de Genève," *Mémoires et documents publiés par la Société d'histoire et d'archèologie de Genève*, III, 1906. The sad remains of the painted wall decoration are very provincial in style and could never have amounted to much.

64. See Th. Pistollet de Saint-Férjeux, "Le chateau et les seigneurs de Pailly," *Mémoires de la Société historique et archéologique de Langres*, I, 188, p. 245.

65. When referring to himself as a goldsmith, Duvet appears to use the form "Jehan Drouhot"; however, when he signs his name as individual identification, he calls himself "Dwet." It may well be that Jean used the patronymic when engaged in that craft which he learned from his father; alternately, the name Drouhot could have distinguished one branch of the Duvet family from another on a professional basis.

66. See Alexis François, *Le Magnifique Meigret*, Geneva, 1947; E. Droz, "Laurent Meigret et la propagande religieuse," in G. Berthoud, et al, *op. cit.*, pp. 155-166; Robert M. Kingdom, *Geneva and the Coming of the Wars of Religion in France*, *1555-1563*, Geneva, 1956, p. 58.

67. François, *op. cit.*, pp. 134-135.

68. Although de Maisonneuve was commendably close-mouthed at the time of his trial, the "evidence" against him provided scholars with important indications of the scope and process of distributing the literature of the Reformation throughout France.
See E. Droz, "Pierre de Vingle, l'imprimeur de Farel," in G. Berthoud et al, *op. cit.*, pp. 38-78, esp. p. 72. For Baudichon de Maisonneuve, see J. G. Baum, *Le procès de Baudichon de Maisonneuve*, Geneva, 1873; H. Ammann, "Uberdeutsche Kaufleute und die Anfänge der Reformation in Genf," *Festschrift Kart Otto Müller*, Stuttgart, 1954, pp. 183 ff.

69. Roget, *op. cit.*, I, p. 28. The quotation is taken from p. 38 of the *Chronique*, according to pp. 27-28, n. 2.

70. *Ibid.*, II, p. 167.

71. For the Treaty of Crespy, see Ernest Lavisse, *Histoire de France*, V, Part 2 (by Henri Monnier), Paris, 1910-1911, p. 116.

72. Perrin's diplomatic mission to the court of François Ier in 1544-45, seeking the *mandement* of Thiez, was a complete failure since he had been completely deceived by the wily monarch. While this diplomatic disaster might have resulted in large political upsets in Geneva, such was not the case, due in part to the opportune death of the leader of the opposition, Claude Pertemps, another associate of Duvet's. See Roget, *op. cit.*, II, p. 123. See also Monter, *op. cit.*, p. 74, p. 123.

73. Roget, *op. cit.*, II, p. 57.

74. *Ibid.*, p. 199.

75. Baptismal registers were not established before 1549. See Naef, p. 137, who also pointed out that the death of the engraver's son in 1575 doubtless accounts for that date being given as that of his father's in the *Dictionnaire des artistes suisses*, *op. cit.*, I, p. 406. According to Jean Laran, *L'Estampe*, Paris, 1959, I, p. 63, Duvet died in Langres circa 1570.

76. See Raymond Lebègue, *Le mystère des Actes des Apôtres*, Paris, 1929. This study, subtitled *Contribution à l'étude de l'humanisme et du protestantisme français au XVIe siècle*, pointed out how the dialogues of mystery plays inevitably reflected the Protestant views of their dramatists. Chapponeau, a priest and associate of Calvin's at Bourges from 1529 to 1531, introduced a sculptor called Demetrius into his adaptation of the *Apôtres mystère* and has the sculptor inveigh against holy images, repeating a sermon the playright had preached at Bourges (p. 133).
See also Roget, *op. cit.*, II, pp. 322-323, Appendix I. According to Caliagnon, p.29, the performance took place on April 16.

77. *Ibid.*, p. 242.

78. However, historical and classical plays were permitted. In 1547 the Latin students were allowed to produce an episode from Josephus, and two years later a comedy by Terence was staged by the same group. Léon Wencelius, *L'Esthétique de Calvin,* Paris, 1936, p. 151. See also Martha Grau, *Calvins Stellung zur Kunst,* Munich, 1917, p. 62.
79. See Armstrong, *op. cit.*
80. E. Egger, *L'Esthétique de Calvin,* Paris, 1936, p. 151. See also p. 214, "Ce quel ne pouvait faire imprimer dans ses ateliers de Paris ou Genève, il trouvait le moyen de publier par les presses d'un confrère."
81. Armstrong, *op. cit.,* p. 219. See also T. Dufour, *Imprimeurs et libraires reçus à Genève, 1550-1557,* Geneva, n.d.
82. See E. William Monter, *Studies in Genevan Government,* Geneva, 1964, p. 25. For a brief account of "Les constitutions de l'art après la Réforme," see the chapter of that title, pp. 296-310, in W. Deonna, *Les arts à Genève des origines à la fin du XVIIIe siècle,* Geneva, 1942.
83. Garside, *op. cit.,* pp. 150 ff.
84. For Zwingli's approach to historical subjects, see *ibid.,* p. 150.
85. The reformer's view of the function of painting and sculpture is given by Wencelius, *op. cit.,* p. 163. For Calvin and architecture, see *ibid.,* Chapter 5.
86. See Henri Zerner, *The School of Fontainebleau, Etchings and Engravings,* New York, 1969, p. 14.
87. See Piépape, *op. cit.,* p. 114. See also App. F.
88. See H. Noel Williams, *Henri II: His Court and Times,* New York, 1910, p. 213, quoted from Theodore Godefroy, *Le Cérémoniale de France,* Paris, 1619.
89. Roget, *op. cit.,* II, p. 320; François, *op. cit.,* Chapter 8, "Ami Perrin," pp. 90-98.
90. Marcel, I, p. 162. The confraternity was revived by Givry, who made several changes in its organization after the same chapter at his Roman church of S. Agnese in Agonia (Piazza Navona), active there since the fourteenth century. For a charter of this confraternity at Rouen (Arch. Seine inf. G9.870), see Marcel, I, p. 167, n.1.
91. Marcel, "Pierre Guyot..., *op. cit.,* pp. 320 ff.
92. See Marcel, I, p. 162.
93. N. Weiss, *La chambre ardente, étude sur la liberté de conscience en France sous François Ier et Henri II,* Paris, 1889, pp. 171-176, 199-208; Marcel, I, pp. 414-417, 421.
94. For the statue in Langres, see Marcel, II, Chapter 9, pp. 408-422. According to a study by Canon Marcel, *Le "Christ" de l'église St.-Martin de Langres: simples notes sur son origins,* Langres, 1925, quoted by Marcel, II, p. 416, the statue was ordered by Matthieu de Cirey, a member of the Confrérie du Saint-Sacrement.
95. For a recent examination of this confraternity throughout Europe, see *Studia Eucharistica,* Antwerp, 1956. For its influence on art, see Colin Eisler, "The Golden Christ of Cortona and the Man of Sorrows in Italy," *Art Bulletin,* LI, 1969, pp. 107-118; 233-246.
96. The membership list of the Langres confraternity is given by Marcel, I, p. 166, II, p. 430, n. 4. He pointed out that Duvet and his wife entered the confraternity after 1547 and before 1552.
97. H. Naef, "La monnaie de la Gruyère," *Revue suisse de numismatique,* XXIII, 1924, p. 467.
98. Naef, "L'alchimiste de Michel, comte de Gruyère," *Mémoires et documents publiés par la Société d'histoire de la Suisse Romande,* Ser. 3, II, 1946, p. 128.
99. Belle, *op. cit.,* p. 10.
100. Lebègue, *op. cit.,* p. 240.
101. With the same technical versatility that has been observed in Duvet's oeuvre, Eskrich senior was praised by Neudörfer for his skill in "silver and gold work, in drawing, engraving, casting, repoussé work, painting, cutting and making portraits; what he cut in stone, cameo and iron earned praise, even from the Italians." (Quoted by Elfried Bock, "The Engravings of Ludwig Krug of Nuremberg," *Print Collectors' Quarterly,* XX, 1933, pp. 89-90. Ludwig Krug was one of the extremely few identifiable engravers active in France in the first quarter of the sixteenth century who

possessed a distinctive style. See Bock, *op. cit.*, pp. 87-115. It was probably from an artist like Krug that Duvet learned print-making.

For information on Pierre Eskrich, see Natalis Rondot, *Les graveurs sur bois de Lyon,* Paris, 1897. Eskrich's first dated work is probably the *Horae in laudem Beatissimae Virginis Mariae,* Lyon, 1548. Elaborate mannerist strapwork borders signed "PV" appear in this publication. Baudrier attributes the Rouillé *Ariosto* woodcuts of 1550 and 1556 to Eskrich, but this seems unlikely. The *Emblèmes d'Alciat,* published at Lyon, "chez Macé Bonhomme" in 1549, with vignettes inferior to the earlier Jean de Tournes edition, has fine woodcut borders initialed PV which should also be given to Eskrich.

102. Rondot, *op. cit.*, p. 39.

103. The 34 woodcuts in Rosier's work, published by Zacharie Durent have been attributed to Eskrich by Rondot, *op. cit.*, p. 102. Two of them are reproduced by E. H. Gaullieur, *Études sur la typographie genèvoise du XV au XVI siècle,* Geneva, 1855, p. 177. Paul Chaix's study of printing in Geneva (*Recherches sur l'imprimerie à Genève de·1550 à 1564,* Geneva, 1954) also attributed the woodcuts of the *Antithèse de faicts de Jésus Christ et du Pape* to Eskrich (p. 99). This is presumably a different version of the title listed by Rondot.

104. See W. Lübke, "Mathias Gerungs Apokalypse," *Beilage zur allgemeine Zeitung,* 1886, No. 124/125. The manuscript is in the library at Gotha. The best study of this master has been made by Campbell Dodgson, "Eine Hozschnittfolge Mathias Gerungs," *Jahrbuch der koniglich preussischen Kunstsammlungen,* XXIX, 1908, pp. 195-216. For further discussion of Gerung, see the article by Alois Wagner, "Mathias Gerung," *Jahrbuch der königlich Vereins Dillingen,* IX, 1896, pp. 69-106. The only known complete set of Gerung's *Apocalypse* was owned by Alfred Huth at Fosbury Manor, Hungerford. It is now in the British Museum. The Huth *Apocalypse* is bound in black morocco with the date 1637, in the same style as Duvet's in Cleveland. Both series may have been owned and bound by Rembrandt. See pp. 107-108n.37.

105. Like the historians who were unwilling to accept the identity of the Calvinist and Catholic Jean Duvets, Nagler postulated that either the monogram of the *Spottbilder* was not that of Gerung, or that the artist's Catholic patron was ignorant of his Lutheran activities, or that the woodcutter was reconverted to Catholicism after a Protestant phase. According to the historian, he repented his brief apostasy, and destroyed his caricatures–the strongest of which is identical in format with his Apocalypse series! Nagler was quoted by Dodgson, *op. cit.*, p. 207.

106. Kingdon, *op. cit.*, p. 2. Comité G. Farel, *op. cit.*, pp. 569-570.

107. A stirring presentation of the most oppressive aspects of life in Geneva is provided by Joseph Lecler, S. J., *Histoire de la tolérance au siècle de la Réforme,* Aubier (Editions Montaigne), 1955, I, pp. 306 ff., "Farel et Calvin: la Réforme en Suisse française," See also Monter, *op. cit.*, p. 88 and R. Mandrou, "Les français hors de France au XVIe siècle," *Annales: histoire, économies, civilisations,* XIV, 1959, pp. 665-666.

108. Marcel, II, p. 430.

109. *Ibid.,* I, p. 166; II, p. 430.

110. Naef (p. 137) suggested that the artist was dead by 1561. Boullaye failed to find any record of Duvet's name in the archives after 1552, with the exception of a reference to "Jean Drouot" who attended a town meeting on taxation in 1562 (App. E, Doc. 76), but the archivist was not convinced that this referred to Jean Duvet.

111. See Natalie Zemon Davis, "The Protestant Printing Works of Lyons," in G. Berthoud et al, *op. cit.*, pp. 247-257; Kingdon, *op. cit.*, pp. 258-275.

112. According to Mrs. Mark Pattison, *The Art of the Renaissance in France,* London, 1877, II, p. 106, the supposed Parisian origin of *La Majesté Royale* (Cat. 63) has "been cited in confirmation of the theory that Duvet passed part of his life in Paris."

113. See Carolyn Shipman, *Researches concerning Jean Grolier, His Life and His Library,* New York, 1907, p. 15.

114. See Noël Valois, "Les essais de concilation religieuse au début du règne de Charles IX," *Revue d'histoire de l'église de France,* XXXI, 1945, pp. 237-276.

115. Quoted by Geoffroy Atkinson, *Les nouveaux horizons de la renaissance française,* Paris, 1935, p. 395.

116. Deonna, *op. cit.,* p. 446, stated that the artist died outside Geneva ca. 1570.

117. Gustave Lanson, *Histoire de la literature française,* 12th ed., Paris, 1912, p. 276;

118. Marcel, I, p. 401.

119. J. Ch. Didier, "Jean Duvet," *Dictionnaire de la biographie française,* XI, 1970, cols. 1047-8.

120. From A. M. Bouchart, IX, verses 1-16; see C.A. Mayer, *La religion de Marot,* Geneva, 1960, p. 97.

II.

THE ALCHEMICAL DIMENSION

Diderot, greatest of Langres' sons, observed "Alchemy has often discovered great truths on the highroad of the imagination." In his *Encyclopédie* entry he noted that the Greek name for alchemy was gold maker or gold worker—the Latin *Aurifaber* was used by Duvet to identify himself on the *Apocalypse* Frontispiece. Diderot distinguished between the true and false alchemist: the former, having studied physics and chemistry, is enabled by special combination of the sciences to reproduce the works of nature, making them more accessible to man. Essentially, he found the alchemist to be an artist, recreating a work even more beautiful than in its natural state. It may seem surprising that the most enlightened of men should show such appreciation for a field so perilously close to the irrational and the occult, but Diderot knew best. Long suspended between witchcraft and astrology, alchemy worked with the same roots as the physical sciences: experimentation, technical analysis, and study of properties. It was also intimately associated with the world of art and imagination, as it intertwined kabbalistic lore and Neo-Platonic mystery with the Eastern and Western magical heritages. As Diderot knew so well, the effect of revelation, the sudden epiphany was critical to the history of science for many of its dramatic break-throughs. The exercise of the unfettered imagination is as important as the scientific method itself. Dedicated to exploring the work of God—nature—alchemy strove to reveal the basis of matter, the process of transformation and interaction which links life at all levels. This beginning of modern science brought together the dense tradition of classical and Christian allegory and symbolism which seemed to point to the hidden truths the alchemist was sworn to uncover.

Recent humanistic appraisals of alchemy have not been kind. Specialists in Neo-Platonism such as the late Edgar Wind, saw the field as a dumping ground for misunderstanding or willfully distorted writings and practices, gounded in a bastardized Neo-Platonism. The scholar's disdain for the alchemist recalls only too appropriately Plato's distrust of the artist, and for the same reason. Both alchemist and artist were often united in pursuit of the same goal—understanding the nature of appearance and the appearance of nature. Much alchemical thought reversed the process of *disegno* by starting with the expressive raw materials and working back to the concept of *idea*. This reversion was criticized by Wind when he noted that "The spiritualization of matter attempted by Plotinus (in the fourth *Ennead*) was understood by the alchemist as a materialization of spirits, to be achieved by a series of concoctions and ceremonious conflagrations that mimicked a mystical purification rite."[1] Imitation rather than mimicry might be nearer the truth for it was through this chemical "copying" that the artist-scientist slowly and often wrongly, attempted to reproduce the process of creation. This approach led to a a heightened sense of awareness and metamorphoses upon which the modern physical sciences are grounded. The alchemical workshop, the laboratory, has never really changed. Nor, for that matter have its goals.

In his "ignorant" application of Platonic wisdom, the artist enjoyed a special role. His lack of humanistic training did not prevent him from participating in the alchemical world, which was especially seductive because of its emphasis upon action as well as knowledge. The practice combined a magical and technical grasp of the secret nature of being. A key alchemical text was the late medieval *Roman de la Rose* by the Burgundian, Jean de Meun. We know is was used in the fifteenth and early sixteenth centuries because the court portraitist Jean Perréal's poem *Complainte de Nature a l'Alchemiste errant,* dedicated to François Ier, was based on de Meun's work. De Meun's source in turn, was Vincent of Beauvais' *Speculum;* the writings of Plato, Avicenna and other hermetic literature.[2]

Surprisingly, for all his maguslike powers, viewed as such by Vasari and his own contemporaries, Leonardo's fundamentally Aristotelian orientation inclined him against aspects of alchemical thought. That major objection to the field was only resolved after Agrippa von Nettesheim brought together both the Platonic (the *Phaedrus)* and the Aristolelian (the *Problemata)* in his *Occulta Philosophia* of 1510. Thereafter, the alchemical, the saturnian, and the melancholic were combined in dynamic fashion, leading the artist to an unexpectedly potent identification with these mystical factors.[3]

Agrippa von Nettesheim conceived of art as a complex talisman, resulting from involuntary creative expression in which the master's astral properties were assumed. These in their way, evoked other planetary properties through color, chiaroscuro, proportion and content, so that the work of art itself exercised a special sympathetic magic. Astrological powers, attracted by the artist-practitioners' command of the ratio of geometry, could result in alchemy—the special pursuit of the understanding of God's art—by contemplation and examination of nature. According to Nettesheim, the astrological concept of melancholy was intimately allied to the creative insight of the artist whose nature depended upon that most complex and ambiguous of the four humors. Art, in the sense of work, was the basis of the alchemical achievement through which man reached an understanding of God. The moment of *melanosi* or *nigredo* was critical to the alchemical process. It was the passage from the black world of Saturn—black was that color which subsumed all others—when he left his realm to enter the golden rule of Jupiter, or the joy and light at the end of the Great Work. Melancholia accompanied him during the first part of the journey to the coronation of the Opus, whose happy ending was often indicated, as in the engraving by Dürer, with a rainbow.[4]

15. A. Dürer, Melencolia I, *1514.*

In Dürer's *Melencolia I* there is an overt alchemical reference present in the crucible and tongs recognized as such at the turn of the century by von Giehlow. Four years before Dürer's masterprint a special alchemist's *Melencolia* was the subject of a woodcut. Hartlaub and van Lennep have illuminated the ties between alchemy and melancholy in several publications.[6]

It would be difficult to imagine an early sixteenth century artist of any speculative inclination who did not in one way or another, contemplate the sources of alchemical thought. Duvet's role as goldsmith and engraver inevitably brought him close to alchemical concerns. The alchemical world, originating with a study of metals, focused on gold in its elaborate allegory of salvation-purification. This allegory impinges upon the greater part of Duvet's *corpus*.[7] Many contemporaries of Duvet, Italian artists including Cosimo Roselli, Giorgione, Jacopo de Barbari, Parmigianino, Beccafumi and probably Dosso Dossi were also devoted to aspects of alchemy.[8]

Shattering one of the time-honored barriers between the liberal arts and the visual arts, Paracelsus stressed the importance of working with his hands. In the *Labyrinthus Medicorum* of 1538, Paracelsus repeatedly wrote of the need to understand God through his creation, nature. God's "book of heavens, book of man, book of alchemy, book of medicine" was not an exercise "out of speculation and theories but practically out of the light of Nature, and experience." The Renaissance artist often shared this goal with the scientist-alchemist who explored and analyzed nature through his meticulous recreations.[9] It was inevitable that Duvet should have been drawn to the new alchemical perspectives of Paracelsus. After oscillating between Calvinism and Catholicism, he discovered in Paracelsus the redefinition, perhaps even the invention of a new concept of the means; in short, the goals of human experience. According to Paracelsus, "Art is a second Nature and a universe of its own." True art for him was alchemy, this same second nature which was "obedient to and imitative of Nature, finishing and fulfilling Nature's course."[10]

The divine creativity of God, seen as the work of an artist, is basic to most faiths. Its corollary—the artist as participating in a divine art through his labors—is accepted by all cultures. With the popularization of the Corpus Hermeticum through the invention of printing, Ficino's translations of the *Asclepius* and the *Pimander* (1463) and the Florentine Neo-Platonists' writings on magic, the artist of the High Renaissance was increasingly equated with Mercury, father of the arts and author of special revelation who gave law and letters to the Egyptians and foresaw the one and only God. The artist like Mercury was sage, prophet and magician. By virtue of his own wisdom, he could prepare for the descent to the grave. In this way, he was able to capture the spirit of the cosmos and use his imagination to prepare the way for a new order. Aspects of such Neo-Platonic thought, which might have come to the engraver from several orthodox sources, elucidate the Frontispiece of Duvet's Apocalypse. A discussion of this can be found in the section devoted to that richly allusive print. The more speculative, mystical, alchemical and astrological literature, so rampant in mid-century, must have played a major role in contributing to the artist's vision. More will be said later about the upswing of astrological literature.

Completing his last and major work, the *Apocalypse,* as an old man, Duvet could hardly have been ignorant of the melancholy associations of this achievement. Wrought under the sign of Saturn, and executed for those who "wholeheartedly and sincerely concentrate on that divine concentration," Saturn was viewed as most conducive to the operation of genius— at that point when the intuitive mind penetrates the secrets of divinity. As has been seen, Duvet's self-portrait and the significance of the surrounding emblems are all cast in a profoundly melancholic mould.

The printmaking process itself, reproducing images in transitions from black to white, with reversals and uses of acids in the etching technique may be seen as rife with alchemical illusions in the *arte nigredo* and in the positive-negative reversals of Basil Valentine. Small wonder that the inventor of etching, Parmigianino, through his research into the properties of acids and metals should himself have been placed in an alchemical cast when much of his art was imbued with magical references.[11]

Demonological concerns involved in much of the alchemical procedure are curiously pervasive in early sixteenth century art. Some printmakers such as Hans Baldung have black magic occupying a major role in their oeuvre. Duvet's own work paid tribute to infernal motifs, as can be seen, for example, in his several renderings of the suicide of Judas. It has already been said that his *Apocalypse* Series may be partly rooted in the great dramatic production performed near Dijon. What is important in this discussion is that the *Diablerie* of Chaumont includes in personified form the whole repertoire of classical and Christian evils. The Apocalypse Frontispiece demonstrates the Neo-Platonic concern with demons which is also rooted in medieval tradition. It is tempting to relate it to the belief that in order to summon demons—good and bad alike—a knife and burin were needed, elements akin to those in Duvet's print.[12] The bellows in the same engraving, entirely appropriate to a demon, is also among the essential furnishings of the alchemist's workshop in which the assistant is usually depicted working his bellows. The bad alchemist is traditionally referred to as a puffer, incapable of anything else.

All classical and Christian symbolism provided grist for the voracious alchemical mill, founded in large part on Kabbalistic, hermetic literature. For all its seeming obfuscation, divination, eschatology, and mystical gibberish, the alchemical study nurtured both chemistry and physics and proved to be a later medieval and Renaissance midpoint between the achievements in these areas in ancient and modern times. Off-putting as its associations with black magic and false claims may make it, alchemy must be re-thought and restored to the position of unique significance which it enjoyed in the sixteenth century when it received special prominence through the widely published writings and translations of Pico and the more recent literature of Agrippa von Nettesheim and Paracelsus.

C.G. Jung's analysis of the religious and psychological elements in alchemy has done much to give this complex movement its due as a major contribution to Western culture. Erwin Panofsky was fond of drawing an analogy between the popularity of Neo-Platonism in the Renaissance and that of psychoanalysis in his own day. He might well have included alchemy under the Neo-Platonic umbrella, where it belongs.

Toward the mid-sixteenth century, a steady swell of astrological literature emerged by Pontus de Tyard, among others. In large part these came from the Lyon presses where Duvet's *Apocalypse* was published with accompanying text in 1561. One of the most elaborate descriptions of mystical revelation was printed there in 1555, the same year that Duvet completed his autobiographical Frontispiece, in Nostradamus' "Preface to his Prophecies"— his *Siècles*. Dedicated to his son, the astrologer's text notes "All is predicted through divine inspiration, and by means of angelic spirit with which the man prophesying is inspired, rendering him anointed with prophecies, illuminating him, moving him before his fantasy through diverse nocturnal apparitions.[14] Born a Jew and obviously fearful of heretical charges, Nostradamus specifically records his own obliteration of all alchemical literature in his possesion. Like Paracelsus, Nostradamus was a doctor and with other physicians and alchemists prepared cosmetics such as those made by Battonat for Diane de Poitiers. Steeped in Neo-Platonic literature, Nostradamus edited a translation of the Horus Apollo in the early 1550's as well as one of Galen's *Paraphrase of the Exhortation of Menodatus for the studies of the fine arts, especially medicine*. Predictably, Nostradamus became a great favorite of Catherine de Medici when he went to Paris in 1556. With Ronsard, Nostradamus derived much of his Neo-Platonic knowledge from the Lyon editions of Iamblichus and Ficino, published in 1549. The year 1548, in which Duvet received his *Privilège* at Fontainebleau to publish the *Apocalypse,* Nostradamus made his first appearance at the French court. They need not have known each other, because the coincidence of date and place simply reflect the currency of mystical interests at the time.

Astrological and alchemical concerns were not out of place in the humanistically inclined episcopal court at Langres. The anonymous advisors referred to on the *Apocalypse* Frontispiece may well have included Richard Roussat, a canon who had published astrological writings in 1550. A personal source of such literature close to Duvet's home is Pierre Turel of Dijon who dedicated his work on astrological computation to a local abbot in

1525. When in Geneva, one of Duvet's outstanding associates, "le magnificque Meigret," a prominent Calvinist from Lyon, had alchemical interests and is cited as such by Bernard Palissy, an artist whose broad competence recalls Duvet's.[15] An ingenius ceramist, Palissy's concerns with firing and the chemical properties of glazes may well have introduced him to the alchemical world, just as Duvet's work as goldsmith could have provided him with a similar orientation. Philibert de l'Orme, architect to Henri II and Diane de Poitiers, is known to have been interested in astrology. His two allegorical woodcuts of the Good and Bad Architects would suggest an awareness of alchemical thought as well.[16]

Alchemical, hermetic thought pervaded the courts of Western Europe. It promised mysterious powers, miraculous healing, sudden revelations of eternal but instantly advantageous truths and last, but not least, the possible conversion of metal from base to precious.. All these potential achievements often proved to be an irresistable concern of emperor and king, prince and count. Not only were men of power drawn to the new alchemical literature, to the assemblages of text and practitioners, but they saw themselves as rightful heirs to the prophecies and profits of these complex, veiled powers to whom the Great Work, should speak most directly and resourcefully, Maximillian for one, felt he was the Hermes Trimegistus, miraculous agent and recipient of magical lore. He is shown on his triumphal arch and in the *Weisskönig* as a special student of White Magic.[17] Francois Ier in search of a way to procure the huge ransom needed to free his hostage sons from Spanish captivity, summoned a German magician to fly them back from Madrid, just as Habacus had been borne by an angel from the lion's pit. The French king was also said to have used mirror-magic (captromancy) to project the Italian military campaigns to Paris, so that his subjects could witness events in Lombardy.[18] Such ventures and voyages involving mysterious solutions were partially legitimized by the academic authority given to hermetic thought in the fifteenth century. Endowed with a certain official cachet by Medici patronage, the renaissance of magical literature, the new popularity of astrology and the deliciously obscure and dubious genre of the Horus Apollo offered all the omniscience of contemporary astrophysics and psychoanalysis. Unprecedentedly abstruse in its symbolism, the Galerie Francois Ier, situated between the library above and the baths below, may itself reflect some of the complexities of alchemical thought, which its painter, Rosso, appears to have been attracted to.[19] An earlier court painter to Francois Ier, Jean Perréal, dedicated to his master a central alchemical text he had prepared. Appropriately, the only certain work by Perréal is a single leaf, devoted to a dialogue between the alchemist and nature (ex. coll. Georges Wildenstein).[20] Another alchemical associate of the king's was Agrippa von Nettesheim, who worked on military engineering and weaponry projects and was a friend of Perréal when they were both resident in Lyon.

Alchemical *studioli* in which the scientifically inclined master of the house could ponder alchemical verities were probably built throughout France. Two of these, located near Burgundy still survive. The Hôtel Lallemant at Bourges has a ceiling with alchemical motifs, as does the one found at Dampierre-sur-Bouton.[21] Manuscripts devoted to the same subject were also illuminated for its owner. So prominent a figure as Jacques Coeur had no qualms about broadcasting his alchemical concerns. His residence at Montpellier employed three alchemical furnace-like forms, resembling those of Nicholas Flamel, to frame the doorways, possibly emblematic of his own financial ability to multiply gold. His house at Bourges also incorporated alchemical references, including an alchemical mass sculpted in the tympanum above the stairway.[22]

A small portrait of François Ier by Nicolas Belin, showing him as a Hermaphroditic summary of the gifts of the gods and goddesses may be seen as an eloquent testimony to the acceptability of the alchemical as well as Platonic concept of the androgen.[23] Hermetic revelation offered an irresistible opportunity to those who felt themselves the inevitable recipients. The fact that the king should have promulgated himself as recipient of alchemical grace is suggested by his choice of a flaming but unburnt basilisk or salamander for his emblem. It is the symbol of rebirth and miraculous survival, representing the chemical sulphur which, with mercury and salt are the three basic substances and is light incarnate. The beast also represents *prima materia*.[24] The salamander in the fire (François Ier's emblem) stood for the philosopher's stone.

As forerunners of physicists and chemists, many conservative alchemists of the sixteenth century did not concern themselves with flamboyant exercises in transmutation-essentially an allegory of the transcendance of the soul—but rather with perfectly legitimate testing of metals by acid. François Ier employed an alchemist for this work in 1540.[25] Apparently, he also applied alchemical views to medical practices, if indeed the two were even separable in his time. As an infant, the future Henri II was forced to eat powdered gold, steel, and iron, a practice not far from those of twentieth century medicine. The same cannot be said for the powered "unicorn horn" he was given, unless it can be equated with gelatin. When he became king, Henri seems to have been more concerned with hermetic thought than was his father, which was probably due to the influence of Catherine de Medici as well as Diane de Poitiers. Rabelais referred to Henri several times as the *Roi Mégiste*, not without satiric intent, but nonetheless indicative of Henri's hoped for status as heir to the mystery of classical wisdom.

Rabelais writing of Henri II as a *magus*, used this term for his patronage of Philibert de l'Orme, who similarly pursued astrological concerns. The king's monogram was associated with that of Hermes and the double D device, romantically interpreted as a reference to Diane, may also have been viewed as *donum dei*![27]

Significantly, it is in conjunction with his patronage of Charles Charmois, a painter, and Philibert de l'Orme, the leading ingenious disciple of Vitruvius, that the king is viewed as the great wise man of antiquity. Alchemy was an extremely lively issue. Consequently, Rabelais' first chapter of Book IV of *Pantagruel* seems in large part to satirize that endeavor, precisely by characterizing Henri II as King Megistus, greatest monarch in Christendom (Pantagruel, III, Chapter XXXV). The young king's alchemical interests were applied to its most "practical" end, the transmutation of metals. It may well have been Diane de Poitiers, whose sophisticated intelligence and mystical orientation—best expressed by her necropolis, Anet—led the young king to an investigation of the uses of alchemy. Diane's enduring liaisons with François Ier and then his son Henri II perpetuated an allegory of the golden sun of the king and the silvery moon of Diana which was an alchemical cliché. Diane's age would also lead to an interest in the quasi-cosmetic aspects of alchemy, with its fountains of youth and restoring unguents. Her physician Jean Fernel dedicated his work *The Natural Part of Medicine* to Henri II in 1542. It was a study that was in large part an alchemical dialogue although the author did not believe in the Philosopher's Stone and the more fabulous aspects of the study.[28]

Diane de Poitiers was in correspondence with an alchemist of aristocratic pretentions named Battonat, who was to cheat a Swiss prince, the Count of Gruyère for a very considerable sum. Duvet was summoned after Battonat's downfall in order to mint a new coinage to replace the fraudulent one struck by Battonat. Diane had given Battonat "beaucoup de biens" in 1547, some of these for compounds to restore her youth and beauty.[29] Several meetings took place with the king, Anne de Montmorency, the *connétable de France*, Diane, and Battonat's misguided patron, the Count de Gruyère, a member of the Order of St. Michael, in attendance.

Duvet's activity in the Geneva mints, and his service to the Comte de Gruyère (who needed his own currency restored after the disastrous expreience with Battonat) indicate his familiarity with aspects of alchemical thought especially pertaining to the transmutation of metals. His early training in Dijon would have brought him in contact with coinmaking. Moreover, he could have spent some of the years we cannot account for in mints at other centers. A major issue in Battonat's Geneva trial of 1552 was the sacrilegious invocation of holy names in the process of preparing the transmutation of metals:

> S'il scait que par le droict, tant divin que humain, est defendu
> d'user divinations, incantations, adjurations et invocations de
> Diables et espritz, et pareillement d'abuser du nom de Dieu,
> des Anges, des sainctz et parolles de l'escripture saincte,
> mesmement pour faire incantations, adjurations des espritz
> et divinations? Ny aussi faire des anneaux pour servir à telles
> divinations, et escrire, porter et garder mémoires et parolles

pour servir a faire telz anneaux, invocations, adjurations et
divinations. Et si cela n'est pas ung crime capital, et digne ce
mort?[30]

Probably similar trials took place in France but in his own country the king considered
himself the legitimate heir to all knowledge. While his enthusiasm for demonology may
have been slight, it was no doubt viewed as a necessary evil, the fruits thereof partially
applicable to charitable deeds. In sum, alchemy was a common factor in the intellectual
and aristocratic life of the sixteenth century. It served to unite such royalty and those
close to them as Francois I, Henri II, Henry of Navarre and Jeanne d'Albret, Catherine de
Medici, Diane de Poitiers, the Comte de Gruyère and Meigret.

Duvet's activity as a goldsmith, maker of rings and reliquaries, his cognizance of
gilding and similar processes must have made him familiar with the goals, the claims and
the props of the negative aspects of alchemy. It is highly unlikely that he indulged in
the fabric of transmutation. However, as we can see from his oeuvre, Duvet knew and
observed the alchemical world, as it pricked his spiritual curiousity. Practicing both
Catholicism and Calvinism, the goldsmith must also have investigated the spiritual imperatives of his own craft.

Often in theological disrepute, the alchemist sought a profound, intimate association
with the divine. They viewed their labors in the same spirit as the Lord's. Concluding
his alchemical treatise, a famous French alchemist of the mid-fifteenth century exhorted
his followers: "Which wilt thou do as I did it, if thou wilt take pains to be what thou
shouldst be– that is to say, pious, gentle, benign, charitable and fearing God."[31] The
true alchemist was not concerned with earthly riches, but like the disinterested scientific
ideal of the present, sought to unlock new truths by understanding nature. In a sense,
man was the subject of Alchemy; the object of its art his perfection or improvement
"The salvation of man – his transformation from evil to good, or his passage from a state
of nature to a state of grace – was symbolized under the figure of the transmutation of
metals."[32]

Rooted in Kabbalistic writings and those of Vincent of Beauvais, alchemy and its
hermetic lore exercised considerable appeal to churchmen. The Medici Pope, Leo X, pre-
disposed to the goals of this branch of knowledge through training in Florence as a student
of Pico, Poliziano and Ficino, had elaborate alchemical treatises dedicated to him in 1515
and 1518.[33]

The entire alchemical process was seen as an allegory of the scale which measured
the perfection of the soul as it ascended from base to pure. The refinement of metal was
parallel to the purification of the spirit with its goal the sun, the divine creative force
present in the soul of God. The ambiguity and interpenetration of alchemical and conservative Christianity may best be appreciated on a visual basis by the centuries–long
misread function of a richly decorated chamber at the Hotel Lallemant at Bourges. This
Renaissance room, wrongly viewed as a chapel, was in fact an alchemical *studiolo*.

Both Old and New Testaments provide bases for alchemical interpretation of Holy
writ. The Tablets of Moses and the Pentacle of Solomon(with Mercury's *caduceus*) are
fundamental to the imagery of the quasi-scientific field.' The tablets, primary graphic
manifestation of the spirit and hand of God, with the star of Solomon and staff of Moses
were linked to the divine Philosopher's Stone, the key to the secrets of the universe.[36]
An inscribed version of The Tablets on a mid-sixteenth century alchemical ceiling at
Dampierre, bear the words EN RIEN GIST TOUT signifying that primal matter is found
in abundance in nature.[37] The hermetic lore of the *Horusapollo*, a manuscript of dubious
antiquity, seized upon Moses' Tablets, Duvet's emblem, as the summary of all knowledge
and to the divine wisdom of East and West, as stated by Acts 7:22, "Erudites est Moses
omni sapientia Aegyptorum."[38] As the primal figure of alchemy, Moses personified the
divine wisdom of the ancients. First he made his caduceus-like staff release the water
in the rock, then he proved his technical skills by dying skins and preparing curtains for
the Tabernacle, and finally he revealed his alchemical expertise by "dissolving" the Golden
Calf, thereby comminuting the gold by fusing it with an alkaline sulphate and by testing
the metals of the Midianites.[39] Alchemical readings of the New Testament equate God

the Father with gold, the Virgin with silver, Christ with mercury, and the evangelists with the four impure metals. [40]

We may best judge how profound a grasp alchemical interpretations had upon sixteenth century religious thought through a Hermetic painting at Saint-Maurice (Reims, Text fig. 16). A Greek inscription states: "I gave birth as a virgin an infant without parents." This enigmatic painting probably dates from the later sixteenth century, the figure at the Virgin's side, next to the personification of *Religio* is perhaps a portrait of a local prelate, with alchemical attributes. O. Wirth (*Le symbolisme hermétique dans ses rapports avec l'Alchimie et la Franc-Maçonnerie,* Paris, 1931) sought to tie this work too closely to

16. Hermetic Panel, *from the Church of Saint Maurice, Reims.*

the Masonic movement. The depiction includes an *adepte* (Alchemical initiate or practitioner) wearing a red chasuble, holding a *caduceus,* a book of secrets and a fiery knife' The alchemical literature viewed as divine truth, was itself cast in a biblical mold so that Nicholas Flamel's early fifteenth century compilation was entitled *Psautier chimique.* Pico della Mirandola revived most of the alchemical literature but no doubt it never completely died out.[41] The massive demonology of the Apocalypse made that mystical, dreamlike text text an alchemical favorite. This is seen in greatest abundance in George Ripley's *Book of the Twelve Gates,* a major treatise written in the late fifteenth century, which also whetted the alchemical appetite. It is based on the concept of Original Sin, wherein the Fall of Lucifer was seen as a signifying the corruption of the basic metals. Ripley even manages to have the Whore of Babylon restored to virginity, undoubtedly through alchemical sub-

42

limation.[42] Saint John, Duvet's patron saint as well as the patron saint of printers, was viewed as one of the first alchemists because of apocryphal accounts of his transforming the pebbles on the riverbank to gold and precious stones and causing the poison serpent to emerge from the cup. The Woman of the Apocalypse, with her miraculous conjunction of sun and moon was equated with the alchemical process of libation; "the infant, deriving sustenance from its nurse, the earth, is an image of the Stone whose mother, in the words of the fourth precept of Hermes, is the Moon."[43] Agrippa von Nettesheim, the leading sixteenth century alchemical writer, was probably a major source for Duvet's knowledge of this area. Nettesheim devoted a chapter of his work to the "Pentacles and Sacred Seals" grounded in the Apocalyse.[44]

To add to the list of alchemical enthusiasts, we may add Luther's name, for though he was wary of the Apocalypse, he was receptive to alchemical thought. His new desire for direct contact with the divine, and his individualistic ideals urged him to dispense with ecclesiastic intermediaries. Alchemist and Protestant alike sought refutation of the need for mediation by church and priest in the union between man and God. For the alchemist it was the "donum Spiritus Sancti," the divine art of his individual "opus," for the Protestant, the divine work of his individual faith. Genesis, according to Paracelsus, was a divine chemical separation which this brilliant scientist, mystic and physician sought to understand in terms of an analysis of his own experience of God's work on earth-nature. Luther characterized alchemy as "good art," not only because it represented "the true philosophy of the ancient sages...of great use in creating metals but because of her allegorical and secret meanings which are very beautiful, signifying the resurrection of the dead on the Day of Judgment."[45]

Paracelsus was himself referred to as the Luther, the Calvin, the Zwingli, the Melanchton of medicine, who used the alchemical method not to make gold but to find the sources of healing.[46] It is tempting to see the concept of the Christian alchemist as one aspect underlying Duvet's scrutiny and experience of the Apocalypse, entirely in keeping with the intensely personal nature of his art and with what is known of his spiritual biography encompassing both Catholic and Calvinist faith. The unicorn, an eloquent mystical reference common to Christianity and alchemy, was equally as prominent in Duvet's small oeuvre because of its uniquely comprehensive symbolism.[47] Those who first called Duvet "The Master of the Unicorn" wrote more wisely than they knew.

1.   Edgar Wind, *Pagan Mysteries in the Renaissance,* London, 1965, pp. 214 ff.

2.   See A. Vernet, *Jean Perréal poéte et alchimiste,* Bibliothéque d'Humanisme et Renaissance, III, 1943, pp. 235 ff.; also, Charles Sterling, "Une peinture certaine de Perréal," *L'Oeil,* No. 103 -104, 1963, pp. ·2-15, 64 -65. Also, F. Walker, "Jean de Meun and Alchemy," *The Journal of Chemical Education,* VII, 1930, pp. 2863 - 74.
     The *Roman de la Rose* was of considerable influence in the fifteenth and sixteenth centuries; a lavishly illuminated page dedicated to Charles IX of 1571, from Baïf, covers a late medieval manuscript of the *Roman* now in the Moıgan Library, New York.
     Albert—Marie Schmidt, *La Poésie scientifique en France au seizième siècle,* Paris, n.d., devotes a valuable study to "Trois Alchimistes—Poètes" in its sixth chapter. See also *Umanèsimo e Esoterismo* edited by Enrico Castelli, Padua, 1960, for much valuable information concerning Hermetic thought in the sixteenth century.

3.   See Raymond Klibansky, Erwin Panofsky and Fritz Saxl, *Saturn and Melancholy,* London, 1964, pp. 352 ff.

4.   Calvesi, *op. cit.,* pp. 50-51.

5.   *Ibid.,* p. 329. First recognized by K. Giehlow, "Dürers Stich 'Melancolia I' und der Maximilianische Humanistenkreis," *Mitteilungen der Gesellschaft für vervielfältigende Kunst (Die Graphischen Künste,* supplement), XXVI, 1903, pp. 29-41, XXVII, 1945, pp. 6-18, 57-78.
     Also J. Read, "Dürer's Melancholy: an alchemical interpretation," *Burlington Magazine,* LXXXVII, 1945, pp. 283 -84.

6.   J. van Lennep, *Art et Alchimie,* Brussels, 1966, p. 98, fig. 10, shows the Melancoly Alchemist from J. Brunswyck's *Distilierbuch* (of 1510).

7.   L. Olschki, *Geschichte der neusprachlichen wissenschaftlichen Literatur,* II, Leipzig, 1922, *Die Geheimwissenschaften,* presents an excellent discussion of the relationship between alchemical studies and metal work. He is very firm about the counter-alchemical views of Leonardo, who separated alchemy from magic, and the equally "unalchemical" orientation of Cellini, but recent studies by outstanding Italian scholars have doubted Olschki's views. Maurizio Calvesi ("A noir Melencolia I"), *Storia dell 'Arte,* 1969, pp. 37-96) and Maurizio Fagiolo dell 'Arco (*Il Parmigianino, un saggio sull'ermetismo nel Cinquecento,* Rome, 1970) have made the major contributions to this complex field. Eugenio Garin, *La Cultura filosofica del Rinascimento italiano,* p. 397, stresses Vasari's characterization of Leonardo as a *magus,* the artist's own citation of Hermes the philosopher and his "close relationship with ficinian-hermetic themes of universal life and animation" which bring Leonardo close to the "white magical" aspects of alchemical thought. Francis A. Yates, "The hermetic tradition," in Charles S. Singleton, *Art, Science and History in the Renaissance,* Baltimore, 1967, pp. 255—74, agrees with Garin on p. 261.

8.   For the artist as alchemist, see Rudolf and Margot Wittkower, *Born under Saturn,* London, 1963, pp. 84-88.

9.   The major scholarly awareness of alchemical components in Renaissance art is Hartlaub's, evidenced by the following publications: G. F. Hartlaub, "Arcana Artis—Spuren alchimistischen Symbolik in der Kunst des 16. Jahrhunderts," *Zeitschrift für Kunstgeschichte,* VI, 1937, pp. 289-324; "Signa Hermetis" *Zeitschrift des deutschen Vereins für Kunstwissenschaft,* IV-V, 1937-8, pp. 93- 112, 144-162; *Der Stein der Weisen, Wesen und Bildwelt der Alchimie,* Munich, 1959; "Albrecht Dürers 'Aberglaube'," *Zeitschrift des deutschen Vereins für Kunstwissenschaft,* VII, 1940, pp. 167-196. See also Allen G. Debus, *The Chemical Dream of the Renaissance,* Cambridge, 1938, p. 11; Erwin Panofsky, "Artist, Scientist, Genius: Notes on the 'Renaissance - Dämmerung'," *The Renaissance, a Symposium,* The Metropolitan Museum of Art, New York, 1952, pp. 77 ff.

10. Quoted by Hiram Haydn, *The Counter-Renaissance,* Gloucester (Mass.), 1966, p. 111.

11. Fagiolo dell'Arco's stimulating study may at times push the alchemical elements in Parmigianino's art too far, but it is indisputable that there is a very considerable concern with the mystical-scientific genre in his oeuvre. For a summary of Valentine's thought, see Fulcanelli, *Les demeures philosophales et le symbolisme hermétique dans ses rapports avec l'art sacré et le ésotérisme du grand-oeuvre,,* Paris, 1930, p. 77.

12. Grillot de Givry, *Witchcraft, Magic and Alchemy,* New York, n.d., p. 103.

13. Jung's largely persuasive reevaluation of the role and substance of alchemy has contributed to a new awareness of its function in the art of the Renaissance. With the most important exceptions of Giehlow and Hartlaub, German scholars have been leary of the alchemical factor. This has been especially true of art historians in the Warburg circle, which is most strange as they, more than any others have concerned themselves with Neo-Platonism. See Jung's *Psychology and Alchemy, Collected Works,* XII, New York, 1968, Chapter III, "Religious ideas in alchemy," pp. 225-466.

14. See Edgar Leoni, *Nostradamus: Life and Literature,* New York, 1971, p. 131. Langres appears in several of his predictions.

15. See his *Discours admirables de la nature, les eaux et fontaines,* Paris, 1580, edited by B. Fillon and Louis Audiat, Paris, II, p. 72.

16. From *Le premier tome de l'Architecture,* Paris, 1567.

17. Giehlow, "Die Hieroglyphenkunde des Humanismus in der Allegorie der Renaissance besonders in der Ehrenpforte Kaisers Maximilian I," *Jahrbuch der kunsthistorischen Sammlungen in Wien,* XXII, 1915, pp. 1–233, Pl. 1. W. Ganzenmüller, *L'Alchimie au Moyen Age,* Paris, n.d., pp. 86-100, noted proliferation of alchemists attached to the courts of Europe.

18. M. Gaillard, *Histoire de François Ier, Roi de France,* Paris, 1819, V, p. 290.

19. See Fagiolo dell'Arco, *op. cit.,* p. 110, "E evidente il tentativo del sovrano di paragonarsi a una divinità ermetica, paragonando a Diana la sua donna."

20. The illumination for the *Complainte de Nature a l'Alchimiste errant* of 1516 was taken from the ms. 3220, Bibliothèque Ste.-Geneviève. See Charles Sterling, "Une Peinture certain de Perréal . . . ," *op. cit.,* fig. 1. The alchemical poem is folio 5, v.

21. Guy de Tervarent, "De la méthode iconologique," *Mémoires de l'Academie royale de Belgique, Classe des Beaux-Arts,* XII, fasc. 4, pp. 1-45. Part II is devoted to "Les motifs alchimiques." See also van Lennep, *op. cit., pp.* 191–92.

22. Fulcanelli, *op. cit.* Both discuss the Lallement vault. See Pierre Clément, *Jacques Coeur et Charles VIII,* Paris, 1873, pp. 146–47. Perhaps the financier's initials led to the crown of thorns motif on the facade which was also embellished with a sun and moon filled with fleur-de-lys representing the solar and lunar stones. The relief is shown by Van Lennep, *op cit.,* fig. 176.

23. See *L'Ecole de Fontainebleau,* Paris, 1972, Cat. No. 27, p. 27.

24. Van Lennep, *op. cit.,* p. 37. See André Chastel, "La Salamandre," *Revue de l' Art,* 16-17, 1972, pp. 150-152 for a fine discussion of the heraldic and emblematic significance of the salamander. Fulcanelli, *op. cit.,* p. 79, does not accept an alchemical interpretation of the being's device.

25. Van Lennep, *op. cit.,* p. 136.

26. Pantagruel, Book III, Chapter XXXV, IV, and Book Chapter 2; *Quart Livre,* IV, line 61, published in 1561.

27. Fulcanelli, *Demeures, op. cit.,* pp. 186, 193.

28. Charles Sherrington, *The Endeavour of Jean Fernel,* Cambridge, 1946, pp. 45-52.

29. Henri Naef, "L'Alchimiste de Michel, Comte de Gruyère," *Mémoires et documents publiés par la Société d'histoire de la France Romande,* 3 Sér., II, 1946.

30. *Ibid.,* pp. 280-281.

31. Quoted by Grillot de Givry, *Witchcraft, Magic, and Alchemy,* New York, n.d., p. 84.

32. E. A. Hitchcock, *A History of Magic and Experimental Science*, IV, New York, pp. 252–3, 534, 547. See also James Campbell Brown, *A History of Chemistry from Earliest Times*, Philadelphia, 1920.
   thought.

33. E. A. Hitchcock, *Observations on alchemy and chemistry*, New York, 1865, pp. 1v, viii, x.

34. See Lynn Thorndike, *A History of Magic and Experimental Science*, IV, New York, pp. 252-3, 534, 547. See also James Campbell Brown, *A History of Chemistry from Earliest Times*, Philadelphia, 1920, for a discussion of receptivity to alchemical thought.

35. Van Lennep, *op. cit.*, pp. 14-18.

36. *Ibid.*, pp. 191-2. Guy de Tervarent, *op. cit.*, does not agree as to the extent of alchemical references but his view is incorrect.

37. See Emil Ernst Ploss, Heinz Roosen–Runge, Heinrich Schipperges, Herwig Buntz, *Alchimia, Ideologie und Technologie*, Munich, 1970, p. 89.

38. Van Lennep, *op. cit.*, p. 190.

39. Fulcanelli *(op. cit.,* p. 269) refers to the tablets as the "Tables de la loi hermétique." For additional, bizarre alchemical interpretation of the Ten Commandments, see A. Volguine, *Symbolisme de la vie legendaire de Moise*, Nice, 1933, and Roger Caro, *Pléiade Alchimique*, Marseille, 1967, pp. 120-123. The Dampierre ceiling also includes a device related to the autobiographical Frontispiece of the Duvet Apocalypse, a swan with an arrow through its neck, inscribed PRO PRIIS. PEREO. PENNIS, stemming from Basil Valentine's alchemical text *The Twelve Keys* (according to Fulcanelli, p. 269).

40. For Moses as prototypical chemist, see M. Berthelot, *La Chimie au Moyen-Age*, Paris, 1893, pp. 29, 37-39, 44-48.

41. See E. J. Holmyard, *Alchemy*, Baltimore, 1957, pp. 63–64.

42. It is signed by both P. Dumont and J. Babinet. See van Lennep, *op. cit.*, pp. 166–7.

43. See F. S. Taylor, *The Alchemist*, New York, 1962, p. 107. For alchemical application of the Apocalypse, see also Eugène Canseliet, *Alchimie - Etudes diverses de Symbolisme hermétique et de pratique philosophale*, Paris, 1964.

44. Van Lennep, *op. cit.*, p. 114.

45. For an exhaustive alchemical interpretation of the Apocalypse, see Fulcanelli, *op. cit.*, p. 79. The resemblance between Duvet's *Martyrdom of Saint John* (Cat. 37) and the concept of *Splendor Solis* in the cauldron, the Holy Ghost overhead, may well be coincidental, but nonetheless striking. See the *Mercurius Senex* Ms. Harley 3469, in the British Museum.

46. Quoted by R. and M. Wittkower, *op. cit.*, p. 85.

47. F. Strunz, *Astrologie, Alchemie und Mystik*, Munich, 1928, p. 71.

48. The alchemical Mortification of the King may also be a reference made by the Duvet engraving of that beast wounding members of a royal retinue in their fatal encounter with the ferocious animal. See John Read, *An Outline of Alchemy, its Literature and Relationships*, Cambridge, 1966, Pl. 61. See Jung, *op. cit.*, pp. 415-451. On pp. 435-471, the author discusses the "Paradigm of the unicorn," divided into section a. The Unicorn in Alchemy (pp. 435 - 8); b. The Unicorn in Ecclesiastical Allegory (pp. 439 - 70); c. The Unicorn in Gnosticism (pp. 449-53) and in the Vedas (pp. 453 ff.). Harold Bayley, *The Lost Language of Symbolism*, London, II, 1909, pp. 14-15, stresses the view of Basil Valentine's early fifteenth century alchemical manuscript in which the purity of the unicorn is so strong that it repells all things noxious in the Triumphal Chariot of Antimony. Bayley sees the unicorn as an Albigensian symbol, "woven" into their papers in watermark form. This seems like a dubious thesis as the beast is found as a watermark all over western Europe, including Langres, without any discernible Albigensian associations.

III.

THE APOCALYPSE

The Apocalypse as Autobiography

For centuries all that was known of Jean Duvet's life was the autobiographical information that he engraved on the Frontispiece (Cat. 65) of his *Apocalypse figurée* dated 1555.[1] The print shows a powerful figure of a bearded, saturnine old man in classical attire, reminiscent of a Michelangelesque prophet, seated on a bench at the left, facing a table bearing an hour glass, a tablet, a burin, and an open book. With his right hand he points to the book, inscribed in Latin, "Book of the Apocalypse of the apostle Saint John." His left hand is raised, grasping the stylus with which he recorded his Revelations. The seated figure might well be a standard representation of the Evangelist on Patmos. His aged appearance however, differs from the youthful Saint John in other plates in the series. A burin lying on the table suggests the activity of an engraver rather than an author, and this is affirmed by the Latin inscription on the tablet, the same shape as the print itself, which reads, "Jean Duvet, goldsmith of Langres, aged seventy, has completed these histories in 1555." By literally "imagining" and recreating the Evangelist's turbulent visions in engraved form, Duvet assumed the prophetic role of his patron saint, who was also the divine protector of printers, an activity Duvet became deeply concerned with as publisher of his own *Apocalypse figurée* in 1561. Thus the print is a self-portrait of the engraver in the guise of his patron saint, conforming with the contemporary genre of dual characterization.

Seated on an island, the visionary artist's stooped shoulders and half-closed eyes suggest great age and exhaustion, accentuated by the presence of an hourgalss with its message of time running out. The frisking mouse, just beyond the reach of the faithful dog at the old man's feet, is another sign of gnawing destruction and slow decay.[2] While the dog keeps his eye on the mouse, the other pet, a cat, cranes its neck suspiciously toward an approaching swan. Rendered in loving detail, the animals of the Frontispiece are aware of their master's imminent death, though he himself is still lost in a creative trance. Although the artist-evangelist is a prophet of the divine, the animals know his demise is inevitable.

French writers toward mid-century were especially interested in animal behavior as portents, first shown in the writings of Cardanus. Rémy Belleau translated Aratus' animal lore, and Ronsard, using both sources, dedicated his beautiful *Le Chat* to Belleau. The ancient text describes the bold behaviors of mice as a harbinger of death. The cat is a prophet of death and the dog, like Apelles', may signify the power of the soul over nature

The popular yet complex concept of the introspective, solitary, melancholic humor, essential for artistic creativity, underlies many aspects of this composition. The cat may indicate choler; the mouse phlegm; the dog melancholy. The print could represent at least two moments—the first prior to its creation, as the good and evil inspiration represented by angel and demon, war over Duvet, the second the moment before the artist's death, when once again, the same forces battle.[3] The aged saturnine figure with an hourglass, his drooping head and hand on cheek are all standard attributes of melancholy.[4]

The sleeping dog "signifies the dull sadness of a creature entirely given over to its unconscious comfort or discomfort."[5] This animal has been linked with the prophets and 'sacras literas,' all associated with the melancholic since Aristotle."[6] Duvet's instruments, emblems of creativity, are also melancholic, as is the bellows near his head. Many of these hieroglyphs of the black humor were known to the French artist from Dürer's greatest *tour-de-force, Melencolia I* of 1514 (Text fig. 15). Duvet's plate, when viewed in reverse, bore very considerable forma. resemblance to Dürer's. As a military engineer Duvet no doubt had recourse to Dürer's publication on that subject. The French *Apocalypse,* concluded by the creation of the Frontispiece, shows frequent dependence upon the splendid German wood-cut series. Both print-makers began as goldsmiths. Many aspects of *Melencolia I* refer to that craft. Both artists knew of alchemy, that black art to which Melancholia's dark complexion may refer.[7]

Bearing an arrow in its beak, the swan (emblematic of the artist's name, "duvet" meaning down) swims toward the island, having just broken the golden chain of life by which it was tied to a tree stump. The latter, with the little bridge leading to the island, are additional emblems of transition from life to death. The Three Fates, shown in antique garb, are in a small boat, floating towards the engraver on a cloud.[8] Atropos holds the shears and is about to cut the thread of Duvet's life, the thread which her sisters spin and wind. The engraver wrote between these annunciations of mortality, the swan and the Fates: "Death is upon me and my hands tremble, my eyes are already beginning to fail, yet the spirit remains victorious and I have completed my great work." The inscription reveals Duvet as an old man in 1555, haunted by images of impending death, agreeing with the description of him as aged and ailing in the Geneva archives of the same year (Doc. 70–72). The *Fata* who are upon him, while bringing death, are unable to deprive the artist of the triumph over age, time, and mortality that enabled him to complete his engraved *Apocalypse* shown before him on tablet-shaped plates. The concept of the victorious spirit, in the sense of the Roman triumph frequently depicted in early French printed Books of Hours, is embodied by the classical guardian angel-muse at the engraver's side. Duvet's imagery of mortality is Christian as well as classical, in part due to the assimilation of the latter by the former. The arrow of death is spoken of in Psalm 7:13, and the engraver's fusion of death and victory is reminiscent of I Corinthians 15:54-55: "When the perishable puts on the imperishable, and the mortal puts on immortality, then shall come to pass the saying that is written: 'Death is swallowed up in victory.' 'O death, where is thy victory? O death, where is thy sting?'" These lines seem to be echoed within Duvet's engraving. The sting of death suggested by the arrow, is mitigated by the victory of the artist's personified spirit, by the triumphant figure at his side and by the exultant inscription.

The inscription at the lower left credits the source of the handsome elegiac couplet above. "The sacred mysteries contained in this and the other tablets following are derived from the divine Apocalypse of John and are closely adapted to the true letter of the text with the judgment of more learned men brought to bear." The episcopal court of Langres was one of the several small, informal centers for humanist thought maintained throughout France in the first third of the sixteenth century. For example, the monastery of Fontenay-le-Comte was one such center where Hellenists, jurists, and other scholars met in a congenial and spontaneous manner, creating the richly classical milieu which formed a point of departure for Rabelais. Rabelais was a monk at Fontenay-le-Comte from 1520 until 1525 when a new wave of repressive orthodoxy disbanded it.

One of the "more learned men," who was most likely to have influenced Duvet is Canon Jean Lefèvre, first French editor of Alciati's *Emblemata.*[9] Richard Roussat, a physician and astrologer, may well have been another adviser on the *Apocalypse* Frontispiece. A humanist at the court of Langres, Roussat's profoundly chiliastic views led to the publication in 1550 of his *Le Livre de l'Estat et Mutation des Temps, Prouvant par*

authoritez de l'Escripture saincte et par raison astrologales la fin du Monde estre Prochaine.
The text was printed in Lyon , where Nostradamus' similarly prophetic writings were to be issued in the following decade. Roussat received the *Privilège* for his work in 1549, one year after Duvet. Both belonged to the same Langres confraternity. In 1542, Roussat published an astrological text in Paris; the *Arcandum . . . . de veritatibus et praedectionibus astrologiae.*

A possible author of the Latin distichs on the *Apocalypse* Frontispiece may have been the poet Nicholas Bourbon. Like Duvet, he was born in the diocese of Langres, was patronized by Cardinal de Givry, became a Protestant, and was associated with Lyon. Bourbon was the tutor of Jeanne d'Albret, the daughter of the Protestant sympathizer Marguerite de Navarre and wife of the governor of Burgundy. One of the great fortified towers of Langres was named in honor of the House of Navarre. Its construction had concerned Jean Duvet.[10]

Still another adviser may have been Antoine Dupinet. One of the few Protestant theologians who addressed themselves to the difficult text for reasons other than producing anti-Catholic propaganda, Dupinet wrote a treatise entitled *Familières et briefve exposition sur l'apocalypse de Saint Jehan l'apostre.* Despite its title signifying brevity, it is over four hundred pages long. This impenetrable, now exceedingly rare book, was first printed in Geneva in 1539 and reissued there in 1543. Its author died a year before the publication of Duvet's *Apocalypse figurée* in 1560.[11]

A partial model for the French engraver's self-portrait—brooding prophetically at the banks of Geneva-Patmos—was the pose and attributes of a monumental winged female figure at the water's edge, Dürer's *Melencolia I.* Facing left rather than right, Duvet, like Melancholia, has a dog at his feet, and the wings of divine inspiration at his side. The bellows' nozzle under Melancholia's skirts is now held next to the evangelist-engraver's ear by a demon. The book in Melancholia's lap is placed before the male figure, her compass is replaced by a stylus, and the hourglass hanging over her head now rests upon the table. The rainbow arching over the bat-bearer of the *Melencolia I* defines the top of Duvet's engraving which, unlike the Dürer, is curved at the top.

The Frontispiece is, in the words of Geoffroy Tory, filled "with devices, riddles, and hieroglyphic writings."[12] It is an anthology of emblems, enclosing within its tablet-shaped confines an extraordinary wealth of puns, and of classical and Christian references. As Tory, a French pioneer in the use of the new emblematic language of humanism, noted in his *Champfleury* of 1529 (the year of Alciati's teaching at the University of Bourges), "Devices are not composed of letters, but of representations which bespeak the imagination of their author. They are sometimes called rebus. Their invention requires imagination, but they also stimulate others to reflection."[13] The same desire for a visual pun or *rébus* which led Tory to "sign" his works by including three ribbons (the Latin plural is *tori*) or by showing a drill (*thoret*), induced Duvet to show the down (*duvet*) plucked by an eagle, a double pun both on the engraver's name and, in the sense of action shown, on death. Another example is the inclusion of the plant known as *tufetum.*[14]

Tory and Duvet have followed Andrea Alciati's approach to symbolic communication. The Italian's "*emblemata* consist of three elements: motto, picture, and epigrammatic stanza."[15] Duvet differed from both Alciati, who taught jurisprudence at Avignon (1518) and Bourges (1529), and wrote the first emblematic treatise, and Tory of Bourges, whose pictures did "not illustrate the motto and vice versa, the two elements complementing one another in a happy marriage."[16] Duvet's visual and verbal images do mirror one another, word reflecting form and form conveying word in a more parallel, explanatory sense than the even more recondite, intricate alliance and duet initiated by Alciati in Italy and Tory in France.[17]

The swan with the arrow of death is quite literally the most poignant symbol of death. More than a visual pun on the engraver's name, the swan reflects the curious mixture of chivalric and Biblical thought with which much of Duvet's art, especially the Unicorn Series, is concerned. In breaking the chain of life, the bird is more than a mere swan-boat repetition of the Ship of Fate; it is taken from a Rhenish legend of the swan-knight, who, although chained to life, cannot escape his divine origin. As the swan-knight's golden chain of love is broken, the spirit leaves, never to return. The chain is an especially appropriate emblem for a goldsmith. Not only does this chain of love link the swan-knight to life, but it calms and controls the lake. Once it is broken, the lake stirs, storms come, the calm waters are troubled. The fishermen who hurriedly pull in their nets and the swimmer, who seems shot out of the water, reflect these passages in the swan legend.[18]

The swan bearing Apollo's arrow of death recalls Socrates' account: "The swan sings most, and most beautifully, when he senses approaching death. For then he will go to the Lord, whose servant he is."[19] Guillaume Guéroult, in his *Second livre de la description des animaux, contenant le Blason des oyseaux*[20] the section devoted to the swan, wrote of the bird's singing sweetly when death approached, for death was not to be feared when it led to eternal life. The engraved *Apocalypse*, whose very creation Duvet regarded as a triumph of the spirit over impending death, must itself be regarded as the engraver's swan song, his most eloquent and inspired graphic vision, recapitulating the revelation according to his patron saint John. Duvet may have found it appropriate with regard to his own profession as a goldsmith, for it is the goldsmith, the maker of rings and chains, who is one of the central figures in the legend. An old Cleves song describes a man's death, "Er lenkte an der Hand den Schwan, ein gulden Kettlein glanzte d'ran. Wer einmal ihn geliebt so sehr, der kann ihn nie vergessen mehr."[21]

Death was linked to swans in art as well as literature. Dürer selected huge birds' wings for his *Arms of Death* (B.101) uniting them with the helmet above the menacing skull of mortality. Other Northern artists used the swan in a less sepulchral context. The Swiss artist Urs Graf, rejected the coat of arms of his ancestors, and employed the swan twice in the blazon he devised for himself.[22] As might be expected, German Neo-Platonists also incorporated the swan in their coats of arms: that of Conrad von Celtes, designed by Hans Baldung, has the bird appearing above the humanist's head as he writes in his study by the fountain of the Muses. The same artist, in his design for Jakob Fröhlich's printer's mark shows a swan playing a violin with the inscription "Musae noster, amor dulcesque, ante omnia Musae."[23] The Pléiade described themselves as "new swans" divinely inspired by Apollo, an appropriate sentiment since their pens were often made of swans' quills.[24]

Platonic imagery of death persisted in France throughout the sixteenth century. An extraordinary document to its currency is the funerary oration delivered by an Augustinian for the burial of Guy du Faur de Pibrac in 1584.[25] After quoting both Socrates' and Cicero's swan symbolism, the Augustinian concluded, "Nous, dy je, fidelles, lavez et nettoyez au sang de Jésus-Christ suivons le naturel du Cygne."[26] Swan symbolism was employed in elegies for Jan Hus and Martin Luther.[27] By the late sixteenth century, the swan was officially associated with the concept of a "happy death" in allegories of mortality such as the one engraved by Jan Wierix. Here, a seated female figure in classical garb rests an arm on the Book of the Seven Seals inscribed *Evangelium* while gazing upward to Heaven. Her other arm, in a Leda-like gesture, embraces a large swan; her foot dangles over a freshly dug grave. Vignettes of a deathbed scene at the left and the Resurrection at the right relate the allegory to the late medieval *ars moriendi*.[28]

Duvet's classical annunciation of death was anticipated in France by a funerary monument commissioned circa 1540 for the tomb of Bishop Jean Olivier of Angers. Only one of the sculptures surrounding the grave is biblical—Solomon, selected for his sagacity. The other figures are classical: Plutarch, Aeschylus, Ovid, Cicero, Diogenes, Pythagoras, Ptolemy, and Boethius, accompanied by consoling inscriptions on the nature of death, led by Apollo and the Muses.[29] The evangelist-engraver's drowsy pose suggests the Neo-Platonic view of sleep: "Since sleep is a form of *vacatio*, that is, a state in which the soul withdraws from the body, during sleep the soul is immediately accessible to divine influence, particularly the soul of a man who has been previously purified and directed toward God . . . A genuine dream, therefore, is also a divine inspiration, given only to those who have already elevated themselves above the body while awake."[30] As written in Plato's *Timaeus*, "No man, when in his wits, attains prophetic truth and

inspiration; but when he receives the inspired work his intelligence is enthralled in sleep."
Ficino's theory of prophecy noted "Many priests under the influence of demons were
delivered into divine transports and made marvellous pronouncements." Holy men, by
removing the mind from the body in sleep were able, at once, to see past, present, and
future at the same time, equalling the three orders of succession of the cosmos—providence,
fate, and nature. This is evident in the engraved Frontispiece. By abstracting the self
from the rational, one may then function through intelligence, the *idolum* or nature.
"With eyes opened and purified they wait especially for what divinely may be shown
them, and this Socrates is said to have advised and practised. These are called pious men
and religious. Their soul is more withdrawn while awake than that of any others, in sleep
it is entirely withdrawn."[31] The first two chapters of Ficino's *Theologica Platonica* are
concerned with man's capacity to transcend and control his animal nature through imagination, the third goes directly to the arts enabling man to compete with nature, which
by extension, would include those of illusion—the visual arts.

A puzzling statue by Bontemps on the tomb of Charles de Maigny, executed in
1557, shows the Swiss captain of François Ier's guards fast asleep but seated in full armor
and holding a pike. It has been suggested that this peculiar pose may represent the sleep
of Mars or that of the Just, but it seems far more likely that, like the drowsy Duvet in
the Frontispiece, De Maigny is depicted just before death, receiving the vision of eternal
life.[32]

"The most learned men" credited in the Latin inscription of the Frontispiece with
providing assistance in "adapting Duvet's engravings to the true letter of the text" must
have either known earlier Latin texts from Ficino or his circle, or availed themselves of
the recent burgeoning French interest in Neo-Platonism that called for reading the works of
Symphorien Champier, or Jean de Tournes' printing of Ficino's treatise on the Daemon,
issued in 1552, three years before Duvet engraved his allegorical print.

The broadest French utilization of Neo-Platonic thought is Rabelais' *Tiers livre* of
1543. Largely a satire of Ficino's works, it is close in content to Duvet's engraving.[33]
For all its burlesque, the description of the poet Raminagrobis' death is a poignant por-
trayal of human folly, and the aged, harried Duvet may perhaps have identified with the
dying poet. Possibly the engraver's scholarly friends provided the ironic analogy. Rabelais
himself compared Raminagrobis to Guillaume du Bellay. The aged engraver invests
Rabelais' words with his own zealous pursuit of antiquity, in a vigorous personal statement of touching, yet triumphant finality.

In the last few pages of Chapter 21 of the *Tiers livre,* Panurge takes counsel with
Raminagrobis. Pantagruel tells Panurge, "The swans, which are fowls consecrated to
Apollo, never chant but in the hour of their approaching death . . . However it passeth
for current that the imminent death of a swan is presaged by his foregoing song, and that
no swan dieth until he have sung." The next lines, all distantly derived from the *Phaedo,*
explain Duvet's appearance in prophetic garb and the general setting: "After the same
manner poets, who are under the protection of Apollo, when they are drawing near their
latter end, do ordinarily become prophets, and by the inspiration of that god sing sweetly,
in vaticinating things which are to come. . . . It hath been likewise told me frequently,
that old, decrepit men upon the brinks of Charon's banks do usher their decease with a
disclosure. . . . For as when being upon a pier by the shore, we see afar off mariners,
seafaring men, and other travelers alongst the curled waves of azure Thetis within their
ships, we then consider them in silence only, and seldom proceed any further than to
wish them a happy and prosperous arrival." Pantagruel's words go on to explain the
presence of the angel and demon in the foreground and the seascape in the background.
"Just so, the angels, heroes, and good demons, according to the doctrine of the Platonics,
when they see mortals drawing near unto the harbor of the grave, as the most sure and
calmest port of any, full of repose, ease, rest, tranquility, free from the troubles and
solicitudes of this tumultuous and tempestuous world."[34] Duvet's garb and placement
are thus not only congruent with those of Saint John, but also with that of the melancholic artist as prophet, and prophet as artist under the protection of Apollo—as an old

man seated by a riverbank, the river of death, having completed his swan song, and ultimate revelation, the engraved *Apocalypse*. Duvet's state of divine communication recalls Ficino's views:

> The prayers of a saintly man . . . connect souls with God
> in such an admirable way that the action of God and that
> of the soul become one in a certain sense, but that of God
> after the manner of an artist, that of the soul after the
> manner of a divine instrument.[35]

The association of death with the sea, the ship of fate, the swan, the troubled waters, was also made by Ronsard, who wrote that as death approached the world was "a ceaseless turmoil, and torment, and shipwreck after shipwreck all the while, and whirlpool of sins, and tears and pain," and that "to all misfortunes there was but one port, and this port was death."[36] Taking place on an islet near a harbor, Duvet's annunciation of mortality recalls the lines of Saint Ambrose's *De bono mortis:*

> That is also excellent which is said in the Bible: "No one
> must be praised before his death"; for every man is known
> only in his last moments . . . Death, then, bears witness to
> life. For if the helmsman cannot be praised before he has
> brought the vessel to port, how can one praise a man
> before he has reached the harbor of death? . . . Death is
> the fulfillment of our service, the sum total of our rewards,
> the grant of our release.[37]

Duvet's victorious muse and guardian angel represent, in Neo-Platonic terms, familiar planetary demons who are "like men without earthly bodies who live in the heavenly spheres; they perform the function of transmitting celestial influences; they can, being both soul and spirit, act on both man's spirit and his soul. The Neo-Platonic hierarchy of demons is identified with the Christian hierarchy of angels. A guardian angel is the same as a familiar planetary demon."[38] The aged engraver-evangelist's two attendants may represent Saturnian and Solar demons. According to Ficino, the former fortified the spirit of contemplation and the latter contributed the gift of prophecy.[39] There is a possibility that the demon with the bellows is being overcome by the winged victorious muse, the latter taking Duvet from the lower to the higher realms.

A direct literary link between Neo-Platonic imagery and the Apocalypse is provided by Ronsard in his *Hymne des daimons,* published in the same year that the engraving was completed, 1555.[40] Ronsard interprets Revelation 10:8, in which the angel brings John the book to eat, as the Platonic concept of prophetic thought, divine revelation. The poet's muse, like Duvet's, is a celestial divinity, an aerial demon, who not only brings the will of God to man but also carries the spirit freed from the body to God.[41] It seems very unlikely that the poet should have known Duvet's works. Among Ronsard's numerous references to the arts, those to printmaking are most perfunctory and routine.[42]

Duvet's Frontispiece is cast in imagery which stems in large part from Plato's *Ion,* translated into French in 1548.[43] In this work, the poet does not compose by art: "But by divine dispensation, each is able to compose only that to which the Muse has stirred him . . . And for this reason God takes away the mind of these men and uses them as his ministers, just as he does soothsayers and godly seers, in order that we who hear them may know that it is not they who utter these words of great price, when they are out of their wits, but that it is God himself who speaks and addresses us through them."[44]

In his *Elégie du roy,* Ronsard compares himself to a priest of Apollo:

> Qui n'est jamais attaint du poignant aiguillon
> Ou soi de Prophète, ou soi de Poésie,
> S'il ne sent son Dieu son âme estre Saisie.[45]

Duvet, inspired by muse and demon, completes his own paean while approached by the *Aiguillon,* the feathered arrow brought by Apollo's messenger, the swan. The engraver-saint's prophetic garb, together with the inscribed reference to the sacred mysteries, suggest that Duvet followed Pontus de Tyard's presentation of Neo-Platonic concepts of the

52

state of grace of creativity. In 1555, Ronsard put these concepts into verse in the *Hymne de l'automne*. The verse was also written in the same year as the engraving of the Front-ispiece:

> Car Dieu ne communique aux hommes ses mystères
> S'ils ne sont vertueux, devots & solitaires.[46]

In the same poem, Ronsard writes:

> Il me hausa de coeur, haussa la fontaine,
> M'inspirant dedans l'âme un don de Poésie,
> Que Dieu n'a concedé qu'a l'esprit agite
> Des poignans aiguillons de sa Divinité.
>
> Quand l'homme en est touché il devient un Prophète,,
> Il predit tout chose avant qu'elle soit faite,
> Il cognoist la Nature et les secrets des Cieux,
> Et d'un esprit bouilant s'eleve entre les Dieux.[47]

Duvet's demon is like those described by Ronsard as Apollo's assistants:

> Quelque Démon par le congé des Cieux
> Qui presidoit à mon ardeur première.[48]

Duvet or his advisers may have consulted Ficino's treaties on *daemons*, published in Lyon in 1552 by Jean de Tournes, three years before the Frontispiece was engraved. De Tournes seems to have lent Duvet the typefaces used to print the Apocalypse with text, in 1561. Louis Le Roy's annotated edition of Platonic texts, presented to Henri II in 1552 and published in Paris the following year, might also have been used.[49] Ronsard's association of the *daemons* with the Muses, in his *Ode à Michel de l'Hospital*, and his view of the *daemons* revealing the mysteries in the *Hymne* of 1555 show how current such images were in the year that Duvet's allegorical self-portrait with both a demon and angelic muse was engraved. Michel de l'Hospital's "restrier honorable" as chancellor was characterized by Ronsard as:

> Demambré en divers pars,
> En Prophète, en Poésies,
> En Mystères, & en Amours
> Quatre fureurs, qui tour à tour,
> Chatouilleront voz fantasies.[50]

Duvet's engraving shows the artist in touch with the divine, affected by the four Platonic furies of Prophecy, Poesy, Mystery, and Love.

The bellows held by the artist-evangelist's demon are symbolic of inspiration (from the Latin "to breathe into"), probably signifying Duvet's being filled with the cosmic spirit "like enough to ours for us to be able to nourish and purify our own spirit by attracting and absorbing it."[51] Ficino believed the cosmic spirit "vivifies everything everywhere and is the immediate cause of all motion, of which he [Virgil] says, 'Spiritus intus alit.' "[52] According to Walker, "the Lyonnais doctor Symphorien Champier was the earliest and most active transmitter of Ficinian Platonism in France . . . His *De quadriplici vita* (1507) is presented as an imitation and extension of the *De triplici vita* and in his *Epistola prohemialis* to it he proclaims himself to be a disciple of Ficino."[53] Ronsard reflects the classical vocabulary of inspiration in his exquisite lines:

> "Je sens en ma bouche, souvent,
> Bruire le soupir de son vent . . .
> Resoufflant l'âme qui pendoit
> Aux lèvres ou ell't'attendoit."[54]

Duvet's aged, drowsy portrait, supported by a guardian angel, recalls a beautiful engraving by the great Italian print-maker Jacopo de Barbari of a similar group (Text fig. 17).[55] The Latin inscription on the Venetian master's work "Guard us while we sleep," comes from the text of the evening prayer of Compline. The line in its entirety reads" Save us, O Lord, while we are awake, and guard us while we sleep; so that we may watch with Christ and rest in peace." From the last of the canonical hours, this prayer is known as the *Completorium*, and would be in special harmony with the Latin line of the Frontispiece in which the engraver announces the completion of his great work with that of his own life. Much of the 91st Psalm is incorporated within the *Completorium;* David's prayer is very close to the imagery of the Frontispiece: "You will not fear the terror of the night, nor the arrow that flies by day, nor the pestilence that wastes at noon-day. . . . For he will give his angels charge of you to guard you in his ways. On their hands will they bear you up, lest you dash your foot against a stone" (Psalm 91; 5–6, 11–12).

17. *Jacopo de Barbari,* Custodi nos Dormientes, *engraving.*

18. Frontispiece, *author-portrait from Grüninger Virgil, Strassburg, 1502, New York, Morgan Library.*

The Venetian and the French prints unite the Christian guardian angel with the Neo-Platonic planetary demon.[56] Jacopo's engraving in some ways recalls Dürer's depiction of an impressive ancient, slumbering on pillows by a stove, a demon's bellows inflating him—possibly with a vision of the Venus Carnalis who appears before him.[57]

Another important visual source for the allegory of spiritual sustenance at the engraver-evangelist's side is provided by the woodcut frontispiece for Grüninger's *Virgil* (Text fig. 18) printed in Strasbourg in 1502. Reprinted in France, it belongs to one of the best known humanistic series illustrated in the North, and was copied extensively by the Limoges enamel workshops. The themes of the woodcut recall those of the *Apocalypse figurée* in many ways. Virgil, writing in an open-air *studiolo* near the water is inspired by a winged nude female figure, clearly labeled *Musa-Calliope,* with three very *bürgerlich* Fates in the background.[58]

Like so many aspects of the engraving, Duvet's victorious angel has several double-edged references: to the present and the past, to the Biblical and the Neo-Platonic. First and foremost, this figure is the angel of God from the first verse of the first chapter of the Apocalypse:

> The Revelation of Jesus Christ, which God gave
> unto him to show unto his servants what must soon
> take place; and he made it known by sending his
> angel to his servant John, who bore witness to the
> word of God and to the testimony of Jesus Christ,
> even to all that he saw. Blessed is he who reads
> aloud the words of the prophecy, blessed are those
> who hear, and who keep what is written therein;
> for the time is near.

The angel also represents the artist-evangelist's *anima,* enlivening him by touch. She is his mind, his intellect, as described in the Corpus Hermeticum: "There is nothing more divine than mind, nothing more potent in its operation, nothing more apt to unite men to gods, and gods to men. Mind is 'the good daemon'; blessed is the soul filled with mind . . ."[59]

As pageant master and military engineer, Duvet, like most of his Northern contemporaries, probably consulted the first lavishly illustrated edition of Vitruvius, prepared by the Lombard architect Cesare Cesariano and dedicated to François Ier when it was published at Como in 1521. The *Apocalypse* Frontispiece may reflect the French artist's interest in the Italian's elaborately hermetic allegorical and autobiographical woodcut (the book's largest), entitled *Mundi electiva Caesaris Caesariani configurative* (Text fig. 19).

19. Cesare Cesariano, Autobiographical allegory: Vitruvius' Mundi electiva Caesaris Caesariam configurativa, *Como 1521.*

While Duvet grasps a stylus, Cesariano holds a compass and ruler, standing between personifications of illness, poverty and cares on the one side and virtue rewarded on the other. The victorious architect is crowned with laurel as he is led by Mercury, the messenger of the gods, pointing with his caduceus to the message *SIC FATA VOLUNT.* To the right is the architect's theophany, a great cloud-bordered rainbow of leaders of church and state in a wheel of artistic good fortune, terminating in a massive cluster of winged animal heads like Ezekiel's vision. Here a crowned female figure with the great forelock of Occasio emerges, extending a bellows inscribed *SORS*—Fate, to the young architect.[60] A lengthy Latin inscription behind Cesariano celebrates his final deliverance by fate from a world of troubles to one of inspired opportunity, reading "At last the man of skill is urged forward away from poverty."

With these higher and lower demons, Duvet as artist-evangelist recalls Michelangelo's characterization. The latter's Jeremiah on the Sistine Ceiling is presented with a similarly conflicting inspiration. Joel, in the same fresco, overcome by sudden emotion is described by de Tolnay as meditating upon his inner vision in ". . . the first stage of the *divinus furor . . .* necessary to inner rebirth and the perception of the truth."[61] Duvet as divinely inspired visionary is shown at the very end of his shared revelation and its engraving just before his death. His achievement may have been made possible by a *psychomachia* between his upper and lower demons, the Saturnian and Solar figures struggling at his side. Victory over lower forces as a prelude to divine revelation is clearly indicated in the engraving which is some ways is the pendant to the Frontispiece of *Saint John's Revelation of the Trinity* (Cat. 38), where Satan is literally underfoot as the divine *afflatus* or *pneuma,* and the wind and breath of the triune spirit of God is communicated by trumpets. Seated in the House of the Lord, the Saint is passionately abandoned to the Holy Spirit—"the mysterious creative power of God, possessing and inspiring man, manifested in ecstatic conditions, prophesying . . ."[62] The stress the evangelist and engraver placed upon the pen and the stylus in recording the vision in word and image, suggests awareness of the contemporary issue of *inspiratio verbalis,* the direct divine guidance afforded the Evangelist Matthew by God's "dictating into the pen."

Duvet as Saint John, with Michelangelo's Prophets and Sibyls (Sistine Chapel ceiling) are supernatural beings in the strength of their corporeal existence and in the superiority of their intellectual life. It is the *spiritualis ignis* which illuminates the total existence, physical and spiritual of these seers who enlightened, are now inwardly reborn. It is a *renovatio* brought about by the contemplation of truth. . . . And wind accompanies the rebirth (John 3:8, The wind bloweth where it listeneth, and thou hearest the sound thereof, but canst not tell whence it cometh, and whither it goeth: so is every one that is born of the Spirit") . . . Michelangelo returned to the ancient belief that those who have given themselves over to the spiritual work participate in the divine."[63]

Duvet as recipient of divine inspiration is shown by the very shapes of the copper plates on which he has engraved his revelations. They resemble the Tablets of Moses. engraved by God himself which "were the work of God, and the writing was the writing of God, graven upon the tables" (Exodus 32:15-16). The French engraver used the Tablets of Moses as the device on which to place his monogram in his early works, recalling God's charge to Moses: "With the work of an engraver in stone, like the engravings of a signet, thou shall engrave the two stones with the names of the children of Israel."

The French goldsmith may have seen himself as spiritual heir to the artist of Exodus, the goldsmith Bezalel, who, "filled with the spirit of God, in wisdom and in understanding, and knowledge, and in all manner of workmanship . . . was able to devise cunning works, to work in gold, and in silver, and in brass" (Exodus 35:31-32). Both were makers of reliquaries, Bezalel having executed the Tabernacle housing the Tablets which proved to be very close to Duvet's art and thought.

The role of the engraver's guardian angel is illuminated by two twentieth century professionals, a theologian and an artist, whose combined vocations equalled Duvet's. "Derrière l'humaine raison," wrote Pourrat, "se tient de même un génie, prêt à l'orienter, si elle vent seulement lui donner sa confiance. L'entendra-t-elle? Ill est la, souriant, secret, immense, lui, lui son ange, le serviteur serviteur de Dieu vivant, le génie de la vie."[64] Answering the question of the completion of the creative art, Picasso replied "No, one doesn't stop by oneself. You work and behind you stands somebody who is not a professional and he makes the decisions: this is all right, this is bad . . . a kind of guardian angel who stops you from continuing to paint."[65]

Even more significant than the Neo-Platonic literature published in France in 1555 is an engraving by Bonasone made for Achille Bocchi's *Symbolicarum quaestionum de universe genere* (Text fig. 20), printed in Bologna the same year.[66] This influential emblem book

20. *Bonasone,* Socrates as Sculptor, *from Achille Bocchi,*
Symbolicarum quaestionum de universe genere, *1555*
Bologna.

was partially dedicated to Henri II (Lib. I, Symbol XXIII). Socrates is shown seated on
the square block of virtue, his genius behind him, as he traces a male figure, his *alter ego,*
on a stele illuminated by an auspicious constellation above. An inscription below, taken
from Augustine's *City of God* (IX, II) and derived from Plotinus, states that those who
are blessed are blessed with a good demon. Duvet's advisor may have consulted the same
text, the twelfth chapter of the *City of God,* Book IX, a sort of Reader's Digest of Neo-
Platonism. Struggling to explain Paul's view that Knowledge (Daemon) puffeth up. but
Charity edifieth (Corinthians I, 8, 1), Augustine returned to Plato's derivation of *daimon*
from *daemon* (knowing). The following passage in Corinthians is purely Socratic "and if
any man think that he knoweth any thing, he knoweth nothing yet as he ought to know."
The sense of these passages is clearly reflected in the inscription on the Italian emblematic
engraving by Bonasone which was a major source for Duvet's print. Bocchi's punning
Latin lines epitomizing the emblematic method, as noted by Lavin, read: "In the painting
of weighty matters the burdens of things are shown, and by this their most hidden meanings are revealed."[67] Socrates seems to be carving his own shadow, cast upon the stone in
a fashion recalling the way in which art was supposedly invented by the Maid of Corinth,
when tracing her lover's shadow on a wall.[68] Both the philosopher and the engraver are
shown as divinely guided carvers.

In this way, the Italian print may present the source, action and consequence of
inspiration in the artistic process, leading towards an understanding of the mystery of
creation. Idea, Invention, and Design are all indicated in Bocchi's complex emblem, no
doubt debated in his own Bolognese academy, built by Vignola.[69] The print also demonstrates the function of representation whether in art or thought: it serves to reveal and
communicate meaning. The Italian image, appearing just when the Apocalypse series was
completed (excluding the Frontispiece), must have given the French engraver or his adviser
a sudden insight into his visionary, representative art. Duvet's self-proclaimed ignorance,
recalls the celebrated "ignorance" of Socrates, prophesying the advent of Christianity.
The philosopher's stele, like Duvet's emblem, the Tablets of Moses, and his tablet-shaped
plates, are all carved by divine will.

Xenophon tells of Socrates' "divine sign"—described by Plato as a voice through

57

which he received revelation; Neo-Platonic and patristic literature referred to this sign as Socrates' "genius" or "daemon."[70] According to Plutarch, ". . . Socrates' sign was perhaps no vision but rather the perception of a voice or else the mental apprehension of language that reached him in some strange way . . . What reached him, one would conjecture, was not spoken language, but the unuttered words of a daemon, making voiceless contact with his intelligence by their sense alone. For speech is like a blow—when we converse with one another, the words are forced through our ears and the soul is compelled to take them in; whereas the intelligence of the higher powers, the gifted soul, which requires no blows, by the touch of its thought; and the soul on its part yields to the slackening and tightening of its movements by the higher intelligence."[71] Once again, the "blow of speech" is a metaphor allied to inspiration. In Duvet's engraving it is the female figure who makes voiceless contact with the dying artist's intelligence, while the figure with the bellows is probably a demon of a lower order.

In the Frontispiece, the sleeping engraver with stylus in hand at the completion of his work, has depicted himself in the state of divination parallel to that of *Saint John's Revelation of the Trinity* (Cat. 39). While the one dreamer "sees" the Trinity of Father, Son, and Holy Ghost, directly inspired by a trumpet blown by a cherub in the dome of heaven, three Fates sail down in a cloud bank. Both men are seated at altarlike tables. John the Divine inscribes his revelation on the open book in his lap, an open pen case and inkpot before him; John the Engraver holds the stylus before his closed eyes. Both prints stem from classical concepts of divination summarized by Cicero.[72] "The souls of men, when released by sleep from bodily chains, or when stirred by inspiration up to their own impulses, see things that they cannot see when mingled with the body." Thus the broken chain freeing the swan bearing the arrow of Duvet's death may also symbolize the long "sleep" during which the *Apocalypse* was imagined and engraved.

The dual portraiture of Duvet's Frontispiece may be extended further. The devotedly detailed engraved city on the lake may well represent Geneva or the artist's projects for it. Describing himself as a native of Langres, Duvet may have compared his final return to France to that of his patron saint's to Ephesus. The very free identification of Northern Europeans with Biblical figures can be seen in many sixteenth century portraits painted in the guise of saints and heroes of the Old and New Testaments. A woodcut portrait by Cranach of his friend Luther refers to the years in which Luther made his translation of the Bible at Wartburg as the "Year on Patmos."[73] Luther saw in the Fall of Babylon the most stirring prophecy of the Fall of Rome and viewed Wittenberg as his own New Jerusalem.

Duvet probably engraved most of his visions of the Apocalypse during his Geneva residence. Returning to France in the same year that he completed the series, Duvet extended his identification with his patron saint and considered the city of his self-imposed exile as Patmos.[74] Rabelais' *Tiers livre,* a likely source for the Ficinian Frontispiece imagery, also reveals an isolation and withdrawal in Rabelais' characterization of himself on the title page of the earliest edition as "Calloir des Isles Hières." As a hermit or monastic recluse—*calloir*—of the Isles Hières, the author shares the sense of exile so strongly felt by his fellow artists of the mid-sixteenth century, for these islands offered asylum to "enemies of the state."[75] Rabelais' dedicatory verses to Marguerite de Valois, among the most important French patrons of Neo-Platonic studies of the time, describe his royal patroness as "esprit abstrait, ravi, & ecstatic . . . qui frequentait les cieux, ton origine."[76]

Duvet probably viewed Geneva as both his Isles Hières and Patmos, but Rabelais could not have included the Swiss city among his places of refuge. Bitterly opposed to Calvin and his followers, Rabelais referred to them as "les demoniades," "les imposteurs de Genève."[77] Duvet's *Apocalypse figurée* of 1561 would scarcely have received a warm welcome in Geneva and the engraver may only have contemplated its publication in Lyon after illness forced him to leave the lakeside city. In his *Institution de la religion chrétienne,* Calvin took to task all arguments for the virtues of religious art. He wrote:

Il appert que ceux qui, pour deffendre les images de

> Dieu et des Sainctes, alleguent les Cherubins, que
> Dieu commanda faire, ne sont pas en leur bon sens.
> Car, que signifoient autre chose ces images-la;
> sinon qu'il n'y a nul image propre à figurer les
> mystères de Dieu?

Calvin made equally short shrift of those defenders of art who urged its recognition as a valuable didactic aid, "leur dernier refuge est, de dire que ce sont les livres des Idiotz."[78] He feared and rejected dependence upon the religious image, scorning the "Papists" who felt removed from God if deprived of His depiction..

Invoking the Second Commandment, Calvin pointed out, "Cognoissions donc que Dieu se manifestant par sa voix, a voulu exclure tout images, non point seulement quant aux Juifs, mais quant à nous . . ." Calvin might be regarded as a prophet of realism, urging his followers to paint only what they saw.

Courbet's famous remark about the angel was anticipated and possibly based on the doctrine of the reformer, who stated with admirable precision exactly what he regarded as legitimate subjects for artistic consideration:

> Quant à ce qui est licite de peindre ou engraver, il
> y a les histoires pour en avoir memorial ou bien
> figures, ou medals de bestes, ou villas ou pais.
> Les histoires peuvent profiter de quelque advertissement,
> ou souvenance qu'on en prend: touchant du reste, je ne
> voy point à quoy il serve sinon à plaisir.[79]

These last instructions to the artist, given a year before the publication of Duvet's *Apocalypse figurée,* show why the place of publication should and does read Lyon rather than Geneva.

All things to all men, the gripping widely diffused vision of Saint John lent itself readily to a revelation of the corruption of the Church. Much earlier, the commentaries of Joachim of Flora in the hands of his Franciscan followers during the thirteenth and fourteenth centures had led to an equation of the pope and the Antichrist. Thus, according to R. H. Charles, "the writers of the thirteenth and fourteenth centuries forged the weapons which the reformers of the sixteenth used against Rome."[80] Whether Dürer's woodcut Apocalypse of 1498 was partially intended at the time of its execution as a protest against ecclesiastical corruption is difficult to determine. That the artist associated his work with this message in later years can be demonstrated by his stirring quotation from Revelation when false rumors of Luther's death reached him in 1521.[81]

In the Preface to his translation of the Apocalypse in 1522, Luther made no attempt to disguise his dislike of the work, objecting to its turgid imagery, and the lack of lucid exposition at such variance with the words of the prophets and apostles. Luther denied its authorship by an apostle,[82] stopping just short of describing the Apocalypse as a fairy tale, although that is clearly the way he felt about it. Revelation's omission of any direct reference to Christ led Luther to exclaim "Meyn geyst kan sich in das buch nicht schicken."[83] After the Sack of Rome, Luther felt somewhat more at one with the text, noting in the preface of 1530 that the central theme of the Apocalypse was the destruction of the Roman Church.[84] The possibilities afforded by Revelation for an anti-Catholic vantage point may be seen in Luther's interpretation of the mysterious figure in Saint John's text who devours a book as an allusion to the pope's consuming interest in profane learning.[85] The German reformer saw a use for the Apocalypse in precisely the form that Calvin regarded as the "livres des Idiotz."[86] In 1545, the very year that the Duvet series was started, Luther instructed artists to use the Roman allusions in Revelation as a basis for antipapal caricatures, as Lucas Cranach did in his woodcut *Wider des Papstum vom Teuffel gestifft.* In 1545 Luther had many prints made after satirical paintings, "so that the lay folk, who were unable to read, could appreciate the evils of the Antichrist, just as the Spirit of God in the Revelation of John had destroyed the scarlet Bride of Babylon . . ."[87]

Having learned his lesson well from Catholic didacticism, Luther's exploitation of the graphic arts for the *propaganda* of his own *fides* was a milestone in the history of what was later known as visual aids to psychological warfare. Indicative of his special concern for the Apocalypse is the fact that this text, and this text alone was accompanied by illustrations in the first two editions of Luther's New Testament of September and October 1523. It showed the Whore of Babylon with the papal tiara seen against a Roman view derived from Schedel's very popular *Weltchronik* of 1493.[88] Even more anti-Catholic were the illustrations provided by Hans Holbein the Younger for the September Luther Bible published by Thomas Wolff in Basle in 1523. Not only is the Whore of Babylon clearly shown as Rome and the Vatican, but the monster vomiting frogs (Rev. 27:13) is the pope. The Holbein series was widely reproduced and reprinted in 1531, 1545, and at other dates.[89] The New Jerusalem is identified in Luther's Wittenberg Bible with Northern European centers of the Reformation, while Holbein has it resembling Lucerne and Basle, where the artist resided for a time.[90]

The complicated, often ambivalent attitude of the reformers toward art can best be seen in Zwingli's views. In 1524, he led an image-smashing expedition, and in April of the following year he decided to codify his views on the legitimacy of art in his *Antwort*. Zwingli makes it clear that he has absolutely no objection to beautiful paintings in themselves, heralding the "art for art's sake" attitude. He insisted that the only ecclesiastical works of art that are to be destroyed are those whose destruction is essential for the reformation of the Mass. In this way, any images located near the altar which might become the object of pious veneration had to go. Stained glass windows could remain since they were not directly in line with liturgical observances. It is the context of the work of art which determines whether or not it may exist. For example, a statue of Charlemagne within the church must be smashed as an idol; outside the church, it may survive. Presumably if any possibility exists or has existed for the work of art to have been the object of any pietistic observances, its contribution to the corrupt practices necessitates its destruction.[91]

In 1525 Luther clearly expressed his views on images in *Wider die himmlischen Propheten von den Bildern und Sakrament,* devoting a section of this work to the question of iconoclasm. Like Zwingli and Calvin, Luther accepted many images unless any aspect of their function or situation could be interpreted as inspiring or conducive to worship. Keenly aware of the propagandistic value of the graphic arts, Luther was loath to lose one of the most effective weapons in his arsenal of reform. Seeking Biblical sanction for the acceptability of images, Luther cited Christ's scrutiny of the tribute money as an argument for the validity of non-idolatrous art:

> 'Show me the money for the tax.' And they brought
> him a coin. And Jesus said to them, 'Whose likeness
> and inscription is this?' They said, 'Caesar's.' Then he
> said to them, 'Render therefore to Caesar the things
> that are Caesar's and to God the things that are God's.'[92]

Probably trained as a coin maker, Duvet may also have found theological affirmation of his art in this text.

As might be expected, Cranach's Apocalypse illustrations are among the most anti-Catholic of all. In the scene of the monster vomiting forth frogs, each frog wears a tiny papal tiara (Rev. 27:13). In Duvet's depiction of the same scene, the only Catholic allusion is episcopal: the false prophet is given a mitre, which could not in itself be regarded as inappropriate (Cat. 53). A considerable degree of presumably optional censorship took place between the September Bible, the first German New Testament translation, and the second one in December. Both the papal tiaras worn by the monster in the measuring of the Temple and by the Whore of Babylon were carefully cut away from the block, leaving a somewhat mystifying but inoffensive nimbus above their respective heads.[93]

Among the most common symbols of papal corruption to be found in anti-Catholic caricatures of the Reformation were the Beast of the Apocalypse, the Whore of Babylon, and the many other images of Revelation which referred to Rome. The seven hills of Rome, the three crowns of the papal tiara, and others offered an ideal opportunity for attacking the Church with visual references that would be widely understood.

While generally conservative in character, Duvet's Apocalypse series did not go as far as Marlin's *Novum Testamentum,* published in Paris in 1554, where Christ is shown with the papal tiara. A year after the completion of the prints for the *Apocalypse figurée,* Woeriot, a brilliant engraver of Protestant sympathies active in the Lorraine, showed the Whore of Babylon wearing a papal tiara as "Abundabit Iniquitas" for the *Emblèmes ou devises chrestiennes* of Georgette de Montenay of 1556 (f. 67).

French artists at the courts of François Ier and Henri II showed great caution and conservatism in their relatively rare treatment of Biblical subjects. An engraving by the Fontainebleau printmaker Jean Mignon of the *Last Judgment* (Herbet, no. 27) is in two states. In the first, a pope is shown in hell tormented by demons, his papal tiara uninscribed. In the second state, Mignon has inscribed the word "Arrius"—Arius, the arch-heretic, making it clear that the print cannot be interpreted as an antipapal image, suggesting that such works of art were under close scrutiny.[94] The preponderance of Protestant sympathizers among the French middle class may partially account for the great popularity of Apocalypse subjects in sixteenth century France. The very ambiguity of the references in the Apocalypse offered the only vehicle through which the Protestant patrons and artists could express their religious sentiments without undesirable consequences. Not only could Apocalypse illustration provide a safety valve for the release of pent-up Protestantism, but it was deliberately encouraged by the traditional interpretation of conservative Catholicism, which viewed the Apocalypse as an expression of the suppression of the encroaching Protestant heresy. Thus, images of the Apocalypse are among the most popular religious subjects in sixteenth century art. The triumph of the Apocalypse, derived from the pageantry accompanying entries of dignitaries in the fifteenth and early sixteenth centuries, was extended to opulent tapestry cycles, splendid stained glass windows, and Limoges enamel salvers.[95] (Text fig. 21). This unique duality of Apocalyptic symbolism explains the possibility of Duvet's having been able to obtain a *Privilège du roi.* as well as a royal endorsement for an illustrated cycle containing the emblematic biography and beliefs of an independent, unorthodox man..

The Libertins, abhorred by Calvin and characterized by him as a "secte phantastique et furieuse des libertins qui se nomment spirituelles" are possibly represented in spirit in Duvet's passionate and powerful art. This group which was active in Geneva worked to liberate their prayer from any ecclesiastical bureaucracy or intervention; they sought an immediate, direct encounter with the Holy Spirit. The French engraver is known to have belonged to the same Geneva circle frequented by major leaders of the Libertins. Although such reasons as age and ill-health are given for Duvet's retirement, it seems almost certain he must also have been depressed by the increasingly authoritarian climate of Geneva following the expulsion of the Libertins. He followed their departure from the restrictive city within a few years. Close to the same desire for individual communion with the divine as the Familists, but without the latter's emphasis upon special prophets, the Libertins reflect the widespread trend among Protestant movements of the sixteenth century toward complete individual independence. Interestingly one of the later Libertin leaders was an artist, David Joris, born in Bruges in the early sixteenth century. Like the Familists, Joris saw himself as a prophet, a new David born free from sin. His *Livre de Miracles* was published in 1537. Joris' vision of himself matches Duvet's surprisingly well.

Duvet may have been attracted to the other group because of its fresh, individualistic approach to religion. The Familists, a mystical movement of the mid-sixteenth century, was founded by Hendrick Niclaes (circa 1502-80); the Netherlandish leader of this new faith known as the House or Family of Love[96] might have matched Duvet in his passion for the Apocalypse. Niclaes' major French sympathizer was Guillaume Postel (1510-1581) whose most cherished holy figure was the apostle of the Apocalypse because he found him "the chief Biblical advocate of unity....above all else [Postel's] imagination was nourished by the Book of Revelation."[97] Two of the main symbolic references of Duvet's art, the Tablets of Moses and the vision of St. John, were equally important for Postel who dedicated his *Candelabri typici in Mosis tabernaculo* of 1548 to expressing his belief in the fundamental significance of Moses and John as parallel figures..

Writing of the Familists, van Dorsten observed, "It is typical of the religious climate of the North that this exalted, hyperindividualistic, utterly undogmatic sect with its insistence on charity and actual righteousness attracted so many cool-headed scholars, enterprising artists and successful businessmen. Theirs was an intimate, secret society of believers, who communicated their faith and experiences in the special idiom of their sect, a mystical language derived from the visions and prophetic utterances of H.N. [Hendrick Niclaes]and the other seers."[98] Among the printers, scholars and artists associated with the movement were Coornhert, Plantin, Ortelius, Galle, Hogenberg and probably Pieter Bruegel.

Duvet's singularly flexible ties with Catholicism and Calvinism anticipate what van Dorsten has characterized as the Familist's "official history of...'conversions' from Roman Catholicism to Calvinism and back...Lipsius and Plantin are notorious examples."[99] The Dutch scholar's somewhat romantic discussion of Niclaes' adherents brings to mind a style of life in faith and work cut very much along Duvet's lines. Such correspondance can be seen in the career of "Dr." John Dee, author of *Monas Hieroglyphica,* who saw himself like Saint John the Evangelist on the Isle of Patmos in his own first spiritual revelation. Writing in Antwerp, Dee's phrases recall those of Duvet's Frontispiece in which he saw his "learned mystery" as leading the willing mind upward to a first riddling glimpse of its Creator.[100] Such Familist imagery also recalls the inscription and the image of Saint John's Revelation of the Trinity in another work by Duvet (Cat. 39). During the French engraver's varied professional life, he prepared the ramparts of Langres and Geneva, designed tapestries, stained glass, coinage, worked in precious metals and created his own revelatory art, all in much the same spirit as that of a later figure, the Italian engineer Jacobus Acontius (born before 1520, died circa 1566-67). Born a Catholic and active as a builder and hydraulic engineer, Acontius joined and was excommunicated from the Dutch Reformed Church. The influence of the Basel Reformers helped feed his drive to reconcile all Christians in his *Stratagematum Satanae* of 1565. Close to the Huguenots, Acontius' life ended in England in Elizabeth's service.[101] One could easily see Duvet in the Familist circle, whose members were characterized by van Dorsten as active "wherever they went...the magic of their many arts...turned to pacify their passionate age and guide the steps of kings and rulers."[102]

NOTES

1. E. Jullien de la Boullaye, *Etude sur la vie et sur l'oeuvre de Jean Duvet, dit le Maître à la licorne*, Paris, 1876, p. 87, regarded the engraving as a self-portrait, in which the swan is "symbole de la victoire emportée sur la vieillesse par le génie du maître."
   A. E. Popham, "Jean Duvet," *Print Collector's Quarterly,* VIII, 1921, p. 143, following Bartsch, catalogued this print as *Duvet Studying the Apocalypse,* which is the traditional interpretation of the frontispiece. H. Naef, "La vie et les travaux de Jean Duvet," *Bulletin de la Société de l'Histoire de l'Art français,* 1935, p. 140, regarded the engraving as an allegorical self-portrait, in which the swan swims toward Duvet after having "arraché les chaines de sa vieillesse et portant au bec la flèche de son inspiration, tandis qu'il a gravé ce distique, 'Fata premūt, etc. . .'"
   F. Courboin, *Histoire illustré de la gravure française,* II, Paris, 1923, Pl. 254, listed the engraving as "portrait de Jean Duvet à l'âge de soixante-six ans, en 1555."
   L. E. Marcel, *Le cardinal de Givry, évêque de Langres,* Paris, 1926, II, p. 426, also considered the print a self-portrait with the swan representing the soul about to rise in flight or symbolizing the completed work, delivered at last to posterity, making the artist immortal, or freeing him from the hands of the Fates. Marcel interpreted Atropos' gesture as one of distress.
   M. R. James, *The Apocalypse in Art,* Oxford, 1931, p. 77, described the figure as a "self-portrait in apostolic garb."
   The disposition of figural, landscape, and textual elements is like that seen in some of the woodcuts by Jakob Kallenberg in Valerius Anshelm's (Ryd) *Catalogus annorum et principum geminus ab homine condito* (Berne, 1540).

2. Erwin Panofsky, "The Mouse that Michelangelo failed to Carve," *Marsyas,* Suppl. I, 1964, pp. 242-251. There is a connection that is curious and hard to isolate between mice and Saint John the Evangelist in Franco-Flemish folklore which may relate to the presence of a mouse on the Apocalypse Frontispiece. In Brabant, mice were supposedly driven away by means of reading from the Apocalypse in each corner of the infested room. See Jozef Cornelissen, *De muizen en Ratten in de folklore,* Antwerp, 1923, p. 31. The cat and mouse are also an emblem of preparation for death in Scève's Emblem XXXIII. See I. D. McFarlane, *The Délie of Maurice Scève,* Cambridge, 1966, p. 279.

3. The links between the Frontispiece and the humours were suggested by Anne Hoy in a seminar report and a letter of January 18, 1970.

4. Raymond Klibansky, Erwin Panofsky and Fritz Saxl, *Saturn and Melancholy— Studies in the history of natural philosophy, religion and art,* London, 1964, pp. 10, 250, 286-89, 315, 321-23, 329.

5. *Ibid.,* p. 323.

6. *Ibid.,* p. 323.

7. For Duvet's alchemical associations, see Chapter II. See also Maurizio Calvesi, "A noir (Melencolia I)," *Storia dell'Arte,* 1969, pp. 37-96, for a comprehensive and recent study of the alchemical references in Durer's engraving.

8. The appearance of the Three Fates in a French funerary context is not unusual, but their nautical conveyance is unconventional. The ship may symbolize life or Fortune. The Fates occur in fifteenth century mystery plays as agents of evil, wrath, and destruction. This characterization of the Fates continues into the sixteenth century, where a woodcut of *The Triumph of the Fates* shows their chariot, drawn by figures of *Maladie* and *Excès,* crushing personifications of Chastity, Youth, and Innocence. (Reproduced by John Carteret, *L'histoire,*

la vie, les moeurs . . . , Paris, 1927, I, Pl. XXV.) See E. Petit de Julleville, *Les Mystères*, Paris, 1880, II, p. 3, where Judas summons the Three Fates together with the monsters of the Iliad and the Odyssey. Only later on in the century, following more accurate humanist investigations of classical allegory does one find such characterizations as Pilon's *Three Fates*, who now become benevolent deities or handmaidens of death. See L. Babelon, *Germain Pilon*, Paris, p. 71,, fig. 76. Three windblown, sail-bearing female figures aboard a dolphin appear similarly placed in Dürer's divinatory allegory, inscribed *Pupilla Augusta* (Windsor), reproduced by Gustav Friedrich Hartlaub, "Divination," *Reallexikon zur deutschen Kunstgeschichte*, Stuttgart, IV, 1958, cols. 92-93, fig. 3.

9. Marcel, *op. cit.*, pp. 216-219.
10. V. L. Saulnier, "Récherches sur Nicolas Bourbon," *Bibliothèque d'humanisme et renaissance*, XVI, 1954, pp. 184 ff.
11. For Dupinet, see Emile Haag, *La France protestante*, Paris, 1886, V, pp. 853 ff. There is a copy of the *Familières et briefve exposition . . .* in the Bibliothèque de l'Arsenal.
12. *Champfleury*, Paris, 1529, f. XLIII.
13. *Ibid.*
14. These meanings were discerned by Boullaye, p. 87.
15. W. S. Heckscher, "Renaissance Emblems," *The Princeton University Library Chronicle*, XV, 1954, pp. 56-57.
16. *Ibid.*
17. For an excellent brief presentation of Alciati's life and work, see *Tra Francia e Spagna (1500-1535)*, (VII of *Storia di Milano*), Milan, 1957, "Andrea Alciati, giure consulto e umanista," pp. 444-447.
18. Paulus Cassel, *Der Schwan in Sage und Leben*, Berlin, 1872, p. 27. Following upon the breaking of the chain which "verbindet nach der Legende das brausende Meer die Lagunenstadt freundlich zu machen."
19. Phaedo, 85 (Harold North Fowler, *Plato*, London-Cambridge, 1940, pp. 294-295).
20. Arnoullet Balthasar, Lyon 1550, p. 7.
21. Cassel, *op. cit.*, p. 30.
22. Emil Major and Erwin Gradmann, *Urs Graf*, London, 1947, Pl. 76, 79.
23. *Verzeichnis der Druckgraphik Hans Baldungs*, Karlsruhe, 1959, II, p. 348, Cat. XXII, p. 392, Cat. XLVII.
24. See Robert J. Clements, *The Critical Theory and Practice of the Pléiade*, Cambridge, 1942, pp. 122-186, for a discussion of swan symbolism. See Joachim du Bellay, *Poésies françaises et latines*, Paris, 1893, I, pp. 116, 467, for swan references. The Lyonnais poet Scève, a Protestant whose works must have interested Duvet, was described by du Bellay as a new swan, divinely inspired by Apollo (from the *Olive* of 1549).
25. The oration was published in the same year with a dedication to Henri de Lorraine, Duc de Guise. See Alban Cabos, *Guy du Faur de Pibrac*, Paris, 1922, pp. 443-449, for quotations from the oration which was first printed in Paris by G. Tigé. The publication is very rare; one copy is in the Bibliothèque Nationale.
26. See Cassel, *op. cit.*, pp. 27-29. Quotation from the poem on Luther is given on p. 27. It was written by a friend of Philip Melancthon, Ludwig Helmbold. Luther is also associated with the swan legend in a poem beginning with the swan's death, in this case that of "Martinus Lutherus cygnorum insuperabilis."
28. Illustrated in B. Knipping, *De iconografie van de contra-reformatie in de Nederlanden*, Hilversum, 1939, I, pp. 20-21, fig. 6.
29. Emile Mâle, *L'art religieux de la fin du moyen âge en France*, Paris, 1908, p. 269, n. 1.
30. Paul O. Kristeller, *The Philosophy of Marsilio Ficino*, New York, 1943, p. 313. During sleep–*synesius*–the *pneuma* can more readily receive messages transmitted by *daemons*.
31. Charles Trinkaus, *In Our Image and Likeness–Humanity and Divinity in Italian Humanist Thought*, Chicago, 1970, II, pp. 480-481.

32. See Anthony Blunt, *Art and Architecture in France 1500-1700*, Baltimore, 1953, p. 87. The first stanza of Luther's *Nunc dimittis* ends with "der Tod ist mein Schlaf worden." (*Martin Luther Sämtliche deutsche geistliche Lieder*, ed. F. Klippgen, Halle, 1912, p. 44.) Edelgard Dubruck noted, "As in all Renaissance epitaphs, the defunct is referred to as being asleep or resting." (*The Theme of Death in French Poetry of the Middle Ages and the Renaissance*, The Hague, 1964, Chapter IV, "Renaissance Contributions to French Poetry on Death," p. 112.) According to Henriette s'Jacob, *Idealism and Realism: A Study of Sepulchral Symbolism*, Leiden, 1954, pp. 177, 188 ff., such figures are known as "morts accoudés"; the bronze effigy of Albertus Pius de Savoie (1531) is the oldest of the group, possibly of French or Italian origin. The author relates the De Maigny statue to funerary portraits of the Sansoverini in Naples.

33. See Robert Marichal, "L'attitude de Rabelais devant le Néoplatonisme et l'italianisme," in *François Rabelais: ouvrage publiés pour le quatrième centenaire de sa mort* (*Travaux d'humanisme et renaissance*, VII), Geneva-Lille, 1953. Marichal pointed out that the word *Platonique* is only used in the *Tiers livre*, of which Chapters 3 and 4 represent a satire of Ficino.

34. Taken from the Urquhart and Motteaux translation of the *The Works of Rabelais*, London, 1845, II, Book III, Chapter 21, pp. 315-316.

35. Quoted by Kristeller, *op. cit.*, pp. 315-316 (*Ficino, Opera Omnia*, pp. 304 f.).

36. Translated, Hillaire Belloc, *Avril, Being Essays on the Poetry of the French Renaissance*, London, 1904, p. 123.

37. VII, 35 (Migne, *Patrologia, latina*, Paris, 1857 ff., XIV, col. 584). Trans. Erwin Panofsky, "*Mors vitae testimonium:* The Positive Aspect of Death in Renaissance and Baroque Iconography," *Studien zur toskanischen Kunst: Festschrift für Ludwig Heinrich Heydenreich zum 23, Marz 1963*, Munich, 1964, pp. 221-236. The Biblical passage is Ecclesiastes 11:30. See also Solon, *Historiae*, I, 32.

38. D. P. Walker, *Spiritual and Demonic Magic from Ficino to Campanella*, London, 1953, p. 47.

39. Raymond Marcel, *Marsile Ficin sur le banquet de Platon ou l'amour*, Paris, 1956, p. 204.

40. See the edition by Albert-Marie Schmidt, Paris, 1939, I, p. 17. Schmidt listed Ronsard's chief Neo-Platonic sources as Ficino, Tritthemius, and Agrippa von Nettesheim (p. 13).

41. *Ibid.*, p. 17, p. 41; II, pp. 204-212.

42. Jean Adhémar, "Ronsard et l'école de Fontainebleau," *Bibliothèque d'humanisme et renaissance*, XX, 1958, pp. 344-348.

43. Walter Mönch, *Die italienische Platonrenaissance und ihre Bedeutung für Frankreichs Literatur und Geistesgeschichte (1540-1550)*, Berlin, 1936, pp. 306-308 (trans. Richard Le Blanc). Etienne Dolet, resident in Lyon from 1535 to circa 1542, may also have been a source for Platonic texts.

44. Trans. W. R. M. Lamb, *Plato* (Loeb Classical Library), Cambridge, London, 1952, III, p. 423.

45. Pierre de Ronsard, *Oeuvres complètes*, ed. Paul Laumonier, *Société des textes français modernes*, Paris, IV, 1925, p. 6.

46. *Ibid.*, XI, 1946, p. 47, lines 25-26.
Robert V. Merrill and Robert J. Clements, *Platonism in French Renaissance Poetry*, New York, 1957, p. 126, traces these lines to Ficino's "Argumentationes" on *Ion*. See also *Oeuvres complètes, op. cit.*, p. 311. For related examples of Neo-Platonic imagery of the artist, see Erwin Panofsky, *Renaissance and Renascences in Western Art*, Copenhagen, 1960, pp. 187-191.
For Occasio, see Rudolf Wittkower, "Chance, Time and Virtue," *Journal of the Warburg Institute*, I, 1938, pp. 313 ff.; also Panofsky, "Good Government or Fortune?" *Gazette des Beaux-Arts,* Ser. 6, LXVII, 1966, pp. 305-326.

47. *Oeuvres complètes, op. cit.*, III, p. 143.

48. *Ibid.*, I, 1914, p. 92. See Merrill and Clements, *op. cit.*, Chap. 7, "Metempsychosis and Daemons," pp. 145-156. Ronsard's verse is discussed on p. 130.

49. Ficino's views on the Daemon are discussed by Kristeller, *op. cit.*, p. 153.
50. *Oeuvres complètes, op. cit.*, III, p. 139.
51. Walker, *op. cit.*, p. 13.
52. *Ibid.*; *Aeneid* VI, 726.
53. Walker, *op. cit.*, p. 166. See also Lyon Thorndike, *A History of Magic and Experimental Science*, New York, 1956, V, Chap. 7, "Symphorien Champier," pp. 111-126; 8, "Agrippa and occult philosophy," pp. 127-138. The same approach is found in the *Délie* of Maurice Scève, although I. D. McFarlane (*op. cit.*) believes it to be anti-Neo-Platonic. See his pp. 32-33 for Scève's view of the soul.
54. Ronsard, *Le baiser de Cassandre,* Odes III, XVI, p. 395, Note 468.
55. See Hind, *op. cit.*, Pl. 707 and Catalogue, Part II, V, p. 153. The source of this inscription is the antiphon for the Nunc Dimittis at Compline: "Salva nos, Domine, vigilantes, custodi nos dormientes: ut vigilemus cum Christo, et requiescamus in pace." Dr. Jay Levenson identified the source of the inscription.
56. See Walker, *op. cit.*, p. 47, for Ficino's views of guardian angels as being the same as "familiar planetary demons."
57. Erwin Panofsky, *The Life and Art of Albrecht Dürer*, Princeton, 1955, pp. 70-72. The print is entitled *The Temptation of the Idler*. In the *Iconologia* of Cesare Ripa, Venice, 1669, Libro Primo, p. 11, the bellows are among the attributes of Adulation:

> "Il mantice, che è attissimo instrumento ad accendere
> il fuoco, ad amorare i lumi accesi, solo col vento, ci fa
> conoscere, che gl'adulatori col vento del parole vane,
> overo accendono il fuoco delle passioni, in chi volontiere
> gl'ascolta, overo ammorzano il lume della verità, che
> altrui manteneva per la cognitione de se stesso."

Panofsky discusses the iconography of Dürer's *Idler's Dream* in "Zwei Dürerprobleme," *Münchner Jahrbuch der bildenden Kunst*, N.F. VII, 1931, pp. 1-45. This research is referred to in his *Studies in Iconology*, New York, 1939, p. 225, where, discussing the role of the main figure, Panofsky pointed out that the devil takes advantage of his sleep to prompt him with a pair of bellows so as to conjure up the tempting vision of Venus Carnalis. See also *Albrecht Dürer*, 1948, II, p. 27, Cat. 183.
George R. Kernodle, *From Art to Theatre*, Chicago, 1944, fig. 51, reproduces a *tableau-vivant* staged for the triumphal entry of Archduke Ernest in Brussels. 1954, in which a chained figure is shown attempting to apply the bellows to the ear of a figure holding out her heart. A clearly negative context for bellows is that of the *Statua Haereticorum* (Cologne, 1526), in which Luther is shown on a column, chained to devils, one of them applying bellows in Luther's ear.
58. As Duvet is known to have been active as an *émailleur*, he may himself have drawn upon the Grüninger illustrations in that capacity. The Frontispiece of the same publisher's *Georgics* of 1502 may also have been of interest to Duvet. See Marquet de Vasselot, "Une suite d'émaux limousins à sujets tirés de l'Eneide," *Bulletin de la Société de l'histoire de l'art français*, 1912, pp. 6-51; Philippe Verdier, *Catalogue of the Painted Enamels of the Renaissance*, The Walters Collection, 1967, pp. 75-76.
The Grüninger cuts were copied in Lyon in 1517 by J. Sacon for C. Hochperg and 1529 (Jean Crespin). See Ruth Mortimer, Harvard College Library, *Catalogue of Books and Manuscripts, Part 1. French 16th Century Books*, II, Cambridge, 1964, pp. 656-57, Cat. Nos. 537-38.
Gerhard Kleiner (*Die Inspiration des Dichters*, Berlin, 1949, p. 44) pointed out that in a fourteenth century Vatican *Virgil*, the writer is shown like Saint Matthew, with a muse resembling the Evangelist's angel, her hands folded in prayer. Of course, the Evangelist's angel, in turn, stems from classical author portraits.
59. *Hermetica*, edited by Walter Scott, I, Oxford, 1924, p. 203, from the *Corpus Hermeticum*, Book X.

60. Liber Sextus, f. 142 r. Cesariano describes his sad early life on f. 141v. See Matthias Winner, "Bernini's 'Verità' (Bausteine zur Vorgeschichte einer 'Invenzione')," *Munuscula Discipulorum-Kunsthistorische Studien Hans Kauffmann zum 70 Geburtstag 1966*, edited by Tilmann Buddensieg and M. Winner, Berlin, pp. 393-413 (p. (p. 406). Winner has shown how Cesariano used Vitruvius' insertion of autobiographical information at the beginning of Book VI to provide some of his own and discovered that many figures in the allegorical woodcut are derived from the *Calumny of Appeles* and from Mantegna's painting for the Studiolo of Isabella d'Este.

61. Charles de Tolnay, *The Sistine Ceiling*, II of the Michelangelo series, Princeton, 1945, pp. 46-7. The same Platonic characterization was employed by Marten van Heemskerck for *Saint Luke Painting the Virgin* in the altarpiece for the Guild of Saint Luke in Haarlem.

62. James Hastings, "Holy Spirit," *Dictionary of the Bible*, New York, 1963, pp. 389-94.

63. de Tolnay, *op. cit.*, pp. 46-47.

64. Henri Pourrat, *Le Sage et son démon*, Paris, 1950, pp. 248-9.

65. Dore Ashton, *Picasso on Art*, New York, 1972. Remark made to Clouzot upon the completion of his film *The Miracle of Picasso*, quoted by *Der Spiegel*, 1956.

66. Bartsch XV, 158, 180. Lib. I, Symbol III, p. VII. Dedicated to Alessandro Farnese, it is inscribed "Pictura gravivium ostenduntur pondera rerum, quaq. latent magis, haec per mage aperta." For the block of virtue, see Bocchi, Lib. V, Symbol CXXVII, which shows a bearded man, with his muse, seated on a masonry block inscribed "Virtuti marito sedes quadrata dicatur."

67. For this engraving see Gert Schiff, *Johann Heinrich Füseli*, Zürich-Munich, 1973, I, p. 458, text for his Cat. No. 492; Irving Lavin, "Divine Inspiration in Caravaggio's Two Saint Matthews," *Art Bulletin*, 1974, LVI, pp. 59-81, p. 71, 79. I am much indebted to the latter for showing me his text prior to its publication, with its study of Bocchi's passage.

68. Robert Rosenblum, "The Origin of painting: a problem in the iconography of Romantic Classicism," *The Art Bulletin*, XXXIX, 1957, pp. 279-290.

69. For *Idea* alone, see the engraving by A. Clouwet of "Idea" for Bellori, *Le vite de' pittori*, Rome, 1672, reproduced by Erwin Panofsky, "Idea," *Studien der Bibliothek Warburg*, Berlin, 1924, V, p. 3.
See also J. K. Schmidt, "Zu Vignolas Palazzo Bocchi in Bologna," *Mitteilungen des kunsthistorischen Institutes in Florenz*, XIII, 1967-8, pp. 83-94.
For links between Bocchi's palace and French art, see Olga Raggio, "Vignola, Fra Damiano et Gerolamo Siciolante à la chapelle de la Bastie d'Urfé," *Revue de l'art*, 15, 1972, pp. 29-52, esp. p. 43.

70. L. F. Lelut, *Du Démon de Socrate*, Paris, 1856. Maurice de Gendillac, "Astres, anges et génies chez Marsile Ficin," *Umanesimo e Esoterismo*, edited by Enrico Castelli, Padua, 1960, pp. 85-109. See also Lavin, *op. cit.*, pp. 71-72, for further literary sources.

71. Plutarch's *Moralia*, VII, translated by Phillip H. de Lacy and Benedict Einarson, 1959, "On the Sign of Socrates," pp. 378-507, 588-590.

72. "De Divinatione," I, xlix, 110-111, lvii, 120-130 (trans. William Armistead Falconer, *De senectute, De amicitia, De divinatione*, London, 1951, pp. 343, 365).

> "The second division of divination, as I said before, is the natural; it, according to the exact teaching of physics, must be ascribed to divine nature, from which, as the wisest philosophers maintain, our souls have been drawn and poured forth. And since the universe is wholly filled with the Eternal Intelligence of the Divine Mind, it must be that human souls are influenced by their contact with divine souls. But when men are awake their souls, as a rule, are subject to the demands of everyday life and are withdrawn from divine associations because they are hampered by the chains of the flesh. . . ."

Moreover, divination finds another and a positive support in nature, which teaches us how great is the power of the soul when it is divorced from the bodily senses, as it is especially in sleep, and in times of frenzy or inspiration."

73. Reproduction in John Grand-Carteret, *L'histoire, la vie, les moeurs et la curiosité par l'image, le pamphlet, et le document*, Paris, 1927, II, p. 17, fig. 23.

74. For a carefully documented account of Duvet's residence in Geneva, see Naef, *op. cit.*, pp. 11-141. He first went in 1539, received the rights of a bourgeois in 1541. In 1544 his presence was recorded in the Langres archives as attending the ceremonies celebrating the Treaty of Crespy. In 1546, the same year in which the *Apocalypse* was begun, he became a member of the Conseil des Deux-Cents in Geneva. His return to Langres around 1550, when he joined the Confrérie du Saint Sacrement, would have permitted his receiving suggestions from the canons of Langres as to the program of his engravings. In 1551 he was active in Geneva, and in 1552 again in Langres where his tax payment is recorded. Until 1556 he is listed in Geneva. His absence from the archives thereafter means that he did not die in Geneva. The Apocalypse title page suggests the possibility of residence in Lyon after his return to France.

75. See the introduction to the *Tiers livre* by Marcel Guilbaud, Paris, 1947, pp. 9-10. Three additional editions appeared in 1545, two in Paris, one in Lyon; in 1547, further printings were made in both cities.

76. *Ibid.*, p. 10.

77. Emile Gebhart, *Rabelais, la renaissance et la réforme*, Paris, 1877, p. 98

78. See *Institution de la religion chrétienne*, Paris, 1911, III, p. 130.

79. *op. cit.*, 1560, I, Chapter XI, 1.12. See also Martha Grau, *Calvins Stellung zur Kunst*, Wurzburg, 1917, p. 148.

80. See R. H. Charles, *Lectures on the Apocalypse*, London, 1923, pp. 4, 6. For the use of the "Apocalypse formula" as a contemporary political vehicle, see Paul J. Alexander, "Medieval Apocalypses as Historical Sources," *American Historical Review*, LXXIII, 1968, pp. 997-1018. Alexander describes such texts as a "pseudonymus historical apocalypse." See also Donald Weinstein, "The Apocalypse in sixteenth century Florence: the vision of Albert of Trent," pp. 313-331 in *Renaissance Studies in honor of Hans Baron*, Illinois, 1971, ed. by Anthony Molho and John A. Tedeschi.

81. Panofsky, *Albrecht Dürer*, 1955, *op. cit.*, pp. 198-199.

82. For the texts of Luther's introductions to his Biblical translations, see *Die deutsche Bibel* (VII of *Martin Luthers Werke kritsche Gesamtausgabe*), Weimar, 1931, pp. 404-412.

83. *Ibid.*, p. 404.

84. *Ibid.*, p. 408. See also Hildegard Zimmerman, "Kunstgeschichtliches und ikonographisches zur Bilderfolge in Luthers Septembertestament," in the same publication, pp. 525-528.

85. Schmidt, *op. cit.*, p. 199.

86. Panofsky, *Albrecht Dürer*, 1948, *op. cit.*, I, p. 39. Luther found the Apocalypse "ein unangenehm zu lesend Buch." *Reformation Writings of Martin Luther*, trans. Bertram Lee Woolf, London, 1956, II, pp. 309-310.

87. See Johannes Muthesius, *Ausgewählte Werke*, ed. Georg Loesche, Prague, 1906, III, ". . . wie er auch diss Jar viel scharpffer gemelde abreysen liess, darinn er den Leyen, so nicht lesen kondten, des Antichrists wesen und grewel furbildet, wie der Geyst Gottes inn der offenbarung Johannis die rote Braut von Babilon hat abcontrefactirt. . ."

88. See P. F. Schmidt, *Die Illustration der Lutherbibel*, 1522-1700, Basel, 1962, p. 191.

89. *Ibid.*, p. 127, figs. 67-69.

90. *Ibid.*, p. 127, fig. 71.

91. For Zwingli's views on art see Charles Garside *Zwingli and the Arts,* New Haven, 1966. Also Hans Freiherr von Campenhausen, "Zwingli und Luther zur Bilderfrage," *Das Gottesbild in Abendland,* ed. Wolfgang Schöne (*Glaube und Forschung,* XV), Witten-Berlin, 1959, pp. 142 ff. Zwingli's views are expressed in Book III of the *Werke* ("De vera e false religione," pp. 905 ff.).

92. Matthew 22:19-21. See the Weimar edition, XVIII, 1908, pp. 67-84. A good bibliography on Luther's comments on art is found on p. 67, n. 1. The reference to the tribute money is given on p. 79. The basic arguments for art as long as it does not become a cult object are given on p. 69.

93. Schmidt, *Illustration, op. cit.,* figs. 51-52, 58-59.

94. André Blum, *L'estampe satirique en France,* Paris, 1913, p. 197. "En France, les artistes n'ont pas cherché à jeter ainsi l'anathème à la grande prostituée. Si l'apocalypse s'est emparée fortement de leur imagination, comme du celles de beaucoup d'hommes du XVe siècle, il ne faut pas voir dans l'emploi de cette figure symbolique les manifestations d'une haine contre Rome. Si l'on represente la grande prostituée, la bête à dix cornes et à sept têtes, il n'y a souvent la que à l'allusion classique à l'empire romain, à ses dix provinces et à ses sept empereurs. Il n'y a pas dans ces images d'intentions subversives."

95. The British Museum, Waddesdon Bequest, enamel dish by Martial Courtois (Text fig. 21) and a similar example in the National Gallery, Washington, Widener gift, are good examples of the decorative application of the Whore of Babylon in French sixteenth century art.

21. Martial Courtois, The Whore of Babylon, *Limoges plate, British Museum, Waddesdon Bequest.*

96. The basic study of Niclaes remains Friedrich Wilhelm Franz Nippold, "Henrick Niclaes und das Haus der Liebe," *Zeitschrift für die historische Theologie,* XXXII, 1862, pp. 323-402; 473-563. The mystic experienced visions as the age of nine and again in 1540, when his sense of prophecy became ever stronger and he established his religious community, moving from Amsterdam to Emdem where he resided from 1540-60. A. van Dorsten (*The Radical Arts,* Leiden/Oxford, 1970) provides a lively presentation of Niclaes and his circle, stressing the role of artists and intellectuals which had already been recognized by Charles de Tolnay in his *Pierre Brueghel l'Ancien,* Brussels, 1935, pp. 9-10, 51. C.G. Stridbeck, *Bruegelstudien,* Stockholm, 1956, p. 42) did not believe in de Tolnay's suggestion that Bruegel belonged to the Familists but G. Jedlicka (*Pieter Bruegel,* Erlenbach-Leipzig, 1938) supports de Tolnay. A most helpful survey of the Familist question is provided by Irmgard Simon,

"Hendrick Niclaes und das Huys der Liefde," *Gedenkschrift für Wilhelm Foerste. Niederdeutsche Studien 18,* ed. by Dietrich Hofmann and Willy Sandes, Cologne, 1970. She too follows Tolnay's views (p. 444).

An important list of Familist publications is given by H. de la Fontaine Verwey, "De Geschriften van Hendrik Niclaes—Prolegomena eener Bibliographie," *Het Boek,* N.S. 26 (1940-42), pp. 161-221.

97. See William J. Bouwsma, *Concordia Mundi: The Career and Thought of Guillaume Postel,* Harvard, 1957, p. 35ff. Another major French adherent of the new mystical movement was the Parisian apothecary Pierre Porret. A Parisian goldsmith was one of the leading contributors to Niclaes' cause. For this group in France see Wallace Kirsopp, "The Family of Love in France," *Journal of Religious History,* III, No. 2, 1964, pp. 103-118. Much of Porret's activity postdated Duvet's life. As the century advanced the new leader of the movement, Barrefelt who had split with Niclaes in 1573, was ever more convinced as to the need for unification within the churches. Valuable information about the movement in France is also to be found in H. de la Fontaine Verwey, "Trois Hérésiarques dans les Pays-Bas du XVIe Siècle," *Bibliothèque d'Humanisme et Renaissance. Travaux et Documents,* XVI, 1954, pp. 312-330. The expansion of the movement into French territory is discussed on p. 316, the groups are known there as Familles de la Charité. Still more liberal than Niclaes himself, Barrefelt (known as HIEL, Hebrew for the unique life of God) was particularly influential in France in the later sixteenth century.

98. Van Dorsten, *op. cit.,* p. 28. For Niclaes' images of Revelations see Nippold, *op. cit.,* pp. 336ff. and pp. 530-535. See also Simon, *op. cit.,* p. 444.

99. Van Dorsten, p. 29.

100. *Ibid,* p. 23.

101. *Ibid,* p. 16.

102. *Ibid,* p. 3.

The Apocalypse as Drama

Published in Lyon in 1561, Duvet's *Apocalypse figurée* contained twenty-three tablet-shaped plates (Cat. 39-60, 64) devoted to images from *Revelations* and their text. The Frontispiece showed the aged artist in the prophetic guise of his patron saint (Cat. 65). Most of these plates had been printed earlier without words. This is indicated by the rich, fresh impressions found apart from the excessively rare six surviving examples of the publication of 1561, five of which have much worn, weaker plates. When the French text edition was issued the title—*L'Apocalypse figurée*—was modeled on Dürer's *Apocalypsis cum figuris* of 1498.

Two additional scenes from the life of the Evangelist are among the eight engravings, identical in size, style and format with the twenty-three *Apocalypse* plates; they represent his Martyrdom (Cat. 38) and Revelation (Cat. 39). Of the remaining six plates, one is from the Apocrypha: the *Marriage of Adam and Eve* (Cat. 35), another, *Moses and the Patriarchs* (Cat. 36), includes the Holy Family, and the third is *The Deposition,*[1] (Cat. 37). The remaining three prints show *Henri II as Saint Michael Slaying the Dragon* (Cat. 64); the crowning of this victorious figure (Cat. 61), and an allegory of kingly virtues, known as *La Majesté royale* (Cat. 63).

Through a study of the expression of the series as a whole and of the circumstances which may have prompted its creation, the eight engravings, long regarded as isolated works, fall into place within an impassioned procession of triumphal and dramatic imagery.[2] They reflect the ceremonial pageantry which Duvet staged at Langres, fusing the sacred and profane.

The tablet-shaped plates may have formed a visual moveable feast, functioning in several contexts. As suggested by Boullaye, the *Marriage of Adam and Eve,* to which one might add the *Deposition,* could have been meant as frontispieces for biblical publications. The plates might have accompanied a series of published mystery plays. They may form an elaborate record of a real or imaginary triumphal entry staged for Henri II. Some of the engravings could have been employed as pairs or in triptych form. The two tablet-shaped plates devoted to the divinations of Duvet and his patron saint could have been meant as a diptych in a dual depiction of revelation, circumscribed by the form of the Tablets of the Law. The engravings may also have been thought of as a triptych, with Moses and the Patriarchs at the center. Some of the plates devoted to Henri II as Saint Michael and related subjects also lend themselves to disposition in diptych and triptych form.

The architectural enclosure for John's vision of the Trinity (Cat. 39) resembles the cross section of a magnificent tripartite ecclesiastical interior like that of the cathedral of Saint Mammès in Langres, which was originally dedicated to John, Duvet's patron saint, here restored to "his" cathedral.[3] *Moses and the Patriarchs* (Cat. 36) are ancestor statues within a great Romanesque portal, probably inspired by the magnificent entrance to Saint-Bénigne at Dijon (Text fig. 22), where the engraver's goldsmith father had been employed in the abbey church treasury. The pronounced contrast between the closed Romanesque portal of the *Moses* with the revealed Gothic interior for the *Saint John*

22. Portal of Saint-Bénigne, *Dijon, engraving of lost manuscript from Dom Plancher,* Histoire générale et particulière de Bourgogne, *Dijon, I, 1749, p. 593.*

23. Saint Matthew, *engraved plaque on back cover of Trier Gospels, donated by Charles V to the Sainte-Chapelle in 1379, Paris, Bibliothèque Nationale, MS., Lat. 8851.*

shows Duvet's continuation of later medieval symbolism in which the first style denoted the Synagogue, and the Gothic, the Church.[4] Portals and arches, gateways and windows to revelation, all holy apertures to sacred sounds and sights relate to the artist's most personal device—the double arch of the Tablets of Moses. Enframing the Word, these curved, engaged structures can also provide the holy confines for the reception of visual inspiration, for the seen as well as the heard. Perhaps works similar to the splendid fourteenth century *niello* presentation binding with Saint Matthew (Text fig. 23) and some of Dürer's works lead to Duvet's selection of an arched enframement for his Revelations. The silver book-binding, though probably unknown to the Renaissance engraver was executed in a technique which he must have known, and presents the engagement of a key theme—the Word revealed—which was especially important in sixteenth century theology. The central figures of *Moses* (Cat. 36) probably reflects a lost bronze lectern of the Lawgiver at the cathedral in Langres, while Joseph and Jesus from the Holy Family at the right of the engraving may be linked to a silver reliquary portraying them, in the cathedral treasury, possibly wrought by Duvet in 1533.[5]

The *Revelations of Saint John* (Cat. 39) reflects a highly conservative theological viewpoint, emphasizing the identity of the author of the Gospel and the Apocalypse. Luther's doubts concerning the authorship of the Apocalypse were first expressed in 1522 by designating him Saint John the Theologian to differentiate him from the Evangelist. This distinction was abandoned in the publication of the reformer's Bible translations in 1534, when to stress the common authorship of both texts, the identical author portrait appeared at the beginning of the Gospel and of the Apocalypse.

Duvet's engraving continues a tradition firmly established in German late fifteenth century Bible illustration, as seen in the introductory woodcut for the Gospel according to Saint John in Koberger's Bible of 1483. The Evangelist is seated in his study with pen in hand and a vision of the Trinity before him, the Father and the Son holding the Apocalyptic Book of the Seven Seals as the Holy Ghost hovers overhead (Text fig. 24);[6] Saint John has an eagle perched on his shoulders, the Trinity above recalls Alcuin's words, "John, in writing, you penetrate heaven with your spirit."[7]

24. *Anonymous,* Introduction to the Gospel According to Saint John, *Koberger Bible, 1483 Nuremberg.*

The inscription on Duvet's engraving, stressing John as special advocate of the Trinitarian doctrine, must have been directed against the contemporary "heresies" comparable to those of the Ebionites, an Essene group, mentioned at the lower left.[8]

Duvet's art is intimately allied with the imagery of contemporary *mystères* and *entrées solennelles*. This is evident from his three engravings (Cat. 27, 37, 72) showing the suicide of Judas, represented in Cat. 72 as an independent subject. For the entry of Charles VIII into Paris in 1484, the *mystère* of the *Passion of Christ* was presented, in which

> C'estoit l'amere Passion
> De Nostre Sauveur Jesus-Christ
> Et sa Crucification,
> Et de Judas le grand delict
> Qui a un arbre se pendit,

73

Par très-grande desesperance,
Donc en Enfer il descendit
Ou pune est de son offence . . . [9]

This is depicted earlier in Jean Fouquet's *Heures d'Etienne Chevalier,* in the background of the *Way to Calvary.* The artist, often a pageant master and designer of royal entries, had the images of the *mystères* very much in mind. His *Martyrdom of Saint Apollonia,* from the same manuscript, presents the most elaborate early record of the contemporary appearance of the Passion Play stage. The death of Judas is also shown in Duvet's tablet-shaped *Deposition* (Cat. 37), where the suicide is included at the left. The engraving is identical in format with the Apocalypse plate, and is inscribed with John's account of the Deposition and the opening lines of one of the best known of the *mystères, La Resurrection.* [10] The unusual specificity of Duvet's setting for the sepulchre, a neatly cut square stone, ready to be pushed into place sealing the tomb, also suggests the scenography of the *mystères.* [11]

The words *tabellis* and *mysteria* are both inscribed on the Frontispiece (Cat. 65) and on the tablet-shaped *Marriage of Adam and Eve* (Cat. 35). They reveal the imagery and associations Duvet had in mind when he undertook the engraving of his *chef-d'oeuvre,* linking its format to the miniature double tablets which he customarily inscribed with his monogram or name. One of the engraver's earliest works, *Christ Driving the Money Changers from the Temple* (Cat. 2), shows the double tablets bearing his monogram hung within the synagogue. It is identified with the Ten Commandments. Such lettered panels found in sixteenth century churches intended to remind the congregation of their Christian duties were referred to as *tabellae.* [12] The double Tablets of the Law are the most direct manifestation of the hand and design of God on earth—this may be why Hildegard of Bingen recorded her vision of the Cosmos on this form in her Liber Divinorum. [13] Perhaps Michelangelo or his patron found the double arched wall of the Sistine Chapel a "preordained" shape for the *Last Judgement,* painted within the confines of the Old Dispensation—the form and content of Divine Obedience. An important depiction of Moses with the Tablets of the Law, printed by Thomas Anshelm in 1505, survives in a unique impression in Munich (Text fig. 25). The unusual *tabellis* is also employed in the *Privilège* where the prints are listed as "tables de cuivre."

Moses (Cat. 36), standing at the center of patriarchs and the Holy Family, raises the Tablets of the Law. He is the forerunner of Christ, deliverer of the Old Dispensation as Christ is of the New. His leadership anticipates that of the triumphant Christ of the Apocalypse. Duvet's illustration of Chapter XIX (Cat. 57) has Moses raising the Tablets of the Law behind the victorious Christ. This was a common scene in sixteenth century representations of the Triumph of Faith. The Frontispiece of the Apocalypse which shows John engraving his Revelations on the tablets placed before him, may also refer to those of Moses which received the divine writing and are described in Exodus as engraved by God and later by Moses.

A French equivalent of *tabellis, tablettes,* appears in the inventory of the cathedral of Auxerre. In 1531, a few years before Duvet began his engravings, the cathedral archives record a reliquary of "deux tablettes de boys fermant a deux charnieres d'argent, appelees les tables de Moyse, ayant plusiers prophetes, garnis de feulages d'argent dore et garnirs de plusieurs pierres de grinatz . . ." [14] As the leading goldsmith of Langres, Duvet might well have made a reliquary of this type, and indeed the engraved *Moses* (Cat. 36) resembles the description of the reliquary of Auxerre. Moses was especially venerated in Dijon and Langres since the Duke of Burgundy prized a reliquary containing fragments from the Tablets. [15]

The form of the tablets of Moses was deliberately extended to objects of everyday use. Thus when the queen of France wanted a mirror of gilded ebony in 1556, she decided to have it "faites à table de Moyse, aux chiffres et devises de ladite dame." [17] What worthier form could reflect the image of the queen than that which had originally received the Lord's Commandments?

It is tempting to consider Duvet's device, the Tablets of Moses, as a talisman warding

25. *Thomas Anshelm (printer),* Moses with the Tablets of the Law, *1505, Munich, Graphische Sammlung.*

26. *Pamplona Bible,* Moses Receiving and Inscribing the Tablets of the Law, *c. 1194-1234, Collection of Prince Oettingen-Wallerstein, Harburg, Ms. I, 2, Lat. 4, 15.*

off the injunction of the commandment against image making. By including a visual reference to the forms upon which the Commandments were placed with his own name, it is as though the artist is declaring both his cognizance of the will of God and the conviction that his engraving cannot be construed as "graven image." Since the tablet-shaped engravings were probably seen in pairs, like Moses,' the religious meaning was both explicit and implicit. Though probably predating the Wittenberg Bible of 1524, Duvet's choice of the Tablets of the Law as his device shares a bond with Luther's use of the same sacred forms for the frontispiece of his translation. Both the engraver and the reformer selected the tablets as signs of the word from God, to be communicated by reproduction–by image or type (Text fig. 26).

The Marriage of Adam and Eve (Cat. 35) is inscribed in a translation from the Latin as:

> The marriage of Adam and Eve consecrated by
> divine benediction and the other mysteries herein
> contained are taken in part from the first chapter
> of Genesis.

Linked by format and Biblical subject matter, Duvet's *Adam and Eve* and the *Apocalypse* plates share common designation as *misteria.* Duvet engraved the word "mystère" on the Frontpiece and on the *Adam and Eve* (Cat. 35). Pico della Mirandola's introduction to the *Heptaplus* records the custom of the ancient sages who, writing of the divine, did so in a veiled fashion. He noted that their term "the mysteries" came from this calculated obscurity, since no mysteries exist where nothing is concealed. Plato was so given to concealing his meaning in the form of enigmas, mythical symbols, mathematical images, and obscure reasoning that he himself declared no one could clearly understand his writings on the divine.[17] The central forces and events of Christian faith are also designated as mysteries that are beyond complete human comprehension in their miraculous depth and magnitude.

By the sixteenth century, the term *mystère* was applied to almost any form of dramatic production, including those of the *entrées solennelles* which combined the features of a mystery play and a Roman triumph. As Frank observed:

> It is obvious that the modern distinction between the words "miracle"
> and "mystery"–the first now usually applied to miracles of the Virgin
> and to miracles or lives of the saints, the second to plays with Biblical
> themes–did not obtain in the Middle Ages. In England, "miracle play"
> came to be the generic term for all religious plays; in France *mystère*
> could refer to saint plays, dumb shows, and later even to non-religious
> texts (in 1548 we hear of *mystères profanes*)... Of dumb shows, *mystères
> mimes,* there are many records...usually given at great festivals or on
> the occasion of visits of royalty.[18]

In Duvet's prints the term signifies a representation of divine revelation, often cast within the dramatic conventions of his time.

The *mystères profanes* allude to the Tablets of the Law, most clearly in the elaborate Bruges entry of the Count of Flanders. A contemporary of Duvet's, Lancelot Blondeel, designed the *échafauds* upon which the *mystères* took place.[19] Viewing the Count as a latter day Moses, the plays in his honor were enacted upon twin tablet-shaped stages, illustrating a parallel between the leader of Israel and that of Flanders. This symbolic architectural enclosure was also employed in painting and sculpture, and seen most clearly in a panel by Gossaert of *St. Luke Painting the Virgin* (Text fig. 27).[20] Gossaert, who

27. Jan Gossaert, St. Luke Painting the Virgin, *Vienna, Kunsthistorisches Museum.*

assisted Blondeel in the planning of the Bruges entries, painted the architectural setting in the form of twin tablets; the one to the right, on Luke's side, had a statue of Moses as prophet of Christ and recipient of the Old Law, to the left, the side of the New Law, were the Virgin and Child. The panel, like Duvet's *Apocalypse*, is devoted to divine inspiration and revelation.

The engraving of *Moses and the Patriarchs* reflects the *tableaux vivants* of mystery plays and triumphal entries which a chronicler, writing of the *èchafaud* for the king's entry at Grand Châtelet, described as presenting several figures "sans parler ne sans signer, comme se ce feussent ymaiges eslevez contre ung mur."[21]

The suicide of Judas, shown by Duvet in two separate engravings (Cat. 27,72) and to the left of the *Deposition* (Cat. 37) was portrayed in gory detail in the *Relation de l'ordre de la triumphante monstre de mystères des Actes des Apôtres,* one of the greatest mystery plays. After Judas' remorse and despair, he hanged himself from a cedar tree, and according to the stage directions, "ouvrant sa chemise, il laisse voir les entrailles d'un animal qu'il avait en soin prealablement d'attacher sur son ventre et les scenario porte ces mots: Icy crève Judas par le ventre et les tripes saillent dehors."[22] His soul was shown emerging from the intestines (probably in puppet form) and carried to hell by devils in the drama just as it is represented in the print where Judas' despair is engraved at the right (Cat. 72). The suicide was first shown in this kind of detailed fashion in the Passion performed at Sémur, not far from Duvet's French centers of activity.[23]

The other Judas engraving's reflection of contemporary dramatic productions is found in its architecture, a temple, surmounted by a statue of Hercules, which is a typical triumphal arch from an *entrée solennelle*. It envelops and dwarfs the other modest buildings in just the way that short-lived festival architecture often screened its surroundings (Cat. 38). The barely discernible three crosses of Mount Calvary, at the extreme left, reveal the suicide's source.

In the late fifteenth century Judas emerged as a major figure in French religious drama where his remorse, despair and death were presented with chilling gusto and verisimilitude. The most elaborate and exciting drama centered upon Judas was the *Diablerie*. Before hanging himself, the traitor summoned all the devils and initiated a vast demonic orgy which included the Furies, Megara, Chimera, Gorgon, Radamathys, the Fates, Hydra, Minos, and Eacus. As a combination of Bacchanalia and Saturnalia, the performance of "pre-Christian" evil was most rousingly staged at Chaumont, in the diocese of Langres as part of the celebration of the Grande Pardon, which was held whenever the Feast of Saint John the Baptist fell on a Sunday. The holiday and its attendant drama commemorated the reception of a papal bull from Sixtus IV by his friend Jean de Montmirel, a canon of Saint-Mammès that granted the foundation of the nearby collegiate church of Chaumont. One of these feasts took place in 1545, the year in which Duvet's Apocalypse was begun.[24]

The *diablerie* concluded a vast cycle of mystery plays beginning on Palm Sunday with a re-creation of Christ's entry to Jerusalem. Special emphasis on the palm or other tree branches was made as a symbol of the special gift of grace—*misericordia*—to which the Pardon was devoted. A mystery play called *Les Rameaux,* in which Saint John the Evangelist described the special properties of the branches offered Christ when he came to Jerusalem, may have been adapted for the Entry.[25] Within Chaumont itself elaborate dramas or *tableaux-vivants* were devoted to the *Annunciation, Nativity,* scenes from the *Life of Saint John the Baptist, The Prophets, Our Lady of the Clouds, The Sybils,* and *Fathers in Limbo.* Many of these subjects, with special dramatic details suggesting participation in mystery plays are found in Duvet's art.[26] The complex machinery and hydraulic effects required in their presentation, especially for the *Fall of the Angels,* may well have been prepared by Duvet, who is also known to have worked in collaboration with a Chaumont goldsmith on a triumphal entry (Doc. 30).

Two of the tablet shaped engravings accompanying the *Apocalypse* are especially close in subject matter to the Chaumont drama, and to other mystery plays such as the *Mystère du Vieux Testament* in which the events of Genesis and the heavenly warriors of the Apocalypse are combined.[27] The theme of *misericordia,* basic to the Chaumont drama is equally evident in the *Moses Surrounded by the Patriarchs* (Cat. 36) and the *Adam and Eve* (Cat. 35), both engravings perhaps having been inspired by the performance of the *Grande Pardon*. In the first print the presence of the Holy Family among the patriarchs with a pelican, lily, crown and sceptre are close to the Chaumont references. The *Adam and Eve* shows their triumphal remarriage in the paradisical New Earth, reunited with and by God, flanked by the warrior angels of the Apocalypse who wave their banner crosses. The redeemed and vindicated parents of Mankind are placed before the Tree of Life, as seen by Saint John in *Revelations*, bearing branches of triumph and forgiveness, a central theme in *Les Rameaux*. The silver *fleur-de-lys* held by the knight at the extreme right fits the description of those Duvet made for Langres to present to François Ier on his triumphal entry. The same flower, topping the banner-poles of the *Moses* (Cat. 36) are probably also references to Duvet's royal patrons.

One of the very few prints made at Fontainebleau which has the same shape as the Apocalypse series, provides a classical complement to the *Marriage of Adam and Eve*. Dated 1547 by the Master L. D., it shows Venus, Hercules, Mars, Minerva, and Apollo bearing arboreal tributes to the seated Jupiter (Text fig. 28). It is nearly twice the size of the Duvet print, and has a quotation from Pliny the Elder inscribed on an *escriteau* below. Like some of the plates *en suite* with the *Apocalypse*, it may have served to celebrate the accession and rule of Henri II.[28]

A contemporary of Duvet named Loys Chocquet, who was probably a priest and organizer of triumphal entries, wrote a mystery play devoted to the Revelation of Saint John which was first printed in 1541. Bringing together his skill as a pageant master and playwright, Chocquet's drama was entitled *L'Apocalypse de Saincte Jehan Zebedee, où sont comprinses les visions et revelations que iceluy Saincte Jehan eut an l'isle de Pathmos, le tout ordonné par figures convenables, selon le texte de la Saomcte Escripture*, and alternated scenes from the life of the Evangelist with performances of his fourteen visions on Patmos. Chocquet's drama provided a showcase for the richly illusionistic staging of the visions, including such effects as thunder, rain, storms, earthquakes, sudden darkness, and falling stars, as well as a vast automated zoo of mechanical monsters and flying beasts. The playwright's selection of fourteen scenes suggests his ultimate dependence upon the Dürer *Apocalypse*, the sole major illustrational cycle reducing Revelation to the same number of representations. It is clear that some such Northern publication determined the program of Chocquet's *mystère* by the fourteen little woodcut scenes which accompanied the printed text in 1541; taken from Luther's Wittenberg Bible, they were reduced inn number for the French publication.

The play contains veiled protests against the censorship and religious intolerance of François Ier and Henri II. The heroes include booksellers, manuscript illuminators, philosophers and wise men, who were persecuted and killed by Domitian. The increasingly rigid censorship by the French Counter-Reformation frowned upon the *mystère de sainctes sainc* whose presentation of the sacred was found too free, almost casual, providing artists with a vehicle to convey Protestant sentiments.[30] As if to document their orthodoxy, both Chocquet and Duvet specified that their *Revelations*—"demonstrances des figures de l'Apocalypse"--and *L'Apocalypse figurée* were strictly in accordance with the text.[31]

The curious swimming figure in Duvet's Frontispiece (Cat. 65) may be a reference to an episode in the supplement written by Loys Chocquet, entitled *Mystère de sainct Jehan l'evangeliste, estant en l'isle de Pathmos*. Here, John triumphs over an "enchanter" called Cynops, who with the aid of demons, performs false miracles. Unmasked by the saint, Cynops ends his life by drowning.

Chocquet's drama is the most important contemporary literary complement to Duvet's engravings of the same subject. Published as a supplement to the Gréban *Actes des Apôtres*, the play presents a parallel relationship between Old and New Testament subjects and those existing in Duvet's tablet-shaped plates. During his residence in Geneva, Duvet may have been directly concerned with the production fo the *Actes des Apôtres* when it was staged in 1546. The *Actes* was the chief source for Chocquet's text; in the unlikely event that the engraver was not familiar with the latter, he would almost certainly

28. *Master L.D.*, Jupiter Surrounded by Other
Gods with Branches. *1547.*

29. Facade, *Saint-Michel, Dijon.*

have been acquainted with the former.[32] The work of a Protestant pastor and associate
of Calvin's, the *Actes* was perhaps the only dramatic religious production to meet with
the reformer's approval. Calvin noted, in giving his consent to its performance, that it
was "bien sainte et sellon Dieu."[33]

The royal patronage of the engraved Apocalypse publication (Doc. 68), coupled with
several symbolic references within the plates themselves to Henri II and the Order of Saint
Michael, place the work within a vast pageant of glorification of king and country, to
which the Apocalypse was traditionally adapted in France.

For a long time, the Apocalypse was an important subject in Burgundian art. It was
especially prominent in Dijon toward the middle of the sixteenth century when Duvet
began his series.[34] The façade of the great church of Saint-Michel was designed as tripartite
triumphal arch devoted to the victory of Saint Michael, the militant angelic protagonist
of Revelation (Text fig. 29).[35] The edifice was carved with quotations from the
Apocalypse and presented an endless drama dedicated to Saint John's prophetic text.
It was among the grandest projects in the Renaissance style undertaken in Burgundy,
largely paid for by Henri Chambellan, *maître général des monnaies de Bourgogne,* who
may have been one of Duvet's first employers.[36] Construction of the interior was completed by 1529, the date of consecration by the bishop of Saint-Bénigne, the employer
of Duvet's father and a close friend of Cardinal de Givry. The dates 1537, 1540, and
1551 appear on the façade, the last is contemporary with the execution of part of the
engraved *Apocalypse.* Like the latter, it depicts the writings of Saint John taken from
both the Revelation and the Epistles, and combines the Last Judgment with Revelation,

putting major emphasis upon the Trinity.[37] The sculpted Saint John is presented in a victorious, visionary pose. His eagle is perched upon his shoulders, thus endowing the saint with great wings, and his foot is placed on the vanquished power of evil, the body of a submerged Satan. This statue is reminiscent of the engraved Saint Michel *Victorious* (Cat. no. 9) and in the *Apocalypse* (Cat. nos. 62, 64). Another major local commission devoted to Saint John the Evangelist was the weaving of a tapestry cycle—six scenes from his life—known to have been completed between 1541 and 1542 by the prominent Parisian *tapissier,* Thomas Sourdy, for the Sainte-Chapelle of Dijon, center for the Ordre de la Toison d'Or.[38] Neither the tapestries nor knowledge of their designer (Duvet?) or donor survive. Since Duvet was known to have prepared tapestries during his residence in Geneva, he must have been keenly interested in the Dijon series; it is significant that Sourdy's delivery is so close in date to the beginning of his own *chef d'oeuvre.*[39]

Bishop Michel Boudet of Langres donated the windows for the Chapelle de Saint-Michel in Paris in 1517, when he was *aumônier* to Queen Claude.[40] This church was the the meeting place of the Order of Saint Michael in the early sixteenth century. The diocese of Langres with its strategic location, had long been associated with the Order. Its Bishop Gui Bernard was the first chancellor of the Order in 1469.[41] In the sixteenth century, the grand seignuer of Dijon was Amiral Chabot. He was a relative of the Bishop of Langres and was a prominent member of the Order.

The many images of Saint Michael in Burgundy have been ascribed to an indication of solidarity with France.[42] The saint's Order was the subject of an extremely handsome relief at the Chartreuse de Champmol (now in the Chambre des Comptes) and another one, carced ca. 1521, for the Sainte-Chapelle of Dijon.[43]

The chapel at Vincennes was begun in the late fourteenth century, but was not completed until a century and a half later under Henri II. It was built to establish a new permanent center for the Order which was officially located at Mont-Saint-Michel. Since 1476, it usually met in Paris at the chapel of the same name, but in 1557 the Order moved to the new chapel at Vincennes, built by Philibert de l'Orme.[44] In 1548 the architect received the commission to vault the nave in a gothic style and in 1550 he designed the west end. A magnificent drawing by Primaticcio (Text fig. 30) of a *Victorious Saint Michael,* probably for a Sainte-Chapelle indicates the style and mood of

30. Primaticcio, St. Michael Victorious, *Louvre, Cabinet des Dessins.*

80

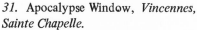

31. Apocalypse Window, *Vincennes, Sainte Chapelle.*

32. Apocalypse Window, *c. 1529, Yonne, Saint-Florentin.*

these centers of royal, militant Christianity. A much restored yet still splendid series of stained glass windows of the Apocalypse remain in the chapel (Text fig. 31).[45]

Duvet's *Apocalypse* Series is comparable to the Vincennes windows. The three additional plates in Duvet's series are also dedicated to Henri II in the guise of Saint Michael, the spiritual leader of France who triumphs over heresy. As *orfèvre du roi,* Duvet's great prints of the Revelation, under the patronage of François Ier and Henri II may have been inspired by contemporary designs for stained glass, perhaps for the lost Sainte-Chapelle in Dijon. The engraver is known to have planned the windows for the Church of the Magdalen in Geneva (Doc. 48). His decorative, swirling Apocalypse series is strikingly close to those of earlier Franco-Flemish *peintre-verriers.* Fitted into a curved, tablet-like space, the Vincennes windows, with their turbulent adaptations of the Wittenberg Bible Apocalypse woodcuts are strongly reminiscent of Duvet's art. Even if knowledge of his activity as a designer of windows was not available, the engraver's interest in this medium becomes readily apparent when Duvet's Apocalypse cycle is compared with the glazed Apocalypse of Saint-Florentin at Yonne (Text fig. 32), within the diocese of Langres. The Saint-Florentin Apocalypse was made by Flemish craftsmen working in Burgundy in about 1529.[46]

Silver tokens of the Chambre des Comptes at Langres, possibly designed by Duvet (Text fig. 3), were stamped with an inscription from the Apocalypse: "To the conqueror, I will give hidden manna, and I will give him a white pebble and on the pebble a new name written which no one shall understand [but] he who receives the pebble" (Revelation 2:17). The Apocalypse itself was one such pebble. As the property of Catholic and Protestant alike, it was equally regarded as the prophecy of Protestant heresy and Catholic corruption. The excerpt that was selected for these Langres *jetons* is appropriate especially in its address "to the conqueror," to whom so much sixteenth century thought and art was devoted. The steady revival of the Roman triumphs and their correlation with that of the Church brought the Apocalypse forward, or perhaps backward to the classical sources of the Evangelist's vision.

Dante initiated the humanistic reunion of classical form and function by combining those images, originally abstracted from imperial triumphs by the Evangelist, with their initial context of Roman victory.[47] His vision provided the model for the Apocalyptic triumphs of the Renaissance.[48]

Through consultation of mystery plays contemporary with the Duvet work, and a consideration of the application of Apocalypse motifs for contemporary royal entries, it is revealed that all Duvet's tablet-shaped engravings form a thematically united series. They reflect both the succession of the *mystères* entitled *Les Actes des Apôtres, L'Apocalypse,* and the *Grande Pardon,* which share the synthesis of Old and New Testament references characteristic of the engravings. Duvet's series also unites the militant, angelic hero of Revelation with his royal patron's Order of Saint Michael.

Among the earliest known dramatic presentations of the Revelation was the 1409 production in Metz of a "jeus de saint Jehan evangeliste, l'on dit l'Apocalice, que duroit III jours . . . en haulte magnificence et triomphe." This *magnificence* and *triomphe,* characterizing the theme of the Apocalypse, account for its popularity in the Renaissance.[49] Less than a hundred miles north of Langres, Metz's drama may well have filtered south to the environs of Dijon. For the entry celebration of Philip the Good of Burgundy, held in Ghent in 1456, scenes from the Triumph of the Lamb were staged in front of Saint-Bavon, the church containing the Apocalyptic van Eyck altarpiece from which the program was derived.[50] At Rouen, a three level stage—very much like the one at Ghent—employed Revelation imagery for the triumphal visit of Charles VIII.[51] Holding the Book of the Seven Seals and the arms of Round, the lamb was ingeniously mechanized. As the king went by, it came forward to greet him accompanied by the Seven Candlesticks which represented both the seven gifts of the Holy Spirit and the seven churches of Normandy. Similarly, the twenty-four Elders also symbolized the local government of Rouen. The king was greeted by two songs of victory from the Apocalypse.[52] Saint John on Patmos was shown within the third arch-shaped level whose setting recalled Duvet's engraving of John with the Trinity (Cat. 39).

The twenty-four Elders of the Apocalypse appear again in a procession at Duvet's Langres, escorting the newly-elected bishop Michel Boudet. Since special Masses were devoted to both Saint Michael and to the Elders of the Apocalypse, it may well be that such religious ceremonies could have concluded an entry whose *Leitmotif* was the imagery of the Apocalypse.[53]

Dijon with its seven parishes may well have regarded itself as the sixteenth century recipient of the Evangelist's seven letters to seven churches.[54] Such identification with the Revelation was prevalent throughout France and was especially evident in the triumphal entries. As has been shown, the twenty-four Elders of the Apocalypse, the Agnus Dei, and many other symbols were appropriated for their use as local references to the twenty-four town councilors, seven provinces, and seven parishes. The Agnus Dei was even regarded as an emblem of the wool industry.[55]

In 1517, triumphal Apocalypse imagery was repeated for the entry of François Ier at Rouen.[56] The Elders, Triumph of David, the Seven Candlesticks, Saint John on Patmos, and the Triumph of the Cross under Constantine were all shown in *tableaux-vivants.* A song linking the Kingdom of God to that of François Ier, in conjunction with an *échafaud* dedicated to the Anointing of Solomon, "Vivat Rex Solomon, vivat Rex noster in seculum," was recited from a stage showing the Anointment of Solomon. As a symbol of royal prudence and justice, Solomon was often represented in the triumphal entries. Both the Judgment of Solomon and the Triumph of David were subjects engraved by Duvet (Cat. 10 and 6). The young hero is shown like a victorious gladiator, crowned with *fleur-de-lys* and framed by a triumphal arch.

The final and most impressive *échafaud* for François Ier's Angers entry of 1518 was a staging of the battle between the Dragon and the Woman of the Apocalypse. It served as an allegory of the power of the royal house of France against the seven heads of the dragon representing the seven great enemies of France. The Child of the Woman, symbolic of the Saviour, was also a reference to the Dauphin. Saint Michael, descending from heaven by an ingenious system of pulleys "un subtil et invisible contrepoids," very diplomatically cut off the dragon's ox head, emblematic of François Ier's victory over the Swiss at Herignac.[57] The Woman of the Apocalypse, appearing as a goddess of victory, gave the palm branch of victory to François:

> On pour mostrer quelle donc ou est moyen de donner
> aux roys et princes les victoires signifiees par la palme.
> Elle estoit environee du soleil et la lune avoit soulz ses
> pied signifait la vision de lapocalipse.[58]

To make her more exclusively French, there were lilies planted at her feet to symbolize both virginity and France. A mechanized Agnus Dei went to the Virgin, then turned around to kneel before the king. Duvet's engraved Apocalypse contains hints of similar flattery in such details as the *fleur-de-lys* halo of the Lamb of God in the plate for Chapter XIV (Cat. 52) and the manner in which God the Father holds his sickle so that it forms the royal crescent over his head (in the other plate for the same chapter—Cat. 53). These regal symbols compliment each other when the plates are placed as in the position of the double tablet. Such juxtaposing of the crown and crescent is not accidental and can be proven by a comparison with the engraving of Henri II (Cat. 64) in which this configuration is crested by the pelican of piety.

Duvet staged several triumphal entries in Langres, and it is likely that his engraving for the *Woman of the Apocalypse* (Cat. 5) reflects a design for one of these. Standing on the sun and moon, she holds a cornucopia in one hand and the Infant in the other. Both form and content reveal a mixture of Christian and classical thought, especially appropriate to the triumphal idiom. The Virgin is derived from a Marcantonio engraving of Lucretia, a figure also repeated on the plinth supporting Saint Michael on the façade of his church in Dijon. While the cornucopia appears to be an equally classical emblem, it stems in this case from its Christian source, the writings of Saint Ambrose, and was selected by Claude de Longvy, bishop of Langres, as his personal device with the inscription *Abundantia diligentibus.*[59]

At Henri II's Rouen entry of 1550 a *fleur-de-lys*, crown, and the Order of Saint Michael emerged from a fiery globe.[60] In Duvet's engraving of *Henri II as the victorious Saint Michael Slaying the Dragon* (Cat. 64), the same background of *fleur-de-lys*, crown, and the Saint's Order emerge from a sky of flames providing an engraved record of the *paille* or cloth of honor, perhaps the most important decoration for the triumphal entry. Another such *paille*, carried by the councilors of Lyon for the arrival of Louis XII in 1507 was composed of three great swaths of red, yellow, and blue satin, studded with a hundred golden lilies with the grand *écusson*, the *fleur-de-lys* and crown above, and crested by the Order of Saint Michael as Duvet showed them four decades later.

Three engravings linked to the Apocalypse by identical size and format are dedicated to Henri II as king and as leader of the Order of Saint Michael. The king is here portrayed as the patron saint of his knightly society. He is crowned by the pelican of piety, wears the Order, is splendidly winged, and is poised delicately before a prostrate devil (Cat. 62). A second print again depicts the king as Saint Michael, this time with a sword in hand about to decapitate Satan (Cat. 64). Wearing both crown and halo as he did in the preceding plate, the angel-king now bears the shield of the Cross. His sword, raised to behead the devil, points to his flaming crown. A typical Duvet cherub pops out to support the royal arms from a crescent of the Order of Saint Michael. To the right, Saint Rémy holds up the *ampulla,* the receptable for ointment while at the left, an angel looks down upon the scene bearing a sword and wreath of triumph. The blank spaces in these engravings reflect the *escriteaux* of the *mystères*, which like comic-strips contained French or Latin lines identifying or clarifying the allegory enacted. These *escriteaux* can still be seen in the unusual Apocalyptic sculpture at Solesmes, which might be described as a "petrified mystère."[61]

The handwritten inscription on the only known impression of Duvet's *Henri II as the Victorious Saint Michael . . .* (Cat. 64) reads in translation: "Henry, we have engraved upon copper the combat where Michael won a glorious crown, because it is under his auspices and under his name that the happy destiny of the Order is dedicated."[62] The engraving almost certainly relates to Henri II's visit to Dijon in 1548. The bulk of Duvet's *Apocalypse* designs may refer to that entry as the major triumphs were on the "grant rue st. Jean que de plusieurs echaffauds qui furent dressez par lad. ville."[63] The engraving's inscription alludes to Rémy's baptisim of Clovis, first Christian king of the Franks. According to legend, Clovis promised his queen Clotilde he would become Christian if he were granted victory over the Alemans. After his triumph, such a crowd followed the king into the Cathedral of Reims that it was impossible for the bishop—Saint Rémy—to get to Clovis with the chrism. Rémy kneeled in prayer for divine aid, whereupon a white dove appeared before him with an ampulla of oil in its beak for the consummation of the sacrament. The bird also bore the *fleur-de-lys* which then became part of the royal arms. In the middle of the sixteenth century this account was of obvious appeal to the king of France. He was once again desirous of divine assurance of military victory against the "Alemans."[64] The Baptism of Clovis was included in the subjects that were performed in the *Miracle de Nôtre Dame*, one of the most popular mystery plays that might well have been performed on one of the *échafauds* of a triumphal entry staged by the engraver in Burgundy.[65]

For the entry of Charles IX at Dijon on May 18, 1561, the king was presented with the costliest gifts given by Dijon to any sovereign. Two goldsmiths were employed to represent:

> le mystère du baptesme du roy Clovis, qui Dieu absoille,
> avec les personnages tant de la Royne Clotilde que de
> monsieur Saint Rémy, évesque, qui seront enlevez sur
> une base d'argent laquelle sera cysellee de demy taille,
> enrichie de figures en six ovalles où seront les histoires
> selon le pourtraiet au'ilz ont. En ontre portraet, lesdites
> figures seront enrichies entour les ovalles d'escripture
> propre de la signification desdites histoires avec les
> armoires et devise de la ville, et de tout bailler de
> modèle et patron en terre à ladicte ville, et lesdictz
> personnages d'un pied de hauteur sur ladicte base avec
> les secretz et ressorts nécessaires pour le sujet de
> mystère . . .[66]

This image is clearly in the tradition of Duvet's *oeuvre* and may even reflect a last project of the aged goldsmith-engraver, whose activity as a pageant master was continued by Hugues Sambin.

Henri II sought to revive the Order of Saint Michael, well-suited as it was to the new militancy of the Counter-Reformation. The Order had lost prestige by the time of François Ier, whose tastes may not have been in accord with its ascetic precepts. The new chancellor of the Order, as always a man of the church, was Charles de Lorraine, Archbishop and duc de Reims. He revived its original garb intending it to be worn for the meeting at Lyon in 1548, and it may have been for this or some other meeting, as suggested by Boullaye, that Duvet's plate was engraved.[67] The frontispiece of Charles' manuscript of the statues of the Order, made in 1548[68] shows the victorious Saint Michael in a medallion enclosed by an elaborate Fontainebleau-style cartouche.[69] Modeled on the School of Raphael painting of the same subject owned by François Ier, the illumination includes Mont-Saint-Michel in the background, as does Duvet's engraving of *Henri II as Saint Michael Slaying the Dragon* (Cat. 64) An early print of Duvet's reproduces the Raphael (Cat. 9). Since the archbishop of Reims played an important part in both the Order of Saint Michael and in Henri II's coronation, at "his" cathedral, the prominence of Saint Rémy in the same print may also be a reference to the chancellor of the Order.

The third engraving of the Henri II trio *en suite* with the *Apocalypse* Series shows three deities above a blank *escriteau* (Cat. 63). The second state of this plate bears the incomplete inscription, "La majesté royale envyronnee de sappience . . ." The central goddess is above the globe of wisdom, and carries the "baton du commandement" in her right arm while *Renommé* and *Sapience* are about to place the crown of eternal fame upon her head. This royal trinity is reminiscent of Duvet's program for the entry of François Ier in 1533, the occasion on which the engraver was probably confirmed *orfèvre du roi*. However, the print is an allegory commemorating the triumph of royalty over time and was probably engraved shortly after the death of François Ier in 1547.

Duvet's triumphal framework for Henri II as Saint Michael and *La majesté royale* follows the traditionally victorious imagery of the period. It recalls the stained glass window commissioned by François Ier which initiated the splendid series devoted to the host desecration at Enghien, for the Chapel of the Sacrament at Saint Gudule. The window was designed by Bernard van Orley, and executed in 1540 (Text fig. 33).[70]

34. Sacreligious Jew, *upper section of central register, 1540,*
Saint Gudule.

33. Window; *Chapel of the Sacrement,*
Saint Gudule, 1540, donated by Fran-
çois Ier

35. François Ier and Eleanor with the Stigmatization of Saint Francis, *bottom register, Chapel of the Sacrement, Saint Gudule.*

Langres' Tour Saint-Jean (Tour de Navarre), possibly designed by Jean Duvet, bears a handsome sixteenth century relief of the Order of Saint Michael (Text fig. 8).[71] Thus far the Henri II series, the *Apocalypse* engravings, and several other prints have been linked to a triumphal *mystère.* The association of the Apocalypse and Henri II prints can be further substantiated by the shattered remnants of the Apocalypse windows at Vincennes, a center for the Order of Saint Michael, which show Henri II wearing the great robes of the Order.[72]

In conclusion, Duvet's description of the plates as *tabellae*, together with his characterization of them as *mystères* confirms their representing a series of scenes from a projected triumphal entry, the Triumph of the Apocalypse. The play by Chocquet, who shared both Duvet's Protestant sentiments and his career as a *facteur,* led the way in using the Apocalypse as a series of imaginary *échafauds* in more elaborate fashion than the earlier known application of Apocalyptic imagery in triumphal entries.

All the engravings with the tablet-shaped format reflect the participation of their maker in the major artistic projects of his day. The reciprocal references between the visual arts and *mystère* production are well known, but in Duvet's oeuvre, the latter appears as the predominant aesthetic determinant, providing the dramatic and iconographic imperative. The form, the content, and the nature of the engraver's major work can only be regarded as the impassioned projection of his role in the many *entrées triomphantes* which, according to the Langres archives, Duvet "guidoit et conduisoit" (Doc. 31).[73]

NOTES

1. Noting its resemblance to a frontispiece, Boullaye suggested that the *Marriage of Adam and Eve* may have been made for an edition of Genesis. E. Jullien de la Boullaye, *Etude sur la vie et sur l'oeuvre de Jean Duvet, dit le Maître à la licorne*, Paris, 1876, p. 71.

2. The major study of the role of the visual arts in the pageantry of the fifteenth and sixteenth centuries is the brilliant work by George Kernodle, *Art to Theatre*, Chicago, 1943. See also René Schneider, "La thème du triomphe dans les entrées solennelles en France à la renaissance," *Gazette des Beaux-Arts*, Sér. 4, IX, 1913, pp. 85-106; François Gébelin, "Un manifeste de l'école néo-classique en 1549: l'entrée de Henri II à Paris," *Bulletin de la Société de l'histoire de Paris, et de l'Ile-de-France*, LI, 1924, pp. 35-45. For a more recent work, see the two volumes *Les fêtes de la renaissance*, ed. Jean Jacquot, Paris, Centre nationale de la recherche scientifique, 1956, especially V. L. Saulnier, "L'entrée de Henri II à Paris et la revolution poétique de 1550," I, pp. 31-60. An excellent bibliography on French triumphal entries is given on pp. 22-23. See also the catalogue of an exhibition sponsored by the Institut pédagogique national, *La vie théatral au temps de la renaissance*, Paris, 1963.

3. Earle Wilbur Dow, "The Roman City of Langres in the Early Middle Ages," *Annual Report of the American Historical Association*, I, 1899, p. 491.

4. Erwin Panofsky, *Early Netherlandish Painting*, Cambridge, 1955, pp. 134-138, p. 412, n. 2.

5. A life-sized bronze statue of Moses was dedicated in 1501 for use as a lectern at the cathedral of Langres (L. E. Marcel, *Le cardinal de Givry, évêque de Langres*, Paris, 1926, p. 310). The statue was donated by a canon of Saint-Mammès, Mathieu Roland, a fellow member of Duvet's confraternity. See also Émile Mâle, *L'art religieux en France à la fin du moyen âge*, Paris, 1908, p. 234; also Godard, "Chaumont en Bassigne," *Mémoires de la Société historique et archéologique de Langres*, I, 1847, p. 100.
"L'image de Saint Joseph, tenait d'une main le saint Enfant Jésus, sur un pied d'estail; le tout d'argent rempli de reliques, qui est un présent de Louis Pithois, chanoine de la cathédrale, en 1533." (Boullaye, p. 6.)

6. See P. F. Schmidt, *Die Illustration der Lutherbibel*, 1552-1700, Basle, 1962, fig. 37.

7. "Scribendo penetras caelum tu mente Johannes." (S. H. Guteberlet, *Die Himmelfahrt Christi in der bildenden Kunst von den Anfängen bis ins hohe Mittelalter*, Strassburg, 1934, p. 244.)

8. The Ebionites—meaning the Poor Men—were severely ascetic Jewish Christians whose sect lived east of the Jordan: "Two of their principal tenets were (1) a 'reduced' doctrine of the Person of Christ, to the effect, e.g., that Jesus was the Human son of Joseph and Mary and that the Holy Spirit in the form of a dove lighted on Him at His Baptism, and (2) over emphasis on the binding character of the Mosaic Law. They are said to have used only the 'Gospel of Saint Matthew' ('the Gospel of the Ebionites') and to have rejected the Pauline epistles." From the *Oxford Dictionary of the Christian Church*, Oxford, 1958, p. 433.

9. François and Claude Parfaict, *Histoire du théâtre français depuis son origine jusqu'à présent*, Paris, 1745, II, p. 176.

10. See Louis Petit de Julleville, *Les mystères*, Paris, 1880, II, p. 221.

11. The reasons for the revival of the archaic four-nail Crucifixion may be the same as those given by Pacheco. Writing in the early seventeenth century, the Spanish artist and theorist stated that the four-nail depiction was preferable because it eliminated the ugly twisting of the body, and showed Christ as though he were standing in a dignified posture, worthy of his majesty. See Manuel Gómez-Moreno, "El Cristo de San Plácido," *Boletín de la Sociedad Española de Excursiones*, XXIV, 1916, p. 182, n. 2; also Emile Mâle, *L'art réligieux après le Concile de Trente*, Paris, 1932, p. 271, for this form in seventeenth century France.

12. See F. W. H. Hollstein, *German Engravings, Etchings and Woodcuts ca. 1400-1700*, Amsterdam, 1954, II, p. 62; Bartsch VII, 487; Passavant III, 299; Nagler, V, 499.

13. Cod. lat. 1942, Biblioteca Governativa di Lucca, reproduced by Emil Ernst Ploss, Heinrich Schipperges, Herwig Buntz, *Alchimia, Ideologie und Technologie*, Munich, 1970.

14. See Walter Gay, *Glossaire archéologique*, Paris, 1928, II, p. 369.

15. Florens Deuchler, *Die Burgunderbeute*, Bern, 1963, p. 166, No. 56.

16. W. Dittman, *Pierre Gringoire als Dramatiker*, Berlin, 1923, p. 5.

17. Gay, *loc. cit.* The reference to the queen's mirror was taken from Arch. Nat. 118, fol. 31. Gay found the Cambrai text in Houdoy, *Comptes de Cambrai*, p. 231.

18. Quoted by André Chastel, *Marsile Ficin et l'art*, Geneva, 1954, p. 141, from Pico's *Omnia opera*, ed. J. F. Picus Mirandula, Bologna, 1496, I, p. 172.

19. For the meaning of the word *mystère*, see E. Littré, *Dictionnaire de la langue française*, Paris, 1885, II, p. 60. The term is believed to derive from the secret cults of classical antiquity. Its meaning is multiple in French and extremely difficult to define in any narrow sense. See also DuCange, *Glossarium mediae et infimae latinitatis*, Graz, 1883-1887, IV, s.v. "Misterium," for a definition within an ecclesiastical context, and p. 594 for its significance in others; also Edmond Huguet, *Dictionnaire de la langue française du seizième siècle*, Paris, 1959, V, pp. 386-387; Edgar Wind, *Pagan Mysteries in the Renaissance*, London, 1958, "Introduction: the Language of Mysteries," pp. 13-19.
    Grace Frank, *The Medieval French Drama*, Oxford, 1960, p. 162, for the quote in text above; also p. 165. The word *mystère* did not exist as such before the fifteenth century, according to Louis Petit de Julleville (*op. cit.*, I, p. 188), when the term denoted plays or *tableaux-vivants*. Later in the century, it was expanded to include the performances, the *entrements* of triumphal entries. By 1563, the accessories designed by François Gentil for the Troyes entry of Charles IX were described as "mistères." See R. Koechlin and J. J. Marquet de Vasselot, *La Sculpture à Troyes*, Paris, 1900, p. 354.

20. See the *Receuil de chroniques . . . publié par la Société d'émulation de Bruges*, Sér. 3, Bruges for Du Puys' *La tryumphante et solennelle entree . . . de Charles duc de Borgogne*, 1515. Paul Clemen ("Lancelot Blondeel und die Anfänge der Renaissance in Brugge," *Belgische Kunstdenkmäler*, Munich, 1923, I, pp. 34-35) described Blondeel's participation in the triumphal entries.

21. See Willy Burger, *Die Malerei in den Niederländer von 1400-1500*, Munich, 1925, Pl. 25, 207, in the collection of the Vienna Gemäldegalerie.

22. Petit de Julleville, II, pp. 213-214.

23. See Hadassah Posey Goodman, *Original Elements in the French and German Passion Play*, Bryn Mawr, 1951, p. 13. "The Sémur Passion is the first of the French plays to elaborate on the theme of Judas' suicide and damnation . . . Judas then summons the devils, Mons Inferni and Clamator Inferni, and hangs himself from a cedar tree. The devils pull the cord about his neck, and when he is dead they seize his soul which emerges through his ruptured abdomen." The print may be based on the *Passion de Jesus Christ* by Jean Michel, written at the end of the fifteenth century, in which Judas' *remords* is followed by *désespoir* and succeeded by suicide. The drama culminates in a great *diablerie*, in which all the demons are summoned (Petit de Julleville, II, p. 414). See also Oswald Boetz, "Hie henckt Judas," *Form und Inhalt, Kunstgeschichtliche Studien*,

Otto Schmitt zum 60. Geburtstag, Stuttgart, 1950, pp. 105-139. Goetz (p. 122) quotes from the Arnould Greban *Passion*, completed in 1452 (verse 21, 889), where Judas encounters *Désespérance*, daughter of Lucifer, and says to her:

> Rage restreinte dedoubtable
> rendant redoublée renforce!
> rouge rage plus ragiable
> que la rage qui me refforce!
> Mort, mort . . .

In Greben's text, it is *Désespérance* who takes a large knife and slices his belly open to let the soul out, so that it is highly dubious whether Duvet had this particular passage in mind. Goetz points out: "Duvet scheint eine bereits mehrfach von ihm benutzte Kupferplatte (vgl. Bartsch 11, de la Boullaye 22, mit falscher Beschreibung; siehe auch Tietze-Conrat, *Der Französische Kupferstich der Renaissance*, Münich, 1925) überzeichnet zu haben" (p. 129, n. 4). He observed in a note that Duvet appears to have known the Valenciennes drama, with its reference to a "grant puis de confusion." performed in 1547, but no text source is given on p. 128.

24. For discussions of the *diablerie*, see Emile Jolibois, *La diablerie de Chaumont*, Paris, 1838; also Jules, comte de Douhet, *Dictionnaire des mystères* (XLIII of *Nouvelle encyclopédie théologique*, ed. Migne), Paris, 1854, cols. 291-295.
    X. Barbier de Montault, *Traité d'iconographie chrétien*, Paris, 1890, I, p. 232, gives a series of symbols of the *pardon* and *misericordia*.
    Godard, *op. cit.*, p. 123, gives the history of the Papal Bull.
    Gustave Cohen, *Mystère de la Passion Joué à Mons en 1501*, Paris, 1926, discusses the elaborate *diablerie* following the suicide. This incorporated Apocalypse symbolism, for the "trébuchment des Angeles" was a major feature of the production. A "Maistre Jehan du Fayr du Fayt" is listed on pp. 476, 480, 485, as having come with a group of seventeen machinists "pour avoir assisté à l'Enfer," manipulating the complex revolving stage, etc', needed for the "servant au secret du trébuchment des Angeles." It is tempting to read this as referring to a very precocious Jean Duvet.
    G. Cohen (*Histoire de la mise en scène dans le théâtre religieux du moyen âge*, Paris, 1951, p. 242) wrote that the play was performed in Langres presumably referring to the diocese rather than the town.

25. See "Les Rameaux, mystère du XVIe siècle." ed. Louis Royer, Extrait du *Bulletin de la Société d'études des Hautes Alpes*, 1927-28, p. 23, lines 382-386. The tree in Duvet's engraving may refer to that of Life: "The tree of life with its twelve kinds of fruits, yielding its fruit each month and the leaves of the tree were for the healing of the nations" (Rev. 22:2). See also *Les rameaux* in Douhet, *op. cit.*, col. 1372). Saint John the Evangelist prescribes the branches to be carried for the entry.

> L'on romp de verdure
> Palmes et mays oliviers
> Cedres, cypresses et lauriers
> Et mays de avellanyers
> Et de aubrespyns.

26. *The Annunciation* could be Cat. 12. Cat. 36 is close to the description on the Chaumont *Pères-aux-Limbes* as well as to the *Prophètes*. The Sibyl is depicted in Cat. 8 and Notre Dame des Nues in Cat. 13. Another *Nativity* (Cat. 28) was first recognized as a reflection of *mystère* iconography by Robert-Dumesnil, who pointed out that "La Nativité à la chandelle" comes from the French sixteenth century phrase "tenir la chandelle." See A. P. F. Robert-Dumesnil, *Le peintre-graveur française*, Paris, 841, V, p. 8.

27. See Petit de Julleville, II, p. 358: "On sait que la Genèse est muette sur la chute des Anges, nôtre auteur emprunt le fond de cette scene à un chapitre célèbre de l'Apocalypse."

28. Dated 1547, this engraving shows the classical deities with their arboreal attributes above a quotation reading,

> "The kinds of trees dedicated to their powers as deities were
> always preserved, as for example the Italian oak for Jupiter, the
> laurel for Apollo, the olive for Minerva, the myrtle for Venus,
> and the poplar for Hercules." (Bartsch XVI, 318, 33.)

Bartsch XVI, 330, 61, is also tablet-shaped. The inscription is from Pliny the Elder, *Naturalis historia*, Book XII.

29. Printed by Angelier, Paris, 1541; performed at Amiens in 1541, 1550, 1560. See Henri Raymond Lebègue, *Le Mystère des Actes des Apôtres*, Paris, 1929, pp. 32, 442. Lebègue, *La tragédie religieuse en France: les débuts (1514-1573)*, Paris, 1929, pp. 41-43, no. 11, gives the title as *L'Apocalypse et les cruautés de Domitien*.

30. Producers of this drama met with difficulty in receiving permission to stage it. A group of traveling players requesting the consent of the bishop of Amiens for the presentation of the work met with objections from both bishop and town council. Permission was finally granted with the proviso that the play be staged indoors, as the councilors were worried about "telle manière de gens jouer publiquement la parole de Dieu." See H. Dusevel, "Variétés." *Revue des société savantes des départments*, Sér. 2, II, 1859, pp. 107-110. This reference is from Petit de Julleville, II, p. 360, who stated that *L'Apocalypse* was staged in Rouen in 1556.

31. Chocquet wrote on his title page, "le tout vu et corrigé selon le vraye verité," and Duvet inscribed on his Frontpiece AC VERAE LITERAE TEXTUS PROXIME ACCOMODATA.

32. Lebègue, *Les Actes de Apôtres*, pp. 29-32. See also Amedée Roget, *Histoire du peuple de Genève*, Geneva, 1873, II, pp. 237-242.

33. Roget, *op. cit.*, p. 237. Two pastors revised the *mystère*, Chaponneau, a former priest and associate of Calvin's at Bourges in 1529-31 before working with Farel at Neuchâtel, and Abel Poupin at Geneva. For the latter, see Roget, p. 322; for Chaponneau, see Lebègue, *op. cit.*, p. 133.

34. Heinrich Göbel, *Wandteppiche*, Leipzig, 1923, I, Part I. Göbel's monumental study includes a brilliant discussion of the Apocalypse in the fifteenth and sixteenth centuries. Aware of the significance of the *mystère*, he wrote, "Die Apokalypse wurde des oftern, ganz oder in selbständig, geschlossenen Teilszenen in den ehedem burgundischen Landen zur Darstellung gebracht: dem Patronenmaler mangelte es nicht an geeigneten Vorlagen" (p. 156).

35. See Henri David, "Le grand portail de l'église St.-Michel de Dijon," *Mémoires de l'Académie des sciences, art et belles-lettres de Dijon*, I, 1923, pp. 225-252; iconography discussed on p. 230. See also the same author's *De Sluter à Sambin*, Paris, 1931, II, p. 52, for history of construction. E. Fyot, *Dijon: son passé evoquée par ses rues*, Dijon, 1928, p. 452, reproduces an engraving of the church by Israel Silvestre which reveals the same fusion of Italian and Northern forms that characterizes the Duvet *Apocalypse*. Most of the façade sculptures of the church were executed by a Flemish sculptor who worked in Dijon in 1550. The incorporation of Apocalyptic subject matter into a triumphal archway extended to domestic as well as ecclesiastical use. The tympanum above the entry to the beautiful mid-sixteenth century Hôtel d'Escoville at Caen encloses a bas-relief depicting a rich synthesis of images from Revelation. The Hôtel was severely damaged during the bombing of Caen in World War II.

36. See David, *De Sluter à Sambin*, II, *op. cit.*, p. 52.

37. The central inscription of the façade, ET TRES SVNT QUI TESTIMONIUM DANT IN TERRA SPIRITUS AQVA ET SANGUIS ET HI TRES VNVM SVNT, an affirmation of the doctrine of the Trinity from I John 5:8, seems similar to the

source of Duvet's inscription on his *Trinity* (Cat. 39): TRES SIMUL AEQVALES PERSONAE SVNT DEVS VNVS PRINCIPIVM ET FINIS RERVM TESTATE IOHANE' David, *De Sluter a Sambin, loc. cit.*, who has made an intensive study of the iconography of the Saint-Michel façade, pointed out the difference between the medieval concept of the Last Judgment based upon Matthew and that of Revelation, seen at Chartres and Saint-Michel. The program of the latter, which he regards as "dans un esprit savant," is close to Duvet's inscriptions. Representations of Isaiah, Ezechiel, Daniel, Baruch, David, and Moses, all of which allude to prophecies of triumph and sacrifice, are found at Saint-Michel.

38. See Marcel, II, p. 338. Marcel gives as source for this information "Arch. Côte-d'Or G. 1524: Compte 8 de Guy Gontault, fabricien de la Sainte-Chapelle (1520-1543) folio 179." Marcel asks, "Quel en fut le donateur? Serait-ce le doyen André de Laval, ami de Givry? Qui les dessina?"

39. Among the few Fontainebleau prints of Biblical subjects is a most impressive one of Saint Michael and the rebel angels (BXVI, 391, 37) in the style of Mignon, probably based on a lost work by Penni. Although not closely related to Duvet's depictions of the same subject, it may stem from a series of Apocalypse illustrations in a French Chapel associated with the Order of Saint Michael which might well have been of interest to Duvet, possibly reflecting the same sources as those of the Dijon tapestries. The print probably dates from the later 1540's, which would coincide with the beginning of Duvet's project. For a helpful discussion of Mignon, see Henri Zerner, "L'eau-forte à Fontainebleau," *Art de France*, IV, 1964, p. 81.

40. Jacques Vignier, *Décade historique de diocèse de Langres*, 1894, II, p. 218.

41. To the right of Louis XI, founder of the Order (in a manuscript, B.N. ms. fr., 19819, f. 1; reproduced in K. G. Perls, *Jean Fouquet*, Paris, 1940, Pl. XI) stands a man identified by Paul Durrieu as Gui Bernard, Bishop of Langres. See "Les Manuscrits des Statuts de l'Ordre de Saint-Michel," *Bulletin de la Société française de reproduction des manuscrits à peinture*, Paris, 1911, pp. 17-47.

42. David, *De Sluter à Sambin*, II, p. 158, n. 5.

43. The Sainte-Chapelle was also associated with the Ordre de Saint-Michel. Girard de Vienne, who founded a chapel within it, belonged to the Order. See Pierre Quarré, *La Sainte-Chapelle de Dijon*, Musée de Dijon, 1962, Cat. nos. 100, 101.

44. See M. Roy, *Artistes et monuments de la renaissance en France*, Paris, 1929, pp. 208-209. Roy states that while the windows resemble the Petit Bernard Apocalypse illustrations for Jean de Tournes' *Les quadrins historiques de la Bible et les figures du Nouveau Testament*, Lyon, 1553, the windows seem to have been completed for a meeting of the Order held in 1544. Henri II, wearing the mantle of the Order, is represented as a donor.
    n.d., p. 54.

45. Roy, *op. cit.*, p. 206. Anthony Blunt, *Philibert de l'Orme*, London, 1958, p. 76, n. 2.

46. Stained glass windows based on the Dürer-inspired Wittenberg Bible Apocalypse are numerous in northeast France, in Champagne, Burgundy, and the Ile-de-France. The best known examples are at Saint-Martin-des-Vignes in Troyes, at Granville and Chavanges in the Aube, at La Ferté-Millon in Aisne, and at Vincennes. For a brilliant discussion of Dürer's influence on Netherlandish art, a development which parallels and predates the German artist's influence in France, see Julius Held's *Dürers Wirkung auf die niederländische Kunst seiner Zeit*, The Hague, 1931. For a discussion of Dürer's influence on French art, see Louis Réau, *Les richesses d'art de la France: la Bourgogne: la peinture et les tapisseries*, Paris-Brussels, 1929, Pl. 29-30. As the first to publish a photograph of the Yonne window, Réau believed it to be by a French *peintre-verrier*, but it may very well have been the work of one of the many itinerant Flemish craftsmen active in this area. The window is also mentioned in L. Ottin, *Le Vitrail*, Paris, 1896, p. 224. The most detailed study of the windows at Yonne has been made by Camille Hermelin, *Histoire de la ville de Saint-Florentin*, Paris, 1912. The same author's *Saint-Florentin: son aspect, ses rues, son église*, Auxerre, 1905, p. 27, points out that

the window which is divided into twelve sections, two of which are devoted to donor portraits, is dated 1529. The high altar at Saint-Florentin, formerly attributed to Jean Goujon but now far more reasonably given to François Gentil, provides a direct link with Duvet, as this sculptor was active in Langres. His great *Christ at the Column* is strikingly reminiscent of Duvet's engraving of the Crucifixion, noted by Marcel, II, p. 410, Cat. 35.

47. See William W. Warren, *Readings on the Purgatorio of Dante*, London, 1897, II, Canto XXIX, pp. 480-516.

48. See Werner Weisbach, *Trionfi*, Berlin, 1919, p. 70.

49. Petit de Julleville, II, p. 8.

50. *Ibid.*, p. 194. See also Lotte Brand Philip's study of *The Ghent Altarpiece*, Princeton, 1972.

51. See Charles de Beaurepaire, *L'entrée du roi Charles VIII à Rouen*, 1485, Rouen, 1902.

52. *Ibid.* The songs were V, 13 and V, 9.

53. See Adolph Franz, *Die Messe im deutschen Mittelalter,* Freiburg-im-Breisgau, 1902, pp. 273-276, for the Mass of Saint Michael, pp. 172-175, for that of the Elders.

54. See A. Daquin, *Les évêques de Langres*, Nogent, 1880-83, pp. 42-45; also Marcel, I, p. 34.

55. See P. LeVerdier, *L'entrée du roi Louis XI et de la reine à Rouen (1508)*, Rouen, 1900, p. 19.

56. C. de Beaurepaire, *L'entrée de François premier, au mois d'août, 1517*, Rouen, 1867.

57. Petit de Julleville, II, p. 151.

58. *Ibid.*

59. According to Erwin Panofsky, *Studies in Iconology*, New York, 1962, p. 157, n. 97, the source of the cornucopia as a symbol of riches can be found in Saint Ambrose: "Non enim augusta, sed dives utilitatem prudentia est" (Migne, *Patrologia latina*, Paris, 1857, XIV, col. 297).
   For a discussion of de Givry's emblem, see Vignier, *op. cit.*, II, p. 229.

60. See S. de Merval, *L'entrée d'Henri II à Rouen*, 1868. The account is taken from a manuscript in the Rouen library. Illustrations from the entry are reproduced by Merval.

61. Reproduced in Paul Vitry and Gaston Brière, *Documents de sculpture française*, Paris, 1904-13, II, Pl. XCII, figs. 1-4. This sculptured altarpiece is actually a monumentalized *mystère*, following the Dantesque program for the Triumph of the Church. The Whore of Babylon is set among the seven virtues. Her monster has seven heads of evil, to contrast with those of the virtues. Above the Scarlet Woman, to indicate the triumph of virtue, there is an inscription from the writings of Saint John: "Ego iohannis mirabor purpurs tam meretrice est abitiola cupida-tuebria de sanguine di martir Iesu." (Revelation 17:6). Above this *écriteau*, the Child of the Apocalypse is shown carried up to heaven, emblematic of the Triumph of the Church in Christ.

62. Another depiction of Henri II as Saint Michael in print form and approximately contemporary with that by Duvet, was executed by Rene Boyvin. Inscribed "Henricus II Gallorum Rex Christianissimus," the print shows the king in armor, wearing the Order of Saint Michael and a laurel wreath. See A. Linzeler, *Inventaire du fonds français*; Paris, 1932, I, p. 187A; see also Robert-Dumesnil, *op. cit.*, VIII, p. 58, No. 105.
   Mrs. Pattison, *The Art of the Renaissance in France*, London, 1879, II, p. 106, linked Duvet's engraving with *La majesté royale* (Cat. 63). She pointed out that "the character of the execution, taken with the youth of the face, would include one to conjecture that both pieces were produced in honour of the King's accession, rather than as a tribute to his memory."

63. Henri Chabeuf, *Entrées d'Henri II à Dijon,"* p. lxxvii (from the Archives de la Ville, Entrées des rois, I, 17. bis, supplément).

64. See Sir Francis Oppenheimer, K. G., *The Legend of the Ste. Ampoule*, London, 1953, pp. 24-25; E. S. Dewick, *The Coronation Book of Charles V of France*, London, 1899 (Henry Bradshaw Society, Vol XVI), col. 68.

65. See Cohen, *Histoire de la mise en scène, op. cit.;* Saint Rémy "reçoit la sainte ampule des mains de l'ange Gabriel pour le baptême de Clovis." The Baptism of Clovis was also performed for the triumphal entry of François Ier, Lyon, 1515, and depicted in a manuscript at Wolfenbüttel, published by Georges Guigue, in 1899.

   See Petit de Julleville, II, p. 555. The unpublished manuscript for this play is at the Bibliothèque de l'Arsenal, no. 3364. An eighteenth century inscription states that the play was written in 1544, but Julleville believed it to date from the fifteenth century. A *Mystère de Saint Michel* was staged at Brou in 1502 for the entry of Margaret of Austria. Like some other Apocalyptic symbolism in France, this *mystère* may have been of Burgundian inspiration. See Jules Baux, *Histoire de l'église de Brou*, Lyon, 1884, p. 26.

66. Louis de Gouvenain and Philippe Vallée, *Inventaire sommaire des archives communales antérieures à 1790, Ville de Dijon*, 1892, III, 10; I, 11.

67. Boullaye, 1876, p. 136.

68. Durrieu, *op. cit.*, pp. 17-47.

69. *Ibid.*, Pl. 10.

70. See J. Helbig, *Oude Glasramen van de Collegiale Sinte-Goedele*, Antwerp, 1942.

71. The Michelin guide states that the Tour Saint-Jean, next to the Long-Porte, was built in 1538. Another relief showing the Order supported by Angels, dating from the end of the fifteenth century, is at the Chartreuse de Champmol. See *La Millénaire du Mont-Saint-Michel 966-1966*, Exposition, Paris, 1966, Cat. no. 402, p. 190.

72. Roy, *Artistes et monuments, op.cit.*, pp. 208-209.

73. For literary equivalents of this genre, see Françoise Joukovsky, *La gloire dans la poésie française et néolatine du XVIème siècle*, Geneva, 1969, "Le Bruit de Gloire," pp. 339-342, and "Les Grandes tombeaux," pp. 415 ff.

The Apocalypse as Publication

The circumstances surrounding the publication of Duvet's engravings and French text seem riddled with contradictions. Only seven copies of the publication are accounted for: two are in the Bibliothèque Nationale, a third is in the Collection Dutuit, and the other four are in the British Museum, the Bibliothèque de la Ville of Langres and of Lyon and the Cleveland Museum of Art.[1] The consensus among scholars is that Duvet must have issued the *Apocalypse* Plates separately before the 1561 publication date. The engraved Frontispiece (Cat. 65) is dated 1555 and the *Privilège* 1556 (Text fig. 9), leaving a curious five year lapse until the publication in 1561. Even the title page (Text fig. 10) presents a problem in its somewhat ambiguous wording "*Lapocalypse figuree—Par Maistre Iehan Duuet, iadis Ofevre des Rois Francois premier de ce nom, & Henri deux ieme—A Lyon—Auec priuilege du Roy pour douze ans.—M.D.LXI.*"

It has been suggested that the "iadis" signifies that Duvet was dead at the time of the publication. But this seems unlikely because the term "feu" rather than "iadis" would have been used. *Iadis* refers to his service as a goldsmith to both François Ier, who died in 1547, and Henri II, who died in 1559. Boullaye has correctly pointed out that in modern French *jadis* is replaced by *ancien*, consequently, he is convinced that Duvet was alive in 1561.[2] Duvet's first biographer and archivist discovered a reference to a Jean Drouot who attended an assembly of Langres residents concerning questions of *Octroi* on November 15, 1562, which suggests that the engraver was still active at the age of seventy-seven.[3] The fact that no publisher's name is given attests to Duvet's existence in 1561, for had he not published this work himself, it would have been issued illegally. Detection of illegal publications was facilitated by a law passed on 11 December 1547, which required that the name of the author and the name and address of the printer be included at the beginning of every religious book. The phrase "A Lyon" offers insufficient identification in itself.[4] The delay in publication may be attributed to the chaotic life Duvet led immediately after receiving the *Privilège* (App. E, Doc. 68).[5]

Further support of the engraver's presence in 1561 is found in the repairs Duvet presumably made during the printing of the *Apocalypse figurée*, where he reworked the edges of some of his plates (Cat. 50, 61). The example at Cleveland is remarkably fresh and was the result of early impressions, bound in with the 1561 text. The six other surviving copies of the publication make it clear that repairs were made at about that time, probably for a final exploitation of the plates in a new literary context. The number "61" scratched in the lower left corner of the "Triumph of the Unicorn" (Cat. 67), also indicates that Duvet was alive and at work in the year his book emerged from the Lyon presses.

The wording of both the *Privilège* and the engraved Frontispiece points to the commencement of the plates, circa 1546, which would coincide with François Ier's last tour of Burgundy; his son's subsequent visit in 1548 could have offered Henri II the opportunity to display an interest in the project. The fact that the plates were primarily the artist's own idea, submitted for royal patronage is made clear by the wording of the *Privilège*, with its emphasis on the fact that no royal financial contribution to the project was ever made, although the project was undertaken at royal command—"par nostre commandement & ordonnances." In obtaining the *Privilège*, Duvet may have utilized the good offices of the Chabot family, who were related to Cardinal Givry of Langres, and known to have possessed a hôtel at Fontainebleau as well as the great chateau at Pagny.

The *Privilège* also states that the plates were initially planned by Duvet, who "portraict & figurs la sacree & saincte Apocalypse" (App. E, Doc. 68). Rather than suggesting an accompanying printed text, this points to the engraved text on the copper plates themselves. Had an illustrated publication been the original plan, the word *illustré* rather than *figuré* would probably have been used. The slovenly appearance of both the typography and the printing and centering of the copper plates (with the exception of the Cleveland *Apocalypse*),indicates a terminal exploitation of the engraving in 1561.

Several of the plates were damaged in the printing process: corners were broken off and surfaces eroded.[6] An examination of the very rare edition shows a clumsy, forced juxtaposition of the plate page and the text page. The suggestion that the artist did not have this format in mind when he first envisaged the series is conceivable from the selection of chapter material; one engraving may contain visual references to as many as three chapters, and two prints are often devoted to a single chapter. Chapters XII, XV, and XVI are only mentioned once and are confined to the same plate. No inscription refers to the second or third chapters. Chapter XII is omitted.[7] All these factors contribute to a free, independent approach towards the Apocalypse, thereby contradicting any theory that the series was originally planned to accompany a chapter by chapter, conventionally illustrated publication.

Jean de Tournes was suggested as the *Apocalypse figurée* printer, but in all fairness this book is far below his normal standards.[8] The grand alphabet of the *Apocalypse* (with ornate capital letters heading each chapter,) corresponds with that of Jean de Tournes' edition of the Chroniques de Froissart (Lyon, 1561), leading Naef to attribute the printing to de Tournes.[9] However, the extremely heavy, coarse typeface used in the title(Text fig. 10)is more like that of a poster or proclamation and could not have come from the de Tournes printshop. Before the use of the Tournes capitals had been proposed, E. Rahir suggested that Jean Marcorelle may have been the printer, as his titlepage for Ioannis Baptistae Donati's *Medici Lucensis* (Lyon, 1566) is similar to that of the *Apocalypse* in its rather irregular and inelegant typography.[10] Marcorelle's biography reinforces the possibility that he printed the work since he was in Geneva from 1554 to 1559 and then in Lyon from 1560 to circa 1576. Like Duvet, he went back and forth between France and Geneva—a typical journey for "the itinerant Protestant artisan."[11]

Marcorelle's later experience in the printing of elaborately illustrated books such as Woeriot's engraved *Emblèmes* of Georgette de Montenay, and woodcuts by a possible associate of Duvet's, Hugues Sambin, makes him a likely candidate as Duvet's printer. It is feasible that Marcorelle borrowed the *grand alphabet* from de Tournes, a fellow Protestant migrating between Lyon and Geneva. As de Tournes' will absolves Marcorelle of debts which may well have been unpaid fees for type rental, it seems almost certain the Marcorelle was the man the aged Duvet employed to finally issue his work and the text in printed form.

The exact source of the Apocalypse translation published in 1561 has not yet been fully identified. Boullaye, the first to study the text, found in comparing it with others published before this date, "légères différences avec la traduction de Le Fèvre d'Estaples, qui du reste a été plusieurs fois remaniée dans cinq ou six editions publiées avant cette année; il est probablement conformé à quelqu'une d'entre elles."[13] Naef believed the translation to have been taken from that of Olivétan, Calvin's cousin, first painted at Neuchâtel in 1535, explaining the delay in publication as due to the engraver's concern over the choice of text.[14] Had Duvet taken Olivétan's (for which Calvin wrote the introduction) he would have alienated his Catholic patrons. Had he taken another based on the Vulgate, he would have estranged his friends in Geneva. After Henri II's death in 1559 and the parley of Poissy, it was once again possible to publish formerly incriminating works. However, Naef's discoveries reveal that the Duvet text was a characterless compromise between the Olivétan version and the Vulgate. Naef's explanation for Duvet's delay is not entirely convincing, as Jean de Tournes issued the Olivétan translation in Lyon in 1545, followed by his illustrated edition in 1553 and 1558, as well as other Lyon works like those of I. Frellon's in 1553 and by G. Rouille's in 1554.[15]

Most indicative of the ambiguity of sixteenth century religious thought is the frequent dependence of German Catholic Bibles on Protestant sources; the one published by Peter Jordan in Mainz, 1534 being a case in point. Here the Old Testament is based on Luther's text and the Vulgate, the New Testament on Emser's translation of 1527 and the Apocrypha on the text of Leo Juda.[16] This Catholic utilization of Protestant sources is paralleled in French art by the Apocalypse illustrations in Lyon Bibles, based upon those for Luther's Wittenberg Bible of 1522.[17]

Theoretically, France entered a new phase of compromise with Protestant thought in the early 1560s, though persecution raged unchecked. Gilles Richebois, a printer who worked for Jean de Tournes in Lyon between 1542 and 1550, then went to Langres to work for Cardinal de Givry, reprinting all the liturgical works of the diocese by 1560. Two years later he was killed in a massacre of Protestants at Sens.[18] Perhaps the fluctuation of political and religious events between the inception of the *Apocalypse* Series and the 1561 publication can help explain the French translation. It is worth remembering that at the time the *Apocalypse* engravings were begun, the very use of French in religious services constituted a sacrilege. Even in 1561, the religious services held by a Carmelite resulted in arrest because the "valets et artisans" who formed the major part of the congregation were singing in French. They were accused of "chantent haultement et scandaleusement en françoy les pseaulmes de David devant le chaire en attendant le predicateur."[19]

Duvet's printed *Apocalypse* appeared at just the time when, according to a prominent French historian, "la protestantisme venait, malgré les efforts opposés à sa diffusion, de se renforcer et d'organiser en églises."[20] It was a banner year for Calvin's negotiations with France, marked by a peak production of Protestant presses in Geneva destined for French consumption.[21] However in 1562, a new flare-up of Protestant persecution occurred in Dijon. Two gunsmiths, who had recently returned from their self-imposed exile, were exiled from Dijon and the City Council initiated rigorous measures for the expulsion of Protestant "valets and artisans."[22]

The Edict of Chateaubriand probably prevented earlier publication of Duvet's book. It not only forbade the importation of books from Geneva (and all other places separated from the Church) but also prohibited the translation of the Bible or any of the patristic texts and prevented the printing or selling of books, commentaries, *scholia*, annotations, tables, indices, or summaries concerning the Holy Scripture and the Christian religion written within the past forty years, in any language without the official approval of the faculty of theology.[23]

All things considered, there may have been less delay in distribution than is generally assumed. The plates broke at least twice in the course of the printing. They lacked the bulk or craftsmanship to bear repeated pressure and were clearly not meant to be issued in large quantities. Were it not for the Cleveland model (whose plates may have been printed in 1556 and bound with the 1561 text), the six other surviving copies might be dismissed as a last minute attempt to extract additional compensation for the great effort which must have gone into the engraving of the plates.

It was not unusual in the sixteenth century for an artist to envision an illustrated series for the Apocalypse with little or no accompanying text. Probably, this concept stems from the popular block books of the mid-fifteenth century. Even Dürer's great work of 1498 does not really lend itself to a conventional "illustrated" format in which the print supplements the word. The earliest sixteenth century printed Apocalypse cycles in France were those forming marginal decorations in Books of Hours, typified by Hardouin's *Heures a lusaige de Rome . . . avec les figures de lapocalipse plusieurs autres histoires* (Paris, 1510). The thirty-nine vignettes accompnaying the Apocalypse text in narrative sequence may occasionally have relied on Dürer's work but could just as well go back to one of Dürer's chief sources, the Grüninger Bible of 1485.[24] It was not until the 1520s that there was a sudden efflorescence of lavishly illustrated German Apocalypse publications. Judging by the editions of that time, *Revelations* was more adaptable to pictorial imagery than any other chapter of the Bible.[25] Schäufelein, Beham, Cranach, Holbein, the Monogrammists H.E. and A.W., Altdorfer, the Master of Jacob's Ladder, and Anton Woesam all prepared Apocalypse illustrations in the 1520s and 1530s.[26] In France, following the decline of the use of Books of Hours, the newly illustrated Bibles of Lyon and Paris reveal themselves to be under complete domination of the German publications.[27] The Parisian printers Frellon and Marlin (1554) produced Bibles similar to those of de Tournes in Lyon, framing their Wittenberg vignettes in Fontainebleau strapwork.

Toward the middle of the sixteenth century, French graphic artists adapted the independent, illustrated Apocalypse production which had long been popular in the North and the Netherlands since the days of the first woodcut Apocalypse block books of the 1440s.[28] There seems to have been a resurgence of interest in a publication stressing a visualization of *Revelations*, starting with the great success of Hans Sebald Beham's *Imagines in Apocalypsim*, printed in Frankfurt shortly before 1539 and reprinted in *1539, 1540, 1551, and 1557-58.*[29] This tendency toward a "Bible in pictures" can also be seen in Virgil Solis' *Biblische Figuren des Alten und Neuen Testaments gantz kuenstlich gerissen* (Frankfurt, 1560). Like most publications of the time, Solis' work had twenty-six Apocalypse illustrations, coupled with four short lines of Latin verse above and a German translation below, placing the main emphasis on the visual rather than a verbal. The same trend toward illustration can be seen in Paris in *Les Figures de l'Apocalipse de Saint Ian apostre a dernier Evangelist, exposées en Latin & vers François*, printed by Estienne Groulleau in 1547,[30] and in a series of six great tapestrylike woodcuts of Apocalyptic subject matter printed by Guillaume Saulce between the years 1550 and 1555.[31]

Closest to Duvet's in date and in number is the Apocalypse by Mathias Gerung, a German printmaker, who, like Duvet, led a double life, executing Catholic and Protestant commissions simultaneously.[32] Consisting of twenty-six woodcuts, Gerung's *Revelations* (Text fig. 36) was begun in 1544 and not released for several years after its completion in 1550.

Thus, Duvet's twenty-one engravings, limited to the text of *Revelations* alone (Cat. 40-61), fall within the mid-sixteenth century convention of an illustrated Apocalypse with a minimum of text. Begun in 1546, its chief source is the Dürer woodcut Apocalypse of 1498—eleven of Duvet's plates are very clearly derived from the corresponding German blocks.[35] The tablet format may have been derived from the artist's woodcut *Life of the Virgin*, in which so many of the scenes take place within an architectural framework of this shape. The Apocalypse cycles published by Dürer (Text figs. 37-41) and Duvet are distinctly similar. In their respective countries, both represent the first books to be designed and published as their artist's exclusive undertakings, appearing as both artist and printer. Duvet could also have been influenced by Italian works after Dürer or prints by Parmigianino and Caraglio of the same format. In fact, Duvet may have derived his forms more from sixteenth century adaptations of the Dürer series rather than from the original woodcuts.

36. *Mathias Gerung,* Revelations: The Four
Horsemen of the Apocalypse, *1541-50.*

37. *A. Dürer,* St. John Sees the Seven Gold Candlesticks,
Apocalypse 1497-98.

38. *A. Dürer,* St. John Summoned to Heaven,
Apocaylpse, 1497-98

39. A. Dürer, The Angel Sounding the Sixth Trumpet, *Apocalypse 1497-98.*

40. A. Dürer, The Angel Gives St. John the Book to Eat, *Apocalypse 1497-98.*

41. A. Dürer, The Babylon Harlot Seated on the Seven-Headed Beast, *Apocalypse 1497-98.*

The most important of these secondary sources was the Wittenberg Bible of 1524. Lemberger's woodcuts expanded the Dürer cycle to twenty and gave it a more conventionally decorative character. Flemish glasspainters often obtained their Apocalypse images for transfer to glass from the Wittenberg series, depicted in vastly enlarged form on church windows throughout the Netherlands and France, such as the one at St.-Florentin (Yonne) in the diocese of Duvet's Langres (Text fig. 32). The illustrations remained popular for a long time and were copied by Anton Woesam von Wurms in 1529 for Peter Quentell's *Das gantz New Testament.* A later, less faithful copy was issued by Hans Lufft, *Das Newe Testament* (Wittenberg, 1552)(Text fig. 42,43).

42. Hans Lufft, The Angel Gives St. John the Book to Eat, *from the* Wittenberg New Testament, *1552.* The British Library.

43. Hans Lufft, The Winepress of the Wrath of God, *from the* Wittenberg New Testament, *1552, The British Library.*

Duvet's androgynous horseman at the extreme left of Cat. 42 is derived from the Lufft Bible's clumsy copy of earlier illustrations. The French engraver's "Woman Clothed with the Sun" (Cat. 50) and his scene of the "Four Angels Holding Back the Winds" (Cat. 44) could have been derived from any one of three versions, although the 1552 Bible, with its swirling, misunderstood adaptions from its predecessors, seems to have been the one most closely consulted. This Bible's extensively classicized approach no doubt attracted Duvet. The Lufft illustrator's innovations in the scene depicting the angel giving Saint John the book shows considerable change from the earlier Wittenberg Bible. Duvet seems to have taken his "cloud-torso" and columnlike legs for Cat. 48 from this anonymous artist who, for all his coarseness, presented a richly black, niellolike surface and an appealing sense of narrative excitement.

The same interest in Renaissance ornament displayed in the Lufft Bible appears in the many printings of small-scale Apocalypse illustrations by Bernard Salomon for Jean de Tournes during the 1540s and 1550s. While they share a common consultation of Italian prints, inserting Michelangelesque figures and Tuscan ornament within the Wittenberg series, neither the Duvet nor the Salomon series seems to have had any effect on the other. They were parallel manifestations of the same tendency toward the use of Italian sources.

In summary, the artist's engraved *Apocalypse* uses the fifteen Dürer woodcuts of 1498 and their expanded versions of 1524, 1529, and 1554, published at Wittenberg. Duvet converts these sources into tablet-shaped compositions, changing the ornament wherever possible in an Italianate fashion. He formalized and schematized the narrative sequences, spreading them over the tablet-shaped plates much as decorative and other elements are distributed over the surface of a shield. The artist uses a Marcantonio-inspired physiognomy wherever possible and frequently turns his adapted figures from a three-quarter to a profile view. The series is filled with countless reminiscences of Italian printmaking, the art of Agostino Veneziano (Text fig. 7), Campagnola, Ghisi, Caraglio, *et al.* Most unusual seem to be the forms reminiscent of the late fifteenth and early sixteenth century Florentine art, such as the engravings after Andrea del Sarto's frescoes of the life of St. Philip Benizzi (Text fig. 44).[34]

Duvet's publication is certainly the most powerful and impressive work to be illustrated with engravings in sixteenth century France. Whether it was the third or fourth identified work to be printed from metal plates seems of relatively little importance.[35] The Cleveland example of the *Apocalypse figurée* contains, in addition to the *Apocalypse* Plates themselves, all the other tablet-shaped engravings with the exception of the unique "Henri II as the Victorious Saint Michael" (Cat. 62).[36] Bound in black morocco with the date 1637 stamped on the cover, this volume has been linked by J.G. van Gelder to other similarly bound and dated works owned by a Dutch collector.[37]

44. Scene from the Life of Saint Philip Benizzi, *engraving after Andrea del Sarto, early 16th century.*

The Bibliothèque Nationale possesses two examples of the 1561 publication. One of these has almost as many plates as the Cleveland example, lacking only Cats. 62 and 64; all the impressions are very late, poorly printed states, including unique final prints of Cats. 38, and 62. [38] The second example at the same library includes only the *Apocalypse* Plates, Frontispiece, and the first state of "Henri II as the Victorious Saint Michael" (Cat. 62); the impressions are all late states but not as carelessly printed as those in the preceding volume. [39] The plates are printed in a warm, rich, dark ink and have very narrow margins. The third example of the *Apocalypse* in Paris is in the Collection Dutuit (Petit Palais). Limited to the plates of Apocalyptic subjects, those of this example are unevenly inked and poorly printed. [40]

The British Museum's example is much stained and has many repairs in the text pages, which have suffered tears and losses on the pages for Chapters 1,3 and 16. [41] The seventh example of the *Apocalypse figurée* is in the Bibliothèque de la Ville, Lyon, overlooked by scholars since 1894. [42] With the exception of a missing title page, the example is complete and has, in addition to the Frontispiece, a unique second state of "Henri II as the Victorious Saint Michael" (Cat. 62), "Revelation of Saint John the Evangelist (Cat. 39) and second states of the "Marriage of Adam and Eve" (Cat. 37), "Moses Surrounded by the Patriarchs" (Cat. 36), and the "Deposition" (Cat. 37), all in very good impressions although not equal of the ones at Cleveland or the Series without the text at the Louvre (Collection Edmond de Rothschild), the Bibliothèque Nationale (Rés. AA2), and the Boston Museum of Fine Arts.

Many major print rooms own single engravings from the *Apocalypse*, which judging from the high quality of the printing and the state of the plate, appear to have been issued prior to 1561. Although most of the known individual impressions of the poorer quality may originally have been printed in 1561 with the text, and later detached from it, the edition could never have been a large one.

NOTES

1. Generally, the fine *Apocalypse* prints, such as those in the Museum of Fine Arts in Boston or the series in the Bibliothèque Nationale (Rés. AA2), have wire lines in the paper running vertically, while the plates in the *Apocalypse* with text, including the brilliant Cleveland example, have horizontal wire lines. The page size of the text version is changes from 386 x 278 mm. to 386/389 x 260 mm.

2. E. Jullien de la Boullaye, *Étude sur la vie et sur l'oeuvre de Jean Duvet, dit le Maître à la licorne,* Paris, 1876, p. 21.

3. *Ibid.,* p. 27 (Archives, art. 619-1).

4. David T. Pottinger, *The French Book Trade in the Ancien Régime,* Cambridge, 1958, p. 214.

5. The honesty of the statement that the work had a *Privilège* for twelve years might perhaps be questioned, as by 1561 six years of the royal protection had already elapsed. Not until 1566 was it legally obligatory to reproduce the text of the *Privilège* in full. See *ibid.,* p. 213.

6. It might seem that the third state of Cat. 61 *(The Fountain of Living Water)* is associated with all examples of the engraved *Apocalypse* of 1561 but this would not be correct, as the Cleveland example, which bears evidence of "type-ghosts" suggesting that it too was printed at the time of the text plates, is a second state.

7. Distribution of Apocalyptic text in Duvet's plates:

Cat. 65	title page	Cat. 51	Chap. XII
Cat. 40	Chap. I	Cat. 52	Chap. XIV
Cat. 41	Chap. IV-V	Cat. 53	Chap. XIV
Cat. 42	Chap. VI	Cat. 54	Chap. XV, XVI
Cat. 43	Chap. VI, IX	Cat. 55	Chap. XVII, XVIII
Cat. 44	Chap. VII	Cat. 56	Chap. XVIII
Cat. 45	Chap. VII	Cat. 57	Chap. XIX
Cat. 46	Chap. VIII	Cat. 58	Chap. XIX
Cat. 47	Chap. IX	Cat. 59	Chap. XX
Cat. 48	Chap. X	Cat. 60	Chap. XXI
Cat. 49	Chap. XI	Cat. 61	Chap. XXII
Cat. 50	Chap. XII		

8. The Jean de Tournes attribution appeared in *Catalogue 65* by Nicolas Rauch, Geneva, March 2, 1953, p. 52; and in the British Museum catalogue *Printing and the Mind of Man,* London, 1963, Cat. 77, p. 27.

9. H. Naef, "La vie et les travaux de Jean Duvet . . . ," *Bulletin de la Société de l'histoire de l'art français,* 1934, p. 135. Naef names Gustave Lebel as the source of the type-study. The capital letters have been tabulated from the editions of both works at the Bibliothèque Nationale.

Apocalypse	Froissart, Book I of the *Croniques*
Chap. II.	Page 35.
Chap. III.	Page 38.
Chap. IV.	Page 405.
Chap. V.	Page 406.
Chap. VI.	In same series as Q on page 4.
Chap. XVI.	Page 219.

10. E. Rahir, *Bibliothèque de l'amateur,* Paris, 1924, p. 412.
J. Baltrušaitis, *Réveils et prodigues,* Paris, 1960, p.274, also assigned the printing to Marcorelle.

11. For Marcorelle's biography and oeuvre, see J. Baudrier, *Bibliographie lyonnaise,* Lyon, 1913, X, pp. 375-378. Baudrier (I, p. 143) was the first to suggest that Duvet was probably the publisher of his own Apocalypse. J.-C.

Brunet (*Manuel de libraire*, Paris, 1861, II, p. 930) follows Senior who, noticing that the plates issued without the text were superior in quality to those with it, believed that there must have been previous editions of the *Apocalypse* plates alone. Boullaye (*op. cit.*, p. 60, n. 1) observed that the heart-shaped *fleuron* on the Apocalypse title page is found in a work printed by Jean Crespin (*Opera Virgiliana . . . ex politissimis figuris et imaginibus illustrata*, Lyon, 1529) and suggested it may have been printed by Crespin or his heirs. Crespin died in 1545.

Jean Marcorelle became an *habitant* of Geneva in 1554, staying there until 1559. He spent the years between 1560 and 1572 in Lyon, returning to Geneva in 1572. He probably died circa 1576 in an unknown location. See Paul Chaix, *Recherches sur l'imprimerie à Genève*, Geneva, 1956, p.204.

12. The information concerning Jean de Tournes' will was most kindly provided by Natalie Zemon Davis. A second printer mentioned in the will, was Claude Chameroi, who came from Langres. His son was apprenticed to Jean de Tournes and went to Geneva with Marcorelle in 1559.

The same difficulty in discerning the print ateliers which produced Duvet's *Apocalypse* is manifested in most French Bible texts published after the Council of Trent. The printers of Lyon, although removed from the supervision of the Sorbonne, nonetheless made it hard to ascertain whether their publications were prepared in Lyon or at Geneva, with a false address in the colophon. See Eugènie Droz, "Bibles français après le Concile de Trente," *Journal of the Warburg and Courtauld Institutes*, XXIII, 1966, p. 211.

13. Boullaye, *op. cit.*, pp. 60, 61.

14. See Naef, *op. cit.*, pp. 135-136. See also E. Droz, "Pierre de Vingle, l'imprimeur de Farel," *Aspects de la propagande religieuse* (*Travaux d'humanisme et renaissance*, XXVIII), Geneva, 1957, pp. 38-78, for an illuminating discussion of French Protestant Bible translation; H. Kunze, *Die Bibelubersetzungen von Lefèvre d'Etaples und von P.R. Olivétan verglichen in ihren Wortschatz*, Leipzig, 1935.

15. In comparing the Duvet and Jean de Tournes' Olivetan text, *Le Nouveau Testament de Nostre Seigneur Jesus Christ*, Lyon, 1553, there are many differences in spelling:

De Tournes		Duvet
Rev. 2	oeuures	ouures
Rev. 3	aureille	oreilles
Rev. 7	quad	quand

The synopses at the head of each chapter are longer in the Duvet than in the de Tournes/Olivétan text. For Rev. 6, de Tournes gives: "Diverses visions à l'ouverture des sept sceaux." The Duvet chapter heading adds the words: "par l'agneau occis." The Eugrammia facsimile of the Apocalypse (London, 1962) gives the Duvet text as Olivétan's.

16. See *The British Museum General Catalogue of Printed Books*, London, 1936, XVI, p. 238. This practice continued throughout the sixteenth century in publications by Quentell's heirs in Cologne. See *Ibid.*, XVI, p. 241, Cat. 3040.r.5; p. 242, Cat. 3049.k.9; p. 242, Cat. 3023.c.2.

17. See Louis Réau, *Iconographie de l'art chrétien*, Paris, 1957, II, Part 2, p.678.

18. See L.E. Marcel, *Le Cardinal de Givry, évêque de Langres*, Paris, 1926 I, p. 282. Two printers who had been established in Dijon by Cardinal de Givry were also Protestants — Jean des Planches and Pierre Grangier. Marcel, unwilling to give the impression that Givry could have known or countenanced such beliefs wrote, "Mais leur adhésion reconnue parait se rapporter tout à la fin de l'épiscopat de Givry" (*Ibid.*, I, p. 355). See also Samuel Mours, *Le protestantisme en France au seizième siècle*, Paris, 1959, p. 134: " . . . l'année 1561 a été la grande année d'expansion du protestantisme en France."

19. Edmond Belle, "La Reforme à Dijon," *Revue bourguignonne de l'Université de Dijon*, XXI, No. 1, 1911, p. 29.

20. Marcel, *op. cit.*, I, p. 811.

21. Robert M. Kingdon, *Geneva and the Coming of Wars of Religion in France, 1555-1563*, Geneva, 1956, p. 58.

22. Belle, *loc. cit.*

23. Pottinger, *op. cit.*, p. 57.

24. Baltrušaitis, *op. cit.*, p. 274, has pointed out the influence of the Cologne Bible of the 1470's on Duvet's *Apocalypse.*

25. Melchior Lotther's *Das Neue Testament deutsch,* printed in Wittenberg in 1522, typifies the trend, as does the New Testament printed by Othmar in Augsburg in 1523, which was illustrated by Burkgmair, who may have also worked for Lotther. Knobloch's Bible, published in Strasburg in the same year, is also limited in its figures to those of the Apocalypse. All of these woodcut illustrations are derived from Dürer and were probably executed by his associates. Twenty vigorous woodcuts, executed by G. Lemberger for the Wittenberg Bible of 1524, may be said to be the most influential Apocalypse illustrations of the sixteenth century. While based upon Dürer's, Lemberger's woodcuts added a certain sinuous, ornate grace, eliminating the last traces of flamboyant Gothic forms from the earlier series. The cuts are dated 1522 and 1523, and signed with the artist's monogram. It was on these illustrations that almost all of the ordinary sixteenth century Apocalypse cycles were based.

26. See Hildegard Zimmerman, *Beiträge zur Bibelillustration des 16. Jahrhunderts,* Strassburg, 1924. For an investigation of the cultural reasons for intense interest in the Apocalypse at this time, see Otto Benesch, *The Art of the Renaissance in Northern Europe,* Cambridge, 1945, pp. 119 ff.
See also Max Dvorák, *Kunstgeschichte als Geistesgeschichte,* Munich, 1928, p. 199. See also Norman Cohn, *The Pursuit of the Millenium,* New Jersey (Basic Books), 1957.

27. See *Le Nouveau Testament,* Basel, 1525, with twenty Apocalypse illustrations; *Novum Testamentum,* F. Gryphius, Paris, 1537, twenty Apocalypse illustrations; and *Biblia Sacra,* Guillaume Rouille, Lyon, 1540, twenty-three illustrations, differing slightly from the others by the addition of a "classical" style background for Rev. 10; *Novum Testamentum,* Regnault, Paris, 1542, twenty illustrations with a slightly Antwerp Mannerist quality but otherwise, like the others, entirely based on the Wittenberg.

28. For a study of this subject with extensive bibliography, see Gertrude Bing, "The Apocalypse Block-Books and their Model-Makers," *Journal of the Warburg Institute,* V, 1942, pp. 143-158. A table inserted between pp. 146 and 147 provides a helpful list of the subjects in these publications. For a survey of Apocalypse illustration, see the entry by Wilhelm Neuss, "Apocalypse," *Reallexikon zur deutschen Kunstgeschichte,* Stuttgart, 1937, I, cols. 751-781.

29. See A. Aumüller, *Les petits maîtres allemands,* Munich, 1888, Nos. 169-195. These illustrations were published under various titles, in 1539 as *Typi in Apocalypsim,* also as *Imaginum in Apocalypsi Iohannes* with a text by "Giorgio Aemilio, C. Egenolphus excudebat."

30 The artist is unknown but may be René Boyvin, according to J. Lieure, *L'École français de gravure* . . . , Paris, n.d., Pl. XXV, figs. 74, 76.
See also Pl. XVII, figs. 45-48. The prints seem to have also been used together with other Biblical woodcuts attributed to Jean Cousin. For the Groulleau Bible of 1547, see the excellent discussion in Mortimer, I, Cat. 75, pp. 101-102.

31. As rare as the preceding illustrations printed by Groulleau, the Saulce woodcuts are listed in André Linzeler, *Inventaire du Fonds Français, II, en Allemagne - en - Aûtriche - en Suisse,* Paris, 1885, II, fig. 96, p. 117. He reproduces *La Pressoir de Nostre Sauveur Jesus Christ.*

32. See Campbell Dodgson, "Eine Holzschnittfolge Mathias Gerungs," *Jahrbuch der königlich preussischen Kunstsammlungen,* XXIX, 1908, p. 908, pp. 195-216. Three woodcuts devoted to illustrating the tenth chapter of Revelation (Nos. 7-10) are the latest in date and seem to have been added by Gerung, enlarging the series, which had already treated that chapter in a single woodcut (No. 11), embracing the subjects later represented individually in the three separate prints. Gerung peopled his *Spottbilder* with the same characters he had created for the woodcut Apocalypse. His satires such as the

Roundtable of Sinners executed in 1546 (Cat. 38) are identical in size, format, and style with the Apocalypse woodcuts. A comparison between the Gerung and Duvet *Apocalypse* plates reveals that while they almost agree in number, the choice of subject matter differs increasingly toward the end of each series.

33. Cat. 40 uses motifs from Dürer B. 62.
    41 uses motifs from Dürer B. 63.
    42 uses motifs from Dürer B. 64.
    43 uses motifs from Dürer B. 60.
    46 uses motifs from Dürer B. 68.
    47 uses motifs from Dürer B. 69.
    48 uses motifs from Dürer B. 70.
    50 uses motifs from Dürer B. 71.
    51 uses motifs from Dürer B. 72.
    52 Partially adapted from B. 67, 74, 79.
    45 uses motifs from Dürer B. 73.

34. A.M. Hind, *Early Italian Engraving,* London, 1948, I, p. 218; II, Pl. 319. Also see the illustrations for Antonio Bettini da Siena, *Monte santo di Dio,* in Max Sander, *Le livre à figures italien,* Milan, 1942, VI, Nos. 489-493.

35. The *Apocalypse* of 1561 is often referred to as the first French book to be illustrated with engravings, but this is not the case. Barring the Breydenbach *Voyages* published by Topie and Herembeck in Lyon in 1488, which had copied the woodcuts of the Mainz 1486 edition on engraved metal plates, all other French fifteenth century metal-based illustrations used relief printing as seen in Jehan Duprê, *Heures à lusage de Rome* (Paris, 1488). For metal-cut illustrations in early French Books of Hours, see Ruth Mortimer, Harvard College Library, *Catalogue of Books and Manuscripts, Part 1. French 16th Century Books,* II, Cambridge, 1964, p. 364. The first sixteenth century publication with engraved illustrations to be generally agreed upon as French is the *Epitome gestorum LVII regum Franciae,* printed by B. Arnoullet in 1546 at Lyon, with fifty-eight portrait engravings by the Monogrammist CC.

See Robert Brun, *Le livre français,* Paris, 1948, p. 60. This identification of the Master CC with Claude Corneille still seems uncertain, yet Corneilles's Netherlandish origin would explain his priority among engravers. See also Mortimer, *op. cit.,* I, Cat. 208, pp. 256-257.

Duvet's biographer, E. Jullien de la Boullaye, dismisses the *Epitome* as an anonymous work in order to stress the unique historical significance of the documented authorship of the engraved *Apocalypse figurée.* Boullaye, pp. 45-49, discusses the position of the "priority" of Duvet's engraved works. Both the *Epitome* of 1546 and Pierre Woeriot's finely engraved *Pinax iconicus* of 1556 are very clearly earlier in publication date, although far less monumental undertakings, than the great plates of the *Apocalypse figurée.* In discussing the emergence of these very few books with engraved illustrations, Robert Brun has pointed out:

> Des précurseurs comme Woeriot, Delaune et surtout
> Duvet, l'auteur d'une Apocalypse pleine de fouge et
> de poésie étrange, n'étaient que des orfèvres et de
> ornemanistes et n'avaient illustré des livres que par
> occasion.

R. Brun, *Le livre illustré en France au XVIe siècle,* Paris, 1930, p. 8. See also Philip Hofer, "Early Book Illustrations in the Intaglio Medium," *Print Collector's Quarterly,* XXI, 1934, pp. 203-227, 295-316. "Therefore, after 1545, I could show you an ever-increasing tide [of intaglio illustrated works]" (p. 307).

36. Harry S. Francis, "The Apocalypse of Jean Duvet," *Bulletin of the Cleveland Museum of Art,* XLI, No. 3, March 1954, pp. 56-58.

37. Several of the volumes containing drawings by Lucas van Leyden and Albrecht Dürer are in the British Museum, given by Hans Sloane in 1754. Another, similarly bound, was formerly in the Huth Collection. See Sidney Colvin,

"Eine Sammlung von Handzeichnungen von Lucas van Leyden," *Jahrbuch der königliche preussischen Kunstsammlungen,* XIV, 1893, pp. 175-176. After showing that the theory that the bound volumes could hardly have been from the collection of Thomas Howard, Earl of Arundel, Colvin pointed out that most of Hans Sloanes's books were inherited from William Charlton (1642-1702), nephew of Sir William Courten (Courteene), the grandson of a partner in the prominent Anglo-Dutch mercantile firm of Courten and Money in Haarlem. It is from Courten's estate that Colvin believed the Dutch-bound volumes to have come.

The Huth volume contains the extremely rare Apocalypse by Gerung. Dodgson, *op. cit.,* p. 202, pointed out the similarity to the Sloane bindings. C. Hofstede de Groot (*Die Urkunden über Rembrandt,* The Hague, 1906, p. 52) related the British Museum collection of Lucas van Leyden drawings, dated 1637, to the documented purchase in that year of "I konstboek van Lucas," bought by Rembrandt's student, Leendert Cornelisz van Beyeren, on March 18 for a very high price. However, it is uncertain whether any of these volumes were ever in Rembrandt's possession. The words FRANSE APOCALIPSE and the indication C8 at the top of the spine and E at the bottom are on the Cleveland binding. The number 6985, written in purple ink, appears on the inside front cover. The book was at one time owned by a *béguinage* at Antwerp; the words "spirito begynage Antwerpegio" are written on the title page. A sticker on the back has an unidentified collector's mark with the number 3180 noted in ink below as well as "Morgand 106, Coll. Beckford 1882, Destailleur 1891 5.93.folio." This copy was first recorded in the *Catalogue of the First Portion of the Beckford Library,* Sotheby, Wilkinson & Hodge, London, 1882, p. 201, Cat. 2740. It was purchased by Quaritch for twenty-three pounds and bought by H. Destailleur, whose collection was sold in Paris on April 13, 1891 (Cat. 72, pp. 16-17) for 7000 francs. Bought by Morgand, it was listed in his own catalogue (Bulletin 31, 1892, Cat. 22201) for 10,000 francs and described as "precieux exemplaire de première emission publiée sans texte." It seems certain that this is the Cleveland copy, despite the "sans texte," in view of the seven additional prints recorded by Morgand. Its subsequent history is somewhat confusing: sold by Ketterer at the Prinzenbau, Stuttgart (according to Lecomte), while the print curator at Fitzwilliam believes it to have been sold at Colnaghi's. Be that as it may, the copy was listed in the auction catalogue of Nicholas Rauch, Geneva, March 2, 1953, Cat. 65, p. 52, where the printing is attributed to Jean de Tournes. It then went to Gutekunst and Klipstein and to the Cleveland Museum the following year. The volume may perhaps have been in Rembrandt's possession in the early seventeenth century, its binding and date corresponding with four folios which seem to have also been in the artist's fine collection.

38. The volume has an unknown collector's mark, the letter A surrounded by scrolls, and is bound in green suede, stamped with the seal of the Bibliothèque Impèriale.

39. The Bibliothèque Royale seal is stamped on the title page. "July 18, 1919 is inscribed in pencil inside the blue morocco binding, which is stamped 3443 on the spine. According to Jean Adhémar, it was formerly in the Bouchet de Villeflix Collection and cost 5 livres in 1848.

40. Listed in Edouard Rahir, *La Collection Dutuit, livres et manuscrits,* Paris, 1899, pp. 8-9, Cat. 23. It is a green binding, probably of the eighteenth century. A page that is bound in with the text is inscribed "Pierre Brigant de Lion 1581"; below this, in a different colored ink, is written "A Pierre de Revoil de Lyon: 1810; The Dutuit example may be the work listed by Boullaye, p. 67, as having been in the Coste Collection at Lyon. This was sold in 1854, according to Boullaye; the latter, quoting Brunet, stated that the Coste volume was sold for 1020 francs.

41. Cat. C.18a.10. Listed in the *Short-Title Catalogue of Books Printed in France . . . from 1470 to 1600 Now in the British Museum,* London, 1924, p. 67. The printing is here attributed to Jean de Tournes, Cat. c.10 e.10. It is bound in blue morocco by Clarke and Bedford. The copy was purchased from the sale of the library of Dr. Philip Bliss (Lot 82) in 1858 and has the British Museum date stamp "2 Aug. 1858."

42. Aimé Vingtrinier, *Histoire de l'imprimerie à Lyon,* 1894, p. 255. The only other example recorded by Vingtrinier was one owned by Antoine Coste, whose sale is said to be listed by Brunet. The Lyon example is stamped on both inner covers and the back of every page with the two seals of the Bibliothèque de la Ville, one of which is dated 1896.

IV.

THE UNICORN SERIES

A mysterious series of six large, unsigned engravings, all concerned with unicorn lore, preserved the identity of Duvet as an individual master long before his oeuvre was drawn together and linked to the autobiographical Frontispiece of the Apocalypse series. Michel de Marolles, the first cataloguer of Duvet's oeuvre, refers to him in 1666 as "Joannes Duvet dit le maître à la licorne."[1] The unicorn prints raise problems of style, significance, and date.

Both classical and Christian, mystical, alchemical, and erotic, it is not surprising that the bizarre legend of the unicorn (especially popular in the late Middle Ages) should have attracted Duvet's talents.[2] The fierce creature of the Old Testament and the Greek bestiary of *Physiologus,* whose horn was credited with miraculous powers of purification, could only be captured by a virgin. The spiraling horn of a sea animal, the narwhal, accepted as that of the unicorn, fetched astronomical prices as a panacea consumed in powdered form, or preserved intact in reliquaries; it was also inlaid in various vessels and swords to protect the owner from poison or other injury.

Since at least the fourteenth century, belief in the purificatory power of the horn led to the manufacture of *touches,* cups with the unicorn horn set in them, rings of the same nature, sword scabbards, and badges bearing the emblem of the beast. Therefore Duvet, in his role as Burgundian goldsmith to the episcopal court of Langres, must have known of its medicinal properties long before he engraved the unicorn series. Cellini's description of the contest with his rival Tobbia for the commission to execute a holder for the unicorn (actually narwhal) horn of Clement III, reveals the sort of work which Duvet may, in more modest fashion, have executed.[3] The medical properties of the unicorn horn were especially popular in Burgundy. There are many references to it in the ducal treasury, where unicorn sword hilts and cups abounded.[4]

The chivalric quality of Duvet's unicorn series reflects the Gothic revival contemporary with the key years of French classicism at mid-century. The romantic, medievalizing spirit can also be found in the *Hypnerotomachia* illustrations and the continued popularity of the *Roman de la Rose* and of *Amadis de Gaule.* It is also found in several projects of Philibert de l'Orme such as the completion of the Chapel at Vincennes for the Order of Saint Michael, and in Duvet's *Apocalypse* which relates in part to the same Order. The *Amadis de Gaule* was first translated into French in 1524, five years after the fourteenth century text's initial Spanish publication.[5] Extremely popular in France, this lengthy romance was published in three different forms within the next twenty years, each of which went into innumerable editions. The motif of the unicorn purifying water is included in a large woodcut for the fourth book of Amadis de Gaule, printed in Paris in 1555.[6]

Their decorative character and horizontal, friezelike format have led some writers to suggest that the unicorn prints were tapestry designs.[7] While Duvet is known to have made such cartoons in Geneva (see Appendix E, Doc. 48), there is no reason to assume the unicorn cycle was intended for such a purpose. However, the elegant tapestries (Text fig. 11-13 ordered by a probable patron of Duvet, Cardinal de Givry, from Jean Cousin in

1543 might also indicate a key date for the prints. The sophisticated manner of these hangings may have introduced the engraver to the court style.[8] Another handsome series of eight tapestries executed for Diane de Poitiers' château at Anet (Text fig. 45) toward the middle of the sixteenth century could also have contributed toward the unicorn engravings' genesis.[9]

45. Fontainebleau Tapestry, Daine traînant Vénus et l'Amour garrottés, *Private collection, New York.*

The possibility that the prints accompanied a text is supported by the impression of *The Capture of the Unicorn* (Cat. 33) in Vienna, which bears a unique contemporary typeset caption below the plate mark, reading, "Le conseil mis en effet, sur le prinse de la Licorne." The series may have depended upon a lost text concerning the miraculous properties of the unicorn (Cat. 68); a hunting party preparing to trap the beast (Cat. 32); the failure to do so by force (Cat. 66); its capture through virginal enchantment (Cat. 33); the transportation of the unicorn on a triumphal car (Cat. 34); and the entering of heaven (Cat. 67).

More copies have survived from the print of *The Unicorn Purifies the Water with his Horn* (Cat. 68), for several reasons. It is one of the only scenes which may be regarded independently of the others, and it contains a popular, commonly understood reference to salvation. *The King and Diana Receiving Huntsmen* (Cat. 32) is also,

46. *Master L.D. after Primaticcio,* Death of the Stag, *Paris, Bibliothèque Nationale.*

somewhat less rare than other engravings in the series and could have been acceptable alone. It can easily belong to the hunting genre that was extremely popular in the mid-sixteenth century.

Duvet's concern with the chase is also manifested in a small print known as *Hallali du cerf* or *Death of a Stag* (Cat. 29), copied in reverse after a Fontainebleau etching (Text fig. 46). Possibly a depiction of the death of Actaeon, the engraving could have belonged with a series devoted to the goddess Diana. The Actaeon story was seen as an allegory of the fleeting nature of life.[10] Actaeon, metamorphosed into a deer, is the quarry of the hunter Nature; his metamorphosis was also subjected to Neo-Platonic interpretation.[11]

All six Unicorn engravings do not result from a single campaign of artistic activity. The stylistic and technical inconsistency indicates production over a long period of time and may also represent the gradual accumulation of several textual sources. The unicorn differs from print to print—its horn changing from smooth to grooved, and its mane varying in luxuriance. The king also changes in facial type and age. Three of the engravings are highly finished and carefully arranged with extensive textural variety and rich flick-work, creating a distinct sense of form in space. They include *A King and Diana Receiving Huntsmen* (Cat. 32), generally regarded as being the scene which initiates the pursuit, *The Capture of the Unicorn* (Cat. 33), and *The Unicorn Borne on a Triumphal Car* (Cat. 34).

A second pair, *The King Pursued by a Unicorn* (Cat. 66) and *The Triumph of the Unicorn* (Cat. 67), is characterized by a hastier, more experimental technique. These prints must be very late works, as they suggest improvisation rather than considered composition, with areas of rather arbitrary shading and curious empty spaces as found in the *Moses and Saint Peter* (Cat. 73).

An early sixteenth century Lombard engraving known as *Poison-contre-Poison* (App. A.1), formerly attributed to Duvet (Text fig. 47), may have provided the artist with a graphic point of departure. This possibly Leonardesque composition of a unicorn and other animals before a warrior, is distinguished by an impressionistic yet powerful technique. The scene of *The Unicorn Purifies the Water with his Horn* (Cat. 68) combines

113

47. *Master of the Beheading of St. John the Baptist,*"Poison-contre-Poison," *early 16th century, Lombard School.*

48.   *Jean Mignon after Penni,* The Temptation, *c. 1543-45.*

characteristics of the first group and final pair, and was probably begun toward the mid-century and completed about two decades later, circa 1560.[12]

It is likely that the Unicorn series began in the late 1540's. This suggestion is based on Duvet's use of several prints after Luca Penni dated by Zerner[13] ca. 1547. Made by

Jean Mignon (Text figs. 48-49), the prints provided Duvet with a sort of pattern book bestiary. From both stylistic and historical view points it is tempting to

49.   *Jean Mignon after Penni,* The Creation of Eve, *c. 1543-45.*

propose the years around Henri II's succession to the throne (in 1547), and the accompanying special prominence of Diane de Poitiers as an approximate starting date for the Unicorn series. The prints reflect in part Henri's dedication to the hunt and the continuing popularity of the chase, manifested in the reissuing of medieval guides to *venerie.* Françoise Bardon and this writer, with reservations, accept the traditional interpretation of some of the Unicorn prints as referring to the love of Henri II and Diane de Poitiers.[14]

Diana imagery abounded in French pageantry long before the prominence of Anet's *châtelaine.* Contemporary references to the chaste goddess of the hunt may have also had the king's mistress in mind; this is always a lively possibility. But to assume a one-to-one correlation between the two in every instance would be erroneous.

The King and Diana Receiving Huntsmen may be the first or second in the group and is cast in the courtly taste. A king (Henri II?) and Diana (Diane de Poitiers?), receive the Master of the Hunt who presents droppings from the quarry collected by the "harborer" and the "lymer," shown to the side of the seated ruler. This presentation was *de rigeur;* Queen Elizabeth I was portrayed receiving an identical offering in the first English illustrated hunting book, *The Noble Art of Venerie of Hunting,* translated from the French.[15]

The Unicorn Purifies the Water with his Horn (Cat. 68), like the scene with the king and Diana, suggests the engraver's attempt to bind his art to that of Fontainebleau. The concentration upon a realistic rendering of the animals and the grotto on the right indicate knowledge of the fashionable Rustic Style, the new extreme naturalism that was to to culminate with Palissy, found at such an early time at Bastie d'Urfé. The last and most freely executed print in the series showing the unicorn leading a triumphal cortège (Cat. 67), repeats some of the elements of *The Unicorn on a Triumphal Car* (Cat. 34), and may well have been engraved as an addition or substitute. It is inscribed *61* in a unique second state (Paris, Cabinet d'Estampes), suggesting completion in 1561, two years after Henri II's death.

Italian prints of triumphal pageantry by or after Giulio Romano and Salviati were immensely popular in the North by the mid-sixteenth century, and were utilized by countless artists and craftsmen. Such frequently consulted "paper friezes," with those done by Mantegna, Dürer and Titian must have helped Duvet in the preparation of his mythological subjects. Two woodcuts by Hans Baldung (Text figs. 50-51), probably served as a source for the unusually dense blacks and thick foliage of the Unicorn Series, especially *The Unicorn Purifies the Water with his Horn* and *The King Pursued by a Unicorn.* One of these German prints showing unicorns, may have been of particular interest to Duvet a Protestant—as it was the title page border used by Johannes Schott in 1523 for Luther's *Dreizehn Predigen.*[16] The other woodcut which is extremely long and narrow in format, depicts a stag hunt in the Loeserwald (Text fig. 51) and was made by Baldung in 1543, very shortly before the Unicorn prints were begun.[17]

50. Hans Baldung, Luther's Dreizehn Heiligen Predigen, *1523.*

51. Hans Baldung, Stag Hunt in the Loeserwald, *1543.*

The only Biblical reference to the unicorn appears in Daniel's vision (Can. 8:3-8) of the he-goat from the West, who had a single horn between his eyes and defeated the invincible ram, relating to Pliny's description of the insuperable one-horned beast. The introduction of the unicorn into Biblical commentaries as an allegory of the battle between Alexander and Darius is of great importance.[18] Its subsequent application, like that of the Apocalypse, unites the celestial with the terrestrial, and is emblematic of victory in heaven and on earth.

Petrarch, who spent much of his early life in France, revived the Roman triumphs in verse form, utilizing them to celebrate the victory of Christianity. This provided a legitimate framework within which classical beauty could be reconsecrated to Christian endeavor. The logical choice of beast to draw the chariot in Petrarch's *Triumph of Chastity* was the unicorn, already firmly established as an emblem of Christian strength and purity. From the second quarter of the fifteenth century onward, illustrations for Petrarch's text depict the unicorn drawing Chastity's triumphal equipage.

Both the Unicorn of Christian Salvation and Apocalypse scenes appear as vignettes in early printed French Books of Hours. Therefore, it is not coincidental that Duvet chose these as the subjects for his two most extensive illustrated cycles, the Unicorn and the Apocalypse. In the *Horae Virginis* published by Tilman Kerver (Paris, 1506), an elaborately illustrated Apocalypse text, containing forty-two very small scenes is followed by the fifteen signs of the end of the earth. One of these, a vignette repeated seven times, depicts animals looking up to a star-studded sky while the unicorn points down with his horn. It alludes to both the end of the world and salvation through Christ.[19]

Medieval interest in the unicorn stems from a reinterpretation of classical accounts of the miraculous healing powers and life of the mythical beast. The unicorn dipping its horn in water, shown in what may be the first subject in the series (Cat. 68), follows the *Physiologus*, which described the miraculous purifying quality of unicorn's horn. When placed in water poisoned by a serpent, the horn renders it potable so that the other animals may drink. This scene was interpreted as an allegory of Christian salvation. The unicorn (Christ) expelled the serpent (the devil) and cleansed the poisoned water (man's sin) by making the sign of the cross with its horn.[20] Reliefs depicting unicorns purifying water surround the Grande Fontaine at the cloister of Fontenay-le-Comte (where Rabelais studied). They were installed in 1542 as part of an elaborate fountain house.[21] Duvet's engraving may relate to a fountain in the little town of Malicorne in Yonne, near Dijon, which was reputed to have miraculous qualities.[22] The nude man on the bridge column could represent Orpheus as the context recalls a *tableau-vivant* staged at the beginning of the bridge for the triumphal entry of Henri II at Rouen in 1550, in which Orpheus enchanted the animals by singing "le chant de Diane." Several of the animals seem to be derived from Moderno's Orpheus plaque, so that Duvet may well have had the classical figure in mind.[23]

The King and Diana Receiving Huntsmen (Cat. 31) initiates the pursuit of the unicorn. Although the print does not reflect any unicorn lore, it introduces the all-important motif of the chase implied by the *Physiologus'* allusion to the beast brought to the palace in a classical triumph (as shown in Cat. 34). The engraving represents an elaboration of the ancient text by way of a late Northern medieval source such as *Parsifal*, in which a king pursues the mythical creature.

In the second engraving, the role of Diana with her nymphs engaged in the capture and triumph of a unicorn, suggests Duvet may have consulted the *Ovide moralisé*. In this fourteenth century Burgundian text, classical mythology is converted into Christian allegory.[24] For example, the very chaste Diana is seen as a prefiguration of the Virgin, her purity symbolized by "la lune sans obscurté," reminiscent of Mary's spotless mirror.[25] Expanding the Christian significance of Diana still further, the *Ovide moralisé* described her as the ruling deity among the Trinity:

> Dyane, c'est la Deité
> Qui regnoit en la Trinité
> Nue, sans humaine nature,

117

Qu'Actaeon vit sans couverture,
C'est il filz Dieu, qui purement
Vit a nu descouvertement
La benoite Trinité
Qui regnoit en eternité
Sans commencement et sans fin.[26]

The setting where the unicorn capture takes place is by a stream in front of a grotto. This could allude to Diana. The lute-playing virgin may be one of her nymphs who needed to be kept wet. Diana was herself a goddess of music (a gold piece from Syracuse shows her with a lyre).[27] Within the garden a three-flowered lily is shown. Like Diana and the moon, the lily represented such different concepts as the French nation and chastity. A traditional representation of chastity was that of a maiden sniffing a lily, accompanied by a docile unicorn.[28] Another early linking of Diana with the unicorn occurs in Francesco Colonna's *Hypnerotomachia Poliphili* in the third of his four Triumphs, that of Danäe in which she is borne upon a chariot drawn by six unicorns consecrated to her.[29] By the later fifteenth century, the association of Diana as the chaste huntress with the unicorn was secure.

In the next print of the series, *The Capture of the Unicorn*, Duvet engraved a much more dramatic subject and one better suited to his expressionistic approach—the rout of the king and his hunting party by a fierce unicorn which had already fatally gored several of the men. The event is found in Northern legends and theological treatises in which the beast's ferocity (in pre-Darwinian Biblical exegesis) causes its own extinction, as it would not enter the Ark.[31] Parsifal, the writings of Thomas of Cantimpré, and the later popular German religious allegory *Der beschlossen Gart des Rosenkrantz Marias* all increased the drama of the *Physiologus* account of the unicorn's capture and triumphal display in the palace, referring to misguided attempts to trap it by force.[32] In the *Rosenkrantz*, the beast's blood is needed to save the life of the king's youngest son, the eldest having already been killed. The king was interpreted as God the Father, the elder son as Lucifer, and the second as Adam and his seed. The maiden who finally captured the unicorn was the Virgin Mary and the huntsman the Holy Ghost, represented as the Archangel Gabriel. The central reference in the allegory is the allusion to the sacrifice of Jesus for the redemption of mankind, with the blood of the unicorn analogous to that of Christ in the Apocalyptic Winepress of the Wrath of God. Even the hounds in the story were given moral significance by being converted from disharmony before the beast's capture to unison, drawing the unicorn's chariot in the ultimate triumph.[33] Similarly, the dogs shown in Duvet's *Hunt of the Unicorn* (Cat. 32, 33) reappear harnessed to draw its chariot (Cat. 34).

Another well-known late medieval retelling of the unicorn legend which may have been among Duvet's sources is that of Thomas of Cantimpré, who asks in rhetorical fashion:

> What shall we understand to be signified in the unicorn,
> that most ferocious animal, if not Christ? . . . Who before
> his incarnation was furious enough to punish angels in heaven
> because of their pride, and men on earth because of their
> disobedience.

Thomas goes on to relate that no one could tame the wild beast until:

> That most beautiful and glorious of women, Mary, a
> virgin of the house of David, in the desert of the world,
> was found by the Son of God through an angel bridegroom.
> Venerating her beauty, virtue, wisdom, and the virtue of
> her chaste body, he was gathered up and humbly bent
> down his head from the heights of his divinity into the
> lap of the Virgin's womb in which, sleeping for nine
> months, he was tamed from his ferocity and moderated
> in spirit to the extent that he allowed himself to be cap-
> tured at the hands of the Jews and thence arising up again

and ascending into heaven, in the sight of his father and the heavenly citizens, in the glory of the solemn victory by which he triumphed over the devils, he wished to be shown as an admirable spectable.[34]

The Capture (Cat. 33), contrasting the futility of violence with the potency of love, shows the conventional seduction of the unicorn by a virgin as described in the *Physiologus* of Eustathius.[35] The dormant unicorn's head is slumped in the lap of the maiden who has attracted him, aided by the sweet strains of her lute. She was planted as a lure by the king and his huntsman. Dogs chased the unicorn toward her so that she might lull him into sleep, allowing the huntsmen to tie him down.

The virginity of the maiden is indicated emblematically by both the beautiful fleur-de-lys and the closed garden in which they grow at her side. The lily is symbolic also of the Valois, as is its setting under a graceful little awning formed by a swag of drapery twisted between two tree trunks, a reference to the Vergier d'Honneur.[36] This floral symbolism also recalls a triumphal entry decoration Duvet designed for the royal family's visit to Langres in 1533. It featured a "lys colossal" suspended between two trees bearing the arms of all the Christian princes.[37] The references to a royal hunt established in the second engraving and emphasized in the following two of the series suggest court patronage. The tribute to the triumph of Christian France over the unicorn is described by Belleau:

> Et la licorne qui vaux mieux.
> Bref je croy que la terre basse
> Et tout ce que le ciel embrasse.[38]

As both a classical and Christian triumphal emblem, the unicorn is often found in French court pageantry. The most frequent combination of a victorious theme with the unicorn appears in early printed Books of Hours illustrations of the Triumph of Caesar, led by a mounted unicorn. Caesar's triumph was equated with that of the Church. This adaptation of classical victory was carried to its most elaborate expression by the recreation of Roman triumphal entries for contemporary royalty.[39]

The earliest French procession consciously performed *all' antica* was a Triumph of Caesar presented by the students of the University of Caen in 1513.[40] Two years later, an elaborate allegory of French campaigns was enacted for the Lyon entry of François Ier. In this procession, a "belle licorne blanche appelée Tranquillité" was shown trying to enter "le jardin de Milan" within the "Parc de France" in order to "reposer au gyron de la vierge Paix, ainsy qu'est la nature de ladicte unicorne . . ."[41] This scene suggests Duvet's engraving of the virgin capture with its prominent Valois lilies. The unicorn's progress is impeded by France's enemies, "l'homme sauvage dicte—More accompaigné de l'ours ravissant"—the Milanese and the Swiss. The author then points out that *Tranquillité* also wanted to enter the closed garden in order to purify the water there, recalling Duvet's print of a similar subject (Cat. 67).

In the tableaux-vivants staged for the Lyon entry, both the religious and national significance of the unicorn are exploited in dramatic fashion to honor François Ier. Eight maidens elevated the letters of their king's name; *Obeissance* held both the "O" and the Tablets of Moses, signifying both royal and divine fealty.[42]

Duvet's first biographer, Boullaye, suggested Duvet's series was probably inspired by a *chasse simulée* held in 1548 for the Lyon entry of Henri II and Catherine de Medici in which the local ladies in the guise of Diana and her nymphs presented the royal couple with a *lyon apprivoisé*. For the wedding of his niece Catherine de Medici, Pope Clement VII presented the groom's father François Ier with a great unicorn horn. Boullaye stressed the significance of Duvet's role as pageant master in the genesis of the Unicorn prints, which he felt might have influenced the tapestry cycle ordered by Diane de Poitiers for Anet in 1552.[43] Primaticcio's projects for French court festivals at about this time included one of a lady riding a unicorn (Text fig. 52). Duvet seems to have been attracted to the very same imagery, if a line drawing after a lost original (Text fig. 53) is based upon a work by the Burgundian engraver (Appendix C.6).

119

52. *Primaticcio*, Design for fête costume: Lady Riding a Unicorn.
Stockholm, Nationalmuseum.

53. *Jean Duvet*, Design for fête costume: Maiden Riding a Unicorn.
Stockholm, Nationalmuseum.

120

54. *Jean Duvet,* Design for fête costume: Winged Warrior Riding a Lion, *Paris, Louvre/Rothschild Collection.*

55. *Jean Duvet,* Design for fête costume: Blackamoor Riding a Griffin, *Paris, Bibliothèque Nationale, Salle des Manuscripts, Collection Rothschild.*

56. *Jean Duvet,* Design for fête costume: Oriental Potentate Embracing Woman in Clouds, *Paris, Bibliothèque Nationale, Salle des Manuscrits.*

57. *Jean Duvet,* Design for fête costume: Siren Holding a Torch, *Paris, Bibliothèque Nationale, Salle des Manuscrits, Collection Rothschild.*

François' new daughter-in-law Catherine de Medici entered Paris in a chariot drawn by two unicorns.[44] He, most implausibly, was assigned a similar equipage accompanied by Diligence, Wisdom, Sobriety, and Virtue.[45] In what was perhaps the most magnificent French triumphal entry ever held outside Paris (accorded Henri II by the city of Rouen in 1550), a float appeared showing the king's coronation by *Vesta-Religio*, with the unicorns' trappings bearing royal insignia with the crescent moon predominant. (Text fig. 58).[46] The priestess held a model of the Saint-Chapelle in one hand, and crowned the king with a laurel wreath with the other. Aspects of this scene are reminiscent of *The Unicorn on a Triumphal Car* (Cat. 34). The maidens shown in illustrations for the Triumph of Victory at Rouen (Text fig. 50) are very much like those in the final engraving—*The Triumph of the Unicorn* (Cat. 66).[47] The spirit rather than the letter of the Rouen entry is shared by much of Duvet's oeuvre.[48]

Many texts linked Diana and the unicorn. In a poem by Luca Pulci, *Driadeo* of 1489, the Renaissance poet tells the story of Severo a dryad, who falling in love with one of Diana's nymphs, was punished by being turned into a unicorn.[49] A direct association between the virgin capturing the unicorn and Diana is seen in the mid-sixteenth century engraving of the Reverdy circle (Text fig. 59).[50] Like the Duvet series, this print relates Diana the huntress to the chase of the unicorn. She is seen in a stag-drawn chariot at the upper left, just above the virgin with the unicorn in her lap. The print appears to be devoid of Christian associations; the unicorn is surrounded by classical hunters on horseback, about to be speared while a figure of Mars (?) emerges from the zodiacal circle engraved in the sky above.

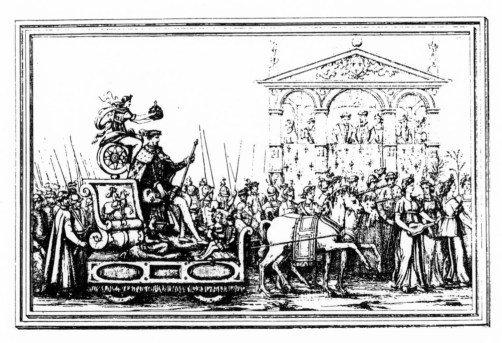

58. Triumphal Entry of Henri II, Rouen, 1550, *facsimile issued by P.P. de Merval, Rouen, 1868.*

122

59. *Reverdy circle,* Diana and the Unicorn, *mid-sixteenth century.*

The horned or crescent moon controlled by Diana, the virgin huntress, was regarded as an agent for the control of poison, relating perhaps to the healing powers of the unicorn.[51]

Diana, appearing in what seems to be the initial engraving of the Unicorn series (Cat. 32), may be seen again in the form of a radiant crescent moon above the mountains over the city—the heavenly Jerusalem—to which the unicorn is brought in triumph (Cat. 34). The martial panoply surrounding the unicorn as it is borne on a chariot with battering rams recalls Dürer and his associates' romantic woodcuts, largely Burgundian in style, of the *Triumphal Procession of Maximilian.* All the major participants in the engraving share triumphal emblems. Below a canopy, the laurel-crowned king holds a wreath of oak leaves over the virgin playing the lute. Her music helped capture the unicorn. The beast is shown with a wreath of oak leaves encircling his horn. The tree is sacred to Jupiter, thus referring in this series to God the Father, as well as Herculean strength or divine force. While the engraving depicts the king's victory and that of the maiden representing mankind, it is also a triumph for the unicorn-Christ, permitting himself to be captured for the redemption of man and about to enter the heavenly Jerusalem. That ultimate entry, in which the unicorn-Christ is borne sacrificially upon the chariot for his reunion with God the Father, is the subject of the next print (Cat. 67).

In this print the three figures are Jupiter—God the Father, his eagle—the Holy Ghost and the unicorn-Christ. The print celebrates the triumph of the Trinity illuminated by the light of the Moon-Church, which in turn derives its light from the Sun-God. Some of Duvet's visual sources appear in the Aldine *Hypnerotomachia Poliphili.* His images may have been guided by Richard Roussat, one of the erudite canons of Langres. Roussat, an astrologer, noted in his *Livre de l'estat et mutation des temps* that "Jupiter signifié et denote nostre Dieu, createur des toutes choses, & la lune l'Eglise."[52] His Nostradamus-like work was published in Lyon in 1550. Nostradamus' own works were printed in Lyon. Duvet's *Apocalypse* was published there in 1561 (Roussat may well have contributed to its complex Frontispiece), which was the same year *The Triumph of the Unicorn* was completed. The putto under the immediate supervision of Jupiter is about to crown the unicorn with a wreath of oak leaves, which again points to divine power, to the tree consecrated to the supreme divinity. All other participants wear wreaths of merit, laurel, and of peace, olive.[53]

The double tablets in *The Triumph of the Unicorn* (Cat. 67) were probably never meant to have been engraved with Duvet's initials in the artist's customary manner, because the Tablets of the Law figure quite consistently within a scene celebrating the triumph of Christ—that of the Word of God. The Tablets of Moses in the Triumph may also follow Roussat who wrote that Moses' sign was Cancer— the glory and exaltation of Jupiter and domicile of the moon.[54] The trinitarian candles borne by the wreathed youths, the maidens with lutes, the hunters sounding trumpets of victory, the hosts of marchers with palms of triumph, all celebrate the coming of the unicorn—Christ into heaven.[55]

The plates devoted to the *Unicorn on a Triumphal Car* and the *Unicorn with God the Father and the Holy Ghost* show how the artist followed the spirit of Thomas of Cantimpré's text. After allowing himself to be captured, the beast arises "and ascending into heaven, in the sight of his father and the heavenly citizens, in the glory of the solemn victory by which he triumphed over the devils, he wished to be shown as an admirable spectacle.[56]

The Burgundian printmaker probably completed the series in France, having set it aside during the years of his self-imposed exile in Geneva, only returning to his homeland in old age. Many of the plates are animated by a turbulent re-creation of the late medieval chivalry of Maximilian's Burgundian *Triumph*. The date is scratched in the corner of a concluding plate indicating the series' completion when the artist was seventy-seven years old. Duvet's reevocation of a splendid, quasi-mythical past assumes special interest in view of van Dorsten's chapter entitled "After Fontainebleau" which states "Geographically and spiritually the exiles' fatherland was Burgundy. The Burgundian state had long ceased to be a political reality, but it continued as a myth of national grandeur and stability. Old cultural roots make themselves felt most acutely when a familiar world falls apart. It was certainly true of the 1560s when change and progress were constantly balanced by a nostalgic sense of loss."[57]

Thus the glory of Burgundy, which was almost reduced to a dream by the time of Duvet's birth, was resurrected by the propagandist fantasies of Maximilian, widower of Mary of Burgundy. It was reborn for very different reasons as a Familist article of faith and belief in a modern Golden Age—*Burgundy Redivivus.* A similar Burgundian revival was taking place at the Valois court in the exuberant, elaborate festivities planned to impress and to influence the course of foreign and domestic policy. Duvet's splendid conclusion to the Unicorn series combining the pageantry he had directed in Langres with the new mystical currents of mid-sixteenth century Europe, is a grand finale to a life-time of victorious imagery in which the mythical beast—symbol of Christian love and sacrifice—may also represent the best of both worlds, heaven on earth as a Burgundian New Jerusalem.

NOTES

1. *Catalogue de livres, d'estampes* . . . , Paris, 1666, p. 137.
2. The major reference work on the unicorn is the brilliant study by Odell Shephard, *The Lore of the Unicorn,* New York, 1930. Other helpful works are A. F. Johnson, "The Unicorn in Early Print and Printed Books," *The Colophon,* Part XIV, 1933; Guido Schönberger, "Narwal-Einhorn: Studien über einen seltenen Werkstoff," Städel-Jahrbuch, IX, 1935-36, pp. 167-247; C.G. Jung, *Psychology and Alchemy* (XII of the Collected Works, New York, 1968), pp. 435-71, "The paradigm of the Unicorn." For unicorn symbolism in France, the most informative article is by de Laborde, *Notice des émaux . . . du Musée du Louvre,* Paris, 1853, Part II, pp. 358-65. Additional material is available in Victor Gay, *Glossaire archéologique du moyen âge et de la renaissance,* Paris, 1887-1928, II, p. 77. Raimond van Marle, *Iconographie de l'art profane,* The Hague, 1931-32, affords a helpful general survey of unicorn symbolism. See also Liselotte Wehrhahn-Stauch, "Einhorn," *Reallexikon zur deutschen Kunstgeschichte,* 1958, IV, cols. 1051-1115; and Jean Avalon, "L'annonciation à la licorne," Pro Arte, V, 1946, pp. 341-348. For animal symbolism, see also Hélène Naïs, *Les Animaux dans la poésie française de la Renaissance,* Paris, 1961, pp. 76, 104, 264.
3. *Memoirs of Benvenuto Cellini,* trans. Thomas Roscoe, London, 1822, I, p. 213. Schönberger, *op. cit.,* p. 205, fig. 215, illustrates a unicorn reliquary which, but for having three instead of four rams' heads, resembles the description of Tobbia's work. Schönberger regards it as dating from the second half of the sixteenth century.
4. In 1388, the king of France paid a goldsmith to manufacture "une esprouve de licorne." See De Laborde, *op. cit.,* pp. 358-65. Entries F, H, M, N, O, P, Q, R, S, T, U, V, X, Y, Z, AA, CC, II are all references to articles of the goldsmith's craft embodying or pertaining to the unicorn; almost all are concerned with the manufacture of objects incorporating a fragment of unicorn horn or of jewelry in the form of this creature for protection from poison. See also Gay, *loc. cit.* For discussions of alleged medical properties of the unicorn horn, see Hermann Meier's and A. Jacoby's notes in Schweizer *Volkskunde,* X, 1920, pp. 14, 78. Jacoby quoted from Stammler (*Die Teppiche des historischen Museums zu Thun,* Bern, 1891) on the medicinal value of unicorn horn. See also Shephard, *op. cit.,* pp. 101-153, "The Treasure of His Brow," E. Jullien de la Boullaye, *Etude sur la vie et sur l'oeuvre de Jean Duvet, dit le Maître à la licorne,* Paris, 1876, pp. 39-42.
5. See Hughes Vaganay, *Amadis en français: Livres I-XII: essai de bibliographie et d'iconographie,* Florence, 1906; J. Boulanger, "Amadis de Gaule," *Dictionnaire de lettres françaises: le seizième siècle,* Paris, 1951, pp. 38-40.
6. Reproduced by Ruth Mortimer, Harvard College Library, *Catalogue of Books and Manuscripts,* Cambridge, 1964, Part 1, I, Cat. 18, "Le plant de l'isle ferme," reproduced on p. 21 (also Vaganay, *loc. cit.*). See the illustration for Livre IV, Chapitre LIV, print No. 292, "Comme le vaisseau ou nauigeoient Lisuart & ses compagnons fut ieté par torment en l'isle des Signes."
7. Two of the most popular French tapestry cycles have been devoted to unicorn lore. See Phylis Ackerman, "The Lady and the Unicorn," *Burlington Magazine,* LVI, 1935, pp. 35-36. A more plausible interpretation is given by A. F. Kendrick,

"Quelques remarques sur les tapisseries . . . ," *Actes du Congrès d'histoire de l'art*, Paris, 1924, p. 662, in which the Cluny series is regarded as representing the five senses. For the unicorn tapestries at The Cloisters, see James J. Rorimer, *The Unicorn Tapestries*, 4th ed., New York, 1962.

8. See L. E. Marcel, *Le cardinal de Givry, évêque de Langres*, Paris, 1926, II, Chapter 4, "Jean Cousin l'Ancien et ses rapports avec le cardinal de Givry"; see also M. Roy, "Les tapisseries de Saint-Mammès de Langres," *Mémoires de la Société archéologique de Sens*, V, 1913; Henri David, "L'esthétique de Jehan Cousin l'Ancien," *Bulletin monumental*, LXXXIX, 1930, pp. 531-536.
   Marcel describes the contract signed by Cousin and Givry for the design of the Saint-Mammès series, on July 14, 1543 (p. 329). Three of the original series of eight survive, two in the cathedral and the third in the Louvre. The tapestries are discussed in Chapter V, "Les tapisseries de la cathédrale de Langres don du cardinal de Givry," pp. 335-352.

9. John Goldsmith Phillips, "Diane de Poitiers and Jean Cousin," *Metropolitan Museum of Art Bulletin*, n.s., II, 1943, pp. 109-117. Of the eight tapestries, four are still at Anet–*Diana Saving Iphegenia, Diana Slaying Orion, The Death of Meleager,* and *Jupiter Turning the Peasants into Frogs. Diana Asking Jupiter for the Gift of Chastity* is at the Rouen Museum. *The Triumph of Diana* is in New York, Private Collection, and *The Drowning of Britomartis* and *The Blasphemy of Niobe* are at the Metropolitan Museum of Art, New York. Phillips bases the attribution to Jean Cousin upon their similarity to the well-documented tapestries designed by the same artist for the Cathedral of Saint-Mammès at Langres.

10. Françoise Bardon, *Diane de Poitiers et la mythe de Diane*, Paris, 1963, pp. 100-101.

11. See the text of an unidentified French poem published by Heinrich Göbel, *Die Wandteppiche*, Leipzig, 1923, I, Part 1, p. 131. The other hunters are entitled *Oultrecuidance, Haste,* and *Vouloir.* The old huntress is *Viellesse* and also pursues the hapless stag. Her dogs are *Aage, Doubtance, Pesanteur, Ennuy, Soucy, Chault, Froit,* and *Peine.* The stag's tongue hangs out at the fatal end of the hunt. Maladi gives the final blow while *Morte* sounds the last trumpet call, heralding the deer's death. The poem accompanying this episode, which may well have been associated with Duvet's engravings, reads:

> Gens de Briefve durée mondaine,
> Qui a chasse mortelle et soudaine
> Estes comme cerf asserois
> Considérez la vie humaine
> Et la vin ou elles vous maine
> Et les metz dont serez servis
> A bien que serez sesserois
> De Jenesse et aurez adviz
> Advisez à tel propos prendre
> Quel quant serez de mort ravis,
> Et les vers seront au corps vifz
> Qui puissons à Dieu l'âme rendre.

12. Wolfgang Wegner, *Fünf Jahrhunderte europäische Graphik*, Munich-Paris-Amsterdam, 1965-66, p. 103, Cat. 93, dates the print ca. 1560.

13. Henri Zerner, *The School of Fontainebleau, Etchings and Engravings*, New York, n.d., p. 24. That by the Master LD is no. 91.

14. Bardon, *op. cit.*, p. 102, n. 1. Clearly Diane de Poitiers, that discerning distinguished patroness, is an important figure in French art and literature. The classical evocations of her name, coupled with her sure taste and intelligence, made Diane a fitting and welcome subject for artistic elaboration. Almost any mid-sixteenth century French representation of a king accompanied by Diana in a forest setting is identified as Henri II with his celebrated mistress; every crescent viewed as a reference to her. But this may not prove correct. The great triumphal arch erected

in honor of Henri II and Catherine de Medici at Lyon in 1548 was crowned by a representation of Diana, placed above such varied classical figures as Romulus and Remus and Mars. To regard this sculptured Diana exclusively as an allusion to Henri II's mistress would be erroneous (George Guigue, *L'entrée de Lyon . . . de Henri deuxième . . . septembre 1548,* Lyon, 1927, p. 31). The birth of Henri II's second son was celebrated in Rome with pageantry in which Diana was also prominent, probably representing the fertility of France, as the goddess did in the earlier Parisian entry of Mary Tudor (Charles Read Baskerville, ed., *Pierre Gringoire's Pageants for the Entry of Mary Tudor into Paris,* Chicago, 1934, p. 12). A detailed description of the Italian festivities was published in Paris in 1549 and may have contributed to the official launching of extensive Diana imagery. *La magnificence des triomphes faicts à Rome pour la nativité de Monseigneur le duc d'Orléans second fils du Roy très chrestien Henry deuxième de ce nom.* According to Bardon, *op. cit.,* p. 81, n.2, this publication was included in an exhibition catalogue *Les français à Rome,* Paris, 1961, Cat. 47.

E. Bénézit, *Dictionnaire des peintres, sculpteurs,* n.p., n.d., II, p. 191, adheres to the traditional interpretation of Diana imagery. While only listing four of the engravings, he stated "Ces 4 pièces sont emblèmatiques et pourroient faire allusion aux amours de Henri II et Diane de Poitiers." P. Darras (*L'oeuvre gravé de Jean Duvet,* Paris, 1938) also discusses the prints as being "consacré aux amours d'Henri II et de Diane de Poitiers." André Linzeler (*Inventaire du fonds français: graveurs du seizième siècle,* Paris, 1932, p. 3) stated that the prints "sont vraisemblablement autant d'allusion aux amours de Henri II et de Diane de Poitiers."

A. E. Popham ("Jean Duvet," *Print Collector's Quarterly,* VIII, 1921, p. 136) noted that "this last well-known series . . . has some reference to the amours of Henri II and Diane de Poitiers between 1546 and 1559. The exact import of the allegory has not been explained. Diane de Poitiers, recognizable by the crescent of the goddess, the unicorn and the King figure bewilderingly as chief characters of the piece." Anthony Blunt (*Art and Architecture in France, 1500-1700,* London, 1953, p. 85, no. 103) concluded that there "seems to be no solid reason" for the view that the series refers to Henri II and Diane. "It is more likely that we have a revival or continuation of the medieval theme of the hunting of the unicorn, though it is here interspersed with classical allusions." The *Diane au bain* (Musée de Rouen) attributed to François Clouet has a Death of a Stag at the upper right. The equestrian figure at the right is thought to represent Henri II and scholarship has interpreted the canvas as a political allegory. For a recent study of complex French sixteenth century portraiture see Roger Trinquet, "L'Allégorie politique au XVIe siècle: *La Dame au Bain* de François Clouet (Washington)," *Bulletin de la Société de l'histoire de l'art français,* 1966, pp. 99-119. This painting has a unicorn.

15. William A. Baillie-Grohman, *Sport in Art,* London, n.d., p. 105, fig. 55. This author refers to the Duvet series as devoted to Henri II and Diane de Poitiers (p. 369).

16. The same printer employed the framing woodcut for Martin Butzer's *An einen christlichen Rat und Gemeinde der Stadt Swissenburg,* printed in Strasbourg.

17. This very rare print is illustrated in C.F.G.R. Schwerdt, *Hunting, Hawking and Shooting,* London, 1928, II, p. 32. It is reproduced in *Hans Baldung Grien* (Ausstellung unter dem Protektorat des I.C.O.M.) Karlsruhe, 1959, p. 387, Cat. 43.

18. "Gesenius, the Biblical scholar, asserted roundly that the *Re'em* of the Old Testament was identical with the unicorn described by Pliny the Elder" (Shephard, *op. cit.,* p. 280, n. 3). Presumably the source would be his *Historia naturalis,* VIII, 33, The association of the unicorn with Persia seems to have begun in the accounts of Ctesias, who was the first author to discuss the beast at considerable length and outline its supposed medicinal properties.

19. Similar illustrations appear in Pigouchet's *Paris Hours* of 1498. The *Horae in usum romanum* printed by Jacques Kerver (Paris, 1519) has a frequently shown vignette of a unicorn, horse, swine, camel, goat, lion, rabbit, and two indeterminate animals

for the text of the fifteen signs of the end of the earth. See also the Tory Hours of 1531, where unicorns draw the chariot for the Triumph of the Virgin.

The celebrated tapestry showing a similar scene, now at The Cloisters, has been described as follows:

> The unicorn, which, kneeling, dips its horn in a stream flowing from a fountain, a symbol of the waters of eternal life. This scene recalls a passage in the records of the pilgrimage of John of Herse to Jerusalem in 1389, where he says, ". . . the unicorn comes from the sea and dips its horn into the stream, and thereby expels and neutralizes the poison, so that the other animals can drink of it during the day." The animals included in the tapestry are a lion, and a lioness, a panther, a civet, a hyena, a stag and two rabbits. These animals are themselves symbolic; for example the lion stands for the strength of Christ, the panther for His sweet savor, and the stag, destroyer of snakes, for His power over evil.

(Rorimer, op. cit., pp. 87-8.) Possibly the seascape in the background and some of the animal symbolism of the unicorn legend quoted by Rorimer may also apply to the Duvet engraving.

20. Shephard (op. cit., p. 81) believes the analogy between horn and cross to have probably been originated by Tertullian but also used by Irenaeus, Adversus Laereses, ii, 42, and Justinus, Dialogus contra Tryphonem Judaeum. Tertullian's Contra Judaeos, cap. 11, is the source of the comparison of the upright beam of the transverse bar in the cross with the unicorn horn (Shephard, op. cit., p. 282, n. 36). Shephard discussed Physiologus texts and referred to Friedrich Lauchert, Geschichte des Physiologus, Strassburg, 1889, as the definitive work on the subject (pp. 46-8).

21. See Pierre du Colombier, Jean Goujon, Paris, 1949, p. 56. Alfred Nock, Journey into Rabelais' France, New York, 1934, pp. 166-67, stated that the inscription on the fountain FELICIUM INGENIORUM FONS ET SCATURIGO (the abundant source of beautiful spirits) was a heraldic one granted by François Ier, but it seems to have been provided by Rabelais himself. The writer is indebted to Naomi Miller for this information.

For medals showing the unicorn purifying water, see G. F. Hill, A Corpus of Italian Medals of the Renaissance before Cellini, London, 1930, p. 294, Cat. 1133, an anonymously designed medal for the Orsini. Georg Habich, Die Medallien der italienischen Renaissance, Berlin, n.d., Pl. LXXVIII, No. I, and Pl. XCV, shows medals by unknown Venetians, the last made for the Bishop of Bitonto, ca. 1544.

22. The Chabot-Charny family, relatives of Cardinal de Givry, probably a major patron of Duvet's, are also linked to Malicorne.

See La grande encyclopédie, Paris, 1886-1903, XXII, p. 1059.

23. Quoted from the publication of the Rouen entry in 1557, Bardon, op. cit., p. 82.

24. See C. de Boer, ed., "Ovide moralisé," Verhandelingen der koninklijke Akademie van Wetenschapen te Amsterdam: Afdeeling Letterkunde, n.d., XV, 1915, n.s. XXI, 1920; n.s. XXX, no. 3, 1931. For the Ovide moralisé, see also the references provided by Bardon, op. cit., p. 8, n. 1.

25. De Boer, op. cit., n.s. XV, p. 11.

26. Ibid., p. 312, Book 3, 11. 632ff. The pursuit and death of Actaeon is dwelt upon at such length that one is tempted to see some connection between Duvet's Unicorn series and his engraving of The Death of a Stag (Cat. 29).

Prescribing the appropriate representation of the deities for the convenience of artists, the editor points out that Diana "est painte en l'espece et figure d'une dame tenant en sa main ung arc et ung saiette, suyvans les cerfs et les bestes sauvaiges." This is followed by a symbolic interpretation of the goddess: "A moralement entendre: par ceste deese nous pouvons prandre la vierge, glorieuse

dame est royne du ciel, laquel pour certaine est armée de l'arc flexible de miseri-
corde et de la saiette d'oroison, par le moien desquelz arc et flèche le cerf cornu,
c'est la dyable, plain d'orgueil, est surmonté . . ." (De Boer, XLIII, 1938, p. 409).

27. C. Daremberg and E. Saglio, *Dictionnaire des antiquités*, Paris, 1892, II, Part 2,
p. 139.

28. See X. Barbier de Montault, *Traité d'iconographie chrétienne*, Paris, 1890, p. 217.
According to Albertus Magnus, pulverized lily was a test for virginity. See Angelo
Gubernatis, *La mythologie des plantes*, Paris, 1882, II, p. 200. For the Parisian
entry of Mary Tudor in 1514 (a year before Diane de Poitier's marriage to Louis
de Brézé at the age of sixteen) an elaborate *tableau-vivant* at Saints-Innocents
represented France as a lily in a closed garden, guarded by Clemency, Force,
Truth, and Grace. It is illustrated on Pl. V of the manuscript at the British
Museum, Cottom Vespasian B.II. Another *tableau-vivant* showed Diana/France
in a moon costume, receiving light from Phoebus Apollo/Louis XII. This metaphor
was to culminate with Louis XIV as the *Roi soleil* in the succeeding century.
Gringoire stated most explicitly that "dyane est france la fertille." See Baskerville,
op. cit., pp. 8-10, 12. This attribution of fertility to the chaste Diana stems from
an ancient correlation between phases of the moon and menstruation. The
Oxford Classical Dictionary, 1953, p. 247, points out, "The central idea of her
[Diana's] function would seem to have been fertility." This conclusion is based
upon archeological evidence of the offerings made to the goddess and of the
nature of processions held in her honor.

29. See the *Hypnerotomachia Poliphili*, Aldus, Venice, 1499; see the edition of
Giovanni Pozzi and Lucia A. Ciapponi, Padua, 1963, I, pp. 161-163, with com-
mentary, II, p. 142. Colonna is creating an involved allegory of the Incarnation,
following the *Ovide moralisé*, in which Danäe, receiving Jupiter in the form of a
shower of coins, appears as a curious prefiguration of Mary. Emphasis is placed
equally upon the chastity of Danäe and her encroaching pregnancy in Colonna's
most explicit text, where the very seat upon which Danäe is placed in this triumph
of chastity is a birth-chair. In the words of Jean Martin's translation, this seat is
"estime ayder aux femmes qui travaillant d'enfant, & rendre la personne chaste,
qui le porte sur soy" (*Discours du Songe de Poliphile*, Paris, Jacques Kerver à la
Licorne, 1546, p. 60). For the translator of the Hypnerotomachia, see Pierre
Marcel, *Jean Martin*, Paris, 1927, esp. pp. 71-84; Anthony Blunt, "The 'Hypnerotomachia Poliphili' in Seventeenth-Century France," *Journal of the Warburg Institute*,
I, 1937-38, pp. 117-137.
As a fertility goddess, it seems appropriate that Diana's presence be suggested by
the unicorn drawing her nymph's chariot. That Diana's aid at childbirth was
known in the sixteenth century can also be seen in Vasari's design for the chariot
of the moon for the celebration of the marriage of Francesco de' Medici. See
Giovanni Milanesi, ed., *Le opere di Giorgio Vasari*, Florence, VIII, 1882, p. 601,
"Carro nonne, della Luna" which was attended by Egeria, "invocata anch'ella in
soccorse alle pregnanti donne." The legend of Danäe, with its similarities to the
life of Saint Barbara and the Virgin Mary, must have offered so many parallels
between the classical and the Christian that one would expect Danäe to have
been a more popular figure in the art of the sixteenth century.

30. The full title runs into ten lines of fine type. Pierre da la Vigne, or Petrum
Lavinium as he is called in the book, had his work published by Etienne
Gueynard at Lyon in 1510. The fourth volume is dedicated to Francesco
Gonzaga and the fifth to Claude de Longvy. See Baudrier, *Bibliographie
lyonnaise*, Lyon-Paris, 1914, Sér. 2, pp. 222-223.
After an Italian journey, during which he seems to have received the patronage
of Francesco Gonzaga, Pierre de la Vigne became affiliated with the Jacobin
cloister in Mâcon, where he dedicated his work to Claude de Longvy, canon of
Saint-Vincent at the time.
Boccaccio's *Genealogia deorum* may have been utilized by Duvet, as this fourteenth century text was extremely well known in France, where it was first

published in translation in 1498 and again in 1531. The imagery of Jean Bouchet's *Triomphes du très chrestien . . . François premier de ce nom* of 1550 is still imbued with Boccaccio's work, according to Bardon, *op. cit.*, p. 5.

31. This subject was depicted by Tobias Stimmer for *Neue künstliche Figuren biblische Historien*, Bible illustrations published in Basle by Thomas Guarin, and shown in a tapestry designed by Michael Coxcie (Barcelona, Palacio de Excema) from a Noah cycle.

32. See Shephard, *op. cit.*, p. 282. *Der beschlossen Gart* was first published in 1505. Thomas of Cantimpré mentions an important unicorn horn in a church at Bruges and seems to have gathered his lore from French, Netherlandish, and German sources, where the expanded unicorn myths originated. The text of *Der beschlossen Gart* by Ulrich Pinder (Nuremberg, 1505) was illustrated by Hans Schäufelein.

   In Parsifal, the essence of the unicorn story is retained, but here the beast is hunted so that the precious carbuncle beneath his horn may be obtained in order to cure the wound of Amfortas. Wolfram's account is a Christian allegory in that the other ingredients of the curative prescription are water from the four rivers of paradise and blood from the wound of a pelican, the traditional emblem of Christian sacrifice and piety. The legend is discussed by O. M. Dalton, *Catalogue of the Ivory Carvings of the Christian Era . . . of the British Museum*, London, 1909, Cat. 368, p. 125 and Pl. LXXXVI, in connection with a fourteenth century ivory chest depicting the Hunt of the Unicorn and the Virgin Capture. Schönberger, *op. cit.*, 190, n. 5, stated that the unicorn passages from Parsifal can be found in the Leitzmann edition, Halle, 1903, Book 9, pp. 114, 482, 483, 485.

33. See Shephard, *op. cit.*, pp. 58-59.

34. From Thomas of Cantimpré, *Miraculorum et exemplorum memorabilium sui temporis . . .* , Douai, 1605, Liber II, cap. XXIX, pp. 313-315. I am very much indebted to Mr. T. Doyle and Mr. L. Richardson for this translation.

35. Carl Cohn, *Zur literarischen Geschichte des Einhorns*, Berlin, 1896. The *Physiologus* of Eustathius, mentioned on p. 21, seems to have been the source for Duvet's engraving, for here, unlike the many other accounts of the capture of the unicorn by a virgin, the importance of a musical instrument is stressed as attracting the unicorn. Eustathius also described the tying of the sleeping animal to a tree. Cohn cited several *Physiologus* texts which discuss the triumphant display of the captive unicorn and its being taken to the palace in an elaborate procession (p. 27). A reproduction of a plaque of supposed classical origin is given in Bernard de Montfaucon, *L'antiquité expliquée et representée en figures*, Paris, 1724, Suppl. III, Pl. XI. Depicting the capture of the unicorn by a maiden, this antique-style medal looks as though it were made in the sixteenth century and like the Duvet engraving, presents what is customarily a Christian allegory in the antique manner. It is also illustrated by Shephard, *op. cit.*, p. 39.

36. See Françoise Joukovsky, *La gloire dans la poésie française et néolatine du XVIe siècle*, Geneva, 1969, pp. 366-7.

37. Boullaye, "Entrées et séjours de François Ier à Langres," *Bulletin de la Société historique et archéologique de Langres*, I, 1880, p. 72. Duvet also made a silver lily and a heart of silver to be presented to François Ier by a beautiful maiden of Langres, imagery which is very much in the spirit of the unicorn series.

38. The unicorn as a being of mystical power is celebrated by Rémy Belleau, a sixteenth century French poet, in a work entitled *Les Cornes*. See *Poètes du XVIe siècle*, ed. Albert-Marie Schmidt, Paris, 1953, p. 562.

39. See such works as Simon Vostre's beautifully printed *Heures à l'usage de Rouen*, ca. 1508 and Philippe Pigouchet's *Heures de Rome* of 1509, both of which present a great Roman triumph which includes a putto riding a unicorn, presented in a

series of marginal vignettes. According to Marcel, the Vostre *Hours* were adapted for use at Langres (I, p. 153, n. 2). C. Fairfax Murray, *Catalogue of Early French Books in the Library of C. Fairfax Murray*, London, 1910, Part 2, provides an extremely useful table listing all the varieties of marginal illustrations in French books of hours.

The heraldic unicorn was also an especially popular emblem among publishers, printers, and paper makers. Harold Bayley believed that the frequently encountered unicorn water mark functioned as a secret symbol for the Albigensian papermakers (*Lost Language of Symbolism*, London, 1909, pp. 98-99). Shephard observed that even if this were to have been true, the watermark must have been widely imitated by those having little if any sympathy with the Albigensians.

40. See Weisbach, *op. cit.*, p. 142.

41. See Guigue, *L'entrée de François Ier roy de France en la cité de Lyon le 12 juillet*, Lyon, 1899. The manuscript is in the Wolfenbüttel Library. Unfortunately, the illumination accompanying the unicorn allegory was stolen.

42. *Ibid.*, p. 52. This publication is especially valuable as one of the best visually documented descriptions of a triumphal entry.

43. Boullaye, *Etude . . . , op. cit.*, p. 36.

44. The traditional late medieval vehicle for the introduction of unicorn symbolism into French triumphal pageantry was as the attribute of Hector, who belonged to the ancient group of the *Neuf Preux*. As an image of invincible strength, the unicorn was appropriate to Hector not only on these grounds but also geographically as being of an Eastern origin, according to Pliny and Ctesias. *Les Neuf Preux*, the nine heroes—three from the Old Testament, three from Roman history, and three from Christian times—including Hector, Alexander, and Caesar, marched along in the triumphal processions, accompanied by the symbolic attributes of a unicorn, griffon, and dromedary. See Charles de Bourgueville de Bras, *Les recherches et antiquitez de la ville de Caen*, Caen, 1858, p. 103. The date of the entry was 1532; Joseph Chartrou gave it as 1539, (*Les entrées colonnelles et triomphales de la renaissance*, Paris, 1928, p. 37).
It was this entry which included so much Apocalyptic imagery in praise of Charles V, uniting his Order of the Golden Fleece with François Ier's Ordre de Saint-Michel.

45. Almanque Papillon's *La victoire et triumph d'argent*, printed in Lyon in 1537 by François Juste, describes the race around the world of Pluto's gold chariot of fornication, and vice, and the chariot of Honor and Love with François Ier at the helm. An illustrated manuscript based on Papillon's text is described by R. Maulde la Clavière, *Les femmes de la renaissance*, Paris, 1898, p. 205, where it is listed as belonging to Baron Pichon. In the *Catalogue de la bibliothèque de Baron Pichon*, Paris, 1897, it is listed as No. 798, ex coll. Duke of Hamilton.

46. See S. de Merval, *L'entrée d'Henri II à Rouen d'après un manuscrit de la Bibliothèque de Rouen*, Rouen, 1868. See also A. Beaucousin, ed., *L'entrée à Rouen de Henri II et Catherine de Medicis*, Paris, 1550 (reprinted by the Société des bibliophiles de Normandie, Rouen, 1882).

47. De Merval, *op. cit.*, folio 17 r.

48. *The Triumph of Fame* at Rouen is strikingly reminiscent of the design of Duvet's little roundel celebrating the *Triumph of the Trinity* (Cat. 12). The costumes, elephants, and the type of musical instruments are all the same. The scene at Rouen is reproduced by De Merval in etchings after the original watercolor drawings, folio 15 r.

49. See Shephard, *op. cit.*, p. 87. See also Luca Pulci, *Poemetti mitologico de secoli d'amore*, Torraca, F. ed. 1888, Part I, pp. 161-319.
The legend suggests the famous Pisanello medal of Cecelia, identified as the "virgo filia" of the Marquis of Gonzaga, the reverse of which depicts a maiden with a unicorn—the conventional virgin capture, but this time with the crescent moon above, an allusion to the chaste Diana.

50. Bartsch, XV, 538, 1. This may be a monogrammist who never existed. The M at the lower left is found on the other engravings that are similar in style and should probably, despite the initial, be placed in the Reverdy (Reverdino) Circle. The initials ZG appear at the lower right and may refer to the man who reissued the plate.

51. Odell Shephard's study of unicorn lore (*op. cit.,*) devotes many pages (242-52) to a discussion of the elusive yet perceptible link between the unicorn and the moon, suggesting that the mythological beast may have been in ancient cultures a symbol of that celestial body. Many associations exist between horns, moons, unicorns, and curses without any one surviving text providing a fully satisfactory explication. Both Diana and the unicorn are agents of healing and purification. See Daremberg and Saglio, *op. cit.*, II, Part 2, p. 140, for a discussion of Diana as a goddess of healing. The authors point out that Mont Corne near Tusculum was consecrated to Diana, providing another link between Diana and the horn (p. 124). Antlers were apparently frequently sacrificed to Diana. Virgil already refers to the crescent moon as horned (*Georgics*, I, 433).
   Shephard points out (p. 132) that the image of Diana, stamped on clay amulets to insure good health, was gradually replaced by that of the unicorn.
   Shephard also suggests that the unicorn was somehow associated with the mountains of the moon, recalling Pisanello's relief of the maiden and the unicorn in a lunar landscape. For example, Mithraic astrological charts describe a moon goddess with a single horn (Shephard, p. 244). French sixteenth century humanism, especially at the episcopal seat of Langres, a center for astrological and antiquarian research where Duvet was often employed, may well have come across some references in which these images were presented.

52. Lyon, 1550, p. 54. This text is largely based upon the *Centiloquium* attributed to Ptolemy Claudius.

53. See De Gubernatis, *op. cit.*, II, p. 65. Zeus chose the oak as his favorite tree; his will was made known through the sounds of the wind rustling through its leaves. The oak was also the divine tree of the Samian Oracles, their "tree of wisdom" (p. 69). De Gubernatis stated that in religious processions at Bologna, crowns of oak and olive leaves were worn. These arboreal attributes point to Duvet's familiarity with L.D.'s print of 1547 (Text fig. 28; Bartsch XVI, 330, 61) showing the deities with branches, illustrating Pliny the Elder's *Historia naturalis*, Book XII. The engraver drew upon the print for *The Marriage of Adam and Eve* (Cat. 35).

54. Roussat, *op. cit.*, p. 54.

55. This scene has been described in medieval terms by Thomas of Cantimpré. See n. 21 above.

56. See Thomas of Cantimpré, *op. cit.*, pp. 313-315.

57. A. van Dorsten, *The Radical Arts*, Leiden/Oxford, 1970, p. 46. See also the new edition of Francis A. Yates *The Valois Tapestries*, London, 1975, pp. XVII-XVIII. Similar stress on the importance of Burgundy as a regal Paradise Lost has recently been asserted in Gordon Kipling's *The Triumph of Honour—Burgundian Origins of the Elizabethan Renaissance* (Leiden, 1977). The Order of the Golden Fleece, with its intricate fusion of Christian, courtly and commercial associations touches upon several of the same bases as the lore and legend of the unicorn so it is more probable than one might first assume that the old Duvet could even have envisaged a market for the ever more mystical cycle of Unicorn prints as the sixteenth century advanced, or perhaps regressed, toward nostalgia for the absolute pageantry of Burgundy.

V.

THE SOURCES; THE OEUVRE;

THE INFLUENCES

Duvet's precociously Italianate engravings of the 1520s place him at the forefront of a most important but now lost generation of French artists who, judging from their few surviving and battered paintings, were the first to turn to Rome, Milan, Antwerp and Nuremberg for High Renaissance inspiration.[1] Dependent primarily upon the prints of Dürer, Marcantonio, and to a lesser degree on those of Northern Italy, these painters, few of whom have been identified, restored an important element to French art—the concern with the Antique. Although Fouquet revived the classical tradition, it was submerged again toward the end of the fifteenth century. French art lost its native clarity to the *retardataire* ornamental styles of the late Gothic and to the Renaissance decorative vocabulary of Milan, Genoa and Naples. Through invasions of these areas under Charles VIII (1483-98) and Louis XII (1498-1515), France was flooded with portable, readily applicable decorative works, prints, small bronzes, medals and plaquettes. Enchanted by the art encountered in his Italian campaigns, Charles VIII resolved upon his return to France in 1498, to recreate the setting he so much admired. "Pour édifier et faire ouvrage à la mode d'Italie," he brought to Amboise twenty-two artists and craftsmen.[2] Few French artists of the turn of the century could resist the tidal wave of ornament which swallowed up or perhaps more accurately determined the otherwise often sentimental, traditional art of the generation of Bourdichon, Colombe, and Bellegambe. Early examples demonstrating the French engulfment of the Lombard ornamental style in the graphic arts are found in the Ovid *Heroïdes*, translated by Octavien de Saint-Gelais in 1496 and probably illuminated in Rouen between that year and 1502 for Louis XII, and in the *Cicero* of 1511.[3]

With the important exception of the 1556 *Privilège* for his *Apocalypse*, there is no contemporary reference to Jean Duvet as printmaker. In the *Apocalypse* Frontispiece, engraved in the preceding year, Duvet described himself near the end of his life, as a gold-worker—*aurifaber*. His father was a goldsmith, and it is from him that he probably learned engraving. Printmaking may have occupied a role in Duvet's many-faceted career as master of the mint, designer of tapestries, stained glass, military and hydraulic engineer, surveyor, accomplished goldsmith, *émailleur* and worker in damascening. His prints are largely a reflection of his activity as pageant master.

Linked to the Netherlands yet not unaffected by the southern, Italian influence, Burgundy was predominantly Flemish in character. In this way, Duvet was trained during his formative years in an area that was connected with a multiplicity of styles. Langres reveals significant examples of the cosmopolitan activities of its native craftsmen.[4] Jean Lefebvre for one, worked as a printer in Turin, Lyon, and Geneva toward the end of the fifteenth century, while another, Philippe Biguerny (Bigarny) was in Spain where his Mantegnesque sculpture at Burgos reflected Italian travels or influence.[5] Duvet's training as a goldsmith and probably as master of the mint may have brought him into contact with Italian medalmakers active in Burgundy.[6]

The engraver's father, a prominent local goldsmith selected to make presentation gifts of *orfèvrerie* for the triumphal entry of Louis XII in Dijon in 1501 (Doc. 3), worked in the terminal style of the fifteenth century, probably fusing a late Gothic aesthetic with a sprinkling of Lombard ornamental motifs—a metallic equivalent of Bourdichon's illuminations which combined the arts of Italy and the Netherlands. The nostalgic conservatism of Burgundian early sixteenth century art can be seen in the partial copy of Sluter's "Well of Moses," commissioned by the Hôpital du Saint-Esprit in 1508.[7] Duvet himself returned to Eyckian sources derived from paintings at the Chartreuse de Champmol in his *Apocalypse* series (Cat. 61) and other works.

Despite many major and minor Italian talents active in France—Benedetto Ghirlandaio, Francesco Laurana, Fra Giocondo, Andrea Solario (1509-11), the Giusti, one of the Gaggini, Andrea del Sarto (1518-19), and the residence of Leonardo at Amboise from 1516 to his death in 1519—the immediate impact of these masters upon French art and architecture was relatively slight. Italian sculptors active in France such as Pacherot and the Juste (Giusti), Girolamo da Fiesole from Florence, and Gaggini from Genoa, were rooted in a rather provincial late Quattrocento aesthetic that had little to do with the new developments early in the next century. Neither Leonardo nor Solario were associated with the new Roman sources employed by Duvet, although Lombard elements in his oeuvre stem from their influence. Fra Bartolommeo's "Holy Family" (Louvre), a major monument of the Italian Renaissance may have been readily accessible to Duvet. It was originally destined for San Marco, but brought to Louis XII by his ambassador to Florence, Jacques Hurault. Other smaller panels by the master were acquired by François Ier. The "Holy Family" seems to have been deposited in the cathedral of Autun at an early date and remained there until the Revolution. Fra Bartolommeo was invited to work at the French court in 1514 but refused to come.[8] Girolamo della Robbia's ware was exported to the North long before the founding of his Northern atelier in 1528.[9] A splendid Benedetto Ghirlandaio "Nativity" is still in France at Aigueperse because the painter is known to have come there in the 1480s or 1490s.[10] A mosaic now at the Musée de Cluny, designed by Davide Ghirlandaio, was brought to Paris and installed at Saint-Merri by the *président* of the *Parlement*.[11] Mantegna's "Sebastian" (Louvre) also came to France in the late fifteenth century.[12]

Whether any of these works, together with those made by Laurana in Marseille were ever seen by Duvet is far from certain. He adapted motifs from readily portable works such as plaquettes rather than working after such monumental masterpieces as the Mantegna "Sebastian." When Duvet utilized Mantegna's art, it was the Mantegna School prints that were consulted; when he needed a model for his own engraved "Sebastian" (Cat. 4), the French printmaker turned to a plaquette by Moderno (Text fig. 1).

The young artist could well have accompanied French troops on the Italian campaigns. Furthermore, as he is known to have been a military engineer and master of damascening, the engraver may have gone to Lyon, there joining the armies bound for the south. Such a journey might have taken place shortly after Duvet joined the goldsmith's guild in Dijon in 1509 or possibly even before, since the artist was already twenty-two at the time of admission.

Of all the obscure Italian artists who may have been associated with early sixteenth century France, none seems less known yet closer to Duvet in style than the painter of an altarpiece now in Nancy, inscribed with two diptychs, and dated 1512 (Text fig. 60).[13] The inscription states that the provost Guido of the noble Auricomi family had commissioned the panel by Francesco del Tatti, probably a member of the Sansovino family of Tuscany and the Veneto who received French patronage. If, as suggested by Suida, the painter of the panel is also the draughtsman of a sheet inscribed "Francesco de Tactis de Varisiis" (Venice, Accademia), then the artist could have had ample opportunity for French patronage in the environs of Varese.[14] The Nancy altarpiece presents a melange of North Italian styles but was probably painted at some remove, judging by its eccentric, awkward, yet provincially forceful style. The physiognomy of the plump, wingless putto holding the tablet in the foreground, together with the appliqué quality of the ornament resemble Duvet's early Italianate style.

Another artist, Amico Aspertini, should also be considered. Only ten years older than the

60. *Francesco Tatti*, Virgin and Child
with Angels, *1512, Nancy, Musée des
Beaux Arts.*

61. *Amico Aspertini*, The Holy Family with Saints, *Paris,
St. Nicholas-des-Champs.*

135

French engraver, Aspertini was also a printmaker. Many of his works resemble late fifteenth century art, and others, though executed mostly in Bologna, point to the aesthetic of Lombardy. A "Holy Family" by Aspertini, in the Parisian church of Saint-Nicholas-des-Champs (Text fig. 61) dating from circa 1516, may prove to have been a French commission. The sinuous, turgid style suggests Duvet's. According to Freedberg, in this work

> "broad forms of bizarre shape and cast of countenance,
> are compelled into a passionate communion by the
> action of a sweeping, knotting rhythm. An effect of
> complex excitement is accentuated by the handling of
> light, which makes a broken coruscation. The work has
> an extraordinary, mostly irrational power, suggesting to
> the spectator the image of what he would expect from
> a demented Michelangelo."[15]

This irrational, mystical Michelangelism is often encountered in Duvet's *Apocalypse,* where as noted by Blunt, prints after the Italian master's "Last Judgment" and the Sistine Ceiling are a major source for the figures.

François Ier's taste in art, set the precedent for ecclecticism which proved so important to Duvet's work. Enthusiastic about almost all foreign art, the monarch brought together Tuscan and Lombard painting with examples from Flanders, drawing artists from all these areas to his employ in the Loire. Pre-Fontainebleau patronage centers like the Cardinal d'Amboise's unusually modern Italianate château at Gaillon and the more modest courts of the bishops of Autun, Bourges, or Auxerre show that François's catholic taste had been the rule rather than the exception in France, ever since the Italian campaigns of Charles VIII (1483-98) and Louis XII (1498-1515). Duvet was about twenty when d'Amboise's château was developed; its cosmopolitan setting gave him a heightened awareness of foreign art.

Duvet was significantly affected by the art of Mantegna and that of Lombardy—both imported and developed on a local scale.[16] In short, as a result of these influences, the artist's job was often primarily that of an organizer of ornament, an amalgamator of motifs who could assemble appropriate emblems, uniting them through formal decorative devices rather than vigorous narrative. A fundamental sense of applied design rather than the creation of original compositions was the basis of native artistic endeavor. Thus, monumental forms such as Marcantonio's "Massacre of the Innocents" appear within the border of a printed *Book of Hours* or a series of Florentine Quattrocento allegorical engravings reappear as *intarsie* on the choir stalls at Gaillon.

The first major French sixteenth century assertion of Renaissance art in prints was, fittingly enough, also the first publication of an illustrated treatise on perspective, based on the oeuvre of Fouquet, the most important French master of the Quattrocento.[17] This publication, *De artificiali perspectiva* by Jean Pélerin, was also appropriately printed in Toul, close to the Alsatian region where so much contact with German artists and craftsmen took place, and dated 1505, the beginning of the great funerary church of Margaret of Austria at Brou. This combination of revival and Northern technical participation is characteristic of the composite nature of French art to come, continually drawing upon both North and South until the middle of the century, when a stable French classical style had been achieved. Also characteristic for France and her rather belated participation in the classicizing currents of the Renaissance is the fact that Pélerin was a canon and that so much of the scholarship related to humanism and science still seems to have been more closely allied to the church than in Italy or the North. The date of Pélerin's publication is also that of the first French printing in Roman type—another international production. This Book of Hours was the work of a German active in Paris, Tilman Kerver.[18]

The most forceful contemporary of Duvet, a graphic artist active in France in the

1520s is Gabriel Salmon.[19]   Although heavily influenced by German printmakers, most importantly Baldung Grien, Salmon tempers his Teutonic heritage with an elegance and sense for the abstract. His twelve woodcuts of the Labors of Hercules, circa 1528, suggest scrutiny of Pollaiuolo and Robetta. Like Duvet's Italianate engravings of the 1520s, Salmon's woodcuts of the same period have a sense of monumental vigor incorporating the different dynamisms of North and South which anticipate Goujon's finest achievements.[20]

Geoffroy Tory, the outstanding French master of the decorative vocabulary of North Italian humanism, was probably only five years Duvet's senior.[21] Since his involvement with the visual aspects of the North Italian Renaissance only asserts itself in the later 1520s, his known works cannot have been of great importance to Duvet's early concern with the same area.

The massive impact of Albrecht Dürer's prints is indicative of a certain lassitude and lack of inventiveness of native artists during this period of general détente in the first quarter of the sixteenth century. Significantly, Dürer's works may have often come to France through a prior transformation in the Netherlands where his art, especially the woodcut *Apocalypse* of 1498, enjoyed a vogue that was to be repeated further South.[22] Receptive to Renaissance currents prior to his first Italian journey, Dürer provided the rest of Northern Europe with a synthesis of Northern and Southern elements. Almost at once his prints became the common property of Germany, the Netherlands, France and Spain.

Duvet's first Italianate works relate in style to those of a Netherlandish master of painted glass windows who was active in Rouen—Arnoult de Nijmègue. French *peintre-verriers* of the early sixteenth century were key figures in the production of paintings of that period.[23] Arnoult's art was based on a combination of native Netherlandish, French and Italian elements. The latter were made available not only through the prints of Agostino Veneziano, Zoan Andrea, and Nicoletto da Modena, sources identical to those of Duvet, but also through possible association with Italian workers for cardinal Georges d'Amboise, a close friend of Arnoult's patron Antoine Bohier. The *peintre-verrier's* early command of Renaissance forms earned him Guicciardini's praise as being the "grandissimo imitatore di disegni d'Italia" in his *Description of the Netherlands* of 1567.[24] Equally at home in his adaptations from Dürer, Arnoult's authoritative eclecticism during the first two decades of the sixteenth century in France presents a notable precedent and model for that of Duvet in the succeeding four.[25]

Replacing windows smashed during the fifteenth century turmoil, Northern glass painters provided France with a fusion of German and Netherlandish currents, adding Italian influence. The latter became increasingly important from 1513-29 when reproductive prints first became a major Roman export.[26] Both Troyes and Bourges produced considerable windows in an advanced Italianate style well before the launching of the Fontainebleau School. The sculptural ateliers of Troyes also incorporated Italianate elements in the quantities of works emanating from that productive area.[27]

In the very first years of the sixteenth century, the environs of Burgundy may have been a patronage center of considerable importance, drawing to it painters and sculptors from Germany and the Netherlands as well as France. The château at Pont d'Ain, where Philibert de Savoie and Marguerite d'Autriche lived at times during their brief marriage, could have provided the point of departure for the eclectic style.[28] Records of elaborate pageantry accompanying the royal couple's comings and goings also indicate many occasions for advanced, classicizing décor which may have involved the cooperation of local artists. A large sculptural atelier, headed by Conrad Meyt (with Vambelli as second in command), was established in 1505 to prepare a magnificent funerary chapel at Brou (Bourg-en-Bresse) following Philibert's sudden death at his nearby château.[29] Marguerite's patronage brought to the Franche-Comté and Burgundy an influx of Netherlandish talents, active until 1532, unequalled in that region since the days of Beauneveu and Sluter.[30]

Describing Marguerite's church, Hilaire Belloc wrote,

"The south and north of our civilization mingled
in it more thoroughly even than on the Loire.
The Walloon and the Italians and the Swiss passed
the chisel to each other; Beughen, Vambelli, Meyt

were at work together; and the French of the plains designed and controlled the whole. The church which surrounds it is Gothic, but the spirit which makes the stones live is the Renaissance."[31]

Few paintings survive in France from the years between 1515 and 1520, when foreign artists and craftsmen worked throughout the country. Those panels which do exist are often of disputed authorship, shifted back and forth between the Netherlands, Germany and France.[32]

A Burgundian triptych (dated 1515) at Autun may be the work of an itinerant artist (Text fig. 62). Saints in grisaille are shown on the exterior, with prefigurations of the Eucharist painted within, to the left and right of the Last Supper. The artist's close study of Renaissance decorative art is reflected throughout: pilasters, the bowl held by the Lombard lady crouching among the manna gatherers, and the flacon at Melchisedek's side are all derived from Italian engravings.[33] A certain sense for the abstract and delight in the clear profiles preclude a purely Netherlandish origin for the Autun triptych; but it has many realistic, intricately wrought details such as the reflection of the Eucharistic still-life in Abraham's helmet.

Even more significant as a parallel to Duvet's style is a "Baptism" at Saint-Omer (Text fig. 63), since the anonymous painter has similarly gone back to Quattrocento sources as well as to the art of the Antwerp Mannerists and of Marcantonio. The nude male figures at the left and right are taken from Raphaelesque and Pollaiuolesque models. The use of the latter, possibly transmitted via Baldung Grien, is seen extensively in the work of Gabriel Salmon.

A triptych dated 1518, devoted to scenes from the life of Saint Jerome, painted for that saint's chapel at Brou (Text fig. 64-66) is sufficiently Northern in feeling to have once been attributed to Dürer's mediocre master Wolgemuth, but is clearly too late in date and too advanced in style for that artist, showing the influence of Lucas van Leyden, Dürer, and Marcantonio, combined with a Lombard finesse.[34]

62. *Burgundian School,* Last Supper Triptych, *c. 1520, Autun, Musée.*

63. *Burgundian School,* The Baptism, *c. 1520, Saint-Omer, Notre Dame.*

138

64. Anonymous, The Altar of St. Jerome, *Bourg-en-Bresse, Musée.*

65-66. The Dream and the Death of Saint Jerome, *wings of triptych, 1518, Bourg-en-Bresse, Musée.*

139

67.　*Anonymous,* Bearing of the Cross, *Retable of Nicholas Chichon and Jacquemette de la Botte, 1523, Bourg-en-Bresse, Musée.*

An example utilizing Dürer's prints may be seen in the wings of a triptych also at Bourg-en-Bresse, dated 1523, where both the scene of "Christ Bearing the Cross" and that of the "Lamentation" are taken from the small woodcut "Passion" of about 1509-11 (Text fig. 67).[35] The adaptation of the first subject (B. 37) is relatively straightforward (excepting the Magdalen's more fashionable appearance); the second combines both Dürer's "Lamentation" and "Entombment" (B. 43-44). The panels are far more suave, generalized and freer in motion than their German models. For all his unabashed use of prints, the French artist has not produced a simpleminded, characterless copy. There is no servility or lack of authority in the paintings, although they are in the strict sense of the word, a pastiche, merging Dürer's woodcuts with an Italianate orientation, viewing the German's art through a Franco-Italian filter. These panels, produced not far from Dijon in 1523, share Duvet's free, often complex appropriation of compositions from Northern and Southern print sources, bringing to them a curious force and individuality that redeem them from shallow plagiarism. A triptych (Nancy, Musée des Beaux-Arts) shows the "Birth of the Virgin" with the "Annunciation to Joachim" and the "Presentation of the Virgin" in the left and right wings (Text fig. 68). All three scenes are derived from Dürer's woodcut "Life of the Virgin."[36] However, some of the figures have a more formal, monumental quality recalling those of the Cardinal Virtues sculpted by the Giusti for the tomb of Louis XII at Saint-Denis. A third source is indicated by some of the fashions and physiognomy, recalling those of the Antwerp Mannerists and Lucas van Leyden. Influence from the graphic art of the Netherlands is also suggested by the *découpage*-like presentation of some of the participants. The complex, almost grotesque *contropposto* of other figures recalls the participants in Rosso's "Deposition" at Arezzo, painted in 1521, close to the date of the Nancy triptych. Such details as the *imago clipeata* of Agrippa shown on the interior reveal knowledge of the designs of Pieter Coecke van Alost from whose circle came the altar for Pagny, the château of Cardinal de Givry's niece and her husband, now in the Philadelphia Museum of Art.[37] Both Like the great Baerze-Broederlam altar of the late fourteenth century, sent from the Nether-

68. *Burgundian School,* Birth of the Virgin, *center panel of triptych, c. 1520, Nancy, Musée des Beaux Arts.*

lands to the ducal chapel at Dijon where it remains, the Pagny retable has a carved cruci-fixion group at the center, surrounded by other scenes from the Passion and the life of Christ, all stamped with the Antwerp guild mark (with Eucharistic subjects painted below and in the wings).

The broad reference of Franco—Flemish art of the early sixteenth century—that of Duvet's generation—is indicated by Jean Lemaire de Belges's "La Couronne Margaritique," dedicated to Margaret of Austria. The poet listed the greatest artists: van Eyck "le roi des peintres," van der Goes, van der Weyden, Bouts and Memling, and Schongauer, and then enumerated those whose "espritz recents et nouveletz" he seemed to rate even higher: Perugino, Leonardo, and Bellini.[38]

While a very small number of paintings survive to reveal the painted world which contributed to and participated in Duvet's early art, no French engravings of approximately the same date may be consulted with equal confidence, as Duvet's are the first to be fully signed and dated. The sole contemporary who can be identified with certainty is Noël Garnier. His only signed and dated work of 1544 ("A Warrior Leading a Horse," after H. S. Beham), stems from the end of his career, which began early in the century with two grotesque, ornamental Gothic alphabets. Duvet may have consulted these for a figure in his "Christ Driving Out the Money Changers" (Cat. 2).[39] His alphabets have a certain *retardataire* conviction and coarse energy, though Garnier's remaining oeuvre is all copied from Dürer and the *Kleinmeister* ["little masters"] significant solely for its revelation of French interest and dependence upon Northern graphic arts.

Several additional printmakers working in France early in the century, might be considered as well. One artist who signed himself "Ioannis Louis E. Avenionensis" engraved a copy of Dürer's "Saint Anthony" (B. 58)[40] in 1519; another, who inscribed a print of Saint Peter Martyr "Cinericius 1516," works in a style which is between that of Garnier and Duvet.[41] His use of Italian ornament is reminiscent of Duvet's "Saint Sebastian" (Cat. 4); the prominence of the crowned *fleur-de-lys* likewise points to French influence.

69. "Cinericius," Saint Dominic, 1516.

70. Anonymous, French School, Virgin and Child.

An engraving of Saint Dominic (Text fig. 69) signed "Cinericius 1516" on a tablet placed by an Italianate column, also has the letters AVI and UN (for Avignon?). The artist's name may be a Latinized Cendre. It is appropriate that Avignon should have provided early examples of Italianate engraving since long after the Babylonian Captivity had ended, Avignon continued to be a leading patronage center for Italian art in France. The Provençal city, during the years of Guiliano de' Medici's domain there, employed numerous Italian artists, although none were of the calibre of their fourteenth century predecessors.[42]

An unusually beautiful engraving (Text fig. 70) which should be assigned French authorship and dated from the end of the first decade of the sixteenth century, shows the Virgin and Child embracing. Jesus' foot rests upon the closed book of the Old Testament, which is placed on an inscribed ledge.[43] Its overt and "disguised" references to the Passion, although found in Italy, are popular in the North.[44] Specifically North Italian in inspiration, the rendering of the print is still delicately Gothic—its combined sources suggesting French origin.

The only engraver who was a contemporary of Jean Duvet, and his technical equal who may prove to be French is the Master of the Mousetrap, signing his prints NA.DAT with a diminutive mousetrap to the side. Although Hind thought him to be a North Italian active between 1500 and 1520, at an earlier date Heinecken regarded this monogrammist as possibly French.[45] The subjects of his three known prints have French associations; their style is exploratory but precise in a manner not then popular in Italy, yet distinctly non-Netherlandish or German. His "Virgin and Child Enthroned with Saint Anne" (B.1) was modelled upon a group carved by Sansovino at San Agostino in 1512, which the sculptor was executing for a German patron, Johan Goritz.[46] Another engraving by the Mousetrap Master commemorates the French triumph at Ravenna under Gaston de Foix.[47] The master's emblem also suggests a Northern origin. There are stylistic parallels in Northern manuscript illumination to the art of the Master Na.Dat.[48] These include Caesar's *Commentaries*, painted by "Godfredius Batavius,"

142

who worked with the Dutch humanist Albert Pigghe for François Ier at Saint-Germain-en-Laye.[49]

The oeuvre of a circle of Netherlandish *peintres-graveurs*, many of whom were linked with both Margaret of Austria at Malines and Phillip de Bourgogne, bishop of Utrecht, may have stimulated or paralleled Duvet's Italianate prints. This accords with André Thevet's text of 1584 on the origin of printmaking in France, which acknowledged the spread of engraving from Flanders where the art was perhaps invented.[50] The fine prints of Gossaert, Crabbe, Hogenberg, Vellert and the Monogrammist A. S.–original and authoritative Netherlandish artists–together with the somewhat lesser achievements of the Master S and the oeuvre grouped about Allaert Claessens, came into France providing a similar aesthetic to that of the *peintres-verriers*. These Netherlandish engravers all display a marked expressionistic quality like many of Duvet's works. Employing a coarse, strong containing line, countered by extreme delicacy of shading, they produced works almost grotesque in their extroverted emotion. Hogenberg's "Man of Sorrows" (B.VII, 547, 3) and Gossaert's "Christ Mocked" (Passavant III, 23, I) reveal precisely the same emotional drive as that of Joseph in Duvet's "Rest on the Flight into Egypt" (Cat. 23) or "Saint John the Evangelist" and "Saint John the Baptist" (Cat. 24).[51]

It is quite possible that Duvet could have come into personal contact with some of these artists. Hogenbert, Vellert, and Gossaert traveled widely–Gossaert with Phillip of Burgundy to Rome, Vellert to England, Hogenberg probably to Bologna.[52]

The seemingly precipitous rise of the Malines engravers, with Lucas van Leyden, from the doldrums of the *fin de siècle* resembles Duvet's own. Popham has suggested that:

> it was apparently as a result of Dürer's visit that a new generation of painters took up engraving. The earliest dates on Flemish engravings are significant: Vellert's first plate is dated August 16th, 1522; what are probably Crabbe's two earliest and one of Gossaert's are dated in the same year. Vallert and Gossaert knew Dürer, and as he came to Malines, Crabbe may have too.[53]

However, Munich-based Hogenberg almost certainly knew the engraver's craft before coming to Malines. Dürer's Netherlandish journey of 1520 hardly seems a sufficient catalyst for the emergence of a brilliant group of engravers, whose oeuvre must date back to the beginning of the century.

Duvet's early engraving style is so similar to that of the Master AC that their oeuvre has been confused.[54] Availing themselves of prints by Dürer, Lucas van Leyden, the *Kleinmeister*, and Italian masters, the prints of both artists share a vital sense of discovery often transcending their graphic plagiarism. Like Duvet, AC probably remained a goldsmith, practicing the craft from which engraving originated. Little is known about the monogrammist, who has been identified as Allaert Claesz, a Utrecht goldsmith. It is highly unlikely that the two hundred or so engravings with the AC monogram were all by the same engraver; the designer must have had several assistants, and must have maintained a print shop–a forerunner of Lafréry and Coecke, affixing his monogram to workshop products. It can be proven that Duvet utilized Claesz's oeuvre from his incorporation of a sword hilt design by the Netherlander in the "Cumaean Sibyl" (Cat. 9). Both the earliest and latest signed prints by Duvet and Claesz coincide in date (in Lyon between 1522-23) the artists exact stylistic contemporaries.[55]

No doubt attracted to Lyon, the cosmopolitan painting center and gateway toward Italy, Duvet may well have seen works there by the prominent Netherlandish painter Joos van Cleves who, like the engraver, designed fortifications in Lyon between 1522–23 before becoming court portraitist to François Ier.

The artist's early work, starting in the first decade, encompasses thirty-four engravings executed before the tablet-shaped Apocalypse series, begun circa 1546. His very first prints were engraved on a very small scale with a highly finished appearance. Planned with great care, and fully thought out before engraving actually began, the silvery tonality and delicate technique of these early prints are in the manner of the *Kleinmeister*, and are reminiscent in some ways of the early Marcantonio when he was studiously imitating Northern models'

What may well be the artist's first known engravings are the two little scenes showing "Christ's Entry into Jerusalem" and the "Expulsion of the Money Changers" (Cat. 1-2). While the "Entry" adheres to the conventional Northern presentation of the subject, as found in Dürer's small woodcut "Passion," the second, with its powerful, expressive figures and the introduction of Italianate participants in the foreground forms a suitable introduction to the artist's vigorous personal style, which may have been shaped by Altdorfer. Duvet conveys an inconsistent yet convincing sense of enclosure and spatial recession through erratic changes of scale. The "Annunciation in a Church" (Cat. 3), probably dating from about 1515 is more fully French in style. Only the drapery, with its abstract energy, and the very unusual, slightly Italianate form of the wingless annunciate angel suggest that the artist's vision extends beyond the art of his own country. He employed Antwerp Mannerist and North Italian sources in the same fashion as Jean Bellegambe. The Virgin is typical of the art of the French détente style: her quiet, almost weary grace like that of the sculpture of Michel Colombe and the painting of Bourdichon. The print relates to the international current at the end of the fifteenth and the early sixteenth centuries, combining Gothic and classical forms, typified by Laurana, who worked from Sicily to Marseille.[56]

A beautiful marble fragment of an angel at Salmaise (Côte-d' Or), believed by David to have been a Saint Michael, has much of the vital fusion of late medieval art with a certain Italianate quality so characteristic of Duvet.[57]

The iconography of the "Annunciation in a Church" is late medieval, exemplified by the Jan van Eyck "Annunciation" (Washington, D.C., National Gallery of Art) which Duvet may have seen at the Chartreuse de Champmol in Dijon. The areas of flick-work and variegated, empirical patches of shading seen in the "Annunciation" reappear in a completely Italianate work, the "Sebastian" (Cat. 4), its composition taken from a Moderno plaque (Text fig. 1). A detail such as the table-fountain design incorporated with the ornament of the pilaster at the right, points to the fundamental importance of the artist as goldsmith. The first evidence of what will prove to be constant adaptation from the Marcantonio circle can be seen in the diminutive Lucretia embedded in the architectural decoration at the lower right. The sculpture on the façade of Saint-Michael (Dijon, Text fig. 29) follows Duvet's Italian sources within the next two decades and parallels his fusion of classical and biblical references in depicting the triumph of Saint Michael. On the plinth supporting the statue of the victorious saint of the Apocalypse, the sculptor included a relief of Lucretia as an *exemplum virtutis*, also based on the Marcantonio engraving.[59]

Duvet's interest in Italian engraving of the late fifteenth century is apparent in the powerfully simplified rendition of the torturers at the left (Cat. 4). It recalls Mantegna's art in its dramatic contrast to the smooth, and that of Lucas van Leyden in the delicate hatching used for the figure of Saint Sebastian. In the "Woman of the Apocalypse with Cornucopia" (Cat. 5), copied after Marcantonio, only the curious contrast between Mary's clumsy hand and the flat, applied look of the cornucopia added by the French engraver point to his authorship.

"The Triumph of David" (Cat. 6) continues the victorious imagery of the preceding engraving. Here, a Pollaiuolesque figure is set within a North Italian triumphal arch, possibly derived from the woodcut title page of a Lombard publication. Its vigorous adaptation of Florentine Quattrocento forms may well predate the adaptation of similar Italian motifs in woodcuts by Gabriel Salmon. The technique used for David is especially close to the Claesz prints.

Duvet's employment of contemporary Northern art becomes obvious in his "Saint Jerome in the Wilderness" (Cat. 7) which is copied from an engraving by Lucas van Leyden (Text fig. 72) dated 1516. The French artist has also consulted Marcantonio's print after the original Lucas (Text fig. 73). Thus Duvet's work represents a fusion of

71. *Marcantonio Raimondi,* Death of
Lucretia, *early sixteenth century, Paris,
Bibliothèque Nationale.*

73. *Marcantonio Raimondi after Lucas van Leyden,*
Saint Jerome in the Wilderness.

72. *Lucas van Leyden,* Saint Jerome Penitent, 1516.

Netherlandish composition with a coarser, blacker engraved line and an emphasis on the profile taken from Italy. Duvet's receptivity to Italian currents, in contrast to contemporary French metalcutters, can be seen by comparing the engraving with the cut used for Saint Jerome's *Introductorium morale*, printed in Paris in 1519 and entirely based on German sources—Dürer and Baldung Grien.[60]

A major combination of North and South can be seen in the artist's "Cumaean Sibyl" (Cat. 8) which amalgamates two separate subjects of Roman High Renaissance art—the engraving after Raphael's fresco at Santa Maria della Pace (Text fig. 2) and the architectural background of Marcantonio's "Lucretia" (Text. fig. 71). What makes the engraving Duvet's own is the infusion of a late Gothic excitement, created by the demonic little Burgundian angels, their setting reflecting those of contemporary mystery plays. Their dramatic pose in a somewhat awkward setting is startling. The great vessel upon which the Sibyl rests her foot may represent an example of the engraver's work as goldsmith.

Duvet's "Saint Michael" (Cat. 9), probably dating before 1520, was a pioneer Burgundian essay in adaptation from the decorative vocabulary of the Italian High Renaissance. It is more than ten years older than the lost statues of the archangel on the retable of Saint-Michael in Dijon, carved between 1530 and 1532.[61] Although the arabesques on the armor could have been copied from Italian or Northern engravings, Duvet's experience as a metal worker no doubt contributed to the convincing rendering not found in its immediate source—a Raphaelesque engraving by Agostino Veneziano (Text fig. 74).

The Judgment of Solomon (Cat. 10) and the *Virgin and Child in the Clouds* (Cat. 11) show Duvet's further interest in the art of Marcantonio. While the latter print is one of the few engravings in which the artist has made a direct copy with only one modifica-

74. *Agostino Veneziano after Raphael*, Cumaean Sibyl.

tion, the former incorporates figures from prints after both Mantegna and Raphael. High Renaissance models are followed in the "Annunciation of 1520" (Cat. 12), and the "Cumaean Sibyl," whose illegible date may be read as 1517. The increasing interest in this style throughout the North may nave resulted from the arrival in Brussels of the Raphael cartoons of 1515 and 1516 to be used for the weaving of the Sistine tapestries. But while borrowing motifs from Rome, Tuscany and Umbria in the figures of the great Gabriel and the kneeling Mary, Duvet still places them in a courtyard recalling Lombard sources of the later fifteenth century. The print is described by Blunt as "a startling work for its date, owing to the pure Italian style which it displays"; he further claims that the "architectural setting [is] more accurately classical than anything to be found in a contemporary French work; [while] the figure has an almost Correggesque sentiment; and the angel reveals a knowledge of current Roman painting."[62] The scene also points to the settings of mystery plays, such as those recorded in 1547 by Hubert Caillau (Text fig. 75).[63]

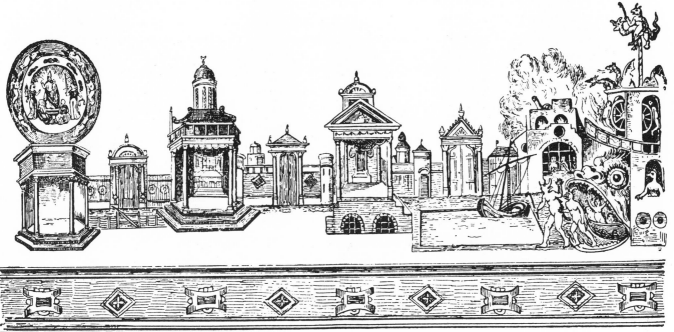

75. *Hubert Caillau.* Staging for 'Le Mystère de la Passion' (drawing after ms.),
Valenciennes, 1547, Paris, Bibliothèque Nationale.

This print is a milestone in the history of French art, the earliest known securely signed and dated engraving which displays the sophisticated assimilation of Italian art of the High Renaissance. Despite its obvious dependence upon foreign sources, the work demonstrated the individual character and precocity of Duvet's art. Neither the many misunderstood borrowed forms nor the confused rendition of space obscure the great power of the provincial French artist. Engraved when Duvet was thirty-five, the print shows him to be at a stylistic crossroads between the careful technique of his first phase—in the execution of Mary and Gabriel—and the hasty, expressionistically scratched putti at the left and right, belonging to his final manner.

Consonant with the irregular emergence of his later works, Duvet's prints always seem to have come in fits and starts. In a single year—1520—he made his first securely dated works, mostly in a Netherlandish or *Kleinmeister* style, but some also evidencing a sudden switch to High Renaissance vocabulary, probably stimulated by a journey he may have made to Italy in that year. However, there is no need to ascribe the change in style to such a voyage since almost all his early Italianate works are copies after prints by Marcantonio or Agostino Veneziano. It may even be the case that the artist began with Italianate works sometime before 1520—and then went to the Altdorfer- and *Kleinmeister*-like "Entry" (Cat. 1) and "Christ Driving out the Money Changers" (Cat. 2).

The first work which indicates the sort of original use of Italian elements that would point to a direct acquaintance with Bramantesque art is the "Annunciation of 1520" (Cat. 12). Although an Italian journey has been postulated as an essential element in the creation of this print, so free in its use of High Renaissance motifs, almost all of them are known to have appeared in reproductive prints.

Some of the expressionistic aspects of Duvet's art may be attributed to his enlivement of the abstract, reduced character of the reproductive prints to recreate the vivacity of the original.

The style of the "Annunciation" seems to have been revived several years later in Duvet's "Nativity with a Candle" (Cat. 28), in which the North Italian architectural motifs are replaced by a more Roman background.

From 1520 on, despite his residence outside the center of court patronage, Duvet was able to maintain his extraordinary primacy in Italianate art. Though many of his works are derivative, Duvet's genius allowed him to utilize and transform the works of others so as to make them his own. His evolution from late Gothic to the timid Italianism of the *Kleinmeister* and their Netherlandish contemporaries, and finally to the full-blown High Renaissance of Marcantonio and Caraglio, is among the outstanding achievements in French sixteenth century art.

In 1524 Duvet executed two engravings for a projected commemorative medal of Adrian VI (Cat. 13, 14) who had died in the preceding year. The papal portrait is derived from Marcantonio and the verso from engravings after coins. At approximately the same time, Duvet prepared most of a series of seven roundels of saints (Cat. 15-21); possibly for adaptation by artisans. Numerous records of the artist's own activities as a versatile craftsman survive. The first in the series may be considerably earlier than the rest, relating to the "Entry of Christ into Jerusalem" (Cat. 1).

"Christ and the Woman of Samaria" (Cat. 22) probably reflects Duvet's oeuvre as goldsmith in the design of the vessel in the foreground and that of the well, which resembles a monstrance. Partially adapted from Dirk Vellert's print of the same subject, the engraving reveals Duvet in repeated contact with Netherlandish printmakers. The crowded figures at the upper right anticipate the frenzied spirit of the artist's later Apocalypse illustrations, while the monumentality of the protagonists points to Goujon's art at mid-century.

The best documented year of Duvet's activity as engraver is 1528, the date of four strikingly Italianate prints (Cat. 23-26). "The Holy Family with Angels" (Cat. 23), based upon an unknown painting of the Roman or Tuscan School, must be numbered among the most impressive engravings of the French Renaissance. Despite the naiveté evidenced in the clumsy handling of the tree at the right and in the distinctly nonintegral quality of the attributes which Duvet appears to have inserted for his own complex symbolic purposes into the Italian source, it is a print of profound spirituality and immediacy, unequalled in Duvet's career until his last works.

Returning to a Northern fifteenth century compositional source, the "Saint John the Baptist and Saint John the Evangelist Adoring the Lamb" (Cat. 24) also shows continued dependence upon the Marcantonioesque physiognomy in the features of the Evangelist. The "Entombment of 1528" (Cat. 25) derived from several Italian sources, is perhaps the artist's most complex essay in the manner of the High Renaissance, with its puzzling motif of the centurionlike figures bearing the dead Christ. Certainly the most classicizing of all Duvet's works is the "Allegory of the Power of Love" (Cat. 26), whose probable literary source, Propertius, points to close contact between Duvet and the humanistic canons of the episcopal court of Langres. The hard, scalloped cloud forms surrounding the corpse in two of the 1528 engravings reappear in the "Suicide of Judas" (Cat. 27). The Judge is somewhat reminiscent of Campagnola. A great triumphal way in the background must spring from such architecture erected by Duvet for the royal Burgundian visits; the suicide of Judas is a theme linked to the dramatic productions of the time.[64]

Although the "Nativity with a Candle" (Cat. 28) may be unfinished, it has a
sketchy, freely rendered quality which points to a new source of inspiration, a more
painterly aesthetic possibly stemming from etching. Following Parmigianino's lead,
Italian printmakers assumed the spontaneity and calligraphic freedom of the etched or
freely drawn line. This was introduced to Fontainebleau by the Italian master's follower
Fantuzzi[65] who used it in the 1540s to reproduce the works of Rosso and Primaticcio.
Duvet adopted the appearance of this technique for the engraving of such courtly sub-
jects as the "Death of a Stag" (Actaeon?) (Cat. 29), copied in reverse from an etching by
LD, the Fontainebleau master also active in the 1540s. The sheer pictorialism of the
Italian landscape eludes Duvet who was untrained as a painter.

Duvet returned to the Quattrocento in the "Entombment" (Cat. 30), engraved
after a Mantegna School print. Dispensing with the landscape background of his model,
the artist concentrated upon the figures alone, which are defined by long, free, scratchlike
lines which betray an emotional involvement in the scene, far from the cautious technique
of the engraver's early works. This increasing sense of experimentation and technical
freedom is seen later in Duvet's use of the counterproof (British Museum) for one of
the Apocalypse plates (Cat. 61). French Renaissance counterproofs are exceedingly rare.[66]

The style of the "Nativity with a Mouse" (Cat. 31) is characteristic of the artist's
middle period. While some areas of the print are engraved with the punctilious care of
his first works, the scene as a whole with its rich use of blacks and the rather sketchily
indicated ceiling point toward the mature style of the *Apocalypse*, as does the essentially
tablet-shaped composition. The classical figure of Mary is still reminiscent of Marcantonio,
yet the print as a whole suggests Aertsen-like Netherlandish artists of the mid-sixteenth
century.

Duvet's Italianism was so far in advance of that of any native French artist ac-
tive around 1520 that it must remain in the category of the isolated phenomenon.
For example, the early work of Jean Cousin, almost contemporary with that of
Duvet remains in obscurity. Furthermore, French sculptural ateliers, especially those at

76.   Master L.D. after Penni? The Death of Adonis.

149

Troyes, although they utilized Italian motifs in piecemeal fashion, never seemed interested in or capable of undertaking any large-scale essay in the spirit of the High Renaissance. The same is true for the sculpture of Burgundy for the greater part of the first half of the sixteenth century.

Related to Duvet's mature Italianism and similarly based upon prints after Cinquecento works is the art of Simon de Chalons, who was born in the Champagne, not far from Burgundy. A signed and dated painting of 1535 (Text fig. 77) executed in grisaille inspired by an Italian work and showing the "Doubting Thomas" (Louvre), has some of the force and fervor of Duvet's prints. Active in Avignon from 1542 until his death in 1561, the painter must have had ample opportunity to see advanced Italian art because of the large Italian colony in that center.[67]

A link between Fouquet's Italianism and that of Duvet's generation was provided by Simon du Mans (Hayeneufve), now known primarily from the inscription of his epitaph and the lines in *Champfleury* in which Tory praised Du Mans as a great designer of letters and as a draughtsman.[68]

Born in 1450, he was not only an artist adept at painting, sculpting, and architecture, but was also a cleric and seems to have spent many years of his youth in Italy, possibly in the study of Law.[69] Returning to Mans before 1495, he was active mainly as architect and supervisor of building, until 1528 when he withdrew to the Abbaye de Saint-Vincent where he continued to work as a designer until his death in 1546.[70] Writing in 1584, LaCroix du Maine compared Simon du Mans to Michelangelo and Dürer, presumably an indication of his sources, if not his quality.[71]

One obscure contemporary of Duvet's was Nicolas Denisot du Mans (1515–59). Under Simon du Mans's tutelage, Nicolas was initially a painter, cartographer, maker of topographical renderings, and calligrapher. Primarily however, he was active as a poet, suggesting the sort of humanistic, Italian-oriented creation which could be achieved in

77. *Simon de Chalons,* Doubting Thomas, *1535, Paris, Louvre.*

150

France during the first half of the sixteenth century, regardless of distance from the chief centers of patronage.[72]

The powerfully Italianate oeuvre long ascribed to Félix Chrestien, a cleric attached to the episcopal court of François II Dinteville and active in nearby Auxerre, has been reassigned by Jacques Thuillier to a Dutch painter.[73] The anonymous master's Romanizing style, so effectively asserted in the "Varzy Triptych" of 1535 (Varzy, Eglise Saint-Pierre) and seen again in the Dinteville family allegory of "Moses and Aaron before Pharaoh" (New York, Metropolitan Museum of Art) of 1537 with its more Northern orientation, shows that a painter of real authority was active in the diocese neighboring Duvet's Langres. The style of the swordsman seen from the back in the "Varzy Triptych" and the figures in the "Stoning of Saint Stephen (Text fig. 78) (Auxerre, Cathédrale de Saint-Etienne), fleshing out linear transcription of High Renaissance works, may well have been of interest to Duvet, whose Unicorn Series utilized related forms.[74]

78. *Pseudo-Chrétien*, Martyrdom of Saint Stephen, *Auxerre, St.-Etienne.*

It is no coincidence that the closest approximation to the engraver's later works is found in stained glass, tapestry, and armor. The increasingly important contribution of a minor arts aesthetic to Duvet's art was first observed by William Ottley who noted in 1838 that even the artist's early work, such as the "Annunciation of 1520" (Cat. 12), "is composed in a way peculiar to the artist's talent in design, which no doubt formed a portion of his labours in the decoration of gold and silver articles of his manufacture."[75] The marked eclecticism and outright imitation of motifs from prints by Italian and Netherlandish masters seen in Duvet's oeuvre is in itself fully consistent with a craft practice. The closest parallels to Duvet's derivative process can be found among the *émailleurs* in their free use of graphic sources. Léonard Limousin, the most famous enameler, was also an occasional printmaker, and his enamels were based upon wide knowledge of the graphic arts.[76] Such applied eclecticism began early in the century, as shown by an enamel triptych made by the atelier of Jean I Pénicaud, where scenes from the life of Christ are based on Mantegna's "Lamentation" and Dürer's "Small Passion."[77] A plaque by Jean II Pénicaud adapts figures from Marcantonio's "David and Goliath," Agostino Veneziano's engraving after Raphael of the "Bataille au Coutelas" and another figure of an angel from Marcantonio's *Santa Felicità.*[78] From Duvet's early "Sebastian" (Cat. 4), it is apparent that he consulted Italian medals as well as prints. His interest in armor, no doubt stimulated by ceremonial regalia he manufactured for the Langres triumphal entries, was evident in the sword hilt design embodied in the "Cumaean Sibyl" (Cat. 8) and in later works such as the "Revelation of Saint John the Evangelist" (Cat.

39), where the form of the eagle is derived from a Milanese helmet design.

In 1524 Duvet completed a great reliquary head of Saint Mammès. Despite this documentation of his activity as sculptor in precious metals, his approach to form was basically two-dimensional. Just as a "rolled-out" rendering of a chalice or other object is more useful to the goldsmith than an illusionistic depiction, so are many of the artist's engravings founded in the disposition of borrowed motifs over the engraved surface. Whether the artist attempts to create depth through a rather erratic perspective construction or through "prefabricated" space copied from another engraving, a decorative, tapestrylike area is the usual result. This fundamental guide to his pictorial approach might best be called the "tapestry style."[79] The tapestry enjoyed a continued vogue in the late Renaissance; due in part to its romantic associations, Ariosto often compared his chivalric text to a woven scene.

Using the formal approach customarily reserved for the ornamentation of *boiserie*, armor, stained glass, weaving, or goldsmith's work, many of Duvet's major engravings spring from the prevalent decorative style.[80] Such publications as *La tapisserie de l'église chrestienne et catholique en laquelle sont depaint la Nativité, Vie, Passion, Mort et Resurrection de . . . Jésus Christ*, a series of 189 woodcuts published by Estienne Groulleau in Paris in 1549, show the metaphoric impact of the tapestry formula. Another book, published in Lyon in 1540, addresses itself to "ymagiers et tailleurs, Painctres, brodeurs, orfèvres, ésmailleurs," urging them to "prendre en ce livre aulculne fantasie comme ilz feroient d'une tapisserie."[81] The wide circulation of the Raphael tapestry cartoons in Northern Europe may have accentuated and reinforced the traditionally popular importance of the oblong decorative format.[82] Perhaps the chief reasons for the currency of this style may be the fact that French artists of the time, almost all of whom sprang from a "craft" rather than an "art" tradition, only felt at home working within a fusion of the two. The undulating, graceful *maniera* approach also worked well within the elegant confines of the tapestry field.

Despite the more austere, classicizing currents entering French art and thought toward the middle of the sixteenth century, the tapestry aesthetic continued in relatively unabated form. Ronsard, in his *Préface sur la Franciade*, commenting on the proper use of the *alexandrine*, praised various poetic devices which, in the hands of a:

> bon artisan, qui les face autant qu'il luy sera possible
> hausser, comme les peintures relevées, & quasi separer
> du langage commun, les ornate & enrichissant de Figures,
> Schemes, Tropes, Metaphores, Phrases et periphrases es
> eslongness presque du tout ou pour le moins separées,
> de la prose trivial & vulgaire (car le style prosaique et
> ennemy capital de l'eloquence poetique) & les illustrant
> de comparaisons bien adaptées, de descriptions florides,
> c'est à dire enrichies de passements, broderies, tapisseries
> & entrelacements de fleurs poetiques, tant pour representer
> la chose que pour l'ornement splendeurs de vers . . .[83]

The establishment in Troyes of Domenico Fiorentino's sculptural atelier in 1541 may have interested Duvet, as the Tuscan master (described by Vasari as Rosso's best pupil) was the most technically adept printmaker in France.[84] With the 1540s production of the Fontainebleau reproductive print ateliers, Duvet was stimulated to a new spurt of graphic activity. The need to reproduce Rosso's unorthodox drawing style at Fontainebleau contributed to the formation of a new linear attack that was far more personal than even the direct etchings by such a great master as Parmigianino. The shortcuts, broken profiles, schematic and abstract approach, renunciation of the completeness of the *maniera*—even when used to recreate it—resulted in a revolutionary austerity. It may be that the aristocratic, Neo-Platonic approach of the *non-finito* so dear to the genius of the High Renaissance—exemplified by Leonardo and Michelangelo—also legitimized aspirations to a new graphism of suggestion rather than completion. It might well have seemed to Duvet that the etchings and engravings of Fantuzzi, the Master LD and many others at the court atelier continued and affirmed aspects of the French goldsmith's vigorous, freely realized style, which through royal patronage, now became the establishment's. There are several examples which demonstrate how Duvet borrowed motifs from the "Palace Style." In one case, he directly copied a work in its entirety—the "Death of a Stag" (Cat. 30). At this point in Duvet's life, he had access to a storehouse of visual imagery that surprisingly matched his own. This source enabled him to increase his imaginative vocabulary in a far more personal and immediate fashion than if he had accepted the foreign influence of Dürer and Marcantonio alone.

While the Unicorn Series is in the Fontainebleau manner, the many changes in style and in the protagonists within the group suggest that it was not a single, continuous project. The complex, mystical allegory is presented in a tapestrylike format.[85] The etchings begun in 1542 by Fantuzzi, after Giulio Romano's Sigismund sequence in Mantua,[86] might have been an important model for the format of the Series.

The sophisticated level of patronage at Langres toward the middle of the century may best be observed in the commission given to Jean Cousin in 1543—the period when Duvet resided in Geneva—for eight tapestries of scenes from the life of Saint Mammès for the cathedral. The three surviving panels (Text figs. 11-13) are according to Gébelin, the earliest documented tapestries showing full French absorption of the Italianate art of Fontainebleau.[87] They represent Duvet's most immediate source for a modified Fontainebleau manner, possibly providing an important stimulus for the genesis of the Unicorn prints.

Duvet might also have been interested in a magnificent tapestry cycle of uncertain authorship (possibly Cousin) depicting scenes from the life of Diana for Diane de Poitier's château at Anet, probably completed by the early 1550s (Text fig. 59)[88] The figure style and detail in the first two engravings of the Unicorn Series, for instance the rendition of the tree-supported canopy (Cat. 32, 33), corresponds with three of the Cousin tapestries, conforming to a prevalent mid-sixteenth century decorative formula.

By the later 1530s the French grasp of Italian sixteenth century art became increasingly strong. Rosso, Rustici, and Primaticcio were fully established; Cellini, Niccolo dell'Abbate, and Salviati came within the next two decades. Castiglione's *Cortegiano* was published in French in 1537, and Serlio's *Primo Libro d'Architettura* printed in 1545. In 1546 the most beautiful of Italian illustrated books, the Aldine *Hypnerotomachia Poliphili* of 1499, appeared in a new, almost equally lovely and indisputably French woodcut version. With the combination of architectural and sculptural creative talent that went into the building of the Louvre in the mid-1540s, French classicism was established as a distinct, superb manifestation of the late Renaissance. This achievement was paralleled in the literary arts of the Pléiade, their language fortified by Du Bellay's *Défense et illustration de la langue française* of 1549. The exquisite fusion of all these elements is seen in the text and woodcuts commemorating the Parisian triumphal entry of Henri II in the same year. At just this time when sculptors, painters, and graphic artists (often Duvet's junior by a generation) were consolidating and reshaping the style he first established in France about thirty years before, the more than middle-aged Duvet embarked upon his masterpiece. The *Apocalypse,* for all its adaptations from Dürer and the High Renaissance stands as a major monument to the new force of French art around 1550.[89] The Apocalypse series, especially the accompanying "Martyrdom of Saint John" (Cat. 38) recalls the windows at Ecouen. Executed in 1541–42, the rich chiaroscuro of painted glass is based upon prints by Caraglio and the Master of the Die after Perino del Vaga.[90]

Both the Unicorn and Apocalypse series fall within the tapestry style. Their visual emphases, despite adaptations from Dürer and the Roman printmakers are confined within a decorative program. The tablet-shaped Apocalypse plates closely resemble heavily ornamented parade shields, swarming with rich, densely packed imagery whose articulation generally depends upon a formal, externally imposed order rather than an internal, pictorial logic. In the Unicorn Series, three of the six prints appear to have been engraved close in date to the early plates of the "Apocalypse," (Cat. 32-34); they are more formal in composition, and finished in technique than the others.

Continuing his stylistic alliance with Northern graphic artists, toward the middle of the century, Duvet turned to the next generation, which included Frans Floris and Jan van Hemessen. The *Apocalypse* engravings are very close in spirit to Floris's "Fall of the Rebel Angels" (Cat. 31), the engraver's adaptations from the School of Fontaine-bleau are tempered by this Netherlandish orientation; they also borrow heavily from prints after Primaticcio (often made by Northerners).

In addition to his adaptations of Marcantonio, the *Apocalypse* is also partially inspired by a later generation of Italian printmakers, such as Ghisi, Bonasone, and Caraglio. Duvet's most important essay in the court style is the engraved "triptych" for Henri II (Cat. 62-64), commemorating his coronation and his father's death. These prints were probably executed around 1548 and may have been devised to interest the young king in the engraved *Apocalypse*, begun two or three years before under François Ier. In these plates Duvet achieves a vigorous elegance and forthright heraldic grace which is close to the most fashionable art of the day. Whatever time could be spared from more immediately remunerative work must have been devoted to the engraving of the *Apocalypse* and its associated prints over a period of about ten years. Duvet probably executed them while engaged in Burgundy and Geneva as mint master, decorative painter, pageant master, military engineer, window and tapestry designer, and goldsmith.

Limiting its narrative scope to a restrained synthesis of the twelfth chapter, Duvet's engraving for the text is perhaps the most beautiful of the series (Cat. 50). Duvet adopted Dürer's woodcut of the same scene (B.71; Text fig. 79, in reverse), confining the composi-

79. *Albrecht Dürer,* Woman Clothed with the Sun, *1497/98.*

154

tion within an arch-shaped area and investing it with an opulent chiaroscuro. Translating Dürer's late Gothic vocabulary into the language of early sixteenth-century Roman ornament, Duvet has created a monument of Burgundian Renaissance art. The artist's passionate character transforms the Dürer derivations, while his fervent vision infuses and unites his eclectic, ornamental creation by assemblage. The abstract, decorative quality of the German woodcut was already close to Duvet's taste and has been intensified by the French engraver through such devices as Mary's mandorla and her star-studded halo. The profound variety of textures that he was able to create in rendering feathers, textiles, hair, and fur enriches the work. Whereas the engraved figure of God the Father is directly dependent upon Italian sources, that of the Son carried to Heaven is copied from Dürer's woodcut—a product of his Italian journey.[91] Unlike most of Duvet's Italianate works, this engraving with its outspoken tonal transitions points more to Florentine printmaking of the Quattrocento than to the School of Marcantonio.

After the completion of the thirty tablet-shaped engravings, Duvet seems to have returned to the projected Unicorn Series. Enlarging the narrative, he engraved three additional plates which were executed in a distinctly looser and more spontaneous style than were the first (much earlier) three. Despite their occasional reflection of French and Italian prints, the "King Pursued by a Unicorn" (Cat. 66), "Triumph of the Unicorn (Cat. 67), and "Unicorn Purifying the Water with his Horn" (Cat. 68) show the increasing sense of technical spontaneity and emotional freedom of the artist's late style. At about the same date, Duvet was printing and repairing the delicate copperplates of his *Apocalypse* for an illustrated French one in 1561.[92] The engraver's concern with the mystical, evidenced in his very earliest signed prints and most elaborately presented in the *Apocalypse* and its Frontispiece, is seen in the last visionary print of the Unicorn Series—the beast's triumph in heaven, probably dated 1561 (Cat. 67). Here the artist's overwhelming concern with immediacy of image results in an expressionistic, impatient technique, to be continued throughout his final works.

"Genius without talent," as was once said of Van Gogh could also characterize Duvet. A visionary without academic training, the French printmaker seized upon others' works and bent them to his own uses. The Frontispiece of the *Apocalypse* is singularly apt as a stylistic self-portrait since the acknowledged degree of collaboration between the engraver and "the judgment of more learned men brought to bear" could also be extended to include the more academically trained artists upon whose works he drew. Duvet found little use for the words "imitation", "derivation" and "eclecticism" in the sense that he considers any source as but another tool, applicable in a pictorial sense toward the full realization of his images.

The curious fusion of technical finesse and coarseness, realism and naiveté of the "Unicorn Purifying the Water with his Horn" (Cat. 68) may be explained by its having been started contemporaneously with the three first engravings in the series, which were set aside for several years and then completed with the concluding plates. "Three Horses Rearing" (Cat. 69) continues the engraver's Fontainebleau manner, recalling an oval print after Primaticcio (Text fig. 80).[93] It may be Duvet's last completed engraving in the courtly style.

The contemporary adaptation of Northern art in sixteenth century Italy and of Renaissance art by the North, although motivated for different reasons, often produced surprisingly similar results. Mannerists seized upon the expressive religious imagery of the late Middle Ages as a documentary and authentic encounter with religious experience before this became an official policy of the Counter-Reformation. Duvet and some of his colleagues, though unschooled in, but keenly aware of the academic achievement, turned to Italy to provide the *dramatis personae* for the show of essentially Gothic visions. Anthony Blunt has made a valuable comparison between Pontormo and Duvet, suggesting that the relationship between the devotional art of the Florentine Mannerist and the official style of the Medici court parallels that of Duvet and the arts at Fontainebleau.[94] He proposed that the relatively liberal personality of Cardinal de Givry of Langres, an active reformer within the Church, could have influenced Duvet's art. This infers that

80. Master L. D. after Primaticcio. Alexander and Bucephalus, *Vienna, Albertina.*

the Confrérie du Saint Sacrement to which the engraver and his wife belonged, was to Duvet what the Roman Oratory of Divine Love was to Michelangelo. However, it is difficult to reconcile the doctrinaire, orthodox focus of the Burgundian chapter to the far broader, more speculative ambience of the Italian religious society. Those painters, sculptors, and other artists Givry is known to have brought to Langres did not differ from the popular courtly trends in French art. This group of artists included Jean Cousin, Jacques Prévost de Gray and François Gentil, who all worked in a modified Fontainebleau manner. Givry's patronage, painstakingly recorded in studies by L. E. Marcel, is not known to have included Duvet, although fortifications (App. G) and a medal (App. D.1) may have been designed for him by the engraver. Many of Duvet's most important early works, clearly establishing his artistic identity were completed before the future Cardinal de Givry came to Langres in 1529; a print (Cat. 5) could reflect his commission.

The personal, fervent late engravings look as though they had been urgently scratched onto the copperplate with a needle rather than by the slower channeling process which used a burin. They reveal some of the passionate intensity of Pontormo, whose art was represented at Fontainebleau by a "Visitation" as well as a "Raising of Lazarus" ordered by François Ier in 1529.[95] Duvet's "Moses and Saint Peter" (Cat. 73) may be traced to Florentine Mannerist sources (Text figs. 81-82).Even in his most evocative late works, Duvet returns to some of his earlier sources—the "Unfinished Entombment" (Cat. 71) revives the Mantegnesque themes employed by him four decades before. The *Pestblatt* of Saints Sebastian, Anthony, and Roche (Cat. 70) also recalls Mantegna and has a curiously Umbrian quality as well. The "Despair and Suicide of Judas" (Cat. 68) is Duvet's last work to use themes of the mystery plays to delineate Judas's final moments, including him twice on the same page, in a cinematic continuum. The print which has been variously catalogued as the experimental, tentative works of a young artist or as the results of an enfeebled hand and mind, definitely must come after the engraved *Apocalypse*. The inflated, awesome grandeur of the heads of "Moses and Peter" (Cat. 73) recall the baloonlike physiognomies

81. *Agostino Veneziano after Bandinelli,* Two Philosophers.　　82. *After Rosso,* Saint Paul and Saint Peter.

by James Thurber and were, like the works of the American cartoonist, produced when, in Duvet's own words (engraved on his "Self-Portrait as Saint John the Evangelist" (Cat. 65) his sight was failing and his hands beginning to tremble.

Undiminished by their creator's physical infirmities, these last engravings have the authority which seems to come at the end of life. "The Moses and Saint Peter," the "Unfinished Entombment," the "Saints Sebastian, Anthony, and Roche," and the "Despair and Suicide of Judas" are statements of such individual apprehension that they defy categorization. With the sketches of the late Titian or Degas, these final prints have an expressive freedom and emotional abandonment that is beyond style. Engraved with the harsh immediacy of a tatoo, their images seem punctured upon the thin skin of the artist's old age, a last visionary will and testament.

Like much else about Duvet, the question of his influence is a most elusive and difficult one.[96] As the engraved *Apocalypse* is itself so derivative, the later sixteenth century works devoted to the same subject, some of which seem to stem from Duvet's, more probably share a common source. Only one obscure later sixteenth century print-maker seems to have recorded reminiscences of the French master's work in his own illustrations, the Netherlandish Master GP (Paludanus).[97] A prominent printmaker from Lorraine named Pierre Woeriot, may also have consulted Duvet's oeuvre. Born around 1531–32, Woeriot was a talented, erudite aristocrat who made several trips to Italy and was one of the first after Duvet to make engraved book illustrations. Duplessis pointed out that some of Woeriot's "Images de la Bible" of 1580 resemble Duvet.[98] The plague scenes are similar to the *Apocalypse*, although Woeriot may also been influenced by Marten van Heemskerk. As Woeriot was in Lyon in 1554 and probably visited Langres in order to engrave a portrait of Jean Roussat, a canon at the episcopal court, it is quite possible that he saw works by Duvet who was then a resident of Geneva.

Another artist who could have been concerned with Duvet's oeuvre was Georges Reverdy, only recently recognized as a Frenchman rather than an Italian.[99] The style of an undescribed roundel by Reverdy, dated 1538 and inscribed ZACCHEUS at the top and

157

LUCE 19 with the engraver's monogram at the bottom, is especially close to that of Duvet who may have been his teacher.[100]

One of the twelve engravings signed FG is remotely similar to Duvet's oeuvre.[101] It has been suggested that the monogrammist is François Gentil of Troyes, who worked in Langres in the 1550s. A letter written by the painter, sculptor, and engraver Jacques Prévost de Gray, active in Langres toward the middle of the century, may refer to Duvet, and led Boullaye to suspect that the latter taught Prévost printmaking.[102]

Despite his primary vocation as a woodworker in Dijon, Hugues Sambin's career closely parallels that of Duvet in the second half of the century as printmaker, military engineer, pageant master, and Protestant. His woodcut designs of terms—fantastic architectural decorations in the Rustic Style— have a protobaroque abandon recalling that of his possible teacher Duvet. The *Livre de Termes* was printed in Lyon by Marcorelle, who may have assisted Duvet in the publication of the *Apocalypse* in 1561.[103]

It is appropriate that the most striking instance of Duvet's influence in the sixteenth century should be found in Spain, where the archaic aspects of his *Apocalypse* must have had great appeal. The Seville sculptor Diego de Pesquera, active in the second half of the sixteenth century, made a relief of the "Adoration of the Whore of Babylon," whose composition depends in large measure on Duvet's engraving of the same subject (Cat. 55).[104]

It was not so unlikely for a Spanish woodcarver to come across Duvet's engravings since there was already a Spanish tradition of Burgundian sculptural activity in the fifteenth century which continued into the sixteenth in the works of Philippe Bigarny, born in Duvet's diocese of Langres, and known in Spain as Felipe de Borgoña. Active in Burgos, Toledo, Valencia, and Granada, before his death in 1543, Borgoña or other French sculptors in Spain may well have brought Duvet's engravings along with them.[105]

Perhaps the greatest influence of Duvet's art may have been exerted upon the restoration of a famous antique statue, the Barberini "Faun." Struck by the similarity between the ecstatic Saint John (Cat. 60) and the Faun, some critics have long suggested that the former depended upon an unknown example of the latter, which was only discovered in the early seventeenth century and found in fragmentary state. The provocative statue was "completed" by a Berninesque artist, the reconstruction similar to the engraved Saint's pose. Seymour Howard, noting Maffeo Barberini's predilection for French culture, proposed that Duvet's print may have provided the model for the Faun's restoration, also suggesting that Bernini may have employed the Apocalypse print for his Sebastian made for the same patron.[106] As Pope Urban VIII, Barberini may have selected the French Christian source for the restoration of his *Faun* as emblematic of his New Rome. Howard emphasized the fact that the statue was excavated on the border of the Old City, on the threshold of the New, analogous to John's situation in the Apocalypse ecstatic as the New Jerusalem was laid bare before him. Tempting as this suggestion may be, it should be remembered that Duvet himself drew upon prints after Rosso (B.XIV, 26) and Giulio Romano (B.XIV, p.83, no. 93), not far removed from the completed *Faun*.

While Roman restorers may have adapted Duvet's ecstatically abandoned poses for the reconstruction of the Barberini Faun, the engraver's art was assiduously assembled at the same time in the North. The Cleveland Museum's splendid *Apocalypse* is thought to have come from the collection of the greatest etcher—Rembrandt van Rijn.[107]

For all the mystical fervor of his oeuvre, Duvet's multifaceted biography implies a certain stoic resilience, a sentiment close to the art of the succeeding century. The inscription provided by one of the artist's humanist friends for the Frontispiece of the *Apocalypse figurée* may well have had this characteristic in mind, since it stems from the lines of Seneca and Plutarch, followed by Tertullian. Appropriately, it was Poussin, the greatest French master of the classical image who employed similar lines to those on the engraving by the first French master of the High Renaissance vocabulary. Blunt recognized the similarity between the words written by Poussin when he was near death, to those on Duvet's engraving. Poussin said that though his servant—the painter's hand—was weak, the master—his mind—could still compel the rendering of the essence of his art.

Duvet had written: "Death is upon me and my hands tremble, my eyes are already beginning to fail, yet the spirit remains victorious and I have completed my great work."[118]

Duvet biographers have pointed out the striking resemblance between his oeuvre and that of William Blake; this has been most recently and eloquently explored by Anthony Blunt.[109] Blake's teacher Fuseli, while making fun of a French mannerist—Bellange—in his writings, shows a very obvious debt to the French Mannerist in his art. William Ottley and other collectors of the period, most notably William Esdaile and William Beckford, were building up brilliant collections of Duvet's oeuvre. The similarity between the work of the two artist-mystics lies mainly in the fact that they were both "primitives" who were endowed with great vision but had little formal training, and who depended upon prints primarily after the art of Raphael and Michelangelo as a point of departure for their highly creative, most individual eclecticism. Separated by more than three centuries, both artists may have utilized the identical prints of the Roman School for their emblem-like transposition of motifs. Had Blake been as seriously interested in the art of Duvet as has been suggested, one would certainly expect such concern to manifest itself in the English artist's Apocalypse illustrations, but there is no similarity whatsoever.[110]

Considering the extraordinary communality of style and spirit between Jean Duvet and William Blake, the following lines from the latter's *The French Revolution* are strangely evocative of the life and faith of his precursor. When the King of France, with the Duke of Burgundy, tells Necker to rise—

> Dropping a tear the old man his place left, and when he was
> gone out He set his face towards Geneva to flee; and the
> women and children of the city Kneel'd round him and
> kissed his garments and wept: he stood a short space in
> in the street,
> Then fled, and the whole city knew he was fled to Geneva,
> and the Senate heard of it.

The whole poem recasts recent French history in the language of the Apocalypse, in a re-creation of the language and vision of Saint John. Blake's theology resembles the mystical manifestations of the Familists to whom Duvet may have belonged. The English artist's emphasis upon freedom and individuality is also close to the spirit of the Libertins of Geneva. His All Religions Are One corresponds to the difficult desire for both unity and independence so characteristic of the late Renaissance. The first principle in Blake's poetry which reads "That the Poetic Genius is the true Man, and that the body or outward form of Man is derived from the Poetic Genius. Likewise that the forms of all things are derived from their Genius, which by the Ancients was call'd an Angel and Spirit & Demon" is founded upon the same profoundly personal, eccentric assimilation of Neo-Platonic thought found in the *Apocalypse* Frontispiece.

Both artists, though separated by two centuries, were autodidacts in art and faith. They invented their own worlds and based the shape of their visions upon those of the Italian High Renaissance. Both were printers as well as printmakers and saw the graphic process as bonded to that of the communication of word and image at one and the same time. All Religions Are One was etched, not type-set in 1788 and was subtitled, "The Voice of one crying in the Wilderness." Doubtless Duvet saw himself in the same prophetic light. Blake's principle 6, "The Jewish and Christian Testaments are an original derivation from the Poetic Genius" is etched within the same confines as Duvet's Apocalypse plates and his monogram, The Tablets of the Law.

Another artist who was drawn to Duvet was Delacroix. Delacroix had a lifelong interest in early engravings and as a result, as Jean Adhémar records, he spent much time time in the 1830s and 40s examining the collection at the Bibliothèque Nationale. His drawings for the Palais Bourbon project of 1833–38 include two (Baltimore Museum of Art, Text fig. 83) and the Louvre (Text fig. 84) inscribed "les anges de Jean Duvet" and "Jean Duvet."[111] In the 1840s, the Romantic master adapted motifs from Rosso and Primaticcio for other projects.[112] Another major mural commission for a chapel at Saint-

83. *Eugene Delacroix,* Studies for the Expulsion of Heliodorus, *Baltimore Museum of Art, on indefinite loan from the Maryland Institute, George A. Lucas Collection.*

84. *Eugene Delacroix,* Studies for the Expulsion of Heliodorus, *1833/8, Paris, Musée du Louvre, Cabinet des Dessins.*

85. *Eugene Delacroix,* Heliodorus Expelled from the Temple,
1849-53, Study for painting in St. Sulpice, Paris; Cambridge,
Fogg Art Museum, Harvard University, Gift of Philip Hofer.

Sulpice, circa 1850, once again led Delacroix to Duvet's oeuvre, due in part to his subject
—the victorious Saint Michael (for the vault)—and an arched format (for the walls) both
of which abound in the engravings. A drawing for the "The Expulsion of Heliodorus"
(Cambridge, Mass., Fogg Art Museum, Text fig. 85) at Saint-Sulpice has written across
the bottom "voir Duvet pour les anges."[113] None of Duvet's prints show angels especially
close to the one in this drawing and Victor Carlson has suggested that the reference may
have been to another drawing cut off from the upper part of the sheet.[114] However, none
of the figures are directly borrowed from Duvet—it is as if Delacroix were acknowledging
the spirit rather than the letter of the engraver's art. He did however, prepare line drawings after at least one of the Unicorn Series—"The King Pursued" (Paris, private collection).[115]

In his Journal for 27 April 1824, Delacroix recorded:

> At Leblond's. Interesting discussion about genius and
> unusual men. Dimier thought that great passions were the
> source of genius. I think that it is imagination alone, or
> better still, what amounts to the same thing, that delicacy
> of the organs that makes one see where others do not see,
> and which makes one see in a different way. I was saying
> that even great passions joined to imagination lead most
> often to disorder in the mind, etc. Dufresne said a very
> true thing: what made a man unusual was, fundamentally,
> a way utterly peculiar to himself of seeing things. He ap-

161

plied it to the great captions, etc., and finally to the great
minds of all sorts. So there are no rules for great souls:
rules are only for people who have merely the talent that
can be acquired. The proof is that they do not transmit
this faculty. He was saying: "How much reflection is needed
to create a beautiful, expressive head, a hundred times more
than for a problem, and yet at bottom, the matter is merely
one of instinct, for it cannot explain what brings it about."
I note now that my mind is never more excited to create
than when it sees a mediocre creation of a subject that is
suitable to me.[116]

This passage provides insight into Delacroix's special fascination for Duvet's genius—his
sympathy for the engraver's passionate, imaginative approach. Despite the damning con-
notation of the word "mediocre," it may nonetheless lead to another clue to Delacroix's
need to acknowledge Duvet's art as a source for his own which significantly, bears no
close resemblance to that of his French forebearer. Obviously, the great painter had no
need for Duvet's figures as specific models. The goldsmith's fiery appropriation of
Renaissance art, invested with a primitive urgency, stimulated Delacroix to revive and
reshape the engraver's figures beyond recognition in an almost mystical transference, creating a Renaissance of his compatriot's art. Without a conservative faith, yet commissioned
by the state to produce devotional art, Delacroix no doubt found Rosso's and Duvet's
pietistic expressionism a point of departure for his own essays in an alien field. His
earlier biblical subjects had stressed the narrative rather than the mystical. Courbet,
Rodin and others were to employ the Images d'Epinal in similar fashion.

In another entry (25 January 1857), written as though he had Duvet's art in mind,
Delacroix observed that

"Engraving is in reality translation, that is to say, the art of
transporting from one art into another, as the translator does
in the case of a book written in one language and which he
transports in his own. The foreign language of the engraver,
and it is here that genius is shown, does not solely consist of
imitating the effects of painting by means of his own art,
which is like another language. He has, if one may say so,
his own language; it gives his works a characteristic stamp
and, in a faithful translation of the work he is imitating, al-
lows his special feeling to shine through."[117]

Part of Duvet's compelling appeal to the present may be due to the apparent
similarity of his creative processes with those of this century—to *assemblage*, surrealism,
expressionism and the black magic of such older masters as Goya, Bresdin, and Redon.
The abstract energy of his sense of pattern, coupled with an almost disturbing specificity
of detail, recall Picasso's "Dreams and Lies of Franco." The sixteenth century master's
entrancing engraved tapestries resemble a cinematic projection of the mystery and passion
of the late Northern Renaissance, made all the more immediate by a certain technical
crudity. The coarseness of his craft has, to twentieth century taste, a virtuoso quality
of deliberate rejection of academic refinement, an old brutalism gratifyingly prophetic
of the new.

Artists and viewers seeking the delineation of the passionate extreme of agony and
ecstasy will find the art of Duvet a triumph of independent vision. Follow Delacroix's
bidding— "Voir Duvet pour les anges."

1. See Alphonse Germain, *Les néerlandais en Bourgogne,* (Brussels, 1909).

2. For Charles VIII in Italy and its art, see M. Sanudo, *La spedizione di Carlo VIII in Italia,* ed. R. Fulin (Venice, 1873); Eugène Münz, *La renaissance en Italie et en France à l'époque de Charles VIII* (Paris, 1888); Eve Borsook, "Décor in Florence for the Entry of Charles VIII of France," *Mitteilungen des kunsthistorischen Instituts in Florenz* X (1961): 106-22; Anatole de Montaiglon, "État des gages des ouvriers italiens employés par Charles VIII," *Archives de l'art français* I, (1851-52): 94-132.
Documents for the transport of works of art from Naples to Amboise in 1495 are reproduced by Ludovic Lalanne, "Transport d'oeuvres d'art de Naples au château d'Amboise en 1495," *Archives de l'art français* II, (1853): 305-6.

3. Ruth Mortimer, Harvard College Library, *Department of Printing and Graphic Arts, French 16th Century Books,* (Cambridge, 1964), vol. I, Cat. 255, pp. 311-12; G. Ritter and J. Lafond, *Manuscrits à peinture de l'école de Rouen* (Rouen-Paris, 1913), p. 18, Pl. XXX-XXXII; P. Renouard, *Bibliographie des impressions et des oeuvres de Josse Badius Ascenius, imprimeur et humaniste* (Paris, 1908), vols. I-III; Paul Durrieu and Jean J. Marquet de Vasselot, "Les manuscrits à peintures de la Bibliothèque Imperiale de Vienne," *Bulletin de la Société française de reproduction de manuscrits a peinture* II (1912): pp. 5-53, esp. 31-33.

4. L.F. and L.E. Marcel, *Artistes et ouvriers d'art à Langres avant la Révolution* (Langres, 1935), p. 75, no. 398.

5. See F. Gébelin, *Le style renaissance en France* (Paris, 1942), pp. 106-7.

6. Nicolas Spinelli, a Florentine medalmaker listed in the Inventory of Charles le Téméraire of 1468 as "tailleur et graveur des sceaux du duc de Bourgogne," was still active in Lyon in 1494. Prosper Valton, "Notice sur une medaille faite au XVe siècle à la cour de Bourgogne," *Revue numismatique,* Sér. 3, V: 76-80, discusses medals by another Italian artist active in Burgundy 1467-72, one of which shows Charles le Téméraire as a Roman emperor. Matteo del Nassaro, who, according to Herbet made three etchings in France, came to Paris in 1515 from Verona to set up a school of lapidary work and *orfèvrerie.* He was listed in 1529 as *graveur du roi,* among the earliest recorded instances of this term. Like Duvet, Nassaro designed medals, tapestries, and triumphal entries, and practiced damascening and engineering. See H. de la Tour, "Matteo del Nassaro," *Revue numismatique,* Sér. 3, II (1893): 517-55. Vasari stated that Nassaro was *maître de la monnaie,* but de la Tour does not believe this to be correct. Nassaro's ninety-two designs for embroideries depicting scenes from Virgil's *Bucolics* (executed in Flanders in 1521) must have afforded an important document of pre-Fontainebleau Italo-Flemish style.

7. Henri David, *De Sluter à Sambin,* II, *La renaissance* (Paris, 1933), p. 125. See also Raymond Koechlin and J.J. Marquet de Vasselot, *La sculpture à Troyes au seizième siècle* (Paris, 1900), chapter 6, "Survivances gothiques et influences de la Flandre et de l'Allemagne," pp. 141-55.

8. For this painting, see Father Marchese, *Lives of the Most Eminent Painters, Sculptors, and Architects of the Order of Saint Dominic,* trans. Rev. C.P. Meehan (Dublin, 1852), vol. II, p. 361. See also Otto Mündler, *Essai d'une analyse critique de la notice des tableaux italiens du Musée nationale du Louvre* (Paris, 1850), p. 87, where the inscription is given. According to Félibien, another work by Fra Bartolommeo, also meant for San Marco, a "Saint Sebastian", was in the possession of Louis XII. See André Félibien, *Entretiens sur les vies et sur les ouvrages des plus excellents peintres, anciens et modernes* (Paris, 1685), vol. I, p. 208. See also Janet Cox Rearick's Louvre exhibition catalogue of 1972-73 on the collection of François I.

9. The tomb of Guillaume Fillastre at the abbey of Saint-Bertin was ordered from Andrea della Robbia in 1469; fragments are at the Musée de Saint-Omer. See Joseph du Teil, *Guillaume Fillastre* (Paris, 1920).

10. An inscription on the "Nativity" states that it was made for a member of the Bourbon-Montpensier family. The date is illegible and has been variously read between 1483 and 1496. See Salomon Reinach, "Le Ghirlandaio d'Aigueperse," *Bulletin archéologique de Comité des travaux historiques et scientifiques* (1918), pp. 201-7; Aby Warburg, "Nativite d'Aigueperse," *Rivista d'arte* VI (1904): 85 ff; Paul Manz, "Une Tournée en Auvergne," *Gazette des Beaux-Arts*, Sér. 2, XXXIV (1886): 375-87; Geza de Francovich, "Benedetto Ghirlandaio," *Dedalo* VI (1925-26): 708-39.

11. For Davide Ghirlandaio's mosaic (Musée de Cluny), see Henri Sauval, *Histoire et recherches des antiquités de la ville de Paris* (Paris, 1724).

12. Mantegna's "Saint Sebastian" at the Louvre came to France in 1481, following Gilbert de Montpensier's marriage to a Gonzaga. See Jacques Dupont, "A propos d'un tableau aux armes de Jacques Coeur," *Bulletin de la Société de l'histoire de l'art français*, (1934), p. 18. The same article pointed out that a school of Filippo Lippi "Annunciation" in Munich has the arms of Jacques Coeur incorporated within the architecture. The "Anunciation" has recently been attributed to the Master of the Barberini Panels. See Federico Zeri, *Due Dipinti, la filogia e un nome* (Turin, 1961), pl. 13, p. 13.

13. First published by P. Perdrizet, *Annales de l'Est: bibliographie Lorraine* (1909-10), pp. 106-7. Perdrizet changes the reading of the date to 1512 and relates the artist "tattorum" to the family of artists originating in Florence and active in the Veneto.

14. Wilhelm Suida, "Leonardo da Vinci und seine Schule," *Monatsheft für Kunstwissenschaft* XIII (1920): 265. See also the unsigned *Thieme-Becker* entry for Francesco de' Tatti (XXXII: 465), connecting the drawing and the painting.

15. S.J. Freedberg, *Painting in Italy, 1500-1600* (Baltimore, 1971), p. 271.

16. For Solario's activity at Gaillon, see Lisa de Schlegel, "Andréa Solario," *Rassegna d'arte* XIII (1913): 89-99, 106-109.
    Elizabeth Chirol, "Le chateau de Gaillon," *Premier foyer de la renaissance en France* (Paris, 1955), pp. 38-39; Roberto Cohen, "The Castle of Gaillon in 1509-1510," *Journal of the Warburg and Courtauld Institutes* XVI (1953): 1-12.
    Gaillon had a "Descent from the Cross" by Perugino, as well as a "Nativity" by Solario, active there 1509-11. See Deville, *Comptes de château de Gaillon* (Paris, 1850), vol. I, pp. 69, 124, 361, 363. A painting by Mantegna was presented to Georges d'Amboise by Isabella d'Este in Milan in 1499.

17. See Otto Pächt, "Jean Fouquet: A Study of his Style," *Journal of the Warburg and Courtauld Institutes* IV (1940-41): 85 ff. For the Viator, see also Mortimer, *French 16th Century Books*, vol. II, Cat. 420, p. 523; also L. Brion-Guerry, *Jean Pèlerin Viator* (Paris, 1962).

18. Paul Lacombe, *Livres d'heures imprimés au XVe et XVIe siècles conservés dans les bibliothèques publiques de France* (Paris, 1907), no. 147 (B.N. Res. 550535). Reference courtesy of Myra D. Orth.

19. George Clutton, "Two Early Representations of Lutheranism in France," *Journal of the Warburg and Courtauld Institutes* I (1937-38): 291, n. 1, related Salmon's strong personality and originality, coupled with an isolation from contemporary artistic developments, to Duvet's life and works. Salmon engraved a depiction of Heresy for Gringoire's *Blazon des hérétiques* of 1524. See Pierre Marot, "Les origines allemandes de Gabriel Salmon, peintre et graveur au monogramme G.S.," offprint from *Mémorial du voyage Rhénanie de la Société nationale des antiquaires de France* (Paris, 1953). See also Albert Ohl de Marais, *Byblis* (Winter, 1931), pp. 139 ff.
    See also Jean Adhémar, *Inventaire du fonds français* (Paris, 1938), vol. II, pp. 92-93; Mortimer, *op. cit.*, vol. I, Cat. 258, pp. 314-19.
    Like Duvet's father, Salmon's father was in the arts, recorded as "Bernard de Heidelberg, painctre", active in Lorraine from the early 1470s onward.
    Gabriel was first listed as working in Luneville in 1514-15 and at Nancy in the early 1530s, both fairly near Duvet's work centers. Woodcuts in his style appeared until the later 1540s.

164

20. For his illustrations for Nicole Volkyr de Serouville's *L'histoire & receuil de la triumphante et glorieuse victoire obtenue contre les lutheriens par Anthoine duc de Lorraine* (Paris, 1526) see Mortimer, *op. cit.*, vol. II, Cat. 553, pp. 677-78.

21. Auguste Bernard, *Geofroy Tory, peintre et graveur, premier imprimeur royal, reformateur de l'orthographie et de la typographie sous François Ier* (Paris, 1865). Bernard estimated Tory to have been born ca. 1480 (pp. 289-92); see also Myra Dickman Orth, "Geofroy Tory: The Illustrations and Decorations in His Printed Books of Hours" (M.A. thesis, New York University, Institute of Fine Arts, 1964), p. 15.
    See Paul Chenu, "Documents des archives sur l'hôtel Lallemant," *Bulletin archéologique du Comité des travaux historiques et scientifiques* (1941/42), pp. 519-55; Paul Vitry, *Hôtels et maisons de la renaissance français* (Paris, n.d.), vol. II, Pl. XX-XXI; Ernest P. Goldschmidt, *Les Heures de Jean Lallemant written by Geoffroy Tory in 1506* (London, 1927). For a similar manuscript belonging to the same family, see Walters MS No. 446 in the Walters Art Gallery, *Illuminated Books of the Middle Ages and the Renaissance* (Baltimore, 1949), Cat. 46, References courtesy of Myra D. Orth.

22. See E. Gavelle, "Les influences de l'art allemand sur l'art champenois au XVIe siècle," *Revue germanique* XV (1924): 265-79; see also Paul Biver, "Modes d'emploi des carton par les peintres-verriers du XVIe siècle," *Bulletin monumental* LXXVII (1913): 3; Louis Réau, "L'influence d'Albert Dürer sur l'art français," *Bulletin de la Société nationale des antiquaires de France* (1924): 101-25. See also Julius Held, *Dürers Wirkung auf die niederländische Kunst seiner Zeit* (The Hague, 1931), and Émile Mâle, *L'art religieuse de la fin du moyen âge en France* (Paris, 1949), pp. 443-56. For the importance of the French *peintre-verrier,* see F. Mathey, *Les trésors d'art de l'école troyenne* (Musée de Valuisant, Troyes, 1953).

23. Trained in Antwerp, the *peintre verrier* Arnoult was active around 1500, working on the stained-glass windows for Tournai cathedral. He then went to Rouen, where he was in the employ of Antoine Bohier, abbot of Saint-Ouen and Fécamp, who was a close friend of Cardinal Georges d'Amboise, perhaps the most important early patron of Renaissance art in France. See Jean Lafond, "Le peintre-verrier Arnoult de Nimègue (Aert van Oort) et les debuts de la renaissance à Rouen et à Anvers," *Actes du XVIIe Congrès international d'histoire de l'art* (The Hague, 1955), pp. 333-44.

24. Quoted by *ibid.,* p. 333.

25. See A. van der Boom, "Un peintre-verrier néerlandais à l'étranger, Arend Ortkens de Nimègue," *Nederlands Kunsthistorisch Jaarboek* II (1948-49): pp. 75-103; Émile Mâle, "Quelques imitations se la gravure italienne par les peintres-verriers français du XVIe siècle," *Mélanges Henri Lemonnier* (Paris, 1913), pp. 140-42.

26. C. Huisman, *Pour comprendre les monuments de Paris* (Paris, 1925), p. 106, fig. 153. Marcel, II, pp. 160-161, 169. This reattribution recalls Jacques Thuillier's discoveries. See his "L'Enigme de Félix Chrestien," *Art de France* I: pp. 57-74.
    A stained-glass window dated 1531 depicting the Judgment of Solomon in Paris (Saint-Gervais, chapel of Saint-Jean-Baptiste), long attributed to Robert Pinaigrier, has been found to be of Netherlandish design, the work of an Antwerp artist.

27. R. Koechlin and J.J. Marquet de Vasselot, *op. cit.*

28. See Ghislaine de Boom, *Marguerite d'Autriche et la pre-Renaissance* (Paris-Brussels, 1935), p. 51. For the château, see Jane de Jongh, *Margaret of Austria, Regent of the Netherlands* (London, 1954), pp. 98-99.

29. Jules Gauthier, "Conrad Meyt et les sculpteurs de Brou en Franche-Comté," *Réunion des sociétés des beaux-arts des départments* XXII (1898): pp. 253 ff. See also his "Les initiateurs de l'art en Franche-Comté au seizième siècle," *ibid.,* XVIII (1893): p. 609; also Wilhelm Vöge, "Konrad Meit und die Grabdenkmäler in Brou," *Jahrbuch der königliche preussische Kunstsammlungen* XIX (1908): pp. 77-118, for a definitive discussion; also the exhibit-

ion catalogue *Margareta van Oostenrijk en haar hof* Mechelen, 1958; *Marguerite d'Autriche,* (Bourg, 1958, Musée de l'Ain).

30. David, *De Sluter à Sambin,* II, Chapter 5, "La resistance gothique," pp. 1-110.

31. Hilaire Belloc, *Avril, Being Essay on the Poetry of the French* London, 1904, p. i. Vambelli was actually from Bruges — Gilles van Belle.

32. A. Blunt (*Art and Architecture in France,* 1500-1700, Penguin, 1953) noted, "After 1500, however, there are few signs of real activity in painting proper, though certain works to be found in the eastern provinces of France suggest that there may have existed a competent school of religious painters yet to be rediscovered and isolated from contemporary Flemish work" (p. 18); on p. 237, n. 19, he wrote that the "Saint Jerome" (Brou) and the "Last Supper" triptych (Autun) "may be genuine French products; but our present knowledge is too incomplete for any definite statement." The Autun triptych is reproduced in Louis Réau, *Les richesses d'art de la France: La Bourgogne,* Fasc. I and II, *La peinture et la tapisserie* (Paris, 1927), Pl. 20-24. Several of these works have been examined with characteristic brilliance by Michel Laclotte ("Quelques tableaux bourguignons du XVIe siècle," *Studies in renaissance and baroque art presented to Anthony Blunt on his 60th birthday* [London-New York, 1967], pp. 83-85).

33. The woman may be derived from an engraving of the Leonardo School. See A.M. Hind, *Early Italian Engraving,* London, 1940, vol. VI, Pl. 622; vol. V, Cat. 15, pp. 91-92. Laclotte (*op. cit.,* p. 84, n. 2) quoted John Shearman as suggesting the artist's adaptation of Marcantonio's "Last Supper."

34. The *Jerome Triptych* is listed in the *Marguerite d'Autriche* catalogue (Bourg, 1958), Cat. 7, p. 16 as Flemish School. Laclotte (*op. cit.,* p. 84, n. 6) included it with works by French painters. Perhaps the work may prove to have been commissioned by the bishop of Bourg-en-Bresse, the humanist Henri Botteus (de Bottis). For his interests, see P.S. Allen, *Opus Epistolarium des. Erasmi Roterodami* (Oxford, 1906-58), vol. VII, 1928, p. 376, no. 1985. Also, Erwin Panofsky, "Erasmus and the visual arts," *Journal of the Warburg and Courtauld Institutes* XXXII, 1969: p. 204.

35. See Alphonse Germain, "L'ancien triptyque de Nôtre-Dame de Bourg," *Gazette des beaux-arts,* Ser. 5, VII 1923: pp. 114-20. Germain has recognized the eclectic sources from North and South contributing to the design of the triptych, assigning it to Franco-Burgundian authorship. The donors of the work were identified by V. Nodet, "Donateurs des tableaux de la sacristie de Notre-Dame de Bourg," *Annales de la Société d'émulation de l'Ain,* 1904, as Nicolas Chichon and his wife Jaquette de la Botte. The triptych was shown in the *Exposition de la Passion* at the Trocadero in 1934, Cat. 174, "The Lamentation", and Cat. 109, "Christ Bearing the Cross."

36. Details such as the three putti above are taken from the Nativity (B.85) in the same series, but presented in classicized form.

37. See David DuBon, *The Chapel of the Château of Pagny,* Philadelphia Museum of Art, Philadelphia, n.d.; also Marcel, *op. cit.,* II, pp. 99-108. Formerly in the collection of George Gray Barnard, the altar was attributed by Martin Weinberger to the studio of Pieter Coeck van Alost in the sale catalogue, New York, 1941, pp. 26-27, Cat. 117, Pl. XXXIII-XXXVI. The altar seems still closer in style to a similar carved and painted retable of the life of the Virgin attributed to Moreau, at the Chapelle Castrale, Enghien. See J. Borchgrave d'Altena, "La retable de Herbais-sous-Pietrain," *Bulletin des musées royaux d'art et d'histoire,* Ser. 3, XIV, 1942: pp. 15-24; see also *Arts religieux* Tournai-Cathedrale, 1958, Pl. XI, Cat. 21, p. 23.

38. See D. Yabsley, *Jean Lemaire de Belges: la plainte de Desire,* Paris, 1932, p. 39. Grete Ring ("An Attempt to Reconstruct Perréal," *Burlington Magazine* XVII [1950]: p. 225) has suggested that "Gentile Bellini" rather than referring to Giovanni's brother, stands for Giovanni, the word *gentile* being used to characterize his art. This seems like a correct interpretation, as Gentile hardly goes along with Perugino and Leonardo, nor was he especially famous at the time of the poem. There is a possibility, which Miss Ring does not mention, that the poet may have been thinking of a painting by Gentile acquired by

Louis XI from the Venetian church of S. Francesco della Vigna.

39. See André Linzeler, *Inventaire du fonds français,* Paris, 1932-35), vol. I, pp. 361-70. Garnier is listed as "graveur au burin, peut-etre aussi peintre, né vers, 1470-75 et travaillant encore en 1544."

40. According to Passavant *(Le peintre graveur,* Leipzig, 1864. vol. VI, p. 272). the engraving is listed twice by Heller, nos. 704 and 707, and dates from the end of the sixteenth century.

41. Paul Kristeller *(Thieme-Becker,* vol. VI, p. 606) thought Cinericius was probably Netherlandish, influenced by the Master S. Passavant *(Le Peintre Graveur* [Leipzig, 1864], vol. V. p. 228) wrote that Cinericius was a Dominican monk named Ascher (in an Italian monastery) and that the kneeling figure with a music scroll in the "Saint Peter Martyr" represents a self-portrait. He omitted the AVI UN inscription. Cinericius engravings are in the Reserve of the Cabinet des Estampes at the Bibliothèque Nationale, where they are listed by their Passavant numbers, 4130 and 4131, recorded by François Courboin in his *Catalogue sommaire des gravures et lithographies comprisant la réserve* (Bibliothèque Nationale, Paris, 1900-1901), as being Italian (AA1 Rés.). Another engraving in the Reserve AA2, inscribed FRATER FRANCISCUS DOMEN ECANUS ADS 1488, a large, coarse print relating the lives of Christ and Mary in many small squared-off scenes, may also be French or perhaps North Italian. A print reproduced by Henri Delaborde, in *La gravure en Italie avant Marc-Antoine* [Paris, 1883], opp. p. 179), described as being by "maitre milanais anonyme" also depicts scenes from the life of the Virgin in a style similar to that of the preceding print and might be regarded as an example of early French printmaking. Two small engraved roundels in the Bibliothèque Nationale may be added to Cinericius' oeuvre; both have been listed by Courboin 693, and "The Death of Lucretia," Courboin 796. They probably date from the teens or early twenties.

42. Franco Simone, *Il rinascimento francese,* Turin, 1961, p. 38.

43. Bibliothèque Nationale 63.B 30308. Ea. 196 rés.pet.fol Anonymous, Courboin *op. cit.,* 348; Passavant, *Le peintre-graveur* (Leipzig, 1864) vol. VI, pp. 78, 31, The words are from the Song of Solomon 1:22, "Let him kiss me with the kisses of his mouth."

44. E. Maurice Bloch, "The Iconography of Andrea Mantegna's Half-Length Pictures of the 'Madonna and Child'," M.A. thesis, New York University, Institute of Fine Arts, 1942. Courboin recognized the print to be French.

45. Hind (*Early Italian Engravings* [London, 1948] vol. V, Cat. Part II, p. 265), wrote: "I am inclined to place the engraver in the School of Bologna, and near to the work of Master I.B., with bird and early Marcantonio." Karl Heinrich von Heinecken (*Idée générale d'une collection d'estampes* [Leipzig, 1771], p. 487) and Alessandro di Baudi di Vesme ("Il Maestro della Trappola," *L'Arte* [1921], p. 175) attempted to link the engraver to a hypothetical Paduan artist.

46. See a note by Kurth Rathe, who revives Heinecken's French view, in the *Mitteilungen der Gesellschaft für vervielfältigen Kunst* (1931), pp. 27-29. The print is illustrated there and in Hind, Pl. 849.

47. The print is reproduced by Hind, Pl. 850. It was copied in reverse by Agostino Veneziano (B.XIV, 313, 415) and reissued by Antonio Salamanca in 1530. A French print dealer in Rome, Salamanca made a practice of buying up plates and often re-engraved them.

48. For an anonymous early sixteenth-century manuscript illuminator who demonstrated a precocious grasp of Italian art of the period, see Paul Durrieu, "Un mystérieux dessinateur de début du XVIᵉ siècle: le Maître du 'Monstrelet' de Rochechouart," *Revue de l'art ancien et moderne* XXXIII (1913): p. 324. Durrieu compared the works of this artist with those of the engraver Master NA DAT; and Myra Dickman Orth, "Geoffroy Tory: The Illustrations and Decorations in his Printed Books of Hours," M.A. thesis, N.Y.U. Institute of Fine Arts, 1964, p. 40, n. 78, has pointed out that the portrait of Louis XII in the manuscript relates to the same engraver's "Virgin and Child". Since some of the illustrations in the three volumes of the *Chroniques de Enguerrand de Monstrelet* of 1510 (Paris, Bibliothèque Nationale, MS.fr. 20360-62 are

inscribed in Flemish, they may perhaps be the work of a Netherlandish artist active in France, in the employ of Francois de Rochechouart, governor of Genoa from 1508 to 1512 and subsequently in the service of François Ier The architectural details and the borders are entirely within the decorative style of Northern Italy and done in a most accomplished manner as is the perspective and general planning of the compositions. Another manuscript by the same master is an *Histoire universelle abregée,* present whereabouts unknown.

49. Léon de Laborde, "Godefroy, peintre de François Ier," *Revue universelle des arts* I, 1855: p. 6. The manuscript is Bibliothèque Nationale MS. fr. 12.429. I-III. A Petrarch *Trionfi* is, according to Franco Simone, *Il Rinascimento Francese,* Turin, 1961, p. 184, n. 1, also illuminated by "Godefroy le Batave." See H. Martin, *Catalogue des manuscrits de la Bibliothèque de l'Arsenal,* Paris, 1889, vol. VI, p. 201. For Albert Pigghe, see Lynn Thorndike, *A History of Magic and Experimental Science,* New York, 1941, vol. V, pp. 279-83.

50. The text (quoted by Jean Adhémar, "Les origines du nom de graveur," *Bibliothèque de l'Ecole des chartes,* L [1939]: p. 234-38) is taken from Thevet's *Hommes illustres,* Part IV. The first French center mentioned by the author is Lyon, which Adhémar, doubtless correctly, interprets as a reference to the engravings of Woeriot, Reverdy, and Gourmont published there in the middle of the century.

51. The major work on these artists is Max Friedländer, "Nicholaus Hogenberg und Frans Crabbe die Maler von Mecheln," *Jahrbuch der preussischen Kunstsammlungen* XLII (1921): pp. 161-68.

52. For Vellert, see A.E. Popham, "Dierick Vellert," *Print Collector's Quarterly* XXV, 1925: pp. 343-68; also E. Bock and J. Rosenberg, *Die niederländische Meister,* Berlin, 1930, pp. 55 ff. The French popularity of Vellert may be seen in the "Judgment of Solomon" window at Saint-Gervais based on a drawing attributed to the engraver, and the use of the latter's "Saint Bernard Adoring the Virgin" for a window in the choir at Conches (Eure). (Gébelin, *Le style renaissance* [Paris, 1942], p. 61.)

53. Popham, *op. cit.,* p. 94. See F.W.H. Hollstein, *Dutch and Flemish Etchings, Engravings, and Woodcuts* (Amsterdam, 1949), Cat. 233, p. 227.

54. Malaspina di Sannazaro in his *Catalogo di una raccolta di stampe antiche* (Milan, 1824), vol. IV, *Scuola francese,* pp. 13-15, attributed Claesz's "Baptism of the Eunuch" and his "Lady with a Dragon" to Duvet. The latter engraving relates in subject matter to "Poison-Contre-Poison," another formerly assigned to Duvet, which was also given to the French engraver in the Italian catalogue. See Appendix A.1 for this print. Hollstein, *op. cit.,* IV, p. 120, recorded these prints.
The monogrammist AC's "David and Goliath" is so close to Duvet's early engravings that were it not for the initials, the print would be attributed to the French artist. B.IX, 117, 20; Hollstein, p. 10 (illustrated).

55. The monogrammist S, among the most prolific and least-known engravers of the first quarter of the sixteenth century, offers another Netherlandish parallel for aspects of Duvet's style. Probably active in Brussels as a goldsmith as well as printmaker, the monogrammist has left only two dated works — from 1519 and 1520 — but his production clearly extends to the mid-century. Dependent upon Dürer and Lucas van Leyden as well as the Kleinmeister, the Netherlandish engraver's large number of prints, like those of his contemporary Allaert Claesz, were consulted by designers throughout the North. See Hollstein, XIII, pp. 121-223.

56. Pierre Quarré, *La Chartreuse de Champmol, foyer d'art au temps des sucs Valois* (Dijon, 1960), pp. 7, 15.

57. David, *De Sluter à Sambin, op. cit.,* II, fig. 51, p. 157.

58. Ernest F. Bange, *Die italienischen Bronzen,* Berlin, 1922, vol. II, pl. 46.

59. See David, "Le Grand Portail de l'église Saint-Michel de Dijon," *Mémoires de la Société des arts de Dijon* I, 1923: pp. 225-52.

60. Mortimer, *op. cit.,* Cat. 269, p. 332. The metal-cut is reproduced on p. 332.

61. David, *De Sluter à Sambin*, fig. 53, p. 160, reproduces a detail from a Saint Michael at Santenay-le-Haut (Côte-d'Or) which he believes to reflect the lost figure from Dijon (p. 161, n. 1). See also pp. 215 ff.

62. Blunt, *op. cit.*, 1970, p. 66.
    "Duvet may have known the Raphael design from the engraving of Agostino Veneziano, but the real understanding of High Renaissance Italian design displayed in these ["The Sibyl," "The Annunciation of 1520," "The Judgment of Solomon"] and other early works leads to a conclusion that he must have visited Italy and have seen the works of Raphael and his contemporaries for himself. It is otherwise hard to see how he should have an understanding of them so much in advance of his fellow countrymen" (Blunt, *Art and Architecture in France, 1500-1700* [London, 1953], p. 71). Blunt also stated that Popham "makes the important point that his engravings after Raphael's "Cumaean Sibyl" agree with the original and not with any of the Italian engravings after it. Duvet must, therefore, either have worked from the original or from a drawing brought back by another artist from Rome" (*Ibid.*, p. 84, n. 102).

63. For Hubert Cailleau, see the exhibition catalogue *La vie théatrale au temps de la renaissance,* Institut pédagogique national, Paris, 1963, pp. 15-19, which refers to two manuscripts of *La Passion de Valenciennes* 1547, Bibliothèque ıe Nationale, MS. fr. 12, 536 (to which Mâle refers) and MS. coll. James de Rothschild 1.7.3. Both were illustrated by the same hand, the first serving as a model for the second. Documents relating to these were published by Petit de Julleville, *Les mystères* Paris, 1880, vol. II, pp. 145 ff.; *Catalogue James de Rothschild,* vol. IV, pp. 368 ff. The first ms. is the better known, the illustrations published by Gustave Cohen, *Le théâtre en France . . .* Paris, 1928, vol. I; also the fine study by George R. Kernodle, *From Art to Theater* Chicago, 1949; J. Jacquot, *Les fêtes françaises de la renaissance* Paris, 1956-60.

64. This engraving is similar in stylistic adaptation to a bas-relief at Saint-Jean, Troyes, showing "The Repentance of Judas" (Koechlin and Marquet de Vasselot, *op. cit.*, fig. 28). Duvet's interest in the iconography of Judas, known from his three representations of the subject, suggests that he may well have known this relief, attributed to the Julliot workshop; it is dated ca. 1530 by Koechlin and Vasselot on p. 240.

65. See Henri Zerner, "L'eau-forte à Fontainebleau: le rôle de Fantuzzi," *Art de France* IV (1964); pp. 70-85.

66. One of the few known counterproofs is of Marc Duval's "Christ and the Woman Taken in Adultery" (Bibliothèque Nationale) (R.D. 1) after Lotto.ɔ. A copy of the Duval print was once attributed to Duvet (App. B.5).

67. See Charles Sterling and Hélène Adhémar, *La peinture au Musée du Louvre, école française, XIVe, XVe, et XVIe siècles* Paris, 1965, Pl.169, Cat. 58. p. 24; *Thieme-Becker* XXIII, p. 574 (listed as Simon de Mailly).

68. Paris 1529, Livre II, folio 14 v.; see also Livre LV, folio 41 v.

69. See LaCroix du Maine, *Bibliothèque générale des auteurs de France* Paris, 1584, pp. 457-58.

70. See Thieme-Becker, *Künstler-Lexikon* XVI, p. 173 (Hayeneufve) for various works that have been attributed to him.

71. No traces have been found of an Italian artist in Orléans employ known as Piètre André, active in the late fifteenth century. See Ulysse Robert, "Piètre André, peintre des ducs d'Orleans (1456-1491)," *Nouvelles archives de l'art français* V 1877: pp. 120-35. For Italian artists active in Lyon, see Natalis Rondot, "Les artistes et les maîtres des métiers étrangers ayant travaillé à Lyon," *Gazette des beaux-arts,* Sér. 2, XXVIII 1883: pp. 157-69.

72. See Clément Jugé, *Nicolas Denisot du Mans* (Paris, 1907).

73. Jacques Thuillier, "L'énigme de Félix Christien," *Art de France* I 1961, p. 69. The triptych is reproduced on pp. 58, 67, 71, 72.

74. *Ibid.*, p. 73, has enlarged the work from the Dinteville patronage to include the brilliant, enigmatic "Three Men in a Wine Cellar" (Städelsches Institut, Frankfurt), also dated 1537 (attributed to Jean de Gourmont) recognizing the Dinteville arms on the post in the foreground.

75. William Ottley, *Facsimiles of Scarce and Curious Prints* London, 1828, p. xxii.

76. See André Demartial, "Léonard Limoisin, émailleur et graveur," *Revue de l'art chrétien* LXII 1912: pp. 18-28. Penicaud and Noailler, also contemporary *émailleurs,* worked after Schongauer and after illustrations to the work of Sebastian Brandt, according to Demartial. For further information on Limoisin's prints, see M.C. Ross, "Léonard Limoisin, Enameller and Engraver," *Print Collector's Quarterly* XXV 1938: pp. 361-64.

77. The triptych is in the Dutuit collection, Petit Palais, Paris.

78. The plaque is in the Victoria and Albert Museum, Inventory no. C.2461-1010.

79. See E.H. Gombrich, "Apollonio di Giovanni: A Florentine Cassone Workshop Seen through the Eyes of a Humanist Poet," *Journal of the Warburg and Courtauld Institutes* XVIII 1955: pp. 16-34, for this style in the preceding century.

80. See the stained-glass window by Laurence Fauconnier of the "Death and Assumption of the Virgin" at Écouen, reproduced by Lucien Magne in *L'oeuvre des peintres-verriers français* Paris, 1886, opp. p. 94. The window dates from 1544, in a church designed by Jean Bullant, who was also active at Anet and at Langres, where he planned the chapel of Pothière for Jean d'Amoncourt, according to Gaston Le Breton (Marcel, II, p. 361). For this chapel, see Blunt, 1957, p. 251, n. 2.
    A tapestry of the "Last Supper," dated 1532, based on the composition by Leonardo, probably made in the Fontainebleau workshop, offers similar stylistic analogies to the mature style of Duvet. Its French origin or patronage is indicated by fleurs de lys surrounded by the Order of Saint Michael. Now in the Vatican, it is reproduced by Goebel, *Die Wandteppiche und ihre Manufakturen . . .* Leipzig, 1928, vol. II, Pl. XXXVII, "Bourguignote de Henri II." The figures of Mars and Bellona are very much in the style of those in the engraved triptych to Henri II (Cat. 62-64). See also the plaque (Pl. LIV, "Plaque de selle en fer repoussé et damasquine. Italie – XVIe siècle"), which belongs with the helmet and may very well have been executed in France by a Milanese armorer at the court of Henri II. It is tempting to think of Duvet himself as the possible author of similar armor. For further examples of the tapestry style in armor, see Stephen V. Grancsay, "The Armor of Henri II of France from the Louvre School," *Bulletin of the Metropolitan Museum of Art* XXVII 1932: pp. 68-80; Thomas Bruno, "Die Müncher Harnisvorzeichnungen des Etienne Delaune," *Wiener Jahrbuch* XX 1960: pp. 7-62.

81. Gilles Corrozet, *Hecatongraphie* Lyon, 1540; quoted by R. Brun, *Le livre illustre en France au XVIe siècle,* Paris, 1930, p. 65.

82. That a state of reciprocity between tapestry and other art forms existed can be seen in the Triumph of Petrarch tapestries in the Vienna collection. According to *Art Treasures from the Vienna Collection,* n. p., 1949-51, the cartoons may have been based on a lost print series.

83. Pierre de Ronsard, *Oeuvres complètes,* ed. Paul Laumonier, Société des textes français modernes, Paris, vol. XVI, pp. 331-32.

84. See A. Babeau, "Dominique Florentin," *Réunion des sociétés savantes des départements* (section des beaux-arts) I, 1887: pp. 108, 140; also documents quoted in "Actes de la paroisse Notre-Dame," in *Nouvelles archives de l'art français,* Sér. 3, II 1886: p. 349. According to Marquet de Vasselot (*Histoire des sculpteurs français* [Paris, 1888], p. 336), Fiorentino's real name was Rinuccini, and he may have been active in Paris since the very end of the fifteenth or beginning of the sixteenth century. Although Vasselot, in his rather chauvinistic boosting of Troyes as a pre-Fontainebleau center of Italian influence, may have been distorting local archival information to come to this conclusion, his views, if correct, might provide a plausible teacher for Reverdy and sources of Italian influence on the early Duvet.

85. Johan G. von Quandt (*Verzeichnis meiner Kupferstich-Sammlung* [Leipzig, 1853]: pp. 176-77) in his sensitive appreciation of Duvet's works, pointed out that the artist was free of the Fontainebleau-transmitted Italian influences because he was a goldsmith rather than painter, but this view is not correct.

86. Zerner, 1964, p. 75, reproduced on p. 76. See also Franca Zava Bocazzi, *Antonio da Trento incisore,* Trent, 1962, for a different view of the Fantuzzi-

Antonio da Trento problem. For the Giulio Romano drawings, see Frederick Hartt, *Giulio Romano* New Haven, 1958, pp. 147-50.

87. Gébelin, *Le Style Renaissance en France*, p. 79; also Maurice Roy, "Les tapisseries de Saint Mammès de Langres," *Mémoires de la Société Archéologique de Sens*, Fasc. V 1914, reprinted in the same author's *Artistes et monuments de la renaissance française* Paris, 1929, pp. 44-51. The tapestry series was still complete in 1768; two, one showing Saint Mammès preaching to the wild animals (including a unicorn), and the other the martyrdom of Saint Mammes, remain in the cathedral. A third tapestry (Louvre) shows the saint in a forest near the gates of Caesarea, preceded by two soldiers, surrounded by wild animals to protect him. He goes to the soldiers, turning himself over to the governor of Cappadocia, seen at the right of the composition. The saint is shown being tortured in front of a great triumphal arch at the upper part of the tapestry. The tapestries were planned for the decoration of the cathedral choir, like the series at Reims. Each tapestry measures 4.35 m x 4.75 m. Roy, p. 29, gave the contract witnessed by the notary at Châtelet, dated July 14, 1543, signed by Cousin and Cardinal de Givry "pour la preparation de patrons devant reproduire en couleurs des scenes de la vie de St. Mammès." Givry's contract with the Parisian tapestry workshop of Blacé and Langlois, dated Jan. 29, 1544, is also given by Roy. Dora Heinz (*Europäische Wandteppiche*, [Brunswick, 1963]) gave other Blacé commissions, listing the workshop as "Pierre Blasse, father and son."

88. Françoise Bardon, *Diane de Poitiers et le mythe de Diane* Paris, 1963, pp. 66-73.

89. See François Gébelin, "Un manifeste de l'école Néo-Classique en 1549: l'entrée de Henri II à Paris," *Bulletin de la Société de l'histoire de Paris et de l'Ile-de-France* LI 1924: pp. 33-45; and V.L. Saulnier, "L'entrée de Henri II à Paris et la Revolution Poétique de 1550," *Les fêtes de la renaissance* Paris, 1956, pp. 31-59.

90. du Colombier, *L'Art Renaissance en France,* Paris, 1950, p. 124, figs. 172-73.

91. According to Erwin Panofsky, *Albrecht Dürer,* Princeton, 1948, vol. I, p. 54, the motif of the child carried by two angels — *commendatio animarum* — comes from classical funerary monuments.

92. See Cat. 49, the lower corner of which was reengraved after a break in the printing. See also Cat. 60 which was also partially reengraved for the printed edition of 1561. The entire unicorn series is dated around 1560 by Jean Laran, *L'estampe,* Paris, 1959, vol. I, p. 313.

93. Zerner (*The School of Fontainebleau, Etchings and Engravings*, New York, n.d.) L.D. 50, Master L.D. (B. XVI, 314, 12); however, the expressionistic force of the figures is far closer to Fantuzzi's equestrian groups such as the series after Romano of 1542 (Zerner 2-9 or even more notable Zerner 31-32).

94. Blunt, *Art and Architecture in France, 1500-1700,* 1957 edition, p. 72. A visual comparison between Duvet and Pontormo was first provided by Ludwig Goldscheider, who juxtaposed their self-portraits in *Five Hundred Self-Portraits,* London, 1937, Pl. 90-01.

95. An old copy of the "Visitation" is in the Louvre; an engraving after it was attributed by Herbet to Jean Vaquet (H.20). Bartsch included it as No. 8 under the *Anonymes,* while Robert-Dumesnil ascribed the print to Dumonstier.

96. Jules Lieure (*La gravure en France au XVIᵉ siècle,* [Paris, 1927], Pl. LXVIII, No. 238) thought Duvet influenced Jean Bullant. The only known engravings by the latter, a prominent architect of Langrois origin, active in the latter half of the sixteenth century, are of ornament and architecture and show no signs of Duvet's tutelage.

97. The initials GP on these and other prints have been linked with an artist active in the second half of the sixteenth century — Gerard P. Groenning. The latter is sometimes identified with a certain Paludanus, most notably by Nagler, who seems to have confused the identities of Groenning and Crispin van den Broek. K. Zoege von Manteuffel has assembled the extraordinary contradictory and obscure data in his Gerard P. Groenning entry (*Thieme-Becker* XV, p. 70). His print for the Apocalypse, Chapter 4, should be compared with Cat. 40;

and the print for Chapter 6 with Cat. 42. The engravings are extremely rare and difficult to locate.

98. G. Duplessis, *Histoire de la gravure en France,* Paris, 1861, p. 64. Duplessis seems to have slightly overstated the case:

> "On s'aperçoit que Woeriot a vu et connait à fond les
> planches de Jean Duvet; la façon de graver de ce maître
> a été imitée par lui-même dans les moindres accessoires,
> et il n'est pas jusqu'a la confusion de certaines compositions
> qu'il n'ait cherché à reproduire . . . et le travail forme
> d'une infinité de tailles croisées et terminées par de petits
> points est tout à fait analogue aux planches de *l'Apocalypse.*"

99. Long known as Cesare Reverdino, the engraver's Italianate style caused him to be considered Paduan by Zani, Gori, Mariette, and Bartsch. Henri Bouchot has shown the French origin of Reverdy in Doubs and discussed the artist's Italian journey in 1530 and his later activities in Lyon toward the middle of the century. See H. Bouchot, "Le prétendu graveur italien Gasparo Reverdino," *Gazette des beaux-arts,* Pér. 3, XXVI, 1901: pp. 102-8, 229-39. The poem discovered by M. Sotzmann was republished in the *Deutsches Kunstblatt,* (April 22, 1850), p. 156. Written by Nicolas Bourbon, it was included in the Nugae poeticae, p. 153, published by S. Gryphius in Lyon, 1538, comparing Hans Holbein in "Hanso Vibio" and "Georgio Reverdio, pictoricus" to a combination of Parrhasius and Zeuxis. The poet probably knew Duvet since he was born in the diocese of Langres and was also patronized by Givry. A canon at Saint-Mammès in Langres, he wrote many flattering poems to his patron, the Cardinal de Givry. See Marcel, vol. II, pp. 199-205. For Reverdy, see also Alessandro Baudi di Vesme, "Reverdino incisore cinquecentista," *Maso Finiguerra* I, 1936-37: pp. 187-205; III: pp. 123 123-55. Baudi di Vesme, disagreeing with Bouchot, does not believe Reverdy to have been born in Doubs but in Piedmont, first working with Marcantonio in Rome and then fleeing to Lyon after the Sack in 1527. The first work to have been executed in Lyon by Reverdy, according to Baudi di Vesme, was the frontispiece to the second edition of the poems of Jean Lemaire for Jacques Mareschal. Although Reverdy's authorship of the frontispiece has been contested, Baudi di Vesme points out that Reverdy was already registered in the Lyon archives in 1529.

100. Uncatalogued at the British Museum, the roundel is on p. 10 of an album of Reverdy's works. Two additional undescribed roundels are at the Biblioteca Marucelliana, Florence, (I, p. 27), showing "Pyramus and Thisbe" and "The Meeting of Solomon and Sheba." An engraving of "Proserpina and Psyche" (B.XVI, 404, 74; Herbet, Anon. 16) might well be attributed to Reverdy. The print is "Jupiter creating the constellation Taurus" (Herbet 2).

101. A Michelangelesque statue of Christ for the church of Saint Martin in Langres, the sculptor's major surviving work, shows slight similarity with Duvet's "Deposition" (Cat. 36). Gentil was an apprentice and assistant to Domenico Fiorentino at Troyes. If he actually was the Monogrammist FG, he must have learned the art of engraving from Barbiere.
For Gentil, see Marquet de Vasselot, *Histoire des sculpteurs français,* Paris, 1888, p. 250; L.F. and L.E. Marcel, *Artistes et ouvriers d'art à Langres avant la Revolution,* p. 20, no. 56. The sculpture at Saint-Florentin at Yonne has been attributed to Gentil. See C. Hermel, *Saint-Florentin: son aspect, ses rues, son église* (Auxerre, 1906), p. 40.

102. Boullaye, p. 23: "Je vous prie m'avertir, combien de cayers de papier vous avez gastez depuis mon despartement de Dijon, car je prophetize en excrip-vant que nos et moy ensemble maistre Jean avons aultant faict l'ung comme l'aultre." The notation accompanies drawings of Prevost's patrons Cardinal de Givry and Jean d'Amoncourt and was reproduced in the *Magasin pittoresque* (1857), pp. 315-18.
The painter and sculptor Jacques Prévost de Gray was brought to Langres in 1551 to execute decorative paintings for the residence of Jean d'Amoncourt,

who was to stand godfather to Duvet's grandson Mammès. Prévost also painted religious subjects in Langres, where he made sculptures for the *jubé* around 1555. The last artist of any note to have worked there during Duvet's lifetime, he is of interest because he executed several engravings, two of which are dated 1541 and 1547. See Herbet and Robert-Dumesnil, V, pp. 4-9; Jean Adhémar, *Inventaire du fonds français,* vol. II, pp. 57-59. The *Magasin pittoresque* (1857, pp. 315-18) reproduces a letter of Prévost's, discussing how pleasant his living conditions were under the generous patronage of d'Amoncourt and Givry; it also contains some drawings. The same letter is more formally published in *Mémoires de la Société d'émulation du Doubs,* 1868, p. 304. See also Marcel, II, pp. 365-78.

103. See David DuBon, "Hugues Sambin as Architect and Designer of Woodwork," M.A. thesis, New York University, Institute of Fine Arts, 1959. His woodcuts were published under the title *Oeuvre de la diversité des termes dont on use en architecture* (Lyon, 1572). A similar work was etched by a Langrois artist, Joseph Boillot, entitled *Nouveau Portraitz et figures de termes pour user au l'architecture, imprimé à Langres par Iehan des prey.*

104. The relief, part of a retable in the Antesala Capitular of Seville Cahtedral, is illustrated in an article by Manuel Gómez-Moreno, "Diego de Pesquera, escultor," *Archivo español de arte* XXVIII, Núm. 112, Pl. XVIII, dated after 1572.

105. See Gébelin, *Le Style Renaissance en France,* pp. 106-7, 114.

106. Professor Howard kindly showed me his forthcoming article for the *Art Quarterly.*

107. See Chapter 3, part 3, n. 37.

108. Anthony Blunt, *Nicolas Poussin, The A.W. Mellon Lectures, 1958,* Washington, D.C., 1960, p. 220. The lines relate to those in Tertullian's *De Anima* (40.2) and *Adversus Marcionem* (I, 24). Poussins's letter is in the *Correspondance,* edited by Charles Jouanny, Paris, 1911, p. 447.

109. Blunt, *Art and Architecture in France, op. cit.,* p. 85, n. 109.

110. Lawrence Binyon, "The Engravings of Blake and Edward Calvert," *Print-Collector's Quarterly* VII, 1917, pp. 319-20, noted the "small likelihood of Blake's ever having seen the rare set of engravings of the Apocalypse by Jean Duvet." Louis Reau, *Iconographie de l'art chrétien,* Paris, 1957, vol. II, Part 2, p. 679, believed Duvet may have influenced Blake's *Book of Job.*

111. See Jack Spector, *Delacroix' Murals at Saint Sulpice,* New York, 1968, pp. 76-79. The Louvre drawing is RF 9300, for "War," related by Spector to RF 9970, "Peace." Before Spector's study, the Baltimore sheet was assumed to have been for Delacroix's wall paintings at Saint Sulpice.

112. See Lucien Rudrauf, "Imitations et invention dans l'art d'Eugène Delacroix: Delacroix et le Rosso," *Acts et commentationes Universitates Tartuensis,* No. 43 (1938): pp. 1-10. Rudrauf noted the painter's utilization of the Rosso Louvre "Pietà" for the canvas of 1844 at St. Denis-du-Saint-Sacrement. The Primaticcio derivations have not been published.

113. See Agnes Mongan and Paul Sachs, *Drawings in the Fogg Museum of Art,* Cambridge, Mass., 1940, vol. I, Cat. 635, p. 367.

114. Letter of June 6, 1972. Perhaps the inscription was addressed to Louis J.B. Boulangé who laid in the background of the Saint Sulpice paintings.

115. Ex-collection Louis Godefroy, Paris.

116. *Journal de Delacroix 1822-1863,* edited by André Joubin, Geneva, 1943, pp. 44-45.

117. *Ibid.,* pp. 344-45.

CATALOGUE

175

1   THE ENTRY OF CHRIST INTO JERUSALEM

76 x 77 mm.

With monogram ID on double tablet on the pilaster at the extreme right.

London, BM (unique).

Le Blanc 16, Duplessis 3, Passavant 67, Boullaye 67, Popham 67, Linzeler 12.[1] Bersier 10.

This engraving, together with its companion piece, *"Christ Driving the Money Changers from the Temple,"* (Cat. 2), is one of Duvet's earliest known works. It has been dated circa 1526 [1] Characterized by a small format, and carefully designed, meticulously executed compositions, these two engravings present Duvet at his most conservative, working primarily in a Northern European style, with but the slightest indications of exposure to Italian Renaissance forms. The somewhat squat proportions of the figures, the very delicate hatching and attention to particular textures, together with an avoidance of that classicizing generalization which will accompany works in a more "Roman" manner, mark this engraving as an early work. The figure of Christ on the ass is freely derived from Dürer's "Small Woodcut Passion" (B.22),[2] and this engraving and its companion piece may stem from a projected "Passion" series. The architectural detailing and cityscape are especially close to those in the "Annunciation in the Church" (Cat. 3), whose somewhat more sophisticated proportions indicate a slightly later work. The design of the gateway may have been influenced by that of a Gallo-Roman portal formerly at Langres.[3] This piece and Cat. 2 should be placed in the early 'teens.

---

1. *Linzeler (I.F.F., p. 333)* quotes Louis Godefroy as dating the engraving ca. 1526. He thought it was meant for sale at church fêtes or for insertion in a book and viewed the tree as derived from Giulio Campagnola's *Recumbent Deer Tied to a Tree* (Hind 14).

2. According to Scherer (1908, p. 232) this series is dated ca. 1509-1511.

3. This engraving was first published by Georg Nagler, *Neues allgemeines Künstler-Lexikon*, Munich, 1837, IV, p. 37, and then by Charles LeBlanc in the *Catalogue des Estampes de M. Pierre Vischer de Bâle*, Paris, 1852, p. 106, No. 802. "*J.-C. entrant à Jerusalem;* la double tablette avec les lettres ID est suspendue à une colonne vers la droite. Larg. 78 Millim. Haut. 80. Non décrite. Très rare.-Très belle." Although these measurements differ very slightly from the example at the British Museum, it is probably the same print. According to a note by Seymour de Ricci at the Bibliothèque Nationale, the print and its companion piece were both purchased at the Vischer sale by Goupil, who presumably then sold them to the British Museum. According to H. Mireur (*Dictionnaire des ventes d'art faites en France et l'étranger pendant les XVIII et XIX siècles*, Paris, 1911, II, pp. 33-35) the prints from the Vischer sale reappeared in the same year at the Delande sale.

2 CHRIST DRIVING THE MONEY CHANGERS FROM THE TEMPLE [1]

79 x 77 mm. [2]
Signed ID on double tablets hanging from second column from the right.
London, BM (unique).
Le Blanc 15, Duplessis 4, Passavant 68, Boullaye 68, Popham 68, Linzeler 13, Bersier 11.

For the style and technique of this engraving, see *The Entry into Jerusalem* (Cat. 1). The Roman soldiers in the foreground offer a more overt form of Italian influence than was perceptible in the latter, and suggest derivation from a sixteenth-century print. The temple interior conforms with contemporary northern Altdorfer-like building styles as shown in prints like the Master CC's *Massacre of the Innocents*. [3] The figure bearing fowl is reminiscent of Noel Garnier's letter Y in his illustrated alphabet. [4]

1. This print was first mentioned by Georg Nagler (*Neues allgemeines Künstler-Lexicon,* Munich, 1837) and later published in LeBlanc, 1852, no. 801. "J.-C. chassent les vendeurs du temple; la double tablette avec les lettres ID est suspendue à une colonne vers la droite. Larg. 78 millim. Haut. 80. Non décrite. Très rare.–Très belle."
2. Another impression was included in the Luigi Angiolini sale, by H. G. Gutekunst, Stuttgart, 1896. Judging by the illustration in the catalogue, no. 1213, it was a fine print, despite being described as "très rogué." Linzeler *(I.F.F.* p. 333) lists the engraving as having been executed circa 1526.
3. Bartsch, IX, 44, n. 1. R.-D., VI, 12, n. 1. Duvet's work might have been inspired by Altdorfer's of the same subject (B.6) of 1520. The interior may be partially based upon Altdorfer's etchings of the synagogue at Ratisbone (B.63-4) of 1519. Should these have been the sources, the the print probably dates from the early 1520s.
4. Reproduced in Courboin *Histoire Illustré de la Gravure en France,* Paris, 1923, I, fig. 253.

3 THE ANNUNCIATION IN THE CHURCH[1]

182 x 114 mm.
Unsigned.
Vienna (A–unique).
B 3, RD 4, LeBlanc 6, Passavant 4, Boullaye 4, Popham 4, Linzeler 15, Bersier 6.

While the engraving adheres to late medieval formulas such as the ecclesiastical Annunciation, the free flow of the figures already appears informed by the achievements of recent Italian art.[2] Reminiscent of the art of Michel Colombe and Jean Bellegambe, the print must be placed among Duvet's earliest works. The tight, carefully planned composition, emphasizing perspective, and using a great deal of flick-work, also points to an early period in the master's oeuvre. Its very delicate hatching and silvery quality show his style before the adoption of more Italianate, expressionistic, rich black surfaces. Mary's face is very much in the manner of the Maître de Moulin, her physiognomy revealing an asceticism and introspection very different from the more sensuous, classical features Duvet takes over from Marcantonio in his later works.

The revival of the fourteenth century Annunciation formula in this engraving reveals an early conservatism which will be abandoned in Duvet's revolutionary representation of the same subject in 1520 (Cat. 12). The *prie-dieu's* open doors refer to the Annunciation as the inception of Christian observance, also stressed by the presence of the chalice within.[3] The Virgin is often referred to as the Open Door or the Door to Heaven, stemming from Psalm 118:19. The left arm of the angel points to the windows, suggesting the passage which the Holy Spirit is to follow in entering the church, while his right hand points to Mary's body, perhaps indicating the Incarnation. The church interior may reverse one by Altdorfer (B.6), the "Expulsion" of 1520.[4] But this print could date in the 'teens of the sixteenth century.

---

1. Linzeler (*I.F.F.*, p. 334) notes, "Louis Godefroy qui émet des doutes sur l'attribution de cette pièce à Duvet, la date approximativement de 1530." The basis for his doubt and reasons for the relatively late date are not provided.
2. See David M. Robb, "The Iconography of the Annunciation in the fourteenth and fifteenth centuries," *The Art Bulletin*, XVIII, no. 4, 1936, p. 500. The curiously wingless angel of Duvet's engraving is seen also in the stage designs for the Valenciennes mystery play by Hubert Caillaux devoted to the Procès de Paradis (circa 1547). However, the same artist's drawing of the Annunciation shows a conventionally winged Gabriel. See Gustave Cohen, *Le théâtre en France*, I, Paris, 1928; the wingless figure is shown on pl. XLI, and the *Annunciation* on pl. XLII.
3. Suggested by Eric Zafran.
4. Certain of the architectural details of the interior, especially the triforium, recall the Cathedral of Saint Mammès at Langres. See Marcel, II, p. 131, for an illustration of the pre-Revolutionary appearance of the choir of Saint Mammès. The porch is similar to that of the Cathedral of Dijon. The interior of the church also bears a certain resemblance to that of Saint Lazare, although the great piers at Autun differ. Should the German print prove Duvet's source, the date of the *Annunciation* would have to be advanced.

4 THE MARTYRDOM OF SAINT SEBASTIAN

183 x 112 mm.
Signed DI on double tablets on the floor between the saint's feet.
London (BM), Paris (BN—cut within plate mark) L—Rothschild—Louvre
RD 23, Passavant 23, Boullaye 23, Popham 23, Linzeler 23, Bersier 49.

The composition of this engraving is derived from a bronze plaque by G. Moderno, copied in reverse (Text fig. 1).[1] Duvet has added the group of torturers at the left. The Parisian print is illustrated here.

The presence of a Gothic monogram on the double tablets, coupled with the meticulous finish, suggest an early dating for this engraving, which is similar to, but probably earlier than, his *Triumph of David* (Cat. 6).[2]

Duvet's later representation of Sebastian (Cat. 70) is also derived from an Italian source. Like the latter, this print may have functioned as a *Pestblatt*. Duvet's work center—Langres—was plague stricken in 1522, and 1526, dates which would correspond with the style of this engraving.[3] The incorporation of a design for a *tazza* here is comparable to Duvet's introduction of a sword-hilt pattern in his *Annunciation of 1520* (Cat. 12). The parrot on the ledge may be interpreted as a symbol of patience.

---

1. This derivation was first observed by A. Oberheide, *Der Einfluss Marcantonio Raimondi auf die nordische Kunst des 16 Jahrhunderts,* Hamburg, 1930, p. 155, n. b.
2. Linzeler, p. 344, dates the engraving ca. 1521. This dating is probably based upon the research of Louis Godefroy.
3. The 1515 plague date is cited in Marcel, II, p. 286, n. 3. Clément-Janin, *La Peste en Bourgogne,* Dijon, 1879. gives 1526 for the date of a plague throughout Burgundy, which would seem close to the very latest date possible for this engraving. In 1522 Langres was ravaged by the most severe plague of all according to Boullaye, 1879, p. 82. Duvet's colleague Jean Richier had the Collège closed. As Richier provided many of the programs for the Langres entries designed by Duvet, he, as a humanist and Italophile, may perhaps have suggested the form of the engraving.

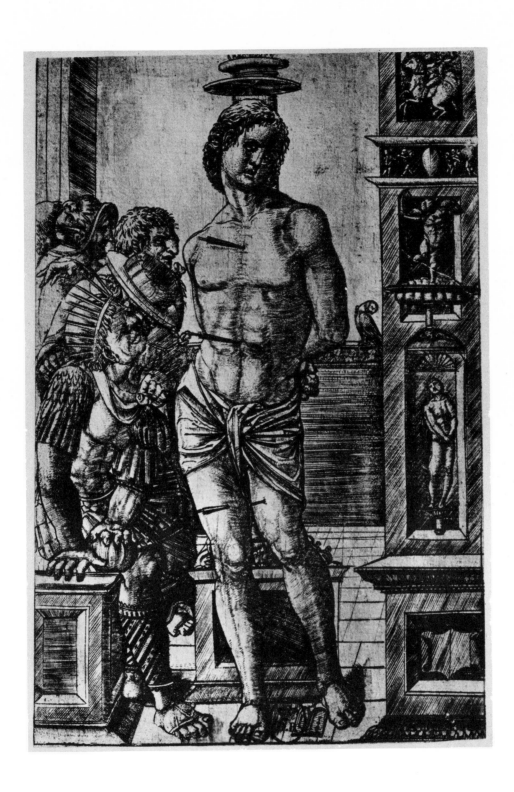

5 THE WOMAN OF THE APOCALYPSE WITH CORNUCOPIA [1]

158 x 64 mm.
Signed ID in Gothic letters on double tablet.
Paris (BN—two impressions), Vienna (A).
B7, RD 17, LeBlanc 22, Passavant 17, Boullaye 17, Popham 17, Linzeler 5, Bersier 42.

The figure in this engraving is identified as "The Woman of the Apocalypse," by the presence of the sun and moon at her feet. This appellation may also have been understood as a reference to both the Immaculate Conception and the Assumption of the Virgin, commonly represented as the Virgin of the Sun and the Moon in the sixteenth century.[2] Duvet has copied Marcantonio's "Lucretia" (B.192, Text fig. 71) for the classical figure of the Woman.[3] With its delicate hatching and scrupulous attention to detail, this engraving should be placed among Duvet's first works under Italian influence. Such a dating would agree with the early form of the artist's signature. The "Woman of the Apocalypse" was a popular French triumphal symbol of the early sixteenth century, several of which were designed by Duvet. For the Rouen entry of François I, she was shown holding a palm of victory rather than a cornucopia.[4]

This print may have been engraved for Claude de Longvy, humanist bishop of Langres and future Cardinal de Givry, whose emblem was a cornucopia with the incription *abundantia diligentibus*.[5] The form of the cornucopia, and the general style of the engraving is close to that of a painting after Jan Gossaert of *Mars, Venus and Cupid* in the collection of Paul Mersch, in Paris. Both the painting and the print display a fusion of northern technique and Italian style typical of Franco-Flemish art of the first quarter of the sixteenth century.[6] Duvet's engraving combines the early, restrained works of Marcantonio with those in the Netherlandish tradition of Lucas van Leyden.

---

1. This engraving is usually known as *The Virgin Standing on a Crescent*, as catalogued by Popham, p. 143.
2. See B. Knipping, *De iconografie van de Contra-Reformatie in de Nederlander*, Hilversum, II, 1940, pp. 37. ff.
3. The Marcantonio derivation was first recorded by Bartsch, VII, p. 496. Oberheide, Plate XIX, fig. 5, compared the figures in the Italian and French engravings.
4. See Charles de Beaurepaire, *L'entrée de François I dans la ville au mois août, 1517*, Rouen, 1867, p. xiv. Mary was shown among the entry images. "On pur mostrer quelle done ou est moyen de donner aux roys et princes les victoires signifiées par la palme. Elle estoit environée du soleil et la lune avec soulz ses pieds en signifat la vision de lapocalipse." Two angels crown her, lilies are planted at her feet, while a mechanized Lamb of the Apocalypse turns and kneels before the king.
5. Jacques Vignier, *Décade Historique du Diocèse de Langres*, II, Langres, 1894, p.229, "Il (Givry) en faisoit son hieroglyphe et sa devise. . . y ad joutant un cornet d'abondance ou de fruits, avec cette inscription. *abundantia diligentibus*, c'est a dire que tout prospere a qui aime notre Sauveur attache à la Croix." A relief of the Virgin and Child (Musée, Langres) in which the pediment is flanked by cornucopias may also have been commissioned by Givry. For a discussion of cornucopia symbolism, see also E. Panofsky, *Studies in Iconology*, New York, 1939, p. 157, n. 9.
6. Several versions after the lost panel by Gossaert exist. M.J. Friedländer, *Die altniederländische Malerei*, Berlin, 1930, VIII, no. 46 illustrates one; another was lent to *Kunstschatten uit Nederlandse Verzamelingen*, Museum Boymans, Rotterdam, 1955, illus. p. 18, Cat. 13. A similar cornucopia is also found in the *Hypnerotomachia Poliphili* of 1499.

6 THE TRIUMPH OF DAVID

140 x 96 mm (BN).[1] Cut well within platemark.
Signed ID on double tablet suspended from a tree at left.
Paris (BN), Parma (Regia Bibliotheca)[2].
RD 3, LeBlanc 4, Passavant 3, Boullaye 3, Popham 3, Linzeler 2, Bersier 3.

The figure has a generalized Pollaiuolesque character, somewhat similar to the adaptations of Gabriel Salmon and Baldung Grien. Dutuit has observed the similarity to Robetta, but the work is actually closer to early sixteenth century engravings of the Allaert Claessens workshop.[3] The engraver's monogram and style place it between dated works of the 1520s, and undated prints presumably from an earlier period. The motif of the victorious David was a popular theme in French sixteenth-century imagery for triumphal entries. David's crown of *fleur-de-lys* may be an allusion to a similar celebration of royal prowess, in the Burgundian entries staged by Duvet.[4]

---

1. The upper left corner is lost. (Here illustrated.)
2. Probably the impression listed in the Massimiliano Ortalli collection in Parma, recorded in 1820 as measuring "5,4.I.3,8." See Pietro Zani, *Enciclopedia Metodica,* Parma, 1820, Parte Seconda III, p. 294.
3. "Claessens" is here used to denote the group of engravers assembled by Hollstein under the name. See F.W.H. Hollstein, *Dutch and Flemish Etchings, Engravings, and Woodcuts,* Amsterdam, n.d., IV, p. 101.
4. For the triumphal entry of Charles VIII at Troyes a statue of David slaying Goliath was erected above the city gates to symbolize Charles's victory over the enemies of France.

7   SAINT JEROME IN THE WILDERNESS

165 x 115 mm.
Signed ID in Gothic characters on double tablet suspended from a tree trunk.
Vienna (A–unique).[1]
RD 24, LeBlanc 50, Passavant 24, Brulliot 2864, Boullaye 24, Popham 24, Linzeler 45, Bersier 50.

This print was first identified as a work of Duvet's by Brulliot, who also recognized it as a copy after Marcantonio's engraving of the same subject (B.101, text fig. 73).[2] The engraving by Marcantonio is in turn freely derived from one by Lucas van Leyden (B.113, text fig. 72), dated 1516. Rather than making a straightforward copy of the Marcantonio, as is generally assumed, Duvet also incorporated details from its Netherlandish source. He retains van Leyden's rustic cottage, rejecting Marcantonio's Roman ruins. On the other hand, he adopts the physiognomy and physique of Jerome as shown by Marcantonio, whose classical strength is very different from the Gothic figure in the Lucas van Leyden. The complex character of Duvet's eclecticism in this relatively early engraving points toward the variety of sources consulted for the *Apocalypse*.[3] The highly finished technique and Gothic monogram point to a date before 1520, after which he generally signed his name in more classical fashion.[4] The plant which grazes the cheek of the lion and which also appears in the foreground may be a signature in the form of a Latin pun, since *duvet* is the French name for the plant, known in Latin as *tufetum*.[5]

---

1. The entire section at the upper left of the Albertina impression has been lost. Fortunately, very little of the missing area (which has been replaced with a patch of old paper) appears to have been engraved. The tree may have extended further to the left, but other than this, the area may very well have originally been as blank as it appears in the present restoration.
2. Franz Brulliot, *Dictionnaire des Monogrammes*, Munich, 1832, II, p. 406, No. 2864.
3. Duvet's engraving is similar to one of the same subject (reproduced in *Cat. of Early French Books in the Library of C. Fairfax Murray*, Second Part, London, 1910, Cat. 461, p. 678), on the verso of the title page of *Protestation de la foix avecques sept cosideratios*, published in Lyon, probably before 1525, in 1519 a related composition was included in Jérôme de Hangest, *Introductiorum Morale*, Paris, Jean Petit (Mortimer 269).
4. Linzeler (I, p. 343) gives a date of ca. 1518, probably based upon studies by Louis Godefroy.
5. This pun was first recognized by Boullaye, p. 87, in the title page of the *Apocalypse* (Cat. 65) and the same plant is identified in the *Jerome* by E. Tietze-Contrat, *Der französicher Kupferstich der Renaissance*, Munich, 1925, p. 9.

8   THE CUMAEAN SIBYL [1]

202 x 141 mm.
Signed ID on double tablet hung from the steps at left, inscribed IOANNES on the ewer under left foot of the sibyl, in the same form as Cat. 12. Inscribed on cornice at upper right PATER NOS[TER (?)].
A series of lines on the house to the right of the sibyl have been interpreted as reading "MDXVII." [2]
Paris (BN) [3], Vienna (A), Washington (NG–Rosenwald Coll. [4]).
B 37, RD 52, LeBlanc 5, Passavant 52, Boullaye 52, Popham 52, Linzeler 68, Bersier 61.

Bartsch first pointed out the Italian derivation of the Sibyl and annunciate angel from an unspecified engraving after Raphael at the Vatican, identified by Popham (Bartsch XV, p. 49, no. 6). But upon comparing Agostino Veneziano's print with Duvet's and their source, Raphael's fresco of 1516 for the Chigi Chapel (Text fig. 2) Popham concluded that the French engraving was taken directly from the fresco or from a drawing by a contemporary artist, rather than from the School of Marcantonio print. Blunt accepted Popham's findings. As two other parts of the French print can be shown to be adapted from other Italian and Netherlandish prints, and since it is extremely close to the Agostino Veneziano, there seems little point in using this work as evidence for an early Italian journey, as has been suggested by Popham and Blunt.

The architectural setting in which the Sibyl is shown is adapted from Marcantonio's "Lucretia" (B.192), an engraving which Duvet drew upon frequently. The curious, ornamented object upon which the large putto at the left rests his elbow is an enlarged design for a sword hilt, which Duvet has taken directly from an engraved sword hilt printed by the Allaert Claessen workshop. [6]

Signed and decorated with *fleur-de-lys,* the great ewer under the Sibyl's foot reflects commissions received by Duvet for royal presentation at triumphal entries. The Sibyl, symbolizing divine revelation to royalty, was a popular image at these entries, which Duvet is known to have designed, affording a convenient fusion of Christian and classical references, a handsome tribute to the imperial and religious virtues of the rulers of France. [7]

The Claessens sword hilt design, van Leyden-like landscape, and engraving technique, point to northern sources; the figures of the Sibyl and angel and general composition are taken with only slight modifications from the School of Marcantonio, revealing the poles of Duvet's early style. Popham, pointing out the similarity of the form of the date to that of similar inscriptions in early Marcantonio engravings, wrote that if the almost illegible date of 1517 is correct, the Sibyl already presents the artist's characteristic style. [8]

---

1. Recent scholarship argues against the specific identification of the sibyls in the Chigi Chapel of S. Maria della Pace. See L.D. Ettlinger, "A Note on Raphael's Sibyls in S. Maria della Pace," *Journal of the Warburg and Courtauld Institutes,* XXIV, 1961, pp. 322-23. See also in the same volume Michael Hirst, "The Chigi Chapel in S. Maria della Pace," pp. 161-185, esp. p. 169.
2. Popham, p. 132, n. 1. "Duvet's engraving has, on the cornice of a house at the back, what one is tempted to read as a date A.D.1517. (Analogous to the inconspicuous dates on some of Marcantonio's earlier engravings)." ' Linzeler, p. 349, dates the engraving circa 1521. The 1517 reading is accepted by François Courboin, *La gravure en France des origines à 1900,* Paris, 1923, p. 48.
3. In very bad condition, much scratched, with lower right and upper left corners lost. (Here illustrated).
4. Considerably repaired.
5. Blunt, p. 71.
6. See F.W.H. Hollstein, *Dutch and Flemish Etchings, Engravings, and Woodcuts,* Amsterdam, IV, Cat. 233, p. 227.
7. See Cyprien Monget (*La Chartreuse de Dijon,* Montreuil-sur-mer, 1898-1905, II, p. 203) for the Dijon entry of François Ier in 1521. Six sibyls were presented on a special stage, one of three prepared for the triumph.
8. Popham, p. 134.

9 SAINT MICHAEL VICTORIOUS

132 x 195 mm. Cut within platemark.
Unsigned.
Paris (BN—Acq. 11531, Album Ed. 16 Rés, unique).
Bersier 44.[1]

The print is copied in reverse from the engraving by Agostino Veneziano (B. XIV 93, 105 Text fig. 7) based upon a design from the School of Raphael. Duvet has omitted the lance shown in the Archangel's right hand and the grotesque helmet of the Italian print, reducing the rocky area and the terrain in the foreground. Buildings Duvet added at the right contribute to the spatial recession. He clothed Veneziano's nude Satan, converting his classical curly coif into a demonic brush-cut. The latter's armor is far more elaborate in the French print, equipped with figured greaves and ornamented cuirass. The lance-bearing hand in the Italian print points to heaven in the French. This early engraving, together with Cat. 4,5,7,8, 11, and 13, represents Duvet's closest early copying of Italian art of the High Renaissance, initiating his process of self-education through imitation.

---

1. The print was first recorded in the sales catalogue of Gutekunst and Klipstein (Auction 91, Nov. 6, 1958, p. 22, Cat. 137) as previously undescribed, attributed to Duvet on a stylistic basis. The paper has the *fleur-de-lys* watermark which Briquet listed as being used in eastern France between 1485 and 1550. Reproduced on pl. 4 of the catalogue. It has been published by Jean Adhémar.

150 x 224 mm (BM), 155 x 226 (BN). All examples cut within platemark.
Unsigned.
Berlin (East), London (BM[2]), Paris (BN[3]), Washington (NG—Rosenwald Coll., ex coll. Friedrich August II[4]).
RD 64, Duplessis 1, Passavant 64, Boullaye 64, Popham 64, Linzeler 1, Bersier 4.

The general composition, the architectural setting, the central figure and the horrified woman by the throne, are all taken from an engraving by Agostino Veneziano, dated 1516 (B. XIV, p. 48, no. 43), after Raphael's tapestry cartoon of "The Blinding of Elymas" of 1515-16. The dead child in the foreground is derived from an engraving by Marcantonio—"The Massacre of the Innocents" (B. XIV, p. 19, no. 18), also after a drawing by Raphael. The two soldiers at the left come from a School of Mantegna engraving of "The Flagellation" (B. XIII, p. 227, no. 1). The woman seen from the back is reminiscent of classicizing Raphael types taken over by Marcantonio.[5] The print's subject was a representation of royal justice, re-created for triumphal entries similar to those known to have been staged by Duvet.[6] It is possible that the engraver may have drawn upon "The Judgment of Solomon" as the subject of one of the tapestries he was commissioned to design in later years for the Geneva Maison de la Ville in 1545.[7]

The print appears unfinished, the indications of modelling too uneven and spotty to qualify as a completed work. It seems to have been engraved shortly after the "Saint Jerome" and the first "Martyrdom of Saint Sebastian" (Cat. 4, 7) which are distinguished by an even tighter, more meticulously worked technique and finer flick-work. It is probably the first engraving in which Duvet draws upon the art of Mantegna, a major source for the development of his mature style.

---

1. First recorded by M. J. Renouvier, *Académie des sciences et lettres de Montpellier*, "Des types et des manières des graveurs," I, 1854. An impression in the Dresden print room was destroyed during the Second World War. Another example was recorded in the *Cat. d'estampes . . . Cabinet de M. le Comte . . . (Harrach) de Vienne*. Paris. 1867, p. 67, Cat. 816. It was purchased by Clément, who had previously, in cataloguing the Harrach collection, attributed it to the Italian School.
2. Poorly preserved. A rather weak example was illustrated in the Boerner Catalogue of August 8, 1932.
3. In poor condition; the lower right margins have been repaired, and the surface is much abraded. (Here reproduced.)
4. The extremely fine example in the Rosenwald collection has a watermark somewhat like those listed in Briquet 7236, as does the British impression.
5. Almost all these adaptations have already been cited by Passavant, Robert-Dumesnil, Popham, Oberheide and Godefroy.
6. See G. R. Kernodle, *From Art to Theatre*, Chicago, 1944, p. 170, fig. 51, "Street theatre for a play of the Judgment of Solomon," which has a composition similar to that of the Duvet engraving.
7. See Appendix E, Doc. 48. According to Blunt (1953, p. 71), it is "undated but probably early."

11 THE VIRGIN AND CHILD IN THE CLOUDS

166 x 116 mm.
Signed ID in Gothic letters on a double tablet at the lower right corner, the only engraving in which this Gothic style lettering appears.[1]
London (BM—unique).
Boullaye 79, Popham 79, Linzeler 9,[2] Bersier 41.

This print was first published by Mrs. Mark Pattison as *The Virgin Surrounded by Cherubs in the Clouds*[3] and may be the *Assumption* given to Duvet by Bellier and Auvray.[4]

A somewhat wooden, coarse copy of a popular Raphaelesque engraving by Marcantonio (B. IV, 30, 47), the print must come from an early stage in Duvet's graphic oeuvre.[5] The hanging string and Gothic lettering of the double tablets are discarded after his first phase.

This print is among Duvet's closest copies after another master; he did, however, add the putto at Jesus' side. It provides evidence of the close study of other masters which the French printmaker must have undertaken before embarking on his own personal venture in the Italian manner, as seen in his *Annunciation of 1520* (Cat. 12).

---

1. Its source was discovered by Popham (p. 150) who pointed out (p. 132) "that the signature in this engraving, while not used in any other of his prints, corresponds closely with the monogram Duvet placed on a receipt formerly in the Archives at Langres." Dated 1533, this monogram is reproduced by Boullaye, p. 13.
2. Linzeler (p. 332) states "Dans un Ier état, les initials ne figurent pas dans la double tablette." He gives no provenance for this "first state," which is unknown to this writer.
3. Mrs. Mark Pattison, *The Renaissance of Art in France*, London, 1879, II, p. 100. She groups this print with "Christ and the Woman of Samaria," "The Judgment of Solomon," and the unfinished *Deposition*, finding these "Marked by the same careful effort after the technic of a foreign school. There is the same endeavour to bring about continuous and equal ruling of level lines, or neatly regulated cross-hatching, in the attempt to come up to the standard of a system which is afterwards entirely put aside."
4. Bellier and Auvray, *Dictionnaire Générale des artistes de l'Ecole Française*, Paris, 1852, p. 508. See Appendix B.3.
5. Also reproduced by Aenea Vico in 1542 (B. XV, 283, 4).

12 THE ANNUNCIATION OF 1520

234 x 173 mm.[1] Cut within platemark.
Signed IOANNES DVVET on cartouche at the center of the foreground, the first name similar in form to the inscription on Cat. 8.
Dated 1520 on a pilaster at the extreme right.
Berlin (East), London (BM), Paris (BN), (Ecole des B.-A.), Vienna (A), Basel.
RD 5, LeBlanc 7, Passavant 5, Boullaye 5, Popham 5, Linzeler 8, Bersier 5.

The Annunciation takes place here on the porch of a church, rendered in the North Italian Renaissance style.[2] The lunette at the center of the porch contains an indistinct sculptural figure– possibly God with an open book, or Moses holding the Tablets of the Law.[3] The powerful High Renaissance figure of Gabriel, who has just descended in a mandorla of clouds with music-making putti, resembles a Roman personification of Victory in the manner of Marcantonio, contrasting with the more Umbrian figure of the kneeling Mary,[4] depicted in late *quattrocento* style. Mary's strange halo, which at first appears to have been abandoned in favor of the crown of stars placed on top of it, may actually represent a prop from the staging of a mystery play. The wire halo was used to provide almost invisible support for the crown above, which was to appear as though floating in space. Gabriel's mandorla may also stem from a theatrical source, recalling Brunelleschi's device for the presentation of the same subject. Duvet was known as a master of theatrical effects in the staging of mystery plays at Langres and this engraving may represent one of the *tableaux-vivants* presented in Burgundy for triumphal entries. The advanced architectural forms may also be partially explained by their possible function as mystery-play settings.[5]

---

1. An impression of this engraving is listed in *A Catalogue of Prints (the property of) Thomas Lloyd, Esq., Sold by George Jones,* London, July 1st, 1825, p. 43, Cat. 547, "The Annunciation, 1520, not noticed by Bartsch," and bought by (George?) Walker. This must have been the source of the reproduction appearing in W. Ottley's *Facsimiles of Scarce and Curious Prints,* London, 1828, p. XXII, and Plate 107. Ottley purchased prints at the Lloyd sale, the probable source of the British Museum impression. The print reproduced is from the Bibliothèque Nationale.
2. Blunt (1953, p. 71) writes, "The architectural setting is more accurately classical than anything to be found in contemporary French work . . ." There are, however, certain similarities between the building and details at Blois. M. J. Renouvier, "Des Types et des Manières des Graveurs," *Académie des sciences et lettres de Montpellier,* I, 1854, p. 741, the first author to discuss the style of this engraving, proposes an Italian journey to account for the advanced architectural forms.
3. Representations of Moses were frequently shown in Annunciation scenes. Duvet, whose adopted emblem was the "tablettes de Moïse," may very well have wanted to include Moses in the print, where, possibly for the first time, the engraver's monogram is on a classical eared tablet instead of the usual double tablet.
4. Blunt, p. 71. Oberheide, p. 156, believed the angel to be derived from Marcantonio's *Athena* (B. 357), providing illustrations of both (Plate XXI, fig. 2), but specific source is not entirely convincing. Popham, pp. 132-33, believed that this engraving, together with *The Nativity with a Candle,* "suggest, in the affected grace of their figures, some late Umbrian prototype." Duvet's eclecticism is far too complex in this engraving to point to any single work as its model. For a somewhat later French sculpture of the same subject, with stylistic affinities to this print, see *La collection de M. E. Foulc,* Paris, 1927, p. 90, Cat. 165, "*L'Annonciation.* Art français, école de Champaigne, XVIe siècle," illus. II, Plate XLI.
5. See Text fig' 75 for a reproduction of a miniature of 1547 by Hubert Caillaux for *Le mystère de la Passion* (B.N. ms. fr. 12536) in which the central structure has certain affinities to the one in the Duvet engraving. Mary with an oddly discontiguous clump of hair waving out to the left is seen again in Duvet's *Apocalypse* (Cat. 50).

13 ADRIAN VI

Ø 81 mm. Cut within platemark.
Unsigned.
Paris (BN—unique).
RD 62, LeBlanc 65, Passavant 62, Boullaye 62, Popham 62, Linzeler 11, Bersier 63.

This engraving was executed in 1524, the year inscribed upon its verso which shows the "Triumph of Divinity" (Cat. 14), with the artist's double tablets.[1] This, together with its style, make an attribution to Duvet incontestable, despite opinions to the contrary.[2] The rather tight, dry technique of this work points to an early date, fully in accord with that of 1524 inscribed on the pendant. This papal medal design is after Marcantonio, copied in reverse from the Italian's engraving of Adrian VI (B. XIV, 368, 494).[3]

Born in Utrecht in 1459, Adrian VI depended upon the friendship and protection of Margaret of York, widow of Charles the Bold of Burgundy. Much of his career was taken up with complex negotiations with the French. Duvet, who executed many commissions as goldsmith for the diocese of Langres, appears to have been selected to design a commemorative medal following the pontiff's death in 1523.[4] ADRIAN SEXTUS PONTIFEX MAXIMUS is inscribed around the papal portrait, each word separated by a fleuron. A missing word was probably inscribed upon the lost left section. The embroidered motifs on the cope are echoed in other works of Duvet.[5]

The medal, showing the profile of Adrian VI and the *Triumph of Divinity* (Cat. 14) emerged briefly at the end of the nineteenth century, when it was described by Barbier de Montault.[6] Active in the Geneva mint, Duvet was probably trained in that genre in Dijon by his uncle.

---

1. The border at the extreme left of the circular print has been lost, as well as parts of the inner ground. It is trimmed within the platemark.
2. Mrs. Pattison, *The Renaissance of Art in France*, London, 1879, II, p. 142, rejects both *The Triumph of Divinity and Adrian VI* as examples of Duvet's oeuvre; Émile Galichon, "De quelques estampes milanaises," *Gazette des Beaux-Arts*, XVIII, 1865, p. 552 attributed them to an unknown Milanese engraver.
3. The discovery of the Italian model for Cat. 13 was made by Louis Godefroy (quoted by Linzeler, p. 349).
4. See C.-F. Chevé, *Dict. des Papers*, Paris, n. d., p. 63.
5. The ornament on the upper part of the papal collar reappears as relief designs on the pilasters in *The Nativity with a Candle* (Cat. 28); that of the lower collar was already used on the gateway for *The Entry of Christ into Jerusalem* (Cat. 1).
6. Barbier de Montault, *Traité d'iconographie chrétienne*, Paris, 1890. I, p. 265. Under the classification of Triomphe de Dieu, the author describes, without mentioning source or maker, "Une médaille d'Adrian VI, datée de 1524, représente, sur un char trainé par quatre éléphants et que montent Saint Paul, Saint Pierre, Saint Jean et Saint Marc, les trois personnes de la Trinité, assises et tenant une tablette sur laquelle est écrit: In principio erat." The only medal of Adrian VI is illustrated in G. F. Hill's catalogue of *The Gustave Drefus Collection of Renaissance Medals*, Oxford, 1931, Cat. 629, p. 292, p. CXXXVII. Made in the Netherlands, this medal is entirely unlike Duvet's, and has no *verso*. Hill suggests it was made by a seal engraver.

14 THE TRIUMPH OF DIVINITY

Ø 81 mm. Cut within platemark.
Unsigned.
Paris (BN—unique).
RD 11, LeBlanc 54, Passavant 11, Boullaye 11, Popham 11, Linzeler 70, Bersier 64.

Dated 1524, this print prominently displays the double tablet, which is almost a Duvet signature in itself.[1]
It is inscribed *IN PRINCIPIO ERAT* (John 1:2).

The engraving is surrounded by the words *ETERNITAS SEV DIVINITAS OMNIA VIN IT.* The fourth
letter of the last word is effaced and the word has been read as either *VINXIT* or *VINCIT.* The first
would render the sentence "Divinity embraces all," the translation provided by Robert-Dumesnil and
LeBlanc. Émile Galichon suggested the VINCIT reading, which would change the sentence to "Divinity
conquers all."[2] In view of the fact that the trinity is shown in a triumphal chariot, the motif of victory
should be expected to be consistent in the quotation, as translated by Galichon.

This engraving is the obverse of the one done for a projected commemorative medal of Pope Adrian VI.
(Cat. 13). Both may have been on the same plate. The two riders appearing to the left of Paul and Peter
may represent Mark and John. The four elephants signify the triumph of fame over death. The engraving
refers to Adrian's participation in the triumph of Faith and to the triumph of his own fame over death.[3]
It is ironic that such a medal should have been designed for a pope who, in his zealous opposition to all
Roman classical imagery, objected to the triumphal arches erected in 1522 upon his elevation to the papacy
as pagan vestiges having nothing to do with Christianity.[4]

While the triumphal chariot drawn by four elephants (symbols of religion, chastity, and loyalty)[5]
may well have been derived from a School of Mantegna engraving, it also appears on the reverse of a medal
of Trajan, executed by the "Medallist of the Roman Emperors" working in Northern Italy in the last quarter
of the fifteenth century.[6] Duvet, known to have designed and executed coins and presumably medals as
well, probably knew the Trajan's Verso.[7] The elephants are also found in Roman coinage, reproduced by Vico
perhaps the French engraver's primary source,[8] associated with apotheosis

---

1. As in the case of Cat. 13, Mrs. Pattison, *The Renaissance of Art in France,* London, 1879, II, p. 142, rejects the attribution. E. Galichon ("De quelques estampes milanaises," *Gazette des Beaux-Arts,* XVIII..1865, p. 552) whose reading
   of the inscription and identification of the four figures as evangelists seem correct, believed both prints to be Milanese.
   That they should have been influenced by Lombard art seems very likely, considering the many North Italian
   stylistic elements in Duvet's art. See note 6.
2. Galichon, p. 552.
3. One of the tapestries in the Vienna collection illustrating *The Triumph of Eternity over Time* shows the Holy Trinity
   enthroned on a car drawn by symbols of the Four Evangelists. See *Art Treasures from the Vienna Collections,* 1949-51,
   p. 257, Cat. 258.
4. See C.-F. Chevé, *Dict. des Papes,* Paris, n.d., p. 63.
5. For elephant symbolism see W.S. Heckscher, "Bernini's Elephant and Obelisk," *Art Bulletin,* XXIX, 1947, pp. 166-182.
   In Cesare Ripa's *Iconologia,* Rome, 1603, p. 430, the elephant is included in the emblem for *religione.*
6. In G.F. Hill's *Catalogue of the Gustave Drefus Collection of Renaissance Medals,* Oxford, 1931, I. p. 187, no. 733;
   illustrated II, pl. 123. Hill believed that this medallist, who signed his works S.C. worked in the region of Milan.
   For a medal showing a Roman triumph in which elephants play a major role, see Graeven, *Römische Mitteilungen,*
   XXVIII, 1913, Plate 8, fig. 9.
7. See Documents 57, 61, 63.
8. B. XV, p. 341, included among Cat. 257-317.

15 SAINT STEVEN

Ø 50 mm.
Signed ID, upside down on the double tablet at the feet of the seated figure on the right.
Amsterdam (Rijksmuseum). Formerly Dresden (destroyed 1944).
RD 25, LeBlanc 53, Passavant 25, Brulliot 2864, Boullaye 25, Popham 25, Linzeler 52-6, Bersier 57.

One of a series of seven roundels, Cat. 15-21. The roundel, generally described as "A Saint in the dress of one of the religious orders" seems to depict Steven or Lawrence, frequently represented young martyrs shown as deacons.[1] The figure at the extreme left (whose shoulder has been partially scratched out in the Rijksmuseum impression) may be another saint. A scene comparable to the engraving is that of Steven brought in captivity before the emperor (Acts 7:2).

The very precise technique and delicate small scale of this engraving, coupled with the monogram in Gothic letters, point to an early time of execution;[2] the series of seven roundels (Cat. 15-20) may perhaps date even earlier than its placement here suggests.

---

1. See Karl Künstle, *Ikonographie der Keiligen*, Freiburg-im-Breisgau, 1926, p. 397.
2. Godefroy dated it "1525," and regarded the engraving together with the others in the series as provisional studies for medals according to Linzeler, p. 345.

16 SAINT JOHN THE BAPTIST

Rijksmuseum.
RD 15, LeBlanc 13, Passavant 15, Boullaye 18, Popham 15, Linzeler 50-4, Bersier 54.

One of a series of seven roundels, Cat. 15-21. The young saint, in classical attire, stands on a hillock. A crossed staff rests on his right shoulder. He holds an open book with his left hand and is seen before a classical arcade.

Shown very young, in the popular Italian fashion, the apostle stands to the left of a female statue (the Virgin?). A votive diptych hangs at the base, like the one so often employed by Duvet to place his monogram.

17   SAINT JOHN THE EVANGELIST[1]

∅ 47 mm.
Unsigned.
Paris (BN—unique).
RD 15, LeBlanc 13, Passavant 15, Boullaye 15, Popham 15, Linzeler 50-4, Bersier 55.

One of a series of seven roundels, Cat. 15-21. The saint's facial type may have been derived from Campagnola. For a discussion of style and dating, see "The Saviour in Heaven," Cat. 21.

---

1. The only known impression is printed to the right on the same sheet as the roundel showing Saint Andrew (Cat. 18) which is signed ID on the double tablet.

18   SAINT ANDREW[1]

∅ 48 mm.
Signed ID on a double tablet, partially obscured by the tuft of grass at the saint's feet.[2]
Paris (BN—unique).
RD 16, LeBlanc 14, Passavant 16, Boullaye 16, Popham 16, Linzeler 51-5, Bersier 56.

One of a series of seven roundels, Cat. 15-21. The most conventionally composed of all seven roundels, Duvet's "Saint Andrew" emerges as the best of the series. The saint resembles a heroic statue which has stepped down from a niche. The handsome loggia and the smaller houses glimpsed between its columns create a convincing space, carefully distributed within the circular confines of the print area.

For style and dating, see "The Saviour in Heaven" (Cat. 21).

---

1. The only known impression is printed on the same sheet as the roundel showing Saint John the Evangelist (Cat. 17).
2. Boullaye, p. 80, observed, "Au milieu du bas, on distingue difficilement les lettres I H D." While the monogram is almost indecipherable, it seems to be on the conventional double tablet, as in Cat. 16.

19   SAINT PAUL

$\emptyset$ 47 mm.
Unsigned.
Paris (BN-unique).
RD 14, LeBlanc 12, Passavant 14, Boullaye 14, Popham 14, Linzeler 49-3, Bersier 53.

One of a series of seven roundels, Cat. 15-21. Paul is identifiable by a great sword held in the right hand, which appears to have a serpent wrapped around it.[1] The scene may have been meant to suggest an Eastern setting.

For style and dating see "The Saviour in Heaven" (Cat. 21).

---

1. While this may only be a sword belt, the caduceus-like appearance of the belt spiralling around the sword may have been suggested by Acts 14:13, where the people of Lystra refer to Paul as Hermes.

20 SAINT PETER

Ø 46 mm.
Signed ID on double tablets below companion roundel showing "The Saviour in Heaven" (Cat. 20).
Paris (BN-unique).
RD 13, LeBlanc 11, Passavant 13, Boullaye 13, Popham 13, Linzeler 48-2, Bersier 52.

One of a series of seven roundels, Cat. 15-21. For style and dating, see "The Saviour in Heaven" (Cat. 21).

21 THE SAVIOUR IN HEAVEN

Ø 46 mm.
Signed ID on double tablet below the roundel, which is printed on the same sheet as "Saint Peter" (Cat. 20).[1]
Paris (BN-unique).
RD 12, LeBlanc 10, Passavant 12, Boullaye 12, Popham 12, Linzeler 47-1,[2] Bersier 51.

One of a series of seven roundels, Cat. 15-21. The print seems to be from a transitional period in Duvet's career, moving away from Northern sources to emulate the late style of the School of Marcantonio, the source for the putti and the remotely Michelangelesque Christ.

This series of roundels was intended for liturgical application. They seem to have been engraved over a considerable time span, as "Saint Steven" (Cat. 15) is earlier in style than "The Saviour in Heaven" and the intermediary roundels.

1. In decorative roundels (B.170) by Lucas van Leyden, the artist placed his monogram between the roundels, so that craftsmen, adapting the design, would not have to draw over the alien name. See Max J. Friedländer, *Lucas van Leyden*, Leipzig, 1924, pl. 15.
2. Linzeler catalogued the engraving as No. 11 but described it under 47.1.

154 x 108 mm.
Signed ID on double tablet in the lower right corner.
London (BM—unique).[1]
RD 2, LeBlanc 16, Passavant 66, Boullaye 66, Popham 66, Linzeler 6, Bersier 9.

The crowded figures at the right are reminiscent of Duvet's very earliest engravings, the architecture and figures in the foreground reveal a new Italian influence. The small block of grassy soil under the feet of Christ continues the landscape convention of the roundels. This print resembles one of the same subject by Dirk Vellert, dated 1523, and was probably engraved shortly thereafter.[2]

The design for the wellhead is very much like those by Jacques Androuet Ducerceau, which were published in the *Second Livre d'Architecture*, Paris, 1561.[3]

---

1. Inscribed on the back "G. Storck à Milano 1799 Tu A^d 9328," it was first published by Pietro Zani, who records another impression in Milan, owned by "Maino," noting "cose tutte che mettono fuor d'ogni dubbio, che questo Maestro era un excellente orefice. Ammirata in Milano nel Gab. dei Sig. Storck, e del Maino." In his *Enciclopedia metodica*, Parma, 1821, Part II, VI, p. 372, Zani gives the measurements of the Storck impression as "5,8 x 4,1." Possibly Sykes, former owner of Cat. 30 from the Storck Collection, also brought *Christ and the Woman of Samaria* to the Museum. For Storck, see F. Lugt, *Les Marques des collections de dessins et d'estampes*, Amsterdam, 1921, II, p. 435.
2. Reproduced in *The Print Collector's Quarterly*, XII, 1925, p. 35. Both engravings may be derived from an unknown common source.
3. The curious well-covering may be an adaptation from the many triumphal arches Duvet designed for royal entries. Both the well, which also reflects pattern-book designs for monstrances, and the two elaborate water vessels also reveal the French engraver's activities as a goldsmith. See also the later design for a monstrance by Ducerceau, reproduced in O. Reynard, *Ornements des ancien maîtres*, Paris, 1845, Plate 14. It is also similar to that shown in an engraving by Duvet's younger contemporary Reverdy, in The *Judgement of Solomon* (Passavant, VI, 109, No. 6).

231 x 171 mm.[1]
Signed IDV below inscribed date, 1528, on wall at extreme right.
Florence (Biblioteca Marucelliana–unique).
Popham 80.[2]

The composition is adapted from a Roman or Tuscan source of the High Renaissance, circa 1510. Duvet converted the Virgin's forearm into a breast by inserting a nipple between the fingers of the hand placed upon the upper arm.[3]   The tree trunk above the wall is clearly intended to suggest its continuation down behind the wall; this is also indicated by the angel's shoulder placed before the tree.   The artist changed his mind, placing the lower part of the tree in front of the wall as a more satisfactory compositional closing at the left.

The technique presents a harsh juxtaposition between the carefully finished, delicate realization of Mary's face, typical of Duvet's conservative early style, and the powerful, hasty rendering of Joseph, characteristic of the artist's expressionistic *Spätstil*.   Mary's elaborate drapery is of a sort that became popular in Northern art toward the middle of the century.   Like so many of Duvet's works, this print is both derivative and avant-garde.

The exact subject of this engraving is difficult to identify.   The figures surrounding Mary seem to have a sudden intimation of the sorrows in store for Mother and Son.   Only the stoical, serene face of Mary, gazing beyond the immediate environment, seems removed from the grief shared by Joseph, Jesus, and the angels.   It is as though Mary is prophetically aware of her ultimate role as Queen of Heaven, shown already endowed with the crown.   She bares her breast in the traditional gesture of intercession for the salvation of mankind at the Last Judgement.   The bitten pomegranate held by Jesus probably refers to Him as the New Adam, and to the Resurrection.   Mary is surrounded by symbols of her sorrows, and the scene as a whole, once identified as a *Rest on the Flight into Egypt*, may suggest this sorrow, among others.[4]   The great tree trunk upon which Mary is seated may itself be interpreted as alluding to the Crucifixion, as does the ointment jar of the Deposition, at the extreme right.[5]   The three bullrushes at the exact center of the composition summarize the disguised symbolism as promise of both the Passion and ultimate reign of Christ.[6]

---

1. First mentioned by Benvenuto Disertori, in "Cronache," *Emporium*, LXXII, no. 1930, p. 323, as a "Nativity." The engraving is mounted in a volume of old prints, Vol. 1, no. 60.   At the bottom of the page on which it is found, there is written, "forse del Douvet Gio."

2. This engraving was originally entitled *The Rest on the Flight into Egypt* by Popham, "An Undescribed Engraving by Jean Duvet," in *Maso Finiguerra*, XV-XVII, 1937, Fasc. I, pp. 92-93.
    The absence of a donkey, a spring, or a fruit tree, all traditionally present in the Rest on the Flight into Egypt, would seem to preclude that subject as a wholly satisfactory identification of the print.

3. Popham, 1937, p. 94, has described the print as being "obviously Raphaelesque in origin," pointing out that the "Roman scarf in her [Mary's] hair, for example, is a stock property in the studios of Raphael and Giulio Romano." Actually, this headress could just as well be of Netherlandish origin.   See the painting by Cornelius Buys of *SS. Ursula and Cunera*, formerly in the Guggenheim collection, N.Y., rep. by G. J. Hoogewerff, De Noord-Nederlandsche Schilderdunst, "S-Gravenhage, II, 1937, fig. 171.   Of the angel at the left, Popham 1937, p. 94, notes, "Perhaps the angel on the left is borrowed, but if so, it has been transformed by Duvet into his own characteristic form."

4. See no. 2 above.   An iconographically complex rendering of this subject, in a wall painting at d'Hauvers-le-Hamon (Sarthe) dating from the very end of the sixteenth century, shows the *Flight into Egypt* with intimations of the Passion.   See the Catalogue of the exhibition, *La Vierge dans l'art-français*, Petit Palais, 1950, Cat. 91 B.

5. A triptych of the *Last Judgement*, attributed to Bernard van Orley in the Jacobskerk, Antwerp, shows Saints Agatha and Margaret on the right shutter, and Christ, Peter, and Paul on the left shutter, with God the Father above.   Christ, bearing a cross, kneels on a great log, not unlike that in the Duvet engraving.

6. The bullrush (Typha latifolia) is listed in the *Dictionnaire de Botanique*, ed. J. P. Migne, Paris, n.d., VIII, of *Nouvelle Encyclopédie Théologique*, under "Massette," p. 865, and is described as signifying "l'emblème de la dignité et du commandement."   In the sixteenth century it was shown thrust into Christ's hands during the Passion as a mockery of his claim to be leader of the Jews (Matt. 27:29-30).   An etching by Gossaert portrayed the same theme.   This lost Gossaert is reproduced in Julius Held, *Dürers Wirkung auf die niederländische Kunst seiner Zeit*, Den Haag, 1931, Plate VII, 2 and 3.

24 SAINT JOHN THE BAPTIST AND SAINT JOHN THE EVANGELIST ADORING THE LAMB OF GOD

140 x 97 mm.
Unsigned. Dated 1528 at the center.
Vienna (A-unique).
B 8, RD 18, LeBlanc 24, Passavant 18, Boullaye 18, Popham 18, Linzeler 53, Bersier 43.

The style of this engraving, with its almost sketchy quality, shows frequent references to Roman and North Italian printmaking—Saint John the Evangelist (who resembles the same figure in the engraved Apocalypse series, Cat. 60-61 is reminiscent of Marcantonio. The composition and iconography may be a remote reflection of Raphael's "Madonna of Foligno" (Vatican, Rome) or of a fifteenth-century Netherlandish work like the Campin panel at the Musée Granet (Aix-en-Provence). Both saints celebrate Christ as the Lamb of God and are shown vernerating this image here.

125 x 136 mm. (BM, BN). Both cut within platemark.
Unsigned. Inscribed 1528 at the upper right on the wall above the soldiers' heads.
London (BM), Paris (BN),[1] Vienna (A) here reproduced.
Duplessis 5, Passavant 69, Boullaye 69, Popham 69, Linzeler 14, Bersier 13.

Like two of the three other engravings dating from the same year (Cat. 24, 26), the "Entombment" is unsigned; the placement of the date on an architectural form is seen in the third print of 1528 (Cat. 23). The composition is derived from both late fifteenth- and sixteenth-century Italian prints—the group at the right, inspired by Mantegna's "Bacchanale with the Vat" (B. XIII, 128, 19), reappears in Cat. 38 and 70, the Saint John suggests a Michelangelesque source. The swooning Mary resembles the same figure in the engraver's "Deposition" (Cat. 37) associated with the *Apocalypse* Series,[2] shown sharing her son's Passion as co-Redeemer.

1. Very poorly preserved.
2. Here, however, the rock-cut tomb appears at the upper right, and it is clear that Joseph and Nicodemus will bear the body to the sepulchre. E. Haverkamp-Begemann has noted a small painting (presumably a fragment) depicting the *Entombment,* by Isenbrandt, in which the body of Christ is carried by two men, apparently Joseph and Nico-demus, into a rock-cut tomb as Mary, John, and the three Marys look on at the left. Exhibited by Kunsthandel P. de Boer (Amsterdam) at the Prinsenhof (Delft) July 7 - August 20, 1951, illustrated in dealer's catalogue, no. 22.

190 x 133 mm.
Unsigned. The date 1528 is engraved in the corner at the lower left.
Vienna (A-unique).
B 38, RD 53, LeBlanc 56, Passavant 53, Boullaye 53, Popham 53, Linzeler 71, Bersier 62.

E. Tietze-Conrat has suggested the title *Allegorie der von Amor besiegten Keuscheit,*[2] interpreting the curious position of the young man's right arm and hand as signifying chastity and modesty, Amor bringing a fetter with which to capture the pure youth. The subject matter is similar to that depicted by Robetta in his *Allegory of the Power of Love.*[3] Duvet's engraving reflects the great popularity of classical and pseudo-classical amorous literature in sixteenth-century France—the *Loves of Cupid and Psyche* were illustrated and discussed ad infinitum; the poetry of Martial, Catullus, Petronius, and Propertius was also extremely popular.[4] The engraving recalls a verse by the latter in which a young man recounts meeting "certain boys . . . some held flambeaux, other arrows, part of them even appeared to be getting ready bonds for me. But they were naked." These "boys" eventually tie him up for delivery to a lady.[5]

The tree in this engraving is almost identical with the one in "The Suicide of Judas" (Cat. 27).[6] 1528 is Duvet's best documented year. With its Dürer-like landscape detail and Campagnolesque tree, the figures freely derived from Marcantonio, Mantegna, and possibly Gossaert, this engraving marks an important stage in Duvet's eclecticism, the richest fusion of Northern and Southern sources to date. It may have begun as a Gossaert-like *Fall* which was then changed to an Italianate allegory.

1. Generally known as "Love, a Man and a Woman."
2. According to E. Tietze-Conrat *(Der französische Kupferstich der Renaissance,* Munich, 1925, p. 31) the engraving is reminiscent of the later illustration for the hieroglyph "Continence et vénérable chasteté" in the Kerver edition of 1543 of the *Horusapollo,* f. 53. See also Denyse Métral, *Blaise de Vigenère,* Paris, 1939, p. 190, n. 2.
3. Reproduced in Hind I, Part I, no. 29. Duvet's engraving belongs to the same genre as a woodcut from Fossa, *Inamoramento di Galvano,* Milan, n.d., reproduced in Kristeller, *Die lombardische Graphik,* Berlin, 1913, p. 34. See also the print now attributed to Gossaert at the British Museum (Passavant, III, p. 320, no. 5—as Baldung).
4. See Ernst Lavisse, ed., *Histoire de France,* Paris, 1900-1911, V, (by Henri Lemonnier) Part 2, pp. 261-2.
5. See the H. S. Phillimore translation of *Propertius,* Oxford, 1906, p. 79, from Book II, xxix.
6. Despite this and many other correspondences between the engraving and Duvet's other works, L. Godefroy is quoted by Linzeler (p. 350) as having questioned its attribution.

174 x 89 mm (BN). Both examples cut within platemark.
Signed DI, Duvet's monogram in reversed order, on double tablets placed on the ground on the lower left.
Dijon (Bibliothèque Municipale), Paris (BN).
RD 21, LeBlanc 20, Passavant 21, Boullaye 21, Popham 21, Linzeler 10, Bersier 16.

Judas is seen from the back, hanging from a tree; his ribbonlike entrails dangle below the knotted, classical drapery. He is placed outside the gates of Jerusalem in an open landscape; a river, flowing along a V-shaped course, converges at the base of the tree. The city gate is shown prepared for a triumphal entry, surmounted by a sculpture of a pagan deity, placed above four other figures in niches. Golgotha is at the extreme left, its three crosses barely visible. A turbulent sky fills the upper part of the print. The horseman is shown in Duvet's later representation of the same subject (Cat. 72).[1] The tree, which also appears in the "Allegory of the Power of Love" (Cat. 26), is taken from Campagnola. The Judas also has certain North Italian qualities. Close correspondence between "The Suicide of Judas" and Duvet's Allegory of the Power of Love, dated 1528, and also between it and the same subject in the upper left of the "Deposition" (Cat. 37), suggests a date between 1528 and 1540 for this engraving.[2] See Cat. 72 for further discussion of the iconography. For the Dijon entry of Charles VIII, the painter Perronet Rousseau was paid for providing wigs and beards for prophets and for "l'omme pendu," the Judas figure frequently hung in effigy outside the city walls for ceremonial entries.[3]

---

1. The horseman is shown in Duvet's later representation of the same subject (Cat. 72). He may represent the Apocalyptic Horseman of Death.
2. Godefroy (quoted by Linzeler, p. 335) dates the print circa 1523.
3. See P. Gouvenain, *Mém. de la comm. des antiquités de la Côte-d 'Or*, XI, 1885-1888, p. 243.

152 x 222 mm (BN). All examples cut within platemark.
Unsigned.
London (BM), Paris (BN), Vienna (A).
RD 7, LeBlanc 9, Passavant 7, Boullaye 7, Popham 7, Linzeler 7, Bersier 7.

In 1841, Robert-Dumesnil suggested that the presence of the candle referred to a mystery play. The laurel wreaths substantiate his view.[1] They symbolize the victory of Christianity while the classical ruins point to the collapse of the pagan world and relate to the religious imagery utilized for Burgundian royal triumphal entries staged by Duvet.[2]

Apparently unfinished, this print is in the style of the 1520s, but whether dating before or after the 1528 series is hard to say. It has a freedom which may be interpreted as signifying a new degree of sophistication and confidence or as reflecting a lesser degree of formal and technical competence than the signed and dated works—the latter view taken in the Bibliothèque Nationale catalogue.[3] It is very close to the subject in Tory's *Metz Hours* of 1525 and 1529.[4]

---

1. Robert-Dumesnil (1841, V, p. 8, n. 1) suggests consulting Guillaume Roger Molé's anonymously published *Observations historiques et critiques sur les erreurs des peintres, sculpteurs et dessinateurs, dans la representation des sujets tirés de l'histoire sainte*, Paris, 1771, in connection with "En tenant une chandelle," derived from "tenir la chandelle," a line from mystery plays. The motif goes back to the revelations of Saint Bridgit; see E. Panofsky, *Early Netherlandish Painting*, Cambridge, 1953, p. 126.
2. Molé (II, p. 35) quotes from Nicolas Denisot's *Cantique spirituelle*, of circa 1545, in which the Nativity is described as taking place in a setting similar to that of the Duvet engraving.

> Ont veu la Vièrge être mère
> Sur ces fourches tout en long
> Quatre perches a l'antique,
> Desceignoient le double front
> D'un double & double portique.

However, as Denisot was trained as a painter before becoming a poet, his literary images may have been inspired by the visual arts. See Clément Jugé, *Nicolas Denisot du Mans*, Le Mans, Paris, 1907, pp. 6 ff. The structure at the right is a more complex version of the *cantoria* seen in Cat. 2. The relief designs on the pilasters are identical to that on the pope's cope in Cat. 13. The composition relates to that of a niello, attributed to Perugino (reproduced by André Blum, *Les nielles du Quattrocento*, Paris, 1950, p. 57, *La Nativité*). The Holy Family, with Joseph holding a lantern, is shown in front of a triumphal arch in a *Nativity* printed by Simon Vostre for the *Heures de Verdun* 1508. Here, however, the family is not in classical garb, their clothes differing in no way from the genre representations of the scene.
3. According to Godefroy (quoted by Linzeler, p. 332) the engraving dates from circa 1519 and this date may prove correct.
4. Observed by Myra Dickman Orth.

29 DEATH OF A STAG (ACTAEON?)

178 x 280 mm.[1]
Unsigned.
Vienna (A—unique).
RD 70, Duplessis 6, Passavant 70, Boullaye 70, Popham 70, Linzeler 75, Bersier 66.

This engraving makes a somewhat unfinished impression, especially in the upper part of the composition, toward the center. It is copied in reverse from a print by the Master L.D. after Primaticcio (Text fig. 46),[2] B.XVI, p. 331, no. 64.While omitting the small figures in the background of the Fontainebleau master's print, Duvet added two huntsmen in the foreground. His source represents the Death of Actaeon.[3] Duvet may have chosen this subject because it had been of considerable theological importance in France since the fourteenth century, when the *Ovide moralisé* reinterpreted the story of Actaeon as a Christian allegory.[4] In view of the contemporary prominence of French neo-Platonism, the subject may have been selected to follow Bruno's interpretation of Actaeon's metamorphosis where the hunter represents man's intellect, the hounds his ideas. Moved beyond himself by the divine beauty of Diana, Actaeon is transformed into his very prey, pursued by his own hounds.[5]

The Fontainebleau source suggests a date in the later 1540s, when printmakers there first became productive on a large scale.[6] The print may resemble a tapestry design which Duvet is known to have made.[7] Scenes of the chase were popular subjects for hangings—the death of the stag was interpreted as an allegory of the brevity of life.[8]

---

1. Boullaye (p. 131) and Popham (p. 149) erroneously give 298 x 280 mm as the size of this engraving.
2. The engraving is signed L. D. Bologna; B.XVI, p. 331, no. 64. Félix Herbet, *(Les graveurs de l'École de Fontainebleau,* Paris, 1896-1902) lists it as no. 38.
3. L. Dimier, *Le Primatice,* Paris, 1900, p. 491, Cat. 34. For a similar Death of Actaeon, see the extreme right of a painting after François Clouet, *Le Bain de Diane,* Musée des Beaux-Arts, Rouen (rep. in P. du Colombier, *L'art renainssance en France,* Paris, 1945, fig. 118). A related composition in enamel from the Leonard Limoisin workshop is given by O. von Falke, *Alte Goldschmiedekunst in Zürcher Kunsthaus,* Zürich, 1928, Cat. 92, p. 45, rep. on plate 28.
4. See C. de Boer, editor of *Ovide moralisé,* in *Verhandelingen der koninklijke Akademie van Wetenschapen te Amsterdam,* Afdeeling Letterkunde, XV- XVI, p. 312, Book 3, line 632 ff.
   > Dyane, c'est la Deité
   > Qui regnoit en la Trinité
   > Nue, sans humaine nature,
   > Qu'Actaeon vit sans couverture.
5. The anonymous and anti-Semitic compiler of the *Ovide moralisé* compares the Jews, called the killers of Christ. with the dogs, killers of Actaeon.
6. See Henri Zerner, "L'eau-forte à Fontainebleau - le rôle de Fantuzzi," *Art de France,* IV, 1964, p. 78. The print was included in the 1972-3 Fontainebleau Exhibition in Paris, Cat. 305, p. 280.
7. See Appendix E, Doc. 48.
8. Heinrich Göbel, *Die Wandteppiche,* Leipzig, 1923, Teil I, Band I, p. 131.

180 x 285 mm (BM).[1]
Unsigned.
Chatsworth, London (BM), Vienna (A).
B 6, RD 10, LeBlanc 17, Passavant 10, Boullaye 10, Popham 10, Linzeler 16, Bersier 15.

The engraving is a free copy, reduced in size, after a print of the School of Mantegna (B.3), possibly by Zoan Andrea or Girolamo Mocetto.[2] Duvet has omitted Mantegna's Latin inscription, replacing it by a swag of drapery. Cutting away the background, he restricts the composition to the space occupied by the participants, creating a scene which in some ways exceeds the dramatic intensity of the original. The sketchy, almost unfinished character of the print presents a radical departure from "The Entombment of 1528" (Cat. 25). The engraving anticipates the frenzied immediacy of works of the artist's *Spätstil*, such as the "Unfinished Entombment" (Cat. 71).[3]

The engraving reflects the continued French interest in Mantegna, whose prints were copied extensively for decorations at Gaillon and elsewhere. Duvet used motifs from Mantegna for the "Judgment of Solomon" (Cat. 10), and later for the "Martyrdom of Saint John the Evangelist" (Cat. 38).

Like the "Death of a Stag" (Cat. 29), this engraving probably represents a brief departure from the artist's more conventional engraving style, in favor of the more rapid, free approach which was becoming current in the etchings of Fantuzzi and other Italian printmakers in the 1540s.

---

1. The impression at the British Museum was originally in the Storck collection at Milan, which possessed several other rare Duvets, including the "Christ and the Woman of Samaria" (Cat. 22).
2. Bartsch was the first to recognize the derivation from Mantegna, which is not, as stated by Popham, p. 134, copied in reverse. Mrs. Mark Pattison (*The Renaissance of Art in France,* London, 1879, II, p. 97) considered the Italian print to be by Mocetto. Hind (V. Part II, 1948, p. 11) includes the Duvet engraving as Cat. 2. b, among the copies after the Italian print, which he treats as being by or after Mantegna. Linzeler, no. 16, confuses the Italian engraving with the Duvet copy, cataloguing the Mantegna as a Duvet and including it as such in the Bibliothèque Nationale. (Cabinet d'Estampes, AA3, Rès.)
3. Popham (p. 134) wrote, "The copy of Mantegna's *Entombment* reproduces on a smaller scale much of the majesty and pathos of the original, with the addition of that sort of almost grotesque intensity which characterizes Duvet; one would be inclined to place it around 1530."

248 x 140 mm.
An uninscribed double tablet, hanging at the extreme left, the engraver's emblem, may be regarded as his signature.
Vienna (A—unique).
B 4, RD 6, LeBlanc 8, Passavant 6, Boullaye 6, Popham 6, Linzeler 17, Bersier 8.

With the exception of such obviously Italianate details as Mary's drapery, the composition is Northern. The exposed cellar was especially popular in German depictions of the first quarter of the sixteenth century; it represents Christ's birthplace.[1] The nibbling mouse is a symbol of the corruption and decay of antiquity, as is the ruined building itself.[2] The figures of Mary and Jesus are reminiscent of those in the central panel of a triptych attributed to Pieter Aertsen at Saint-Sauveur (Bruges) whose *oeuvre* is also close to Duvet's "Revelations of Saint John the Divine" (Cat. 39). The pose of the figure of Mary is almost identical to that of the artist's Magdalen embracing the cross in the "Deposition" (Cat. 37), probably dating from about 1540. This print, with its tablet-shaped format and architectural details— both of which point to the *Apocalypse* plates —may have been executed shortly before the initiation of that great series, its relatively freer technique indicative of a prior period of experimentation and discovery. The artist has momentarily abandoned the triumphal imagery of his other, more characteristic treatment of the same subject (Cat. 28). Note the cross hidden among the beams above the Christ child, indicating the Passion.

---

1. See Gert von der Osten, "Der Blick in die Geburtshöhle," *Kölner Domblatt,* XXIII-XXIV, 1964, pp. 341-358.
2. Erwin Panofsky, "The Mouse that Michelangelo Failed to Carve," *Essays in Memory of Karl Lehmann,* ed. Lucy Freeman Sandler, New York, 1964 (Marsyas Supplement I), pp. 242-51. The type of broken columns and the emphasis on the subterranean structure are similar to those in the *Apocalypse.* Cat. 51, 56, 59.

32 A KING AND DIANA RECEIVING HUNTSMEN [1]

224 x 396 mm (BN). All examples cut within platemark.
Unsigned.
Amsterdam (Rijksmuseum), Berlin, Cambridge (Fogg Art Museum), Chicago (AIC—two impressions, ex colls. Dresden and Fürstenberg), Cincinnati (AM), Cleveland (MA), Detroit, Dresden, London (BM, V & A), Paris (BN, L, Petit Palais, ex Coll. Jean Ehrmann, sold by Kornfeld 1970, pc.), Vienna (A), Washington (NG—Rosenwald Coll.).
B 39, RD 54, LeBlanc 59, Passavant 54, Boullaye 54, Bénézit 5760, Popham 54, Linzeler 60-1, Bersier 67.

One of a series of six, Cat. 32-34, 66-68. The engraving is based upon the text of a popular fourteenth-century work on the hunt, *Le Livre du Roy Modus et du la Royne Racio,* by Henri de Ferrières.[2] It was consulted for the numerous tapestry cycles devoted to the hunt in the early sixteenth century.[3]

On the basis of similarity of format and subject, this print has long been linked with five other Duvet engravings devoted to the medieval allegory of the unicorn hunt. The king and Diana may represent Henri II and Diane de Poitiers.[4] Duvet dedicated three engravings to the sacred and profane virtues of Henri II, under whose protection the artist completed the engraved *Apocalypse.*[5]   The young king's love of the hunt and of Diane de Poitiers are well known, and there is considerable facial resemblance between figures in the engraving and reliable portraits of the king and Diana.[6]

With the exception of "The Death of the Stag" (Cat. 29), this engraving brings Duvet closer to the School of Fontainebleau than any other print in his œuvre. The composition reflects Duvet's familiarity with the etchings of Fantuzzi after Rosso which were executed shortly after 1540.[7] Duvet's interest in the Fontainebleau manner may well have been aroused by a series of eight tapestries designed by Jean Cousin, which were hung in the Cathedral of Langres in 1543 (See text figs. 11-13).

---

1. The title generally given this engraving, "A King Receiving a Present from a Huntsman," has been changed; the "present" consists of animal droppings. See C.F.G.R. Schwerdt, *Hunting, Hawking, Shooting,* London, 1928, III, p. 57. An impression of this print was in the Schwerdt ill. Cat. 1, p. 57.
2. See the edition edited by Elzéar Blaze, Paris, 1839, fol. viii v⁰ . "Pour cognoistre grand cerf par les froyers," also fol. viii, "Pour cognoistre les fumées de cerf," which states, "Et si les treuves de grosse forme et en grosse torches et bien moulues, c'est bien signe qu'il est cerf dix cors chacable." The circular objects held out by the scout would correspond to these "fumées de cerf." An early illuminated manuscript of de Ferrière's text, dated 1379, is in the Bibliothèque Nationale (Fr. 12399).
3. The print corresponds to that of a tapestry representing the month of February in the series of the Chasse de Maximilian, entitled "L'assemblée au Palais du Roy." Instead of the living Diana, the tapestry shows a seated king and queen, with her statue displayed in a niche. See Paul Alfasse, "Les tapisseries des 'Chasses de Maximilian,' " *Gazette des Beaux Arts,* 5 éme pér., I, Feb. 1920, pp. 127-40. J. Destrée. *Industrie de la tapisserie à Enghien,* 1900, pp. 12-16, illustrates an additional tapestry series devoted to Roy Modus and Royne Racio. See also Gaston Migeon, *Les tapisseries des Chasses de Maximilian,* Paris, 1920, p. 6. The scene which corresponds to the Duvet engraving is Février-Signes de Poissons, for which *L'assemblée au Palais du Roi* is shown.
4. For the problem of this identification, see pp. 115-122 above.
5. See Cat. 61-63, and the Privilège text, Appendix E, Doc. 68.
6. See the reproduction of the François Clouet portrait in Blunt, 1953, pl. 50(B). The resemblance may be fortuitous. The ring so prominently displayed in the king's ear tends to substantiate the traditional identification with Henri II, whose protraits emphasize the earring. See the portrait medal by Germain Pilon reproduced by Pierre du Colombier, *L'art renaissance en France,* Paris, 1945, fig. 129, opp. p. 94. The king's baton is designed somewhat along the same lines as the *baton du justice* in the Hôtel de Ville at Geneva, supposedly the one executed by the French engraver and goldsmith during his residence in Geneva for the town council in 1555 (Appendix E, Doc. 65). See fig. 14).
7. The Fantuzzi closest to the Duvet is B.XVI, p. 348, no. 27. Duvet may well have consulted triumphs engraved after Salviati (B.XVI, p. 385, no. 22) and Giulio Romano (B.XVI, p. 49, no. 16), as well as an undescribed engraving in the British Museum after a facade by Polidoro da Caravaggio for the Via della Maschera d'Oro (Sloane Collection, Cat. V8-74).

33 THE CAPTURE OF THE UNICORN

237 x 394 mm (BM),[1] 230 x 395 (A).
Unsigned.
Berlin, Dijon (Bibliothèque Municipale), London (BM), Vienna (A).
RD 56, Duplessis 8, LeBlanc 61, Passavant 72, Boullaye 56, Bénézit 5760, Popham 56, Linzeler 63-3 and 64-3a,
Bersier 70.

One of a series of six, Cat. 32-34, 66-68. The impression in the Albertina has a type-set caption printed immediately below the plate: "Le conseil mis en effect, sur la prinse de la Licorne." (Council effected for the capture of the Unicorn.)[2]

Showing the all-important episode of the capture of the unicorn, this engraving is generally regarded as being the fourth scene of the series. The episode is taken from Greek Bestiaries—the Physiologus texts.[3] In relating the conventional capture of the unicorn, classical accounts stress the importance of music in attracting the ferocious animal to the virgin. The latter, after the unicorn has placed its head in her lap, ties the sleeping animal to a tree with a rope given to her by a hunter. The virginity of the maiden is stressed by the traditional symbols of purity—the lily and the enclosed garden, both shown at her side.[4] The proximity of stream and grotto may indicate that the maiden is one of Diana's nymphs; the goddess is shown in the preceding print. The swag of drapery covering the lily is reminiscent of the drapery shading the king and Diana in the latter. The lily in a closed garden was a traditional emblem for the kingdom of France and may well substantiate theories of real or projected royal patronage for the Unicorn Series.

The horizontal disposition of the composition, coupled with its decorative quality, has suggested its use, together with the rest of the Unicorn series, as engraved tapestry designs.[5] Of the six prints, the "Capture of the Unicorn" belongs with the two which are the most highly finished (Cat. 32, 34) It lacks the sketchy, improvisational quality of the three other engravings, and appears to have been executed considerably earlier, and in a very different spirit from that of its narrative predecessor, "The King Pursued by a Unicorn" (Cat. 66).

The same dogs who are here depicted in pursuit of the unicorn will be shown again in "The Unicorn Borne on a Triumphal Car" (Cat. 34), pulling their quarry into the heavenly Jerusalem, while a maiden similar to the one who is here ensnaring the unicorn, sings a song of praise.

The style of this engraving is close to that of the more formally composed plates in the *Apocalypse* Series, especially Cat. 56 and 60. In the latter, the handling of the verdure, and in the former the king and his retinue resemble "The Capture of the Unicorn." The storks and their setting recall those of the Master LD's "Christ in Limbo"; some of the poses relate to the same print.[6]

---

1. The British impression may well have come from the Paignon-Dijonval (Cat. 5766, 3523), Buckingham, and Ottley Collections. The Berlin print probably stems from the Brentano-Birckenstock Collection sold in Frankfurt, 1870 (Cat. 1764), to Damlos, described as being in poor condition.
2. This impression with printed caption was first recorded by Passavant, VI, 1864, Leipzig, p. 258.
3. See Carl Cohen, *Zur literarischen Geschichte des Einhorns,* Berlin, 1896. On p. 27 Cohen cites the *Physiologus* of Eustathius. (*Spicilegium Solesmense, Sanctorum Patrum,* ed. J.B. Pitra, Paris, 1855, III, p. 355.)
4. According to Albertus Magnus, *De secretis mulierum,* a girl's virginity can be determined by her coloring after eating pulverized lily. See Angelo da Gubernatis, *La mythologie des plantes,* Paris, 1882, II, p. 200.
5. Duvet is known to have designed tapestries in Geneva. See Appendix E, Doc. 48.
6. Observed by Eric Zafran.

236 x 381 mm., complete engraved surface. 234 x 387 mm.
Signed emblematically by the fighting swan plucking down—*duvet*—from the swan below, in an enclosure at the upper left.
Berlin, London (BM).[1]
RD 57, LeBlanc 62, Passavant 57, Boullaye 57, Bénézit 5760, Popham 57, Linzeler 66-5, Bersier 71.

(One of a series of six, Cat. 31-33, 65-67.) The design of the great city in the background of this engraving is derived from Dürer.[2] The subject matter derives from a Northern European, late medieval reworking of the *Physiologus* text, in which, after the capture of the unicorn, the royal hunters' victory is celebrated by a triumphal procession carrying the prize quarry to the palace.[3]

The hunting dogs now draw the chariot, upon which either Diana or one of her nymphs—virgins instrumental to the unicorn's capture—rides. Paired, the hounds' union symbolizes the new concord of virtues. Dogs, given names such as Veritas, Justitia, Pax and Misericordia in tapestries and manuscripts illustrating the Holy Hunt, at war with one another before the triumph of the unicorn, now function in harmony, united by the unicorn's sacrifice.[4] While this engraving depicts the king's victory, it is also that of the unicorn—Christ, who, permitting himself to be captured and suffering for the redemption of mankind, is about to enter the Heavenly Jerusalem for his reunion with God, the subject of the concluding engraving (Cat. 67).

The wreaths of oak—sacred to Jupiter—with which the maiden and the unicorn are crowned, symbolize the participation of the Holy Spirit, since Jupiter was viewed as a pagan parallel of the Holy Spirit. The oak, whose rustling leaves made Jupiter's will known to the Samian oracles, is here an indication of his participation in the victory of the unicorn.[5]

The late Middle Ages identified the Triumph of Caesar with that of the Church, and French early sixteenth-century Books of Hours can be found in which the Triumph of Caesar is led by a putto riding a unicorn, the symbol of Christ. Christ—the unicorn—is carried in triumph to the heavenly Jerusalem—the city in the background whose sanctity is indicated by the moon illuminating it by night and day. The moon refers to Diana, goddess of chastity, prototype of the Virgin Mary, just as the unicorn, another emblem of chastity, was considered symbolic of the purity of Christ. By attaching the unicorn to Diana, a complex new allegory involving pagan and Christian references was achieved. It is this fusion which the engraving depicts.

Duvet's triumphal car, with its winged battering ram over the wheel, is, like Dürer's woodcut of "Maximilian's Marriage to Mary of Burgundy," rooted in the Burgundian tradition. Duvet himself participated in the staging of many triumphal entries. No records show his having used unicorn imagery in triumphal processions in Dijon and Langres, but there is abundant documentation for the prominence of this mythical beast in contemporary pageantry.

The unicorn's horn is grooved in this print, differing from the smooth horn depicted in the "Capture" (Cat. 33). The king's face is also markedly different—heavier and squarer, more like that of idealized representations of Francois I[er] than like those of his son. These variations in important details must cause us to question the probability of the existence of a single, consistent literary source for the engravings of the Unicorn Series.

---

1. Probably first listed in *A Catalogue of Prints [the property of] Thomas Lloyd, Esq., Sold by George Jones, July 1st, 1825,* London, Cat. 545, B. 41, the print may have entered the Molteno collection from this sale. In 1834, presumably the same impression reappeared in the sale of the Buckingham Collection in London, Cat. 2523, where it was acquired by Ottley. Both of the above probably refer to the example listed by Bénard in the "Catalogue de Paignon-Dijonval," Paris, 1808, p. 201, as this collection is known to have been dispersed in England.
2. Popham, p. 147, has pointed out that part of the cityscape is taken from the background of Dürer's "Virgin with the Pear," 1511 (B. 41).
3. See Carl Cohn, *Zur literarischen Geschichte des Einhorns,* Berlin, 1896, p. 10. Cohn quotes from the *Physiologus* of Eustathius *(Spicilegium Solesmense, Sanctorum Patrum,* III, ed. J. B. Pitra, Paris, 1855, p. 355). On p. 27 other Physiologus texts are listed as stressing the importance of the displayed animal in a triumphal procession.
4. See O. Shephard, *The Lore of the Unicorn,* New York, 1930, p. 59.
5. See Angelo Gubernatis, *La mythologie des plantes,* Paris, 1882, II, P. 65, for further discussion of Jupiter's "arbre de la sagesse." See also Cat. 67, Note 3.

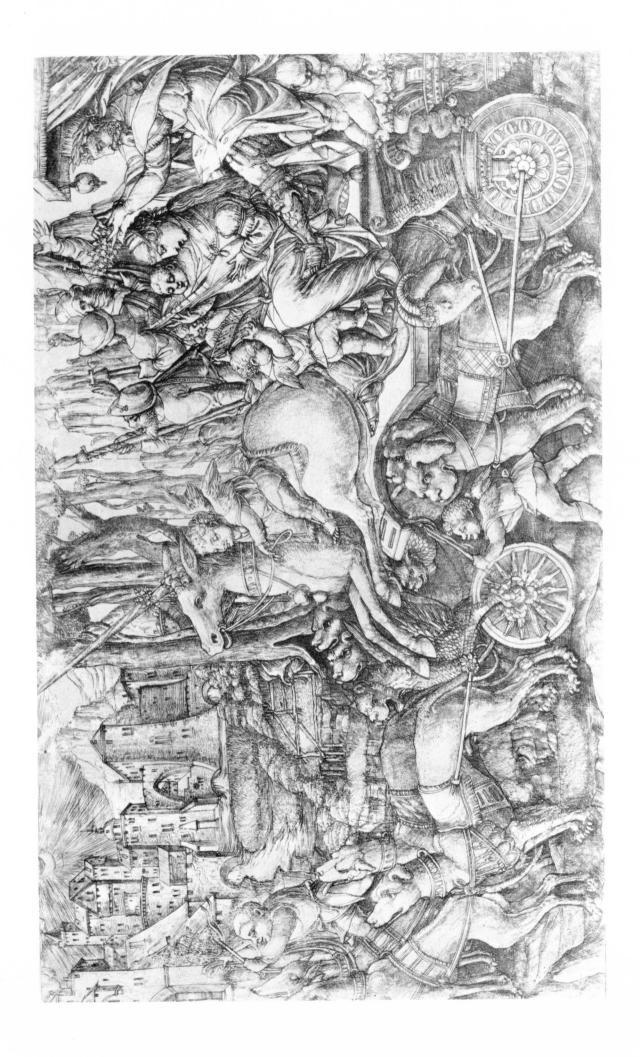

35. THE MARRIAGE OF ADAM AND EVE

305 x 216 mm.

Signed IOHANNES DVVET FAC on ground at left between feet of Adam.

Inscribed: ADE ET AEVE CONIVIGIVM EORVMQVE
DIVINA BENEDICTIO ET ALIA HIC
CONTENTA MISTERIA EXPRIMO
GENESIS CAPITE PENE SVMVNTVR[1]

First state: Dijon, (Bibliothèque Municipale—unique). Proof sheet with increased hatching in brown pen lines indicating strengthening of the shading at Adam's feet.[2]

Second state: Berlin, Boston (MFA), Budapest, Chantilly (Musée Condé), Chicago (AIC–BM duplicate), Cincinnati (AM), Cleveland (MA-in *Apocalypse figurée*), London (BM), Louvre Fonds Rothschild, Lyon (Bibliothèque de), New York (MMA-two impressions), Paris (BN-two impressions in Cabinet des Estampes-one in *Apocalypse figurée* Inv. Rés. A1587 Imp., L), Vienna (A), Washington (NG-Rosenwald Coll.), Zurich. Dijon, Dresden.

The increased shading indicated in the unique Dijon proof by pen lines has been engraved in the hatching below Adam's feet. The full sheet on which the brilliant Louvre impression is printed measures 411 x 280 mm.

B 1, RD 1, LeBlanc 1, Passavant1, Boullaye 1, Bénézit 5756, Popham 1, Linzeler 3, Bersier 1.

The composition is ultimately derived from Dürer's woodcut "Marriage of the Virgin" (B.82) which is also the source for the figure of God the Father, shown as a priest but for the cross on his mitre. It may have been transmitted via Caraglio's print after Parmigianino,[3] which places the scene within an arch-shaped setting similar to Duvet's. The Adam is derived from Dürer's "Adam and Eve" (B.1) of 1504; Eve is taken from the figure at the extreme left of Marcantonio's "Three Graces" (B.340). Together with the twenty-nine other tablet-shaped plates by Duvet, "The Marriage of Adam and Eve" is representative of the master's mature style, and probably dates between 1540-55.

The blessing of Adam and Eve (Genesis 1:28) is linked to the triumphal imagery of Duvet's engraved *Apocalypse*. The major participants and heavenly witnesses carry branches or banners of the cross, symbolizing the victory of Christ and the resulting state of peace and grace.[4] Eve's conquest of original sin through the New Eve's Son may be indicated by her wreath of lilies at the right and by Satan at her feet crushed under the banner of the Cross. The fallen angels of the Apocalypse are alluded to by the shields trampled upon by the victorious armed angels at the left. The sword and lily indicate divine justice preceding this heavenly, visionary "remarriage" of Adam and Eve. The sacrament takes place before a new tree of knowledge.

The iconography and inscription of this engraving reflect Duvet's staging of the mystères, such as *Les Rameaux (The Branches)*, the *tableaux-vivants* presented for triumphal entries. The branches echo those carried at Christ's entry into Jerusalem—the triumphal entry which initiated the Passion and the Redemption of Adam and Eve.

The lily at the extreme right, together with the *fleur-de-lys* capped banner staves, may refer to the royal patronage acknowledged in the *Privilège* of the engraved *Apocalypse* (App. E., Doc. 68). While this plate was not included with all the late published examples of the Apocalypse with text, its style, format, and fusion of images from Genesis and Revelations prove that it was conceived together with the *Apocalypse* Series.[5]

---

1. "The marriage of Adam and Eve and their blessing from God and other mysteries here contained are taken for the most part from the first chapter of Genesis." The inscription is a partial paraphrasing of Gen. 1:28.

2. It is hard to isolate distinct successive states, other than that differentiating the Dijon proof from the second state. Boullaye (p. 71) proposes two states for this engraving based upon impressions at the Bibliothèque Nationale: "1' exemplaire du recueil (AA.2) a subi dans un second tirage (recueil Ed,I.b) quelques retouches qui notamment ont fait disparaître certain detail trop libre en sa naiveté." Popham (p. 42) writes that there are two states, probably basing this view on Boullaye. H. Hilberry (New York University M.A. thesis, *Jean Duvet*, 1938, p. 72) noted a re-working of the plate after it had been worn down.

3. B. XV, 66, 1. It was very popular in sixteenth century France; J.A. Ducereau copied it in reverse. Reverdy also made a copy; an undescribed state is in the British Museum Print Room, Reverdy Album, p. 6.

4. X. Barbier de Montault, *Traite d'iconographie chrétienne*, Paris, 1890, I, p. 232. Misericordia is symbolized by branches, "symbols de paix et de pardon." The tree and branches may also be a reference to John 15:4 where interdependence of the Lord (the tree) and his people (the branches) is stressed.

5. Boullaye, p. 71, regards the engraving as a possible frontispiece for a projected illustrated Genesis. E. Tietze-Conrat, (*Der französische Kupferstich der Renaissance*, Munich, 1925, p. 8) agrees with this theory. Boullaye considers the engraving to have been planned in association with the Moses (Cat. 36).

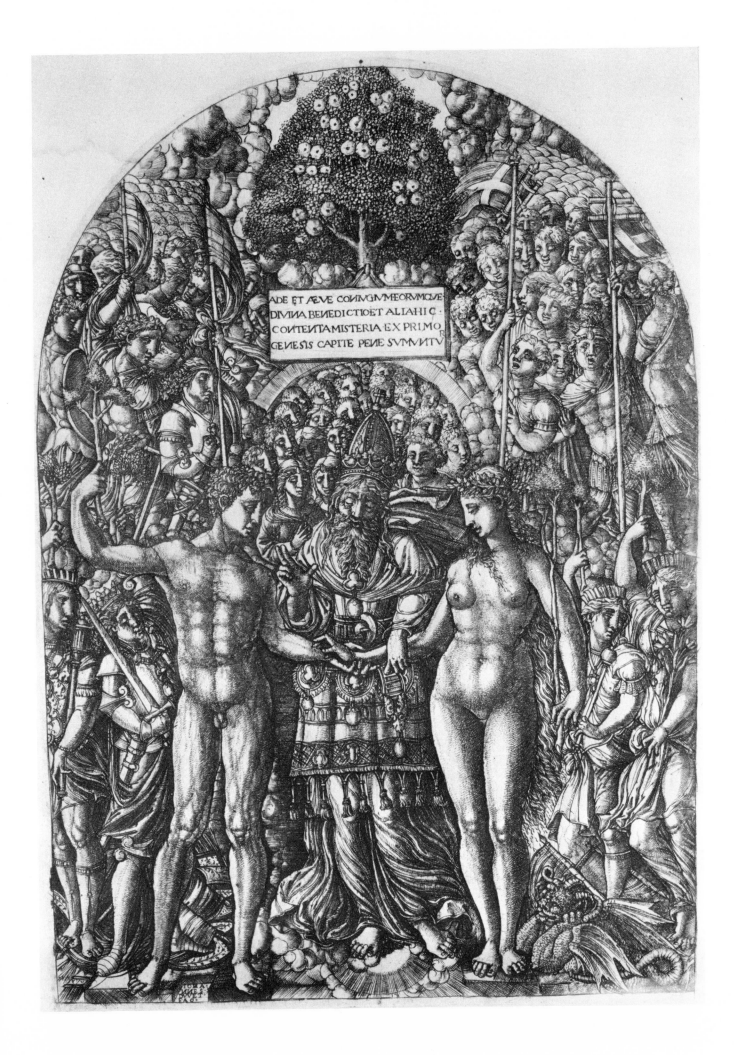

298 x 212

Signed DVVET on floor at lower left.

The tablets are inscribed: NO-ERIT IN TE DEUS RECENS. NEQ. ADORABIS. DEV. ALIENVM EGO. SVM DNS DEVS. TVVS QVI EDVXI. TE. DE TERRA. AEGIPTI.[1]

Reading from left to right, the columns are inscribed: NOE, ABRA, ILAC, IACOB, MELCHE (sedek), MOYSES, IESSE, DAVID, IOSEPH, MARIE IESVS.

First State: Langres (Musée des Beaux-Arts), Paris (BN–AA2 Rés). The tablets held up by Moses are blank. Columns uninscribed. Signature absent.[2]

Second State: Baltimore (MA), Berlin, Boston (MFA–two impressions), Chantilly (Musée Condé), Cleveland (MA–in *Apocalypse figurée*), Lyon (Bibliothèque de la Ville–in *Apocalypse figurée*), Middletown, Ct. (Davison Art Center), Paris (BN, L-Coll. Rothschild), Petit Palais, Ecole des Beaux Arts, Vienna (A–two impressions), Washington (LC, NG–Rosenwald Coll., ex coll., d'Arenberg). The tablets are inscribed, as are the columns. Engraving is signed.

Third State: Paris–in *Apocalypse figurée*, Rés. A1587 Imp., Petit Palais–in *Apocalypse figurée*–Coll. Dutuit. The plate surface has been damaged at the lower right, so that it looks as though a bomb had dropped among the Apostles on the Mount of Olives.

B 2, RD 2, LeBlanc 2, Passavant 2, Boullaye 2, Bénézit 5757, Popham 2, Linzeler 4, Bersier 2.

Seen behind Moses' columnar support, is a relief of the Burning Bush. The Holy Family, at the extreme right is placed above a relief depicting the Visitation and the Agony in the Garden. Parallel to the Holy Family at the extreme left, are Noah raising the Ark, and Abraham and Isaac. Abraham's upraised sword, restrained by an angel above, is opposite Joseph's sprouting rod, just as Isaac is opposite Jesus. Reliefs of the Drunkenness of Noah, and a male figure (holding a book?) are seen below. Jacob is above a relief depicting his dream. Jesse and David (who wears a crown and holds a harp) are at the right with reliefs of Saint Christopher and the Angel of the Annunciation(?) below.

The print's program is inspired by Romanesque portals such as that of Saint-Bénigne at Dijon (Text fig. 22) devoted to the ancestors of Christ and other Old Testament personae displayed for typological reasons, as prefigurations of salvation, with Moses the chief prophet and recipient of the Old Law as the chief forerunner of Christ, the New Law.[3] The key role of Moses in the context of the engraving follows Heb. 8:5-13 and John 1:17,45

The association of this print with Duvet's *Apocalypse* Series–identical in size and format–suggests a reference to Rev. 15:3 in which divine victory is celebrated by "the song of Moses, the servant of God, and the song of the Lamb . . ." The emphasis on triumphal imagery points to the possible application of the design to a *tableaux-vivant* for a royal visit. Since Abraham's sword ends in a *fleur-de-lys* and the Virgin is also shown with lilies, her attribute and the French royal emblem, the flower may be a dual reference to the first families of Heaven and France. The patronage of the latter is acknowledged in the *Privilège* of the printed Apocalypse (Appendix E, Doc. 68).

The depiction of Moses may reflect a lectern at the cathedral of Langres supported by a life-size bronze statue of that patriarch;[4] the group of Joseph and Jesus recalls the description of a lost silver reliquary which Duvet may have executed for the cathedral treasury circa 1533.[5] The Noah and Abraham re-appear in the engraving of the *Revelations of Saint John the Divine* (Cat. 39), whose architectural setting is also reminiscent of Langres cathedral.

---

1. "Thou shalt have no other gods before me. I am the Lord thy God who brought thee out of the land of Egypt." (Ex. 20:3,2).

2. The Langres impression has four pale, rubbed numerals at the lower left of the page below the plate mark read by Boullaye, p. 73, as 1517. F. Courboin, *Histoire illustré de la gravure en France*, 1923, I, p. 119, and Naef, p. 119, and Marcel, II, p. 435, accept this as the date of the engraving. I have examined the "date," and found it illegible. The impression at the Bibliothèque Nationale, AA2 Rés. has the names added in brown ink.

3. Blunt, *Art and Architecture in France, 1500 to 1700*, London, 1957, p. 248, n. 105, pointed out Romanesque influences in this print, suggesting such sources as Chartres, Souillac, and Moissac. The artist's father was appointed abbey goldsmith (of St.-Bénigne). Dom Plancher, *Histoire générale de la Bourgogne*, Dijon, 1749, I-II, reproduces the destroyed portal. Many other lost Romanesque monuments may also have influenced the artist.

4. The lectern is described in Marcel, II, p. 310. See also E. Mâle, *L'art religieuse en France à la fin de moyen âge*, Paris 1908, p. 234.

5. For the reliquary, see Boullaye, p. 6; Marcel, II, p. 431, n. 3.

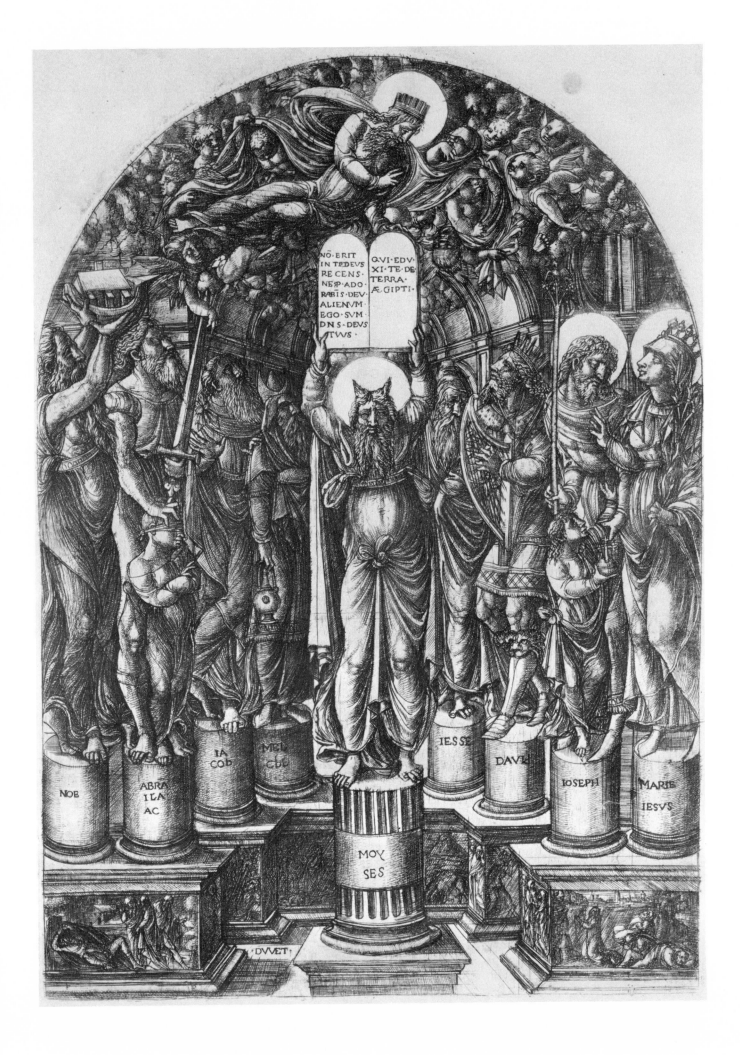

301 x 212 mm.

Signed IOHANNES DVVET FAC across double-tablet at the extreme lower left.

A tablet at the foot of the cross is inscribed:

>ROGAVIT PILATVM IOSEPH
>AB ARIMATHIA VT TOLLERET
>CORPVS IESV ET PERMISIT
>PILATVS   IOH 19[2]

A plaque nailed to the top of the cross bears the initials INRI in Hebrew, Greek, and Latin (John 19:21). First State: Dijon (Bibliothèque Municipale—unique). The shadows cast upon the cross by the Magdalen are indicated by pen lines. Shading is indicated in the following areas: below the feet of Christ; on the cross of the thief at the right; to the right of the thief's head; to the right of his hand; and below his feet. The Dijon impression has additional pen-drawn shading on the Magdalen's halo, on her knee towards the cross, as well as heavier shading over the Virgin's stomach, which were never engraved on the plate.

Second State: Berlin, Boston (MFA), Chantilly (Musée Condé), Chicago (AIC-ex coll. Gallice), Cleveland (MA—in *Apocalypse figurée*), Dijon (Bibliothèque Municipale), Langres (Musée des Beaux-Arts), Lyon (Bibliothèque de la Ville—in *Apocalypse figurée*), New York (MMA), Paris (BN—two in Cabinet des Estampes—one in *Apocalypse figurée*, inv. Rés. A1587 Imp.), Vienna (A), Washington (NG—Rosenwald Coll. ex Coll. d'Arenberg). The shadows indicated in the first paragraph above are added. B 5, RD 8, LeBlanc 17, Passavant 8, Boullaye 8, Bénézit 5758, Popham 8, Linzeler 20, Bersier 12.

In an unusual form for this time, Christ and the thieves are all crucified with four nails, their feet resting on ledges.[3] The Holy Sepuchre is hollowed out of the living rock,[4] the stone table nearby. The sumptuously dressed, bearded old man wearing a mitre-like hat who holds the shroud up to the man at the top of the cross is probably Joseph of Arimathea who, according to Mark (15:46), brought a linen shroud.[5]

Like so much of the engraver's oeuvre, "The Deposition" reflects his participation in the production of the *mystères*. The quotation from Saint John is the opening line of one of the major dramas of Duvet's day.[6] The suicide of Judas, another popular scene in the mystery plays, is shown in two other engravings by Duvet (Cat. 27, 72). The juxtaposition of Judas' suicide with the Crucifixion is typical of contemporary drama.[7]

The figure of Christ, as well as those of the group surrounding the swooning Mary, are similar to those seen in the sculpture of François Gentil and Ligier Richier.[8] All of these French works were probably influenced by the Marcantonio "Deposition" after Raphael.

The kneeling Evangelist closely resembles the same figure in the concluding plate of the *Apocalypse* (Cat. 61). The complete stylistic congruence of these works suggests a date of circa 1550. The drama that is Saint John's relation of the Deposition and the ensuing suicide of Judas is a prelude to the sustained *mystère* of John's Revelation (Cat. 39, 61).

---

1. Usually known as the *Crucifixion*.
2. "Joseph of Arimathea asked Pilate for permission to take down the body of Christ, and Pilate granted it to him. John 19." (John 19:38).
3. This curious reversion to Romanesque formula can also be seen in the School of Fouquet triptych at Loches and Fouquet's *Pietà*, formerly in the Beatty collection. It can also be seen in an early altarpiece by Hans Holbein the Younger, at Basel, and in a rather mysterious engraving, apparently left incomplete by Albrecht Dürer, circa 1523, known as the *Great Crucifixion* or *Crucifixion with Many Figures* (M. 25, T. 913, D. 107) discussed by Erwin Panofsky, *Albrecht Dürer*, Princeton, 1941, II, p. 65, Cat. 534. The earliest known surviving impression was printed circa 1550/60. For another four-nail crucifixion, see Geoffroy Tory, *Heures à l'usage de Metz*, 1525. Two early sixteenth century depictions of the four nail Crucifixion are reproduced by M. Horster ("Eine unbekannte Handzeichnung der Kreuzabnahme im Cinquecento," *Wallraf-Richartz-Jahrbuch*, XXVII, 1965, pp. 191-234) one by Filippino Lippi (Horster, Fig. 149), the second by Signorelli (Horster, Fig. 151).
4. John 19:39-41; Mark 16:3-4. A similar rock-cut tomb appears in Fouquet's *Heures d'Etienne Chevalier;* see Perls Pl. 17, p. 49. It has been identified as the palace of Joseph of Arimathea by Mrs. Pattison, *The Renaissance of Art in France*, London, 1879, II, p. 105.
5. For the problem of the identification of Joseph and Nicodemus see Wolfgang Stechow, "Joseph of Arimathea or Nicodemus?" *Studien zur toskanische Kunst*, Munich, 1963, pp. 289-302.
6. Entitled *La Résurrection*, it is discussed by L. Petit de Julleville, *Les mystères*, Paris, 1880, II, p. 221.
7. See E. Parfait, *Histoire du théâtre français*, Paris, 1745, II, p. 176, for a description of the *tableau vivant* staged for the entry of Louis XII in Paris, 1498. In the Fouquet *Heures d'Etienne Chevalier*, Christ goes past the hung body of Judas on his way to Calvary, rep. in Perls, fig. 4
8. The head of the woman comforting Mary is close to that of the same figure at Saint-Mihiel by Richier, see Paul Denis, *Ligier Richier*, Paris, 1911; dated circa 1530. The head of Christ resembles that of a sculpture attributed to Gentil at Langres, commissioned by a fellow-member of Duvet's confraternity. A plate comparing both heads can be found in the limited edition of Marcel, II, opp. p. 410. Mary's fainting represents the "co-passio" of the Virgin—her sharing of Christ's suffering.

298 x 209 mm.

Signed IOHANNES DVVET FAC at the left; between the cauldron and barrel.

Inscribed: IN FERVETIS OLEI DOLLIO MISSUS IOH APO ROMAE
             DOMITIA IMPER ILLOESUS EXIIT AC IN PATMOS INS
             RELEGAT VBI ET APOCALYPSIM SCRIPSIT.[2]

First State: Dijon (Bibliothèque Municipale, unique). No shadow cast to the right by the third ewer from the left. The right hand and wrist of John are free of shading. No shadow cast by the arm of the torturer at the right on the upper right of John's chest. Area on ground at the bottom of print between knee and toe of kneeling fire-tender at left lacks shading.[3]

Second State: Berlin, Boston (MFA), Brussels, Chantilly (Musée Condé—two impressions),[4] Detroit, Cleveland (MA–in Apocalypse figurée), London (BM), Lyon (Bibliothèque de la Ville–in Apocalypse figurée), New York (MMA), Paris (BN–three impressions, L–Coll. Rothschild), Ecole des B.-A., Vienna (A), Zurich. The shadows cited above are engraved.

Third State: Paris (BN–in Apocalypse figurée, Inv. Rés. A1587 Imp.). The corners of the plate at the lower right and left have been broken off and coarsely repaired.

B 36, RD 51, LeBlanc 26, Passavant 51, Boullaye 51, Popham 51, Linzeler 56, Bersier 47.

The engraving records John's martyrdom before his exile to Patmos.[5]   The elaborate gateway above the Saint's head represents the Porta Latina, as described by Tertullian.[6] The three handsome ewers, used to fill the cauldron and the vat, suggest the engraver's designs for goldsmith's work. His activity as pageant master is shown in the triumphal gateway, probably resembling some of the many royal entries designed by Duvet in Burgundy. The group of Saint John and his torturers is taken from Mantegna's *Bacchanal with a Vat* (B.19), also adapted in the *Entombment of 1528* (Cat. 25) and the *Saints Sebastian, Anthony and Roche* (Cat. 70).

This relatively rare subject, included by Dürer in his *Apocalypse* (B.61) was represented on a reliquary of St. John, the oldest in the treasury of the Cathedral of Langres which was first dedicated to that saint.[7]   One of Duvet's most successful engravings, the *Martyrdom of Saint John* has the richness of mid-sixteenth century painted glass windows, which Duvet is known to have designed in Geneva (Appendix E, Doc. 48).

---

1. Listed as the *Martyrdom of Saint John the Baptist* by Popham, p. 147.

2. "In Rome, by order of emperor Domitian, the apostle John, placed in a vat of boiling oil, leaving it safe and sound, was sent to the island of Patmos, where he wrote the Apocalypse." In the Boullaye transcription of the text, p. 118, he gives RELEGATUS, while on the print itself only RELEGAT is legible, followed by a scratched, blurred form. Bartsch, in his transcription (VII, p. 498, no. 36) omits the word ROMAE.

3. In the Dijon impression, all the areas enumerated above are filled with brown pen lines to guide the engraver in his subsequent activity. Several figures in the upper section of the print have additional pen-drawn hatching, but this was never engraved.

4. The sales catalogue of the W. Drugulin collection (London, 1866, p. 30, Cat. 330) lists this engraving and describes it as "first state, before the retouch, and with large margin, extremely rare." It is a curiously pale, but fresh example of the second state. A similar impression is listed in Katalog Nr. 29, H. Gilhofer and H. Ranschburg, Lucerne, p. 70, Cat. 137, described as a "Brilliant early impression in faultless condition with margins," (illustrated on p. 71).

5. A comparable use of the subject appears in the Besançon *Heures* of Simon Vostre (Paris, circa 1512) where the Martyrdom follows the Almanach as an introduction to the *Apocalypse*. Votre's work was also adapted for Langres (Marcel, I, p. 153).

6. Karl Künstle *(Ikonographie der Heiligen*, Freiburg-im-Breisgau, 1926, I, p. 344) gives the source as Tertullian, *De praescript.*, xxxvi. The subject may have been of special interest to printers and engravers since John was their patron saint. The burning oil of his "martyrdom" was similar to that used by sixteenth-century printers in their inks, according to D. Bourquin, "La gravure en France des origines à la fin du XVème siècle," *Le courrier graphique*, LXXXI, Sept.–Oct., 1955, p. 27.

7. H. Brocard, "Inventaire des reliques et autres curiosités de l'église cathedrale de Langres," *Bull. soc. hist. et archéol. de Langres*, 1880, p. 160.

IOHA
NNES DV
VET

INFE   RVETIS OLEI
DOLIO   MISSVS IOH
APO   OMAE DOMITIA
IMPER   ILLOESVS EXIITAC
IN PATMOS INS RELEGAT
VBI ET APOCALIPSIM SCRIPSIT

39 THE REVELATION OF SAINT JOHN THE EVANGELIST[1]

293 x 207 mm.

Signed IOHANNES DVVET FAC on double tablet on floor at right of bench.

The three following inscriptions appear on the engraving: An aureole surrounding the Trinity at the top of the plate is inscribed: TRES SIMVL AEQUALES PERSONAE SVNT DEVS VNVS + PRINCIPIUM ET FINIS RERVM TESTATE IOHANE +[2]. On the open book on the Evangelist's lap is written: IN PRINCIPIO ERAT VERBVM.[3]

On a pedestal at the lower left below Noah is inscribed: B IOH APOS SVB PERTINACE PRINCIP AB EXILIO REDIIT EPHESU VBI EVAGEL OIM NO VISSIMO SCRIPSIT QUOD A XPI DIVINA ILLA NATIVITATE INCHOAVIT VT EBIONITARV HERESIM MALA REFELLERET.[4]

First State: Dijon (Bibliothèque Municipale, unique). Top of column under foot of Saint John free of shadow; no shading on table cloth below row of books facing him; no diagonal lines of shading present along side and base of bench; no cross hatching engraved on top of bench. In the Dijon impression, all the areas indicated above are drawn in with a brown pen line, corresponding to the engraved lines on the second state.[5]

Second State: Berlin, Boston (MFA), Chantilly (Musée Condé), Chicago (AIC), Cleveland (MA-two impressions), Langres (Musée des Beaux-Arts),[6] London (BM—lower right corner restored), New York (MMA), Paris (BM—three impressions, a fourth in *Apocalypse figurée,* Inv. Rés. A1587 Imp., L—Coll. Rothschild), Ecole de B.-A. Vienna (A), Washington (NG—Rosenwald Coll., Berlin duplicate).

The table cloth under the books facing the Evangelist and the bench upon which he is seated are shaded. Lines of shading on the column upon which John's foot rests have been intensified.

B 13, RD 50, Le Blanc 25, Passavant 25, Boullaye 50, Bersier 36, Bénézit 5759.2, Popham 50, Linzeler 57.

The scene represents Saint John in the House of the Lord and refers to Rev. 1:10, "I was in the spirit on the Lord's day, and heard behind me a great voice, as of a trumpet." Saint John, his eyes closed, is in communication with the Trinity, three seated young male figures of equal size appearing above in an inscribed glory.[7] Their unity is accentuated by their copes, knotted together below the central Apocalyptic Book of the Seven Seals which indicates that this is a Trinitarian revelation peculiar to John. A second Apocalyptic image is shown below in the Fall of Satan. The great wings rising from the eagle perched on the Saint's shoulders reflect the Greek theological concept of his revelations, of his "spirit"–as flights into the divine.[8] He holds a book inscribed with the first line of his gospel, confronted by the other three. Above and below are inscriptions pertaining to his Epistles and Apocalypse.

The pedestal supporting Noah bears an inscription stating that Saint John, upon his liberation from Patmos, was returned to Ephesus, where he wrote his final work. This negates the traditional title of the engraving as "Saint John on Patmos." The visual references to the Apocalypse and the Trinitarian Epistles do not restrict the locale to Ephesus where John wrote his gospel refuting the heresy of the Ebionites. Duvet's inscription is based upon texts of Jerome and Irenaeus which identify the heresy of the Nicolaites (Rev. 2:6, 14 f) with that of the Ebionites (not specifically referred to in any of John's works).[9]

Duvet's engraving, stressing John as special advocate of the Trinitarian doctrine, must have been directed against some of the contemporary "heresies" of the Reformation, comparable to the unorthodox Christology of the Ebionites.[10] In view of the Trinitarian controversies, this print should be regarded as a monument of conservative Catholic theology. Since the architectural setting recalls the Cathedral of Langres and its relic of Saint John, this print may be related to its confraternity of the Holy Sacrament.[11] The figures of Noah and Abraham are symbolic of salvation through faith.[12]

The print was probably planned in immediate conjunction with that of "Moses and the Patriarchs" (Cat. 36). Moses and John occupy parallel positions as prophet of the Redeemer and as witness to the Redemption through the Trinity, the Mosaic tablets of the Old Law paralleling the Apocalyptic Book of the Seven Seals of the New Law.[13] Both John and Moses appear in dramatic architectural settings which may in themselves suggest a contrast between Church and Synagogue, the Romanesque and Gothic symbols of Old and New Dispensations.[14] Just as Moses is represented as the focal point of his prophecy, given the Tablets of the Law as the New Covenant, John is presented at a synthetic moment in which he is in simultaneous communication with the sources of his Epistle, Revelation, and Gospel. Bartsch, the first scholar to catalogue this engraving, was also the first, and last, to identify it correctly as "S. Jean en extase, inspiré de ses visions divines."[15]

The components of the engraving appear in the introductory woodcut of the *Kobergerbibel* of 1483 for the Gospel according to Saint John (Text fig. 24), where the Evangelist is shown seated in his study, pen in hand, with a vision of the Trinity appearing before him—Father and Son hold the Book with Seven Seals, with the Holy Spirit hovering between their heads.[16] Saint John's proximity to divinity—his annunciation by and of the Trinity in Duvet's engravings—suggests the characterization of this evangelist by Saint Jerome. In his preface to the Gospels, Saint Jerome points out that while Matthew wrote for the Jews and Mark and Luke were respectively the interpreter of Peter and the disciple of Paul, John "super pectus domini recumbens purissima doctrinarum fluenta potauit."[17]

The style of the engraving is completely in accord with that of the artist's other tablet-shaped engravings relating to the Apocalypse. Duvet has adapted the figure of Saint John from a print by Marcantonio.[18] The eagle who "lends" his wings to the Evangelist is derived from a North Italian print of a parade helmet.[19] As designer for triumphal entries, Duvet was certainly familiar with Italian renaissance motifs for such occasions. The extremely complex imagery of this engraving, together with that of the "Moses" (Cat. 36), would indicate a date of execution close to that of the "Jean Duvet as Saint John the Evangelist" (Cat. 64) of 1555 which also shows a prophetic figure, of the artist as evangelist, with his eyes closed, in final revelatory ecstasy.

---

1. Generally known as *Saint John on Patmos.*
2. "Three equal persons are a single God, beginning and end of all, as John testifies." A free transcription from "And there are three who give testimony in Heaven, The Father, The Word, and the Holy Ghost. And these three are one." (John 5:7).
3. "In the beginning was the Word." John 1:1.
4. "Saint John apostle, under prince Pertinax, delivered from exile, returned to Ephesus where he wrote a Gospel, the last of all, which he began with the birth of Christ in order to refute the bad heresy of the Ebionites." As pointed out by Boullaye, p. 116, Prince Pertinax could not be the Roman emperor of the same name, who lived almost a century later. Boullaye suggests that Duvet may have been alluding to a proconsul called Pertinax.
5. In addition to the pen lines already mentioned, the Dijon impression also has shading indicated by Abraham's feet and Noah's feet, to the right of the pediment containing the inscription at the extreme lower left, at the feet of the Trinity. None of these areas were engraved however. Dutuit's own manuscript catalogue, II, *Ecole anglaise, Ecole française,* p. 267, records the existence of a first totally uninscribed state, but does not give its location.
6. With an indistinct group of numerals at the lower left which have been deciphered as 1517, and have led certain writers to believe that this is the correct date for the engraving. In point of fact the numerals are illegible; they appear to have been scratched in, rather than engraved. The date was first published by Boullaye, p. 117. *Moses Surrounded by the Patriarchs* (Cat. 36) at Langres has a similar illegible date.
7. This representation of the Trinity was far more common in French fifteenth century art. It is shown twice in manuscripts illuminated by Jean Fouquet. See K. G. Perls, *Jean Fouquet,* Paris, 1940, figs. 27, 213.
8. See Alben Butler, *The Lives of the Fathers . . . ,* London, n.d., II, p. 845.
9. See the *Douay Holy Bible,* ed. James Carey, Douay Bible House, New York, 1938, "Introduction to the Gospel of Saint John," p. 112. If the engraving actually represented Saint John at Ephesus, this too would follow Irenaeus. See *Catholic Encyclopedia,* New York, VIII, p. 493.
10. According to the *Oxford Dictionary of the Christian Church,* Oxford, 1958, p. 433, the Ebionites were poor, severely ascetic Jewish Christians whose sect lived on the East of the Jordan. "Two of their principal tenets were (1) a 'reduced' doctrine of the Person of Christ, to the effect, e.g., that Jesus was the human son of Joseph and Mary and that the Holy Spirit in the form of a dove lighted on Him at His Baptism, and (2) over-emphasis on the binding character of the Mosaic Law. They are said to have used only the 'Gospel of St. Matthew' ('the Gospel of the Ebionites') and to have rejected the Pauline Epistles."
11. For the Confraternity of the Holy Sacrament, see pp. 47-70 above.
12. See Heb. 11:7, "By faith Noah, being warned of God of things not seen as yet . . . prepared an ark to the saving of his house: by which he condemned the world and became heir of the righteousness which is by faith." Also Heb. 11:17, "By faith Abraham, when he was tried, offered up Isaac . . ."
13. The Gospel of Saint John regards Moses as major prophet and prefiguration of the coming of Christ. See John 1:4, 6, 18, 3:15; 6:32; 7:19.

14. See Erwin Panofsky, *Early Netherlandish Painting,* Cambridge, Mass., 1953, pp. 132-134.
15. Bartsch, VII, p. 504, No. 13.
16. Schmidt, *Die Illustration der Lutherbibel, 1522-1700,* Basel, 1962, fig. 37.
17. *Nouum Testamentum,* ed. by J. Wordsworth and H. J. White, Oxford, 1889-98, I, p. 12.
18. Noted by Popham, p. 147. He suggests the Marcantonio is in turn "after Parmigianino, B. 460." A. Oberheide, *Der Einfluss Marcantonio . . . ,* Hamburg, 1933, Plate XLI, fig. 3, points out the source for Duvet's work and illustrates both. This pose may have been known to Duvet from engravings after the *Stoning of Saint Steven* from Raphael's *Acts of the Apostles* tapestry series (woven in the Netherlands) or from a painting of *Saint John the Baptist in the Wilderness* (now in the Louvre) painted for Cardinal Gouffier de Boissy.
19. The helmet design is reproduced by Ludwig Goldscheider, *Leonardo da Vinci,* London, 1944, p. 14.

301 x 214 mm.
Signed IOHANNES DVVET FAC on double-tablet between the two candlesticks to the left of the Evangelist.
Inscribed HISTORIA I. CAPIT. APOCAL. above signature.
Represented in major print collections.
B 14, RD 28, LeBlanc 28, Passavant 28, Boullaye 28, Popham 28, Linzeler 23-2, Bersier 19.

The composition is freely adapted from Dürer's woodcut *Apocalypse* (B.62) (Text fig. 37). Duvet has reversed the composition, adapting it to fit the tablet-shaped format. The mannered, late Gothic elaborations seen in the German woodcut have been eliminated in the French engraving, which partially replaces a northern vocabulary with that of the High Renaissance. The kneeling evangelist is converted from a Gothic figure to one of the School of Raphael. The Lord now appears *all'antica*, in a Michelangelesque pose. Duvet intensifies the form of Dürer's implied rainbow and introduces the clearly-defined mandorla and halo giving his composition symmetry.[1]

Dürer's design of flaming eyes—Rev. 1:14, ". . . and his eyes were as flames of fire"—is changed from a twisting flamboyance to triangular fields of light rays converging at the eye. Audaciously converting the text, of which verse 16 states, "And He had in His right hand seven stars," Duvet shifts these to the mandorla, leaving the Lord's hand free to grasp the trumpet of inspiration which is thrust down to John's ear—a brilliantly literal way of presenting, "I was in the Spirit on the Lord's day, and heard behind me a great voice as of a trumpet" (1:10).

The engraver's activity as goldsmith is reflected in the ornate girdle worn by the Lord, as well as the classical ornament which now replaces Dürer's Gothic tendrils on the candlesticks.[2]

As stated in the *Privilège* (Appendix E, Doc. 68), the engraved *Apocalypse* was under royal patronage, and the *fleur-de-lys* on the sword handle and within the Lord's halo may well reflect the king's crest.

Duvet's engraving incorporates a wider range of references from the first chapter of the Apocalypse than does the Dürer woodcut. The French print unites the images of verses 12 to 20 of the first chapter, investing them with a graphic vitality and dramatic immediacy worthy of the text.

---

1. The mandorla may have been borrowed from Dürer's next woodcut in the series (B.63).
2. For the sole classical motif within the Dürer woodcut—the ramshorn and acanthus scrolls on the base of the candlestick nearest the Evangelist—Duvet has substituted ox-skulls and swags.

HISTORIA
·I·CAPIT·
APOCAL

IOHA DV
MESNIL
FAC

303 x 215 mm.
Signed IOHANNES DVVET FAC on double tablet at the center of the foreground.
Inscribed HIST CAP 4 APOC ET 5 on base of throne at lower right.
Represented in major print collections.[1]
B 15, RD 29, LeBlanc 29, Passavant 29, Boullaye 29, Popham 29, Linzeler 24-3, Bersier 20.

The engraving unites all events in the fourth and fifth chapters of the Apocalypse by including the figure of the Lord (Ch. 4) with that of the Lamb (Ch. 5). The kneeling Evangelist is at the lower left, in the clouds, next to a detailed rendering of a fortified cityscape similar to that of the frontispiece (Cat. 65). At the center of the composition is the door of Heaven (4:1). An angel flies before it bearing the trumpet, which calls the Evangelist to heaven (4:1). Immediately above is the Lord's "throne set in Heaven" framed by a mandorla-like rainbow (4:3). The sides of the composition are lined by the twenty-four enthroned, Elders (4:4, 10, 11; 5:8, 9, 10); some cast their crowns before the throne (4:10); others harp or bear the golden vials. The throne is crested by the seven lamps (4:5) and flanked by the four living creatures (4:6). The Lord holds the Book of Seven Seals (5:1). Facing the Evangelist and pointing to the Lamb above is the Elder of 5:5. The Lamb is shown taking "the book out of the right hand of him that sat on the throne" (5:7). The heads of "the many angels" are shown clustered "around about the throne" (5:11).

The composition is a reversed, freely adapted and classicized version of the Dürer woodcut *Apocalypse* (B.63) (Text fig. 38). The French engraver introduces an original, much smaller landscape and reduced Dürer's gates of Heaven to a very small, emblematic doorway at the very center, rather than at the sides of the composition. Of all the woodcuts in Dürer's "Apocalypse," this was the most influential for Duvet, as the composition, framed by the great portal of heaven, resembles the tablet-shaped confines of the French series. The engraver's name appears in the identical portion as that of the author of his German source. Duvet heightens the excitement and sense of immediacy by his emphasis on formal rather than rational figural relationships, and by the intimacy engendered by the crowded composition. The engraved print incorporates a far more ambitious repertoire of Apocalyptic incidents than does its woodcut counterpart. The angel with the trumpet is adapted from a running angel of the Annunciation, which Duvet places on its side. Such free use or relocation of a motif is typical of the French engraver's emblematical, ornamental application of form.

---

1. In an early impression at the Bibliothèque Municipale, Dijon, Duvet added brown ink shading on the Evangelist's foot, but this was never engraved.

300 x 213 mm.
Signed IOHANNES DUVVET FAC on double table at the upper left, overlapping the horseman's bow.
Inscribed HISTORIA CAPIT 6 APOCAL on square tablet at the upper left.
Represented in major print collections.
B 16, RD 30, LeBlanc 30, Passavant 30, Boullaye 30, Popham 30, Linzeler 26-5, Bersier 21.

The engraving is limited to the events surrounding the opening of the first four seals (6:1-8). At the top center of the plate, an angel in a glory flies toward the haloed horseman at the upper left. Representing the First Horseman, this androgynous figure wears the crown and holds the bow and arrow mentioned in 6:2. The halo identifies him as the divine figure of Christ, "conquering that he might conquer" (6:2) with Duvet's signature to the left. Below the head of his white horse is the identifying plaque. A personification of evil, a Michelangelesque *ignudo,* is under the horse's hooves; similar figures are seen at the lower left. At the center of the plate, the Second martial Horseman (6:3) is shown riding a prancing steed. His left arm raises a sword in the air, about to decapitate a passive, apostle-like figure, apparently a representation of Peace which is to be removed from the earth by the Second Rider—War. To the right of the Second Rider, mounting his horse, is the Third, Hunger (6:5), waving his empty scales wildly in the sky.[1] The Fourth Rider, Death (a skeleton as opposed to Dürer's emaciated elder), on a starved nag, appears at the lower right, raking the prostrate figure of a king, with many other people, into the mouth of Hell.

Duvet's engraving echoes the major aspects of Dürer's woodcut (B.64) in reverse; it may reflect other, later adaptations of the German master's work. The personification of Peace appears to be an iconographical innovation of the French artist. The Michelangelesque figures are typical of the engraver's eclecticism, adapting and applying figures with a freedom usually reserved for ornament.[2] The group of heads below probably come from a Lamentation. The outstretched figure at the bottom is close to one in the Unicorn Series (Cat. 66). Several other figures are common to both prints.

---

1. Derived from Dürer's First Horseman. While the comparable woodcut by Dürer shows a figure wearing a tiara or mitre with his head in the mouth of Hell, Duvet inserts a crowned head, a change probably motivated by the rigorous prosecution of Protestant views in mid-sixteenth century France. A late fifteenth-century French Book of Hours—*Heures a l'usage de Rouen de 22 aout,* 1498, is similar in composition to Duvet's plate (See F.Courboin, *Histoire illustrée de la gravure en France,* Paris, 1923, I, fig. 127). It also recalls Reverdy's *Marcus Curtius* (Passavant VI, 112, 25).
2. These figures may depend upon engravings after Raphael and his School's "Building of the Ark" in the Vatican Loggia.

306 x 216 mm.

Signed IOHANNES DVVET FAC at the center of the left margin.[1]

Inscribed HIST CAP 6 ET 9 APOC on the plaque at center of altar. The upper half of this engraving illustrates the ninth through eleventh verses of the sixth chapter, while the lower half shows the first eleven verses of chapter nine.

First State: Dijon (Bibliothèque Municipale—unique[2]). The right shoulder of a crowned male figure seen from the back at the bottom of the composition has pen-drawn indications of increased shading at left hand. The recumbent figure at the lower right corner has increased pen-drawn shading on the upper foot.

Second State: Represented in major print collections. The right shoulder of the crowned male figure at lower left has increased shading, as does the area near the left hand of the kneeling figure at bottom, and the upper foot of the recumbent figure at the lower right corner.

B 17, RD 31, LeBlanc 31, Passavant 31, Boullaye 31, Popham 31, Linzeler 25-4, Bersier 22.

The kneeling Evangelist points to the inscription on the altar front. The dead (6:9) are like the naked *gisants* of contemporary French tombs. The opening of the sixth seal is indicated by the personifications of the dark moon and sun below the altar (6:12). The arched upper half of the composition is filled by angels dispensing robes to the resurrected souls (6:11) while the Lord, seated on a rainbow, is at the center. A cadaverous couple may be the same as the couple shown before the altar.

Duvet in the lower portion of the plate combines the end of chapter six representing the "kings of the earth and the great men and the generals and the rich and the strong and every one, slave and free hid in the caves and among the rocks of the mountains" (6:15) with the first eleven verses of the ninth chapter. The latter relates the events following the fifth angel's sounding of the trumpet, the falling of a star from heaven upon the earth, and the opening of the bottomless pit (1:1-2). A crowned Satan is seated at the right holding up the key to the pit, the fallen star on his shoulder, as he points down with his scepter to the pit, filled by a writhing mass of miserable, locust-ridden souls whose foreheads had not been crossed with the sign of God (9:14).[3] The depiction of the locusts follows the Apocalypse description closely (9:7-10).[4] Anguished figures at the lower left, "seeking death and not finding it" (9:6), attempt to hurl themselves into an abyss in order to escape the locusts. The maelstrom of tormented figures includes that of a semi-recumbent king, whose form seems to have been derived from an Italian print. Below him, in the left corner, is a reclining nymph-like figure, copied in reverse from Dürer's "Meerwunder" (B.71). The huge figure at the lower right may be derived from a "Drunkenness of Noah" or from the Caraglio engraving of "The Dream of Saint Jerome" after Parmigianino.[5] Duvet repeats Dürer's tormented figures (B.65), omitting the church officers of the woodcut so as to remove overt anti-Catholic reference.

---

1. Just as the signature in the preceding plate was placed in the close proximity to the presence of Christ, it is here seen immediately below the figure of a kneeling nude male about to be clad in heavenly rainment, perhaps suggesting an identification with this figure.

2. The Dijon impression has + 20 added in ink at the end of the engraved text reference. Almost certainly in Duvet's own hand, this curious indication suggests the artist's having included subject matter from the twentieth chapter, but such is not the case; the numerals were never engraved. Nor were the additional pen-drawn indications of shadow on the right half of the arc supporting Christ; the left upper-arm of the falling figure at lower left; between the legs of the kneeling figure on the ledge at the bottom. Increased pen-drawn shading on the drapery on the thighs of the recumbent, baton-bearing figure at the lower left was not engraved. Late impressions such as those at the Bibliothèque Royale de belgique (Brussels) and in the bound *Apocalypse figurée* at Lyons have numerous minor repairs and alterations, seen for example, in the star of the seated monster at the right with key and scepter.

3. He is the king of 9:11, "the angel of the bottomless pit; whose Hebrew name is Abbadon (the destroyer) . . ."

4. "And the shapes of the locusts were like unto horse prepared unto battle: and on their heads were, as it were, crowns, like gold: and their faces were as the faces of men. And they had hair as the hair of women; and their teeth were as lions: and they had breastplates as breastplates of iron, and the noise of their wings was as the noise of chariots and many horses running to battle. And they had tails like to scorpions, and there were stings in their tails; and their power was to hurt men nine months" (9:7-10).

5. The innumerable nude male figures may have been partially inspired by a print after Michelangelo's "Battle of Cascina" (B.XIV, p. 191, no. 487). The woman at the lower right, bent over her child, relates to Marcantonio's engraving of "The Massacre of the Innocents" (B.XIV, p. 11, no. 18).

299 x 211 mm.
Signed IOHANNES DVVET FAC on double tablet at the feet of the second angel from the right.
Inscribed HIST CAP 7 on a Roman-style plaque at the upper left.
Represented in major print collections.[1]
B 18, RD 32, LeBlanc 32, Passavant 32, Boullaye 32, Popham 32, Linzeler 27–6, Bersier 23.

The first eight verses of the seventh chapter are illustrated. Four angels hold back the winds (7:1), while another raises a head in benediction and still another makes the sign of the cross on the brows of the servants of God. With the exception of the angel at the upper right (in combat with one of the four wind-gods), the angels hold down their swords, obeying the heavenly Tau-bearing messenger near the top who orders them to cease hurting the earth until the servants of God have been designated (7:2–3). A great sea of countless crossed heads flows through the landscape at the left, even filling the distant mountain ridges, indicating the 144,000 who were signed. At the left foreground, Duvet invents a group in frantic disputation, anxiously awaiting the sign of salvation. Their introduction provides a dramatic contrast to the swelling sea of the saved who fill out the composition.

While the configuration of the angels and the tree is, in its broadest outlines, adapted in reverse from Dürer's woodcut of the same scene (B.66), the German print only provides a point of departure for the chaotic grandeur of the Duvet engraving. Where Dürer is content with a small group awaiting salvation, Duvet saturates his landscape with infinite numbers.

This engraving, together with many others in the series, suggests that Duvet may have consulted an early sixteenth-century Florentine set of engravings showing scenes from the life of Saint Philip Benizzi (Text fig. 44).[2] The similarity between Duvet's art and that of slightly earlier Italian mannerist artists' fusion of Gothic and Renaissance motifs is striking. The unknown Florentine engraver's disposition of a complex historiated landscape confined within an arched form identical to that of Duvet's plate is too close to seem coincidental. It is also possible that the Italian engraver, working after Andrea del Sarto frescoes which may themselves have been influenced by Dürer, was indirectly reflecting the same sources as the later work of Duvet.

---

1. An early impression at the Bibliothèque Municipale in Dijon has brown ink-line shading added to that on the feet of the angels at the lower right. This additional hatching, presumably in Duvet's hand, was never engraved.
2. The five Andrea del Sarto frescoes are in the Florentine cloister of the Servi. (A.M. Hind, *Early Italian Engraving*, London, 1948, I, Cat. Part 1, p. 218). The engraving measures 329 x 220 mm. Hind dates the print circa 1500–1520, pointing out that it is "not unlike the work of Agostino Veneziano." See also John Shearman, *Andrea del Sarto*, Oxford, 1965, II, Cat. 7–11, pp. 198–202.

45 CHAPTER 7 (b) (AN INNUMERABLE MULTITUDE WHICH STANDS BEFORE THE THRONE)

299 x 211 mm.
Signed IOHANNES DVVET on double-tablet at the lower left margin.
Inscribed HIST CAP 7 APOC on plaque resting on the lower margin, just below the Evangelist. The halo surrounding the heads of the Trinity, at the top of the composition, is inscribed SALUS DEO NRO QUI SEDET SVPER TRONV ET AGNO.[1]
Represented in major print collections.[2]
B 19, RD 33, LeBlanc 33, Passavant 33, Boullaye 33, Popham 33, Linzeler 28-7, Bersier 24.

The Ancient at the left tells the Evangelist that the white-robed figures above are the saved (7:13-14). A group of crowned angels at the very center of the composition are flanked by the saved, whose palm-bearing ranks are continued on up the sides of the plate, framing the throne of God (7:15).[3] A great nimbus surrounding the altar throne bears the symbols of the four Evangelists.[4]

Rather than showing God as the Lamb, as described in the seventeenth verse, and as Dürer showed him in his woodcut of the subject (B.67), Duvet engraved a formally enthroned Trinity. The Father and Son, profiles confronted, are seated on an altarlike bench, the Holy Ghost's wings sheltering their crowned heads, united by the Latin inscription which borders their common halo (7:10). The figures on either side of the altar represent Mary, and probably John the Baptist.

While some of the general groupings in this engraving may have been partially inspired by Dürer's woodcut of the same subject (B.67), the consistently classicizing ornament, landscape, and individual figures point firmly to Italian or Northern mannerist intermediaries. Duvet's substitution of a powerful image of the Trinity for Dürer's Lamb may perhaps be attributed to the French engraver's desire to place his work securely within the most orthodox Catholic interpretation of the scene.

---

1. 7:10, "Salvation to our God, who sitteth upon the throne, and to the Lamb."
2. An early impression in the Bibliothèque Municipale, Dijon, has pen-drawn brown lines of slight changes, presumably in Duvet's hand, at the right arm and stomach of Christ that were never engraved.
3. These are presumably the angels of the first verse, who are also shown in the preceding plate.
4. This nimbus was already shown in Cat. 41 and is derived from Dürer's woodcut *Apocalypse* (B.63).

302 x 220 mm.
Signed IOHANNES DVVET FAC on double-tablet by the tower at the extreme left.
Inscribed HIST CAP 8 APOC on a plaque set in the earth at the center of the lower margin.
Represented in major print collections.[1]
B 20, RD 34, LeBlanc 34, Passavant 34, Boullaye 34, Popham 34, Linzeler 29-8, Bersier 25.

The consequences of opening the seventh seal are depicted (8:1). The upper half of the composition shows the Lord at the center, distributing the trumpets to the surrounding angels side (8:2,13). An angel immediately below the Lord fills the censer with altar fire (8:3,5).

The angel at the lower left is blowing the first trumpet, which resulted in the burning of earth, trees, and grass (8:7). The second angel, below the altar, casts the mountain burning with fire into the sea, causing the destruction of the sea and its creatures (8:8-9), represented by the capsized and storm-tossed boats below. The third angel, at the extreme right, blows his trumpet, causing the star Wormwood to fall from heaven, destroying the waters and its drinkers. The fallen star is in the right corner, in a square basin, surrounded by the mortally poisoned bodies of its drinkers (8:10-11). One of these, cowering at the right angel, is taken from engravings after Michelangelo's *ignudi*. The blower of the fourth trumpet, presumably the angel at the left, shatters the sun, moon, and stars (8:12). Duvet follows Dürer's ambiguous presentation of this episode (B.68) by placing the sun and moon at either side of the altar. The angel at the very center of the composition, his mouth open as if in speech, is perhaps taken from illustrations for Luther's Apocalypse. where he mistranslates the Vulgate eagle as angel, having an angel flying in the midst of heaven, rather than an eagle, screaming, "Woe, woe, woe to the inhabitants of the earth: by reason of the rest of the voices of the three angels, who are yet to sound the trumpet" (8:13).[2] The latter are the three angels at the very top, shown receiving their trumpets from the Lord.

In its very broadest outlines, this engraving is taken from Dürer's woodcut *Apocalypse* (B.68), probably by way of a sixteenth-century adaptation, such as the Wittenberg Bible of 1524, or the 1552 edition. Unlike the other engravings of the *Apocalypse* which are freely adapted from Dürer, this print is not consistently in reverse. Duvet has added the corpses seen below, changed the half-length figure of the Lord to a full-length, and provided a far more crowded, eventful scene with greater narrative complexity and dramatic excitement than its German source.

---

1. An unusually fine impression is at the Cleveland Museum (30.531).
2. See E. Panofsky, *Albrecht Dürer*, Princeton, 1945, II, p. 36. See also Georg Stuhlfauth, "Kleine Beiträge zu Dürer," *Monatshefte für Kunstwissenschaft*, XV, 1922, pp. 57–64. Dürer's illustration is based on the Koberger Bible. The *Novum Testamentum*, published by Gryphius in Paris, 1552, also shows an angel, with the words "We, We," coming from its lips.

298 x 211 mm.
Signed IOHANNES DVVET on double tablet under the title plaque.
Inscribed HIST CAP 9 APOC on plaque attached to altar of the Lord.
Represented in major print collections.
B 21, RD 35, LeBlanc 35, Passavant 35, Boullaye 35, Popham 35, Linzeler 30-9, Bersier 26.

This plate continues the presentation of the ninth chapter, the eleven verses of which had been shown in Cat. 43. The scene begins with the angel blowing the sixth trumpet, shown at the upper left, by the altar of the Lord, who holds out two trumpets in each hand—the "four horns of the golden altar, which is before the eyes of God" (9:13). The sounding of the sixth trumpet releases the four angels who are to kill a third of mankind (9:14-15).

The orphrey of the bearded pope is decorated with a male (Peter) and a female who is derived from Marcantonio's *Lucretia* (B.192). The great angel is also taken from Marcantonio.[1]

The army mounted on horseback seems doomed, pursued by the armor-clad legions of fire-breathing horses with lion-heads and serpent tails who appear above them (9:16-19).

Some of the details are derived from Dürer's woodcut of the same scene (B.69) (Text fig. 39) such as the three wind gods (Dürer shows all four). Dürer's lion-headed, serpent-tailed horsemen are copied in reverse; his Gothic altar has been refashioned in the Renaissance manner. While Dürer placed a prostrate pope and king in the right corner, Duvet greatly increases the drama of their violent demise by toppling them from their thrones. The motif of Dürer's horseman at the right may have stimulated Duvet to attempt a similar figure, whose articulation is as different as it is unsuccessful. Drawing upon both German and Italian sources for his presentation of his unique vision, Duvet's plate for the ninth chapter of the Apocalypse typifies his audacious, creative eclecticism.

---

1. This was first pointed out by A. Oberheide, *Der Einfluss Marcantonio . . .* , Hamburg, 1933, p. 15, "Der linke Engel mit den erhebenen Schwert wurde B. 18 entnommen." Illus. Pl. VI, fig. 1. Duvet has clothed the figure in toga and greaves.

304 x 215 mm.

Signed IOHANNES DVVET FAC on double tablet below right knee of Evangelist.

Inscribed HIST CAP 10 APOC on rectangular tablet at right hand of angel.

First State: Dijon (Bibliothèque Municipale—unique). The Bible is free of any shading, which is indicated here in brown ink hatchings. Additional rows of hatched shading to the immediate right and far left of the angel's spinal column are also indicated in brown ink. Further shading is drawn in with pen-lines along the ground parallel to the drapery on the right leg of the evangelist, but this was never engraved.

Second State: Represented in major print collections. Shading added to Bible, and shading on Angel's back increased at immediate right and far left of spinal column.

B 22, RD 36, LeBlanc 36, Passavant 36, Boullaye 36, Popham 36, Linzeler 31–10, Bersier 27.

The composition is dominated by the great, centrally placed figure of the "mighty angel come down from heaven, clothed with a cloud, and a rainbow was on his head, and his face was as the sun, and his feet as pillars of fire" (10:1). The figure strides on its column-legs, the left on the Evangelist's island, while the right is in the sea (10:2). A lion-like head emerging from the sea between the angel's wings may illustrate the description of the angel who "cried with a loud voice, as when a lion roareth" (10:3).[1]

A small angel, flying down from the upper left toward the Evangelist, is probably the personification of the voice from heaven which instructed the Evangelist to request the great angel's book (10:8). The kneeling saint grasps the book, which the great angel thrusts toward him, placing a corner of it in the Evangelist's mouth, so that he may literally eat the book of prophecy (10:10–11). The great angel's right arm points up to heaven, while his left hand holds the book, thus shown in the act of swearing by God that "Time shall be no longer"(10:6).

Duvet has adopted many of Dürer's suggestions from B.70 (Text fig. 40) but has heightened the drama and immediacy of the event. The disembodied angel is given a muscular torso of clouds, and wings. The angel's head is in profile rather than three-quarter view and fittingly resembles that of an Apollo, possibly due to a humanistic reinterpretation of the verse where the angel's face is described "as the sun" (10:11). The head is surrounded by the same rainbow as Dürer's, but Duvet has directed three streams of light from it, rather than showing the more generalized radiation of the German woodcut.

In keeping with Duvet's process of formalizing and classicizing Dürer's inventions, he shows the altar above converted from a late Gothic design to that of contemporary Italian High Renaissance architecture. The casual clump of bullrushes at the lower left of the woodcut appears in emblematic fashion at the lower right of the engraving.[2] The elaborate seascape with fishermen pulling in their nets is more ambitious in the engraving than in the woodcut.

The direct source for this engraving is the woodcut illustration of the same subject in Hans Lufft's *Das Newe Testament,* Wittenberg, 1552 (Text fig. 42).

---

1. The lion-head and the group of fishermen in the background are derived from a woodcut illustration in the *Zürich Foliobibel,* dated 1531, showing Jonah and the Whale' See Paul Leemann-Van Elck, *Die Zürcherische Buchillustration,* Zürich, 1952.
2. See Cat. 23 for meaning of bullrush.

305 x 222 mm.

Signed IOHANNES DVVET FAC on double-tablet below left arm of central figure at bottom.

Inscribed HIST CAP 11 APOC on rectangular plaque attached to the altar.

First state: Dijon (Bibliothèque Municipale—unique) The Lord's thigh is shaded by very slight hatching. The sixth figure from the left—the innermost one of the group at the lower left—is not yet differentiated from its companions by over-all parallel hatching. The arm and shoulder of the figure to the left also lack the hatching which will be added in the second state. The cloud-cluster immediately above the heads of both figures is not yet appreciably darker than the nearby clouds. These areas are all indicated in brown ink in the Dijon proof. This impression also has pen-drawn shading on the signature tablet which was never engraved.

Second state: Represented in major print collections. Most pen-drawn indications of further shading on the Dijon proof engraved. The two innermost figures of the group at the lower left corner have increased over-all hatching, and the cloud groups over their heads have been intensified. The Lord's thigh covered with a series of slightly curved parallel strokes of engraved shadow.

B 23, RD 37, LeBlanc 37, Passavant 37, Boullaye 37, Popham 37, Linzeler 32–11, Bersier 28.

Saint John, a small figure at the upper left, is shown near the angel who gave him the reed with which to measure the temple of God (11:1–3). Below, to the right of the saint, appear the two bearded, kneeling witnesses to whose adventures the chapter is devoted, who receive rays of divine power from the mouth (11:3) of the Lord who appears in a nimbus filled with the heavenly host. The two olive trees and two candlesticks of the fourth verse are placed symmetrically at each side and in front of the altar. The witnesses appear again in the foreground, devoured by "the beast that ascendeth out of the abyss" at the completion of their testimony (11:7). To the upper right of the monster, the witnesses reappear; "their bodies shall lie in the streets of the great city, which is called spiritually Sodom and Egypt, where their Lord also was crucified" (11:8). This reference is illustrated at the center of the composition, where Golgotha, the three crosses on the mount—is showered by stone.

It is difficult to determine whether or not Duvet has specifically represented the important scene of the witnesses's resurrection (11:11–12). The first view of the witnesses at the upper left may have been intended to show both their initial reception of instruction and their later resurrection. The groups at the lower left, and above the head witnesses are the Gentiles (11:2): "they of the tribes, and peoples, and tongues, and nations" (11:9). The resurrection of the witnesses was followed by an earthquake, depicted by the destroyed city at the center of the plate (11:13). The concluding verses (11:14–19) are not illustrated in this plate, which is already extraordinarily comprehensive, presenting the first fourteen verses of chapter eleven.

294 x 221 mm.

Signed IOHANNES DVVET FAC on double-tablet within the right end of the crescent moon.[1]

Inscribed HEC HISTORIA APOCALIPYSIS CAP 12, on plaque held in the mouth of dragon on left.

First State: Dijon (Bibliothèque Municipale—unique). Brown ink lines indicate additional delicate hatching on the wings of the angel to the right of the Lord. The Dijon proof also has additional hatching drawn on the drapery of the Lord and the Woman of the Apocalypse, but this was never executed.

Second State: Represented in major print collections. Delicate additional hatching engraved on the angels' wings at the upper right.

Third State: Paris (L—Coll. Rothschild). The broken corner at the lower left has been partially re-engraved so that the dragon's foot comes over the rock.

Fourth State: London (BM—in *Apocalypse figurée*), Paris (BN—in *Apocalypse figurée*, Inv. Rés. A1587 Imp., Petit Palais—Coll. Dutuit—in *Apocalypse figurée*). The broken corner at the lower left has been re-engraved so that the dragon's foot comes over the rock.

B 24,[2] RD 38, LeBlanc 38, Passavant 38, Boullaye 38, Popham 38, Linzeler 33–12, Bersier 29.

At the right is the "woman clothed with the sun, and the moon under her feet, and on her head a crown of twelve stars" (12:1). She is confronted by the "great red dragon, having seven heads, and ten horns; and on his heads seven diadems" (12:3). His magnificent tail curls up the left side on the print, "drawing the stars from heaven and casting them to earth" (12:4). The dragon is frustrated in his plan "that, when she should be delivered, he might devour her son" (12:4). Instead of showing the defeat of the dragon (12:10) to which Dürer and Duvet devote the next print in their series—both artists omit these verses (12:7–12), going on to the thirteenth, in which the dragon decides to persecute the Woman, and the fourteenth, where she is given wings with which to escape. One dragon head is shown casting out water "as it were a river; that he might cause her to be carried away by the river" (12:15). The proud figure of Mary as the personification of Christian Victory, the world at her feet, evil held at bay and her Son delivered, looks beyond the angry dragon. An additional reason for separating the scenes may have been for the preservation of image unity. Verses 7–12 shift in reference from the dragon to Satan and the the fallen angels, from the seven-headed monster to an army of devils, calling for a change in representation if textual fidelity and interpretation were to have been preserved. Dürer attempts ("Saint Michael and the Dragon," B.72) to amalgamate both images by slicing his dragon into several seemingly independent monsters, while Duvet depicts an army of demons.

Limiting its narrative scope to a restrained synthesis of the twelfth chapter, this engraving is perhaps the most beautiful of the *Apocalypse* series. Duvet adapted Dürer's woodcut of the same scene (B.71) (Text fig. 74) in reverse, confining the composition within an arch-shaped area and investing it with an opulent chiaroscuro. Translating Dürer's late Gothic vocabulary into the language of early sixteenth-century Roman ornament, Duvet has created a monument of Burgundian renaissance art. The abstract, decorative quality of the Dürer woodcut was already close to Duvet's taste and has been intensified by the French engraver through such devices as Mary's great mandorla and her star-studded halo. The profound variety of textures that he was able to create in wings, drapery, hair, and the scales of the dragons enriches the work. The great figure of God the Father is entirely dependent upon Italian sources. The Son carried to heaven is taken unchanged from the Dürer woodcut, derived from his Italian journey.[3] Unlike most of Duvet's Italianate works, this engraving, with its outspoken tonal transitions, points more to Florentine printmaking than to the School of Marcantonio.

---

1. The curious handles attached to the plaque appear to be swordhilt designs.
2. Popham, p. 45, gives the Bartsch number as 38.
3. According to E. Panofsky, *Albrecht Dürer*, Princeton, 1948, I, p. 54, the motif of the child carried by two angels ["commendatio animarum"] comes from classical funerary monuments.

270

298 x 214 mm.
Signed IOHANNES DVVET on double tablet at lower left, on low circular wall.
Inscribed HIST CAP 12 APOC on plaque at the upper right.
Represented in major print collections.[1]
B 25, RD 39, LeBlanc 39, Passavant 39, Boullaye 39, Popham 39, Linzeler 34-13, Bersier 30.

This plate illustrates the seventh through twelfth verses. With the exception of a highly detailed, fortified landscape in the lower part of the composition,[2] the entire plate is given over to the "great battle in heaven: Michael and his angels fought with the dragon, and the dragon fought and his angels" (12:7). The dragon is shown as "the devil and Satan" (12:9). Saint Michael is presumably the angel at the left who raises his sword, preparatory to the decapitation of the prostrate devil underfoot. Satan and his angels are about to be cast down to earth (12:9).

Excepting the angel with bow and arrow at the extreme left, copied in reverse from Dürer's woodcut of the same subject (B.72), there is no close link between the German and French artists' works. The print has all the ornamental *richesse* and density which one would associate with Duvet's apprenticeship as a goldsmith in the fusion of decorative motifs and devices.

---

1. An early impression at the Bibliothèque Municipale, Dijon, has pen-drawn hatching for additional shading on the wall against which the double-tablet rests, but this was never engraved.
2. The engraver was a designer of fortifications (see Appendix E: docs. 36, 37, 39, 42) and Appendix G. The *Apocalypse* commission relates to the Order of Saint Michael, which, dedicated to militant Christianity, might well have been interested in the detailed representation of fortifications.

305 x 222 mm.
Signed IOHANNES DVVET on double-tablet at the extreme lower left, just below inscribed plaque.
Inscribed HIST CAP 14 APOC on rectangular plaque at lower left above double-tablet.
First State: Langres (Musée des Beaux-Arts), Paris (B–Cat. AA2, Rés.). Both the rectangular tablet and
the double-tablet at the lower left are uninscribed.[1]
Second State: Represented in major print collections. Double tablet and plaque above inscribed.
B 26, RD 40, LeBlanc 40, Passavant 40, Boullaye 40, Popham 40, Linzeler 35–14, Bersier 31.

Although inscribed CAP 14, the bulk of the composition depicts events from the preceding chapter. The center and lower left are occupied by the "beast coming up out of the sea, having seven heads and ten horns" (13:1). Each beastly head is endowed with a great halo; the upper one at the extreme left is the head seen "as it were slain to death: and his death's wound was healed. And all the earth was in admiration after the beast" (13:3). The angelic would-be assassin is shown alone, flying with upraised sword and cross, while a crown of crowned figures prostrate themselves before the seven-headed beast. Several of its mouths are open to utter blasphemies (13:5-10).[2]

The upper part of the plate is devoted to the first verses of the fourteenth chapter, as stated in the plaque at the left. The Lamb, bearing the symbols of the Four Evangelists, appears on top of Mount Zion, surrounded by the harping Saved (14:1-5). At the upper right, showing a book to those people at the extreme right who are not worshipping the beast, is the "angel, flying through the midst of heaven, having the eternal gospel to preach unto them that sit upon the earth . . ." (14:6).[3] The book may also be "the book of life of the Lamb" (13:8). The angel at the upper left, immediately above the horns of the tallest monster-head, is probably the third angel of 13:9, who warns against adoring the beast.

While the immensely crowded plate, with its entanglement of episodes and chapters, uses the same elements which contributed to a sense of excitement in preceding prints, these elements seem to nullify each other here. The white areas make a spotty impression, especially along the left margin, which may still be incomplete. The beast itself is very freely inspired by Dürer's woodcut (B.74), as is the cross-bearing angel. Both Dürer and Duvet combine the thirteenth and fourteenth chapters, but select different verses for illustration.

---

1. The tablets have had the inscription added in black ink at Langres; in Paris "15 and 14" is written in brown ink.
2. The second beast (13:11), illustrated by Dürer is omitted by Duvet.
3. The woman wearing a turban, with one child over her shoulder and another by the arm, resembles Lucas van Leyden's figure style. The upturned head at the lower left is also found in Cat. 47.

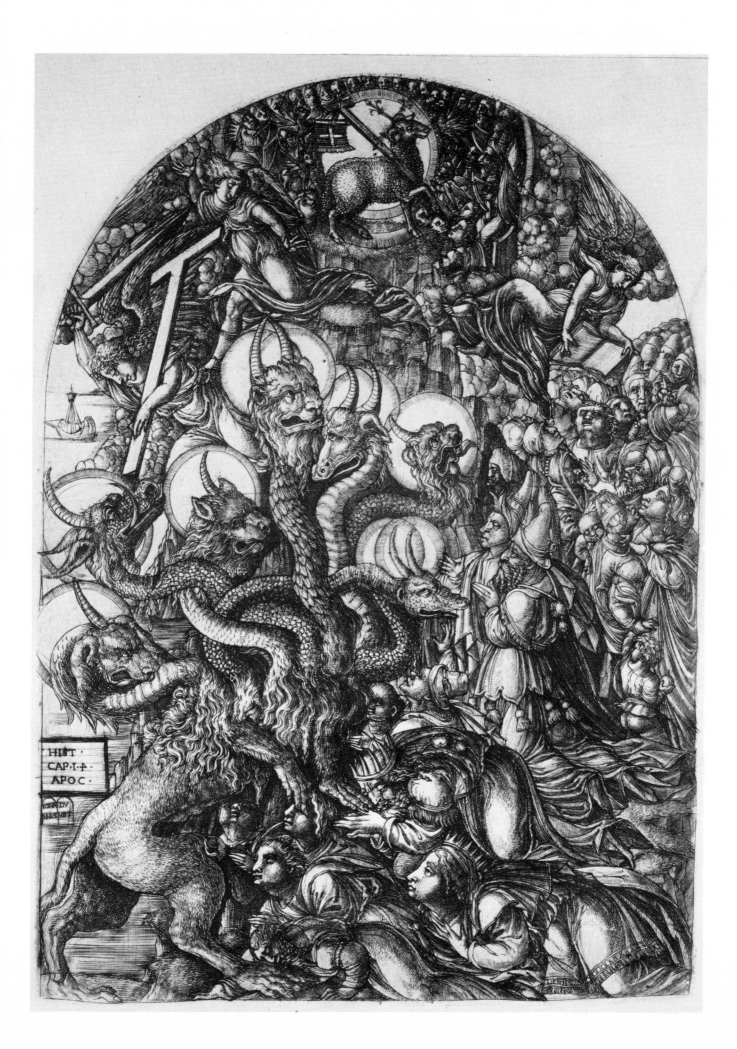

HIST·
CAP·I·4·
APOC·

303 x 220 mm.

Signed IOHANNES DVVET on double tablet at lower right above the vat.

Inscribed HIST CAP 14 APOC on rectangular plaque on ground at lower left.

First State: Dijon (Bibliothèque Municipale—unique). The horses' heads in the stream at the center of lower part of composition are not engraved, but drawn in brown ink as is the upper horse in the section of the stream beyond the second footbridge. The footbridge above the bottom wine-vat and between the feet of the third angel from the right is unshaded. Shading in the face, right arm, and torso of the angel, who is third from the left in the group at the lower left, is indicated by pen-lines alone. Similar shading is indicated on the clouds at the Lord's feet. The first state lacks any shading whatever to the immediate right of the Lord's heel. Additional shading, indicated by ink-lines in the Dijon proof on the left arm and below the right hand, was never engraved.

Second State: Represented in major print collections. The additional hatching, indicated in the Dijon proof by brown pen-lines, has been added to the footbridge under the angel who is third from the right and to the angel who is third from the left. The horses' heads in the stream at the center have been engraved. Shading is added in clouds below the Lord and appears for the first time to the immediate right of His heel.

B 27, RD 41, LeBlanc 41, Passavant 41, Boullaye 41, Popham 41, Linzeler 36–15, Bersier 32.

The plate is devoted to the concluding eight verses of the fourteenth chapter of the Apocalypse. The Lord is shown at the top, facing left (14:14), seated upon a cloud-cluster, encircled by a great halo in front of the triumphal-arch-like temple of heaven. The angel facing the Lord at the left, who points to the harvest scene below, tells him to "thrust in thy sickle, and reap, because the hour is come to reap, for the harvest of the earth is ripe" (14:15). Raising his sickle, preparatory to thrusting it into the earth, the Lord holds it in such a way as to resemble a crescent moon topped with the *fleur-de-lys* of his halo. The crowning device, similar to that displayed in Duvet's engraving of "Henri II as the Victorious Saint Michael" (Cat. 64) is another of the indications that the Apocalypse series and the triptych of engravings devoted to Henri (Cat. 64-66) were planned in unison to glorify the Order of Saint Michael, one of whose symbols was the crescent moon.[1]

Striding in front of the temple altar of heaven at the upper right is the angel "who had power over fire"; he orders his companion at the upper left to "thrust in thy sharp sickle, and gather the clusters of the vineyard of the earth . . ." (14:18).[2] Four angels below operate a wine press, "the great press of the wrath of God" (14:19). Wheatfields and vineyards stretch back to the fortified walls of a city in the background (14:20). Horses' heads, appearing in the stream between the two largest angels, show that "the press was trodden without the city, and blood came out of the press up to the horses' bridles, for a thousand and six hundred furlongs" (14:20). Duvet mistakenly shows liquid running from the stream *into* the wine vat.

The harvesting scene in this engraving is derived from a woodcut in Hans Lufft's *Das Neue Testament*, Wittenberg, 1552, showing the "Winepress of the Wrath of God," (Text fig. 43) an episode in the Apocalypse which was of exceptional popularity in the sixteenth century as a symbol of Eucharistic Salvation.

---

1. See Cat. 61, no. 3.
2. The angel at the extreme left of the temple of heaven must be the one referred to in 14:17.

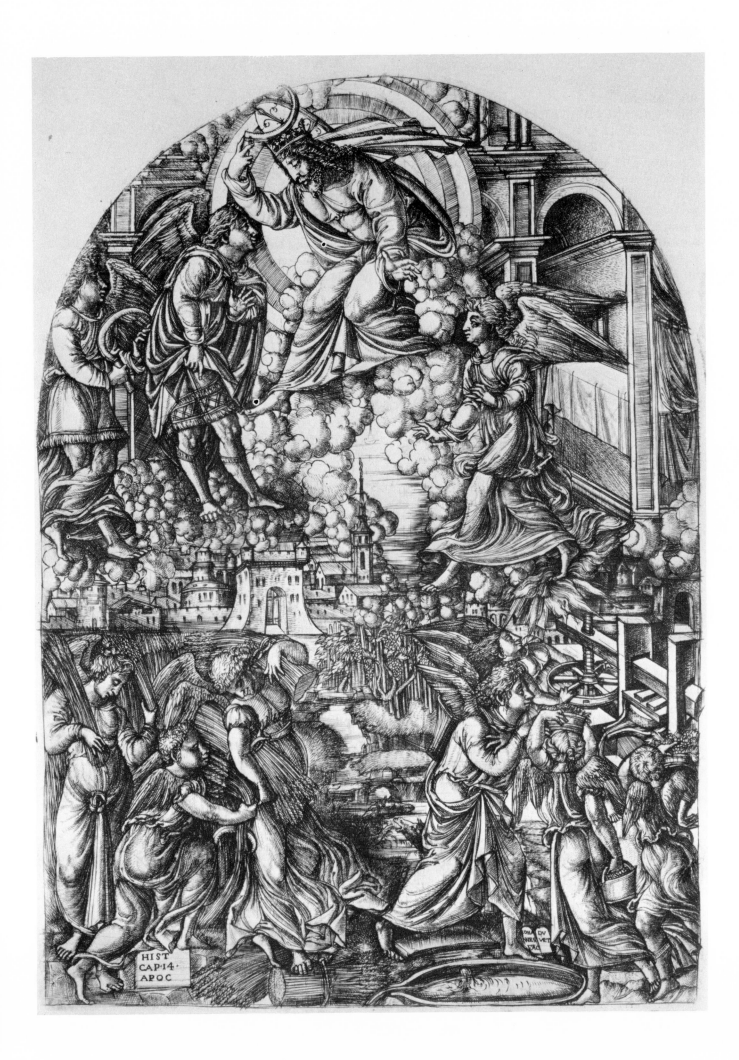

54. CHAPTERS 13, 15, 16 (THE DRAGON WITH TWO HORNS AND THE BEAST WITH SEVEN)

304 x 218 mm.

Signed IOHANNES DUVVET FAC on double-tablet at lower left by the dog.

Inscribed HIST 15 CAP 13 ET 16 APOC on rectangular plaque at the center of the bottom margin.

First State: Dijon (Bibliothèque Municipale), Paris (BN–Cat. 1b, Rés.). No shadow cast by leg of beast at extreme right on base upon which it is seated. Shading on isolated head of man immediately above left shoulder of standing man at extreme left of composition is pale, similar to that of next head to the right. The Dijon impression has the additions which were engraved in the second state indicated in brown ink. Increased shadow drawn on the Dijon print on the angels surrounding the Lord was never engraved.

Second State: Represented in major print collections. A cast shadow is engraved running down the left side of the block upon which the beast with two horns is seated and along the ground reaching as far as the beast's other foot. The isolated male head to the immediate right of the standing man at the extreme left of the composition is so shaded as to distinguish its tonality from that of the adjacent heads.

B 28, RD 42, LeBlanc 42, Passavant 42, Boullaye 42, Popham 42, Linzeler 37-16, Bersier 33.

The upper part of the composition shows God turning from his book to distributing the seven gold vials filled with the seven last plagues (15:1, 6, 7).[1] His great halo is filled by the might of "them that had overcome the beast . . . having the harps of God" (15:2, 3). While the angels at the top center and at the extreme right are just receiving their vials, five others have already cast theirs toward the earth. The vials are shown in mid-air in an almost straight line crossing the plate near the horizon line (16:1). The nude central figure is the fourth angel, who "poured out his vial upon the sun, and it was given to him to afflict men with heat and fire" (16:8). The second angel from the right is probably the fifth, who "poured out his vial upon the throne of the beast" (16:10). The lower angel at the left, emptying his vial over the nude back of a grimacing man below, is the first angel, whose vial brought a "sore and grievous wound" (16:2). The angel immediately under God is probably the seventh, who will "pour his vial upon the air" (16:17).

The two great beasts occupying the lower right of the composition are taken from chapter thirteen. The seated dragon at the extreme right of the composition is the third beast of the chapter, who "had two horns like a lamb, and he spoke as a dragon" (13:11). The lionlike beast at the left is "like to a leopard, and his feet were as the feet of a bear, and his mouth as the mouth of a lion" (13:2). The beast-dragon seems to expel the false prophet, a bishoplike figure, who in turn vomits out "three unclean spirits like frogs" (16:13). These, "the demonic spirits," leap toward the richly clad kneeling figures at the left foreground, "the kings of the whole earth," who will "battle against the great day of the almighty God" (16:14).[2] This battle has already begun, initiated by the casting down of the vials. The great tower of the city in the background has begun to topple, showing the fall of the cities of the Gentiles (16:18). The "great hail, as large as a talent" (16:21), falls just above the dragon at the right.

Both the Rosso-like man with his arms folded at the extreme left, and the adjacent draped warrior to the right are of Italian derivation.[3] The curious fusion of elements from three chapters, as represented in this engraving, make it unlikely that the plate was designed to accompany a printed text.

---

1. Duvet's illustration is textually inaccurate in that he shows the Lord himself, rather than "one of the four living creatures," i.e., one of the Evangelists, giving out the vials, as stated in 15:7.

2. Compressing three chapters into one plate, Duvet also reduces his *dramatis personae*, as the original passage reads, "And I saw issuing from the mouth of the dragon, and from the mouth of the beast, and from the mouth of the false prophet, three foul spirits. . . ." (16:13).

3. A. Oberheide, *Der Einfluss Marcantonio . . .*, Hamburg, 1933, p. 156, writes of the latter figure that it is copied from Marcantonio, B.18, which he illustrates and compares with the Duvet warrior on p. 5, fig. 8. The comparison is not convincing.

HIST·15·
CAP·13·ET·16·
APOC

303 x 219 mm.
Signed IOHANNES DVVET FAC on double-tablet at middle of bottom margin.
Inscribed HIST CAP 17 ET 18 APOC on rectangular tablet to the immediate left of the Whore of Babylon.
Represented in major print collections.[1]
B 29, RD 43, LeBlanc 43, Passavant 43, Boullaye 43, Popham 43, Linzeler 38-7, Bersier 34.

The composition is dominated by the great figure of the Whore of Babylon "sitting upon a scarlet-colored beast . . . having seven heads and ten horns" (17:3), the same beast that has already appeared in the plates for chapters 12 and 14 (Cat. 49, 51). The beast's tail is twisted and knotted around the Whore's right arm, which supports the golden cup "full of the abomination and filthiness of her fornication" (17:4). The kings of the earth crowd the lower half of the plate (17:2), those at the lower left so blinded by their love for the Whore that they are crushed under the feet of the beast, those at the right already aware of the fate in store for her. The kings, recognizing the burning of the great city in the background as a sign of the Whore's impending destruction, turn to her with gestures of concern (18:9, 10). The Woman, "drunk with the blood of the martyrs of Jesus" (17:6), is oblivious to her burning city, because "she saith in her heart . . . sorrow I shall not see" (18:7). The sea bordering upon the heavily fortified city in the background is filled with boatmen who have taken refuge from the burning of Babylon (18:17-19). Two angels flying over the heads of the crowd below point to the complete destruction of Babylon; the angel on the right is the one who "took up a stone, as it were a great millstone, and cast it into the sea, saying: 'With such violence as this shall Babylon, that great city, be thrown down and shall be found no more at all' " (18:21).

The general grouping for the composition and the Seven-Headed Beast are freely adapted in reverse after Dürer (B.73) (Text fig. 41). The Harlot, no longer Dürer's Carpacciesque courtesan, resembles a dissolute Fontainebleau nymph.[2] Duvet omits the horsemen which appear in the sky of the German woodcut, as well as the regal figure seen from the back, sometimes identified as the Antichrist,[3] the latter is shown in Cat. 58).

The young king at the lower right resembles a figure in a woodcut of the same subject in the Vorsterman Bible, printed in Antwerp in 1528, with illustrations by Jan Swart whose Northern mannerist style has stylistic affinities with that of Duvet.

The highly detailed rendition of the burning city of Babylon may indicate some of the engraver's activities as architect and military engineer. He is known to have been active in these areas in Geneva, and it is assumed that he also was connected with the fortifications of Langres, which played such an important role on the occasion of the royal visits there. The triumphal entries staged by Duvet were due primarily to royal interest in the town as a fortification.

The composition is divided almost in two by the reverse curve of the line formed by the beast, beginning at the lower left, and continuing to the upper right, carried on by the undulating body of the angel with the millstone. The plate possesses the same sort of precarious balance as that of the drunken woman who manages to remain astride the beast by embracing its several necks. Through this use of moving line to articulate the great mass of figures below, coupled with the mushrooming quality of the composition, Duvet unites essentially disparate scenes, covering a range of two chapters, and many events.

The popularity of this theme extended to the sumptuary arts, often found on splendid Limoges platters (Text fig. 21) of the period.

---

1. The early impression at Dijon, Bibliothèque Municipale, has pen-drawn indications of increased shading on the Woman's breasts, the uppermost angel's wings, and on the drapery to the right of the right food of the figure second from the left at the bottom of the composition.
2. The Woman was adapted by Woeriot for his *Emblèmes ou Devises Chrestien,* by Georgette de Montenay, Lyon, 1556, no. 68, with the inscription ABUNDABIT INIQUITAS REFRIGERESCET CARITAS'
3. This is the view of C. Sommer, quoted by E. Panofsky, *Albrecht Dürer,* Princeton, 1945, II, no. 293.

300 x 211 mm.
Signed IOHANNES DVVET FAC on double-tablet at the lower right between the hoofs of the second horse from the right.
Inscribed HIST CAP 18 APOC on rectangular plaque above two broken columns at right.
First State: Langres (Musée des Beaux-Arts), Paris (B-N–Cat. AA3 Rés.). The double-tablet and the plaque above the two broken columns at the lower right are uninscribed.
Second State: In major print collections. Plaque above broken columns inscribed; double-tablet at lower right signed.
Third State: Cleveland. Lower right corner much repaired; lower left corner lost.
B 30, RD 44, LeBlanc 44, Passavant 44, Boullaye 44, Popham 44, Linzeler 39–18, Bersier 35.

The angel at the upper right tells the people of Babylon to leave the fallen city (18:4); they are shown at the upper right, streaming from destroyed Babylon, symbolized by a great devastated building, and at the upper left, fleeing in ships. Further down, along the right side of the plate are the "merchants of the earth" with their casks and camels, lamenting their destroyed goods (18:10–16). "The kings of the earth" are shown as three crowned figures on horseback at the lower right behind the two broken columns in the foreground; they mourn the fall of the Woman of Babylon. The harpists, trumpeters, and pipers who "shall no more be heard at all" (18:22) huddle over their silent instruments at the upper left.

The composition is dominated by the Fall of the Woman of Babylon, whose monumental form is derived from the figures from the Sistine Ceiling, turned upside-down. The great mass of drapery that envelops her legs is also taken from that of a figure seen from below. Her cup of sin also spills; its lid and liquid about to be caught by the nearest of the adoring kings (18:6). The seven heads and necks of her beastly mount are visible as Medusa-like extensions behind the Whore's head. The Fall, heralded by the angel with the millstone on the preceding plate (18:21), takes place before a destroyed classical archway, supported by pairs of columns which confine the seven heads of the beast.

Essentially an independent composition, despite its many borrowed forms, the print has unusual three-dimensionality. Both the horsemen at the lower right and the musicians at the upper left are reminiscent of the engraver's Unicorn series. The structure with a niche containing a female figure, framed by pilasters at the very center of the composition, is close to the triumphal entries that Duvet is known to have produced.[1] Despite the plate's intensely violent and confused subject matter, narrative clarity is maintained through the monumental rendering of the Woman and the structure of Babylon behind her.

---

1. According to E. Haverkamp-Begemann, an impression of this engraving at the Museum of Fine Arts, Budapest, has the words "Monsieur" and "Madam" written in old French on the left and right plinths of the archway. This suggest the possibility of the archway's having been adapted for a triumphal entry arch, perhaps by the engraver himself.

301 x 218 mm.
Signed IOHANNES DVVET FAC on double-tablet on the ground at the left, next to the dog.
Inscribed HIST CAP 19 APOC on a drum-head at extreme left of the foreground. The figure of Christ at the center has the words REX REGO ET DNS DOMINANTIUM I inscribed on the thigh.[1] The upper hem of His robe is inscribed FIDELIS ET VERAX.[2] 19:2
First State: Dijon (Bibliothèque Municipale). All the shading on the earth surface at the foreground is horizontal. The impression has pen-drawn vertical lines.
Second State: Represented in major print collections. Vertical hatching is added to the shading on the ground in the foreground.
B 31, RD 45, LeBlanc 45, Passavant 45, Boullaye 45, Popham 45, Linzeler 40-19, Bersier 36.

The composition is dominated by the great, centrally placed figure of the Christ mounted upon a white horse (19:11). Flames emerge from his eyes. Eight superimposed halos surrounded his crowned head. (19:12). His alb, studded with spots resembling open wounds—the "garment sprinkled with blood" (19:13)—is crossed by a *stola*. The stigmata are prominently displayed on his outstretched hand and foot. The latter "treadeth the winepress of the fierceness of the wrath of God and the Almighty" (19:15), shown immediately below. The sword of conquest emerges from his mouth. He holds the rod of iron in the left hand (19:15). Christ is surrounded by a swarm of figures, representing "the armies in heaven" who "followed him on white horses" (19:14). The chief heavenly soldier is at the right of Christ, holding a sword in one hand and a book in the other.[3]

Among the vast crowd of trumpeting angels and bearded Elders, Saint James Major and Saint Peter are discernible to the immediate left of the large sword at the upper right. Moses is shown at the top of the print, his flamelike horns extending beyond the margin, raising the tablets of the law.[4] The book held by the large man wearing an oriental-style hat is probably the Koran. Christ's sword points down to him "the false prophet, who wrought signs before him, wherewith he seduced them who received the character of the beast . . ." (19:20).[5] The lower section of the composition is occupied by "the kings of the earth and their armies gathered together to make war" with Christ (19:19).

The abrupt transitions in scale are less satisfactory in this engraving than in others of the Series. The front legs of the horse at the upper right have no relationship to the rest of the animal, and a similar awkwardness characterizes the entire composition, whose naturalistic, small-scale grouping of horsemen below contrasts with the huge figure of Christ above. The composition lacks the considerable psychological and ornamental unity of the rest of the Series.

---

1. 19:16: "And he hath on his garment, and on his thigh written: King of Kings, and Lord of Lords."
2. 19:11: "And I saw heaven opened and behold a white horse; and he that sat upon him was called faithful and true, and with justice doth he judge and fight."
3. The position of the sword, directly over the horse's brow, suggests the form of the unicorn—symbol of Christian purity—with which Duvet was extensively concerned (Cat. 32-34, 67-68).
4. His presence may be explained by the victorious angels who celebrate their triumph, "singing the canticle of Moses" (15:3). The eight trumpeters at the top, together with the heavenly host, may be singing another canticle of triumph (19:1-8), appropriate to this scene of the victory of Christ.
5. Dürer shows the false prophet—the Antichrist—in his woodcut of the "Whore of Babylon" (B.73). The oriental headdress and elaborate chain seen from the back on the Dürer Antichrist may have determined Duvet's concept of the same character, with his scimitar and rich chain.

58. CHAPTER 19 (THE ANGEL IN THE SUN CALLING THE BIRDS OF PREY)

300 x 217 mm.
Signed IOHANNES DVVET FAC on banner at upper left.
Inscribed HIST CAP 19 on the slightly curved plaque at the center.
First State: Chantilly (Musée Condé). Blank area below the heads of the birds at the upper right, between them and the plumed helmet of the warrior below.
Second State: Represented in major print collections. The area below the heads of the birds at the upper right is filled with parallel lines of shading.[1]
B 32, RD 46, LeBlanc 46, Passavant 46, Boullaye 46, Popham 46, Linzeler 41-20, Bersier 37.

The uppermost part of the composition is dominated by "an angel standing in the sun, and he cried, with a loud voice, saying to all the birds that did fly through the midst of heaven: come gather yourselves together to the great supper of the Lord" (19:17). Placed in a great double glory, the angel is flanked at right and left by flocks of vultures, who prepare to swoop down upon "the great supper of the Lord," the bodies of his enemies below. Driving the warriors from their mounts, the ferocious birds are shown already devouring "the flesh of kings and the flesh of tribunes, and the flesh of mighty men, and the flesh of horses, and the flesh of them that sit upon them . . ." (19:18). To the left, the falling bodies of the beast and the false prophet—the Antichrist—are shown "cast alive into the pool of fire, burning with brimstone" (19:19).[2] The same kings who were martialing their ranks in the previous engraving are now seen in utter defeat.

The striking contrast between the radiant Marcantonio-style angel at the top of the composition and the scene of utter chaos below is used to maximum effect. The arch-shaped outline of the engraving provides a brilliantly placed window, isolating the conflicts of the chapter in such a way as to capture the moment of battle in monumental fashion.

---

1. Dijon, Bibliothèque Municipale, has an impression of the second state in which additional pen-drawn lines of shading are placed all around the angel at the top, but these lines were never engraved.
2. The figure of the fallen Antichrist, like that of the fallen Whore of Babylon, was created by turning a figure upside down or on its side. The falling nude was at the center of the lower part of the composition seems also to have been created by inverting a figure that was designed to be seen from below.

302 x 220 mm.
Signed IOHANNES DVVET FAC on double-tablet at lower right corner.
Inscribed HIST CAP 20 APOC on square tablet at lower right.
Represented in major print collections.
B 33, RD 47, LeBlanc 47, Passavant 47, Boullaye 47, Popham 47, Linzeler 42-21, Bersier 38.

The composition is divided into three registers, the uppermost occupied on the left by a fortified castle, while at the right, the angel receives the key and chain to the bottomless pit from the Lord (20:2). In the central register, the great figure of an angel (Saint Michael (?) bends over a prostrate monster. This is the angel of the second verse, who came from heaven with the key to the bottomless pit and the great chain, and who "laid hold on the dragon, the old serpent, which is the devil and Satan, and bound him for a thousand years" (20:1-2).

The lower register shows another great angel. Unlike the one above, clad in military attire, this angel wears classical drapery. He fastens a ball and chain on the dejected Satan preparatory to locking the lid on the pool of fire and brimstone at the lower left. The angel's body is surrounded by a froth of clouds streaming down in serpentine fashion from the upper right, connecting all three registers, which may represent the "fire from God out of heaven" (20:9) which destroyed the followers of Satan a thousand years after his first liberation (20:7). The second and final imprisonment of Satan (20:9, 10) is depicted below the first.

The architectural details may refer to the four quarters of the earth (20:7) and to "the breadth of the earth . . . the camp of the saints, and the beloved city" (20:7, 8) invaded by Satan following his first thousand-year imprisonment.

This print has the same decorative quality and rhythmic repetition of form as "Henri II as Saint Michael Slaying the Dragon" (Cat. 64). Order and narrative sequence are attained through the treatment of the composition in terms of an ornamental surface, clearly divided in three distinct zones, united by the serpentine curve that wends its way from upper right to lower left. The heraldic, emblematic character of the engraving represents Duvet's most successful style, congruent with his goldsmith's training and tradition.[1]

---

1. Perhaps in some of its very broadest outlines, this engraving may have been partially derived, in reverse, from Dürer's woodcut Apocalypse (B.75). Duvet appears to have also consulted a woodcut Apocalypse by Dürer's associate, Hans Schauffelein (B.52).

302 x 219 mm.
Signed IOHANNES DVVET FAC on double tablet above eagle's claw on bottom margin at left.
Inscribed HIST CAP 21 APOC on rectangular plaque between the angel's feet at bottom margin.
Represented in major print collections.[1]
B 34, RD 48, LeBlanc 48, Passavant 48, Boullaye 48, Popham 48, Linzeler 43-22, Bersier 39.

The composition is divided into two chief areas: the upper, curved section is occupied by the Heavenly Jerusalem, while the lower part shows the haloed Saint John on the island of Patmos.[2] While in ecstatic slumber, he is approached by the angel who tells him "Come, and I will show thee the bride, the wife of the Lamb" (21:9). The angel's staff points up toward "the holy city, the new Jerusalem, coming out of heaven from God, prepared as a bride adorned for her husband" (21:2). John's annunciation takes place within a rustic structure of twisted apple trees—"living architecture" especially appropriate for the theophany.

At the upper left, Saint John kneels at the feet of the pointing angel: "and he took me up in spirit to a high mountain: and he shewed me the holy city of Jerusalem coming out of heaven from God" (20:10). The handsome city, inspired by architectural prints of the Renaissance, presents a multiplicity of classical walls, gates, colonnades, combined with Northern dormer windows and crenellations (21:12-14, 18-19, 20-21). The many angel-filled portals represent the twelve described in 21:12. The complex structure of the city illustrates the twelve foundations upon which it was built, containing the names of the apostles (21:12-14).

In front of the central gate, an angel with a rod is measuring "the city and its gates and walls" (21.15). To the right, another angel writes, presumably in the book of life of the Lamb, recording names of the saved—the infinite number of figures who dot the city in the background, gazing up at the miniscule figure of the Lord at the top left of the plate. John's elevation to a mountain top from which he sees the Heavenly Jerusalem is shown at the upper left. He reappears walking in the clouds, recording the angel's measurements of the city (21:15-17). The angel wears peaceful garb in heaven, which is a classical city recalling temporary triumphal architecture. The seashore at the extreme right may represent the sea and earth which will vanish from the Evangelist's vision during the spirtual elevation (21:10). The chain of clouds crossing the plate reinforces the barrier between the new and the old.

The exact source for the classical figure of Saint John has aroused considerable speculation. Mrs. Tietze pointed out that Saint John is astride his eagle in the manner of Jupiter on the Paris Cameo. also finding the pose reminiscent of the "Barberini Faun."[3] However, the figure of John stems either from an engraving by Caraglio after Rosso (B. XIV, 26) or from one by Agostino Veneziano after Giulio Romano showing Saint John the Evangelist (B.XIV, 83, 93). Paganum's *Testament Novi*, Lyon, 1548, shows a scene of similar subject, shape and organization.

An ultimately classical source for the group of Saint John and the Eagle would be iconographically as well as stylistically correct, for in the medieval *Ovide moralisé,* Ganymede was interpreted as a prefiguration of the Evangelist, with the Eagle symbolizing Christ. The eagle was also representative of the subline clarity which enabled Saint John to reveal the secrets of Heaven. This interpretation was still referred to in the sixteenth century.[4]

---

1. Dijon, Bibliothèque Municipale, has an early impression with brown pen-drawn indications of increased shading on the plaque and by the eagle's claws on the ground. These lines were almost certainly drawn by the artist himself, but never engraved.
2. A curiously pale yet fresh impression at Chantilly is probably the example in the W. Drugulin Sale Catalogue, London, 1866, p. 30, no. 329, described as "first state, before the retouch, and with broad margins, extremely rare."
3. Erika Tietze-Conrat, *Der französische Kupferstich der Renaissance*, Munich, 1925, p. 8. See p. 158 for further discussion.
4. An amusing letter from Sebastiano del Piombo to Michaelangelo describes his own Christian metamorphosis of antiquity, converting Ganymede into Saint John of the Apocalypse simply by adding a halo for his decoration of the cupola of the Medici Chapel.

297 x 218 mm.

Signed JOHANNES DVVET FAC on double-tablet between the angel's feet.

Inscribed HIST CAP 22 APOC on square plaque at lower right corner. The words EGO SVM ALPHA ET Ω are inscribed around the halo surrounding the head of Christ at the center of the upper part of the plate.[1]

First State: Dijon (Bibliothèque Municipale). The knot of drapery on the right shoulder of the Evangelist, immediately above the hand of the angel resting on his shoulder, is absent. It is drawn in brown ink, presumably by the engraver.

Second State: Represented in major print collections. A knot of drapery is engraved on the right shoulder of Saint John, immediately above the angel's hand.

Third State: Brussels (Cabinet des Estampes), London (BM—counterproof[2] —*Apocalypse figurée* examples), Paris (BN, Petit Palais—Coll. Dutuit). The rectangular patch at the top, to the right of the Lord's throne, previously filled with small clouds, now shows these clouds transformed into cherubs' heads, by adding facial features in a rather coarse engraved line.

B 35, RD 49, LeBlanc 49, Passavant 49, Boullaye 49, Popham 49, Linzeler 44-23, Bersier 40.

Saint John kneels at the lower left, his shoulder grasped by the angel at the right, who points up toward the New Jerusalem, illustrating the first verse of chapter 22: "And he [the angel] showed me a river of water of life, clear as crystal, proceeding from the throne of God and of the Lamb." The tree of life, bearing twelve fruits, is immediately behind the angel; its highest bough reaches up to the source of the river of life streaming from the Lord into a rectangular pool below.[3] The enthroned Sluter-like figure of God the Father is derived from the Burgundian Throne of Grace in which the Father holds the crucified Son and from the Eyckian figure in the "Foundation of Living Water" (Oberlin, Ohio and the Prado) both well known in Dijon. In the engraving the cross is replaced by a solar disk with its trinitarian *fleur-de-lys*.[4] The tree below may also refer to the *lignum vitae*—the source of the cross.[5] God holds a paten-like disk bearing a bust of Christ (22:4). The curved top of the plate is filled with the heavenly host, many of whom wear crowns or wreaths. Peter, Paul, and James are discernible at the left, while David and Louis (?) appear among the saints to the right.

Although there is no reference to the architecture of the New Jerusalem in this chapter, Duvet has introduced a view of a great imaginary lakeside city which stretches across the center of the composition. John and the Angel are separated from the heavenly city by a body of water whose source appears to be the river of life above, the water flowing down through a passage that opens behind the tree of life. The lake, filled with the water of life, is banked by a semicircle of retaining clouds, in front of which Saint John and the angel appear in the extreme foreground.

The figure of John in this, the concluding plate of the *Apocalypse* proper, probably dating from the 1550s, is reminiscent of the same figure engraved about a quarter of a century earlier in "Saint John the Baptist and Saint John the Evangelist Adoring the Lamb" (Cat. 24). The style of the figure of the angel points to that of "Henri II as the Victorious Saint Michael" (Cat. 62), part of a triptych glorifying both Saint Michael of the Apocalypse and the patron of the engraved *Apocalypse*—Henri II.

---

1. "I am Alpha and Omega" (22:13). The line also appears in the preceding chapter, 21:6.
2. Inscribed on the back F. Rech[berger] 1802. Cat. 1842-8-6-132. This is the only example of a counterproof by Duvet.
3. They may represent the Twelve Fruits of the Holy Spirit 5:22-23 (Vulgate), see also Thomas Aquinas, *Summa theologica*, II, i, q. 70, a. 3.
4. See Henri David, *De Sluter à Sambin*, Paris, 1933, I, pp. 36ff.
5. See Frederick Hartt, "Lignum Vitae in Medio Paradisi. The Stanza d'Eliodoro and Sistine Ceiling," *Art Bulletin*, XXXII, 1950, pp. 115-45, 181-218.

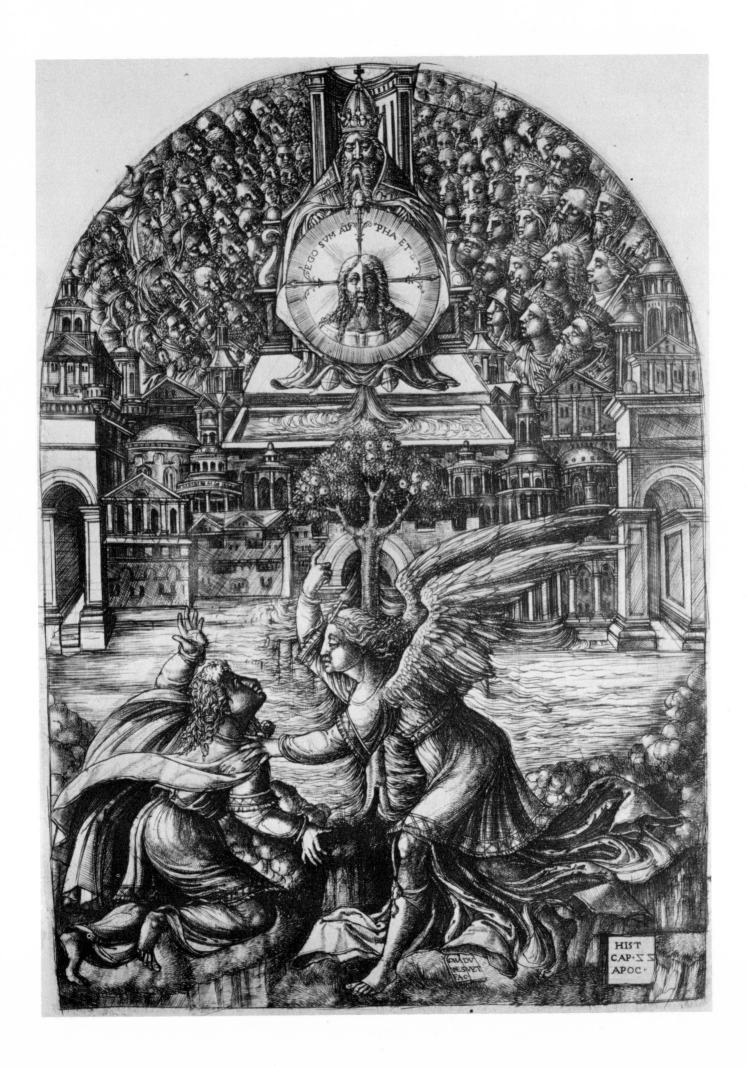

62. HENRI II AS THE VICTORIOUS SAINT MICHAEL [1]

296 x 209 mm.

Unsigned. A rectangle at the lower right, planned for an inscription, remains blank.

First State: Boston (MFA), Cleveland (MA—in *Apocalypse figurée*), London (BM), New York (MMA), Paris (BN—two impressions, L—Coll. Rothschild), Vienna (A), Washington (NG—Rosenwald Coll., ex Coll. d'Arenberg).[2] The prostrate demon sprawled at the feet of the three standing figures has a claw-hammer in his hand.[3]

Second State: Lyon (Bibliothèque de la Ville—in *Apocalypse figurée*), Paris (BN—in *Apocalypse figurée*). Made after the plate had undergone extensive repairs, noticeable in the L-shaped patch at the lower right. The claw-hammer in the demon's hand has been changed into a cleaver in this clumsy repair. The banner at the right seems to have been worked over.

B 45, RD 63, LeBlanc 66, Passavant 63, Popham 63, Bénézit 5763, Boullaye 63, Linzeler 72, Bersier 59.

The three triumphant, haloed figures support a crescent moon initialed H and surmounted by a crowned orb and Pelican of Piety over the crowned head of the central winged armor-clad figure who brandishes a sword with a *fleur-de-lys* pommel and wears the Order of Saint Michael. The winged figure at the left holds an escutcheon with the Valois *fleur-de-lys*. The figure at the right supports a grand banner of the *oriflamme*—the French national emblem of Saint Martin.[4] The central figure combines the attributes of Saint Michael and Henri II, as victorious leader of Catholic France.

Both the *oriflamme* and the triple crescent were emblems of the Order of Saint Michael, chosen at the rededication of the Order by Henri II in 1548, the year after his coronation, in which this plate and the two others relating to Henri II were probably engraved.[5]

---

1. This print is listed, usually, as "Henry II, King of France," as in Popham, p. 149. Linzeler (*I.F.F.*, p. 141) entitles it "Henri II couronné par un ange et par un génie." He identifies the bird at the top as the Holy Ghost. Naef, p. 136, describes this engraving as an *Apothéose allegorique du roi Henri II*. A. Hyatt Mayor (*Prints and People*, New York, 1972, fig. 359) entitled the print *Henry II between France and Fame*, dating it circa 1548. According to H. Mireur (*Dict. des ventes d'art*, Paris, 1911, II, p. 633), an impression was listed in the Rossi Sale—presumably Marseille Rossi (Lugt I, no. 10229, Apr. 16–19, 1822).
2. Very fine impression.
3. The claw-hammer held by Satan also appears in the Raphael School "Saint Michael" (Louvre), ordered by Leo X in 1518, presented by Lorenzo de'Medici to his aunt the Queen of France (Jean Adhémar, "The Collection of Paintings of Francis I," *Gazette des Beaux-Arts*, Sér. 6, XXX, July 1946, pp. 5–16). The painting was engraved by Beatrizet. A similar subject was painted by Sebastiano del Piombo for François I. M. Dutuit's annotated *Bartsch* (Paris, Petit Palais) states that Duvet's demon symbolizes envy or calumny. The figure recalls Florentine fifteenth-century Dante illustrations. See Cat. 9 for a Raphael-like "Saint Michael" which Duvet engraved approximately thirty years before.
4. Claude Paradin, *Devises Heroiques*, Lyon, 1557, illustrates the triple crescent, with the accompanying text: "DONEC TOTUM IMPLEAT ORBEM. La Devise a present du Treschrestien & victorieux Roy Henri II de ce nom, est la Lune en son croissant: Est sacrées escritures donques la Lune préfigure L'Eglise, quasi en tous passages, a quoy se conform l'histoire recitée par Paul Emil du Pape Calixte II . . . lequel la nuit précédent sa creacion eut vision d'une ieune enfant qui lui apporter & mit une Lune sur le giron. La Lune aussi est sugette à mutacions, croissant & decroissant de tems en tems; ainsi veritablement est l'Eglise militante, laquel ne peut demourer long tems en une estat, que maintenant ne soit soutenue et defendue des Princes Catholiques, & tantot perfectuée des tirans & hérétiques; au moyen de quoy est en perpetuel combat, auquel néanmoins le Royal Majesté. où Roy premier fils de l'Eglise promet de tenir main de proteccion iusques à ce que reduite sous un Dieu, un Roy, & une Loy, aparoisse la plenitude & rotondité de sa bergerie, régie par le seul Pasteur." Robert-Dumesnil, *Le peintre graveur français*, Paris, 1841, V, p. 32, quotes from a poem by Louise Labé, *Ecriz de divers Poètes à la louenge de Lovise Labé Lionnoize*, Jean de Tournes, Lyons, 1556:

   Du tresnoble roy de france
   la croissant nvve acroissance
   de iour en iour reprendra,
   iusques à tant que ses cornes
   iontes sans aucunes bornes
   en un plein rond il rendra.

   For the political significance of the crescent moon under Henri II, see "Numismatic Propaganda in Renaissance France," by W. McAllister Johnson, *Art Quarterly*, XXXI, 1968, pp. 123–53, esp. pp. 127 ff.
   For the iconography of the *oriflamme*, see E. Panofsky, *Abbot Suger*, Princeton, 1946, pp. 232–33.
5. A date before 1548 is proposed for this print as so many French Protestants fled to Geneva in that year. C. Pannier, "Encore un artiste française peu connu, Jean Duvet (1485-1570?)," *Bulletin historique protestante française*, LXXXVII, 1938, p. 216. Hennin (*Monuments de l'histoire de France*, Paris, 1856, VIII, p. 403) believed that Cat 62 commemorated the death of Henri II in 1559. He dated *La Majesté Royale* (Cat. 63) 1550 without giving any specific reason. In Hennin's day *Henri II as Saint Michael Killing the Dragon* (Cat. 64) had not yet been discovered.

302 x 209 mm.

Signed IOHANNES DVVET on double-tablet at lower left corner. Five banners attached to trumpets are inscribed RENOMME (Fame) as is a cartouche at the upper left. A book held by a female figure at the right is inscribed SAPIENCE (Wisdom).

First State: Paris (BN–Cat. AA3, Rés). Vienna. Unsigned and uninscribed.[1]

Second State: Boston (MFA), Brussels (Bibliothèque Royale), Chantilly (Musée Condé), London (BM), Vienna (A), Washington (NG–Rosenwald Coll.).[2] The tablet supported by angels at the base of the three central figures is now inscribed with the artist's name.

Third State: Cleveland (MA), London (BM), New York (MMA), Paris (BN, L–Coll. Rothschild), Gutekunst and Klipstein Auction 91 (Nov. 6, 1958, Cat. 136). The incomplete inscription IA MAIESTE DV ROY (Royal Majesty) has been erased and the large tablet remains blank.

B 43, RD 60, LeBlanc 58, Passavant 60, Boullaye 60, Popham 60, Bénézit 5761, Linzeler 74, Bersier 58.

In this allegory of the enduring triumph of royalty over time, the three seated women in classical garb represent, from left to right, Justice, Royalty, and Wisdom. This victory is made possible through the ruler's divine inspiration, indicated by the centrally placed trumpet coming from heaven down to the haloed head of Royalty, who has a crown of *fleur-de-lys*–emblem of the Valois dynasty–above her.[3] Two mourning angels hold a rectangular plaque inscribed "Royal Majesty" in the print's third state. This may refer to the sealing of a monarch's tomb. The king's death is also indicated by the perforation of an orb–signifying earthly dominion–by a snake, its intertwined body, possibly symbolizing eternity.

The print was probably prepared after the death of François I in 1547. The tomb resembles that of Christ in Cat. 37, which was prepared *en suite* with this plate. It provides a throne-like base for the figures above–the general grouping may have been adapted from prints after Raphael's "Stanza della Segnatura." Symbolic triads often appeared in the imagery of triumphal entries.[4] The female trinity of secular virtues act as a counterpart to the male trinity of spiritual values in Cat. 62. Delaborde wrote that the print depicted Justice, Royalty and Wisdom, and viewed *La Majesté Royale* as its collective title.[5] Boullaye agreed and suggested that it, with *Henri II as Saint Michael Slaying the Dragon* (Cat. 64), and the *Victorious Saint Michael* (Cat. 62) were prepared for a book commemorating the coronation of 1547 and the royal re-dedication of the Order in Lyons the following year.[6] The engraving may be partially derived from two Fontainebleau prints, one of 1547 (Text fig. 20) by Master L. D. (B.XV, 318, 32). Duvet adapted figures from another print after Rosso by Fantuzzi (B.XV, 359, 37) for the angels at the base.[7] The inscriptions may represent a confused recollection of a celebrated Rosso decoration at Fontainebleau.[8]

---

1. Perhaps this is the impression listed as "Epreuve de Ier état" in "Chevalier S" Sale in 1855; a first impression was also included in the Lady St. Aubin Sale (1856) and that of Borlunt de Noordonck, Ghent, 1858.
2. The Washington impression has a handwritten inscription ICONES VARIAE APOCALIPSIS and "Dinja Laforix, A.D. 3 Juillet 1641."
3. Here Duvet may have followed Bocchi's emblem of God creating the earth by inspiration (B. XV, 166, 317) by inspiration, engraved by Bonasone. He used another print from the same series completed in 1555 for Cat. 65.
4. A Troyes goldsmith prepared *Justice, Force and Prudence* for Charles IX's entry in 1564. See R. Kocchlin and J. J. Marquet de Vasselot, *La Sculpture à Troyes*, Paris, 1900, p. 345. The group was designed by a local painter.
5. Delaborde, *Le Départment des Estampes à la Bibl. Nat.*, Paris, 1875, p. 345, no. 170.
6. Boullaye, 1876, p. 136.
7. A bust of François I, supported by putti was flanked by large figures representing Victory and Fame, described by F. Herbet in his "Les graveurs de l'Ecole de Fontainebleau," *Annales du Gâtinais*, 1902, p. 72. The Fame engraved by Domenico Fiorentino (B.7) was based upon the same figure in the above project.
8. Duvet adapted the putto on horseback from the same print for his "Unicorn Borne on a Triumphal Car" (Cat. 33).

310 x 220 mm.

Signed IOHANNES DVVET FAC on double-tablet at the extreme right.

The print has three blank plaques, evidently intended for engraved inscriptions, inscribed in pen and brown ink, presumably in the engraver's hand.[2]   The inscription at the upper left is illegible.   At the upper right is written:

> Pretendit sacrum officiosa columba liquorem
> Tuque novis rex es (Galle) renatus aquis.[3]

A large horizontal plaque, at the foot of the plate, is inscribed:

> Hoc Henrice tibi signavimus aere duellum
> Unde Michaeli parta corona fuit.
> Illius auspiciis nimirum nomine certo
> Pendet foelici sorte monile tibi.[4]

Dijon (Bibliothèque de la Ville—unique).   A proof sheet, the print has a series of brown, pen-drawn indications of increased shading on the throat and upper profile of the saint.[5]

Boullaye 72a, Popham 72a, Linzeler 73, Bersier 60.

Saint and devil fight upon an islandlike plaque at the base of the print, with Mont-St.-Michel rising at the left.   A dominant cluster of ornament begins at the top with a crescent studded with crowned letter "H" 's, supporting a flaming *fleur-de-lys* crested crown.   The head and arms of a little angel are seen below; straddling a great shield inscribed with three *fleur-de-lys* and framed by the encircling *Ordre de Saint Michel.* To the left, a second angel leans upon the square plaque filled with an illegible, hand-penned inscription, a triple crescent over his wreathed head.   A second triple crescent in a parallel position at the right is shown above the head of a bishop, standing behind the inscription plaque.   He points to the *Ordre de Saint Michel* descending from the cloud-clustered heaven, as he raises an appointing flask.   Both flask and the dove are alluded to in the Bishop's inscription, directed to Henri II, "The duteous dove has proffered the holy oil, and you are born again a Gaul and king, in this new anointment."   These words identify him as Saint Rémy holding the miraculous ampulla with which he baptised Clovis, first Christian king of the Franks, for the anointment of Henri II at his coronation.[7]   The triple crescent was adopted by Henri II as the emblem of the Ordre de Saint Michel in 1548.[8]

The engraving, as Boullaye suggested, was planned in conjunction with Cat. 62 and 63 to celebrate the coronation of Henri II in 1547 and his rededication of the Order of Saint Michel in the following year.[9] The most likely date for the three engravings is circa 1548.   Close in format and style to those devoted to the illustration of the Apocalypse text proper, the engraving provides a link between those plates and the patronage of Henri II, alluded to in the *Privilège* of 1555 (Appendix E, Doc. 68).

The Order commissioned works of art illustrating the victory of its patron saint as described in the Apocalypse of Saint John and shown in this print: Rev. 12:7, "And there was a great battle in heaven, Michael and his angels fought with the dragon."   The stained-glass windows of the Order's chapel at Vincennes (Text fig. 31) which were installed at about the time of the Duvet prints, also celebrate the events of the Apocalypse and the Order's royal leader.   A magnificent Primaticcio drawing, recently acquired by the Louvre, may have been a design for the altar at Vincennes (Text fig. 30).

Duvet may have planned this print for royal presentation during a triumphal Burgundian entry of Henri II in 1548, engraving the plate to conform with and complement the *Apocalypse* which he had begun under the patronage of the young king's father.   Together with the other two plates of the "triptych," the engraving celebrates the spiritual and secular virtues of Henri II and reflects the victorious pageantry Duvet staged for royal visits.

The presence of Saint Rémy, the emphasis on the coronation, the saint's "Valois" sword, and the great H-monograms in heaven, all show Henri II as participating within the Saint's victory as celebrated in contemporary *mystères.*[10]

---

1.   Generally identified as "Saint Michel and the Dragon." For a fine reproduction, see P. de Neveux and E. Dacier, *Les richesses des bibliothèques provinciales de France,* Paris, 1932, I, Pl. XLVII.

2.   The handwriting on the engraving is close to that of an autograph receipt of Duvet's discovered by Naef in the Geneva archives, dated 1544.

3.   "The duteous dove has proffered the holy oil, and you are born again a Gaul and king, in this new annointment."

4.   "In this plate, Henry, we have engraved the combat whence arose the crown of Saint Michael: with his patronage, and under his name, a happy fortune hangs Saint Michael's order about your neck."

5. According to the catalogue by P. Darras for the Jean Duvet exhibition held at the Bibliothèque Nationale in 1938, the engraving was found in a print-album assembled by a councilor of the Parliament of Burgundy—J. B. Jehannin de Chamblanc. Since the unique engraving probably represents a municipal project for the decoration of a triumphal entry of Henri II in 1548, it is tempting to assume that it may have been originally discovered in some archival material. However, this print is probably the one included in the Rossi Sale, 1822, listed as "Portrait de Henri II, foulant aux pieds un monstre renversé."

6. The Battle of Saint Michel and Satan was already shown as taking place by Mont St.-Michel in the *Très riches heures de Jean de France,* Duc de Berry (Chantilly).

7. For a discussion of the significance of this event, see E. R. Vaucelle, *La Collégiale de Saint-Martin de Tours des origines à l'avènement des Valois,* Paris, 1908, Appendice II, "La baptême de Clovis," pp. 411–23. By the sixteenth century the account of the dove seems to have fallen into disfavor. Gerolamo Siciolante's "Baptism of Clovis" for the chapel of Saint-Rémy (Rome, San Luigi dei Francesi) shows the event in an airy, neoclassical interior. See Olga Raggio, "Vignola, Fra Damiano et Gerolamo Siciolante à la chapelle de la Bastie d'Urfe," *Revue de l'Art,* 15, 1972, p. 50, fig. 64. French publications of the turn of the century omit the dove too. See Colin Eisler, *Catalogue of French, German, Netherlandish and Spanish Paintings,* London, 1974, entry for the Maître de Saint Gilles' p. 242. Duvet may have revived the dove for its Burgundian significance. The Baptism of Clovis was shown for François Ier's Lyon entry of 1515. See the Guige edition of 1899.

8. See Cat. 62, n. 4, for the symbolism of the triple crescent. Boullaye, p. 135, points out that it, together with the *oriflamme,* were selected by Henri II at the rededication of the *Ordre* in Lyon in 1548, the year following his coronation.

9. Boullaye, p. 135.

10. See pp. 73-74, 76-78, 83.

65 JEAN DUVET AS SAINT JOHN THE EVANGELIST [1]

301 x 226 mm.

The plate is signed IOH. DVVET AURIFAB. LINGON. ANOR. 70. HAS. HIST. PER FECIT. 1555. "Jean Duvet, goldsmith of Langres, aged seventy, has completed these histories in 1555."

An inscription on the left page of an opened book on the desk reads: LIB. APOC. BEAT. IOH. APO. "Book of the Apocalypse of the Apostle Saint John."

A second inscription at the lower left corner reads:

SACRA IN HAC ET ALIIS SEQUĒTIBUS
TABELLIS CONTENTA MISTERIA EX_
DIVINA IOHANNIS APOCALIPSI DESŪPTA
SUNT AC VERAE LITERAE TEXTUS
PROXIME ACCOMODATE ADHIBITO
ETIAM VIRORUM PERITIORVM IVDICIO.[2]

"The sacred mysteries contained in this and the other tablets following are derived from the divine revelation of John and are closely adapted to the true letter of the text with the judgement of more learned men brought to bear."

At the lower right, immediately above the figure of a swan, a final inscription in elegaic couplets reads:

FATA PREMŪT
TREPIDANT
MANVS IAM
LUMINA FALLUNT
MENS RESTAT
VICTRIX GRĀ
DE SVADET
OPUS.

"Death is upon me and my hands tremble, my sight fails, yet the spirit remains victorious and I have completed my great work."

First State: Dijon (Bibliothèque Municipale). The artist has indicated ten areas with a brown pen line for further shading. Five of these were engraved in the second state: on top of right half of bridge, drapery to right of angel, on side of desk facing swan, on top of desk cover, below left arm of Evangelist. Five additional areas of pen-drawn hatching were never engraved: on Evangelist's right arm, below the drapery on bench, between dog and cat on corner of block at lower left, to right of prow of Fates' ship, on Evangelist's left foot.

Second State: Berlin, Boston (MFA), Budapest, Chantilly (Musée Condé), Chicago (AIC), Cleveland (MA—in *Apocalypse figurée*), London (BM—in Print Room and in *Apocalypse figurée*), Lyon (Bibliothèque de la Ville—in *Apocalypse figurée*), Ottawa (National Gallery of Canada), Paris (BN—in *Apocalypse figurée*—Ecole des B.-A, two in Cabinet des Estampes, L—Coll. Rothschild, Petit Palais—Coll. Dutuit—in *Apocalypse figurée*), Vienna (A), Washington (NG—Rosenwald Coll., ex Coll. Behague), Zurich. The first five changes, enumerated above, are engraved following the pen-drawn indications of the Dijon trial proof.

B 12, RD 27, LeBlanc 27, Passavant 62, Boullaye 27, Bénézit 57591, Popham 62, Linzeler 22-1, Bersier 18.

At the extreme left, a saturnine old man, resembling a Michelangelesque prophet, is shown in right profile, seated on an island by a lake. Holding a stylus in his left hand, he points to an open book on the desk before him, "Book of the Apocalypse of the Apostle Saint John," a burin is next to the Apocalypse manuscript. An inscribed tablet—Duvet's customary format for his signature—provides the most important surviving biographical information.

The demon with his bellows of infernal inspiration and the winged genius at the engraver's side are derived from Platonic texts, probably those of Ficino, possibly taken from their largely satirical restatement by Rabelais in his *Tiers Livre,* Book III, Ch. 21,[3] which mocks the fashionable, often fatuous Neo-Platonism of the day, derived in part from Agrippa von Nettesheim's concept of Melancholy. The Raphaelesque guardian angel, a winged genius, illustrates the prophetic engraver's victorious spirit which beat death to the finish of his *Apocalypse figurée.* The artist's triumph over approaching death—symbolized by the oncoming ship of Fate and the swan with an arrow in its beak, dual annunciations of mortality in classical guise—is inscribed on a "square of virtue"[4] at the lower left. Just as the swan has broken the chain of life in order to approach the engraver with his emblem of death, so Atropos is shown about to cut the thread of life. The swan is frequently shown in Duvet's prints as a rubric of his name. The eagle in the foreground, plucking the down from his prey, may be another visual pun on Duvet, and still another to the left of the eagle provides a third *rebus* on Duvet.[5] Duvet has substituted the swan for the Evangelist's eagle in this scene, providing himself with Apollo's messenger of death.[6] The fishermen drawing in their nets as the swimmer emerging from below a bridge may also be interpreted symbolically.[7] In the lower left corner, a dog is shown at his master's feet, while a mouse frisks under the desk seat. A cat peers at a swan, who, having broken the chain which moored it to a tree stump (another emblem of death) swims toward the old man. The four animals refer to the Humours—the dog to Melancholy; the cat to Choler; the mouse to Phlegm and the swan to the Sanguine. Symbolic of destruction and decay, the mouse under the bench is barely restrained by the faithful dog.[8] The swan is seen first by the cat, traditional prophet of death.[9] Symbol of sacred letters, the dog is placed above a reference to the "true letter of the text."

The seated figure is that of the engraver, Jean Duvet, shown in the guise of his patron saint, John the Evangelist. The engraver's burin is on the table. Like all the other engravings in the Apocalypse series, this print is in the shape of a tablet and is described as such—*tabellis*—in the inscription at the right. The tablets themselves become areas for recording the experienced revelation.[10]

This dual biographical image fuses Duvet's life with that of his patron saint, relating John's exile on Patmos to Jean's self-imposed exile in Geneva. The lakeside city in the background bears considerable resemblance to the latter, and its fortifications may well represent the engraver's projects as municipal supervisor of military engineering.[10]

The latest of Duvet's signed and dated prints, the Apocalypse frontispiece was also the final plate in the Series. Engraved in his mature style, it combines the fine shading of the early Marcantonio with a more expressionistic chiaroscuro. The composition is inspired by such classicizing "author-portraits" as those depicting Socrates, Virgil and Cesariano (Text figures 18-19) earlier in the century.[11] While retaining much of the intricate texture of his early style, dependent upon the graphic discoveries of Northern print-makers of the first decade of the century, Duvet also employs the urgent, rapid linear communication and coarse, almost dry lines of his Fontainebleau contemporaries.

---

1.   Usually listed as "Duvet Studying the Apocalypse" or as "Saint John on Patmos." First correctly identified in F.-L. Regnault Delalande, *Catalogue raisonné du Cabinet de feu M. de Silvestre*, Paris, 1811.

2.   For a discussion of who these learned men might have been, see Marcel's survey (II, p. 434, n.3) of the erudite canons attached to the cathedral of St.-Mammès at the time of Duvet's residence in Langres—"Claude Félix, versé dans l' Ecriture, Jean Lefèvre, secrétaire du cardinal Givry, François Mangeard, son coadjuteur, et les chanoines artistes et érudites, Jean Tabourot, Richard Roussat." See n.8 below.

3.   For Duvet's textual sources, see p. 58. The angel is after a School of Raphael figure. Duvet may also have consulted Jacopo da Barbaris' *Custodenos dormientes* (Text fig. 17).

4.   See R. Wittkower, "Space, Time and Virtue," *Journal of the Warburg and Courtauld Institutes*, II, 1932-38, pp. 313-21.

5.   See Boullaye, p. 87. E. Tietze-Conrat (*Der französische Kupferstich der Renaissance*, Munich, 1925, p. 8) interprets the eagle plucking down (duvet) in the foreground as an emblem of self-sacrifice.

6.   For swan symbolism, see pp. 48-53 above. For the role of Apollo as a bringer of death, see Pauly-Wissowa, *Real-Encyclopädie*, Stuttgart, II, 1896, p. 17. Dürer's engraved Arms of Death of 1505 appears to be a clear allusion to the swan of Apollo as harbinger of death; see pp. 50-51 above. The swan carrying an arrow was also the emblem of Louise de Savoie, mother of François I.

7.   E. Tietze-Conrat believes that the draught of fishes is taken from Jacques Kerver's translation of the *Horapollo*, published in 1553, fol. 105, p. 211, "Quo modo eum qui rerum honestarum amore flagit." The illustration shows two fishermen pulling in a squid-like creature. It is hard to see any relationship between this and the Duvet. Duvet may well have consulted Dirk Vellert's engraving of the "Calling of Peter and Andrew" (B.VIII, 27, 3). The motif of the fishermen may relate to an illustration appearing in a sixteenth-century illustration to an Aesop fable—"Quod ars negat fortuna prestat." See L. Lalanne, *The Book of Fortune*, Paris, 1883, Pl. CLVII.

8.   In Andrea Alciati's *Emblemata* (Leyden ed., 1591, p. 306, Emblema LXXIX) "Lascivia," the mouse is listed as a symbol of destruction. Duvet's familiarity with this source is certain since the first French translation was by Canon Jean Lefèvre of Langres. The first edition of 1536 was dedicated to Amiral Chabot, and the second, expanded edition of 1548 to Duvet's patron Cardinal de Givry (Marcel, II, pp. 216-19). Secretary to Givry, Lefèvre was famous for his erudition, known as "curieux des arts mécaniques, surtout l'horlogerie et peinture." He, with Roussat, are the most likely candidates for the role of "more learned men" referred to by Duvet in this print.

9.   The cat is described as "representative of Hebe [sic] goddess of Death . . . a widely respected omen of approaching mortality," in M. Oldfield Howey, *The Cat in the Mysteries of Religion and Magic*, Philadelphia, n.d., p. 192.

10.   The third plate of the *Apocalypse* (Cat. 41) shows a similar series of lakeside fortification. Both resemble the view of Geneva reproduced in Sebastien Münster's *Cosmographie*, Basle, 1554. For Duvet as fortifications designer, see Appendix G.

11.   For these portraits, see pp. 54-55 above.

FATA PREMVT·
TREPIDANTQ·S·
MANVS·IAM·
LVMINA·EAIVNT·
MEVS·RESTAT·
VICTRIXGRÄ·
DEQ·SVADET·
OPVS·

SACRA IN HAC ET ALIIS SEQVÈTIBVS·
TABELLIS CONTENTA MISTERIA EX·
DIVINA IOHANNIS APOCALIPSI DESVPTA·
SVNT AC VERÆ LITERÆ TEXTVS·
PROXIME ACCOMMODATA ADHIBITO·
ETIAM VIRORVM PERITIORVM IVDICIO·

66. A KING PURSUED BY A UNICORN

235 x 390

Unsigned.

Amsterdam (Rijksmuseum), Berlin, Boston (MFA), Brussels, Budapest, Cambridge (Fogg Art Museum), Chicago (AIC–two impressions, ex Colls. Dresden and Fürstenberg), Dresden, Langres (Musée des Beaux-Arts), London (BM, V & A), Ottawa, Minneapolis (Minn. Institute of Arts), New York (MMA), Paris (BN–two impressions, Petit Palais–Coll. Dutuit, pc, Ecole des B.-A.), Vienna (A–two impressions), Washington (NG–Rosenwald Coll.).

B 40, RD 55, LeBlanc 60, Passavant 55, Boullaye 55, Bénézit 5760, Popham 55, Linzeler 61-2, Bersier 69.

(One of a series of six, Cat. 32-34, 66-68.) The landscape is somewhat like that for the "Unicorn Purifying the Water" (Cat. 68). With the exception of the carefully executed unicorn, this engraving approximates the more painterly, sketchy style of the Fontainebleau printmakers. Duvet may have consulted a Milanese engraving entitled *Poison et Contre-Poison* (Text fig. 47). Both format and depiction of the leaping, smooth-horned unicorn point to the anonymously engraved print which was often attributed to Duvet's hand.[1] The expressionistic character of this crowded, ambitiously conceived scene has much of the immediacy and excitement of the Apocalypse plates.[2]

The nude figure holding a shield at the lower right is clearly taken from an Italian source.[3] A print by the Fontainebleau Master LD seems to have provided the point of departure for this engraving. Probably after a painting by Luca Penni, it depicts the death of Adonis (Text fig. 76).[4] It is very close in size to Cat. 66. An engraving by Giorgio Ghisi (B.60), distributed by Cock in 1555, shares many of the characteristics of the Duvet print, as does a print by Frans Floris of "Victory" (B.47), dated 1552. These similarities suggest that the Duvet probably dates circa 1555.

There is no completely satisfactory textual source for this scene,[5] which illustrates the legendary ferocity of the unicorn–the invincible strength which can only be subdued by a virgin. The print displays the power of the unicorn so as to make his eventual conquest by virgin capture and the accompanying triumphal procession all the more meaningful.

---

1. See Appendix A.1 for a discussion of this engraving.
2. The left quarter is reminiscent of Cat. 56, while the figure at the lower right is identical with another *Apocalypse* plate (Cat. 55).
3. Perhaps via the Claessen engravings after Pollaiuolo. See F. W. H. Hollstein, *Dutch and Flemish Etchings . . .* , Amsterdam, IV, n.d., pp. 144–45, Cat. 153-55.
4. An Adonis sarcophagus in Mantua appears to be one of the sources for the Fontainebleau composition adapted by Duvet. See Aldo Levi, *Sculpture greche e romane del Palazzo ducale di Mantova*, Rome, 1931, Pl. CV, CVI.
5. R. Van Marle (*Iconographie de l'art profane*, The Hague, 1932, p. 452) mentions this engraving in a discussion of unicorn symbolism without giving any interpretation of the subject matter.

235 x 392 mm.

Unsigned. Blank double tablet of Moses appears at extreme upper left.

First State: Amsterdam (Rijksmuseum), Berlin, Cambridge (Fogg Art Museum), Chicago (AIC), Cincinnati (AM), Dijon (Bibl. Mun), London (BM, V&A), Paris (BN, Ecole des B.-A. L–Coll. Rothschild, Petit Palais–Coll. Dutuit, Coll. Jean Ehrman, pc), Washington (NG–Rosenwald Coll., ex Coll. Behague).[1]

Second State: Paris (BN–Cat. AA2 Rés). The numerals 61 are engraved at the extreme lower left. The plate appears to have been left unfinished by the engraver, as all known impressions have a curiously blank area in the sky at the upper right.

B 41, RD 58, LeBlanc 63, Passavant 58, Boullaye 58, Popham, 58, Linzeler 65–4, Bersier 72.

(One of a series of six, Cat. 32-34, 66-68.) A freely restated Roman triumph, Duvet's engraving draws upon previous representations of the subject, which was extremely popular in sixteenth-century France, such as Fantuzzi's print after Rosso.[2] The style may be influenced by that of the tapestries ordered by Diane de Poitiers for Anet. The maidens with their pointed little noses and rather thin faces move away from the classical assurance of the Marcantonio types toward Campagnola and the North.

The plate has an uneven quality, suggesting that it is either unfinished or that it was worked on erratically over a long period. The firmly outlined, very three-dimensional, crowning putto seems unrelated to the much sketchier rendering of the other figures. The sky at the upper right, especially in the blank area of the palm branches, makes an incomplete effect.

This, perhaps the last engraving of the series, represents the apotheosis of the grooved horned unicorn, who is coming toward, or is already in, heaven. God the Father, shown as Jupiter, flies with the Holy Ghost–the eagle–to watch the Son, the unicorn, receiving the crown of Heaven, Jupiter's oak wreath. The crescent moon is an emblem of the Church.

The identification of Christ with the unicorn was a common one in the late Middle Ages, and that of Jupiter with God only slightly less so. Duvet's familiarity with this interpretation can be proven by the writings of an erudite canon of Langres, Richard Roussat.[3] Emblems of the Old Testament–the tablets of Moses at the upper left–and the New–the Trinitarian candles at the lower left–are displayed in this triumphal procession celebrating the victory of Christianity.

---

1. An impression was in the C.F.G.R. Schwerdt collection, *Hunting, Hawking, Shooting,* London, 1928, III, p. 57, Cat. 3.
2. Passavant 27, in the British Museum (Cat. 11.2.8115).
3. Richard Roussat, *Livre de l'Estat et Mutation des Temps, Prouvant par authoritez de l'Escripture saincte et par raisons astrologales la fin du Monde estre prochaine,* Lyon, 1550, p. 54, "Jupiter signifie et denote nostre Dieu, créateur de toutes choses, la lune, l'Église." See Marcel, II, pp. 237–45, for a brief biography of this canon.

226 x 395 mm (BN). 227 x 401 mm (BM).
Signed emblematically with swan plucking down *(duvet)* at lower right.
First State: Boston (MFA), London (BM). A rectangle at the upper margin of the plate, immediately above
the monkey on the tree at the right, is left blank.
Second State: Amsterdam (Rijksmuseum), Berlin, Boston, Brussels, Fitzwilliam Museum, Chicago
(AIC–Berlin duplicate), Cincinnati (AM), London, New York (N.Y. Public Library), Paris (BN,
Ecole des B.-A. L–Coll. Rothschild), Vienna (A), Washington (NG–Rosenwald Coll, ex Coll.
Béhague, Zurich. The rectangle is filled in with sketchily indicated foliage, completing the upper
part of the tree.
B.42, R.D.59, Le Blanc 64, Linzeler 67-6, Bersier 68

(One of a series of six, Cat. 32-34, 66-68.) This engraving illustrates the purity of the unicorn,
analogous in its healing powers to that of Christ. The episode shown, based on the *Physiologus*,
depicts thirsty animals at the water's edge, unable to drink because the water has been poisoned by
a serpent. They await the unicorn, who will purify the water by immersing its horn in the water and
making the sign of the cross.[1] The theme is seen in French consultation of Greek rather than Latin
bestiaries.[2]

This print, like the rest of the series, presents a curious fusion of naturalism and formalism, combining
courtly elegance, heraldic and emblematic references with close observation and almost grotesque realism.
The proportions and style of the engraving suggest the format of a tapestry; Duvet is known to have
designed such works (Appendix E, Doc. 48).

The classical column may point toward the Roman triumph with which the capture of the unicorn
will be concluded; it may also allude to Orpheus. The goat on the mountain top at the upper right is
derived from Dürer's engraved "Adam and Eve" (B.1). The posture of the unicorn and the beasts' sequence
resemble those shown in G. Bonasone's engraving of the "Animals entering the Ark" dated 1544 (B.XV,
p. 113, no. 4). Duvet's animals and setting are freely adapted from Jean Mignon's "Creation of Eve" and
"Temptation," based on compositions by Penni (Text figs. 48-49) probably executed between 1543 and
1545.[3] The leopard and boar may have been derived from a tapestry designed by Jean Cousin for the
Cathedral of St.-Mammès at Langres in 1543. See Text fig. 11..

The carefully engraved animals, with their Rousseau-like naïveté, reflect the artist's work. However, the appliqué-like relationship of elements, together with a technique emulating the etched line of the
mid-century Italian printmakers of the School of Fontainebleau, point to a later date, perhaps contemporary
with the last plates of the *Apocalypse.* The ridge-like black lines and the dense, flat crowding belong to
the artist's late style.

1. Mrs. Pattison, *The Art of the Renaissance in France,* London, 1879, II, p. 110, "The subject is, perhaps the opening
   prelude to the drama which commences in the next plate, in which Diana appears, sitting enthroned under a canopy,
   with the king at her side and her dogs at her feet . . ."
2. See Odell Shepard, *The Lore of the Unicorn,* New York, 1931, p. 60. The single horn represents the Holy Cross, the
   serpent the devil and the poisoned waters the sins of mankind.
3. Henri Zerner, *The School of Fontainebleau, Etchings and Engravings,* New York, n.d. Jean Mignon, Cat. nos. 56 and
   57.

∅   176mm[1]
Unsigned.
London (BM, unique).
The far right section of this impression is lost, cutting off the man's arm at the shoulder and part of the horse's tail.
RD 9, Duplessis 9, Passavant 75, Boullaye 78, Popham 75, Linzeler 76 and 77, Bersier 65.

This ornamental plate is reminiscent of designs for metalwork, possibly armor or enamel. A *rondache* by Giorgio Ghisi signed and dated 1554 has a similar motif at the center. His prints share many of the characteristics of Duvet.[2] Probably a pupil of Giulio Romano, Ghisi brought to France an approach to handsome, applied classical ornament close in spirit to that found at the Palazzo del Tè. Duvet's roundel follows the Fontainebleau reflection of this Mantuan decorative style in the 1540s.

Duvet is known to have designed heraldic trappings for triumphal entries, and this roundel may well relate to a design he executed for ornate ceremonial armor. The print is close in style to the late engravings of the Unicorn series (Cat. 66-68).

---

1. First recorded by F.-L. Regnault Delalande, *Catalogue raisonné du cabinet de feu M. de Silvestre*, Paris, 1811, Cat. 790, p. 241, "Deux Hommes, trois chevaux et deux Chiens. Sujet attribué à J. Duvet. Composition dans une forme ronde. Diamètre, 6 p. 61." It was next published in 1856 by G. F. Waagen ("Uber einige seltene, neuerdings in der Kupferstich Sammlung des britischen Museums erworbene Blätter," *Archiv für die zeichnende Künste von Dr. Robert Nauman,* Leipzig, 1856, II, p. 248) who pointed out that not even Robert-Dumesnil had been able to examine an impression.
2. British Museum, ex-collections Demidoff and Rothschild.

248 x 164 mm (BN).

Unsigned.

Berlin, Boston (MFA—two impressions), Cambridge (Fogg Art Museum), Chicago (AIC—ex Coll. Seasongood), Dijon (Bibliothèque Municipale), Dresden, London (BM), New York (MMA, N.Y. Public Library), Paris (BN—two impressions, L—Coll. Rothschild, Petit Palais—Coll. Dutuit), Saint Louis (City Art Museum), Vienna (A), Zurich.

Several impressions are found printed in ink with a purple or brown cast.

B 10, RD 20, LeBlanc 52, Passavant 20, Boullaye 20, Popham 20, Linzeler 54, Bersier 48.

In this unfinished engraving Sebastian is the only completed figure. Roch is shown older than usual, in left profile, leaning on an unfinished staff. Presumably the sore on Roch's thigh has already been healed by the little angel (often shown with him) who blesses him at the left and seems to be handing Roche a small, strand-like object.

The print is like a sketch, its figures still tentative in placement. All impressions are covered with very fine scratch-like lines. The animal head at the lower left seems to be a study for Roch's dog at the right; it certainly cannot represent Anthony's pig. Deprived of a formal setting, the figures seem to step all over each other.

The large print, depicting three saints venerated for their healing powers, is one of the few known French examples of a *Pestblatt*.[1] The only full-page impression of this sheet, showing it as it must have appeared as a poster or broadside, was at Dresden (destroyed in World War II).[2] Other French *Pestblätter* are coarse woodcuts, such as the one inscribed *Aux carmes de Paris,* dating from circa 1510, which also shows a Mantegna-inspired figure of Sebastian.[3]

Here Duvet again borrows motifs from Mantegna's work, as he had already done in "The Entombment" (Cat. 30) and the "Martyrdom of Saint John the Evangelist" (Cat. 38). Like the latter, this engraving is derived from Mantegna's "Bacchanal with the Vat" (B.19); Sebastian is copied in reverse from this work. The composition seems to have been suggested by the Italian artist's "Risen Christ between Saint Andrew and Saint Longinus" (B.6).[4]

There was a great plague throughout Burgundy in 1554, which may well be when this print was engraved.[5] Duvet could have been influenced by sculptures at the nearby church of St.-Florentin at Yonne, where the figure of Saint Roche resembles that in the engraving.[6]

The print is typical of the artist's *Spätstil,* its extremely rich, expressionistic quality achieved by a strange fusion of a coarse, rapid line contrasted with a dense, dramatic chiaroscuro.[7]

---

1. See Karl Künstle, *Ikonographie der Heiligen,* Freiburg-im-Breisgau, 1926, p. 526, and the chapter in L. Réau, *Mathias Grünewald,* Paris, 1920, entitled, "Iconographie des saints antipesteux," for the specific healing qualities attributed to these saints. A print showing the same three saints in a roundel was executed by Master S (Passavant 320, Hollstein 320, reproduced in Hollstein, *Dutch and Flemish Early Engravings and Woodcuts,* Amsterdam, n.d., XIII, p. 187.

2. The sheet is reproduced in facsimile in Paul Heitz and W. L. Schreiber, *Pestblätter des XV Jahrhundert,* Strasbourg, 1901, Pl. XXX2. It measures approximately 348 x 168 mm. Most impressions are cut down around the platemark. Those at the Louvre, Berlin, and the New York Public Library are on large sheets of paper, but in comparison with the Dresden example were probably cut down.

3. This woodcut is reproduced in Heitz and Schreiber, Pl. XXV. The date for it, given above, is taken from Campbell Dodgson's review of the publication, in *The Library,* Jan. 1902, p. 11. An Italian *Pestblatt* by Caraglio, showing Mary, Jesus, Roche, and Sebastian (B.XV, p. 71, no. 7), bears a slight formal resemblance to the French engraving.

4. These Italian sources were discovered by Popham, p. 143.

5. See M. Brocard, *La grande peste de Langres au XVII siècle,* Langres, 1926. Between 1560–65 rigorous means were taken to prevent the entry of plague carriers. See Marcel, II, p. 286, n. 3.

6. Reproduced in Marcel Aubert, *Les richesses de l'art de la France,* Fasc. I–II, *La Bourgogne,* Paris, 1921, p. 113, fig. 3.

7. Jean de Foville, "Jean Duvet," *Le Musée,* 1909, p. 82, believes that this engraving together with Cat. 71 and 72 are all early works. Boullaye, p. 82, considers the engraving late, as being by "une main défaillante." Popham, p. 136, believes that the print "must be placed with the mature engravings."

245 x 165 mm. Cut within platemark.
Unsigned.[1]
London (BM);[2] Paris (B.N.).
RD 9, LeBlanc 18, Passavant 9, Boullaye 9, Popham 9, Linzeler 18, Bersier 14.

In this engraving Mary's profile confronts that of Christ for the Last Farewell, her hand touching his breast.[3] The unfinished composition is for the most part only lightly incised; none of the figures are completed. With the exception of Christ and the Holy Women, the figures are not as yet fully worked out. Those at the extreme right and left run one into the other, each form blending with the next. The artist is evidently still experimenting with different solutions to the ultimate. unrealized work.

While the composition dimly reflects Raphael's Borghese "Entombment," Duvet probably consulted a School of Fontainebleau adaptation.[4] He may also have used a plaque by Andrea Riccio which affords a similar synthesis of Mantegnesque and Raphaelesque motifs.[5]

The preliminary sketch is scratched upon the plate in lines resembling drypoint, but was almost certainly engraved with a burin.[6] Although the articulation of the figures is bizarre, the work's personal authority and power transcend its obvious shortcomings. The print's passionate immediacy and freedom are akin to Titian's late style.

---

1. First identified by F.L. Regnault-Delalande, *Catalogue raisonné du cabinet de feu M. de Silvestre*, Paris, 1811, p. 241. This probably is the same impression recorded in the *Vente Robert-Dumesnil*, Paris, 1843, Cat. 34, measuring 230 x 167mm. The Parisian print is reproduced here.
2. The example in the British Museum has been cut down, measuring 218 x 165 mm.
3. For this theme, see Erwin Panofsky, *Early Netherlandish Paintings*, Cambridge, 1953, I, pp. 273-274.
4. The anonymous engraving (B.M. duplicate 385, no. 24, 50.5.27.114) is probably after a work by Luca Penni, which was derived in turn from a School of Marcantonio engraving (B.37). Jean de Foville ("Jean Duvet," *Le Musée*, 1909, p. 18) wrote that Duvet's engraving is based upon a drawing by Raphael in Florence, without further data.
5. Reproduced by L. Planiscig, *Andrea Riccio*, Vienna, 1927, Pl. 326. The mourning women engraved at the upper right are similar to those in the plaque.
6. Linzeler, p. 335, writes, "Cette planche inachevée parait avoir été esquissée à la point sèche. Date approximate 1540."

72. THE DESPAIR AND SUICIDE OF JUDAS [1]

248 x 164 mm (BM), 245 x 160 mm (BN).[2]
Unsigned.
First State: Berlin, London (BM—two impressions, one in rust-red ink,[3] Paris (BN), Vienna (A).
(Upper left and lower right without scratch-like parallel lines). Oxford, Ashmolean
Second State: Freely drawn scratch-like parallel lines are added at the upper left and lower right.
B 11, RD 22, LeBlanc 21, Passavant 22, Boullaye 22, Popham 22, Linzeler 19.

Judas, the desperate, bent-over man at the upper right, is shown walking toward the bank of a rushing stream near a bridge, as though contemplating casting himself into the water. He is shown again on the left side of the stream, hanging from a tree, suspended by a rope around the neck. A demon, standing at the rim of a flaming well below the hung man, pulls his soul (in the form of a small naked body) down from Judas' dangling entrails.[4]

The engraving is incomplete—only the two large figures and that of the demon may be finished. The tree and cloak, at the left, the hell-pit, and the landscape, are all indicated by very thin, scratch-like lines, reminiscent of those in Cat. 70, 71, 73. The main figures are engraved with a heavy black outline and a rich overall texture seen in the works here associated with the artist's late style, in which formal backgrounds and silvery hatching are abandoned in favor of isolated expressionistic forms and a dramatic chiaroscuro.

Judas' suicide had been engraved twice (Cat. 27, 37) before the artist undertook this final version, executed late in life when his eyesight was failing. Judas' spirit emerges from his entrails (Acts 1:18) so as not to desecrate the lips kissed by Christ; this aspect is combined with Matthew's account of Judas' hanging (Matt. 27:3–10). The bridge at the center, crossed before the suicide, is that of life. The stream may represent the river of death and the rider the Horseman of the Apocalypse.

Mrs. Tietze-Conrat suggested that the print was influenced by mystery plays, where the suicide was often elaborately staged.[5] Animal guts were bought to suspend below Judas' skirts, and the actor was frequently hung so realistically that he almost died.[6] Duvet was himself a master of stagecraft, participating in the *mystères* produced at the episcopal court of Langres for the triumphal entries of visiting dignitaries. Judas' suicide was staged to accompany such entries in France.

In the late fifteenth-century mystery play *La Passion de Jésus-Christ* by Jean Michel, a large part of the drama is devoted to scenes entitled "Remords de Judas," "Désespoir et Suicide de Judas," "Diablerie." These are the three scenes synthesized in Duvet's engraving. The tree in the Judas engraving, with its somewhat exotic appearance, may very well be intended as a cedar, as described in the Sémur Passion play.

---

1. Usually known as "Judas Hanged." Popham, p. 143, lists an impression at Oxford. There are no works by Duvet recorded at the Ashmolean, so this reference is apparently incorrect. An impression was listed in *A Catalogue of Prints . . . [the property] . . . of Thomas Lloyd, Esq., Sold by George Jones, London, July 1st, 1825*, p. 43, Cat. 543, and is almost certainly the print now in the British Museum (listed as sold to Walker).
   Another impression of this engraving was listed in the sales catalogue of *Borlunt de Noortdonck*, Gand, 1858, Cat. III, No. 21018. From this sale it is known to have entered the collection of Ad. van der Meersch of Ghent. The third and final appearance of this print in a sales catalogue is that of Luigi Angiolini (Milan), sold by H. G. Gutekunst, Stuttgart, 1895, Cat. 1202, where is is described as being "rogué tout autour."
2. Inscribed at the upper left in a later, probably seventeenth- or eighteenth-century hand, "Jean Danet, ou Duvet, dit Maître à la Licorne."
3. This use of colored ink seems to reflect an Italian print practice, seen in the work of Fantuzzi, active at Fontainebleau toward the middle of the century, whose, print, after Rosso, is also in the British Museum (B.M. 57.2.8.163). Duvet is known to have consulted works by Fantuzzi for Cat. 33 and 62.
4. According to O. Goetz, Judas hanged himself above a well or a spring, as these afforded the shortest route to hell. See his study "Hie henckett Judas," *Form und Inhalt. Kunstgeschichtliche Studien. Otto Schmitt zum 60. Geburtstag*, Stuttgart, 1950, pp. 105–37. On n. 64, it is suggested that Duvet knew the Valenciennes play, and on p. 128 a date of circa 1555 is proposed for the print.
5. See E. Tietze-Conrat, "Zur Ikonographie des Judasstiche von Jean Duvet," *Graphischen Künste*, 1930, LII-LV, no. 1, part 1. Mrs. Tietze does not recognize that the figure at the upper right is the same as that at the left.
6. Germain Bapst, *Essai sur l'histoire du théâtre*, Paris, 1893, p. 53, describes the scene in *Les Actes de Apotres*, with which Duvet was probably familiar, as it was published in conjunction with Chocquet's *mystère* of the *Apocalypse*.

250 x 162 mm. (Cut within platemark,[1] lower left corner restored, upper left corner slightly repaired.)
Unsigned.
London (BM),[1] Paris (BN).
B 9, RD 19, LeBlanc 3, Passavant 19, Boullaye 19, Popham 19, Linzeler 55, Bersier 45.

The engraving is unfinished. Much of the left half, most noticeably the back of Peter's head, is not yet drawn in. The wall below is indicated by a single, tentative line near Moses' hand.

The print represents the confrontation of the Old and New Dispensations, Moses with the tablets from God of the Old Testament and Peter with the key and book from Christ of the New Testament. The dramatic juxtaposition of the deeply engrossed, patriarchal figures was a popular Renaissance motif, where the physiognomy and hair-dress of the two figures remain surprisingly constant and probably originated in the symbol for Dialectic.[3] A Bandinelli-inspired engraving (B.XIV, 330, 439), showing two disputing philosphers (Text fig. 81), may have provided Duvet with a physiognomical point of departure for Moses and Saint Peter. Lucas van Leyden's "Peter and Paul" (B.106) of 1527 or the print after Rosso of the same subject (B.XIV, 389, 33) (Text fig. 82) may have influenced Duvet's composition and characterization. The latter could have been Duvet's chief source, since it includes a depiction of the *Ordre de Saint Michel,* with which Duvet was much concerned. Rosso's "Peter and Paul" was also adapted by Boyvin who substituted the tablets of Moses for the *Ordre de Saint Michel.* Since the tablets were Duvet's emblem, this print may also have been of particular interest for him.

The church of Saint Florentin at Yonne (near Duvet's residence at Langres), has a series of sculptured portrait roundels whose great, powerful heads have much of the isolated intensity of those in this print.[4]

Perhaps Duvet's most powerful and personal work, the passion and immediacy of this engraving place it among his very late works. Disregarding technical or other refinements, the artist, with unforgettable conviction, has hurriedly engraved his great apprehension of the founders of the faith.

---

1. In the Paris impression, a seemingly unengraved section in the hair above Saint Peter's ear is due to the scraped surface of the paper in this area. Here reproduced.
2. The example in the British Museum has been cut down still more and measures 235 x 162 mm. An impression of this engraving was listed in the Vente Brisart, Ghent, 1849, included in a lot.
3. For an early Renaissance example, see Luca della Robbia's *Dialectic* on the Campanile of the Duomo, Florence (A. Venturi, 1908, VI, fig, 373, facing p. 558). A drawing in the Uffizi entitled "La Disputà" (Barocchi, *Il Rosso Fiorentino* Rome, 1950, fig. 162, attributed by her to Rosso), shows a confrontation similar to that of Duvet's composition. The same drawing has been given to Pontormo by L. Becherucci (*Manieristi Toscani,* Bergamo, 1949, p. 65). However, the graphic style precludes the latter view and seems far closer to that of the Bandinelli circle than to either of the artists mentioned above.
4. The sculpture is reproduced in Marcel Aubert, *Les richesses de l'art de la France—Bourgogne,* Paris, 1921, I-II, Pl. 113, fig. 1.

APPENDICES

A1   POISON ET CONTRE-POISON (Text fig. 47)
By the Master of the Beheading of St. John the Baptist

318 x 225 mm.
Unsigned
3.44 RD 61 LeBlanc 57, Bénézit 5762, Linzeler 78.

This engraving was first attributed to Duvet by Bartsch, who viewed the man as protecting himself from the noxious exhalations of the dragon by shielding himself with the buckler. Bartsch believed the unicorn was included for its purifying powers.[2] Passavant, accepting the Bartsch attribution assigned another engraving, catalogued by Bartsch among anonymous engravings of the sixteenth century *The Beheading of Saint John the Baptist*—to Duvet as well.[3] Fully aware of the pronounced Italianate characteristics of both engravings, Passavant, pointing out that *Poison et Contre-Poison* was based upon a drawing by Leonardo da Vinci in the British Museum (a copy, the original is in the Louvre), concluded that Duvet was very much under the influence of North Italian artists. The German scholar believed Duvet to have received the Leonardesque motifs by way of an Italian follower of Leonardo's at Gaillon presumably Andrea Solario.[4]

The following year, Emile Galichon [5] reattributed the prints to an anonymous Milanese of the sixteenth century. Kristeller[6] named him the Master of the Beheading of Saint John the Baptist.

Hind's interpretation of the print as a political allegory seems reasonable.[7] Despite the very delicate use of flick work, the engraving achieves a powerful sense of three-dimensionality. Its draughtsmanship is most accomplished; clearly the work of a highly skilled artist, trained as a painter rather than as a goldsmith.

While the engraving is no longer considered part of Duvet's oeuvre—and has been unanimously agreed to by all recent students of the French artist—it is most important to recognize *Poison et Contre-Poison* as a possible influence on Duvet's art. Its format, technique and subject matter relate closely to those of the Unicorn series, for which it may very well have provided a point of departure.

1. See Hind, *Early Italian Engraving,* London, 1948, Cat. Part II, pp. 97–99 for collections.
2. B. VII, 1808, 495 ff.
3. B. X, 23, 1808, 42.
4. Passavant, p. 255.
5. The Louvre drawing is the original from which the one in London was copied (Berenson No. 1064). Emile Galichon, "De quelques estampes milanaises," *Gazette des Beaux-Arts,* XVIII, 1865, p. 552. Galichon also disputed Duvet's authorship of the roundel depicting Adrian VI (Cat. 13). Galichon regarded all these works as the oeuvre of an anonymous Milanese engraver somewhat inferior to Cesare da Seste.
6. *Die lombardische Graphik der Renaissance,* Berlin, 1913, pp. 21–22. These views are repeated in his excellent *Kupferstich und Holzschnitt in vier Jahrhunderten,* Berlin, 1921, p. 333.
   The attribution of *Poison-Contre-Poison* was accepted by the editors of later editions of the Bartsch catalogue—A.P.F. Robert-Dumesnil in 1841 and George Duplessis in 1871, and by Pattison in 1879. Boullaye lists the engraving within Duvet's oeuvre.

7. Hind, VI, p. 7 and Plate 579 discusses an engraving by Zoan Andrea copied in reverse after a Leonardo drawing showing a lion attacked by a dragon. A similar engraving was also executed by Lucantonio degli Uberti. See also Hind, V, Cat. Part II, p. 65, Cat. Part I, Plate 309, p. 214 for similar engravings, all of which appear to be early sixteenth century, based upon Leonardo drawings and interpretable as political allegories.

A beautifully inlaid pavement in the Capella di Santa Caterina in the church of San Domenico, Siena, usually identified as *Orpheus and the Wild Beasts* is strikingly similar to *Poison et Contre–Poison.* For a highly convincing discussion of subject matter closely related to that of *Poison et Contre–Poison,* see André Chastel, *Art et humanisme à Florence,* Paris, 1959, p. 274 ff. It is probably this engraving that prompted Alfredo Petrucci to find the entire Unicorn series "tutta infusa di spirito leonardesco." (*Gli incisori dal secolo XV al secolo* XIX, Rome, 1958, pp. 52, 80).

A2 THE BEHEADING OF SAINT JOHN THE BAPTIST
By the Master of the Beheading of St. John the Baptist[1]

209 x 166 mm.
Passavant 65, B 1, 23, 42 (as anonymous German), Linzeler 59 (Duvet attribution not accepted)

The attribution of this engraving to Duvet by Passavant has never been accepted by any other scholar.[2] Even Boullaye who was anxious to preserve and enhance the reputation of Duvet was reluctant to accept Passavant's attribution.[3] Following Galichon, the print is generally agreed to be the *chef d'oeuvre* of an anonymous Milanese engraver known as the Master of the Beheading of Saint John the Baptist.[4]

1. See Hind, *Early Italian Engraving,* London, 1948, Cat. V, Part II, pp. 97-99 (ill. on Plate 629) for collections in which it is represented.
2. Passavant, p. 257, Cat. 65.
3. Boullaye, p. 30.
4. E. Galichon, "De quelques estampes Milanaises," *Gazette des Beaux-Arts,* XVIII, 1865, p. 552.

A3 THE STAG BROWSING

161 x 128 mm.
Passavant 73, Linzeler 79 (by Master of the Beheading of Saint John the Baptist), Hind 4 (by Master of the Beheading of Saint John the Baptist)[1]

Passavant's attribution of this engraving and its companion piece (A4) to Duvet has not been accepted by other scholars. He catalogues the engravings twice as the works of Giulio Campagnola and as copies by Jean Duvet after Giulio Campagnola.[2] As pointed out by Hind, the flick work in Campagnola's engravings is very different from that seen in this print and its companion piece, *The Doe Resting.* He attributes them to the Master of the Beheading of Saint John the Baptist. This grouping had already been suggested by Galichon and Kristeller.[3]

Rather than attributing the two little engravings to the Master of the Beheading of Saint John the Baptist, it would be preferable to regard them as anonymous North Italian engravings, executed near the beginning of the sixteenth century.

1. See Hind, *Early Italian Engraving,* London, 1948, V, Cat. Part II, Plate 631.
2. Passavant, V, p. 116, No. 6. as Campagnola; VI, p. 258, No. 73 as Duvet.
3. Galichon, "De quelques estampes milanaises", *Die lombardische Graphik,* Berlin, 1931, p. 21.

A4 THE DOE RESTING[1]

180 x 137 mm.
Passavant 74, Hind 3 (by Master of the Beheading of Saint John the Baptist).
Linzeler 80 (by Master of the Beheading of Saint John the Baptist).

The engraving appears to be unfinished, part of the tree and ground are left unshaded and the background, present in its companion piece, *The Stag Browsing* (A3), has not been engraved. Only Passavant has regarded this engraving as a Duvet, cataloguing the same print as a Giulio Campagnola and a copy by Duvet after Campagnola.[2]

1. Catalogued under this title by Hind, *Early Italian Engraving,* London, 1948, Cat. Part II, p. 97-99. Illustrated on Plate 631.
2. J. Passavant, *Le peintre-graveur,* Leipzig, 1864, V, p. 166, No. 17 as G. Campagnola and VI, p. 259, No. 74, as Jean Duvet.

A5 CHRIST APPEARING TO THE MAGDALEN

410 x 294 mm. The Chatsworth impression has been cut down, without margins.
Signed at the left; initials BF at the right. Inscribed *NOLI ME TANGERE NONDUM ENIM ASCENDI AD PATREM IO XX* at the foot of plate.
LeBlanc No. 26. Probably by a German monogrammist.

The Chatsworth impression has been cut down, without margins. According to Mr. Thomas S. Wragge, Keeper of the Devonshire Collections, the print is tentatively attributed to Duvet in the Chatsworth Catalogue.

A6 CORIOLANUS OUTSIDE THE WALLS OF ROME

19 x 16 mm.
Unsigned
Uninscribed

The only known impression is in the print room of the Victoria and Albert Museum[1] Catalogue E. 1760-1927. This very decorative etching, with its "Limoges-platter" style border resembled a design that was planned for transfer to a metal. Reminiscent of Milanese damascened armour, the attribution to the "School of Duvet" was listed by the Victoria and Albert Museum Print Room Catalogue.[2] The style is a coarser version of that seen in a series of unpublished roundels attributed to Reverdy in the British Museum Print Room. As no etchings are known to have been made by Duvet, it is hard to accept a work of his hypothetical school executed in a technique which he may never have mastered.

1. Acquired from Gilhofer and Ranschburg, in their sale of November 16-17, 1927, when it was purchased in a lot of 50 decorative sixteenth and seventeenth century prints.
2. A damascened mirror, presumably of Milanese origin, also in the collection of the Victoria and Albert Museum, Cat. 7648-1861, is similar in both style and subject matter to the etching, as is a magnificent shield from a suit of parade armour in the Wallace Collection. The parade shield, bearing the arms of Henri II and Diane de Poitiers shows Scipio Africanus receiving the keys to Carthage. Known as the Piccinino shield, it is of Milanese craftsmanship.

A7 THE GOD MARS

79 x 54 mm.
Passavant 76, Le Blanc 55, BN 81 (not accepted as Duvet), Boullaye 82, B. VIII, 541, 2.
Listed as German, a copy after Aldegrever in reverse.
Signed ID
Inscribed 1530 at the lower left.

Attributed to Duvet by Huber, Joubert, and Passavant.[1] While the engraving and its companion piece, *Intemperance* are clearly not Duvet's, they are attributed to him on the erroneous assumption that the initials ID related to his monogram. The style of both fuses Northern European and North Italian engraving techniques similar to that of Duvet.

1. F. E. Joubert, *Manuel de l'amateur d'estampes,* Paris, 1821, II, p. 19. Huber, *Cat. Rais. du Cabinet de Monsieur Brandes,* Leipzig, 1794, II, p. 326. While listing the engraving under Duvet (Jean), Huber, recording the inscribed date, 1530, and monogram ID, observes "Ald. Exoud." It is listed in Nagler, *Die Monogrammisten,* III, 2177.1.

A8 INTEMPERANCE

79 x 54 mm.
Passavant 78. BN. 82, as Monogrammist ID. Popham 76, as Monogrammist ID.
B., VIII, 540, 132 as anonymous German engraver after Aldegrever.
Signed ID on little plaque at top.
Inscribed 1530 near monogram.

See *The God Mars* for a discussion of the style of this print.(A7).

A9 ELEVEN WOODCUT ILLUSTRATIONS FOR THE "TRACTATUS BREVIS AC VALDE UTILIS DE ARTE ET SCIENTIA BENE MORIENDI"

No date or publisher given. (Pétit in 4, goth) Bibliothèque Nationale, Cabinet des Estampes (Ed. 7a. Rés).

First attributed to Jean Duvet by Johann Christ in 1750.[1] This belief was repeated by A. Claudin, when he catalogued the work for a sale held in Paris in 1873. He believed the book was printed in Lyon between 1505-10.[2] Boullaye has shown conclusively that the monogram appearing on the woodcuts has nothing to do with Duvet's engraved monograms, or another manuscript monogram that he discovered within the archives at Langres.[3] The woodcuts are totally alien to Duvet's art, being a *fin de siècle* version of a Netherlandish block-book style. They are by a master who is now known as the Master I. D. who was, as Claudin rightly suspected, first active in Lyon at the end of the fifteenth century. Master I.D. worked in Barcelona in 1492, Granada in 1495, and Logroño in 1517. A woodcut of his appeared as late as 1546 in a publication by Olivier Arnoullet.[4]

It may be due to mistaken belief in Duvet's designing the *Tractatus* that both J. M. Papillon and Diderot write of the French engraver as having also made woodcuts.[5]

1. *Dictionnaire des Monogrammes,* Paris, 1750, p. 173.
2. *Catalogue des livres de MM. Randin et Rostain,* Paris, 1873, Cat. no. 122. The book is now in the Cabinet des Estampes.
3. Boullaye, pp. 32-33.
4. For an excellent discussion of Master I. D.'s life and woek, see Claude Dalbanne, "Le Maître I. D.," *Maso Finiguerra,* IV, 1939, pp. 215-252. Dalbanne cites Desbaneaux-Bernard as also giving the *Tractatus* woodcuts to Duvet.
5. *Traité historique et pratique de la gravure sur bois,* Paris, 1766, I, p. 1720 Denis Diderot, "Graveurs sur bois," *Encyclopédie,* VII, 1757, p. 890.

Lost Engravings Attributed to Duvet

B1 SAINT EUSTACE

353 x 258 mm.
Unsigned
Bénard, 5764. RD 26, Le Blanc 23, BN 58.

This engraving, which has not been seen since Bénard père listed it in his *Catalogue de Paignon-Dijonval,* Paris, 1810, p. 201, No. 5764 as "St. Hubert ou St. Eustache à la Chasse; pièce copiée d'apres Albert Dürer: h. 13 po. sur 9 po. 6 li. Sans nommes ni marque, mais parfaitement dans la manière du J. Duvet."

The Collection Paignon-Dijonval was sold and dispersed in England. The extremely scholarly character of the great Paignon-Dijonval catalogue makes the attribution worthy of attention.[1]

1. Popham, 1921, p. 143, doubts the accuracy of Bénard's attribution of this engraving to Duvet.

B2 THE MAGDALEN

M. J. Renouvier lists "La Madeleine à des formes plus arrondis et plutôt imitées des Allemands."[1]

Without giving any information as to the size or location of this engraving, M. Renouvier included it in his otherwise reliable list of the French engraver's works. As Renouvier's scholarship and connoisseurship are of a high order, it would be capricious to doubt this attribution until the print comes to light. Recent archival research has shown Duvet to have designed windows for the church of the Magdalen in Geneva, which may support the acceptability of the Renouvier proposal.

1. "Des types et des manières des graveurs," Académie des sciences et lettres de Montpellier, I, 1854, p. 741.
2. H. Naef, "La vie et les travaux de Jean Duvet le 'Maître à la Licorne' " *Bull. de la soc. de l'hist. de l'art française,* Année 1934, p. 126.
   Archive d'Etat de Genève, Registre du Conseil, 40, fol. 249, Oct. 1, 1545.

B3 ASSUMPTION OF THE VIRGIN

Nothing of this engraving is known other than a reference to it made by the anonymous author of of the "Essai biographique de la Haute-Marne," *Annuaire de la Haute Marne,* 1844, p. 92, repeated by Bellier and Auvray in 1852, republished by Émile Jolibois in 1858.[1]

1. According to Bellier and Auvray, *Dictionnaire général des artistes de l'école francaise,* Paris, 1852, p. 508, Luigi de Angelis' additions to Gori Gandinelli's *Notizie degli intagliatore,* Siena, 1811, part 9, pp. 214-224 include an *Assumption,* but there is no reference in the latter to such a print. Emile Jolibois, in his *La Haute-Marne ancienne et moderne, Dictionnaire,* Chaumont, 1858, p. 200, lists an *Assumption* among Duvet's most remarkable works. It is possible that these authors may be referring to either *The Woman of the Apocalypse with Cornucopia* (Cat. 6) or to *Virgin and Child in the Clouds* (Cat. 11). M. Dutuit's annotated edition of Bartsch, in his library at the Petit Palais, lists "Les Notices sur les graveurs, de Besançon" as including "Ier une assumption."

B4 CHRIST AND THE WOMAN TAKEN IN ADULTERY

8 pouce, 5 lignes x 10 pouce, 8 lignes

Attributed to Duvet by F. L. Regnault-Delalande, *Catalogue raisonné du Cabinet de Feu. M. de Silvestre,* Paris, 1811, p. 241. The engraving is described as showing, "Une femme surprise en adultère, amenée à Notre-Seigneur. Composition de sept demi-figures. Au fond, vers la droite, MARC DVVAL."

It seems unlikely that Duvet would have copied the fine engraving by Duval (RD 1), which is after the Lotto painting from the French royal collection. Had Duvet copied the print, he must have done so late in his career. The Duval engraving has at least 18 figures in it, so that the lost print must be a reduced, simplified version. A work, perhaps by a German engraver, in the Zurich Print Room, answers Regnault-Delalande's description and seems to have been the print attributed to Duvet.

APPENDIX C

Drawings Attributed to Jean Duvet

Since no drawing survives that is indisputably linked with any of Duvet's documented works, all attributions to the engraver are extremely uncertain.

C1 CHRIST IN LIMBO

Brown ink
236 x 231 mm.
British Museum, ex coll. Lanna, where it was attributed to Domenico Campagnola.

This drawing was tentatively ascribed to Jean Duvet by Sidney Colvin in 1912,[1] but the French engraver's authorship was rejected by Popham.[2] It has since been given to the circle of Lelio Orsi, an equally unlikely attribution, and by Philip Pouncey to Benvenuto di Giovanni.

The drawing is characterized by a coarse, expressionistic brown ink line. Its style suggests the work of a Northern Italian artist working in the manner of Bandinelli or Passarotti. Its frenzied emotional quality, coupled with a flat rendering in decorative, planimetric line, explain Colvin's Duvet attribution, of which Popham wrote, "The subject is one which he might have treated, but the style is hardly his."

1. Sidney Colvin, *Guide to an exhibition of drawings by Old Masters,* British Museum, London, 1912, Cat. 193. "This drawing, formerly attributed to D. Campagnola, so much resembles the engraved designs of Duvet. . . as to suggest at least the possibility that it may be by his hand."
2. Popham, p. 150.

C2 THE CREATION OF THE EARTH

Pen, brush, and ink.
282 x 202 mm.
Musée du Louvre, Cabinet des Dessins.[1]

According to Erika Tietze, who attributed this drawing to Jean Duvet, it was formerly placed with anonymous Italian fifteenth-century drawings, after having entered the Louvre with the confiscated property of an émigré.[2] The name Pietro Perugino is written on it in a recent hand. A note on the back of the mat states that J. Byam Shaw attributed it to Amico Aspertini.

Tietze believed it to be preparatory to a lost engraving, for which the *Annunciation of 1520* (Cat. 12) would provide a *terminus post quem.* The Louvre drawing is done in a more flexible, less mannered fashion than that of Duvet's oeuvre after 1520, according to Tietze, and for this reason she places it relatively early in his career.[3] Her view is very tentatively accepted by de Hévesy.[4]

The Louvre drawing does not appear to be preparatory to an engraving since it is squared off in a fashion suggesting transfer to a wall or ceiling.

The quality of the drawing seems somewhat low to sustain Byam Shaw's attribution to Amico Aspertini. While it would be tempting to accept this drawing as an autograph Duvet, its style is too generalized to make this certain.[5]

1. Shown at the Bibliothèque Nationale in an exhibition of forty of Duvet's works celebrating the 25th exhibition of the Soc. des peintres-graveurs français, May 4-23, 1938. See *L'oeuvre gravé de Jean Duvet* (Cat. 40) by P. Dàrras, Paris, 1938.
2. "Un dessin de Jean Duvet," *Gazette de Beaux-Arts*, Sér. 6, XX, 1938, pp. 127-129. The drawing is illustrated on p. 129. fig. 3.
3. Of all the French engraver's work, it is closest to the *Virgin and Child in the Clouds* (Cat. 11) not known as being by Duvet at the time of Tietze's publication. This is presumably the work which J. Adhémar had in mind when he wrote that there was one drawing which may be by Duvet in *French drawings of XVI century*, London, 1953, p. XXIV.
4. The Italian attribution was first contested in an inventory by Morel d'Arleux who ascribed the drawing to a German artist. André de Hévesy, "Un dessin de Jean Duvet," *La Revue des Arts*, IV, 1954, p. 108, says, "Pourtant sur le dessin du Louvre, les angelots ne s'ébattent pas sur de nuages en boule, à la manière de Duvet, et les traits à la plume n'ont pas la précision caractéristique du graveur. Serait-ce un croquis de jeunesse? On peut supposer que la majestueuse face du Créatur est due au pinceau de quelque maître italien, copié par Duvet lui-même?"
5. Geneviève Monnier, following Tietze's arguments, included the drawings as Duvet's in *Le Seizième Siècle Européen, Dessins du Louvre*, Paris, 1965, Cat. 136, p. 61, Plate XXXIII.

C3 SEATED FIGURE IN THE CLOUDS

Sanguine.
No measurements given
Private Collection (France?)

This drawing was attributed to Duvet by André de Hévesy in 1954, who believed the depiction of a seated man praying in the clouds to have been a preparatory study for an unexecuted engraving of the Apocalypse series.[1]

Despite a certain physiognomical resemblance between the male head in the sanguine drawing and that of the Whore of Babylon from Duvet's *Apocalypse* (Cat. 56), the drawing is much closer to Flemish art of the late sixteenth century. It has the appearance of a copy—the curious articulation of the crossed legs being especially characteristic of a misunderstood drawing after a completed work of art. The unknown author of this drawing and Jean Duvet both depended upon the same sources for their art.

1. "Un dessin de Jean Duvet," *La Revue des Arts*, IV, 1954, pp. 103-108, illustrated on p. 107, fig. 7.

C4 THE UNICORN PURIFIES THE WATER WITH ITS HORN

Pen and brown ink with brown, green, black, and orange wash.
209 x 545 mm.
Ex. coll. C. R. Rudolph, sold at Sotheby's May 21, 1963, Cat. No. 45 and again there Nov. 21, 1974, Cat. No. 41.

The attribution seems to have been made by J. Q. van Regteren Altena, quoted in the 1974 catalogue, p. 19. Clearly the work of a highly accomplished, probably Northern *animalier*, possibly active in France, the drawing may reflect a lost source which was also consulted by Duvet, perhaps a work by Luca Penni. The latter's Old Testament subjects (Creation, *Fall of Adam*—Herbet 1 & 2, Zerner 56 and 57), reproduced in print form by Jean Mignon, were adapted by Duvet for his Unicorn series.

C5 DESIGN FOR A FETE COSTUME: WINGED WARRIOR RIDING A LION (Text fig. 54)

Pen and water color.
266 x 379 mm.
Louvre (Edmond de Rothschild bequest), linear copy in the National-museum, Stockholm,
Sweden (Tessin collection). Inventory No. 83/1874: 286.

The knight is in elaborate armour, with a seated cupid holding two arrows and a bow riding on
his helmeted head. Holding an apple (?) in the raised left hand, and the lion's bridle in the right, the
warrior rides his richly-caparisoned lion mount to the right. C5-C9 were attributed to Duvet by Per
Bjurström, the Nationalmuseum, Sweden.

C6 DESIGN FOR A FETE COSTUME: MAIDEN RIDING A UNICORN (Text fig. 53)

Pen.
Linear copy of lost original, in the Nationalmuseum, Stockholm, Sweden (Tessin collection)
inventory No. 83/1874: 287.

The maiden, with an elaborate headdress and costume in which her breasts are exposed, rides to
the right on a unicorn who turns his head toward her. She looks down to the unicorn, whom she is about
to suckle at her bared breast, which she holds with the right hand.

C7 DESIGN FOR FETE COSTUME: BLACKAMOOR RIDING A GRIFFIN (Text fig. 55)

Pen and water color.
250 x 360 mm.
Bibliothèque Nationale (H. de Rothschild collection), Salle des mss., Cat. II-1460,
fol. 1 v. Linear copy in the Nationalmuseum, Stockholm, Sweden (Tessin collection),
Inventory No. 83/1874: 288

Seen in left profile, the right arm raised with lance-like arrow, the blackamoor rides to the
left on a rampant griffin. The blackamoor wears a fantastic, plumed helmet and a pantalooned
costume with a sword, holding a shield with a lion mask on it. The griffin is colored with a faded
yellow; his caparison is green. The blackamoor's garb is a faded red; his shield is also red and the
line running down the torso, light blue. [79a, 79b].

C8 DESIGN FOR A FETE COSTUME: ORIENTAL POTENTATE EMBRACING A WOMAN IN THE CLOUDS (Text fig. 56)

Pen and water color.
260 x 390 mm.
Bibliothèque Nationale (H. de Rothschild collection), Salle des mss., Cat. II-1460, fol. 1.
Linear copy in the nationalmuseum, Stockholm, Sweden (Tessin Collection), Inventory No. 83/1874: 289.

Seated on a cloudbank, his legs crossed, an Oriental potentate embraces and kisses a kneeling woman. Two crescents of drapery spring from a knob at the center of the man's exotic crowned headdress, forming arcs to the left and right. This headdress is colored yellow and reddish-purple. The band across his shoulder is blue; his costume's upper sleeve is yellow and the lower one green. The band across his knee is blue, his greaves are yellow, and the bands across his feet red. The woman, seen from the the back, has a knotted, turbanlike coiffure; her skirt is red and her upper robe violet.

C9 DESIGN FOR A FETE COSTUME: SIREN HOLDING A TORCH (Text fig. 57)

Pen and water color.
280 x 365 mm.
Bibliothèque Nationale (H. de Rothschild collection), Salle des mss. Cat. II-1460, fol. 39.
Linear copy in the Nationalmuseum, Stockholm, Sweden (Tessin collection), Inventory No. 83/1874: 285. Reproduced on cover of La Vie theatrale au temps de la renaissance. Institute Pedagogique National, 1963.

The siren is turned to the left, holding an elaborate *torchère* with an abstract leaf pattern. She wears a plumed, horned headdress of shells. Dragonlike wings are attached to her sleeves; an additional pair of wings are joined to her skirts which terminate in a curled, finned, fishtail covered with scales. The flame is red, the upper wings yellow, and the lower ones blue. The tail is tinted violet with a pale pink bow. Like most of these costumes, this figure was probably equestrian.

Surviving Works in Metal and Glass By or Attributed To Jean Duvet

D1 SILVER MEDAL FOR CHAMBRE DE COMPTES OF LANGRES (Text fig. 3)

Cabinet des Médailles, Bibliothèque Nationale.

The arms of Cardinal de Givry are on one side, and Saints Agnes, Mammès and Claude on the other. The Lord is seen in half-length, flying above the central figure. The Cardinal's arms are surrounded by an inscription, "Pro. camera comptorum. D. R. cardi. de Givri, episc. L. G." The three saints are contained within an inscription reading: "Vincenti dabo calculum candidum." This is taken from the *Apocalypse* (2:17), "To the conqueror, I will give hidden manna, and I will give him a white counter, and on the counter a new name written, which no man shall know but he who receives the counter."

The medal is a reduced version of a great seal, probably designed by Duvet as well, described by Douë d'Arcq[1] and dated after 1533, the year in which de Givry was made cardinal and assigned the Church of Sant'Agnese in Agone.[2] Marcel believes that the "Vincenti" of the Apocalypse quotation is an allusion to the church of Saint Vincent in Maçon, where Givry was canon. In view of the cardinal's important role on a royal committee to combat the diffusion of Protestant thought, the quotation from the Apocalypse seems most appropriate, since "the conqueror" of 2:17 was interpreted as one who would overcome heresies, such as those of the Nicolaites, referred to in the lengthy quotation on Duvet's engraving of *The Revelation of Saint John the Evangelist* (Cat. 39).[3]

It is likely that this silver medal for the town of Langres was made by Duvet in view of his having already received a municipal commission to make a silver casket in which to preserve local seals in 1525.[4]

Two engraved designs for a commemorative roundel of Adrian VI by Duvet, executed ca. 1524, share certain stylistic similarities with the medal. The verso, showing the *Triumph of the Trinity* (Cat. 14), has a disposition of figural elements within a circular area similar to that of the medal. A line is drawn across the lower part of the inner circle, and the figures are placed upon this line, making no attempt to articulate them within a circular program, in both the silver token for the Chambre des Comptes and the engraved *Triumph of the Trinity* of 1524. In medal and print, parts of the figures impinge upon, or extend beyond the encircling margin. Both medal and engraving have very coarse lettering. The drapery on the medal is reminiscent of that shown in a series of seven early engraved roundels by Duvet of which the *Saviour in Heaven* (Cat. 20) and *Saint Peter* (Cat. 19) are especially close. It is most probable that the engraved roundels were to be applied to metal work. Another circular print, *Three Horses Rearing* (Cat. 69) may also have been engraved for transfer to metal.

1. "Sceau ogival de 115 mm. sur 76. Dans un monument à trois arcades d'architecture de la Renaissance richement ornementé 3 personnages nimbés, posés sur un entablement. Au milieu, Saint Mammès soutenant de la main droit ses entrailles dechirées, à ses pieds un lion. A gauche Saint Claude tenant une croix et un livre' A droit Sainte Agnès en riche costume, ayant près d'elle l'agneau, son emblème. Au dessous de Saint Mammès, un écusson à bords contournés chargé d'une bande, timbré d'un chapeau de Cardinal. Légende: Sigillum: magnum: Rmi Domini: Cardinalis: de: Givry: tituli: sanctae: Agnetis: in: agone." Described by Douë d'Arcq, *Arch. nat., inventaires et documents: Collection de sceaux,* Paris, 1867, II, Cat. 6221.
2. According to Marcel, II, p. 477, n. 3, the medal is catalogued by Roy-Chèvrier, "Numismatique bourguignonne; Chalon métallique," *Mém. de la soc. hist. et arch. de Chalon-sur-Saône,* 1919, pp. 302-307.
3. It was the belief of Irenaeus that the Gospel was written against the heresies of Cerinthus and the Nicolaites, whom Saint Jerome classified with the Ebionites. See *The Holy Bible,* ed. by James Carey, The Douay Bible House, N. Y., 1938, p. 112.
4. See Claudon, in "Lettres de Dijon," Séance de fév. 12, *Mém de l'académie des sciences, arts et belles lettres,* 5 Sér., II, 1919, p. LXXXIX. See also Doc. 16.

D2 SEAL FOR GIVRY, WITH THE CARDINAL'S HAT ABOVE THE FAMILY ARMS

Inscribed *CARD. DE. GIVRY.*
Reproduced by Marcel, II, p. 179. The manuscript is in the Bibliothèque Nationale, ms. fr. 26, No. 112.

This work must date after 1533, when Duvet's patron was made a cardinal. The seal appears on a testimonial for Jean de Gand.

D3 STAINED GLASS BEARING CITY ARMS OF GENEVA

Dated 1547
Geneva, Musée d'art et d'histoire, ex. coll. Engel-Gros.

The commission, given to Duvet in 1545 to design stained glass windows for the Eglise de la Madeleine in Geneva, has led Naef, who discovered the documents (see Doc. 48) to attribute the design of an unsigned window displaying the arms of Geneva, dated 1547, to the French engraver. Naef wrote, "La disposition des armoires, le dessin du demi-aigle et de la clef, le texte et les caractères employés sont très proches de l'art de Duvet."[1] A coat of arms cannot reflect the individual style of any artist, since a coat of arms in its form and meaning are independent of stylistic variations. The window has little apart from its subject and date to recommend Duvet's authorship. It has been remarked that the inscriptions on the windows point to Duvet's authorship, but since most official writings of the time were in French, this is hardly conclusive.

The window was published in 1922 by Paul Ganz, "Die feingetönte Gläser von zarter, seltener Farbung und die sorgfältige, miniaturartig modellierte Zeichnung lassen die Scheibe als ein Werk des Zürcher Glasmaler Virtuosen Karl von Áegeri erkennen, der damals wohl als der beste Meister des Handwerk galt."[2] It was first published by Jacques Mayor in 1897 who made the same attribution.[3]

The window was most probably designed and executed by Pierre Favre, described as "peintre, né à Genève, fut rehabilité gratuitement en la bourgeoisie le 30 dec. 1546."[4] His name has been associated with the windows for the Eglise de la Madeleine, on which Duvet was also employed, and he received numerous commissions to execute stained glass windows for the Hôtel de Ville. Like Duvet, Pierre Favre also was entrusted with surveying. In 1562, he made a "portrait du pays des Genève à Jussy" which seems to have been a bird's eye view. Nine years before, Favre received an order for six "panneau à plombe à aveqz les armoyries de ceste oyté de Genève," which were to be installed within two chambers of the Hôtel de Ville. He was also associated with window designs for S. Pierre.

The Geneva window, which is here given to Favre rather than to Duvet, was described by Henri Deonna: "Dans un encadrement architectural de style Renaissance à pilastres feuillages et linteau en-guirlandé sont disposés trois écus: deux accolés, aux armes de Genève, et le troisième qui les surmounter, aux armes de l'Empire couronées."

"Sur le fond bleu, la banderolle porte la devise génevoise: 'Post tenebras Lux;' sur le linteau du portique une cercle avex J. H. S. à sa parte inférieure, dans un cartouche ornemental sur fond bleu on lit: 'La parolle de Dieu demeure éternellement' entre les deux écus la date 1547."[5] The biblical quotation comes from Isaiah 40:8. According to E. William Monter the window is the "earliest iconographical representation of the Genevan motto, 'Post Tenebras Lux' (1547)"[6]

1. Henri Naef, "La vie et les travaux de Jean Duvet, le maître à la licorne," *Bulletin de la Société de l'histoire de l'art francois,* 1934, pp. 114-141, p. 126.
2. Paul Ganz, "Zwei Standesscheiben der Stadt und Republik Genf," *Archives héraldique suisses,* 1922, p. 95, with illustration. See also W. Deonna, "Les arts à Genève des origines à la fin du XVIII siècle," *Geneva,* XX, 1942, pp. 366-369. Illus. on p. 370, fig. 246.
3. Jacques Mayor, "Un vitrail aux armes de Genève," *Fragments d'archéologie Génevoise,* 1897, p. 170. See also *Collection Engel-Gros, Catalogue de vitraux anciens,* 1922, p. 24, Cat. 47.
4. For Pierre Favre, see Carl Brun, *Schweizerisches Künstler-Lexikon,* I, 1905, p. 446.
5. W. Deonna, "Vitraux aux armes de Genève," *Geneva,* I, 1923, pp. 145-147, with illustration.
6. E. William Monter *Calvin's Geneva,* New York, 1967, p. 78.

D4 COINAGE FOR MICHEL, COMTE DE GRUYERE

Geneva, 1552

The letter from the count to the Geneva council, requesting permission to use the services of Jean Duvet to execute his coinage is given in Doc. 56-57.[1]

The coins Duvet executed for Michel, Comte de Gruyère are in no way different from typical Swiss currency of the mid-sixteenth century.[2]

The Gruyère coat of arms appears on one side; a bird emblazoned on a shield, the date 1552 above, and an inscription in a double circle around the arms that reads *MYCHAEL PRIN ET CO GRUER*. The reverse shows a Greek cross terminating in fleuron-like extremities. The words *TRANSVOL NVBILA VIRTUS* surround the cross. This coinage, which was recalled by the Berne government within two weeks after it had been issued by the Comte de Grüyère in 1552, is extremely rare. Eighteen coins are known, of which two, in the British Museum, still bear traces of gilt.[3]

1. See Naef (1924) and Naef (1947), also Eugène Demole, "Histoire Monétaire de Genève de 1535 à 1792," *Mém. de la Soc. d'hist. et d'arch. de Genève,* Sér. 40, I, 1887, p. 28, Plates II-III.
2. See Léodgar Cornagioni *Münzgeschichte der Schweiz,* Geneva, 1896, Plate IV for a representative assortment of local coinage of the period.
3. For illustrations, see Reginald S. Poole, *A descriptive catalogue of the Swiss coins in the South Kensington Museum,* London, 1878, pp. 247 and 632. The two Gruyère coins came to the Museum from the Townshend collection. Since Poole's publication, they have been transferred to the British Museum. See also Naef (1947) for eight reproductions of Duvet's Swiss coinage. There are two very slightly different forms of the Gruyère currency.

D5 BATON DE JUSTICE (Text fig. 14)

1555
Silver niello and enamel.
Inscribed: *Post Tenebras Lux.*
In the Maison de la Ville, Geneva (Text fig. 14)

The silver baton head bears the motto of Geneva, POST TENEBRAS LUX engraved at its base within three little mannerist strap-work cartouches distributed around a broad ring. The ring is surmounted by a pommel bearing three shields of Geneva heraldry executed in enamel and separated from one another by silver acanthus leaves in relief. At the very top is a typically Northern European decorative detail— three converging S-shaped volutes crested by a rosette.

First recognized as a work of Duvet by Naef, the baton head may well be the one listed in the Geneva council on October 31st, 1555, when "syre Jehan du Vett dic Dro" received seven florins for having "racoutré le bâton de justice que porte sgr. lieutenant" (Doc. 65).[1]

The identification of this baton head with the one listed in the Geneva archives was made largely on the basis that only Duvet among the artisans present in Geneva would have had the ability to combine engraving and enamel in a single work. While there is as yet no absolute proof that the piece is by Duvet, in the Apocalypse series he did engrave similar batons in the hands of the rulers of heaven and hell. The key held by Peter (Cat. 73) is conceived in exactly the same curious fashion, with a cross-shaped incision on the side, as though it were still a raw block of metal, waiting to be cut along the incised or enameled line to its ultimate form.

The leaves in relief are masterfully executed, and the work as a whole reflects the mind and touch of a mature craftsman.

1. Henri Naef, "Un artiste français du XVIe siècle, bourgeois de Genève: Jehan Duvet, le Maître à la Licorne," *Bulletin de la Société d'histoire et d'archéologie de Genève,* V, 1925, p. 39.
   W. Deonna, *Les arts à Genève des origines à la fin du XVIIIe siècle,* Geneva, 1942, "Le Vitrail," pp. 366-369.

D6 SILVER-GILT CHURCH SERVICE FOR THE ABBEY OF SAINT ETIENNE, DIJON

Duvet may have been the goldsmith responsible for the manufacture of a church service bequeathed by Cardinal de Givry to the Abbey of Saint-Etienne. According to an inventory of 1571, the cardinal gave "un autre calice d'argent doré d'or ciselé, en la pomme duquel sont les treize apôtres, au bas les armoires du cardinal de Givry emaillées, avec la platine . . . deux grands chandeliers d'argent doré ciselé aux armes du cardinal de Givry . . . deux chainettes dorées, ciselées, aux armes du cardinal de Givry . . ." (Archives Côte-d'Or G. 169, folio 18, 19; cf. ff. 20, 21: Mémoire de l'inventaire des reliques, chapes, et ornements de l'église Saint-Etienne (1627)). He may also have manufactured the "basins d'argent doré niellé" listed in the codicil to Givry's will (Archives Côte-d'Or G. 135, folio 258, 169, folio 16, 17).

Marcel, II, p. 82.

D7 LOST RELIQUARIES

Marcel suggested that Duvet might have made the reliquary of St. Joseph for Langres cathedral presented by Chanoine Louis Pithois in 1533 and a reliquary of St. Steven presented by Chanoine Antoine Bouvier.[1]

1. Marcel, II, p. 431, n. 2.

APPENDIX E

The Documents

The following abbreviations to archival entries in Geneva will be used:

AEG - Archives d'Etat de Genève

ISACD - Inventaire sommaire des archives communales . . . de Dijon, de Gouvenain and Ph. Vallée.

RC - Registre du Conseil

c. 1485	Year of Jean Duvet's birth according to inscription on his self-portrait as Saint John, dated 1555, Cat. 65. See Doc. 66.
1. 1495	Dijon. Drouhot de Vay, and four other goldsmiths at Dijon request tax reduction "qu'ils gagnaient peu de leur métier."
	ISACD, III, p. 189, L. 672.
2. 1495	Dijon, June 4. Drouhot Duvet commissioned to make sculpture in precious metals for the Abbey of Saint-Etienne'

> "Marché passé par les abbé et couvent de Saint-Etienne avec Huguenin
> Humbelot et Drouhot du Vay, orfèvre à Dijon, pour la façon d'un chief
> de vierge en l'honneur et en la figure de Madame saincte Coronnes, le
> tout d'argent blanc et marque, ensemble le pied sur six lyons de cuyvre
> moyennant la somme de 4 francs par marc de l'ouvrage, qui pèsera 18 à
> 19 marcs et dont le métal sera fourni par l'abbaye."

Archives Côte-d'Or, G. 169, fol. 14.
Marcel, II, p. 424, n. 2.

3. 1500	Langres. Date of beginning of manufacture of the reliquary head of Saint Mammès by Jean Duvet at Langres according to Chanoine Henriot's manuscript of 1563. The date may be a clerical error, since Duvet was fifteen years of age at the time. It could also refer to the goldsmith's father, who might have begun the reliquary at that date, assisted by his apprentice-son. For description of completed reliquary, see Doc. 17. *ir*
4. 1500	Dijon. "Philibert Duban, orfèvre se pretendant exempt on sa qualité d'éssayeur et tailleur en la monnaie de Dijon."
	ISACD, III, p. 191, L. 677. Prost, "Le trésor de l'Abbaye Saint-Bénigne," *Mém. de la soc. bourguignonne de géog. et d'hist.*, p. 190, has interpreted this reference to a "Duban" as pertaining to a worker in precious metals, Philibert Duvay, at whose address Jean Duvet may have resided in 1506.
5. 1501	Dijon, April 23. Drouhot du Vay commissioned by the city of Dijon to execute two silver-gilt *drageoirs* in precious metals to be given to Louis XII and Anne de Bretagne.
	ISACD, III, p. 111, L. 619.
6. 1506	Dijon, Philibert Duvet recorded as being "éssayeur de la monnaie" and "orfèvre" in Dijon, residing at the "rue tirant devant la porte St.-Etienne."
	ISACD, III, p. 193, L. 682, 730. Prost, p. 190, has concluded from the above that "Enfin Jean Duvay, probablement fils de Droux, était orfèvre et éssayeur de la monnaie de Dijon de 1506 et vers 1520."
7. 1509	Dijon, May 11. "Louis et Jean Du Vay, fils de maître Drouhot Du Vay, demeurant à Dijon" were listed together with four other young men who were received as *maître orfèvres*. As goldsmith's sons, the customary fee was waived for Louis and Jean.
	ISACD, IV, p. 212, M. 436, fol. 132.
8. 1512	Dijon. Accounts of Abbey of Saint-Etienne.
	"20 francs payés à Drouhot Duvay, orfèvre, en déduction" for a silver statue of Saint Augustine.
	Archives Côte d'Or, G. 530, cf. 531, Marcel, II, p. 424, n. 2.
9. 1513	Dijon. "Drouhot Du Vay, orfèvre, paroisse Saint-Médard, rue tirant droit devant la porte de Saint-Etienne qui n'avait, disait-il ni ceuses, ni rentes dont de puisse norrir eui, sa femme, et son mesnaige, sinon de son mestier au jour de la journée'."
	ISACD, III, p.195, L.686.
10. 1517	The unclear letters on *The Cumaean Sibyl* (Cat. 8) have been read as this date.

11. 1520   Dijon, November 15. "Drou Duvay, argentier, demeurant à Dijon," worked on the inventory of the treasury at Saint-Bénigne.

    This reference to Jean Duvet's father was published by Prost, p. 29, n. 3. He found the text written in the margin of the inventory of the treasury.

12. 1520   Jean Duvet signed and dated his engraving of the *Annunciation* (Cat. 12).

13. c. 1520   Dijon. Tax list of parish of Saint-Medard lists "Drout Du Vay, orfèvre, près les prisons imposé à 32 gros."

    ISACD, III, p. 212, L. 730, fol. 36.

    The same manuscript (fol. 36) lists "Jean Du Vay, orfèvre, rue tirant devant Saint-Etienne, à 12 gros." This passage has been quoted by Prost, p. 190, n. 2, as listing Jean Duvet "essayeur de la monnai de Dijon." Since Duvet lived at the same address as Philibert Duvay, who is known to have been a master of the mint, Prost may have made a correct assumption.

14. 1521   Langres, April. Preparations for the Entry of François Ier

    "Les 14 et 15 Avril furent assemblez plusieurs notables personnaiges en l'hostel de ville, assavoir les officiers du roy, de monseigneur de Langres, et les officiers de la Ville, avec plusieurs autres bourgeois, pour adviser ce qui estoit à faire pour l'entrée et venue du Roy. Le 19 Avril furent derechiet assemblez audit hostel de la ville les dessus dits et avec eulx M. Nicole Ladmiral, facteur, Jehan Drouet, Perrenot l'argentier et Guyot filz dudit Perrenot, orfévres, pour marchander à eulx de la façon du présent que l'on etendoit faire au Roy."

    Jean Duvet, together with the two other goldsmiths, as well as Nicole Ladmiral, a painter called Estienne Thomas, and several merchants met again to "assemblez pour adviser les mistères qui se fereient à l'entrée du Roy nostre Seigneur." They also took part in a "disné" which was offered by the town.

15. 1522   Dijon. "Diro" is recorded as repairing a statue of Saint Mark, which had been taken to him from the treasury of Saint-Bénigne.

    Published by Prost, p. 47, n. 4, as referring to Drouet Duvet, the engraver's father.

16. 1524   Dijon. Payment was "donnés à Drouhot Du Vay, orfèvre, pour avoir redressé et ressoudré la trompette de la ville."

    ISACD, IV, p. 40.

17. 1524   Langres, March. Jean Duvet completed the reliquary *Head of Saint Mammès* for the treasury of the cathedral of Saint-Mammès at Langres, according to a manuscript written by Claude Demongeot in 1563 and transcribed by Canon Henriot of Langres.

    "Le chef de Saint Mammès est dans un buste à demi-corps, avec une couronne, le tout de vermeil doré, enrichi de plusieurs pierres fines, entre lesquelles est une émeraude d'une grandeur considerable, qui a été estimée par un joaillier 1800 livres, donée par Guy Bernard (évêque de Langres), mort en 1481. Jean d'Amboise le vieil (aussi évêque, mort en 1496), donna 1200 livres pour orner ce chef. Il y a à la main, un sceptre surmonté d'un oiseau, avec une croix où il y a cinq pierres. Il y a aussi un camayoul avec trois grosses perles fines dessous, attachées à la couronne, avec une houppe pendante, couverte de perles. De ce chef pend une petite croix d'or à quatre diamants, avec une chaisne de vermeil donnée par Pierre de Balaveine, chanoine, et une autre petite croix d'argent avec quatre pierres. Il y a aussi un château d'argent doré representant celuy de Grancey, que le seigneur du lieu voua à Saint Mammès dans un incendie. Ce précieux chef fut commence à Langres par Jean Drouet, orphevre, en 1500, et ne fut achevé qu'en 1524, au mois de mars. Il est orné en tout de soixante-dix-sept pierres précieuses. Suivant le chanoine Claude Demongeot, de ces temps-la (1563), il pèse deux cent vingt-trois marcs six onces d'argent fin, qui est à raison de 12 livres 15 solz; et pour la façon, à raison de 8 livres le marc, vaut 1801 livres 18 solz, qui est on tout le dit chef et façon 4,721 livres 13 sols."

    The text was first published by Boullaye (pp. 4-5) who believed the date 1500 for the beginning of the reliquary to be a clerical error, suggesting that 1510 may have been intended.

18. 1524   Langres, August. List of contributions for supplies for civil defence

    "Ce sont les dixsaines du canton du Marchier soubs la charge de Nicolas Boucher le jeune cartenier et de Philipes de Deilloncourt cinquantenier, fait le dernier jour du mois d'aoust 1524. Dixaine de Jehan Roussat: Jehan Drouet faict (ou fournit) deux emyne, une hache, 1 pelle ferée et hotte."

Archives de Langres, art. 513. Boullaye, p. 8.

19. 1524 Langres, October 1, September 30 - Jean Duvet received payment at some time between these dates for a silver box bearing the arms of Langres, used to contain the town seals.

"A Jehan Drouet, orfèvre dudit Langres, la somme trante solz tournois pour avoir achapte de luy ung petit cachet d'argent où sont pourtraictes les armes de la lad. ville, servant à seeler et cacheter les lettres que l'on escript pour les affaires de la ville, et ce tant pour l'argent que pour la façon d'icelluy cachet, comme par le mandement et quictance cy rendus appert, pour ce XXX s.t."

Written in the margin is the note, "Le procureur de la ville a lad. cachet et le rapportera en la chambre."

The text was found in the "comptes quatrième de honneurable homme Symon Noyrot, receveur des derniers commungs de la ville et cité de Longres" covering the period between Octover 1, 1524 through September 3, 1525.

Archives de la Haute-Marne, cinquième chapitre de la dépense, fol. 19 v°. Published by H. Claudon, *Mémoires de l'academie des sciences, arts, et belles-lettres de Dijon*, 5e Sér., II, Feb. 12, 1919, lxxxix.

20. 1524 Two engraved designs for a medal commemorating Adrian VI, here attributed to Jean Duvet, are dated 1524 (Cat. 13 and 14). The date is only inscribed on *The Triumph of Divinity* (Cat. 14), the verso of the medal, on which the double tablets also appear.

21. 1527 Langres. List of contributors to ransom fund of François Ier

"La rue Sainct-Didier à prandre au querre près ledit Sainct Didier, tyrant du i costé Guiot Genevois procureur de la Ville, tout à l'entour: Maistre Thibault Le Goux controlleur, 7 livres, - Guyot Genevois, procureur de la Ville, et Gille son fils, 12 livr. 10 solz. - Guillaume le Tondeur, 6 solz. - Jehan Drouet, orfévre, 50 solz. - Jehan Fayl, 100 solz. - Bartholemin de Lespine, 15 solz. - Jehan Roussart et son fils, 8 liv."

26. 1533 Langres, January 2. Order of the Corps de la Ville, giving Jean Duvet funds for a gift to be presented to Eléonore d'Autriche.

" . . . a maistre Jehan Duvet, dit Drouet, orfebvre, la somme de cent unze livres dix solz, pour l'achat de sept marcs et demy d'argent . . . pour employer au présent, ordonne pour la Reyne."

Archives de Langres, Art. 1157 (?), destroyed.
Boullaye, pp. 13-14.

27. 1533 Langres, January 3. Jean Duvet signed a receipt for the funds with his monogram.
Archives de Langres, Art. 1157 (?), destroyed.
Boullaye, p. 14.

28. 1533 Langres, January 9. Order of the Corps de la Ville giving Jean Duvet additional funds for gifts for the queen and for the sons of François Ier by Claude de France.

" . . . a maistre Jehan du Vet dit Drouot, orfebvre, la somme de quarante-cinq livres pour l'achapt de dix-neufz ducatz pour dorer les présens ordonnez pour la Royne et mes-? seigneurs les Dauphin, ducz Dorléans et Dangoulesme."

Archives de Langres, Art. 1157 (?), destroyed.
Boullaye, p. 14.

29. 1533 Langres, January 10. An additional order for funds for the gifts.
"Item plus donne deux ducatz d'or pour parachever de dorer, oultre le contenu cy dessus."
Archives de Langres, Art. 1157 (?), destroyed.
Boullaye, p. 14.

30. 1533 Langres, January 12. Jean Duvet signed a receipt for both the above grants from the Corps de la Ville with his monogram. Jacques Bouler, a goldsmith from Chaumont, who was called in to help with the making of the gifts, received ten livres "pour ses peines et vacations par luy faictes à avoir besoingné au présent ordonné pour la Royne."
Archives de Langres, Art. 1157 (?), destroyed.
Boullaye, p. 14.

31. 1533 Langres, January, no day given. Account of three *échafauds* erected in honor of the triumphal entry of François Ier, Eléonore d'Autriche and their three sons January 12, 1533. Duvet is credited with the invention, design and partial execution of the elaborately staged tableaux-vivants. According to the menuisiers, who built the stages, "A messieurs les procureur et eschevins de la ville . . . le marchié fait par le Conseil, délibéré en la Chambre de

la dite ville, en présence de Jehan Drouot qui guidoit et conduisoit ledit affaire."
According to a cloth merchant, " . . . cinq aulnes taffetas noyr pour acoustrer ung petit
garson qui menoist le personnage de Paix . . . par le devys de Drouhot l'argentier."
Archives de Langres, Art. 1157 (?), destroyed.
Boullaye, pp. 14-15.
Presumably all the above quotations, transcribed by Boullaye from the Langres archives, and printed on
pp. 12-14, are taken from Art. 1157.

32. 1533   Langres, January 26. Order by the Corps de la Ville and receipt for funds for the manufacture of gifts for the queen, Eléônore d'Autriche, presented on the occasion of her visit
to Langres with François Ier. The latter also received presents as did his three sons, the
Dauphin François, duc de Bretagne, Henri, duc d'Orléans (the future Henri II), and Charles
duc d'Angoulême.

"Les procureurs et commis aux affaires communs de la ville et cité de
Langres, à vous Jehan Bouchard reçeveur des deniers de ladite ville,
baillés et délivres à maistre Jehan Duvet dit Drouot, orfebvre, la somme
de quarante-six livres tournois, pour parpayé du présent de la Reyne.
Et en rapportant ce présent mandement avec quictance dudit Drouot,
ladite somme de quarante-six livres tournois sera allouée en voz comptes
sans difficulté. Fait en l'hostel de ladite ville le xxvie jour de janvier
l'an mil ccccc trente et trois. G. Thieery; Maignen; P. Genevoys; A.
Noirot; De Lecey; Nicolay; A. Boursault; Noirot."

"Jehan Duvet dit Drouot, orfebvre demeurant à Langres, confessé avoir
eu et receu de honnorable homme Jehan Bouchart, recepveur des deniers
commungs de la ville et cité de Lengres la somme de quarante-six livres
tournois, mon. courant et ce pour la parpaie du présent de la Reyne,
comme appert par le présent mandement dont il se tient pour comptant.
Et de laquelle somme de xlvi l. ts; il a quictée et quicte ledit recepveur,
ladite ville et tous aultres qu'il appartiendra.
Faicte audit Lengres le cinquiesme jour du moys d'apuril, l'an mil cinq
cens trante-trois avant Pasques. Signé dudit Duvet et du notaire soub-
scrit les ans et jour que dessus J. D.; Botechou."
Archives de Langres, Art. 1157, destroyed.
Boullaye, pp. 12-13. Duvet's monogram is reproduced on p. 13; it resembles the engraved initials on
The Virgin and Child in the Clouds (Cat. 11).

33. 1534   Dijon. " . . . la veuve de Drouhot Du Vay, orfèvre, et Didier Maney son gendre, imposés
à 3 fr."
Record of taxes in the parish of Saint-Médard.
ISACD, III, p. 212, L. 730.

34. 1540   Geneva, September 17. By this date Duvet had already been appointed *tailleur de le
monnaie* by the Petit Conseil of Geneva, probably active as such since 1539.
"Jo. Drouot, taillieur" told the Petit Conseil "comment il az fayct les cuing des testons
qu'il az encore entre ses maiens" and hopes that he will be paid "de saz poienne."
AEG, RC, XXXIV, fol. 446. Naef, pp. 120-121, notes that by this date Duvet had already engraved
the *coins de testons.* According to Eugène Demole, "Histoire monétaire de Genève," *Mém. et
documents de la soc. d'hist. et d'arch. de Genève,* Sér. 4, I, 1887, p. 28, Louis Guillard was listed
as "graveur à la monnaie de Genève" from August 2 to August 29, 1539. Duvet was appointed
before September 17, 1540, and was probably already active as "graveur" in 1539.

35. 1540   Geneva, October 12. Work on coinage for Geneva. "Noble Henrys Gule" advanced to

"honorable homme Jehan Drooz, talleurs . . . , dix escus d'or de cuing
de Roy au soleil, az bons comptes, moyennant que ledit sire Jehan soit
tenus de le servir az la facture des cuing de la monoye, continuellement
pour luy, jusques à ce que soient estés achevés lesdictz cuings de la
dicte monoye . . ."

A contract was signed in which "noble Amed Perrin," the future captain general of the
Seigneurie, vouched for Duvet.
AEG, RC, XXXIV, fol. 475. Naef, p. 121.

36. 1541   Geneva, February. Duvet had not yet been paid for his work at the Mint for the Seigneurie.
The *Magnifique Petit Conseil* called the;

"maystre de monoye qu'il l'aye az contenter icelluy. Et pource qu'il
est homme expers az deviser des forteresses, et deyjaz az servye apprès,

ordonné que il luy soyt fayct ung present de demy dozanne d'ecus . . . . . .
Ayant viheuz les escus par nostre maystre de monoye fayct, az esté
ordonné que icelluy les doyge fere fayre de poys et de loys des escus
soley."
AEG, RC, XXXV, fol. 91 v°. Naef, p. 121.

37. 1541   Geneva, June 29. Work on the fortifications of Geneva.

"Ediffication du Belluard vers Pallex. Az este Resoluz ordonne et arreste
que leditz Belluard soyt ediffie et que promptement les ouvriers il soyent
mys et az este prinse et ordonne Laz longueur et laz larguer dung bon
accord consentant/ Et lon az hiez les bons advys des N baudechon de laz
moysonnovaz, Laurent mogret dict le magniffique et de J. droz expers en
tel cas."
RC, XXXV, fol. 248, v°. Naef, p. 122, n. 1.
N is the abbreviation for Noble, the title given to the councillors and syndics of Geneva.

38. 1541   Geneva, August 13. Order to treasurer to give Duvet funds to make a ring for presentation
by the city to Pierre Cullier of Bâle.
" . . . de lyvrer aut sire Jehan Droz, orpheuvre, pour la fasson d'ung aneau qu'il az fayct au
sire Pierre Cullier, de Ballo" two and a half écus.
RC, XXXV, fol. 277. Naef, p. 124.

39. 1541   Geneva, November 15. Duvet completed fortification studies and a wall painting for the
Hôtel de Ville and received rights of citizenship.

"Jehan Droz, orpheuvre, Lequelt az vacqué az plusieurs journées az
comprendre les forteresses de laz ville et en peintures en laz moyson
de laz ville sans estre satisfayct; dequoy resoluz que pour ceste foys
q   il luy soyt ballié six coppes de froment. Et pource qu'il est home
d'esperit et sort bien en laz ville, resoluz qu'il soyt admys az borgeoys
et juré de Geneve, gratis. Et az promys et juré."
AEG, RC, XXXV, fol. 398, v°. Naef, p. 122.

40. 1541   Geneva, November 15. Register of Foreigners.
"Jehan Duvet, filz de deuz Loys Duvey, alias Drot de Dijon."
First published by A. Covelle, *Livre des bourgeois de l'ancienne république de Genève,* Geneva, 1897,
p. 122. The text is discussed by Naef, p. 116; Marcel, II, p. 430; and Edmond Belle, "La Réforme
à Dijon," *Revue bourguignonne de l'Université,* 1911, p. 17.

41. 1542   Geneva, August 6. Record of a theological discussion at a tavern, the Logis de la Rose,
between Duvet, Loys Guillard, his predecessor at the Mint, and a monk, Frère Noël of
Cluse.

"Frère Noel, religieulx de Cluse. Sus quelque propos qu'il a tenu avecque
Jehan Droz et Loys Guillard, hier a soyer aut logis de la Roze touchant
l'evangele; et ayant aoys lesd^es parties, resoluz que mons^r Calvin et altres
predicans doybge converser avecque luy et l'instruyre à vraye verité, affin
de le povoyer retyre à Dieu et à sa s^te parolle."
RC, XXXVII, fol. 120. Naef, p. 124.

42. 1543   Geneva, June 8. The Seigneurie sent a commission to Dôle to study the fortifications there.

"Pource que, avant que parachevé les murailles de la ville, il seroy bon de
voyer, les forteresses des aultres villes . . . ordonné de envoyé à Dosle . . .
les sg^rs Claude Pertemps, Amyed Perrin, Pernet de Fosses et Jehan Dro.
Et ce aux despens de la ville . . ."
RC, XXXVII, fol. 120. Naef, p. 124.

43. 1544   April 3. The "Scindicques et Conseyl de Geneve" order the treasurer to give "à Jehan
Droz, orpheurvre, en deduction des deux emaulx, qu'il fayct pour la ville, troys escus
soley."
AEG, Finances P. 5, mandats, 2e liasse. Naef, p. 124.

44. 1544   April 5. Receipt for funds cited above, written by Duvet.

"Jehan Drouot, orffevre, confece avoier receu de Monsr le treszorier de
sete cité la somme sy derriere hecripte an dedussion de deux hemaux
que je fet pour mes manifique seigneur. De la quelle somme, que sont 3
equs, je le quite, temoien mon sygnet manuel sy mis ce 5e d'avril 1544.
J . Dwet."
AEG, Finances P. 5, mandats, 2e liasse. Naef, p. 124, with facsimile of ms. on p. 127.

45. 1544   Geneva, September 16-18. Duvet was commissioned to make three enameled insignia for the *hérauts à cheval de la Seigneurie.*

"Jo. Dro, dorier . . . par comandement à luy fayct, a apportee troys esmaulx bien fayct des armes de la ville pour les heraulx, et a demandé pour ch(aque) emaulx dix escus soley. Ordonné qu'il soyt contenté gracieusement."
RC, XXXVIII, fol. 375, 377; 16 and 18 September, 1544. Naef, p. 125.

46. 1544   Geneva, September 18. Duvet is given an order for three enamels for which he received "wingt et deux escus soley."
AEG, Finances, P. 5, mandats, 2ᵉ liasse. Naef, p. 125. See also Eugène Demole, *Journal suisse d'horlogerie,* Année 41, 1916, p. 159, where the name is given as "Jean Duvet de Dijon" and the sum as 25 écus.

47. 1544   Langres, October 10. The name of Jean Duvet is included among those taking part in a *cortège* formed by the *procureur général* and *échevins* of Langres, at the time of the issuing of the treaty of Crespy.
Archives de Langres, Art. 753. Boullaye, p. 17.

48. 1545   Geneva, October 1. Duvet received payment for designs he executed for the stained glass windows of the Madeleine and tapestries for the Maison de la Ville.

"Jehan Dro orpheuvre. Sus la supplication qui a presenté pour estre satisfaict des pourtrays des veirreires du temple de la Magdeleine et des tapisseries que l'on faict fere pour la mayson de la ville: ordonné qui luy soyt donné deux escus soley."
RC, XL, fol. 249. Naef, p. 126. See App. D. 3.

49. 1545   Geneva, October 9. Duvet received a boy from the *procureurs de l'hôpital* as an apprentice for four years, "pour apprendre le mestier." The artist was given a grant of "vingt florins et quatre coppes de froment et, pour ces accoustremens, douze florins."
RC, XL, fol. 256 vᵒ. Naef, p. 125.

50. 1545   Geneva, November 5. Duvet, recorded Drouot and Droz, presented himself as candidate for a confidential post generally reserved for citizens of Geneva. He was nominated at once with a temporary appointment, which was then confirmed with an annual salary of forty florins which he retained for two years.

"Resoluz que si lya quelque citoyen que soyt prepice à tel office, soyt preferu, synon pour à présent icelluy office soyt ballieé aud. Dro . . ."
RC, XL, fol. 248 vᵒ. Naef, p. 128.

     1546   Jean Duvet received the patronage of Henri II in the undertaking of his engraved Apocalypse, according to the Privilège of 1556, which was published in 1561 (See Doc. 68).

51. 1546   Geneva, February 9. Duvet was elected to the Conseil des Deux-Cents, to which he belonged intermittently until 1556. He is listed as living "en la Reviere dessous."
RC, XLI, fol. 7. Naef, p. 128.

52. 1546   Geneva, March 8. Duvet is listed as both *éssayeur* and *graveur* at the Geneva Mint, from March 8, 1546 to March 8, 1547.
AEG, RC, XXX, fol. 223. Eugène Demole, "Histoire monétaire de Genève de 1535 à 1792," *Mém. de la soc. d'hist. et d'arch. de Genève,* Sér. 4ᵒ, I, 1887, p. 28.

Geneva, March 16. Continued work on city fortification projects. Duvet executed "le modelle du belluars a le tout compassé. Ordonné que les sgʳˢ Claude Du Pan conscindicque, Jaque des Ars et Pierre Tissot consellers, doybgent appointer avecque luy de sa poienne."
RC, XLI, fol. 52. Naef, p. 128.

54. 1549   Geneva, April 19. Duvet requests the Conseil's authorization to purchase for 7 écus, "les pailles et trosseaulx du feux duc de Savoex, en nombre de 66 pièces," for use in his office as *tailleur de la monnaie.*
RC, XLIV, fol. 73, vᵒ. Naef, p. 128.

Geneva, May 10. Documentation concerning the "retaillon" (the Mint-sweep) connected with his activity as *tailleur de la monnaie.*
RC, XLIV, fol. 96, 365 vᵒ. Naef, p. 129.

55. 1550   Geneva, April 18. Request for the "coings gastés" similar to that of May 10, 1549, in connection with Duvet's capacity as *tailleur de la monnaie.*
RC, XLIV, fol. 96, 365 vᵒ. Naef, p. 129.

56. ca. 1550   Langres, The names of "Jehan Duvet dict Drouot orphebure; Jeanne sa femme." inscribed on fol. x in a manuscript membership list of the Confrairie du Sainct-Sacrement de l'autel

(Langres, Bibliothèque Publique). The order was instituted in 1547 at the church of the Frères Prêcheurs. Folios v-x list members admitted between 1547-1572, without specifying date of admission. The archives (art. 511) did not include Duvet or his wife as having paid their *cotisation* to the Confraternity, and for this reason Boullaye believes the artist and his wife were absent from Langres between 1547-1550, a date of admission of c. 1550 proposed on pp. 17-18.

57. 1551 Geneva, September 15. The Conseil de Genève took cognizance of a letter from the comte Michel de Gruyère requesting that Duvet be permitted to execute coinage for him. The coin was struck in 1552, and is illustrated by Naef, 1946, Plate 1.

> "L(ett)re de Gruyre. - sus la 1re ja hyer receue du comte de Gruyre et
> ce que proposa N. Martina son ambassadeur de permettre Jehan Droz
> luy faire des cuing pour sa monoye battable en Gruyre. Ce que luy est
> oultroyé et arresté de comander à Jean Droz que moyennant son moderé
> salaire, il luy en face."

RC, SLVI, fol. 58. Naef, p. 129, n. 2. The letter is reproduced by Naef, 1946, Plate VII, opp. p. 224.

58. 1551 Geneva. Jean Duvet recorded as living "en la Reviere dessous," according to Naef, p. 128, no text source given.

59. 1552 Geneva. Jean Duvet listed as residing "sus le pont de Rosne" where he was still recorded as living on February 11, 1556.
RC, SLVI, fol. 154. Naef, p. 128.

60. 1552 Langres, July 2. Jean Duvet, living in the quartier du Moulin à vent, is listed as having paid his share of a tax. Jehan Drouot, orphebvre taxé à quatre bichetz."
Boullaye, p. 17, Naef, p. 133.

61. 1552 Geneva, September 26. Jean Duvet testified in a trial against a counterfeiter, Battonat, held in Geneva.
AEG, P. C. I., No. 477. Naef, p. 133, n. 5.

62. 1554 Geneva, May 18 and 21, July 3 and 9.
"Honneste Jean Dro monstré le portray de aulcunes pieces" of coinage which he proposed to strike. These were designs for a thaler, four sols, and three liards. It was decided to mint them in July.
RC, SLVI, fol. 96, 365 v°. Naef, p. 129.

63. 1555 Geneva, February 28. Jean Duvet was reappointed as *tailleur de la monnaie*, during an election of officers.
RC, XLIX, fol. 19 v°, Naef, p. 129.

64. 1555 Geneva, October 11. Jean Duvet requested the use of "deux chambres en la Monoye pour son habitation . . . et pour se tenir." The request was granted on October 15.
RC, L, fol. 7 v°, fol. 10 v°. Naef, pp. 129-130.

65. 1555 Geneva, October 31. "syre Jehan du Vett dic Dro" received seven florins for having "racoutré le baton de la justice que porte le sg^r lieutenant."
AEG, Finances I, mandats et parcelles, No. 20, fol. 11. Naef, p. 130.

66. 1555 Dated and inscribed engraved Apocalypse Frontispiece *Self-Portrait as Saint John the Evangelist*. See p. 301, Cat. 65, for text of inscriptions.

67. 1556 Geneva, February 11. Jean Duvet lists his residence as "sus le Pont," presumably du Rosne, as on February 11, 1552.
RC, LI, fol. 4 v°. Naef, p. 128.

68. 1556 Fontainebleau, June 3. Privilège du Roi, signed by Robillart, published in Lyon in the 1561 edition of *L'Apocalypse figurée*.

> Henry par la grace de Dieu Roy de France à noz amis & seaux conseillers
> les gens tenans nostre court de parlement de Paris, Provost dudit lieu,
> Seneschal de Lyon, Bailly de Vermandois ou son Lieutenant, & Langres,
> Bailly D'auxerre, & à tous noz autres iusticiers & officiers, leurs lieutenans,
> & à chacun d'eux ai comme a lui appartiendra Salut & dilection, Comme
> de la part de nostre bien amé Jehan Duuet, maistre orfeure de feu nostre
> treshonoré Sieur & père & de nous, demeurant en nostre ville de Langres:
> Nous ait faict dire & remonstrer, que par nostre commandement &
> ordonnance, tant de nostre dit feu sieur & Père que de nous, il ha puis
> dix ans en ça, portraict & figuré en table de cuyure, & caractaires pour
>
> Imprimer, liures des hystoires de la sacrée & saincte Apocalypse a
> grans frais, & mises, & par longue espace de temps. Et pour aucune-

ment le recompenser de son temps, frais & mises, il nous ha faict supplier & requerir, luy permettre vendre lesdits portraicts & figures en tous lieux, & places de nostre Royaume, païs, terres & seigneuries, & partout ou il verra bon estre sans que nul autre en puisse faire vente ne distribution sinon par son congé & consentement: nous humblement requérant sur ce luy donner prouision, & lettres à ces necessaires. Nous à ces causes inclinans liberallement à la supplication, & requeste dudit suppliant fair Imprimer ledits histoires d'Apocalypse en tel nombre & partie de ses peines, & qu'il ait fruict de son labeur & trauil, & pour autres considerations a ce nous mouuans, auons permis & octroye, permettons & octroyons de grâce especiale par ces presentes à iceluy suppliant fair Imprimer lisdits histoires d'Apocalypse en tel nombre & quantité qu'il verra bon estre, & qu'il les puisse vendre & distribuer par tout nostre Royaume, & ailleurs, ou bon liu semblera, par lui ou ses commis & deputez, & ce par l'espace de douze ans. Sans ce que nul autre pendant & durant ledit temps soit orfeure, graueur, painctre, libraire, ou autre de quelque qualité que se soit, en puisse faire vente ne distribution en aucune manière: Sinon que se fust du vouloir & consentement dudit suppliant. Ne aucunement le contrefaire ne contretirer: ce que nous leur deffendons très expressement sur peine de confiscation des portraicts figures & liures, ou autre plus grosse amende arbitraire a tous ceux qui contreuiendront ausdites deffenses. Si vous mandons, & à chacuns de vous si comme à luy appartiendra, que de noz present octroy & permission, & de toute le cotenu cy dessus ilz facent, souffront, & laissent iouir & user plainement & paisiblement, cessans ou faisans cesser tous troubles, ou empeschement au contraire. Car tel est nostre plaisir. Donné a Fontainebleau le troisieme jour de Juing, lan de grace mil cinq cens cinquante et six & de nostre regne le dixieme.

Par le Roy en son Conseil.
Robillart."

Quoted in part by Boullaye, pp. 18-19.

1558   Jean Duvet has been "identified" by Duplessis with a goldsmith called Danet, known to have been active in Paris in 1558 for the church of S. Pancrace d'Avallon.

See Duplessis, *Bull. du comité des beaux-arts,* II, p. 544. The suggestion has not been accepted.

69. 1556   Geneva, August 5. Jean Duvet's *deposition* is recorded. His name is given as Jean Drouot, "tailleur des cuings des monnoyes."

AEG, Registre des affaires criminelles, I, fol. 147. Naef, p. 131.

70. 1556   Geneva, September 14. A grant of assistance was made to the artist who was,

"a esté mis en avant de ses maladie et necessités. A esté arresté que luy soit assisté de dix florins, oultre deux testons de son louiez . . . balliés par le sgr scindique, ung de 5 deniers: de quoy soit faict mandement de xii ff. 3 s., inclus lesd. 2 testons."

RC, LII, fol. 7. Naef, p. 131.

71. 1556   Geneva, September 25. Record of assistance to the artist and his wife.

"Jehan dro et sa femme. - Lesquelz ont fait presentee supplication proposans estre tombez tous deux au lit malade, requerans leur faire quelque bien et aulmosne. Arresté en consideration de sa pauvreté qu'on luy donne encor six florins, et deux copes de bled oultre ce que desjà luy a esté donné."

RC, LIII, fol. 22. Naef, p. 131.

72. 1556   Geneva, November 5. A new request for assistance.

"Jehan du Vet dict Droz. - Ayans esté presentée sa requeste . . . de le subvenir à sa grande necessité et indigence, comme plus applain est contenu en lad. requeste, a esté arresté qu'on luy donne pour aumosne, au nom de Dieu, dix ff. d'argent et deux coppes de froment, pour le subvenir à sad. necessité, et de ce luy soit faict mandement, avecq bonnes remonstrances."

RC, III, fol. 82. Naef, pp. 131-132.

November 16, 1556 is given as the terminal date of Duvet's function as "tailleur de la monnaie" by Eugène Demole.

73. 1557   Langres, May 21. Baptismal register of the parish of Saint-Pierre, records the baptism of the son of Mammès Duvet (presumably Jean Duvet's son), named after the patron saint of Langres Cathedral whose reliquary was Duvet's chef-d'oeuvre. Jean d'Amoncourt, the infant's godfather was a friend and associate of Jean Duvet's, a prominent art patron and future bishop of Poitiers.

> "Le vendredy xxie de mai à une heure, fut baptizé Jehan filz de
> honorable homme Mammès Duvet orfebvre, et l'ont tenu sur les
> fondz révérend pere en Dieu monsieur de Poictiers et damoyselle
> Francoyse Talbourot, Vefue de feu Philippe Viard contrerolleur
> au grenier à sel de Lengres."

Boullaye, who discovered and transcribed this record on p. 19, states on the next page that the baptismal entries were generally summary, as evidenced by the omission of the mother's name, concluding that the absence of Jean Duvet's name is insignificant.

74. 1561   Lyon. Title page of published *Apocalypse.*

Lapocalypse
figuree
Par maistre Iehan Duuet, iadis Orfevre des Rois,
François premier de ce nom, &
Henry deuxieme.

A LYON

avec priuilege

M. D. LXI.

75. 1561   Date inscribed on impression of *Triumph of the Unicorn* (Cat. 67), if the "61" at the lower left refers to a year.

76. 1562   Langres, November 15. "Jean Drouot" attended a meeting of the Assembly General at Langres, concerning *octrois,* tolls or grants.

Archives de Langres, art. 619-1°. Boullaye, p. 21, notes "Serait-ce encore Jean Duvet, qui, a cette époque âge de soixante-dix-sept ans, aurait pris part aux délibérations des affaires communales?"

77. 1563   Date of Chanoine Demongeot's transcription of the St.-Mammès inventory. Doc. 17.

78. 1570   Geneva, November 23. The widow of Jean Duvet appealed to the Petit Conseil for a tax exemption, which was granted.
"Jehanne, relaissée de Jehan Droz, a presenté requeste pour estre examptee du guaict. Ce que luy a esté accordé."
RC, LXV, fol. 173 v°. Naef, p. 138.

79. 1575   Geneva, April 11. Jean Droz, presumably Jean Duvet's son, citizen of Geneva, informed the Council that he wished to return to settle his debts, but was afraid to do so because he feared violence at the hands of his creditors.
RC, LXX, fol. 68, v^o. Naef, p. 137.

80. 1576   Geneva, April 2. The name of "Jean Duvet dict Droz" appears in the archives.
RC, LXXI, fol. 49°. Naef, p. 137.

81. 1576   Geneva, July 10. The Council ruled "que led. Droz tiendra les arrestz en ceste cité où il est de present."
RC, LXXI, fol. 96. Naef, p. 137, gives additional text.

82. 1576   Geneva, August 10. Jean Duvet takes a partner, a fellow goldsmith, "Bonadventure Berthon, d'Austung, orphevre, habitant en ceste ville . . . lequel s'afferme au service de syre Jehan Duvet dict Droz, citoyen de ceste cité."
AEG, Min. J. Cusin, VII, fol. 102. Naef, p. 137.

83. 1576   Geneva, September. Jean Duvet was condemned to die in October for having extorted funds from a draper, Jean Joly.
AEG, RC, LI. Naef, p. 134.

APPENDIX F

Chronological List of Recorded Works

All documents cited are in Appendix E

1. 1517 (?)   Date inscribed on the *Cumaean Sibyl* (Cat. 8).
2. 1520   *The Annunciation of 1520* (Cat. 12).
3. 1520   Langres. Gifts in precious metals for royal presentations. See Doc. 14.
                 Duvet also participated in the plans to stage the triumphal entry.
4. c. 1524   Two engraved designs for a commemorative medal of Adrian VI. (Cat. 13, 14).
5. 1524   Langres, the *Reliquary Head of Saint Mammès*. For a full description, see Doc. 17.
6. 1524   Langres. A silver casket, bearing the arms of Langres, for the town seals. See Doc. 19.
7. 1528   Dijon. Bowl of *laiton,* damascened in silver and gold. Lost.
                 Bowl made of an alloy of copper and zinc *(laiton),* sometimes known as yellow copper, damascened in silver and gold, purchased by François Ier in Dijon on January 28, 1528, following his triumphal entry there on January 21. The bowl is described as being "ouvré d'or et d'argent à la moresque sur laiton" in the accounts of Claude Haligre, royal treasurer in a manuscript at the Archives nationales (kk, 100, fol. xii, ms. sur parchemin).
                 For text, see Doc. 23.

                 The record of this bowl was discovered by Jules Labarte, who stated that Jean Duvet was one of the first French goldsmiths to have practiced the art of damascening *(Histoire des arts industriels au môyen âge et à l'epoque de la Renaissance,* Paris, 1872-75, IV, p. 38). This may not be correct, as damascened objects were already popular in France at the time of the early crusades, when they were brought back from the East. This popularity resulted in the manufacture of imitations of Near Eastern damascened ware in France.
8. 1528   *Rest on the Flight into Egypt* (Cat. 23).
                 Saint John the Baptist and Saint John the Evangelist Adoring the Lamb of God (Cat. 24).
                 The Entombment of 1528 (Cat. 25).
                 An Allegory of the Power of Love (Cat. 26).
9. 1533   Langres. Gifts in precious metals for royal presentation. Planning and staging of the accompanying triumphal entry. See Docs. 26-32.
10. 1540   Geneva. Coinage executed for the city. See Doc. 34.
11. 1541   Geneva. Fortification projects for the city. See Doc. 37, 39.
12. 1541   Geneva. Paintings for the Maison de la Ville. See Doc. 39.
13. 1541   Geneva. A ring. See Doc. 37.
14. 1543   Geneva. Fortification projects. See Doc. 42.
15. 1544   Geneva. Enamels for the city heralds. See Doc. 43-45.
16. 1545   Geneva. Designs for stained glass for the Eglise de la Madeleine. See Doc. 48.
17. 1545   Geneva. Designs for tapestries for the Maison de la Ville. See Doc. 48.
18. 1546   Geneva. Fortification projects. See Doc. 51.
19. 1547   Geneva. Design for stained glass window bearing arms of Geneva. The attribution to Duvet, made by H. Naef, is not accepted. See App. D3.
20. 1549   Geneva. Recorded activity as *tailleur de la monnaie.* See Doc. 53-54.
21. 1552   Coinage struck for the Comte de Gruyère. See Doc. 57, and App. D4.
22. 1554   Designs for coinage: a thaler, four sols, and three liards. See Doc. 62.
23. 1555   Geneva, Baton de Justice. Reproduced in Text fig. 14. See App. D5.
24. 1555   Completion of the engraved *Apocalypse.* See Doc. 66 and Cat. 65.
25. 1556   Duvet received *Privilège du Roi* for Apocalypse publication. See Doc. 68. Text fig. 9
26. 1561   Duvet published his own *Apocalypse figurée,* in Lyon. See Doc. 74. Text fig. 10.
27. 1561   The number 61 is inscribed on the *Triumph of the Unicorn* (Cat. 67).

APPENDIX G

Duvet as Architect

The artist, after working in Burgundy as a goldsmith and producer of triumphal pageantry, is documented in Geneva from 1540 on. There he is known to have been associated with fortification planning. There is a possibility that Duvet had prior activity as a military architect in his native Dijon and the nearby episcopal court of Langres, as it is unlikely that he would have been entrusted with important commissions in Geneva without considerable previous experience.

Perched on top of a steep hill, the heavily fortified town of Langres had been of strategic importance since pre-Roman times. Francois Ier's military interest dictated his lifelong scrutiny of the episcopal seat, commanding the key position on the eastern borders of his realm. It was no coincidence that the locations selected for the erection of the three stages designed by Duvet for the king's triumphal entry of 1521 were placed at bases of the three chief fortified towers of the town. The king made an exhaustive survey of the defenses, decreeing in 1517 and in 1524 that they be planned along the most advanced lines.[1] Duvet held the title of *ordonnateur* for the entry of 1521 and in earlier unspecified ones.[2] According to Boullaye, "les fonctions d'ordonnateur des fêtes publiques, que étaient ordinairement remplies a Langres par le maitre des oeuvres, furent confiées exceptionellement a Duvet."[3] From his discussion it is clear that the *maitre des oeuvres* was a Commissioner of Public Works, a municipal architect, and a military engineer. Boullaye pointed out that among the later *maîtres des oeuvres* were several painters, architects, and sculptors.[4] A prominent Dijon architect, printmaker, and furniture designer, Hugues Sambin, thought to have been a student of Duvet's, staged triumphal entries and also designed the fortifications of that city.[5] In the sixteenth century many artists such as Leonardo, Grunewald, Hirschvogel, were also designers of fortifications and expert military and hydraulic engineers. Two opposite influences on Duvet's art, Dürer and Michelangelo, proved to be experts in fortification design.

Dürer's *Unterricht zur Befestigung der Stadte Schlosser und Flecken* was printed in 1527; a Latin translation was published in Paris by Wechsel in 1535. There is a question as to how closely the French followed Dürer's text. Wechsel's introduction provides a passage from Ovid's *Metamorphoses* with the charming injunction: "Here, gentle reader, thou hast the most elegant description of which, so soon as Dürer's precepts prove at all tedious to thee, thou mayest run unto and read."

In view of both Duvet's later activities in Geneva, where even before he received citizenship, the town council noted respectfully that the artist was "homme expers a deviser des forteresses" (App. E, Doc. 36), and of the lovingly detailed renderings of fortifications in his Apocalypse series, the engraver may have been chosen as *ordonnateur des fêtes,* precisely because he had functioned as *maître des oeuvres* in fact if not in title.

Duvet probably completed the major fortification known as the Tour de Navarre (Text figs. 86-87) which loomed so large in all royal entries.[7] It was one of the most important feats of Northern European military engineering and among the first of its kind in France, with enormously thick walls to support a spiral inner masonry ramp sustaining the great weight of the new cannons. This permitted them to be moved up and down the fortifications with greatest efficiency. Military historians differ as to the dates of the Tour's construction. According to Boullaye, it was begun as early as 1511 and enlarged in 1516.[8] Boullaye noted that by August 1515, the tower was already 58 feet high, when Jean d'Albret ordered that it be elevated another six feet. Whatever the exact circumstances of the tower's building history may prove to be, the major part of its construction took place after 1521,[9] when Francois Ier climbed the first part of the ramp tower on horseback; he celebrated its completion in 1547 with a similar ascent.[10]

Major work on the fortifications of Langres was undertaken under Cardinal de Givry's direction in the years between 1530 and 1545 and may well have involved Duvet's participation. These projects included the building of the Saint-Gengoulph and Guise towers, with extensive enlargement and repair of those known as La Fromagerie, La Dizaine (also called Baudricourt), Orval, and De la Chapelle. The town's entrances of Louot and Moulin Avant were rebuilt, as was the Arsenal du Roi.

Duvet may have been drawn to Geneva by requirement of his fortifications' expertise as well as by his sympathy with Calvin's cause. Threatened from all sides, the city could not expand and devoted its resources to ever-increasing fortifications. What roads and residential sections lay outside the

86. Tour de Navarre, *Langres.*

87. Interior view, Tour de Navarre, *Langres.*

347

major part of the old city were town down and converted into defenses for the urban perimeter. Duvet worked on the fortifications with distinguished citizens who had also left France. Outstanding among these was Laurent Meigret who, with another member of the mercantile aristocracy from Lyon, Baudichon de Maisonneuve, was assigned to work with Jean Duvet (App. E, Doc. 37) on the building of a great earth work *(belluars)* toward Pallex.[11]

Throughout 1542 a major building campaign was under way, directed by Pernet DesFosses, "the maistre des murailles de la ville" for the construction of fortifications near Saint-Gervais, especially "ung belloard fort et puissant, affins qu'ils puisse battre a tous cotes." The large sum of 24,000 *écus* was borrowed from Basel and "les citoyens plus aises furent invites a preter a la Seigneurie a 5%." All citizens were ordered to work on the project.[12]

On June 8, 1543, Duvet joined a "commission d'étude," including Perrin, Claude Pertemps and Pernet DesFossé, appointed by the Conseil to study the fortification at Dole, preparatory to designing additional ramparts for Geneva (App. E, Doc. 42). Claude Pertemps and Pernet DesFosses were also among the Calvinist *avant-garde* of Geneva. Appointed Treasurer in 1534, Pertemps joined the Petit Conseil two years later. Described in Bonivard's *Chronique* as "homme d'ung grand esprit commun, sans soy estre adonne a l'estude des lettres, mais principalement en art de bastiment ou d'architecture," he sounds much like Duvet in character. The campaign to shore up the fortifications of Geneva continued throughout 1543. By the end of the year, two great *courtines* stretching from the Rhone to Saint-Léger were completed, and construction of the Porte Neuve undertaken. In 1544 Claude Pertemps was appointed Capitain-général, as was Duvet's guarantor Ami Perrin.[13]

In 1546, Duvet worked on further fortification projects for Geneva (App. E, Doc. 52). He was probably in Langres the following year for the completion of the Tour de Navarre[82a, 82b] and the rampart construction prepared for what was to be Francois Ier's last visit there in 1547. 1555, the year which marked the realization of Duvet's major graphic work, also witnessed the commencement of what may prove to have been his most important architectural undertaking, the great ramp of the Maison de la Ville of Geneva, the design of which was in large part derived from that of the Langres' Tour de Navarre.[14] Shortly thereafter, the construction costs were found to be excessive, and by November it was decided to reduce expenses by having no more than "six ouvriers et des meilleurs."[15] The construction reached at least as far as the upper part of the entrance, where the date 1556 is carved on a tablet. Not until twenty years later did the Conseil decide to have the project completed, between 1577 and 1580. Although Camille Martin, architectural historian of the Maison de la Ville, observed in 1906 that no one then known from the archives could have been the designer of the ramp, he very tentatively proposed Pernet DesFosses as a possible candidate.[16] A prominent magistrate and *maître d'oeuvre* of fortifications, DesFosses was listed in 1555 as presenting a model of the ramp tower to the Conseil. However, Duvet, first associated with DesFosses in 1543 seems the most probable source for the tower's design.

Martin, searching for the ramp's author, posed the question, "Et parmi les innombrables refugies, recus habitans ou bourgois au milieu du XVIe siècle, ne se trouvait-il pas également des gens experts en architecture?"[17] Specifically Burgundian details in the applied sculptural decorations within the ramp also point to a designer from that region. Identical palmettes can be seen on both the ramp vaulting and the decorative stone work of the Château de Pailly, the residence of the Lieutenant de Bourgogne, within the diocese of Langres. The chateau's architect, Nicolas Ribonnier, may have been a student of Duvet's.[18] Its construction was probably begun toward the end of the 1550's and, together with Ancy-le-Franc, was the major Renaissance chateau of Burgundy.

It seems more than mere coincidence that the halt in construction of the ramp tower and Duvet's illness and departure from Geneva should occur simultaneously, and more than chance that when building was resumed after an interval of twenty years, it was completed by an architect from Langres, Nicholas Bogueret.[19] The upper story of the ramp is Bogueret's only surviving work, and he altered the original plans to include a skylight. The architect's younger brother Jean came to Geneva from Langres in 1574 and assisted Nicholas in completing the tower. Both had sons who became *Maitres orfèvres,* suggesting the alliance of these skills. Nicholas' son Jean was a member of the Conseil des Deux-Cents, all of which suggests the repetition of a previously established cycle.[20]

Another important building constructed during Duvet's Swiss residence is the Collège de Genève, also known as the Collège de Calvin. Built between 1558 and 1562, this renaissance structure is also of a distinctly Burgundian style, found in the *nouvelle enceinte* at the ramp tower. In view of this common vocabulary, Martin suggested that the College and ramp tower were by the same architect.[21] Responsible for much of the ramparts and, in all likelihood the tower's designer, Duvet could have been the architect of the College as well.[22] One of the regents of Dijon's Collège des Martins, Antoine Franchot, fled to Geneva in 1545 and may have provided Duvet with an entrée to the Collège de Calvin.[23] Center of humanistic studies in Geneva, it may have been of particular interest to Duvet as he probably had worked in Langres for the similar institution there.[24] The Collège de Genève was also the only place in that city where dramatic performances were allowed.[25]   The artist, an experienced pageant master, would certainly have been consulted for the College's theatrical presentations.

It is tempting to link Duvet's name to the design of a centrally planned chapel built by his grandson's godfather, Jean d'Amoncourt, in Langres in 1549.[26] The artist is known to have returned to France in 1548 when he joined the Langres Confraternity of the Holy Sacrament to which d'Amoncourt also belonged.

1. Theodore Pistollet de Saint-Ferjeux, "Anciennes fortifications de Langres," *Mémoires de la Société historique et archéologique de Langres,* II, 1887, pp. 231-252. Joseph Garnier, "Notes sur quelques debris de comptes de la recette générale de Bourgogne," *Mémoires de l'Académie des sciences, arts et belles lettres de Dijon,* V, 1895-6, pp. 1-11. For the fortifications, see also L. E. Marcel, *Le Cardinal de Givry, évêque de Langres,* Paris, 1926, I, pp. 412 ff., II, pp. 296 ff. He cites *Inv. Arch de Langres,* Nos. 947, 949-51, 994.

2. E. Jullien de la Boullaye, "Entrées et séjours de François Ier à Langres," *Bulletin de Société historique et archéologique de Langres,* I, 1880, pp. 68-100, p. 68 f.

3. E. Jullien de la Boullaye, *Étude sur la vie et sur l'oeuvre de Jean Duvet dit le maître à la licorne,* Paris, 1876, p. 16.

4. Boullaye, 1880, p. 95.

5. Garnier, *op. cit.,* p. 9.

6. See Ruth Mortimer, Harvard College Library, *Catalogue of Books and Manuscripts, Part 1. French 16th Century Books,* I, Cambridge, 1964, No. 184, p. 226.

7. The Tour de Navarre is discussed by Viollet-le-Duc in his *Dictionnaire d'architecture,* Paris, 1875, II, pp. 177-179; Léonce de Piépape, *Histoire militaire du pays de Langres,* Langres, 1884, pp. 112 ff.; Boullaye, 1880, p. 77; Th. Pistollet de Saint-Ferjeux, *op. cit.;* Marcel, *op. cit.,* I, p. 412, n. 3; II, p. 190, n. 1-4. Most of Piepape's material is drawn from the Annuaire de 1808, p. 503. According to the Guide Michelin, *Bourgogne, Morvan,* Paris, 1963, p. 112, the Tour de Navarre was built in 1519 and the adjacent ramp tower, listed as the Tour d'Orval, was first climbed by Francois Ier in 1521. Perhaps Duvet worked on this tower (de Navarre) in conjunction with the Dijon architect Pierre Tabourot, who is known to have been concerned with the fortifications of that city, like Tabourot's father, who in 1474 had been *controlleur des ouvrages des fortifications.* These architectural interests were passed on to the third generation, evidenced in the career of Canon Jean Tabourot of Langres.

8. Piépape (*op. cit.,* p. 112) wrote that the ramp tower was begun following François Ier's visit to Langres in 1519, its building initiated under Jean d'Albret, Comte d'Orval, the governor of Champagne. Since the latter died in 1516, the tower named after him (or called Navarre after the quarter of Langres in which it is located) must have been started well before 1516. Another tower was begun in 1517, the Tour Brouault, which may have been the structure which Piepape had in mind, rather than the Tour de Navarre.

9. Boullaye, 1880, p. 77.

10. Piepape, *op. cit.,* p. 114.

11. I am indebted to Professor François Bucher for explaining that the term *belluars* or *belloard* is the forerunner of the boulevard, the latter being nothing less than the urban incorporation of the *belluars* converted into avenues by the burgeoning city. According to Dr. Bucher, the *belluars* toward Pallex is the one big fortification toward what today is known as the Place Plain Palais (letter of December 26, 1966).

12. Amedée Roget, *Histoire du peuple de Genève,* Geneva, 1870, II, pp. 58-59, 120-121.

13. *Ibid.,* p. 122.

14. According to Martin ("La Maison de la Ville de Genève," *Mémoires et Documents publiés par la Société d'histoire et d'archéologie de Genève,* III, 1906), the only other European structure that can be compared with the ramp tower in Geneva is the tower of Munoth at Schaffhausen, which was only begun in 1564. See also W. Deonna, *Les arts à Genève, des origines à la fin du XVIIIe siècle,* Geneva, 1942, pp. 323 ff. Louis Blondel (*Le développement de Genève à travers les siècles,* Geneva-Nyon, 1946, pp. 68 ff.) gives Pernet DesFosses as architect, relating the ramp to those found earlier at Amboise, Meaux, Schaffhausen, Langres and the Château de Montmort (Haute-Marne). Adolf Reinle (*Kunstgeschichte der Schweiz,* III, *Die Kunst der Renaissance, Des Barock und des Klassizismus,* Frauenfeld, 1956, p. 88) cites Pernet DesFosses as designer of the ramp and the Collège de Calvin, describing him as a "Baudilletanten".

15. Martin, *op. cit.,* p. 75 (R.C., L, f° 27 v. (Nov. 5, 1555)).

16. *Ibid.,* p. 77.

17. *Ibid.,* p. 78.

18. The palmette from Pailly is illustrated by Charles Sauvageot, *Palais, châteaux, . . . de France,* Paris, 1867-68, II, fig. 5, p. 14). It should be compared with those reproduced in Martin (Pl. XIV, figs.

40, 55). Boullaye lists Nicolas Ribonnier, who was architect to the "Duché de Bourgogne" in the 1560's , as a pupil of Jean Duvet, seemingly without documentary evidence. Marcel's authoritative discussion of Ribonnier's oeuvre concludes, "Mais rien de précis, rien que nous renseigne sur cet artiste et sur son oeuvre, sur sa formation, sur les caracteristiques de son genre." He was first listed as a "Nicolas Ribonier, maçon en nostre ville de Dijon," and then received the appointment of "visiteur des ouvrages des places fortes, villes et chasteaulx de notre pays de Bourgogne" (Marcel, II, Chap. 11, p. 445). He belonged to the same important Langres confraternity as Duvet and at the end of the century is listed as supervising reconstruction work on the fortifications there. Reconstruction of the Château de Pailly was begun in 1563, according to a letter from the Maréchal de Chavanne written on the subject in that year (Marcel, II, p. 549, n. 5). See also Pistollet de Saint-Ferjeux, "Le château et les seigneurs de Pailly," *Mémoires de la Société historique et archéologique de Langres*, I, 1880, pp. 241 ff. Ribonnier was considerably younger than Duvet; even if his death took place at an advanced age in 1605, he would still have been about thirty years the engraver's junior.

19. Martin, *op. cit.,* p. 77.
20. The main information on Nicolas Bogueret is given by Martin, *op. cit.,* p. 77. There is also a short monograph (Louis Dufour-Vernes, *Nicolas Bogueret, une des victimes de l'Escalade,* Geneva, 1896), devoted to an account of his heroic death in the defense of Geneva in 1602. Bogueret was active in Geneva many years before 1568, the date of his marriage and the first record of his residence there. *Thieme-Becker* (IX, p. 219) says that Bogueret received the rights of a bourgeois of Geneva in 1571. Karl Brun, (*Schweizerisches Künstler-Lexikon,* Frauenfeld, 1905, I, pp. 169-170) gives a detailed description of the ramp, but errs in attributing its entire design and construction to Bogueret.
21. Martin, *op. cit.,* p. 77, n. 5.
22. A bas-relief at the Collège de Genève, occasionally placed within the oeuvre of Goujon, is discussed by W. Deonna, "Un relief de Jean Goujon a Genève?" *Gazette des Beaux Arts,* Sér. 6, II, 1929, pp. 356-371. At best, this inferior work could only be associated with the School of Goujon, or as M. Deonna put it, "C'est le travail d'un disciple de Goujon." Although Goujon's name is absent from Geneva records, he could very possibly have stopped there on his way to Italy. See also Anatole de Montaiglon, "Jean Goujon," *Gazette des Beaux-Arts,* Sér. 2, 1885, p.15.
23. Marcel, I, p. 368.
24. Marcel, II, pp. 216-219.
25. Roget, *op. cit.,* p. 236; Bernard Gagnebin, *A le rencontre de Jean Calvin,* Geneva, 1964, pp. 53-54.
26. See Anthony Blunt, *Art and Architecture in France, 1500-1700,* Baltimore, 1957, p. 251, n. 2, and the same scholar's *Philibert de l'Orme,* London, 1958, p. 39.

BIBLIOGRAPHY

Adhémar, Jean. 1946. *Les graveurs français de la renaissance Encyclopédie Alpine illustrée*, Paris, plates XII, XIII.

————. 1939. *Inventaire du fonds français*, Paris, II, p. 313.

Alvin, L. 1856. Les graveurs anciens, *Revue universelle des arts*, III, p. 254.

Angelis, P. Luigi de. 1811. *Notizie istoriche degli intagliatori..da Gori Gandinelli*, Part 9, Siena.

Aubert, Marcel. 1921. *Les richesses de l'art de la France-Bourgogne*, Paris.

Auguis, A. n.d. Duvet, *Biographie universelle*, XII, p. 174.

Austin, Stanley. n.d. *The History of Engraving*, New York.

————. 1903. Ninth article in a series on the history of engraving, *The Printseller*, Sept., pp. 393ff.

Baltrusaitis, Jurgis. 1960. *Reveils et prodigues: Le gothique fantastique*, Paris.

Barbier de Montault, X. 1890. *Traité d'iconographie chrétienne*, Paris.

Bardon, Francoise. 1963. *Diane de Poitiers et le mythe de Diane*, Paris.

Barocchi, P. 1950. *Il Rosso Fiorentino*, Rome.

Bartsch, Adam. 1808. *Le peintre graveur*, VII, p. 496.

————. 1854-76. *Le peintre graveur,* nouvelle édition, Leipzig, VII, p. 497ff.

Basan, F. 1791. *Supplément au dictionnaire des graveurs*, Brussels, p. 63.

Baudrier, J. 1853. *Bibliographie lyonnaise. Récherches sur les imprimeurs libraires, relieurs et fondeurs de lettres de Lyon au XVIe siècle*, Lyons, I, p. 143ff.

Becherucci, L. 1949. *Manieristi Toscani*, Bergamo.

Belle, Edmond. 1911. La reforme a Dijon, *Revue bourguignonne de l'Université de Dijon*, XXI, no. 1, p. 17.

Bellier, E., and L. Auvray. 1882. *Dictionnaire général des artistes de l'école française*, Paris.

Bénard père. 1808. *Catalogue de Paignon-Dijonval*, Paris, p. 201.

Benesch, Otto. 1948. *The Art of the Renaissance in Northern Europe*, Cambridge, Mass.

Bénézit, L. 1913. *Dictionnaire des peintres, sculpteurs*, Paris, II, p. 191.

Bersier, Jean E. 1977. *Jean Duvet, Le Maître à la Licorne, 1485-1570?* Paris.

————. 1947. *La gravure, les procédés, l'histoire*, Paris.

Binyon, Laurence. 1917. The Engravings of Blake and Edward Calvert, *Print Collector's Quarterly*, VII, pp. 307-332.

Blondel, Spire. 1884. La damasquinerie, *Gazette des Beaux-Arts*, XXX, p. 276.

Blum, André. 1936. Un musée de la gravure — La collection Edmond de Rothschild, *L'Art et les artistes*, XXXIII, pp. 12-13.

————. 1913. *L'estampe satirique en France*, Paris.

Blunt, Anthony. 1953. *Art and Architecture in France 1500-1700*, London.

Bock, Elfried. 1849. *Gravure en France*, Paris.

————. 1930. *Geschichte der graphischen Kunst*, Berlin.

Boivin, Jean. 1925. *Les anciens orfèvres français et leurs poinçons*, Paris.

Bonnardot, Alf. 1849. *Histoire artistique et archéologique de la gravure en France*, Paris.

Bouchot, Henri. n.d. *Pièces choisies de l'école française*, Paris, Plate 10.

Boullaye, E. Julienne de la. 1876. *Étude sur la vie et sur l'oeuvre de Jean Duvet dit le maître à la licorne*, Paris.

————. 1880. Entrées et séjours de François Ier à Langres, *Bulletin de la société hisorique et archéologique de Langres*, I, pp. 68-100.

Bourchand, G. 1903. *A travers cinq siècles de gravures*, Paris.

Bourquin, D. 1956. La gravure en France au XVIe siècle, *Le courrier graphique*, LXXXIII, January, p. 19ff.

Brocard, H. 1880. Inventaire des réliques et autres curiosités de l'eglise cathedrale de Langres, *Bulletin de la société historique et archéologique de Langres*, pp. 152-178.

Brulliot, Franz. 1833. *Dictionnaire des monogrammes*, Munich, I, 1832, p. 203; and II, p. 406.

Brun, Charles. 1901. *Dictionnaire des artistes suisses*, I, p. 406.

————. 1917. *Dictionnaire des artistes suisses*, Supplément, IV, pp. 504-505.

Brun, Robert. 1948. *Le livre français*, Paris.

————. 1930. *Le livre illustré en France au XVIe siècle*, Paris.

Brunet, Gustave. 1861. *Manuel du libraire*, Paris, II, Iere partie.

Brunet, Jacques Charles. 1842. *Manuel du libraire et de l'amateur de livres*, Brussels.

Bryan, Michael. 1806. *Dictionary of Painters and Engravers*, London, I, p. 444.

Burty, Philippe. 1861. Mouvement des arts, *Gazette des Beaux-Arts*, X, April, p. 54.

Cassirer, Kurt. 1922. Ein Replik nach der Barberinischen Faune, *Münchner Jahrbuch der bildenden Kunst*, XII, pp. 90-97.

Chabeuf, Henri. Jean Duvet ou Du Vai, le maître à la licorne, *Journal des arts*, No. 41, March 19.

————. Jehan Duvet était-il dijonnais ou langrois? *Mémoires de l'academie des sciences, arts et belles-lettres de Dijon*, 5 Sér., II, pp. 7-12.

————. 1915. Jean Duvet, *Archives de la Côte-d'Or*, 5 Sér., XIII, p. 7ff.

Chapuis, A. 1906. Les anciennes corporations dijonnaises, *Mémoires de la société bourg. de géogr. et d'hist.*, XXII, 1906, pp. 1-507.

Christ, Johann Friedrich. 1750. *Dictionnaire des monogrammes*, Paris, p. 173.

Claudin, Anatole. 1873. *Catalogue des livres de MM. Randin et Rostain*, Paris, 1873, Cat. 122.

————. 1894. *Histoire de l'imprimerie en France au XVe et au XVIe siècles*, Paris, IV, p. 445.

Claudon, H. 1919. "Séance de fév. 12," *Mémoires de l'academie des sciences, arts, et belles-lettres de Dijon*, 5 Sér., II, p. LXXXIX.

Clayton, Muriel. 1930. *The Print Collector*, New York.

Clément-Janin, V. 1889. *Les orfèvres dijonnais*, Dijon.

Clutton, George. 1937-38. Two Early Representations of Lutheranism in France, *Journal of the Warburg and Courtauld Institute*, I, pp. 297-98.

Colombier, Pierre du. n.d. *L'art renaissance en France*, Paris.

Colvin, Sidney. 1912. *Guide to an Exhibition of Drawings by Old Masters*, British Museum, London.

Comstock, Helen. 1941. French Engraving, *The Connoisseur in America*, CVIII, Sept., pp. 124-25.

Coppier, M.A.-C. 1932. Qu'est-ce qu'une gravure precieuse? *L'Illustration*, année 90, Aug. 20, p. 508.

Courboin, Francois. 1923. *Histoire illustrée de la gravure en France*, Paris, II, pp. 247-48; I, p. 131.

————. 1923. *La gravure en France des origines à 1900*, Paris.

Covelle, A. 1897. *Livre des bourgeois de l'ancienne république de Genève*, Geneva.

Dacier, Emile. 1944. *La gravure française*, Paris.

Dalbanne, Claude. 1939. Le maître I.D., *Maso Finiguerra*, IV, pp. 215-252.

Darras, P. 1938. *L'oeuvre gravée de Jean Duvet*, Catalogue of Exhibition at the Bibliothèque Nationale, Paris.

Delaborde, Henri. 1875. *Le département des estampes à la Bibliothèque Nationale. Notice historique*, Paris, p. 344.

————. 1882. *La gravure précise élementaire*, Paris, p. 160.

Delen, A. J. J. 1956. *De grafische Kunsten door Euwen Heen*, Antwerp.

Demole, Eugène. 1916-17. *Journal suisse d'horlogerie*, XLI.

————. Histoire monétaire de Genève de 1536 à 1792. *Mémoires de la société d'histoire et d'archéologie de Genève*, Sér. 40, I, 1887.

Deonna, W. 1937. Artistes à Genève au temps de la Réformation, II, Jean Duvet, la Maître à la licorne, *Genava*, XV, pp. 128-130.

Diderot, Denis. *Les Arts à Genève des origines à la fin du XVIIIe siècle*, Geneva.

————. 1757. Graveurs sur bois, *Encyclopédie*, VII, p. 890.

Didier, J. -Ch. 1979. Duvet, Jean, *Dictionnaire de biographie française*, XII, cols. 1047-8.

Dilke, Lady E.P., See Pattison, Mrs. Mark.

Disertori, Benvenuto. 1930. Cronache, *Emporium*, LXXII, Nov., p. 323.

————. 1949. *Dix siècles de livres français*, Lucerne, July 9 - Oct. 2, Cat. 124.

Duchesne, Jean. 1855. *Notice des estampes exposées à la Bibliothèque Royale*, Paris.

Duplessis, George. 1861. *Histoire de la gravure en France*, Paris, also editions of 1869, 1880.

————. 1869. *Merveilles de gravures*, Paris.

————. 1871. *Le peintre-graveur français*, Paris, XI.

————. 1873-80. *Eaux-fortes et gravures des maîtres anciens . . .*, Paris. Contains a heliogravure after Duvet cat. 64.

————. 1875. *Histoire de la gravure du portrait en France*, Paris.

Duvet, Jean. 1962. *L'Apocalypse figurée* (facsimile), London.

Edwards, H. 1941. Jean Duvet's Saint Sebastian, Saint Anthony and Saint Roch, *Chicago Art Institute Bulletin*, XXXV, Sept. - Oct., pp. 74-75.

Eisler, Colin. 1953. The triumphal entry and 'mystère': as leit motif for the form and content of his art, *Actes du XIXe congrès international d'histoire de l'art*, Paris.

————. 1960. Jean Duvet, ce grand graveur français du XVIe siècle n'est pas assez connu, *L'Oeil*, no. 70. Paris, Oct., pp. 20-27, p. 65, p. 76 and 8 reproductions.

Eméric-David, Toussaint B. 1808. *Discours historiques sur la gravure en taille-douce et sur la gravure en bois*, Paris.

————. 1955. *L'Europe humaniste, Palais des Beaux-Arts*,

Brussels.

Fagan, L. 1904. *Handbook to the Department of Prints,* British Museum, London.

Forrer, L. 1904. *Biographical Dictionary of Medallists,* London, I, p. 618.

Foville, Jean de. 1909. Jean Duvet, *Le Musée,* VI, pp. 113-122.

Francis, Henry S. 1954. *Bulletin of the Cleveland Museum of Art,* 42st year, No. 3, March, pp. 56-58.

Frauenfelder, Reinhart. 1917. *Dictionnaire des artistes suisses. Supplément,* IV, pp. 504-505.

Frenzel, J. G. A. 1854. *Die Kupferstich Sammlung Friedrich. August II,* Leipzig.

Furst, Herbert. 1931. *Original Engraving and Etching,* London.

Galichon, Emile. 1865. De quelques estampes milanaises, *Gazette des Beaux-Arts,* XVIII, p. 552.

Garnier, Joseph. 1889. *Les anciens orfèvres de Dijon,* Dijon.

Garnier, Noel. 1892. Seance du 8 janvier 1892, *Mémoires de la société bourg. de géographie et d'histoire,* VIII, pp. XXXVI-XXXVIII.

Gébelin, F. 1942. *Le style renaissance,* Paris.

Godefroy, Louis. 1935. L'Apocalypse de Duvet à Langres et à Dijon, *Bulletin trimestriel de la Chambre internationale des experts d'art,* No. 3, Jan.

————. 1935. Séance du 23 janvier 1935, *Mémoires de la comm. des antiquités de la Côte-d'Or. Acad. des sciences de Dijon,* XX, fasc. 3, p. 325.

Goetz, Oswald. Hie hencktt Judas, *Form und Inhalt. Kunstgeschichtliche Studien. Otto Schmidt zum 60 Geburtstag,* Stuttgart, pp. 105-137.

Goldscheider, Ludwig. 1937. *Five Hundred Self Portraits,* London.

Gonse, Louis. 1877. Review of E. Julienne de la Boullaye, *Étude sur la vie . . . de Jean Duvet* (Paris, 1876), *Chronique des arts,* No. 6, February 10, pp. 52-53.

Gutekunst, H. K. *Kat. der Sammlung des vers. Luigi Angiolini zu Mailand, Kunst-Auktion in Stuttgart. No. 47.*

Heine, Maurice. n.d. Prodiges, *Minotaure,* No. 10, pp. 45-48.

Heinecken, G. *Idée générale d'une collection d'estampes,* Leipzig.

Heitz, Paul, and W. L. Schreiber. 1901. *Pestblätter des XV Jahrhunderts,* Strasbourg, Plate XXXII.

Heller, Joseph. 1831. *Monogrammen-Lexikon,* Bamberg.

————. 1823-36. *Praktisches Handbuch für Kupfterstich Sammler,* Bamberg, III, pp. 189-191.

Hennin, M. 1862. *Les monuments de l'histoire de France,* VIII, Paris.

Hévesy, André de. 1854. Un dessin de Jean Duvet, *La revue des arts,* IV, pp. 103-108.

Hilberry, Harry I. 1938. Jean Duvet, unpublished M.A. thesis for New York University, Institute of Fine Arts, June.

Hind, Arthur M. 1948. *Early Italian Engraving,* London, V, Catalogue, Part II, p. 11.

Hourticq, Louis. 1925. *Encyclopédie des beaux-arts,* Paris, I, p. 202.

Huber, Michel and C.C.H. Rost. *manuel des curieux,* Zurich, VII, p. 51.

Ivins, W.H., Jr. 1926. Jean Duvet, *The Arts,* IX, May, pp. 261-271.

————. 1945. French XVI Century Prints, *Bulletin of the Metropolitan Museum of Art,* n.s. III, January, p. 132.

James, M.R. 1931. *The Apocalypse in Art,* Oxford.

Jansen, Hendrick. 1808. *Essai sur l'origine de la gravure,* Paris.

Johnson, A.F. 1933. The Unicorn in Early Print and Printed Books, *The Colophon,* Part XIV.

Jones, George. 1823. *A Catalogue of Prints . . . Thomas Lloyd, Esq., Sold by George Jones, July 1st, 1823,* London.

Joubert, F.E. 1821. *Manuel de l'amateur d'estampes,* Paris, II, p. 19.

Kristeller, Paul. 1913. *Die lombradische Graphik der Renaissance,* Berlin.

————. 1921. *Kupferstich und Holzschnitt in vier Jahrhunderten,* Berlin.

Labarte, Jules. 1872-75. Histoire des arts industriels au moyen-âge et à l'époque de la Renaissance, Paris, IV, p. 387.

Laborde, L. de. 1853. *Notice des emaux, bijoux et objects divers, exposés dans les galeries du Musée du Louvre,* Paris.

Laprade, J. de. 1938. Les peintres graveurs français et l'oeuvre de Jean Duvet à la Bibliothèque Nationale, *Beaux-Arts,* n.s. année 75, May 13, p. 3.

Laran, Jean. 1959. *L'Estampe,* Paris.

LeBlanc, Charles. 1852. *Cat. des estampes de M. Pierre Vischer de Bâle,* Paris, p. 106, Cat. 801-805.

————. 1856-88. *Manuel de l'amateur d'estampes,* Paris, II, p. 66.

Lieure, L. n.d. *L'école française de gravure des origines à la fin du XVIe siècle,* Paris.

Linzeler, Andre. 1938. Un dessin inédit de Jean Duvet, *Bulletin de la société de l'histoire de l'art français,* No. I, année, p. 84.

————. 1939. *Inventaire du fonds français. I. Graveurs du XVIe siècle,* Paris, 1932-1936, pp. 329-352. See also II, *Supplément,* p. 313.

Lippman, F. 1896. *Der Kupferstich,* Berlin.

LoDuca, G.M. 1932. Duvet et gli incisori alla Bibliothèque Nationale, *Emporium,* LXXXVIII, p. 332.

Malaspina di Sannazaro, Luigi. 1824. *Catalogo di una raccolta di stampe antiche,* Milan, IV, pp. 13-15.

Marcel, L.E. 1926. *Le Cardinal de Givry,* Paris, I-II.

Marcel, L.F. 1917. Pierre Guyot de Giey - Sa vie, sa maison - ses collections, *Bulletin de la société historique et archéologique de Langres,* Nos. 98-99, pp. 300-302.

Marcel, L.F. and L.E. 1935. *Artistes et ouvriers d'art à Langres avant la Révolution,* Langres.

Marguery, H. 1933. Jean Duvet, *Cahiers d'art*, V.III, Nos. 5-6, pp. 173-177.

Marolles, Michel de. 1872. *Livre des peintres et graveurs*, Paris. Reprinted from the 1666 edition, No. 280.

Mazerolle, F. *La grande encyclopédie*, Paris, XV.

Menzies, W.G. 1908. Some French Line Engravers, *The Connoisseur*, XXII, Part 6, pp. 175-178.

Michel, André. 1912. *Histoire de l'art*, Paris, V, Part I.

Millin, Aubin Louis. 1806. *Dictionnaire des beaux-arts*, Paris, I.

Mireur, Hippolyte. 1911. *Dictionnaire des ventes d'art faites en France et à l'etranger pendant les XVIII et XIX siècles*, Paris, II.

Mongan, Elizabeth. 1950. *The Rosenwald Coll. An Exhibition of Recent Acquisitions*, Washington.

Mortet, Charles. 1924. *Le livre français des origines à la fin du second empire*, Paris.

Naef, Henri. 1947-53. La frappe de Michel comte de Gruyère, *Revue suisse de numismatique*, Nos. 33-35, pp. 35-50.

—. 1924. La monnaie de la Gruyère, *Revue suisse de numismatique*, XXIII, p. 467.

—. 1925. Un artiste français du XVIe siècle, bourgeois de Geneve: Jehan Duvet, le Maître à la Licorne, *Bulletin de la société d'histoire et d'architecture de Genève*, V, 1925, p. 39.

—. 1934. La vie et les travaux de Jean Duvet le Maître à la Licorne, *Bulletin de la société de l'histoire de l'art française*, Annee, pp. 114-141.

—. 1946. *L'Alchimiste de Michel, Comte de Gruyère, Mémoires et documents publiés par la société d'histoire de la Suisse Romande*, 3 Sér., II, Lausanne.

Nagler, George. 1837. *Neues allgemeines Künstler Lexikon*, Munich, 1835-41, IV.

Neveux, Pol and Emile Dacier. 1932. *Les richesses des bibliothèques provinciales de France*, Paris, I, Plate XLVII.

Oberheide, Albert. 1933. *Der Einfluss Marcantonio Raimondi auf die nordische Kunst des 16 Jahrhunderts*, Hamburg.

Ohl des Marais, Albert. L'Art de la gravure en Lorraine jusqu'au XVIe siècle, *Bulletin artistique de L'Est*, June, No. 2.

Ottley, W.Y. 1828. *Facsimiles of Scarce and Curious Prints*, London.

Ourcel, Charles. 1953. *L'Art en Bourgogne*, Paris.

"P.M." 1921-22. Jehan Duvet, orfèvre du roi, dit le Maître à la Licorne, *Byblis*, Winter, pp. 19-23.

Pannier, J. 1938. Encore un artiste huguenot peu connu, Jean Duvet (1485-1570?)," *Bulletin historique protestante française*, LXXXVII, pp. 215-218.

Papillon, Jean Michel. 1766. *Traité historique et pratique de la gravure sur bois*, Paris, I.

Passavant, Johann. 1864. *Le peintre-graveur*, Leipzig, VI.

Pattison, Mrs. Mark (Lady E.P. Dilke). 1879. *The Renaissance of Art in France*, London, II.

Popham, A.E. 1921. Jean Duvet, *The Print Collector's Quarterly*, V.III, No. 2, July, pp. 122-150.

—. 1937. An Undescribed Engraving by Jean Duvet", *Maso Finiguerra*, XV-XVI, Fas. I, pp. 92-93.

Prassé, Leona R. 1931. Engraving by Jean Duvet, *Cleveland Museum Bulletin*, 18th year, January, pp. 13-16.

Prestel, C.E.G. 1819. *Catalogue raisonné de . . . Clemence Aloys Hohwiesner*, I.

Prost, B. 1894. Le trésor de l'abbaye Saint-Bénigne, *Mémoires de la société bourg. de géographie et d'histoire* X, p. 190.

Quandt, von, Johann. 1853. *Verzeichnes meiner Kupferstich-Sammlung*, Leipzig.

Rahir, Edouard. 1899. *La collection Dutuit, livres et manuscrits*, Paris.

—. 1924. *Bibliothèque de l'amateur*, Paris.

Rauch, Nicholas. 1953. *Auction Catalogue, March 2, 1953*, Geneva, Cat. 65.

Réau, Louis. 1957. *Iconographie de l'art chrétien*, Paris, II, part 2.

Regnault-Delalande, F.L. 1811. *Catalogue raisonné du . . . feu M. de Silvestre*, Paris.

Renouvier, M.J. 1854. Des types et des manières des graveurs. *Académie des sciences et lettres de Montpelier*, I, pp. 739-741.

Ricci, Seymour de. *Manuscript Catalogue of the Oeuvre of Jean Duvet*, Paris, Bibliothèque Nationale, Cabinet des Estampes (YB 3-2061-13).

Robert-Dumesnil, A.P.F. 1841. *Le peintre-graveur français*, Paris, V.

Rondot, Natalis. 1897. *Graveurs sur bois à Lyon au XVIe siècle*, Paris.

Rosenthal, Leon. 1909. *La gravure*, Paris.

Rossiter, H.P. 1952. Duvet's Engravings of the Apocalypse: with comments on Naef's Findings, *Boston Museum Bulletin*, L, June, pp. 15-18.

Roy-Chèvrier. 1919. Numismatique bourguignonne: Chalon métallique, *Mémoires de la société historique et archéologique de Chalon-sur-Saône*, pp. 302-307.

Schwerdt, C.F.G.R. 1923. *Hunting, Hawking, Shooting*, London, III.

Strutt, Joseph. 1785. *A Biographical Dictionary of All the Engravers*, London, I.

Swope, Horace M. 1935. Notes on the Print Collection, *St. Louis Museum*, XX, Jan. p. 10.

Thausing, M. 1880. Kunstliteratur, *Zeitschrift für bildende Kunst*, XV, p. 88.

Tietze-Conrat, E. *Der französicher Kupferstich der Renaissance*, Munich.

—. 1930. Zur ikonographie des Judasstiche von Jean Duvet, *Graphischen Künste*, Vienna, Jahrgang 52-5, No. 1, Part I, Associated with *Gesellschaft für vervielfältigende Kunst*, pp. 3-4.

—. 1938. Un dessin de Jean Duvet, *Gazette des Beaux-Arts*, Sér. 6, XX, pp. 127-129.

Vallée, P. and L. de Gouvenain. 1900. *Inventaire sommaire des archives communales antérieures à 1790*, Dijon, III, 1892, IV.

Vallet. 1844. Essai biographique de la Haute-Marne, *Annuaire de la Haute-Marne,* p. 62ff.

Van Marle, Raimond. 1933. *Iconographie de l'art profane,* The Hague.

Venturi, A. 1908. *Storia dell'arte italiana,* Milan.

Vingtrinier, Aimé. 1894. *Histoire de l'imprimerie à Lyon,* Lyon.

Vloberg, M. 1954. *La Vierge et l'Enfant dans l'art français,* Paris.

Waagen, G.F. 1856. Über einige seltene, neuerdings in der Kupferstich Sammlung des britischen Museums eworbene Blätter, *Archiv. für die zeichnenden Kunste. Herausgegeben von Dr. Robert Naumann,* Leipzig, II, 248.

Weigert, Robert. 1933. Review of *Les Richesses des bibliothèques françaises, L'amateur d'estampes,* Annee 12, p. 74.

Willshire, W.H. 1871. *An Introduction to the Study and Collection of Ancient Prints,* London.

Wilson, Thomas. 1821. *A Catalogue Raisonné of the Select Collection of Engravings of an Amateur,* London, 1828.

Zani, Pietro. 1821. *Enciclopedia Metodica,* Parma, Part 1, VIII.

Zerner, Henri. 1969. *The School of Fontainebleau, Etchings and Engravings,* New York.

INDEX

A. NAMES AND PLACES

Woeriot, Pierre, 14, 28, 30 n.48,
96, 157
Wolff, Thomas, 60
Wolgemut, Michael, 138

X

Xenophon, 57

Z

Zurich, city of, 18
Zwingli, Huldreich, and art, 15,
18, 41, 43, 60

B. SUBJECTS

A

Actaeon, 113, 226
Adam and Eve (Dürer), 240
*Adoration of the Whore of Bab-
ylon* (de Pesquera), 158
Adrian VI (commemorative medal),
6, 148, 200, 202
Agnus Dei, 82, 83, 278
Alchemy 16, 21, 22, 35-43, 48
　as spiritual quest, 41-43
　classical and Christian symbol-
　ism in, 38, 41-43
　kinship to physical sciences of,
　35, 38
　modern appraisals of, 35, 38,
　45 n.13
　and religious thought, 41-43
　and sixteenth century art, 36-38
　transmutation of metals in, 37,
　39-40
　"true" and "false" in, 35
　and Unicorn Series, 111
Allegory, 37, 113, 300
　of Christian salvation, 117, 118,
　226, 237, 280
　of brevity of life, 226
　fusion of classical and Christian,
　35, 226
　in *tableaux-vivants*, 5, 10-11
　see also Christian symbols; clas-
　sical symbols
Allegory of the Power of Love
　(1528), 7, 9, 148, 220, 222
　humanism of, 7, 148
　fusion of northern and southern
　sources in, 220
Allegory of the Power of Love
　(Robetta), 220
*Angel Gives Saint John the Book
　to Eat, The* (Chapter 10), 270
*Angel Shows Saint John the Foun-
　tain of Living Water, The* (Chap-
　ter 22), 296
*Angel Shows Saint John the New
　Jerusalem, The* (Chapter 21),
　158, 294
　influence on Barberini of, 158
*Angel in the Sun Calling the Birds
　of Prey, The* (Chapter 19), 290
Angels, 52, 55, 262, 264, 266, 270,
　272, 278, 280, 282, 284, 286,
　290, 292, 294, 296

guardian, 294, 296
animal behavior, in French literature, 47
animal symbols,
　cats as prophets of Death, 47
　308
　dog as Melancholy, 47, 48, 118
　308
　dogs and unicorn, 234, 237
　dragon or beast, as Satan, 278,
　282, 284, 286, 292
　eagle as Divine Inspiration, 73
　251, 294
　elephants as Fame, 202
　and Four Humours, 308
　locusts, 260
　mouse as Corruption, 47, 230,
　308
　mouse as Phlegm, 308
　parrot as Patience, 182
　pelican as Piety, 83, 298
　snakes as Eternity, 300
　swan as Death, 48, 49-50, 51
　52-53, 307
　as Sanguine, 308
　vultures, 290
　see also: Unicorn
Animals Entering the Ark (Bon-
　asone), 314
Annunciation (Jan van Eyck),
　144
Annunciation in the Church, The,
　144, 180
Annunciation of 1520, 196, 198
　use of Italian form in, 3, 4,
　147, 148
　and Duvet as goldsmith, 151
　revolutionary nature of, 180
Antichrist, 284, 288, 290
Antwerp Mannerists, 138, 140, 144
Antwort (Zwingli), 60
*L'Apocalypse de Saincte Jehan
　Zebedee* (1514, Chocquet-
　Mystère), 78, 90 n.30
Apocalypse, as anti-Catholic, 59-
　60
　in art and literature, 48, 49, 52,
　59-61, 73, 78, 79-80, 81-83,
　86, 91 n.39, 97, 98-102, 106
　n.25, 117, 159, 280, 284
　Four Horsemen of, 258
　imagery of 42-43, 52, 60, 79-
　80, 81, 82, 92 n.61, 251-308

Luther's translation of, 59-60,
　264
　and triumphal entries, 61, 82-83
　and the unicorn, 117
Apocalypse figurée (1555), 47
　see also *Apocalypse* Series
Apocalypse illustrations (Blake),
　159
Apocalypse Series 2, 18, 19-20, 21,
　38, 148, 153-54, 157, 232, 240,
　242, 243, 251-308, 310
　architectural elements in, 71-72,
　147, 270, 284, 286, 292, 294,
　296
　Christian and classical imagery
　in, 48, 49, 51-53, 54, 71, 77, 78,
　82, 83, 294
　conservatism of, 61, 78, 97
　copies without text, 103, 104
　n.1
　dating of, 95, 96, 103, 155, 303
　distribution of Apocalyptic text
　in, 104 n.7
　Dürer, and, 48, 49, 71, 72, 98-
　102, 107 n.33, 254, 258, 260,
　262, 264, 266, 270, 274, 276,
　278, 292
　as Duvet's ultimate work, 52, 54
　format of, 71, 74, 82, 96, 98,
　102, 153
　and François I, 19, 95, 154, 303
　and Henry II Series, 303
　history of surviving examples of,
　107-109, ns.37-42
　iconography of, 251-308
　Lyon publication of, 25, 38, 59,
　95, 123
　imagery in pageant and mystère
　in, 71, 74, 77, 83, 284, 286
　plates as diptychs or triptychs,
　71, 83, 303
　reflects pageantry at Langres, 71
　source of 1561 translation, 96
　sources of forms of, 98, 101,
　102, 106 n.25, 134, 136, 154-
　55, 188, 251-308
　Tablets of Moses in, 56, 71, 74,
　153
　typography and printing quality
　of, 25, 53, 95, 96, 103
　Frontispiece (155), 2, 71, 74,
　78, 95, 103, 155, 307-8, advi-
　sors referred to on, 39, 48-49,

363

PHOTOGRAPH CREDITS

A.C.L. Brussels: Text figs. 33,34,35; *AGRACI, Paris:* Text fig. 61; *Albertina, Vienna:* Text fig. 2; *Archives Photographiques, Paris, S.P.A.D.E.M.:* Text figs. 11,29,31,32,77, 79,80; *Autun, Musée:* Text fig. 62; *Baltimore Museum of Art:* Text fig. 81; *Bibliothèque Nationale, Paris:* Text figs. 70,55,56,57,52; *British Library, London:* Text figs. 42,43; *British Museum, London:* Text figs. 21,44; *Cleveland Museum of Art:* Text figs. 4,5, Catalogue figs. 35-65; *L. Dentan, Geneva:* Text fig. 14; *Documentation Photographique de la Réunion des Musées nationaux, France:* Text figs. 12,13; *P. Dumond & J. Basinot, Reims:* Text fig. 16; *Graphische Sammlung, Munich:* Text fig. 25; *Harvard University Archives:* Text figs. 3,83; *Kunsthistorisches Institute, Vienna:* Text fig. 27; *Musée du Louvre, Paris:* Text figs. 30,54, 82; *Morgan Library, New York:* Text fig. 18; *Nancy, Musée des Beaux-Arts:* Text figs. 4,5; *Photographie Bulloz, Paris:* Text figs. 60,64,65, 66,67; *Photohaus Hirsch, Nordlingen:* Text fig. 26; *Stockholm, Nationalmuseum:* Text fig. 53; *Victoria and Albert Museum, London:* Text fig. 1; *Warburg Institute, London:* Text figs. 7,15,20,28,36,37,38,40,41,46,48,49,59,71,72,73,74,75,76, 84,85.

Eisler	Bartsch	LeBlanc	Robert-Dumesnil	Passavant	Boullaye	Popham	Linzeler	Bersier
1		16		67*	67	67	12	10
2		15		68	68	68	13	11
3	3	6	4	4	4	4	15	6
4			23	23	23	23	46	49
5	7	22	17	17	17	17	5	42
6		4	3	3	3	3	2	3
7		50	24	24	24	24	45	50
8								44
10			64	64	64	64	1	4
11					79	79	9	41
12		7	5	5	5	5	8	5
13		65	62	62	62	62	11	63
14		54	11	11	11	11	70	64
15		53	25	25	25	25	52-6	57
16		13	15	15		15	50-4	54
17		13	15	15	15	15	50-4	55
18		14	16	16	16	16	51-5	56
19		12	14	14	14	14	49-3	53
20		11	13	13	13	13	48-2	52
21		10	12	12	12	12	47-1	51
22		16	2	66	66	66	6	9
23						80		
24	8	18	18	18	18	18	53	43
25				69	69	69	14	13
26	38	56	53	53	53	53	71	62
27		20	21	21	21	21	10	16
28		9	7	7	7	7	7	7
29			70	70	70	70	75	66
30	6	17	10	10	10	10	16	18
31	4	8	6	6	6	6	17	8
32	39	59	54	54	54	54	60-1	67
33		61	56	72	56	56	63-3	70
34		62	57	57	57	57	66-5	71
35	1	1		1		1	3	1
36	2	2	2	2	2	2	4	2
37	5	17	8	8	8	8	20	12
38	36	26	51	51	51	51	57	47
39	13	25	50	25	50	50	57	36
40	14	28	28	28	28	28	23-2	19
41	15	29	29	29	29	29	24-3	20
42	16	30	30	30	30	30	26-5	21
43	17	31	31	31	31	31	25-4	22
44	18	32	32	32	32	32	27-6	23
45	19	33	33	33	33	33	28-7	24
46	20	34	34	34	34	34	29-8	25
47	21	35	35	35	35	35	30-9	26
48	22	36	36	36	36	36	31-10	27
49	23	37	37	37	37	37	32-11	28
50	24	38	38	38	38	38	33-12	29
51	25	39	39	39	39	3·	34-13	30
52	26	40	40	401	40	40	35-14	31
53	27	41	41	41	41	41	36-15	32
54	28	42	42	42	42	42	37-16	33
55	29	43	43	43	43	43	38-17	34
56	30	44	44	44	44	44	39-18	35
57	31	45	45	45	45	45	40-18	36
58	32	46	46	46	46	46	41-19	37
59	33	47	47	47	47	47	42-20	38
60	34	48	48	48	48	48	43-30	39
61	35	49	49	49	49	49	44-31	40
62	45	66	63	63	63	63	72	59
63	43	58	60	60	60	60	74	58
64					72a	72a	73	60
65	12	27	27	62	27	62	22-1	18
66	40	60	55	55	55	55	61-2	69
67	41	63	58	58	58	58	65-4	72
68	42	64	59	59	59	59	57-6·	68
69				75	78	75	76,77	65
70	10	52	20	20	20	20	54	48
71		18	9	9	9	9	18	14
72	11	21	22	22	22	22	22	19